"This Is My Doctrine"

"This Is My Doctrine"
The Development of Mormon Theology

Charles R. Harrell

Greg Kofford Books
2011

Copyright © 2011, Charles R. Harrell

Cover design copyright © 2011 by Greg Kofford Books, Inc.
Cover photo courtesy of Andrea Chemelli

European Printing, 2015
Paperback ISBN 978-1-58958-506-5
Hardcover ISBN 978-1-58958-103-6

All rights reserved. No part of this book may be reproduced in any form or by any means without permission in writing from the publisher, Greg Kofford Books. The views expressed herein are the responsibility of the author and do not necessarily represent the position of Greg Kofford Books, Inc.

>   Greg Kofford Books
>   P.O. Box 1362
>   Draper, UT 84020
>   U.S.A.
>   www.gregkofford.com
>   facebook.com/gkbooks

Library of Congress Cataloging-in-Publication Data

Harrell, Charles, 1950-
  This is my doctrine the development of Mormon theology / by Charles Harrell.
       p. cm.
  Includes bibliographical references and index.
  ISBN 978-1-58958-103-6
  1. Church of Jesus Christ of Latter-Day Saints—Doctrines—History. I. Title.
  BX8635.3.H37 2007
  230'.9309--dc22
                                                2007021768

Contents

Preface vii
1. Theology, a Divine-Human Enterprise 1
2. The Great Apostasy. 31
3. Joseph Smith and the Restoration. 47
4. The Restoration of the Priesthood and the Church. 73
5. Doctrinal Truths Restored 91
6. The Godhead and Plurality of Gods. 105
7. God the Father 125
8. Jesus Christ. 149
9. The Holy Ghost 185
10. Satan 193
11. The Preexistence 199
12. The Creation 227
13. The Fall and Nature of Humanity 251
14. The Atonement 273
15. The Gospel Plan 293
16. Salvation for the Dead 343
17. The Priesthood. 373
18. The Gathering of Israel and Establishment of Zion . . . 397
19. The Second Coming and Millennium. 427
20. The Resurrection. 455
21. Final Judgment. 473

Epilogue 501
Bibliography 509
Scripture Index 547
Index. 563

Preface

"There are more things in heaven and earth, Horatio, than are dreamt of in your philosophy." (Hamlet, Act 1, Scene 5)

As an active Latter-day Saint and avid student of Mormon doctrine, I have long been impressed by the breadth and depth of Latter-day Saint (LDS) theology. Few religions provide such definitive answers to so many of life's important—and not so important—questions. Latter-day Saints derive their doctrinal beliefs primarily from the standard works (the Bible, Book of Mormon, Doctrine and Covenants, and Pearl of Great Price) and the pronouncements of Church leaders—especially those of the First Presidency and Quorum of the Twelve Apostles, whom members sustain as prophets, seers, and revelators. It is generally taken as axiomatic that their words, like those recorded in scripture, are divinely inspired and thus reflect a consistent and objectively true theology.

Beginning as early as 1828, two years prior to the organization of the Church, Mormonism's founding prophet Joseph Smith began issuing doctrinal pronouncements with the voice of divine authority declaring, "This is my [God's] doctrine" (D&C 10:67). Such divine authentication should not necessarily be taken to mean that the doctrines that followed are absolute and immune to change. Indeed, a close examination of scriptural and authoritative teachings, both ancient and modern, indicates that God's word is not always static, neither is it entirely free of human input. For example, the nature of the Godhead is expressed differently in the Old Testament, New Testament, Book of Mormon, and later LDS scripture—suggesting that doctrines are dynamic and change with time (see Chapter 6). This does not mean that ancient and modern prophetic teachings are not inspired—only that they should not be understood as the final and inalterable word of God. Twentieth-century LDS apostle Bruce R. McConkie, though known for his doctrinal authoritarianism, observed that "the last word has not been spoken on any subject" and "there are more things we do not know about the doctrines of salvation than there are things we do know."[1]

Because God's word is mediated through finite and fallible humans, it is never perfect, and therefore never final. President Brigham Young, successor to Joseph Smith, remarked that "revelations, when they have passed from God to man, and from man into his written and printed language, cannot be said to be entirely perfect."[2] The apostle Paul included himself when declaring that, while in mortality, "we see through a glass, darkly," and "know [only] in part" (1 Cor. 13:12).

This book traces the development of Mormon theology by examining how doctrines taught today appear to have been understood in early Mormonism and earlier Old and New Testament times. The *New Standard Dictionary of the English Language* defines doctrine as "that which is taught or set forth for acceptance or belief," and lists as synonyms "article of belief, article of faith, belief, dogma, precept."[3] Accordingly, I use the term "doctrine" throughout to refer to *beliefs* about ultimate reality and not to ultimate reality itself.[4] Thus, it can be said that doctrines change and evolve, even if truth itself remains constant.

It would be overly ambitious and even presumptuous to attempt to provide a definitive—much less an exhaustive—treatment of prevailing doctrinal beliefs for all periods of Judeo-Christian history, or even of early LDS history. Historical records, including the scriptures, show evidence of both multiple and mixed theological perspectives, which are often lacking in doctrinal detail. The intent of this work, therefore, is to focus only on select traceable developments that would likely be of interest to an LDS audience.

The interpretation of theological history presented herein is based primarily on critical scholarship and contextual analysis, which sometimes lead to different conclusions than those found in traditional LDS narratives. My purpose in calling attention to these differences is not to refute or disparage LDS beliefs, but rather to stimulate reflection on how the narratives promoting these beliefs developed. Certainly the doctrines of the Restoration need not always conform to modern scholarship to be divinely inspired. However, just because they are inspired doesn't necessarily mean that the narratives developed to frame them are always correct.

This book has its genesis in an article I wrote over twenty years ago for *BYU Studies* on the development of the doctrine of preexistence in early Mormon thought.[5] My research led me to conclude that this distinctive LDS doctrine went through at least four major transitions during the first fifteen years of the Church, none of which was completely congruous with the others, and all of which had tenuous biblical grounding. They did, however, have recognizable precedents in the religious environs of Joseph Smith. As I began examining other LDS doctrines it became apparent that they also initially paralleled teachings in contemporary religious movements and only gradually took on more distinctive forms of expression. This is not to say that Mormon doctrines are simply products of their environment, but that environmental influences arguably helped shape their formulation.

According to modern biblical scholarship, the Bible itself reflects, in large part, the culturally conditioned understanding of its authors. In 1994, the Pontifical Biblical Commission under Pope John Paul II endorsed the approach of Catholic scholars who, like many of their Protestant and Jewish counterparts, view scripture as "the work of human authors." According to the commission, "The texts of the Bible are the expression of religious traditions which existed before them. The mode of their connection with these traditions is different in each case, with the creativity of the authors shown in various degrees." The commission further explains that these "biblical traditions bore the mark of the socio-cultural milieu which transmitted them."[6] The premise of this work is that the development of Mormon theology, like that of ancient Israel and early Christianity, can best be understood when examined in light of its contemporary cultural influences, especially during its formative years.

Mark S. Smith, professor of Bible and Ancient Near Eastern Studies at New York University, describes theological development as a process of "convergence" followed by "differentiation."[7] In the case of Israelite religion, convergence involved both the coalescence of various Canaanite notions of deity into the makeup of Israel's perception of Yahweh (e.g., a tribal and warrior God), and the bringing together of different Canaanite worship practices and ritual forms. "The second major process," he explains, "involved differentiation of Israelite cult from its Canaanite heritage."[8] Thus Smith, along with many other Near Eastern scholars, sees the religious beliefs and practices of ancient Israelites as having been largely appropriated from their "pagan" neighbors, but then gradually transformed into a distinctive Israelite religious tradition.[9]

Religious historians observe that Christianity, too, came along initially as one of many first-century Jewish movements and reflected ideologies and practices found within the fragmented Jewish world of the Greco-Roman period.[10] The first Christians were Jews who naturally held to traditional Jewish ideas of God and the hereafter. Only over time did Christianity carve out its own distinctive theological tradition—or, rather, traditions.

Scholars of early American religion tend to view Mormonism, which emerged during the revivalism of the Second Great Awakening, as having also adopted many of the beliefs and perspectives of the time.[11] W. H. Oliver, in his study of prophetic and millennial movements in early American history, goes so far as to say that "there was nothing in [Mormonism] that had not been anticipated over the preceding half-century."[12] In less than two decades, however, Mormonism distinguished itself so much from mainstream Christianity that many traditional Christians now label Mormonism as "non-Christian."[13] Some scholars have even characterized Mormonism as an emerging new world religion taking its place alongside Christianity and Judaism.[14]

This work is meant to be neither apologetic nor polemic, and aside from rejecting the unwarranted (and unofficial) notion of doctrinal immutability, I neither attempt to defend or refute the truth claims of Mormonism. Furthermore, I make no attempt to elevate the teachings of one era over another. The notion that LDS doctrines have merely progressed in a linear and progressive fashion (so that those taught today are more correct than those taught in previous eras) is an appealing, but difficult, idea to corroborate—except perhaps for doctrines that lend themselves to scientific investigation, such as the age of the earth or the nature of the cosmos. Theological historian Karen Armstrong notes that, historically, religious ideas have "not evolved from one point and progressed in a linear fashion to a final conception. Scientific notions work like that, but the ideas of art and religion do not. Just as there are only a given number of themes in love poetry, so too people have kept saying the same things about God over and over again."[15] Mormon theology is now more systematized and codified than it has ever been, but it isn't clear how much of that is due to increased enlightenment or to nearly two centuries of doctrinal harmonizing.

I am indebted to many individuals whose insights have been invaluable in writing this book. I express thanks to Kevin L. Barney who critically reviewed an early draft and provided many helpful suggestions. Appreciation also goes to my colleague, A. Brent Strong, and my brothers, Daniel and Thomas, for their thoughtful feedback. I am especially indebted to my editors, Lavina Fielding Anderson and, later, Loyd Ericson for their encouragement and professional guidance in crafting what *finally* became the final work. Lastly, I am grateful for the constant love and unselfish support of my wife, Yvonne. It is to her that I dedicate this book.

Notes

1. Bruce R. McConkie, "A New Commandment: Save Thyself and Thy Kindred!" 11.
2. Brigham Young, July 13, 1862, *Journal of Discourses*, 9:310.
3. *The New Standard Dictionary of the English Language*, s.v. "doctrine."
4. I recognize that many LDS expositors equate doctrine with truth itself. Bruce R. McConkie, for example, writes, "Gospel doctrine is synonymous with the truths of salvation." Bruce R. McConkie, *Mormon Doctrine*, 204. For a discussion of the problems involved in defining Mormon doctrine, see Loyd Ericson, "The Challenge of Defining Mormon Doctrine," 69–90.
5. Charles R. Harrell, "The Development of the Doctrine of Preexistence," 75–96.
6. Joseph A. Fitzmyer, *The Biblical Commission's Document: "The Interpretation of the Bible in the Church,"* 132–34.
7. Mark S. Smith, *The Early History of God: Yahweh and the Other Deities in Ancient Israel*, 75.
8. Ibid. The general LDS explanation for similarities between Old Testament theology and that of Canaanite religions is that the Canaanites had a degenerate form of what was originally revealed in its purity to Adam and Eve. See, for example, Glen L. Leonard, *Nauvoo: A Place of Peace, a People of Promise*, 315. Many Hebrew scholars argue, however, that Canaanite traditions actually provided the original basis for Israelite beliefs, and only after years of historical struggle to understand themselves did the Israelites differentiate their theology. Mark S. Smith notes that "while early Israel recorded some traditions not shared by its neighbors, these distinctive features are relatively rare and hardly indicate a wholly different culture or religion." Mark S. Smith, *The Origins of Biblical Monotheism: Israel's Polytheistic Background and the Ugaritic Texts*, 14.
9. For a chronicled history of this transformation, see Karen Armstrong, *The Great Transformation: The World in the Time of Buddha, Socrates, Confucius and Jeremiah*.
10. See ibid., 382–83.
11. That non-LDS scholars tend to view Joseph Smith as a product of his time was acknowledged by both LDS and non-LDS participants in the 2005 academic conference commemorating Joseph Smith's birth. Papers from this conference were printed in a special issue of *BYU Studies*. See John W. Welch, *The Worlds of Joseph Smith: A Bicentennial Conference at the Library of Congress*.
12. W. H. Oliver, *Prophets and Millennialists: The Uses of Biblical Prophecy in England from the 1790s to the 1840s*, 218; quoted in Grant Underwood, *The Millenarian World of Early Mormonism*, 137.
13. See, for example, Craig L. Blomberg, "Is Mormonism Christian?" 315–32.
14. See, for example, Jan Shipps, *Mormonism: The Story of a New Religious Tradition*.
15. Karen Armstrong, *A History of God: The 4000-Year Quest of Judaism, Christianity, and Islam*, xxi.

1

Theology, a Divine-Human Enterprise

Theology, coming from the Greek *theos* (God) and *logos* (word or discourse), has been defined as that area of study "which treats of the being and attributes of God, his relations to us, the dispensations of his providence, his will with respect to our actions, and his purposes with respect to our end."[1] Latter-day Saints derive their theological understanding primarily from the standard works (the Bible, Book of Mormon, Doctrine and Covenants, and Pearl of Great Price), which comprise the LDS canon of scripture. When clarification of the scriptures is needed, Saints generally turn to the sermons and writings of Church leaders or to other generally accepted doctrinal works such as the *Encyclopedia of Mormonism* or the Church-published *Gospel Principles*.

Although LDS leaders seek to ensure that the doctrines taught in the Church are orthodox and consistent, the Church has never published an "official" exposition of Mormon doctrines. James Faulconer, the Richard L. Evans Professor of Religious Understanding at Brigham Young University, describes Mormonism as being "a-theological," meaning that it is "without a church-sanctioned, church-approved, or even church-encouraged systematic theology."[2] Joseph Smith, the founding prophet of the Church, decried creedal pronouncements, claiming that they "set up stakes" and prevent one from further advancing in truth and understanding.[3] Rather than having a static doctrinal creed, Latter-day Saints are to let the revelations speak for themselves on doctrinal matters while continuing to remain open to further light and knowledge from the Lord.

Though Mormonism bases its teachings on divine revelation, this does not mean that Church teachings are entirely free of cultural influences. LDS scholar Terryl L. Givens explains, "We too often think that Joseph started with a clean slate, repudiating the entire

Christian past and starting out fresh, only teaching that which came to him direct from the Heavens; but he emphatically resisted any such expression."[4] Givens suggests that "syncretism" played a role in the development of Mormon thought, with many ideas being drawn from Joseph's own environment. This chapter looks at the divine-human interplay in the revelatory process and the significance this has had on theological development in both ancient and modern times.

Theological Conservatism and Liberalism

A spectrum of theological perspectives can be found in the Church ranging from conservative to liberal.[5] The late apostle Bruce R. McConkie, who exemplified the more conservative end of the spectrum, taught that correct beliefs on matters such as evolution and individual progression from one kingdom to another after the resurrection were crucial to one's salvation.[6] LDS scholar Lowell Bennion, whose writings were often characteristic of those near the liberal end, confided: "The two greatest contributions of religion, for me, are faith—faith in God, faith in Christ, faith in the meaning and purpose of life—and a clarification of life's values. . . . So instead of trying to get my description of reality out of the scriptures, as far as the nature of creation and the age of the earth go, . . . I decided those things have nothing to do with religion."[7] Both of these individuals led exemplary lives and served faithfully in the Church, and yet both held divergent views regarding the relevance of doctrinal teachings in the scriptures.

Latter-day Saints closer to the conservative end of the theological spectrum tend to view scripture as the infallible word of God and, therefore, doctrinally sound. Mormons towards the liberal end accept the scriptures as inspired, but may at the same time also perceive them to be human-informed and, therefore, not to be taken indiscriminately as the absolute truth. Consider, for example, scriptural passages indicating that there was no death on the earth prior to the fall of Adam, which, according to the Bible's chronology, occurred around four thousand years before Christ. The Book of Mormon states that if Adam had not fallen, "there would have been no death" (Alma 12:23), and "all things which were created must have remained in the same state in which they were after they were created; and they must have remained forever, and had no end" (2 Ne. 2:22). The book of Moses likewise attests that "by [Adam's] fall came death" (Moses 6:48, 59). Those who view scripture as the inerrant word of God either accept these declarations at face value, dismissing scientific evidence to the contrary, or look for ways to harmonize them with scientific evidence.[8] For example, some may argue that it was only in the Garden of Eden that there was no death prior to the Fall. On the other hand, those who are more liberal in their interpretation of scripture might be more inclined to see a human influence manifesting itself in these passages, perhaps reflecting the author's own literalistic understanding of the Genesis account.

Conservative Latter-day Saints, therefore, tend to take an inerrantist view of scripture, maintaining that, aside from translation and transcription errors,[9] the doctrinal teachings of scripture are without error or variation. The syllogistic reasoning seems to be:

God's word is without error or variation.[10]
Scripture is the word of God.
Therefore, scripture is without error or variation.

On the other hand, Mormons who are more liberal in their doctrinal thinking tend to take a less rigid stance toward scripture, seeing it as mediated through humans and, therefore, not entirely free from misconceptions and inconsistencies. This is not to say that they reject the inspiration of scripture, but rather that they reject the notion that inspiration necessarily implies inerrancy and uniformity. In other words, while a liberal perspective may accept the scriptures as the word of God, it does not see the scriptures as being literally God's words.

The Myth of Scriptural Inerrancy

Modern biblical scholarship generally agrees that the mediation of scripture through finite and fallible humans necessarily presents a limited and imperfect view of ultimate reality. In his massive work, *On Being a Christian*, Catholic scholar Hans Küng gives his assessment that the Bible "is unequivocally man's word: collected, written down, given varied emphasis, sentence by sentence by quite definite individuals and developed in different ways. Hence, it is not without shortcomings and mistakes, concealment and confusion, limitations and errors."[11] According to LDS theologian Blake T. Ostler, "The inspiration of scripture is not experienced by the prophet/writer free of human interpretation, cultural biases, and conceptual limitations."[12] Ostler notes that the consensus among critical biblical scholars is that, judging by the New Testament record, even "Jesus' teachings were culturally and temporally conditioned," and that "he had a human range of understanding and consciousness."[13]

In some instances scriptural writers themselves admit to expressing their own "judgment" (1 Cor. 7:25) and personal "opinion" (Alma 40:20) that may be subject to error. The Book of Mormon prophet Nephi acknowledged his own susceptibility to err in relating sacred truths "because of the weakness which is in me, according to the flesh" (1 Ne. 19:6). The Book of Mormon itself, which Joseph Smith called "the most correct book,"[14] has a disclaimer in its Title Page ascribing any imperfections it may have to man and not to God (see also Morm. 8:17).

It should be noted that when Church members vote to canonize inspired writings (i.e., add them to the official standard works), these writings become officially binding. However, this does not necessarily mean that they are without error. For example, the presiding councils and general assembly of the Church voted unanimously on August 17, 1835, to accept the *Lectures on Faith* as part of the Doctrine and Covenants,[15] even though the *Lectures* present the Godhead as consisting of only "two personages" (the Holy Ghost is depicted as an impersonal force) and regard only the Son, not the Father, as "a personage of tabernacle."[16] In 1921, well after it had become generally accepted that the Holy Ghost is also a personage and that God the Father has a physical body, the *Lectures* were removed from the Doctrine and Covenants, effectively becoming decanonized.[17]

Ostler suggests that, rather than viewing scripture as the pure word of God dictated to passive humans, scripture should be understood as the product of "creative coparticipation" with both divine and human imprint.[18] This is not to say that scripture is necessarily a heterogeneous mixture of divine and human voices. It may be that God works in and through the mind of his prophets so that the resultant Word is, according to LDS historian Grant Underwood, "both fully divine and fully human."[19] Princeton theologian Benjamin Warfield refers to this model of revelation as "concursus," which means that "the Scriptures are the joint product of divine and human activities, both of which penetrate them at every point, working harmoniously together to the production of a writing which is not divine here and human there, but at once divine and human in every part, every word and every particular."[20] Yale professor of divinity Brevard Childs gives a similar assessment:

> The divine and human dimensions of Scripture can never be separated as if there were a kernel and a husk, but the heart of the Bible lies in the mystery of how a fully time-conditioned writing, written by fragile human authors, can continually become the means of hearing the very Word of God, fresh and powerful, to recipients open to faithful response.[21]

Thus, many faithful scholars see evidence of culturally conditioned teachings in scripture without precluding them from also being God inspired.

The Myth of Doctrinal Uniformity

In addition to viewing the scriptures as essentially inerrant, there is also a tendency among many Latter-day Saints to view them as being uniformly consistent in the doctrines they teach. LDS religious scholar Philip Barlow notes that most Saints assume that "inconsequential details aside, all Bible theology is perfectly compatible with itself and with twentieth-century LDS conceptions."[22] Accordingly, Latter-day Saints are accustomed (and often encouraged) to interpret the Bible through the lens of modern LDS theology.

More discriminating LDS students of the scriptures frequently see variation in the doctrinal teachings of the scriptures and find that different prophetic authors had different theological perspectives. According to Barlow, these Saints are able to "give broad leeway to the human element in both ancient and contemporary scriptures."[23] They have come to believe, as many biblical scholars have long asserted, that scripture is human-conditioned and that therefore doctrinal paradigms may vary from author to author.

Biblical scholarship affirms that, far from presenting a single unified theology, the Bible contains a kaleidoscope of doctrines reflecting multiple theological perspectives. Felix Just, professor of theology at the University of San Francisco, writes:

> Deuteronomistic Theology is very different from Biblical Apocalyptic, and the theology of the Books of Kings contrasts sharply with that of the Prophet Jeremiah. The same is true within the New Testament: there are significant differences between Pauline and Johannine theologies, the theology of the Letter to the Hebrews differs from that of the Book of Revelation, and so forth.[24]

Blake Ostler similarly observes that "while the fundamentalist speaks of the biblical view of God or the biblical concept of justification, the more informed person speaks of biblical concepts [plural] of God, or concepts of justification, and views of humanity."[25]

Scholars see doctrinal change going back to the earliest Old Testament writings. As described by Catholic Bible scholar Gerald O'Collins, "Old Testament religious themes often remained fluid and not very sharply defined. Over the centuries, in response to new circumstances, key themes could be interpreted, reinterpreted, emphasized and marginalized."[26]

Many LDS scholars have similarly found that Mormonism also exhibits a changing theology, particularly during the first two decades of the Church. According to Philip Barlow, "Mormon perceptions evolved with astonishing rapidity through the 1830s and 1840s."[27] There is a sense among some scholars that this evolution of doctrine wasn't always linear or consistently cumulative, but that theological change was occasionally disruptive, with previous doctrines being overridden or even reversed. According to LDS historian Thomas G. Alexander,

> Perhaps the main barrier to understanding the development of Mormon theology is an underlying assumption by most Church members that there is a cumulative unity of doctrine. Mormons seem to believe that particular doctrines develop consistently, that ideas build on each other in hierarchical fashion. As a result, older revelations are interpreted by referring to current doctrinal positions. Thus, most members would suppose that a scripture or statement at any point in time has resulted from such orderly change. While this type of exegesis or interpretation may produce systematic theology and while it may satisfy those trying to understand and internalize current doctrine, it is bad history since it leaves an unwarranted impression of continuity and consistency.[28]

One example of doctrinal turn-about pertains to the priesthood ban for blacks. President Brigham Young stated in 1854 that blacks would never hold the priesthood until "all the other children of Adam have had the privilege of receiving the Priesthood . . . and have received their resurrection from the dead."[29] Elder Joseph Fielding Smith, eighty-one years later, similarly stated that this curse would continue "while time endures."[30] However, when the revelation opening the door for blacks to receive the priesthood was received in 1978, Bruce R. McConkie said, "Forget everything that I have said, or what President Brigham Young or President George Q. Cannon or whomsoever has said in days past that is contrary to the present revelation. We spoke with a limited understanding and without the light and knowledge that now has come into the world."[31] An inference which can be drawn from this is that Church leaders sometimes speak with "limited understanding" and that doctrines held at one period of time may later be superseded.

The authority to change doctrine is actually inherent in the calling of Church president. President J. Reuben Clark, a counselor in the First Presidency under David O. McKay, told Church members that "only the President of the Church . . . has the right to receive revelations for the Church, either new or amendatory, or to give authoritative interpretations of scripture that shall be binding on the Church, or change in any way the existing doctrines of the Church."[32] To state that the president has the right to "change" church doctrines implies that they are not necessarily fixed. Accordingly, a May 2007 release on the Church's LDS Newsroom website entitled "Approaching Church Doctrine" states, "The Church does not preclude future additions or changes to its teachings or practices."[33]

Those who view the teachings of scripture as absolute and unchangeable undoubtedly find the notion of theological change and discontinuity a bit unsettling. Others see changes in theology as the natural consequence of having a living, dynamic church guided by continuing revelation. James Faulconer notes, "One of the spin-offs in a belief in continuing revelation is an implicit refusal to allow theology to be set once and for all."[34] Continuing revelation, therefore, does not just fill in gaps of an incomplete but otherwise perfect theology; it also revises and sometimes even overturns previously held theological beliefs.

The Myth of Prophetic Infallibility

The myths of scriptural inerrancy and doctrinal uniformity are both part of the more general myth of prophetic infallibility. Significantly, the Church has never officially endorsed the doctrine of prophetic infallibility. "Consider the irony," quipped LDS scholar Keith Norman, "Roman Catholic doctrine proclaims the pope to be infallible, but most Catholics don't really believe it; whereas Mormon doctrine rejects the idea of infallible leaders, but we Mormons refuse to accept that."[35]

When considering the doctrinal teachings of General Authorities of the Church, it should be noted that the calling to be a general ecclesiastical authority does not automatically make one a doctrinal authority. Bruce R. McConkie explained, "Though general authorities are authorities in the sense of having power to administer Church affairs, they may or may not be authorities in the sense of doctrinal knowledge. . . . A call to an administrative position of itself adds little knowledge or power of discernment to an individual."[36] President George Q. Cannon asserted that even "the First Presidency cannot claim, individually or collectively, infallibility," and that "infallibility is not given to men."[37]

But, one might ask, isn't it better for Latter-day Saints to always defer to Church leaders and give them the benefit of the doubt than to be tentative or perhaps even skeptical? While there may be a certain virtue in respecting the authority of Church leaders in doctrinal matters, blindly accepting their teachings as the absolute truth may be more of a sign of credulity than genuine faith. President Hugh B. Brown, counselor to President David O. McKay, counseled that "while all Mormons should respect, support, and heed the teachings of the authorities of the Church, no one should accept a statement and base his or her testimony upon it, no matter who makes it, until he or she has, under mature examination, found it to be true and worthwhile."[38]

Much of the more vicious anti-Mormon literature written to date has been dependent upon this fallacious assumption of prophetic infallibility, and Saints who base their faith on this faulty assumption run the risk of painting themselves into a doctrinal corner. As the entry on "apostate" in the *Encyclopedia of Mormonism* states, "Apostasy may be accelerated by a faulty assumption that scripture or Church leaders are infallible. . . . Neither the Church nor its leaders and members claim infallibility."[39] Therefore, erring on the side of over-belief can cause one to stumble just as erring on the side of disbelief.

Proof-Texting

As shown above, one's outlook on the inerrancy and uniformity of scripture has a decided impact on how one interprets scripture. Additionally, one's own theological biases and presuppositions also color the way scriptures are read, which can sometimes lead to scriptural proof-texting. A proof-text is a scriptural passage lifted out of its original context and given an interpretation other than that which was originally intended—or at least as can be determined by the most reasonable reading of the text. BYU religion professor Stephen Robinson notes that even Latter-day Saints have a tendency to read Mormon beliefs into the Bible as proof-texts, largely because they assume that the doctrines of the Restoration are all corroborated in the Bible.[40] Most occurrences of proof-texting are the innocent result of careless or uninformed reading of the scriptures, though they can still be detrimental. When, however, one deliberately twists the meaning of a passage in order to justify a personal belief or bias, it is condemned in both the New Testament and the Book of Mormon as "wresting [i.e., twisting] the scriptures" (2 Pet. 3:16; Alma 13:20, 41:1).[41]

An example of proof-texting familiar to many LDS missionaries is the appeal to Revelation 22:18 to criticize the Mormon canonization of additional scriptures. This objection is based on the latter half of this verse which reads, "If any man shall add unto these things, God shall add unto him the plagues that are written in this book." Mormon missionaries correctly point out, however, that the first part of this verse makes it clear that "these things" refer to "the words of the prophecy of this book" (i.e., the book of Revelation) and not to the entire Bible, which had not yet been compiled. Thus, this proof-text requires the passage to be taken out of context in order to have its purported meaning.

Some biblical proof-texts are attributable to known errors in the King James translation and become exposed once the correct (or better) translation is rendered. One such example is Isaiah 28:10: "For precept must be upon precept, precept upon precept; line upon line, line upon line; here a little, and there a little." This passage is frequently quoted in LDS gospel discussions to show that God imparts knowledge incrementally. While God may indeed reveal truth "precept upon precept" and "line upon line," scholars note that this isn't what the original Hebrew conveys. LDS Bible scholar Kevin Barney explains that the Hebrew actually expresses "either baby talk ('goo goo gah gah') or, even more likely, a portion of a child's spelling lesson."[42] Whichever the case, it is not saying that the Lord will give unto the leaders of Ephraim (to whom Isaiah is speaking) "precept upon precept," but rather the foreign babble of the Assyrians who will soon invade their land. This is, in fact, the explanation given in verse 11: "For with stammering lips and another tongue will he [the Lord] speak to this people." Notably, the modern proof-text usage of this passage seems to appear in the Book of Mormon when, following the Isaiah chapters in 2 Nephi, the Lord is quoted as saying, "I will give unto the children of men line upon line, precept upon precept, here a little and there a little" (2 Ne. 28:30; see also D&C 98:12; 128:21). The way in which the Book of Mormon abbreviates and reverses ("line upon line" appearing before "precept upon precept") the wording of KJV Isaiah 28:10 also happens to correspond to the way this passage was commonly paraphrased in Joseph Smith's day to describe the manner in which God imparts knowledge.[43] This, of course, leads to the logical question of whether the Book of Mormon is perpetuating this modern proof-text in its use of Isaiah 28:10, or if Joseph Smith was merely "adapting" the KJV language of Isaiah 28:10 to express Nephi's thought.

A Christian proof-text popularized in post-New Testament times is Zechariah 13:6: "And one shall say unto him, What are these wounds in thine hands? Then he shall answer, Those with which I was wounded in the house of my friends." Latter-day Saints, like many other Christians, interpret this passage as a prophecy of Christ.[44] The Doctrine and Covenants (D&C 45:51–52) alludes to Zechariah 13:6 in this way and even adds wounds to the "feet," which makes the fit more obvious. According to most biblical scholars, the wounds referred to in Zechariah are actually in the chest (the Hebrew reads "between" the hands) and, in the context of Zechariah 13:2–6, were inflicted on "the [false] prophets" in Israel (v. 4).[45] The NRSV uses the pronouns "they" and "them" throughout verses 2–6, making it clear that verse 6 is speaking of the same false prophets alluded to in verse 4. Pagan prophets were often self-lacerated (Lev. 19:28; Deut. 14:1; 1 Kgs. 18:28) for reasons that are not entirely clear. Methodist Bible commentator Adam Clarke censured popular Christian applications of this verse to Christ noting that it was clearly referring to false prophets who alleged that they had received these marks in their own families when, more likely, the wounds "had been dedicated to . . . idols."[46] From a purely contextual reading, this passage is recognized by scholars (LDS and non-LDS) as a prophecy of the destruction awaiting the false prophets in Israel because of their lies and deceit (see Zech. 13:2–4).[47]

Critical scholars see numerous proof-texts in the Bible itself, a result of later scriptural writers interpreting earlier scriptural texts to suit their own purposes. Scores of Old Testament passages, originally having other meanings, are interpreted in the New Testament as having reference to Christ's ministry. Describing what he saw as a veritable pattern among New Testament writers, Franciscan scholar Bellarmino Bagatti wrote, "The method of procedure adopted consisted in this: first take a deed or saying in the life of Jesus, and then proceed to find the biblical text which could explain it."[48] Matthew, for example, alludes to Hosea 11:1: "When Israel was a child, then I loved him, and called my son out of Egypt"; he then applies it as a prophecy of Christ's infancy in Egypt (Matt. 2:15), even though in its original context it had reference to the historical exodus of Israel from Egypt.[49] Matthew also cites Jeremiah 31:15 ("A voice was heard in Ramah, lamentation, and bitter weeping; Rachel weeping for her children refused to be comforted for her children, because they were not") as a reference to Herod's slaughter of Bethlehem's male children, while the original context referred to the slaughtering of Jerusalem's inhabitants and the Babylonian exile of the children of Israel (Jer. 31:16). There is perhaps no harm in finding shadows and types of Christ in these passages, but one should not confuse later allegorical meanings with the originally intended meaning.

A final and somewhat amusing proof-text draws on Zechariah 9:9, which speaks of Israel's "king" entering Jerusalem "riding upon an ass, and upon a colt." Matthew cites this passage to show that Christ's triumphal entry into Jerusalem was foretold in prophecy (see Matt. 21:2–7). He mistakenly assumes, however, that Zechariah was claiming that the person would be riding on both an ass *and* a colt. As Old Testament scholar W. Sibley Towner explains, Matthew "fails to take into consideration the parallelism of the Hebrew poetry (*donkey* is equivalent to *colt*) when it has Jesus riding on two donkeys at once."[50] In the Church's official magazine, *Ensign*, Kevin Barney suggests that Matthew probably improvised the historical account of Christ's entry, adding both colt and ass, so that it would fulfill the language of Zechariah.[51] The imagery of a king riding into Jerusalem makes it suitable for appropriation into the gospel narrative; however, in Zechariah, the event has an end-time setting with judgment poured out on the wicked (Zech. 9:1–8), the king taking over worldly governments, and peace reigning universally (Zech. 9:10). Thus, this passage doesn't really fit the time and situation of Jesus.[52] What this proof-text illustrates is that New Testament writers not only drew on Old Testament passages as proof-texts to bolster their witness of Christ, but they sometimes embellished events to better accommodate these proof-texts. New Testament scholar James Dunn cites several examples in the New Testament where Old Testament passages are taken out of context, substantively altered to fit a different context or used to create a new context.[53]

The fact that New Testament writers found new significance in Old Testament prophecies (and even in historical references that weren't prophecies at all), doesn't mean that they were deceitful or even necessarily ignorant of Old Testament meanings. Scholars explain that it was a common practice among the more than twenty-four Jewish sects active at the time of Christ to use Old Testament proof-texts to legitimize their own particular religious movements.[54] Biblical scholar Joachim Becker notes, "The New Testament proceeds by means of an exegetical [i.e., interpretive] method common in late Judaism, which undertakes a concrete application to the present situation without regard for the original statement and its concomitant historical consciousness."[55] The appropriation of Old Testament scriptures to support New Testament Christianity is found throughout the New Testament and even in many of the teachings attributed to Jesus.[56]

The history of theology is thus best understood when it is recognized that scriptural texts have been reinterpreted with each successive era to create new scripture and new theological ideas. Evangelical Bible scholar Dewey Beegle writes, "There are numerous biblical examples of theological interpretations of one generation being revised slightly or even rejected by another."[57] The 1994 Catholic Pontifical Biblical Commission expressed a similar view: "From its very inception the Bible has been itself a work of interpretation. . . . In the course of the Bible's formation, the writings of which it consists were in many cases reworked and reinterpreted so as to make them respond to new situations previously unknown."[58]

LDS scripture and authoritative commentary seem to follow this same tradition of reinterpretation and reformulation to accommodate new times and changing paradigms. The Book of Mormon, for example, contains numerous Old Testament and even New Testament passages, sometimes with subtle changes, to reinforce the message of the Restoration. Mark Thomas, whose expertise lies in the interface of the Book of Mormon and its nineteenth-century milieu, observes that "the Book of Mormon uses the Bible as proof text, as a springboard to new revelation and creativity."[59] Joseph Smith frequently appropriated biblical texts to establish scriptural grounding for the doctrines he introduced. Noteworthy is the fact that many of the passages he appropriated are considered by scholars to be themselves proof-texts from yet more ancient texts.

Because Joseph Smith appears to have used biblical proof-texts to support some of his teachings, many critics of Mormonism have labeled him as a false prophet. But as New Testament scholar Anthony Hutchinson puts it: "It seems that if anything, the presence of imaginative midrashic technique, pseudonymous authorship, and the reworking of doctrines and texts in Joseph Smith tends to ally him more with the ancient prophets of Israel and authors of the Bible than it separates him from them."[60] There is arguably nothing inherently wrong with finding new applications and secondary or typological meanings in scripture. Indeed, many see this as being God's way of breathing new meaning into older texts. The challenge, of course, is knowing when it is God who is doing the breathing.

Mining the Theology of the Scriptures

This book examines how LDS doctrines taught today were understood in early Mormonism and even earlier biblical times. In ferreting out the doctrinal beliefs expressed in the Old and New Testaments, I rely heavily on the interpretations of critical biblical scholars, realizing that many Latter-day Saints are skeptical and even dismissive of the way in which these scholars interpret the Bible—especially when these scholars disagree with traditional LDS interpretations. Admittedly, biblical scholars are not always correct, nor do they always agree among themselves. They do, however, provide informative insights that can add measurably to our understanding of the theological world of the Bible. BYU religion professor Brian Hauglid observes,

> Some Latter-day Saints may fear that biblical criticism means calling into question significant saving doctrines or even the divinity of Jesus Christ. Perhaps some biblical scholars tend to approach the discipline of biblical textual criticism in this way. However, one caution in the field is to recognize and beware of our own set of presuppositions and biases. Ideally, the idea is to try to let the text speak for itself, to avoid prooftexting.[61]

Critical Bible scholars have been trained to interpret the records of the past in much the same way skilled archeologists make sense of artifacts while sifting through successive strata of the earth. While one goal of both the theologian and the archeologist is to look for similarities and unifying characteristics among different periods, another is to identify the distinctive features of each period. When attempting to characterize a particular era, precaution is used to keep artifacts and data sorted by era and avoid making artificial assumptions about one period based on findings from other periods. Of course the reverse precaution is to avoid making artificial distinctions between artifacts of different periods when no such distinction actually exists.

Not surprisingly, the older the period, the more difficult it is to make correct assessments about the world view and theological beliefs of that period. Catholic scholar Raymond E. Brown observes: "No matter how earnestly modern Christians may affirm that they hold nothing except what is found in Scripture, they are so far from the worldview of the Old Testament and New Testament authors that they cannot look at spiritual realities the way those authors did."[62] Even scholars must rely on inference and conjecture for many of the conclusions they draw regarding biblical theology.

To avoid (as much as possible) imposing later doctrinal beliefs on earlier religious texts, the doctrines surveyed in this book will be examined chronologically, starting with the Old Testament and progressing through the New Testament, early nineteenth-century evangelical Protestantism, early Mormonism, the Nauvoo period, and current LDS commentary. What follows is a brief overview of some of the theological assumptions and tendencies that critical scholars believe characterize each of these periods.

Old Testament Theology

"The Old Testament did not come to expression in a vacuum," notes Protestant biblical scholar Greg Herrick.[63] The Israelites were influenced by Canaanite worldviews and adopted many Canaanite customs and beliefs—even when they strenuously denounced many of them as idolatrous.[64] Strands in Old Testament theology developed gradually over many centuries, paralleling ideas and practices found in neighboring Near Eastern religions; these include temple building, sacrificial offerings, circumcision, and the belief that one's local tribal gods were more powerful than those of neighboring tribes. According to Arvid Kapelrud, professor of Old Testament and ancient Near Eastern religions at the University of Oslo, "Over and over again the Old Testament shows that the Israelites did not only borrow from the Canaanite ways of worship but constantly relapsed into them."[65] As for doctrinal uniformity, many biblical scholars contend that there is hardly a doctrine in the Old Testament that is articulated consistently throughout the text of the Hebrew scriptures, including the nature of God, the creation, the hereafter, humanity's duty to God, and Israel's covenant relationship with God.[66]

The impression one gets from reading the Old Testament is that the early Israelites and Hebrews had a naïve, parochial view of God and the universe, which reflected their tribal, nomadic culture.[67] Ronald Hendel, a professor of Hebrew Bible and Jewish studies at the University of California, Berkeley, observes that "the portrayal of the natural world in Genesis . . . belongs to the worldview of its time—a geocentric [earth-centered] universe with light and the earth created before the sun, and with the stars, sun, and moon attached to the surface of the dome of heaven."[68] In the Old Testament, people are blessed for obedience to God, but only in this life. (The idea of an afterlife was a late development in Hebrew thought.) Not only does much of the theology expressed in the Old Testament lie outside the framework of current LDS thinking, but it also lies outside the larger Christian theological tradition. Though the Old Testament speaks of God's dealings with his covenant people and the importance of obedience to his laws, there are no clear and explicit references to Jesus Christ and his gospel. Thus, many scholars suggest that to get at Old Testament theology, one should refrain from imposing modern Christian paradigms onto Old Testament narratives.

Another assumption of many today is that the Old Testament prophets had a clear view of the distant future and spoke directly of events in modern times. Furthermore, it is often thought that these ancient prophets foretold all of the significant events in the history of God's dealings with humankind. Critical scholars note, however, that the Old Testament prophets were more forthtellers than foretellers, with their attention being focused on immediate times and situations, preaching hard-to-hear truths about the inevitable consequences of sin. They explain that Amos's pronouncement that "the Lord God will do nothing, but he revealeth his secret unto his servants the prophets" (Amos 3:7) has more to do with the Lord forewarning the wicked of imminent punishment (see vv. 1–6; 7:10–17) than with foretelling every act of God. John Barton, professor of interpretation at the University of Oxford (U.K.) explains that Amos 3 specifically addresses God's condemnation and judgment on the wicked and that Amos 3:7 merely "makes the point that the Lord always reveals impending judgment in advance."[69] The Old Testament prophetic model is perhaps best epitomized in the Lord's calling of Ezekiel: "I have made you a sentinel for the house of Israel; whenever you hear a word from my mouth, you shall give them warning from me" (NRSV Ezek. 3:17).

Critical Bible scholars see little evidence that Old Testament prophets had a view of distant future events, including the life and mission of Christ. Prophets, they contend, spoke to people in their own day addressing contemporary issues and making sense of their current situation—much the same way Latter-day Saints view their prophets today.[70] According to Raymond Brown,

This conception of prophecy as prediction of the distant future has disappeared from most serious scholarship today, and it is widely recognized that the New Testament "fulfillment" of the Old Testament involved much that the Old Testament writers did not foresee at all. The Old Testament prophets were primarily concerned with addressing God's challenge to their own times. If they spoke about the future, it was in broad terms of what would happen if the challenge was accepted or rejected.[71]

Critical scholars further note that when prophets spoke of events that would take place in the *last* days, they weren't speaking of *our* day, but rather perceived themselves as living at or near the last days of the world when the events they spoke of would be fulfilled.[72]

Scholars suggest that it is much easier to understand and make sense of biblical prophecies when they are considered in the ancient setting in which they were given. David P. Wright, a professor of biblical and ancient Near Eastern studies at Brandeis University, notes, "Much of [the] perception of complexity and obscurity in the prophets can be seen as due to the imperfect fit between contemporizing interpretation and the actual, original, and full contextual meaning of the prophetic passages."[73] Prophecies may have typological application to distant future (and even multiple) events, but their original meaning is best understood when read in light of the historical context in which they were given and with sensitivity to the more immediate concerns they expressed.

Traditional understandings of prophecies that identify specific people and places well into the future—such as Isaiah 44:28, which names Cyrus as the liberator of Israel 150 years prior to his birth—have also come under the scrutiny of modern scholarship. Both critical and many conservative scholars categorize these types of prophecies as pseudepigraphic—meaning that they weren't really uttered or written by the individual credited with them but were composed by pseudonymous authors well after the lifetime of the prophets whose names were attached to the prophecies.[74] Also referred to as *vaticinium ex eventu* ("prophecy after the fact"), these writings present historical events as though they were prophecies of the future in order to convince readers that, just as prophecies of events up to the time of the real writer had been fulfilled to the minutest detail, so will prophecies of yet future events (usually an assurance of rescue on the immediate horizon of the actual time of writing) likewise surely come to pass.

Critical scholars note that when Old Testament prophets actually did speak of future events, many of these prophecies never materialized. Wright notes that, although Old Testament prophets foretold Israel turning from its sins and returning from captivity to a glorious kingdom, "the propensities of the people to sin remained the same; only some, not all, of the Israelites returned to the land; the Judeans remained dominated by foreign nations; the rebuilt temple and Jerusalem were not as glorious as expected; Ezekiel's ideal temple was not built; [and] the Davidic dynasty was not restored."[75] According to Robert Carroll, a lecturer in Old Testament at the University of Glasgow,

> Attempts to revive that [Davidic] dynasty supported by the prophets Haggai and Zechariah came to nothing. The larger hopes for peace and prosperity also were substantially unrealized. The two nations [Judah and Israel] did not merge but rather the survivors of both became more sharply separated. The only elements of the general hopes that could be said to have been realized in any sense were the survival of a community centred on Jerusalem and a rebuilt temple as its focus.[76]

Those who acknowledge a human dimension in scripture are content to allow for what appears to be lapses in prophetic fulfillment. Those who see scripture as the infallible word of God, however, prefer to believe that some form of typological, if not literal, fulfillment is still on the horizon.

New Testament Theology

The New Testament builds on Old Testament and intertestamental teachings, expanding and reinterpreting them in light of the Christ message. While Latter-day Saints and conservative Christians tend to view Christianity as a new and higher belief system brought to earth by Jesus, critical scholar Richard Hooker points out that Christianity "was continuous with a variety of traditions, philosophies, and religious practices, and synthesized all of these into a new structure."[77] The predominant influence on earliest Christianity was first-century Judaism, which was the tradition and background of the first Christians.

An understanding of contemporary Jewish beliefs can shed light on many New Testament teachings and imagery. With the exception of Luke, the authors of the New Testament were all Jews who wrote from a Jewish perspective. Jesus himself was a Jew who naturally would have thought and taught in Jewish categories. Although Jesus denounced the sanctimoniousness of the Pharisaic Jews, religious historian Karen Armstrong notes that "many of his sayings, recorded in the gospel, were similar to the teachings of the Pharisees."[78] Judaism was such an integral part of early Christianity that for the first few decades of the church it was believed that a non-Jewish convert must first become a Jew to become a Christian (Acts 15:1–5, 24).

Greco-Roman culture was another influential element on the New Testament writers who spoke Greek and lived in a largely Hellenized world. "We should not forget," reminds Dunn, "that a significant section of the earliest Jerusalem community spoke, worshipped and theologized in Greek from the start."[79] Such concepts as the afterlife, the logos (the "Word" of John 1:1), gods having offspring, and the potential for a mortal to achieve divine status at death—which was Paul's explanation of how Christ became divine—were all familiar to the Greeks. The early church father Justin Martyr, a second-century philosopher converted to Christianity, saw striking parallels between Christianity and Greek philosophy. These included Christian teachings about Christ being "born of God in a peculiar manner," being called the "word of God," and "being born of a virgin." He noted that these were the same assertions that the Greeks made about the sons of their gods.[80] Critical scholars suggest that the New Testament authors likely picked up or adapted some of these ideas from their Greek culture. On the other hand, those who view early Christianity as an entirely revealed religion may see ideological similarities as either intending to prepare people for Christianity or perhaps an attempt by Satan to discredit Christianity.

Though a consistent theme in the New Testament is "Jesus Christ and him crucified" (1 Cor. 2:2), the doctrines of the New Testament, like those of the Old Testament, are not always consistent. Ostler identifies three conflicting views on divorce alone which, he notes, "hardly touch the tip of the proverbial iceberg."[81] Scholars see much of the diversity in New Testament doctrines as symptomatic of different underlying theologies. A different theological framework, for example, is said to exist between the teachings of Paul, which are the earliest available writings, and the later Gospels. The latest writings are generally considered to be those of John, who wrote near the end of the first century and expressed some of the most esoteric theological ideas found in the New Testament.

Critical scholars note that New Testament prophecies, like those in the Old Testament, appear to be near-sighted, addressing pressing issues of the time instead of events that would take place two millennia in the future. For example, according to most critical scholars, Christ's prophecy on the Mount of Olives (Mark 13; cf. Matt. 24), which most Christians (including Latter-day Saints) believe predicts modern-day events, doesn't actually go beyond the events surrounding the destruction of the Jewish temple at the hands of the Romans near A.D. 70.[82] Moreover, many argue that it may have actually been written after the temple had been destroyed, making it yet another prophecy given after the fact.[83]

The book of Revelation likewise speaks of events already in progress and of impending retribution on the Roman persecutors. James Charlesworth, a professor of New Testament language and literature at Princeton University, observes that there is unanimous consensus among critical scholars, "whether it's Roman Catholic, Protestant or Jewish," that John the Revelator was addressing "a community at the end of the first century, and he's trying to give them meaning for their lives."[84] The angel forbade John to even seal up his prophecy because the time of its fulfillment was "at hand" (Rev. 22:10). The anticipated immediacy of events to take place and urgency in tone of New Testament writers suggest that they perceived themselves as living in the last days of the world. Their predictions focused primarily on God's rescuing the church from its current persecution before Christ's imminent return. Like Old Testament prophecies, many New Testament prophecies appear to have lapsed and were therefore recast by later Christians to refer to yet future times.

Early Nineteenth-Century Christian Theology

A burgeoning Christian movement in Joseph Smith's day was Protestant evangelicalism—not to be confused with modern-day conservative evangelical Protestantism. According to Mark Noll, a historian of American Christianity, "evangelicalism . . . [was] the nation's dominant faith by the early decades of the nineteenth century."[85] The doctrines of evangelicalism had their roots in New Testament theology but were also shaped by centuries of theological debates and the religious controversies emerging from the Reformation. Evangelical theology and practice had a recognizable influence on early Mormonism. Just as ancient Israelite beliefs were influenced by other Near Eastern ideas, and early Christianity was influenced by Jewish and Hellenistic thinking, early LDS thought was partially shaped by nineteenth-century American evangelicalism. Many early Mormon converts came from these Protestant movements, and Joseph Smith, who was personally drawn to Methodism in his youth (JS–H 1:8), claimed to have had "intimate acquaintance"[86] with their activities and preaching.

Grant Underwood characterized this general evangelical movement as being primitivist (attempting to restore the original Christian doctrine and church), millenarian (looking forward to the imminent return of Christ, the destruction of the wicked, and the reign of righteousness on the earth), and charismatic (given to the outward gifts of the Spirit such as healing, the gift of tongues, and prophecy).[87] In May 1836, early Mormon apostle Parley P. Pratt wrote a letter from England describing the Irvingites and their striking parallels to early Mormonism, noting that they preached the gathering of Israel,

Christ's second coming and personal millennial reign on the earth, the apostasy of the Gentile church, the need for an organization with authority from God, and the need to revive spiritual gifts.[88] The Irvingites, like many other reformers and restorationists at the time, believed that a universal apostasy had followed the death of the apostles. They further saw themselves as the select body that would restore Christ's church with a foundation of twelve apostles.[89]

Similarities between nineteenth-century evangelicalism and Mormonism can be (and have been) explained in a number of ways. First, they may be attributable to the cultural influences common to the Second Great Awakening. Most secular historians point to this explanation, stating that economic, political, and cultural forces all combined to produce similar religious movements. Alternatively, evangelical teachings may be viewed as counterfeit doctrines in which Satan imitated the truth to keep people from the true restored gospel. Joseph Smith, for example, remarked that the Irvingites (discussed above) "counterfeited the truth perhaps the nearest of any of our modern sectarians."[90] A third possibility is that these movements were all inspired by the same spirit that was being "pour[ed] out . . . upon all flesh" (Joel 2:28; proof-text intended), leading different people to the same truth along different avenues. In a related sense, evangelicalism may have been a preparatory movement to the restoration of the fullness of the gospel. Thomas Ward, editor of the *Millennial Star*, the Church's newspaper in England, wrote in 1843 that "the Lord permitted the propagation of those principles [i.e., the teachings of Primitivist sects such as Campbellism] as a forerunner to the fullness of the gospel, though its advocates knew it not."[91]

As a final explanation of Mormon and evangelical similarities, Joseph Smith may have consciously or unconsciously borrowed familiar evangelical beliefs to fill in the theological gaps which had not yet been elucidated by revelation.[92] This explanation sees Mormonism as an eclectic religion—the result of Joseph Smith's composite experience with religion. While freely appropriating familiar doctrines to build this new faith, he also liberally modified and sometimes contradicted them to fit his own developing doctrinal understanding. Obviously, these explanations are not all mutually exclusive and a combination of factors may have come into play.

Early Mormon Theology

The earliest LDS theological ideas (1828–30) are articulated most plainly in the Book of Mormon and are not unlike many evangelical doctrines being taught in Joseph Smith's own community. Initial attacks against Mormonism were not directed so much at its theology as they were at the claim that Joseph had received ancient gold plates from God. The Book of Mormon employs familiar early nineteenth-century rhetoric to address doctrinal issues being debated during Joseph Smith's day, prompting Alexander Campbell's cynical comment that the Book of Mormon "decides all the great controversies," including "infant baptism," "the trinity," "the fall of man," "the atonement," and many others.[93] In spite of the impressive evidence assembled by LDS apologists linking the Book of Mormon to ancient Judaism, Mark Thomas has contended that "on all major theological issues (the doctrines of god, humanity, and salvation), . . . the Book of Mormon consistently takes the nineteenth-century position most foreign to the ancient Jewish thought from which the book purports to spring."[94]

An increasingly popular theory used to explain the presence of nineteenth-century evangelical rhetoric in what otherwise appears to be an ancient religious history is the view that the Book of Mormon is the co-creation of both God and Joseph Smith. In his version of this theory, called the "expansion theory" of the Book of Mormon, Blake Ostler states, "It seems to me that the Book of Mormon makes most sense if it is seen as both a revelation to Joseph Smith and as Joseph's expansions of the text."[95] Explaining the concursive nature of these textual expansions, Ostler writes,

> The presence of translator anachronisms or expansions in the book show that Joseph imposed an interpretation on the text which was foreign to the ancient text, but not an interpretation alien to his revelatory experiences which produced the book. In other words, he did not perceive the ancient text and then consciously interpret it as he pleased; rather, the text is the revelation he experienced within his own conceptual paradigms.[96]

Terryl Givens, in his study on the Book of Mormon, writes that he finds this expansion theory "appealing," and cites Richard Bushman's observation that it is "attracting more and more fairly faithful church members."[97] Givens adds that "New Testament scholar Krister Stendahl, one of the few non-Mormon academics to look closely at LDS scripture, . . . clearly sees the text [of the Book of Mormon] as a nineteenth-century expansion and application of ancient material."[98]

It is noteworthy that the doctrines expressed in the Book of Mormon tend to bear closer similarity to those found in early nineteenth-century Protestantism than to those in later Mormonism. For example, the Book of Mormon and original *Book of Commandments* (the precursor to the Doctrine and Covenants) say nothing about the need to comply with higher ordinances necessary for exaltation—such as ordination to the Melchizedek Priesthood, the temple endowment, and the rite of eternal marriage. On the contrary, the Book of Mormon expressly states that faith, repentance, baptism, and the gift of the Holy Ghost are alone sufficient for salvation and that "whatsoever is is more or less than this cometh of evil" (3 Ne. 11:40). There is no explicit concept of different Aaronic and Melchizedek Priesthoods in the Book of Mormon (only different "holy callings")—even after Christ's visit in which he established his church in its fullness among them. There is no doctrine about differing degrees of glory (only a traditional heaven and hell). And not only is there no hint of vicarious work for the dead, but the Book of Mormon teaches that those who die without hearing the gospel automatically inherit eternal life—just like little children who die before being baptized (Mosiah 15:24; cf. 3:11; Moro. 8:22). These are all teachings that were espoused by various evangelical denominations in Joseph Smith's day. It is certainly conceivable that the people of the Book of Mormon didn't have all the gospel teachings that Saints have today (even though they presumably had the "fulness of the gospel"), but one wonders why virtually none of the doctrines that would later distinguish Mormonism from other Christian faiths is to be found in the Book of Mormon.

The specificity with which the Book of Mormon prophesies of the Christian era, the colonization of America, and Joseph Smith's work relative to the Book of Mormon is also noteworthy. Robert M. Price, professor of theology and scriptural studies at Johnnie Coleman Theological Seminary and editor of the *Journal of Higher Criticism*, has observed that the Book of Mormon has the markings of a pseudepigraphic work in that it prophesies of events in great detail up to the time of the coming forth of the Book of Mormon itself—events of which Joseph Smith would have obviously had knowledge—but then treats events after the time of its publication in terms that are general, vague, and in some cases different from the way history has actually played out.[99] Mormon critics point out, for example, that the Lamanites have not trodden down the gentiles as prophesied (3 Ne. 21:12–13). As we shall see in Chapter 18, apologists account for such apparent lapses with explanations that to them seem perfectly reasonable.

Nauvoo-Period Theology

Beginning with the Kirtland era and accelerating into the Nauvoo period (1835–44), Joseph Smith began advancing bold new doctrines that went well beyond (and sometimes against) his own earlier teachings. It is during this period that Mormon theology really began to diverge from its evangelical roots. The fact that members were able to remain faithful during such turbulent theological times is a testament to their implicit faith in being led by a living prophet.

Marvin Hill, an LDS historian of early Mormonism, observed that "it was not disturbing to most Mormons when some initial ideas were brushed aside, and the Saints were generally more concerned that the process of revelation continue than that old ideas be harmonized with the new."[100] Notwithstanding the theological adaptability of many, however, "each time a new stratum of theology and doctrine was imposed on existing belief and practice, a substantial number of Smith's followers were disturbed enough to leave."[101]

It is noteworthy that early in Joseph Smith's prophetic career his teachings reflected a more figurative interpretation of the scriptures. Later in life, however, he seems to have favored a more literal interpretation.[102] For example, in 1832 he interpreted the four beasts in Revelation 4:6 to be "figurative expressions" (D&C 77:2); but in 1843 he asserted that John saw "actual" beasts in heaven, and that "the four beasts were four of the most noble animals that had filled the measure of their creation, and had been saved from other worlds." In the same sermon, he insisted that "there is no revelation . . . to show that the beasts meant any thing but beasts."[103] Similarly, he initially clarified that the beast spoken of in Revelation 13:1 was a "sign, in the likeness of the kingdoms on earth" (JST Rev. 13:1). A decade later, however, he declared, "The beast John saw was an actual beast to whom power was to be given . . . to destroy the inhabitants of the earth."[104] The Book of Mormon speaks of the gentiles becoming "numbered" as the seed of Abraham (1 Ne. 14:2; 2 Ne. 10:18; 3 Ne. 16:13, 30:2), but in 1839, Joseph Smith speaks more literally: "The effect of the Holy Ghost upon a Gentile is to purge out the old blood & make him actually of the seed of Abraham."[105] In answer to the question, "What is the rule of interpretation [of scripture]?" his 1843 response was, "Just no interpretation at all; it should be understood precisely as it reads."[106]

This later literalistic propensity of the Prophet may partially account for some of the more radical teachings he later began introducing—such as serpents having legs in the Garden of Eden,[107] the need to restore blood sacrifices,[108] and the corporeality of God. This doesn't mean that such teachings weren't inspired, only that their emergence seems to have been facilitated by the development of more literalistic interpretive tendencies.

LDS teachings on temple worship, preexistence, and the cosmos during the Nauvoo era seem to resonate with ideas in contemporary Masonry and hermetic traditions which were publicized in Joseph Smith's day.[109] The Prophet's quotations from the apocrypha and Jewish midrash are evidence that he was intrigued by legendary and sometimes mystical ideas. Several of his innovative teachings pertaining to Elohim and the idea of a head God seem to be linked to his growing knowledge of Hebrew, in which he received tutoring during the Kirtland and Nauvoo periods.

Like ancient Biblical prophecies, prophetic utterances of Joseph Smith also tended to address more pressing issues of immediate interest than events that would happen in the more distant future. And while many of his predictions had recognizable fulfillment, others appear to have gone unfulfilled. For example, on April 14, 1842, the Prophet told the newly organized Relief Society, "I now deliver it as a prophecy that before ten years shall roll round, the queens of the earth shall come and pay their respects to this Society—they shall come with their millions and shall contribute of their abundance for the relief of the poor."[110] As it so happened, no such visits or contributions were ever made by "the queens of the earth" in the next "ten years." On December 16, 1843, the Nauvoo City Council heard the Prophet say, "I prophecy [sic] by virtue of the Holy Priesthood vested in me [and] in the name of Jesus Christ that if Congress will not hear our petition and grant us protection they shall be broken up as a government and God shall damn them. There shall nothing be left of them, not even a grease spot."[111] Congress ignored the petition, and yet the government withstood the Civil War twenty years later. What these and other examples illustrate is that modern prophetic utterances, even when spoken in the name of the Lord, are not always to be taken as the infallible word of God. LDS President of the Seventy B. H. Roberts explained one such apparently errant prophecy Joseph received through a seer stone stating, "The Prophet, overwrought in his deep anxiety for the progress of the work, saw reflected in the 'Seer Stone' his own thought, or that suggested to him by his brother Hyrum, rather than the thought of God."[112] The implication is that prophets may not always be able to discern between their own thoughts and impressions that come from God.

Later Mormon Theology

In the mid 1800s, after the Saints migrated west, radical doctrines continued to be advanced by President Brigham Young and other Mormon leaders, including his teaching that Adam is God the Father and that God continues to advance in knowledge and power (see Chapter 7). Young expected the Saints to embrace these teachings, proclaiming in 1870, "I have never yet preached a sermon and sent it out to the children of men, that they may not call scripture."[113] Today, these same teachings, including this self-proclaimed canonization of his sermons, are generally dismissed as being Young's own opinion and not given as "official" pronouncements.

During the end of the nineteenth century and into the twentieth century, several of the more radical doctrines of Mormonism, such as

God's ongoing progression in knowledge and power, the identification of Adam as God the Father, plural marriage, and the sealing of men to prominent Church leaders,[114] were abandoned. Many of the distinctive doctrines introduced by Joseph Smith have persisted, however, which continue to set Mormon theology apart from mainstream Christian theology. Over the past century and a half, doctrinal expositors in the Church have focused largely on synthesizing the teachings of the scriptures and Church leaders into a single, unified theology.

One trend evident in modern doctrinal discourse is a return to the more Protestant-like theology of early Mormon scripture (particularly the Book of Mormon). Kendall White points out that modern LDS scholarship "has disclosed the essential Protestant flavor of earliest Mormon beliefs"[115] and that current LDS theological discourse is more consistent with its original Protestant roots. BYU religion professor Robert Millet, for one, welcomed this return to "the Book of Mormon and the redemptive theology set forth therein" calling it "long overdue."[116]

A growing tendency among LDS scholars is to view biblical prophecies, particularly in the Old Testament, as actually referring to more contemporary events and only typologically applicable to events in the distant future such as the Atonement, the coming forth of the Book of Mormon, and the restoration of the gospel. This trend provides more accommodation to—and hence more fruitful dialogue with—modern biblical scholarship; however, it raises concerns among more conservative Latter-day Saints who see it as diminishing the impact that prophecies have traditionally had in reinforcing the message of the Restoration.

Notes

1. Charles S. Buck, *A Theological Dictionary*, 436.

2. James E. Faulconer, "Rethinking Theology: The Shadow of the Apocalypse," 179.

3. Andrew F. Ehat and Lyndon W. Cook, *The Words of Joseph Smith*, 256.

4. Quoted in Molly Farmer, "Premortal Existence is not a New Concept, Author Says," *Deseret News*, March 12, 2009, M3.

5. Borrowing Book of Mormon imagery, Richard D. Poll has aptly labeled conservatives "iron rodders" and liberals "liahonas." Richard D. Poll, "What the Church Means to People Like Me," 1–13.

6. Regarding such issues, McConkie states, "There is no salvation in believing a false doctrine." Bruce R. McConkie, "The Seven Deadly Heresies," 74.

7. Lowell L. Bennion, Oral History, 80–81, 193.

8. The LDS Bible Dictionary (s.v. "death") states unequivocally, "Latter-day revelation teaches that there was no death on this earth for any forms of life before the fall of Adam." See also William E. Evenson and Duane E. Jeffrey, eds., *Mormonism and Evolution: The Authoritative LDS Statements* and Howard C. Stutz, *"Let the Earth Bring Forth": Evolution and Scripture.*

9. The LDS Eighth Article of Faith states, "We believe the Bible to be the word of God as far as it is translated correctly" (AoF 8). Joseph Smith declared, "I believe the Bible . . . as it came from the pen of the original writers." Ehat and Cook, *The Words of Joseph Smith,* 256. Thus, evangelical inerrantists aren't really any different from Mormons in this regard since, according to the 1978 Chicago Statement on Biblical Inerrancy, which was signed by nearly 300 noted evangelical scholars, inerrancy applies "only to the autographic [i.e., original] text of Scripture." See "Chicago Statement on Biblical Inerrancy with Exposition," reprinted in G. K. Beale, *The Erosion of Inerrancy in Evangelicalism: Responding to New Challenges to Biblical Authority,* 267–79.

10. While it is often taken for granted that God is unchangeable, James Barr, professor of the interpretation of holy scripture at the University of Oxford (U.K.), argues that this assumption is at best a conditioned presupposition because "there is no biblical or exegetical ground upon which it can be made." He goes on to say that "in the Bible God . . . can change his mind, he can regret what he has done, he can be argued out of positions he has already taken up. . . . The picture of God which presents perfection as the essence of the doctrine of God is clearly of Greek origin and is well represented in the Platonic and Aristotelian traditions. It was incorporated into Christian thought at a very early date and has remained extremely influential." James Barr, *Fundamentalism,* 277.

11. Hans Küng, *On Being a Christian,* 465.

12. Blake T. Ostler, "Bridging the Gulf," 125.

13. Blake T. Ostler, *Exploring Mormon Thought: The Attributes of God,* 418. Latter-day Saints must weigh these scholars' claims regarding Jesus's finite understanding with the traditional Christian and LDS perceptions of his infallibility. Joseph Smith seemed to believe, for example, that Jesus was not swayed by human teachings because "he knew all things" (JST John 2:24). Additionally, the Gospels were written several decades after Christ's crucifixion, so they may not be a completely accurate representation of his teachings.

14. *History of the Church,* 4:461.

15. Ibid., 2:243–46.

16. *Lectures on Faith,* 5:2.

17. See Richard S. Van Wagoner, Steve C. Walker, and Allen D. Roberts, "The 'Lectures on Faith': A Case Study in Decanonization," 71–77.

18. Ostler, "Bridging the Gulf," 125.

19. Grant Underwood, "Revelation, Text, and Revision: Insight from the Book of Commandments and Revelations," 79. Underwood suggests that the Lord not only tolerates but actually accommodates cultural paradigms stating that "the Lord . . . treats his chosen servants not as puppets or pawns but honors their agency and understanding and teaches them, according to the Doctrine and Covenants [1:24], 'in their weakness, after the manner of their

language (cultural as well as verbal).'" Grant Underwood, "A 'Communities of Discourse' Approach to Early LDS Thought," 34.

20. Benjamin Warfield, "The Divine and Human in the Bible," 278–79.

21. "An Interview with Brevard S. Childs."

22. Philip L. Barlow, *Mormons and the Bible: The Place of Latter-day Saints in American Religion*, 223.

23. Ibid.

24. Felix Just, "New Testament Theology: Introductory Glossaries."

25. Blake T. Ostler, "The Book of Mormon as a Modern Expansion of an Ancient Source," 113.

26. Gerald O'Collins, *Christology: A Biblical, Historical, and Systematic Study of Jesus*, 24.

27. Barlow, *Mormons and the Bible*, 68.

28. Thomas G. Alexander, "The Reconstruction of Mormon Doctrine: From Joseph Smith to Progressive Theology," 24.

29. Brigham Young, December 3, 1854, *Journal of Discourses*, 2:143.

30. Joseph Fielding Smith, *The Way to Perfection*, 101.

31. Bruce R. McConkie, "All Are Alike unto God."

32. J. Reuben Clark Jr., "When Are Church Leader's Words Entitled to Claim of Scripture?" 9–10.

33. LDS Newsroom, "Approaching Church Doctrine."

34. James E. Faulconer, "Review of Francis J. Beckwith and Stephen E. Parrish, *The Mormon Concept of God: A Philosophical Analysis*," 187.

35. Keith E. Norman, "The Mark of the Curse: Lingering Racism in Mormon Doctrine," 131.

36. Bruce R. McConkie, *Mormon Doctrine*, 309.

37. Jerreld L .Newquist, comp. and ed., *Gospel Truth: Discourses and Writings of President George Q. Cannon*, 162.

38. Edwin B. Firmage, *An Abundant Life: The Memoirs of Hugh B. Brown*, 139. Likewise, the apostle Paul advised the saints in his day to "test everything" (NRSV 1 Thess. 5:21).

39. Gilbert W. Scharffs, "Apostate," 1:59.

40. Craig L. Blomberg and Stephen E. Robinson, *How Wide the Divide? A Mormon and an Evangelical in Conversation*, 94.

41. As a point of clarification, proof-texting goes beyond "likening" (1 Ne. 19:23) or applying the language of a passage to a new situation while still recognizing its originally intended meaning. A passage can be legitimately *adapted* to fit a number of situations well outside of what the author originally intended. For any given usage of scripture, therefore, one should determine when an interpretation is being rendered or an adaptation is being made.

42. Kevin L. Barney, "Footnotes: 'Line upon Line,'" email to Scripture-L.

43. See, for example, Jonathan Edwards, *The Works of Jonathan Edwards: With an Essay on His Genius by Henry Rogers and Memoir by Sereno E. Dwight*, 1:403.

44. The 1979 edition of the King James Bible published by the LDS Church makes this interpretation explicit in the chapter heading for Zechariah 13. These headnotes were written by Elder Bruce R. McConkie. "Elder Bruce R. McConkie: 'Preacher of Righteousness,'" 15–21.

45. See NET Bible, s.v. Zechariah 13.

46. Adam Clarke, *Commentary on the Bible,* s.v. Zechariah 13.

47. See Thomas L. Constable, *Notes on Zechariah*, 74–75. BYU Old Testament scholar Kent Jackson acknowledges that this passage refers to the condemnation of false prophets in Israel, but suggests that, since it is referred to as a prophecy of Christ in D&C 45:51–52, the surviving manuscripts must have been corrupted. Kent P. Jackson, *Lost Tribes and Latter Days: What Modern Revelation Tells Us about the Old Testament*, 134.

48. Bellarmino Bagatti, *The Church from the Circumcision*, 138.

49. The entire passage reads, "When Israel was a child, I loved him, and out of Egypt I called my son. The more I called them, the more they went from me; they kept sacrificing to the Ba'als, and burning incense to idols" (RSV Hosea 11:1–2). In context, the Lord is simply saying that he "called" (past tense) Israel out of Egypt. Notice that the more he called them, the more unfaithful "they" (i.e., the Israelites) became. This obviously wouldn't apply to the faithful Jesus. Biblical scholar Dewey M. Beegle notes that given the sense of the passage and intention of the prophet, "there isn't the slightest hint that the statement was intended as a prophecy." Dewey M. Beegle, *Scripture: Tradition and Infallibility*, 237.

50. W. Sibley Towner, "Zechariah," 1421.

51. Kevin L. Barney, "Understanding Old Testament Poetry," 51–54.

52. Paul Hanson, professor of divinity at Harvard University, explains that this passage echoes "a very ancient tradition within Israel, the tradition of the ideal kingdom which Yahweh had promised Israel as an inheritance." Paul Hanson, "Zechariah 9 and the Recapitulation of an Ancient Ritual Pattern," 50.

53. James D. G. Dunn, *Unity and Diversity in the New Testament: An Inquiry into the Character of Earliest Christianity*, 102–109.

54. Raymond E. Brown, *The Birth of the Messiah*, 146, note 39. The Qumran community is an obvious example of Old Testament accommodation. Jews at Qumran read the scriptures in such a way as to see themselves as the fulfillment of end-time prophecy.

55. Joachim Becker, *Messianic Expectation in the Old Testament*, 94.

56. If the conclusions of the Jesus Seminar are correct, more than 80 percent of the sayings of Jesus recorded in the Gospels were likely not uttered by Jesus himself; Funk and Hoover, *The Five Gospels*, 5. Thus, we can't really be sure whether Jesus used proof-texts.

57. Beegle, *Scripture: Tradition and Infallibility*, 195.

58. Pontifical Biblical Commission, "The Interpretation of the Bible in the Church."

59. Mark D. Thomas, *Digging in Cumorah: Reclaiming Book of Mormon Narratives*, 17.

60. Anthony A. Hutchinson, "A Mormon Midrash? LDS Creation Narratives Reconsidered," 70.

61. Brian Hauglid, "Searching for God's Word in New Testament Textual Criticism," 101.

62. Raymond E. Brown, *Introduction to the New Testament*, 33.

63. Greg Herrick, "Baalism in Canaanite Religion and Its Relation to Selected Old Testament Texts."

64. Mark S. Smith, *The Early History of God: Yahweh and the Other Deities in Ancient Israel*, 22–23.

65. Arvid S. Kapelrud, *The Ras Shamra Texts and the Old Testament*, 78.

66. F. Deist and I. Du Plessis, *God and His Kingdom*, 19.

67. Karen Armstrong, *A History of God: The 4000-Year Quest of Judaism, Christianity, and Islam*, 12–13.

68. Ronald Hendel, "Genesis," 4.

69. John Barton, "Amos," 1284.

70. Prophecies of specific times and events have greatly diminished since the death of Joseph Smith. More recent LDS prophets have preoccupied themselves with guiding the Church rather than prophesying about the Church.

71. Brown, *Birth of Messiah*, 146.

72. Robert P. Carroll, "Eschatological Delay in the Prophetic Tradition?" 47–58.

73. David P. Wright, "Joseph Smith's Interpretation of Isaiah in the Book of Mormon," 206.

74. Even *The Eerdmans Bible Dictionary*, which is conservative in tone, follows "the majority of critical scholars" in asserting "that only the first portion [chapters 1–39] can be ascribed to the eighth-century B.C. prophet Isaiah, a contemporary of Amos, Hosea, and Micah. Isaiah 40–46, the second section, is attributed to an unknown prophet, commonly designated Second or Deutero-Isaiah, living among the Jews in Babylon toward the end of the Exile (ca. 550–538)." *The Eerdmans Bible Dictionary*, 531.

Because Lehi brought portions of Isaiah beyond chapter 39 with him to the Americas, many conservative LDS scholars dispute the Deutero-Isaiah theory. LDS apologist Marc Schindler notes, however, that this still doesn't necessarily mean that Cyrus's name was in the original Isaiah text. He observes that the Isaiah chapter (45) containing the name Cyrus, is never cited in the Book of Mormon, and could therefore very well be a later insertion into the text. Marc Schindler, "Deutero-Isaiah in the Book of Mormon?"

75. David P. Wright, "Historical Criticism: A Necessary Element in the Search for Religious Truth," 32.

76. Robert P. Carroll, *When Prophecy Failed*, 39.

77. Richard Hooker, "Backgrounds." This website provides an excellent overview of the influences that helped shape New Testament Christianity.

78. Karen Armstrong, *The Great Transformation: The World in the Time of Buddha, Socrates, Confucius and Jeremiah*, 383.

79. Dunn, *Unity and Diversity in the New Testament*, 35.

80. Justin Martyr, "First Apology," vol. 1, chap. 22.

81. Ostler, "Bridging the Gulf," 111.

82. See, for example, Dunn, *Unity and Diversity in the New Testament*, 359–360.

83. Morna D. Hooker, *A Commentary on the Gospel According to St Mark*, 297–303; Duling, "Matthew," 1857.

84. Planet News, "A discussion with Dr. James H. Charlesworth."

85. Mark A. Noll, "The Enlightenment and Evangelical Intellectual Life in the Nineteenth Century," 43.

86. Dean C. Jessee, *The Papers of Joseph Smith: Autobiographical and Historical Writings*, 5.

87. Grant Underwood, *The Millenarian World of Early Mormonism*, 137.

88. Parley P. Pratt, "To the Editor of the Latter Day Saints Messenger and Advocate," 318.

89. Underwood, *The Millenarian World of Early Mormonism*, 135.

90. Joseph Smith, "Try the Spirits," 746.

91. "Caswall's Prophet of the Nineteenth Century," 197. Milton V. Backman explains that, in the early nineteenth century, "the beliefs of many were being brought into harmony with the teachings of the still-future restored Church. These changes in belief would later make it easier for many to receive the fulness of the gospel." Milton V. Backman, "Preparing the Way: The Rise of Religious Freedom in New England," 18.

92. Grant Underwood gives several examples in which Mormonism borrowed doctrinal ideas from contemporary religions and notes that, as "a wise and loving father," God "does not immediately correct all his children's mistaken notions nor attempt to teach them all at once." Grant Underwood, "A 'Communities of Discourse' Approach to Early LDS Thought," 34.

93. Alexander Campbell, "Delusions," 93.

94. Mark D. Thomas, cited in "Lecture Series Explores the Book of Mormon," 55.

95. Ostler, "The Book of Mormon as a Modern Expansion," 66–123.

96. Ibid., 112.

97. Terryl Givens, *By the Hand of Mormon: The American Scripture that Launched a New World Religion*, 173.

98. Ibid., 138. Conservative Mormons are generally opposed to the expansion theory because it repudiates the more accepted view of a literal translation of the Book of Mormon. For example, see Stephen E. Robinson, "The Expanded Book of Mormon?"391–414.

99. Robert M. Price notes: "What Joseph Smith did, as historical critics understand the matter, is exactly what all ancient pseudepigraphists did, and he belongs to an illustrious company including authors of the Book of Daniel, the Book of Deuteronomy, the Book of Zohar, the Pastoral Epistles and other epistles (1 and 2 Timothy, Titus), not to mention a greater or lesser number of other epistles attributed to Paul: 1 and 2 Peter; 1, 2, and 3 Enoch; 1, 2, and 3 Baruch; the Apocalypse of Moses, Madame Blavatsky's Book of Dzyan, and a number of 'rediscovered' Tibetan Buddhist texts." Robert M. Price, "Joseph Smith: Inspired Author of the Book of Mormon," 327.

100. Marvin S. Hill, *Quest for Refuge: The Mormon Flight from American Pluralism*, 47.

101. Jan Shipps, *Sojourner in the Promised Land*, 296.

102. Underwood observes that Joseph's turn of mind came, in part, from his distaste for the "spiritualizing interpretations" of the Millerites, a contemporary movement that had constructed an elaborate symbolic reading of biblical prophecies by which they anticipated Christ's imminent return. Underwood, *The Millenarian World of Early Mormonism*, 195–96 note 52.

103. Ehat and Cook, *The Words of Joseph Smith*, 188–89.
104. Ibid., 186–87.
105. Ibid., 4.
106. Ibid., 161.
107. Oliver Cowdery said that Joseph Smith learned that serpents had legs while translating the book of Abraham. Oliver Cowdery, "To John Whitmer Esq.," 236.
108. Ehat and Cook, *The Words of Joseph Smith*, 43.
109. See Lance S. Owens, "Joseph Smith and Kabbalah: The Occult Connection," 117–94; critiqued in William J. Hamblin, "Joseph Smith and Kabbalah: The Occult Connection," 251–325.
110. Quoted in D. Michael Quinn, *The Mormon Hierarchy: Origins of Power*, 634.
111. Ibid., 641.
112. B. H. Roberts, *A Comprehensive History of the Church of Jesus Christ of Latter-day Saints*, 1:165.
113. Brigham Young, January 2, 1870, *Journal of Discourses*, 13:95.
114. This wasn't just a practice, but a doctrine known as the "law of adoption," by which living men were sealed to other unrelated men through a sacred ordinance. Indeed, Brigham Young called it "a great and glorious doctrine." April 6, 1862, *Journal of Discourses*, 9:269. Young was sealed to Joseph Smith and had dozens of other men sealed to him. The belief was that this would increase their kingdom in the hereafter and that it would secure the salvation of those being sealed. Wilford Woodruff, who performed many adoption ceremonies, wrote in his journal in June 1896, "I officiated in adopting 96 Men to Men." Wilford Woodruff, *Wilford Woodruff's Journal, 1833–1898*, 9:408. As Church president, Woodruff abolished the ordinance in 1894 after expressing concern that it diminished the role of the biological father in the family.
115. O. Kendall White, *Mormon Neo-orthodoxy: A Crisis Theology*, 139.
116. Robert L. Millet, "Joseph Smith and Modern Mormonism: Orthodoxy, Neoorthodoxy, Tension, and Tradition," 66.

2

The Great Apostasy

Fundamental to Mormonism is the belief that a universal or "great" apostasy occurred within the first few generations of the Christian era resulting in the withdrawal of God's authority from the earth. Todd Compton, writing in the *Encyclopedia of Mormonism* states, "Latter-day Saints see a historical 'great apostasy' and subsequent loss of authority beginning in the New Testament era and spreading in the centuries immediately following that era."[1] It is this loss of authority and closing of the heavens that many Latter-day Saints believe brought on the perceived cultural decline of what has been popularly called "the Dark Ages." According to LDS teachings, this apostate condition prevailed until the time of Joseph Smith and was the reason why a restoration of the gospel was necessary. A revelation given in October 1830 declares, "And my vineyard has become corrupted every whit; and there is none which doeth good save it be a few; and they err in many instances because of priestcrafts, all having corrupt minds" (D&C 30:4). Thus, Mormonism came forth "out of obscurity and out of darkness, the only true and living church upon the face of the whole earth" (D&C 1:30). It was the lone light piercing the "gross darkness" (D&C 112:23; cf. Isa. 60:2) of an apostate world. Here we look at the apostasy in biblical and LDS narratives.

Biblical Prophecies of the Apostasy

According to traditional LDS teachings, Old and New Testament prophets expressly prophesied of the Great Apostasy. However, as recent LDS scholars affirm,[2] at least some biblical passages typically cited as prophecies of the apostasy appear to actually be referring to other times or to less dire situations. This is not to say that there was no apostasy, only that it may not have been fully anticipated by biblical writers. Of course, Latter-day Saints assert that certain prophecies, such as those predicting a loss of priesthood authority, may have been suppressed by heretical groups and therefore never found their way into the Bible as passed down. Mormons also point to historically documented changes in doctrines and worship practices that have crept into Christendom since New Testament times. Whether these changes are indicative of an apostasy or simply a natural progression of the Christian faith—similar in many ways to how Mormonism itself developed—is a theological question, not a historical one.[3]

Old Testament

Passages in the Old Testament referring to ancient Israel's apostate condition are seen by many Latter-day Saints as referring to the much later Great Apostasy and Dark Ages presumed to have followed the deaths of the apostles. For example, Isaiah laments, "The earth also is defiled under the inhabitants thereof; because they have transgressed the laws, changed the ordinance, [and] broken the everlasting covenant" (Isa. 24:5). This same language appears in Doctrine and Covenants 1:15 to describe the situation at the time of Joseph Smith, suggesting that the "everlasting covenant" spoken of by Isaiah refers to the everlasting gospel. Latter-day Saints, therefore, commonly infer that Isaiah must have been speaking of apostate Christianity leading up to the time of Joseph Smith.[4]

The Old Testament itself gives no clear indication that the "everlasting covenant" equates to the gospel of Jesus Christ. According to biblical scholars, the "everlasting covenant" in Isaiah 24 has reference to the law of Moses, which ancient Israelites understood would stand "forever" as an "everlasting" or "perpetual covenant" and would remain in effect "throughout generations" (Ex. 12:14, 17, 24; Lev. 3:17; 16:34; 17:7).[5] The Israelites were guilty of violating this law, particularly its regulations prohibiting murder (see Ex. 20:13; Num. 35:31–34; Gen. 9:1–7). According to Mosaic law, murder defiles the land and brings upon it the curse of God. The Israelites' shedding of innocent blood had defiled the land (see Isa. 1:15, 21; 4:4), "therefore, hath the curse [spelled out in the law] devoured the earth" (Isa. 24:6). In short, Isaiah 24:5 is seen by most Old Testament scholars as a direct commentary on Israel's flagrant violation of the law of Moses in Isaiah's day, though certainly the language may have been well suited to describe the perceived situation in Joseph Smith's day.

Another Old Testament passage frequently cited as a prophecy of the Great Apostasy is Amos 8:11–12:[6]

Behold, the days come, saith the Lord God, that I will send a famine in the land, not a famine of bread, nor a thirst for water, but of hearing the words of the Lord:

And they shall wander from sea to sea, and from the north even to the east, they shall run to and fro to seek the word of the Lord, and shall not find it.

Biblical scholars explain that, in its historical context, the "famine" alluded to in this passage refers to the imminent consequence of the wickedness and apostasy of ancient Israel as seen in the Assyrian conquest (see Amos 7:11).[7] Similar mention of this state of spiritual depravity in ancient Israel can be found in other writings in the wake of the Babylonian captivity (e.g., Isa. 29:10). Amos is telling the Israelites that, although at present they have prophets to tell them the word of the Lord, "the days [will] come" (in their captivity) when they will no longer have access to God's words. This prophecy was uttered around 760 B.C. and Israel was invaded by the Assyrians about 40 years later. Echoing the view of other Old Testament scholars, BYU religion professor D. Kelley Ogden comments, "Amos's mission was to warn Israel of its *present* disastrous state and forewarn it of *impending* captivity." He further notes that "Amos's prophecies [including this one] were fulfilled, soon by the Assyrians and then later by other conquerors."[8]

While the language of these Old Testament prophecies may contain apt descriptions of the spiritual depravity of our modern day—and for that matter almost any other period of history—the scholarly consensus is that in their original context, these prophecies were expressly directed at ancient Israel's apostate condition.

New Testament

Though New Testament writers lived during the initial throes of what Latter-day Saints think of as the Great Apostasy, there is little evidence that these writers perceived any terminal threats to the church. The sense one gets from a contextual reading of the New Testament is that the first Christians saw themselves as living in the last days of the world and being among the faithful who would witness Christ's second coming, which they were convinced was near at hand. Writing near the end of the first century, bishop Clement of Rome observed that the apostles had gone forth "with full assurance of the Holy Ghost . . . proclaiming that the kingdom of God was at hand."[9] Although New Testament writers spoke of a current rebellion and persecution that would continue to rage, the saints were to find solace in knowing that their Savior would soon return in glory to quell this rebellion and rescue the righteous.

On careful examination, none of the New Testament passages referring to heresies within the church or persecution from without seems to predict a wholesale departure from the faith; all seem to assume that there would be faithful saints who remain on the earth until Christ comes. Miami University New Testament professor Roy Ward observed that every prediction of an apostasy in the New Testament and other apocalyptic literature "always assumes that the righteous will have a continuing existence until the end, despite the *apostasia*."[10]

While from a modern vantage point it may seem unimaginable that first-century Christians would have seen themselves as living at the very end of the world, their perception isn't too surprising when one realizes that Christianity emerged in the wake of heightened Jewish expectations that the final kingdom of God prophesied in the Old Testament was about to be ushered in. Anglican New Testament Scholar N. T. Wright reminds us that "first-century Judaism, and Jesus as firmly in it, can only be understood in a climate of intense eschatological [end-time] expectation."[11]

That New Testament writers saw themselves living in the last days is evident from many of their writings. John writes, "It is the last time" (literally "the last hour") (1 John 2:18).[12] Likewise, Jude told his readers that they were living in the "last time" (Jude 1:17–19). Paul told the Corinthians that the scriptures were written for their day "upon whom the ends of the world are come" (1 Cor. 10:11). The author of Hebrews 9:26 explains how God "hath in these last days spoken unto us by his Son." Peter's first epistle proclaims that Jesus "was manifest in these last times" (1 Pet. 1:20). All of these portray Jesus's ministry as the inauguration of the last days with the end of the world in sight.

James reprimanded the materialistically minded of his day, stating, "Ye have heaped treasure together for the last days" (James 5:3). This may sound like punishment stored for a later time, but scholars point out that the Greek preposition *en* here is better translated "in" rather than "for"; thus, *Today's English Version* reads, "You have piled up riches *in these* last days" (emphasis mine). Continuing, James tells the saints to brace themselves, "for the coming of the Lord draweth nigh" (James 5:8).

Paul reminds Timothy that "in the last days perilous times shall come" (2 Tim. 3:1) in which there would be evil men "having a form of godliness, but denying the power thereof" (v. 5). Though Latter-day Saints commonly assume that this passage alludes to the time of Joseph Smith, it is Timothy whom Paul is warning: "From such turn away" (v. 5). When this passage is read in context (vv. 1–9), one realizes that it is Timothy who was living at the time when these teacherous people would be posing a threat to the church. Paul seems to be trying to get Timothy to come to grips with the fact that the reason he and others were being persecuted on all sides (vv. 8–12) was precisely because they were then living in the last days.

With New Testament saints anxiously anticipating Jesus's imminent return, it seems unlikely that they would have anticipated the church falling into a complete state of apostasy. Indeed, there are several indications that they believed the church was here to stay. Consider Christ's words to Peter: "Thou art Peter, and upon this rock I will build my church; and the gates of hell shall not prevail against it" (Matt. 16:18). Many scholars view the pronoun "it" as having reference to the apostolic church, others to the invisible church or body of believers, and still others to revelation or the inspired witness of Christ on which the church is built.[13] Often the interpretation given is influenced by one's religious tradition: Catholic, Protestant or Mormon. In the traditional Mormon interpretation, "the gates of hell should never prevail against the rock of revelation."[14] Whatever the interpretation, most commentators agree that there was some essential aspect of the church that was to persevere or endure. In Christ's last commission to his disciples to preach the gospel to all nations, he reassured them saying, "Lo, I am with you alway, even unto the end of the world" (Matt. 28:20), or as rendered in several modern translations, "to the end of time." Warnings of apostasy, therefore, need to be weighed against assurances of perseverence and continuity. New Testament scholar Paul Barnett explains, "While many warnings are given of the dangers of falling away, there are also encouragements about the mercy of God shown in these situations (e.g. Heb. 4:14–16) as well as the strength and faithfulness of God to 'keep' his children from falling away from the true path of faith (e.g., 1 Pet. 1:5; 2 Pet. 2:9; 1 John 4:4; Jude 1:24; Rev. 3:10)."[15]

A New Testament passage often seen by Latter-day Saints as referring to the Great Apostasy is Jesus's parable of the wheat and the tares in Matthew 13. Jesus states,

> The kingdom of heaven is likened unto a man which sowed good seed in his field:
> But while men slept, his enemy came and sowed tares among the wheat, and went his way.
> But when the blade was sprung up, and brought forth fruit, then appeared the tares also. (Matt. 13:24–26)

The "servants of the householder" offered to gather out the tares but the man said:

> Nay; lest while ye gather up the tares, ye root up also the wheat with them.
> Let both grow together until the harvest: and in the time of harvest I will say to the reapers,
> Gather ye together first the tares, and bind them in bundles to burn them: but gather the wheat into my barn. (vv. 28–30)

The idea of the parable as it stands seems clear. Just when Christ begins bringing disciples into the kingdom of God during his mortal ministry, Satan comes along and stirs some of them up to do evil. Those that are evil are permitted to coexist with those that are good until both grow to maturity. In the end, however, the evil ones are separated out and destroyed, thus sparing the kingdom from any fatal harm. BYU religious scholar John W. Welch observes that this parable, "which was written at a time when many disciples believed that the second coming of the Savior would happen within the first or second generation of Christianity, leads readers to expect that the wheat and the tares will grow together continuously until the final judgment (Mat. 25:30), which need not have been understood in the days of Matthew as being a very long time away."[16]

Doctrine and Covenants 86:3, recorded in December 1832, recasts this parable as a reference to the apostasy, explaining that "the tares choke the wheat and drive the church into the wilderness." The revelation continues, "But behold, in the last days, even now . . . the Lord is beginning to bring forth the word, and the blade is springing up and is yet tender" (D&C 86:4). This altered rendering changes the sense of the parable from the biblical account—preserved also in JST Matthew (revised in the spring of 1832)—where the wheat wasn't choked, but continued to grow and was gathered safely into the barn. There is never any mention, even in the New Testament interpretation of the parable (Matt. 13:37–43), that "the children of the kingdom" would be overcome or that a second growing season (i.e., restoration) would be necessary. The parable as it stands consistently fits the New Testament perspective that the kingdom would survive any perils until the Savior's return. Interestingly, Joseph Smith reverted to this more natural reading of the parable in December 1835, stating that the Savior was essentially telling his disciples, "The Church is in its infancy, and if you take this rash step [i.e., remove the tares], you will destroy the wheat or the Church with the tares: therefore it is better to let them grow together until the harvest, or the end of the world."[17]

Other parables in Matthew 13 convey a similar idea of the kingdom's gradual, uninterrupted growth. The parable of the mustard seed (Matt. 13:31–32), for example, indicates that the kingdom Christ set up was to begin small but would gradually grow into a large, mature tree. Joseph Smith, however, interpreted the parable as representing "the Church as it shall come forth in the last days," with the mustard seed symbolizing the Book of Mormon sprouting out of the earth.[18] Finally, there is the parable of the leaven which was put into three measures of meal "till the whole was leavened" (Matt. 13:33). This seems to convey the same idea as the other parables—a gradual, spreading growth of the kingdom Christ established. According to Joseph Smith, however, this parable refers to the latter days as "the Church of the Latter-day Saints, has taken its rise from a little leaven that was put into three witnesses."[19] Later still, he saw other meanings in the three measures of meal, including, in December 1842, "the three in the Grand Presidency."[20] In recent years, LDS scholars have offered various explanations for why Joseph gave a restoration orientation to these parables. One explanation is that he was merely adapting rather than interpreting the parables.[21]

Another New Testament passage cited to show that the early apostles anticipated a universal apostasy is Acts 20. Here Paul warns the elders at Ephesus, "After my departing shall grievous wolves enter in among you, not sparing the flock. Also of your own selves shall men arise, speaking perverse things, to draw away disciples after them" (Acts 20:29–30). Does the phrase "not sparing the flock" refer to a complete overthrow of the entire flock, or simply the flock not being spared from attacking wolves? Consider a similar remark Paul made concerning the Israelites: "God *spared not* the natural branches" (Rom. 11:21; emphasis mine). Paul clearly doesn't mean here that all of the natural branches (Israelites) were removed because, in verse 17, he specifically states that only "some" of the natural branches were broken off and that the wild branches (gentiles) would be "grafted in among them [that remain]." Furthermore, in understanding Paul's comment to the Ephesians in Acts, it is significant that he would later write to Timothy at Ephesus prophesying that only "*some* shall depart from the faith" (1 Tim. 4:1; emphasis mine).[22] Even assuming that Paul anticipated an entire overthrow of the flock at Ephesus, it isn't clear that he intended his comment for the entire church. His precaution to the elders of the church of Ephesus was that "grievous wolves" would enter among "you" (Acts 20:29).

2 Thessalonians 2:2–3 is another scripture frequently cited as a prediction of the Great Apostasy. Here Paul counsels the Saints to:

> Be not soon shaken in mind, or be troubled, neither by spirit, nor by word, nor by letter as from us, as that the day of Christ is at hand.

> Let no man deceive you by any means: for that day shall not come, except there come a falling away [Greek *apostasia* = rebellion] first, and that man of sin be revealed, the son of perdition.

Significant is the fact that, in modern translations, Paul isn't dispelling a rumor that Christ's coming is "at hand," but rather that it "is already here" (NRSV 2 Thess. 2:2). (No wonder verse 2 says they were "shaken" and "troubled.") Paul explains that two things must occur before Christ comes. First, there must be a period of rebellion (which Paul indicates in verse 7 was already at work); and second, the man of sin, whose identity is undisclosed,[23] must appear. Once this has happened, the Lord will come, consume the rebellious (v. 8), and save the righteous (vv. 13–14). It is instructive to note that the rebellion spoken of here is to culminate in the second coming of Christ, not in a complete apostasy followed by a much later gospel restoration. As Roy Ward explains, "In this text the *apostasia* is an eschatological event linked with the man of lawlessness, immediately preceding the Day of the Lord. There is no suggestion that a restoration movement in history is to take place after the *apostasia* and prior to the Day of the Lord."[24] Paul perceived the second coming as imminent and appears to have anticipated being among the righteous who would still be alive at that day as indicated in his pronouncement: "We" who "are" alive shall be caught up to meet him (1 Thess. 4:17; cf. 1 Cor. 15:51–52).

Another New Testament passage that Latter-day Saints read as prophesying the Great Apostasy is Revelation 12. Here the author describes "a woman clothed with the sun, and the moon under her feet, and upon her head a crown of twelve stars" (v. 1). This woman was about to give birth to a male child who would "rule all nations with a rod of iron" (v. 5), but a great red dragon appears "to devour her child as soon as it was born" (v. 4). When the child is born, he is "caught up unto God, and to his throne" (v. 5). Meanwhile "the woman fled into the wilderness, where she hath a place prepared of God, that they should feed her there a thousand two hundred and threescore [1,260] days" (v. 6). A war ensues in heaven in which the dragon is cast down to earth with "the third part of the stars of heaven" (v. 4). The dragon then begins persecuting the woman (v. 13) and seeks to destroy her with a flood (v. 15), but the Lord protects the woman (v. 16). This makes the dragon "wroth" causing it to "make war with the remnant of her seed, which keep the commandments of God, and have the testimony of Jesus Christ" (v. 17).

Joseph Smith, like other restorationists at the time, saw the woman as "the church of God" (JST Rev. 12:7) and the wilderness as spiritual darkness. A revelation he received in March 1829 speaks of "the coming forth of my church out of the wilderness" (D&C 5:14).

Nearly two centuries before Smith, Roger Williams of Rhode Island taught that the "church" had been "put to flight" and had "retired into the Wilderness of Desolation."[25] Williams had similarly looked forward to the day when the church would come "out of the Babylonian apostasy and wilderness."[26] Congregationalist minister Joseph Lathrop was even more specific in his interpretation of this passage when he wrote in 1812: "We here learn . . . that after St. John's time, there would be, in the Christian church, a great apostasy from the truth, and that pure religion would be succeeded by the worship of images and departed saints; that Christian liberty would be subverted by spiritual tyranny and cruel persecution, and that this afflicted state of the church would continue, in a greater or less degree, for 1,260 years."[27]

Joseph Smith, following this popular millenarian understanding that "days" was biblical code for "years,"[28] changed verse 6 to read 1,260 "years" instead of "days," thus giving the prophecy a much later projected fulfillment. Indeed, Latter-day Saints cleverly calculated this point in time to be the year 1830.[29] Latter-day Saints since the time of Joseph Smith have continued to view this passage as referring to the loss of the church. In one LDS explication of this passage, Joseph Fielding Smith writes,

> The woman is the church; she is glorified by the light of heaven. The twelve stars are the apostles. The son born to her is the Priesthood which is to rule the earth by the truth of the gospel, which is the rod of iron. Because of the persecution and power of the dragon, the Priesthood is taken back to heaven, and the woman is forced to flee from the face of the earth. The dragon is Satan who rebelled in heaven and prevailed upon one third of the spirits to follow him. He with his followers was cast out of heaven into the earth where he made war on the church and drove it into the wilderness. . . . In the year 1830, this woman—the church—with her man child returned to the earth.[30]

While most non-LDS scholars would agree that John was speaking of the intense persecution of the Church in his own time, they don't see a universal apostasy or latter-day restoration in John's imagery. Indeed, most scholars view the woman's fleeing "into the wilderness" (v. 14) to mean that the Church went underground or dispersed from the area to escape Roman persecution.[31] It should be noted that, after she fled into the wilderness, the dragon, who had been "cast unto the earth" (v. 13), pursued her with a flood of water; but "the earth helped the woman," and thus protected the Church (vv. 15–16). The scene John paints is not unlike that portrayed elsewhere in the New Testament—that the Church would continue to suffer Satan-led persecution, but would remain protected on the earth and ultimately triumph over evil.

Protestant Views

Protestants in Joseph Smith's day generally believed that greed and corruption had caused a universal apostasy from Christ's church and that a restoration, or at least a reformation, was sorely needed. The reformers of the Enlightenment (1500–1800) were quick to point out clear signs evidencing this apostasy. John Wesley, co-founder of Methodism, commented that "the extraordinary gifts of the Holy Ghost were no longer to be found in the Christian church; because the Christians were turned heathens again, and had only a dead form left."[32] Roger Williams, a seventeenth-century religious seeker, claimed that there was "no regularly constituted church on earth, nor any person authorized to administer any church ordinance; nor could there be, until new apostles were sent by the great Head of the Church"—a development Williams didn't anticipate would occur until Christ's millennial advent.[33] Such commentaries on the woeful state of the Christian church were, by no means, lone voices in the perceived apostate darkness, nor did they require any special revelatory insight. They reflected what many saw as a glaring discrepancy between religions of the day and the church of the New Testament.

Not only did reformers and restorationists believe that the Catholic Church had become corrupted and significantly altered from Christ's primitive church, but they felt that biblical prophecies vindicated this belief. Alexander Campbell, a popular Baptist preacher and later leader of the Disciples of Christ, wrote in 1825 that the "great apostasy [was] foretold and depicted by the holy apostles."[34] As justification for their beliefs, Campbell, Wesley, and others appealed to the same biblical proof-texts that would later be used by Latter-day Saints.

Protestants at large believed that the Catholic Church was "the beast" and "the mother of harlots and abominations of the earth" spoken of in Revelation 17:5.[35] The *Geneva Bible*, which reflected the Protestant theology of its translators, identified the pope as "the angel of the Bottomless pit" in a marginal note for Revelation 9:11. Nathan Hatch, professor of American religious history at the University of Notre Dame, explains that this general "quest for the ancient order of things" was characterized by a "common conception that Christian tradition since the time of the apostles was a tale of sordid corruption in which kingcraft and priestcraft wielded orthodoxy to enslave the minds of the people."[36] Primitivists and restorationists recognized that if Catholicism had become thoroughly corrupted, a mere reformation was insufficient to lay again the foundation of primitive Christianity. For them, a complete restoration of the primitive gospel was necessary, and many claimed to provide just such a restoration. Alexander Campbell, for example, claimed to have fully restored the "ancient order of things."[37]

Early Mormonism

In his search for the true church of Christ, Joseph Smith was no doubt aware of the sentiments of many in his immediate vicinity, including members of his own family, that the Christian world was in a state of complete apostasy. His paternal uncle Jesse, his parents, and both grandfathers believed that none of the existing churches was patterned after the primitive church of Christ. His mother, Lucy Mack Smith, had difficulty bringing herself to join any of the existing churches, having concluded that "the [primitive] Church of Christ was not like any of them."[38] She related that her husband, Joseph Sr., refused to join any "system of faith" that was not of the "ancient order, as established by our Lord and Saviour Jesus Christ, and his Apostles."[39] Although the Prophet recalls, in his 1838 account of the First Vision, that "it had never entered into my heart that all [churches] were wrong" (JS–H 1:18), his prior autobiographical sketch, written in 1832, states that, as early as 1818, he had concluded that all "had apostatised from the true and liveing faith and there was no society or denomination that built upon the gospel of Jesus Christ as recorded in the new testament."[40] Given his family and environmental influences, it is little wonder that Joseph had essentially already rejected the Christian denominations of his day before going into the grove of trees near his home to pray for guidance.

The earliest recorded LDS teachings give little indication of a universal apostasy, especially in the way it is currently understood. At first, Mormonism shared the popular evangelical sentiment that the apostasy simply consisted of a departure from gospel teachings and practices, and not the withdrawal of priesthood authority. The Book of Mormon, for example, makes no prediction of an apostasy which involves either the priesthood or the Church being taken from the earth; nor does it mention that important ordinances pertaining to exaltation (e.g., temple ordinances) would be discontinued and need to be restored. Rather, the earliest Mormon teachings of an apostasy, like those from other contemporary restorationists, spoke only of moral corruption, a clouding or perversion of the basic teachings of Christ causing "an exceedingly great many . . . to stumble" (1 Ne. 13:29), and a denial of the power of the Holy Ghost—which includes the working of miracles (2 Ne. 28:4–15; Morm. 8:26–31).

The Book of Mormon refers to the "formation" after the time of the apostles of a "great and abominable church" (1 Ne. 13:6–9, 26–28), which early Saints understood as referring primarily to the Catholic Church. But since the Book of Mormon further defined it non-denominationally as any group opposed to "the church of the Lamb of God" (1 Ne. 14:10), Saints also came to see it as referring to any religion or government opposing God's work. Notably, the Book of Mormon doesn't ever suggest that the church of the Lamb would be taken from the earth, only that in the latter days, "its numbers . . . [would be] few, because of the wickedness and abominations of the whore who sat upon many waters" (1 Ne 14:12).

Prior to 1834, there is no mention of priesthood being taken from the earth—or restored for that matter (see Chapter 4). Instead, the Lord tells the Saints in December 1832, "The priesthood *hath continued* through the lineage of your fathers . . . therefore your life and the priesthood *have remained*" (D&C 86:8–10; emphasis mine). It isn't until several years after the restoration of the Church that apostasy narratives began to include a loss of authority along with essential saving ordinances, thus paving the way for the current LDS understanding of the Great Apostasy.

Throughout the nineteenth century and well into the twentieth century, the apostasy continued to be defined primarily as a period of gospel perversion, spiritual darkness and loss of priesthood authority. Catholicism continued to be seen by many as being the principal culprit in corrupting the church.

Contemporary Mormonism

Current LDS historians note a cultural bias underlying early Mormon characterizations of Christianity as a corrupt morass of false teachings; moreover, there is still considerable inertia which keeps these legacy teachings alive. In his historical survey of LDS literature on the apostasy, BYU history professor Eric Dursteler observes that early LDS treatises on the apostasy were "clearly" influenced by "the highly polemical, popular, confessional, historical literature of the nineteenth century and the anticlerical literature of the eighteenth-century enlightenment." He further notes that, although the characterization of the Middle Ages as a dark and decadent era and the Renaissance as an era of spiritual awakening has been repudiated by virtually all modern historians of the past century, "Latter-day Saint treatments of the apostasy . . . have retained much of their binary vision of the Middle Ages and Renaissance."[41]

With modern scholarship having an increasing influence on Mormon perceptions of history, Dursteler observes that there seems to be a growing tendency among LDS writers to "move away" from depicting the apostasy as bringing on a long period of darkness followed by the dawning of the Reformation. "Instead," he notes, "the apostasy is depicted simply as an age in which priesthood authority did not exist."[42] Thus, the concept of the apostasy has shifted from a loss of spiritual gifts and truths to primarily a loss of priesthood authority.[43]

LDS characterizations of other religions as the "church of the devil" have significantly diminished. In 1990, for example, the mock representation of Protestant ministers as hirelings of Satan was removed from the LDS temple ceremony. All of this has gone a long way toward promoting greater mutual respect between Mormons and fellow Christians.

Notes

1. Todd M. Compton, "Apostasy," 1:56.

2. See, for example, John A. Tvedtnes, "Review of Michael T. Griffith, One Lord, One Faith Writings of the Early Christian Fathers as Evidences of the Restoration," 33–42. LDS Philosopher Ryan C. Christensen notes that even Hugh Nibley's classic LDS defense of the apostasy *When the Lights Went Out*, "has attracted criticism" for its "lush assortment of prooftexts." Christensen observes that "many of the passages he cites do not seem to prove his points; many of them seem to be taken out of context or even to be irrelevant to his thesis." Ryan C. Christensen, "Appendix D: Bibliographical Note on LDS Writings," 377–78.

3. Given a belief in continuing revelation, changes in religious doctrines and practices alone can't be taken as conclusive evidence of an apostasy.

4. See James E. Talmage, *The Great Apostasy*, 24–25; Bruce R. McConkie, *The Millennial Messiah: The Second Coming of the Son of Man*, 531; Tad R. Callister, *The Inevitable Apostasy and the Promised Restoration*, 387.

5. There are other "everlasting covenants" made in the Old Testament, such as the Noahic, Abrahamic, and Davidic covenants (Gen. 9:8–17; 17:1–8; 2 Sam. 23:5); however, these were all grant covenants or covenants of promise. As such, they were unconditional and therefore unbreakable. The Mosaic covenant, on the other hand, was a treaty covenant stipulating blessings and curses based upon compliance. This is the covenant that was "broken" in Isaiah 24:5. For a lengthy discussion of the identity of this covenant, see Chisholm, "The Everlasting Covenant and the City of Chaos," 23–53.

6. Talmage, *The Great Apostasy*, 26–27; *Gospel Principles* (2009), 95; and Callister, *The Inevitable Apostasy*, 383.

7. Francis I. Andersen and David Noel Freedman, *Amos: A New Translation with Introduction and Commentary*, 824–26; Donald E. Gowan, "The Book of Amos: Introduction, Commentary and Reflections," 7:419

8. D. Kelly Ogden, "The Book of Amos," 57; emphasis mine.

9. Clement, "The Epistles of Clement," 9:241.

10. Roy B. Ward, "The Restoration Principle: A Critical Analysis," 198. For examples of apocalyptic literature depicting only a partial apostasy, see 1 Enoch 91:7; Jubilees 23:14; 4 Ezra 5:1; and Matt. 24:10.

11. Nicholas Thomas Wright, *Jesus and the Victory of God*, 96.

12. Authorship of the books of the New Testament is widely disputed. For purposes of this book, I have chosen to assume traditionally attributed authorship except where it may have a bearing on the discussion at hand.

13. For a history of different interpretations of Mathew 16:18 see Jack P. Lewis, "'The Gates of Hell Shall Not Prevail Against It' (Matt 16:18): A Study of the History of Interpretation," 349–67.

14. Bruce R. McConkie, *Mormon Doctrine*, 304.

15. P. W. Barnett, "Apostasy," 75.

16. John W. Welch, "Modern Revelation: A Guide to Research about the Apostasy," 122.

17. Joseph Smith, "To the Elders of the Church of the Latter Day Saints," 227.

18. Ibid.

19. Ibid., 228.

20. *History of the Church,* 5:207.

21. For a scholarly summary of the parables in Matthew 13, see Warren Carter, "Matthew," 1769. For a discussion of alternative ways LDS scholars reconcile Joseph Smith's interpretation of theses parables with the general scholarly view, see John W. Welch, "Modern Revelation: A Guide to Research about the Apostasy," 122-23.

22. Modern scholarship suggests that this letter may have actually been written by an associate of Paul. In any case, it reflects the author's anticipation of only a partial apostasy of the Ephesian saints.

23. Though the exact identity of the "man of sin" eludes scholars, there is general agreement that it is probably a human being. Paul in 2 Thessalonians 2 refers to "that Man of Sin," "The Son of Perdition," "he that opposeth and exalteth himself," and "he whose coming is after the working of Satan." These terms all seem to refer to a devious human being. Leon James Wood, *The Bible & Future Events: An Introductory Survey of Last-day Events*, 111–112. Joseph Smith seems to have believed that the "man of sin" was Lucifer himself, an interpretation with which Bruce R. McConkie agrees. *History of the Church* 1:175 note; Bruce R. McConkie, *Mormon Doctrine*, 467–68.

24. Ward, "The Restoration Principle: A Critical Analysis."

25. Roger Williams, *The Hireling Ministry None of Christ's*, 2; quoted in Dan Vogel, *Joseph Smith: The Making of a Prophet*, 537.

26. Roger Williams, *George Fox Digg'd out of His Burrowes*, 66; quoted in Vogel, *Joseph Smith: The Making of a Prophet*, 537.

27. Joseph Lathrop, *The Angel Preaching the Everlasting Gospel*, 7.

28. The 1,260 days of Revelation 12:8 were commonly interpreted in Joseph Smith's day as 1,260 *years*. Adding to 1,260 the roughly 500+ years some thought it took for the apostasy to be fully realized, many Christian writers, including John Wesley and Roger Williams, fixed the year John spoke of to a date that had particular significance for their own movement such as 1827, 1835, 1866, or, in the case of early Latter-day Saints, 1830. See, for examples, Elias Boudinot, *The Second Advent*, iii, 186, 282, 296; Ethan Smith, *Dissertation on the Prophecies Relatives to AntiChrist and the Last Times; Exhibiting the Rise, Character, and Overthrow of That Terrible Power; and a Treatise of the Seven Apocalyptic Vials*, 101–2; John Greenhow, "To the Editor of the Times and Seasons," *Times and Seasons* 4, no. 15 (June 1, 1843): 231; and George Reynolds and Janne M. Sjodahl, *Commentary on the Pearl of Great Price*, 74 note 3.

29. Grant Underwood, *The Millenarian World of Early Mormonism*, 123–24.

30. Joseph Fielding Smith, *The Restoration of All Things*, 83. Interestingly, McConkie disagreed with (his father-in-law) Joseph Fielding Smith's explanation that the child represents the priesthood, stating, "The church did not bring forth the priesthood, but the priesthood is the power that brought the church into being." Bruce R. McConkie, *Doctrinal New Testament Commentary*, 3:516.

31. Raymond E. Brown, *Introduction to the New Testament*, 779.

32. John Wesley, *Sermons on Several Occasions*, 2:266.

33. Quoted in William Cullen Bryant, ed., *Picturesque America*, 1:502.

34. Alexander Campbell, "A Restoration of the Ancient Order of Things—No. 1," *Christian Baptist* 2 (February 1825): 126–28.

35. Craig J. Hazen, "The Apologetic Impulse in Early Mormonism: The Historical Roots of the New Mormon Challenge," 42.

36. Nathan O. Hatch, *The Democratization of American Christianity*, 167. Thomas Jefferson repeatedly denounced the "priestcraft" he saw among the clergy who used religion as "an engine for enslaving mankind" and as "a mere contrivance to filch wealth and power to themselves." Cited in Gordon S. Wood, "Evangelical America and Early Mormonism," 359.

37. See Alexander Campbell's series, "A Restoration of the Ancient Order of Things," *Christian Baptist* 2–7 (1824–30).

38. Lavina Fielding Anderson, ed., *Lucy's Book: A Critical Edition of Lucy Smith's Family Memoir*, 257.

39. Ibid., 294.

40. Dean C. Jessee, comp. and ed., *The Personal Writings of Joseph Smith*, 11.

41. Eric R. Dursteler, "Inheriting the 'Great Apostasy,'" 53.

42. Ibid., 64.

43. Recent LDS general conference talks show a persistence of the LDS perception of the apostasy as a period of spiritual depravity and gospel ignorance. See Russell M. Nelson, "The Gathering of Scattered Israel," 79–82; M. Russell Ballard, "Learning the Lessons of the Past," 31–34; and Boyd K. Packer, "The Twelve," 83–87.

3

Joseph Smith and the Restoration

Just as early Mormons identified prophecies in the Bible supporting the apostasy, they also saw references to the latter-day restoration of the gospel. The calling of the Prophet Joseph Smith, the restoration of priesthood authority, and the coming forth of the Book of Mormon are all events presumed to have been predicted in the Bible. This chapter looks at prophecies that Latter-day Saints traditionally interpret as foretelling the calling of Joseph Smith. It also examines the biblically prophesied "dispensation of the fulness of times" and "restoration of all things" in the light of both traditional LDS and scholarly commentary.

Zealous Protestants in the early 1800s sharply criticized leaders of the Reformation for not going far enough in effecting a complete return to what they believed was the biblical pattern of Christ's church. According to Richard Hughes, a scholar of early American religious history, "The restoration vision which so thoroughly informed the work of Joseph Smith flourished in antebellum America in ways that it has seldom flourished at any other place or any other time in the past two thousand years."[1] The "plea for restoration" at the beginning of the nineteenth century was being heard throughout New England, and numerous religious groups claimed to be God's response to that plea. In the late 1700s, movements led by James O'Kelly, Abner Jones, Elias Smith, John Wright, Walter Scott, and Barton W. Stone positioned themselves as the Lord's restored church; and in the early 1800s, restorationist enthusiasm reached a peak with Alexander Campbell's claim to have restored "the ancient order of things."

Restorationist scholar Robert Mallet notes that, between 1794 and 1835, at least six different restoration churches sprang up in America, all claiming to be Christ's restored church.[2] Contrary to the assertion that no other church in Joseph Smith's day bore Christ's name,[3] all six of these churches incorporated "Christ" in their title—such as the "Christian Church" and the "Church of Christ."[4] They, like the Book of Mormon (see 3 Ne. 27:8), advocated that if it be Christ's church, it should bear his name and be built on the principles of the gospel he taught. In 1825, an article appeared in Campbell's *The Christian Baptist* sharply criticizing churches of the day for deviating from this pattern. "Look into the New Testament," it read, "There the church is the Church of Christ, and his disciples are Christians. Look out of the New Testament, and look into the creeds and confessions. Here we see a Baptist church, a Methodist church, and a Presbyterian church, etc."[5] Restorationists decried sectarian creeds and recognized only those ordinances found in the New Testament, such as baptism by immersion and regular partaking of the sacrament.

Like other early nineteenth-century restorationist movements, the church organized in 1830 by Joseph Smith was, following the Book of Mormon, simply called "the Church of Christ" (D&C 20:1). Three years later, the *Book of Commandments* from start to finish would continue to refer to the Church as "the Church of Christ," with the book itself bearing the title: *A Book of Commandments for the Government of the Church of Christ.*[6] A year later, however, Joseph Smith presided over a Church vote in Kirtland to change the name to "The Church of the Latter-day Saints,"[7] thus dropping "Christ" from the name. This name change created no small reaction and many Saints called for reform and a return to the original name. According to B. H. Roberts, "These 'reformers' insisted that the regular authorities in Kirtland had departed from the true order of things by calling the church 'The Church of the Latter-day Saints.' They proceeded therefore to repudiate this title and adopt what they considered to be the proper one, 'The Church of Christ.'"[8] It wasn't until April 26, 1838, that the name of the Church was changed to its current name with "Jesus Christ" reinstated into the title.

Many scholars reject the notion that there was a well-defined, original Christianity that reformers and restorationists could actually reclaim. In his book, *Unity and Diversity in the New Testament*, James D. G. Dunn argues that "there was no single form of normative Christianity in the first century."[9] He maintains instead that "primitive Christianity was a living, moving process, developing all the time in different ways and different directions in response to diverse influences and challenges."[10] New Testament scholar Bart Ehrman also contends that diversity was characteristic of Christianity from the very beginning and that some of the appearances of a unified Christian tradition in the New Testament are only due to the fact that the Christian movement that eventually became "orthodox" suppressed or destroyed the writings of conflicting Christianities, even "texts claimed to have been written by Jesus' closest followers."[11]

Dunn states that the Reformers' "vision of the purity of the primitive church before the post-Apostolic 'fall'" is nowhere justified in the New Testament.[12] According to Euan Cameron, a professor of Reformation church history at Union Theological Seminary, the ideal image reformers created in their minds of Christ's primitive church "was a mirage" and that "the reformers projected their own ideals back on to the primitive Church."[13] Though all from Protestant traditions themselves, Cameron, Dunn, and Ehrman essentially view any project that attempts to return to a presumed pure, primitive Christianity established by Christ himself as being misguided and ultimately unachievable.

The First Vision

The Mormon story of the Restoration has its beginning in the spring of 1820 when Joseph Smith, age fourteen, received—what he would later report in 1838 as—a vision of the Father and the Son telling him that the Christian world lay in apostasy and that he should join none of the existing churches because "they were all wrong" (JS–H 1:19). This vision has become heralded in Mormonism as the inaugural event signaling the beginning of the restoration of the gospel and the kingdom of God in the last dispensation.[14]

Although Latter-day Saints have come to view the First Vision as a powerful witness of the apostasy and restoration, historians note that it appears to have held only minor significance for early Mormons. There are ten separate accounts of the First Vision recorded during Joseph Smith's life time, and many see a theologically significant difference between earlier accounts and later ones. Although in 1838 Joseph records that his "object in going to inquire of the Lord was to know which of all the sects was right" (JS–H 1:18), his earlier 1832 account simply states that he went to "cr[y] unto the Lord for mercy" for his own sins.[15] In response to this plea, he recounts, "I was filled with the spirit of God and the Lord opened the heavens upon me and I saw the Lord and he spake unto me saying Joseph my son Thy Sins are forgiven thee."[16] This earliest narrative is not unlike numerous other Christian conversion stories of Smith's contemporaries. LDS scholar Mark Thomas notes that "in a typical conversion vision, one or more beings would appear and pronounce the sinner forgiven. These beings might be an angel, Christ, Christ on the right hand of the Father, or God on his throne."[17]

LDS historian James B. Allen could find no evidence that missionaries referred to the First Vision or that it played any role in conversions during the 1830s.[18] He notes specifically that "none of the available contemporary writings about Joseph Smith in the 1830's, none of the publications of the Church in that decade, and no contemporary journal or correspondence yet discovered mentions the story of the first vision."[19] Mormon missionaries were more disposed to reason from the Bible and point to the Book of Mormon as a tangible witness of the prophetic calling of Joseph Smith.

Prophecies Concerning Joseph Smith

The notion of a modern-day prophet who communicates with God was not unknown in early American Christianity, and several movements, like Mormonism, laid claim to their own prophetic leader. Members of the Jerusalem Community in western New York accepted Jemima Wilkinson as God's mouthpiece for declaring his words to all humankind; the Rappites of Indiana believed that their leader, George Rapp, was instructed by God; and converts to the True Inspiration Society or Amana Community near Buffalo, New York, declared that their prophet, Christian Metz, revealed God's will.[20] One of the early leaders of the Seventh-day Adventists, Ellen G. White, professed numerous visions and revelations. Another prophetess was Ann Lee, leader of the Shakers (alluded to in D&C 49), whom her followers regarded as God's spokesperson and whose revelations were seen as the words of God. LDS historian Richard Bushman notes that "the Free Will Baptists, the Universalists, [and] the Shakers all had founders who received open visions of God when they were called to their work."[21] With so many prophetic figures that lived contemporaneously to Joseph Smith, the challenge for Mormons was to point out what it was that set Smith apart from others who claimed similar divine appointments.

Early Latter-day Saints identified several differentiating achievements of Joseph Smith that singled him out as God's prophet, including the restoration of priesthood keys and the bringing forth of new scripture. Another important distinction made with respect to Joseph Smith's calling was the claim of his prophetic career being a fulfillment of ancient prophecy—although other movements made similar claims regarding their founders.

Old Testament

Latter-day Saints traditionally regard Isaiah 29 to be a prophecy of the coming forth of the Book of Mormon with specific reference to Joseph Smith in verses 4 and 12. The prophecy speaks of a people who will be destroyed, but will "speak out of the ground," and their voice will be "as of one that hath a familiar spirit" (v. 4). To speak of one as having "a familiar spirit" (v. 4) was an archaic way of referring to a necromancer or medium who communicates with the dead (see 1 Sam. 28:6–9). Such individuals were said to "peep and mutter" (Isa. 8:19), which was "a disparaging comment about the necromancer's customary manner of speaking during the consultation of the dead."[22] The Book of Mormon depicts Joseph Smith as being like one having a familiar spirit because, in a figurative sense, the deceased ancient inhabitants of America would speak through him (2 Ne. 26:16; cf. Morm. 8:15–16).[23]

Non-LDS Bible commentators make two observations that preclude the "one that hath a familiar spirit" from having direct reference to Joseph Smith.[24] First, they point out that Isaiah 29 is specifically addressing the current situation of wickedness in Jerusalem or "the city where David dwelt" (Isa. 29:1).[25] There is no mention of any other people or place. Second, it doesn't say that this nation will speak through some actual person, such as Joseph Smith. Rather, the voice of the nation would be "as" (v. 4) a person who has a familiar spirit. That is, the voice of Jerusalem's inhabitants will be no more than a peep and mutter. The NRSV captures this sense stating that the voice of the nation of Israel shall be "like the voice of a ghost."

The other verse in Isaiah 29 presumed to be a reference to Joseph Smith speaks of a "book [that] is delivered to him that is not learned, saying, Read this, I pray thee and he saith, I am not learned" (v. 12). Latter-day Saints tend to interpret the "book" as the gold plates and the one "not learned" as Joseph Smith. This interpretation derives from a rewording of this passage in the Book of Mormon which speaks of the gold plates coming forth in the latter days as a sealed book that "shall be delivered unto a man [i.e., Joseph Smith]" (2 Ne. 27:9; JS–H 1:63–65). The problem with this interpretation is that Isaiah is not prophesying of an actual book delivered to a real person. Rather he is reprimanding the Jews for their spiritual blindness—"For the Lord hath poured out upon you the spirit of deep sleep" (Isa. 29:10) —and *likens* the nation to an unlearned person trying to read a sealed book. Thus, Isaiah's words are, to them, "*like* the words of a book that is sealed" (NRSV Isa. 29:11; emphasis mine). When read at face value, Isaiah seems to be merely comparing Israel's inability to discern the word of God to an unlearned person's inability to read a book.

Given these obstacles to the traditional LDS interpretation, some LDS scholars now concede that Isaiah 29 has reference to the spiritual condition of ancient Jerusalem and that the prophet Nephi was only drawing on the language of Isaiah to construct his "own prophecy" (2 Ne. 25:7).[26] Thus Nephi wasn't interpreting Isaiah, but merely "likening" (1 Ne. 19:23; 2 Ne. 6:5) or adapting the words of Isaiah to the

Nephite situation and the latter-day coming forth of the Book of Mormon.[27] "In 2 Nephi 26:12," notes BYU Old Testament scholar Paul Y. Hoskisson, "Isaiah is paraphrased and applied to the Nephites, who will, like the inhabitants of Jerusalem, be destroyed."[28] This explanation resolves the difficulties associated with the traditional LDS interpretation of Isaiah noted above, but it leaves a few loose ends. First, Nephi explains elsewhere that Isaiah prophesied specifically of the Gentiles inhabiting the land of America in the latter days and the coming forth of "a marvelous work" [i.e., the Book of Mormon] which "shall be of great worth unto our seed" in making known to them "his [the Lord's] covenants and his gospel" (1 Ne. 22:1–11; see also 3 Ne. 20:11). Moroni also exhorted readers to "search the prophecies of Isaiah," saying, "behold . . . those saints who . . . have possessed this land [i.e., America], shall cry . . . from the dust," and the Lord "will bring these things [i.e., the Book of Mormon] forth" (Morm. 8:23–25). It is noteworthy that Joseph Smith's inspired revision of Isaiah 29 virtually replicates Nephi's version of Isaiah's prophecy in the Book of Mormon verbatim, confirming at least his perception that Isaiah actually prophesied the coming forth of the Book of Mormon in the latter days.[29] Additionally, the angel Moroni reportedly told Joseph Smith in 1823 that this passage in Isaiah "must be fulfilled before it [i.e., the Book of Mormon] is translated."[30] Finally, the Prophet explicitly referred to the translation of the Book of Mormon as a literal fulfillment of Isaiah 29: "I commenced translating the characters and thus the prop[he]cy of Is<ai>ah was fulfilled which is written in the 29 chapter concerning the [sealed] book."[31] It seems apparent that Joseph Smith saw his work in bringing forth the Book of Mormon as the direct fulfillment of Isaiah 29. The Book of Mormon reflects a similar understanding.

Latter-day Saints also cite Malachi 3:1, which speaks of a "messenger" who would be sent "to prepare the way before . . . the Lord," as another Old Testament passage referring to Joseph Smith. This passage is even included in the LDS Topical Guide to the scriptures under Joseph Smith.[32] It is interesting to note, however, that the "messenger" spoken of in Malachi was first interpreted in early LDS writings as the gospel (D&C 45:9; 133:57–58, 64). It is only gradually that Saints came to associate the messenger of Malachi 3:1 with Joseph Smith. For example, in his 1855 *Key to the Science of Theology*, Apostle Parley P. Pratt referred to Joseph as "*a* messenger in the spirit and power of Elijah, to prepare the way of the Lord."[33] Saints thereafter seem to have increasingly seen the Prophet as fulfilling the role of this messenger. Joseph Fielding Smith reinforced this interpretation stating, "Joseph Smith was sent to prepare the way for this second coming."[34]

Scholars explain that, when read in context, the "messenger" in Malachi appears to be an allusion to Elijah whose appearance would prepare the way before the Lord's coming in judgment as prophesied in Malachi 4:5.[35] The purpose for sending this messenger was to purge Levitical priests from what Malachi believed to be evil practices; thus enabling them to once again offer sacrifices in righteousness when God comes in judgment (Mal. 3:2–4). Like other Old Testament prophecies, this one appears to have been uttered with the expectation that it would soon be fulfilled. Biblical scholars suggest that this prophecy of impending purification and judgment was intended to instill a sense of urgency as well as hope among ancient Israelites. Old Testament scholar W. Sibley Towner explains, "It is the task of this late prophetic book to bring two messages: God is displeased with the lack of piety in the community gathered around the temple (1:6–2, 16; 3:6–12); and God is about to send a messenger who will reunite and purify all of Israel prior to the 'great and terrible day of the Lord' (4:5)."[36]

In the New Testament, the "messenger" of Malachi's prophecy is reinterpreted as being a reference to John the Baptist coming in the "spirit and power" of Elijah (Matt. 11:10, 14; 17:11–12; Luke 1:17) to prepare the way before Jesus. "Elijah" is thus understood as John the Baptist, while "the Lord God" is understood as the Lord Jesus Christ. These early Christians believed that the judgment and kingdom promised in the Old Testament was nigh at hand and saw John as being the very messenger spoken of by Malachi.

While the New Testament interprets Malachi's prophesied "messenger" as a forerunner to the first coming of Christ, by the nineteenth-century, many Christians believed that Malachi's messenger also referred to a forerunner preceding Christ's second coming. Mark Thomas notes that "at least three early nineteenth-century prophetic movements saw the Malachi prophecy as referring to a person in their own movement. . . . Ethan Smith [a Congregationalist minister] was probably typical. . . . He saw the coming of Elijah as having a double fulfillment—first, in John the Baptist, [and] second, the preaching of the gospel by the missionary angel of Rev. 14 prior to the Millennium."[37] Latter-day Saints have likewise adopted the view that Malachi's prophecy of a forerunner had multiple fulfillments: first with John the Baptist, second with the gospel, and later with Joseph Smith. What Saints generally haven't done is link the prophecy of the forerunner in Malachi 3:1 with the prophecy of the coming of Elijah in Malachi 4:5. Thus, unlike the New Testament and most Bible commentaries, Mormons typically identify the messenger sent to prepare the way before the Lord (Malachi 3:1) as someone different from Elijah who would come to turn the hearts of the children to the fathers before the day of the Lord (Malachi 4:5).

A prophecy invoked by Joseph Smith to quell Church skeptics who questioned his divine calling[38] is Isaiah 11:1: "And there shall come forth a rod out of the stem of Jesse, and a Branch shall grow out of his roots." The Prophet interpreted the "stem of Jesse" as a reference to Christ (D&C 113:1–2). Then, in response to the question, "What is the rod . . . that should come of the Stem of Jesse?" he answered: "It is a servant in the hands of Christ, who is partly a descendant of Jesse as well as of Ephraim, or of the house of Joseph, on whom there is laid much power" (D&C 113:3–4). Doctrine and Covenants commentaries interpret this "servant" to be Joseph Smith. In fact, the LDS Topical Guide to the scriptures also lists Isaiah 11:1 under references to "Joseph Smith." As to the identity of the "roots" of Jesse (Isa. 11:10), Joseph Smith stated that "it is a descendant of Jesse, as well as of Joseph, unto whom rightly belongs the priesthood, and the keys of the kingdom, for an ensign, and for the gathering of my people in the last days" (D&C 113:6). Thus, some Latter-day Saints have equated the roots with Joseph Smith, making the rod and roots identical. Other commentators view the roots as yet a future descendant of the Prophet.[39] Joseph Smith himself identified this individual as someone "by the name of David in the last days, raised up out of his [king David's] linage."[40] Some of the Prophet's associates understood this David to be a direct reference to Joseph Smith's son David Hyrum Smith, who was born shortly after the Prophet made the above identification.[41]

Scholars sort out the meaning of these symbols in Isaiah (rod, stem, branch, and roots) by explaining that there aren't four figures represented here, but only two. LDS Old Testament scholar Sidney B. Sperry explains, "We have synonymous parallelism in these lines, so that 'rod' [Hebrew = shoot] corresponds to 'branch' and 'stem' [Hebrew = stump] corresponds to 'roots.'"[42] So it is simply a rod (i.e., a branch) coming from the stem (i.e., the root) of Jesse. The rod or branch, therefore, is a descendent of Jesse who would come to rule with all the wisdom and righteousness described in verses 2–5.[43] For ancient Jews, as well as for most Old Testament scholars, this descendent was an eschatological Davidic king.[44] For most Christians, including most LDS expositors, this Davidic king is perceived to be Christ coming to reign during the millennium.[45]

Many LDS commentaries on Isaiah 11:1–13 seem to disregard its poetic parallelism and consequently read multiple identities into the symbols. In addition to identifying Christ as the stem (D&C 113:1–2) and Joseph Smith as the rod (D&C 113:4), one can find LDS commentaries which equate Christ variously with all four symbols. Joseph Smith has even been identified with all four symbols except for the "stem," and this only because the "stem" is explicitly identified in LDS scripture as Christ (D&C 113:4).[46] As already noted, the "root" has also been interpreted as a future descendant of Joseph Smith or as a future, yet-to-be identified Davidic king. The table below summarizes the various major interpretations of Isaiah 11:1. Where traditional readings see two individuals, LDS readings vary as to both quantity and identity.

Interpretations of Symbols in Isaiah 11:1

Symbol	Scholarly Interpretation	Christian Interpretation	LDS Interpretations
Rod	Davidic king	Christ	Christ, Joseph Smith,
Stem	Jesse	Jesse	Christ
Branch	same as "rod"	same as "rod"	Christ, Joseph Smith
Roots	same as "stem"	same as "stem"	Christ, Joseph Smith, Smith descendant, latter-day Davidic king

An Old Testament passage that Saints were initially reluctant to interpret as a reference to Joseph Smith is a prophecy attributed to Moses in Deuteronomy 18:15; "The Lord thy God will raise up unto thee a Prophet from the midst of thee, of thy brethren, like unto me; unto him ye shall hearken."[47] The image of a "prophet" being "raised up" who would be "like unto Moses" certainly fits Joseph Smith who has been likened to Moses (D&C 28:2, 107:91). Interpreting this prophet as Joseph Smith was initially seen as problematic since the New Testament identifies the prophet in this passage as Christ (Acts 3:22–26, 7:38), an identification that is reinforced in the Book of Mormon (1 Ne. 22:21) and by Moroni during his first visits to Joseph Smith (JS–H 1:40). More recently, LDS scholars have deemed it appropriate to invoke the principle of multiple fulfillment and interpret it as also being an allusion to Joseph Smith. For example, BYU religion professor Frank Judd writes, "Moses's prophecy has dual fulfillment: Jesus Christ and Joseph Smith."[48]

This notion of a secondary fulfillment in Joseph Smith derives from another prophecy Joseph attributed to Moses that sounds remarkably like the one in Deuteronomy 18:15—except that it seems to explicitly refer to Joseph Smith. In this prophecy, the Lord tells Moses that many of the things he had been commanded to write regarding the creation would be lost over time as they are passed down. He then consoles Moses saying, "I will raise up another [i.e., Joseph Smith] like unto thee; and they [i.e., the lost teachings about the creation] shall be had again among the children of men" (Moses 1:41). Joseph Smith even attributed a similar prophecy to the Old Testament Joseph whom the Lord tells: "And he [i.e., Joseph Smith] shall be great like unto Moses, whom I have said I would raise up unto you, to deliver my people, O house of Israel" (2 Ne. 3:9–10). Thus, the "prophet" that was to be "raised up" and become "like unto Moses" is, in modern LDS scripture, a prophetic expression that applies to Joseph Smith as well as to Christ.

Many biblical scholars interpret Deuteronomy 18:15 as referring to Moses's immediate successors and providing instructions on what constitutes a true prophet, rather than as referring to a specific individual in the distant future such as Christ.[49] These scholars see Moses as essentially telling the Israelites that when they enter the promised land, they are not to listen to the pagan soothsayers of the land, but rather only to one like Moses, a fellow Israelite (Deut. 18:9–22). According to one scholarly Christian commentary, "From the context (opposition to the pagan soothsayers) it seems that Moses is referring in general to all the true prophets who were to succeed him."[50] In this sense, one could view the passage as having an eventual fulfillment in Christ (and even in Joseph Smith), but it is questionable from the context alone whether the prophecy was initially uttered specifically with either Christ or Joseph Smith in mind.

New Testament

There are no prophecies in the New Testament that can reasonably be construed as direct references to Joseph Smith. The Prophet did, however, alter Matthew 24:14 to provide such a reference. The KJV reads, "And this gospel of the kingdom shall be preached in all the world *for* a witness unto all nations; and then shall the end come" (emphasis mine). In Nauvoo, Joseph stated that this passage should read: "the Lord in the last days would commit the keys of the Priesthood *to* a witness over all people."[51] This change from "for" to "to" alters the sense of the passage from the gospel being preached *as* a witness, to the gospel being restored *to* a witness. Notably, the Prophet had earlier approved the KJV rendering, which is preserved this way in the Pearl of Great Price (JS–M 1:31). With two different versions and meanings of the same passage, Latter-day Saints must determine whether it is more appropriate to use the earlier canonized meaning of this verse or the meaning later given by the Prophet.

Book of Mormon

Prophecies regarding Joseph Smith in the Book of Mormon are primarily adaptations and reformulations of Old Testament prophecies. We have already examined the Book of Mormon interpretation of Isaiah's "one who is not learned" and "one having a familiar spirit," which were originally intended as merely figurative descriptions of Israel's spiritual depravity and not as actual individuals. We also saw the Book of Mormon disclosure of a prophecy given to Joseph of old, the great-grandson of Abraham, which refers to Joseph Smith by name and even gives the name of his father, Joseph Sr. (2 Ne. 3:14–15). Joseph Smith would later interject this same prophecy into his translation of the Bible (JST Gen. 50:26–32).

A somewhat surprising passage interpreted in 3 Nephi 20 as a reference to Joseph Smith is Isaiah 52:13–14, which speaks of the Lord's servant who would be "exalted and extolled," though "his visage was . . . marred" (3 Ne. 20:43–44). The Savior explained to the Nephites that this prophecy would be fulfilled at the time of the coming forth of the Book of Mormon when a latter-day servant would rise up whom the Gentiles would persecute:

> But behold, the life of my servant shall be in my hand; therefore they shall not hurt him, although he shall be marred because of them.
> Yet I will heal him, for I will show unto them that my wisdom is greater than the cunning of the devil. (3 Ne. 21:9–10)

John Taylor, who would become the third president of the Church, interpreted this passage in an editorial on September 2, 1844 as being a reference to Joseph Smith. He described how Joseph, in fact, fulfilled this prophecy twice, having been *physically* "marred" and healed on two separate occasions.[52]

What makes this interpretation surprising is that the "marred" servant spoken of in Isaiah 52:13–14 is generally regarded as the same suffering servant spoken of in Isaiah 53. Indeed, biblical expositors have long maintained that the suffering-servant song of Isaiah 53 actually begins at Isaiah 52:13 and continues through the end of chapter 53. Since this suffering servant is traditionally understood by Christians, including Latter-day Saints, as having reference to Christ,[53] it is somewhat unexpected that Joseph Smith would be identified in the Book of Mormon as the servant alluded to in Isaiah 52:13–14 (3 Ne. 20:43–44, 21:9–10), especially when Jesus is earlier identified as the suffering servant of Isaiah 53 (Mosiah 14:1–12).

A current explanation for this apparent inconsistency is that Isaiah 52:13-14 has a "dual fulfillment," one in Jesus Christ and the other in Joseph Smith.[54] As BYU religion professor Joseph Fielding McConkie explains, although Isaiah 52:13–14 is "a prophetic description of the promised Messiah," the Book of Mormon gives "a dual meaning to these words by applying them to another servant of the Lord in the last days (see 3 Ne. 20:44). We understand that servant to be Joseph Smith."

According to McConkie, however, Joseph wasn't physically marred like the Savior, but rather "the distortion of image spoken of by Isaiah may refer to the manner in which the promised servant and his labors were to be misinterpreted and misperceived."[55]

Dispensation of the Fulness of Times

Latter-day Saints view the restoration of the gospel as ushering in the "dispensation of the fulness of times" spoken of by Paul in which God would "gather together in one all things in Christ, both which are in heaven and which are on earth" (Eph. 1:10).[56] The LDS Bible Dictionary (s.v. "dispensation") defines a dispensation as "a period of time when the Lord has at least one servant on the earth who holds the keys of the priesthood and is authorized to administer the gospel."[57] The "dispensation of the fulness of times" is believed to be the final such gospel period bringing together the gospel truths and powers of all previous dispensations as well as things that have been reserved exclusively for the last days. In a letter to the Saints in Nauvoo on September 6, 1842, Joseph Smith wrote,

> It is necessary in the ushering in of the dispensation of the fulness of times; which dispensation is now beginning to usher in, that a whole, and complete, and perfect union, and welding together of dispensations, and keys, and powers, and glories should take place, and be revealed, from the days of Adam even to the present time; and not only this, but those things which never have been revealed from the foundation of the world, but have been kept hid from the wise and prudent, shall be revealed unto babes and sucklings in this the dispensation of the fulness of times. (D&C 128:18)

Joseph understood "the fulness of times" to mean "the dispensation of all the times,"[58] which is to say it is a gospel period that includes those things revealed in all former dispensations.

The concept of a dispensation as a period of gospel blessings on the earth was an idea held by many at the time of Joseph Smith.[59] Usually attributed to John N. Darby, a Plymouth Brethren minister, dispensationalism is the belief that the earth's history can be divided into seven major dispensations, or periods of time, with the seventh or last dispensation to be the millennial kingdom of Christ. By 1833 Darby had fully developed the idea that seven dispensations were distinguishable in scripture.[60] Early Mormonism developed a similar concept of seven major dispensations, with Joseph Smith teaching that "he was chosen for the last . . . or Seventh dispensation."[61] At a Church conference held in Ohio in November 1840, Elder Zebedee Coltrin spoke "on the seven dispensations . . . [which was] of great interest to the church."[62] For Latter-day Saints, the gospel restoration marked the beginnings of the seventh and final gospel dispensation ushering in the millennial reign of Christ. Of course, with the belief that the gospel was also preached to the Nephites, most LDS writers currently recognize more than just seven dispensations. The 1979 LDS Bible Dictionary (s.v. "dispensations") states, "There have been many gospel dispensations since the beginning."[63]

Within the context of the Pauline epistles, the "dispensation of the fulness of times" spoken of by Paul does not refer to a specific period, much less a final period ecompassing all previous periods. *Vine's Expository Dictionary* explains, "A 'dispensation' is not a period or epoch (a common, but erroneous, use of the word), but a mode of dealing, an arrangement or administration of affairs."[64] The Greek word translated "dispensation" in Ephesians 1:10 is *oikonomia* (from which we get the word "economy") and literally means household management. In Ephesians 1:10 it is used on a larger scale to denote God's ultimate "plan" (NRSV) for all creation. As the *Expositor's Bible Commentary* states, "Here Paul uses it to suggest the administration or putting into effect of God's far reaching redemptive plan."[65] The final end is the bringing together and subordination of "all things in Christ, both which are in heaven, and which are on earth" (Eph. 1:10).

As to when this "plan" would be put into effect, modern translations render "the fulness of times" in Ephesians 1:10 along the lines of "when the time was ripe" (*New English Bible*) or "when the times will have reached their fulfillment" (*New International Version*). Significantly, the phrase "fulness of time" is used elsewhere in the New Testament to refer to Christ's first coming (Gal. 4:4; Heb. 1:2, 9:10; 1 Peter 1:20). Even the Book of Mormon speaks of Christ's first advent as occurring "in the fulness of time" (2 Ne. 2:3, 26). It is for other reasons, however, that scholars see the dispensation or plan of redemption spoken of in Ephesians as having its commencement with Christ's first advent.

Paul notes that "in other ages" this plan "was not made known unto the sons of men," but "it is now revealed unto his holy apostles and prophets by the Spirit" (Eph. 3:5). For Paul, there was the old dispensation of the Mosaic law (Rom 7:1-5) and the new "dispensation of the grace of God" (Eph. 3:1), which he saw commencing with Christ's resurrection and glorification. All that remained was its final consummation when all things, including believing Gentiles (Eph. 3:6–8), would be gathered together in Christ. After giving an exhaustive treatment of Paul's teachings regarding the dispensation of the fulness of times, New Testament scholar Herman N. Ridderbos concludes, "time and again . . . the whole of Paul's preaching is determined by the all-important fact that in Christ's advent and work, especially in his death and resurrection, the divine work of redemption in history has reached its fulfillment and the redemptive dispensation of the great future promised by God and foretold in prophecy has become present time."[66] Noting the generally held scholarly view that Ephesians 1:10 refers "to the time of Christ, [and] not to the latter days," LDS biblical scholar John Tvedtnes acknowledges that "the passage contains no internal evidence that a restoration is intended."[67] The "dispensation of the fulness of times" in Ephesians 1:10 thus appears to be simply a reference to God's redemptive work which had begun to be put into effect through Christ's ministry.

The Restoration of All Things

The book of Acts gives an account of the apostle Peter prophesying of a "restitution of all things," stating that it was "spoken of by the mouth of all his [God's] holy prophets since the world began" (Acts 3:21). This restitution of all things is popularly understood today in LDS discourse as the return of the gospel and its associated blessings in the latter days. For example, in an October 2005 general conference address, Elder Merrill Bateman concluded his remarks by saying, "I testify that the gospel restored through the Prophet Joseph Smith is Peter's 'restitution of all things.'"[68] Although several different restorations are predicted in both the Old and New Testaments as well as in the Book of Mormon, none of them speaks specifically of a gospel restoration in modern times.

Old Testament

The only restoration spoken of in the Old Testament is the restoration of the kingdom of Israel. In Isaiah, the Lord tells scattered Israel:

> And I will restore thy judges as at the first, and thy counsellors as at the beginning: afterward thou shalt be called, The city of righteousness, the faithful city.
> Zion shall be redeemed with judgment, and her converts with righteousness. (Isa. 1:26–27)

This prophesied restoration gives no indication of a return of priesthood authority, lost ordinances, or gospel teachings, but rather speaks only of a return to righteousness and to the days of splendor enjoyed by ancient Israel. This restoration would include rebuilding both the city of Jerusalem and the temple, restoring them to the glory they had possessed in King Solomon's day. The splendor of this restored kingdom was expected to be greater than the former and even incorporate the paradisiacal state of Eden. According to religious studies historian Jan Shipps, "Again and again Hebrew psalmists and prophets speak of returning to a paradisiacal situation wherein the earth will be renewed, the blind will see, the lame will leap for joy, hunger will be satisfied, righteousness and truth will prevail, and the covenant between God and his people will be reinvested with meaning."[69] As will be seen, this is the very restoration early Latter-day Saints initially spoke of when referring to the "restoration of all things."

New Testament

The New Testament essentially expands the Old Testament notion of a restoration of Israel and all creation by adding a spiritual dimension to it. Biblical scholars generally interpret the "restoration of all things" spoken of by Peter (Acts 3:21) as an end-time redemption of all creation from the ravages of sin.[70] Beverly Gaventa, Princeton Seminary professor of New Testament interpretation and exegesis, explains that this "universal restoration is . . . roughly the equivalent of salvation itself."[71]

That this passage refers to some sort of end-time restoration from sin, rather than the latter-day restoration of the gospel, is evident from the two verses preceding verse 21 in which Peter admonishes the sinful Jews:

> Repent ye therefore, and be converted, that your sins may be blotted out, when the times of refreshing shall come from the presence of the Lord;
> And he shall send Jesus Christ, which before was preached unto you. (vv. 19–20)

The promise is that a time of refreshing would come, and that, as part of this renewal, their sins would be remitted. Furthermore, it includes a promise of Jesus's return. Verse 21, which follows, seems to merely reiterate the fact that Christ would not come until this time of restitution, or, as the *Living Bible* takes the liberty of translating, "until the final recovery of all things from sin."

To illustrate how "all his holy prophets" spoke of this restitution, Peter cites Moses's prophecy (Deut. 18:15–20) of a prophet that the Lord would raise up like unto him (i.e., Moses), and explains that God fulfilled this promise, "having raised up his Son Jesus, [and] sent him to bless you, in turning away every one of you from his iniquities" (vv. 23, 26). Peter doesn't allude to Moses's prophecy to show that prophets spoke of the restoration of the gospel in the latter days; instead, he uses it to argue that these prophets all spoke of Christ's redeeming work or "times of refreshing [i.e., spiritual renewal] . . . from the presence of the Lord" (v. 19). It is this restoration from sin that, according to Peter, was spoken of by Moses and other holy prophets.

For Peter, this restoration was currently in progress and was not something that would occur some two millennia in the future. Verse 24 places the time of this restoration in "these [i.e., Peter's] days," or, as rendered in the *New English Bible*, "this present time." New Testament writers thought they were living in the last days, which wouldn't have allowed for a protracted period of apostasy followed by a gospel restoration. What they seem to have envisioned was an imminent return of the Savior to fulfill his promise of refreshing and restoring all creation from the ravages of sin.

Early Nineteenth Century Christianity

Christians have traditionally understood the "restoration of all things" spoken of in Acts 3:21 as this promised restoration of God's creations from the effects of sin. However, exactly how this universal redemption was to apply to the wicked was hotly debated in Joseph Smith's day. On one side of the debate, Universalists argued that everyone would be completely redeemed (both physically and spiritually), including the wicked. In 1805, Universalist Hosea Ballou explained that "the restitution of all things, which is to be accomplished in the fullness of times, [is] a restitution or restoration from mortality and sin, to a state of immortality and righteousness."[72] Two years earlier, the Universalist declaration of belief, the *Winchester Profession*, called this "restoration of all things" a complete restoration of the entire human family "to holiness and happiness."[73]

On the other side, Protestants holding to a limited salvation accused Universalists of "wresting the scriptures"[74] with their liberal interpretation of Peter's "restitution of all things." While anti-Universalist interpretations of Peter's expression varied, they all avoided any kind of exoneration of the wicked from sin. One interpretation in common with that of the Book of Mormon was that all things would be restored only in the sense that they would return to their natural order, either to righteousness or to wickedness. An article published September 1805 in the *Connecticut Evangelical Magazine* explained that "the restitution of all things, which God hath spoken by the mouth of all his holy prophets, is an event contemporary with judgment" and may be understood to mean that "things will all then be restored to order . . . [and] every creature will have his proper place assigned to him. . . . The righteous will be admitted to heaven" while the wicked will "be left in a state of impenitence and wrath."[75] The article goes on to explain that, contrary to Universalist claims that physical *and* spiritual death would be universally overcome, there would instead only be "a universal destruction of natural death."[76]

Book of Mormon

The Book of Mormon deals similarly with those in ancient America who also happened to hold a Universalist interpretation of the scriptural "restoration of all things." The prophet Alma makes reference twice to "the restoration of which has been spoken by the mouths of the prophets" (Alma 40:22, 24)—seemingly referring to the same restoration spoken of in Acts 3:21—and states that "some have wrested the scriptures" (Alma 41:1) supposing it to mean that all men would "be restored from sin to happiness" (Alma 41:10). Alma explains that what it really means is that "all things should be restored to their proper order" (Alma 41:2, 4). For the righteous it means being restored to "righteousness" and "happiness" (Alma 41:4, 6), while those who are evil are restored to "evil" and "endless misery" (Alma 41:4). Alma explains that only physical death is universally overcome (Alma 41:2).

It is worth noting that the only other restorations alluded to in the Book of Mormon are of (1) the plain and precious truths of the Bible and (2) the House of Israel to the lands of their inheritance, both through the instrumentality of the Book of Mormon. There is no mention of a restoration of priesthood authority or of the Church. In the Book of Mormon, "Joseph Smith . . . is not the prophet of the Restoration but the translator of the Book of Mormon. He is a seer rather than the first elder. Joseph's calling, as described in the Book of Mormon, is connected solely with the Book of Mormon."[77]

Early Mormonism

Early LDS literature subsequent to the Book of Mormon shows a shift in meaning from the idea of the "restoration of all things" as a return to one's proper state to more of the traditional Christian idea of the return of all creation to its Edenic state. In August 1830, just four months after the organization of the Church, Joseph wrote to the Coleville Saints: "The wicked must soon be destroyed from off the face of the earth . . . for the day is fast hastening on when the restoration of all things shall be fulfilled. . . . Then shall [it] come to pass that the lion shall lie down with the lamb."[78] Here, the destruction of the wicked and reign of universal peace are the events signaling the prophesied restoration of all things. It was not generally perceived as the restoration of the gospel, though the gospel restoration would have undoubtedly been seen as playing a preparatory role in this restoration of the earth.

For at least the first decade of the Church, LDS interpretations of Peter's prophesied "restoration of all things" continued to mirror the traditional view of restoring all creation to its Edenic state in connection with Christ's second coming. In December 1835, the Prophet wrote a letter to the elders of the Church explaining that the "end of the world is the destruction of the wicked . . . which shall precede the coming of the Son of Man, and the restitution of all things spoken of by the mouth of all the holy prophets since the world began."[79] Here the second coming and accompanying restoration of all things was to be preceded by the destruction of the wicked or end of the world. Parley P. Pratt's interpretation of Peter's prophecy in his popular 1837 *Voice of Warning* continues to echo this perception. After citing Peter's prophecy, Pratt states,

> It appears from the above that all the holy prophets, from Adam to Christ, and those that followed after, had their eyes upon a certain time, when all things should be restored to their primitive beauty and excellence. We also learn, that the time of restitution was to be at or near the time of Christ's second coming; for the heavens are to receive him, until the time of restitution and then the Father will send him again to the earth.[80]

As late as 1842, an article entitled "The Millennium" in the *Times and Seasons* also interpreted Peter's restoration as the millennial renewal of the earth: "When we speak of . . . the great restitution of all things spoken by the mouth of all the holy prophets since the world began, we mean to be understood that wherein the earth has been changed in the least from its primeval state, it will be restored, and the curse taken away; and in a word any derangement, or degenerated condition of the works of God, which will add to his glory and to the happiness of the saints by being restored, will be."[81]

Though the general LDS perception seems to have been that Peter's prophesied restoration referred to the redemption and renewal of the earth at Christ's coming, there also developed a sense that certain priesthood keys would be needed to help bring about this event. Doctrine and Covenants 27:6, a verse not added until the 1835 edition, reveals that an ancient prophet named "Elias" held "the keys of bringing to pass the restoration of all things spoken by the mouth of all the holy prophets since the world began." Joseph's association of Elias with Peter's "restoration of all things" can be further seen in his revision of the New

Testament, where he may have first made this connection. Matthew 17:11, for example, states that "Elias truly shall first come, and restore all things," to which the JST appends "as the prophets have written" (JST Matt 17:10, 14), thereby echoing the language of Peter in Acts 3:21 ("spoken by . . . all his holy prophets"). The stated meaning of this passage, as given by Jesus himself in the very next verse, is that the prophecy of the coming of Elias to restore all things was fulfilled in the mission of John the Baptist. The disciples had just seen Moses and Elias (i.e., Elijah) talking to Jesus on the Mount of Transfiguration, which prompted them to ask him what was meant by the teaching that Elias should come (an apparent reference to Malachi 4:5). Jesus responds:

> Elias truly shall first come, and restore all things. But I say unto you, That Elias is come already, and they knew him not, but have done unto him whatsoever they listed. Likewise shall also the Son of man suffer of them.
> Then the disciples understood that he spake unto them of John the Baptist. (Matt. 17:12–13)

As to the sense in which John the Baptist was to effect a restoration, Adam Clarke notes that the word "restore" is used in this passage because Christ was quoting from the Septuagint, which states that Elijah will "restore" the hearts of the fathers to the children (Mal. 4:5–6).[82] Thus, the restoration to be effected by John was a restoration of family solidarity and a return of Israel to righteousness, which was understood anciently to be Elijah's mission (see the apocryphal Ecclesiasticus 48:10).

The Prophet also makes the connection between Elias and the restoration in JST John 1:22–26. Thereafter "the restoration of all things" in Joseph Smith's teachings is frequently associated with this mysterious Elias whose identity is never made quite, or at least consistently, clear. The Elias of the restoration was variously identified in early LDS teachings as some unknown ancient Hebrew prophet (who is oddly given the Greek name Elias in D&C 110:12),[83] John the Baptist (Luke 1:17), Jesus Christ (JST John 1:21–28), John the Revelator (D&C 77:14), the angel Gabriel (D&C 27:6; cf. Luke 1:19), one of the angels of the apocalypse (D&C 77:9), and even Joseph Smith.[84]

In the New Testament, *Elias* is simply the Greek form of the Old Testament prophet Elijah's name. Therefore, all occurrences of *Elias* are either direct or indirect references to Elijah. Modern Bible translations actually use "Elijah" instead of "Elias" to remove this unnecessary confusion. In Luke 1:17, Christ referred to John the Baptist as Elijah, because "he shall go before him [i.e., Christ] in the spirit and power of Elias [i.e.,

Elijah], to turn the hearts of the fathers to the children." Even the footnote for this verse in the LDS Bible identifies Elias as Elijah.

Joseph Smith's scriptural alterations and later commentary on Elias, which seem to overlook or disregard its Greek etymology, obscures the simple New Testament idea that Elijah came in the person of John the Baptist who was filled with the spirit of Elijah. The Prophet draws a distinction between Elias and Elijah, stating, "There is a difference between the spirit & office of Elias & Elijah."[85] In the KJV, no such distinction exists, nor would it make sense because Elias and Elijah are one and the same.[86]

Nauvoo Period

At a conference of the Church in October 1840, Joseph Smith spoke of the restoration of all things exclusively in terms of the restoration of the priesthood with its rights and privileges. "All things had under the Authority of the Priesthood at any former period," he said, "shall be had again—bringing to pass the restoration spoken of by the mouth of all the Holy Prophets."[87] The Prophet would even go so far as to state that this restoration necessarily included the return of certain Old Testament practices such as animal sacrifice.[88] This is in spite of the fact that the New Testament and Book of Mormon both teach that sacrificial offerings were done away in Christ (Heb. 7:27; 10:8–9; 3 Ne. 9:19–20), who was to be the absolute "last sacrifice" (Alma 34:14). Joseph himself had earlier (January 1834) taught that "the ordinance or institution of offering blood in sacrifice, was only designed to be performed till Christ was offered up and shed His blood."[89] Nevertheless, now he would assert that the "offering of sacrifice has ever been connected [with] and forms a part of the duties of the Priesthood.... We frequently have mention made of the offering of sacrifice by the servants of the Most High in ancient days, prior to the law of Moses; which ordinances will be continued when the Priesthood is restored with all its authority, power and blessings."[90] If animal sacrifice is to be restored because it was practiced prior to the law of Moses, one wonders if perhaps the Prophet might have envisioned the pre-Mosaic practice of circumcision being restored as well.

Modern LDS Teachings

The common LDS perception today is that the restoration of all things spoken of by Peter has reference primarily, if not exclusively, to the latter-day restoration of the priesthood, the gospel, and all of its ordinances. Even with this perception, however, Latter-day Saints have been, and continue to be, reluctant to embrace the Prophet's vision of the restoration of the "ordinance of [blood] sacrifice," which Joseph said would continue to be performed "after the coming of Christ, from generation to generation."[91] Twentieth-century LDS authorities have downplayed the extent and nature of the restoration of blood sacrifice. Joseph Fielding Smith asserted that the return of blood sacrifice would last only a short while.[92] Bruce R. McConkie went even further saying it would only be on a "one-time basis."[93] John A. Widtsoe described this sacrifice as altogether of a spiritual nature.[94] In contrast to these later explanations of fulfillment, Joseph Smith, himself, envisioned temples erected in the city of Zion solely for the lesser priesthood where ordinances such as blood sacrifice might be performed on an ongoing basis.[95]

Notes

1. Richard T. Hughes, "Joseph Smith as an American Restorationist," 33.
2. Robert Mallett, "What Do You Mean, Restoration Movement?"
3. First Presidency counselor Marion G. Romney, for example, stated: "Of all the churches then claiming to represent Christ, not one of them bore his name." Romney, "Why the Church of Jesus Christ of Latter-day Saints," 31.
4. Mallett, "What Do You Mean, Restoration Movement?"
5. "Christian Union—No. 1," *Christian Baptist* 2 (July 4, 1825): 237.
6. Richard L. Bushman, *Joseph Smith: Rough Stone Rolling*, 172–75.
7. B. H. Roberts, *A Comprehensive History of the Church of Jesus Christ of Latter-day Saints*, 1:405–6.
8. Ibid.
9. James D. G. Dunn, *Unity and Diversity in the New Testament: An Inquiry into the Character of Earliest Christianity*, 407.
10. Ibid., 6.
11. Bart Ehrman, *Lost Christianities: The Battle for Scripture and the Faiths We Never Knew*, 1–2.
12. Dunn, *Unity and Diversity in the New Testament*, 408.
13. Euan Cameron, *Interpreting Christian History: The Challenge of the Churches' Past*, 161.
14. Rand H. Packer, "Dispensation of the Fulness of Times," 1:387.
15. James B. Allen, "The Significance of Joseph's 'First Vision,' in Mormon Thought," 39.
16. Ibid., 40. The earliest recorded reference to the First Vision (April 1830) emphasizes only that Joseph "received a remission of his sins" (D&C 20:5).
17. Mark D. Thomas, *Digging in Cumorah: Reclaiming Book of Mormon Narratives*, 52–53. For specific examples of others who claimed to see the Father and the Son, see D. Michael Quinn, *The Mormon Hierarchy: Origins of Power*, 69 note 13. See also Greg Kofford, "The First Vision: Doctrinal Developments and Analysis."

18. Allen, "The Significance of Joseph's 'First Vision,'" 29–45.

19. Ibid., 30.

20. This list of early nineteenth-century prophets and prophetesses is in Milton V. Backman, *Joseph Smith's First Vision: The First Vision in Historical Context*, 138. Historian Susan Juster notes that there is record of some 300 prophets between 1750 and 1820 and many others that are undocumented. Susan Juster, *Doomsayers: Anglo-American Prophecies in the Age of Revolution*, 64.

21. Richard L. Bushman, "A Joseph Smith for the Twenty-first Century," 166.

22. J. J. M. Roberts, "Isaiah," 1025.

23. Oddly, many LDS commentators don't see an allusion to necromancy in the expression "familiar spirit" as used in the Bible and the Book of Mormon, and instead assert that "familiar" means to be recognizably similar. BYU religion professor Daniel Ludlow remarks, "Some biblical scholars have maintained that witchcraft is being referred to in that portion of Isaiah 29:4. . . . However, a careful reading of this scripture . . . would indicate that the term . . . means that this record (the Book of Mormon) would speak with a 'familiar voice' to those who already have the Bible. In other words, . . . the Book of Mormon would seem familiar to people who had already read and accepted the Bible." Daniel H. Ludlow, *A Companion to Your Study of the Book of Mormon*, 146. Likewise, McConkie writes, "The spirit and tone and tenor of the message shall be familiar. A like account, one dealing with the same truths, the same laws, and the same ordinances, is found in the Bible." Bruce R. McConkie, *The Millennial Messiah: The Second Coming of the Son of Man*, 152. Of course, this interpretation precludes Joseph from being the one metaphorically possessed by a familiar spirit.

24. See, for example, Roberts, "Isaiah," 1051. See also Susan Ackerman, "Isaiah," 994.

25. Some LDS commentators interpret the "me" in Isaiah 1:2 to be a personification of America: "And it shall be unto me [i.e., America] as Ariel." See, for example, James E. Talmage, *Articles of Faith*, 250. The more obvious referent of "me," however, is God who is doing the talking. Scholars explain that "Ariel" simply means "hearth (or altar) of God" and is a poetic reference to Jerusalem. Thus, the meaning is: "It [Jerusalem] shall be unto me [God] as Ariel [a hearth or altar]." This becomes clear in the NRSV which reads, "Jerusalem shall be to me like an Ariel." Interestingly, the JST rephrases v. 2 so that "me" refers to Isaiah: "for thus hath the Lord said unto me [i.e., Isaiah], It shall be unto Ariel." This revision evidently doesn't see Ariel being used as a simile (it shall be *as* Ariel).

26. Richard G. Grant, "Isaiah in the Book of Mormon."

27. Robert Cloward, "Isaiah 29 in the Book of Mormon," 191.

28. Paul Y. Hoskisson, "Update: The 'Familiar Spirit' in 2 Nephi 26:12," 7.

29. Royal Skousen has established that the 1830 edition of the Book of Mormon was the source for most of Joseph Smith's later translation of Isaiah. Royal Skousen, "Textual Variants in the Isaiah Quotations," 387–88. The current official LDS publication of the Bible doesn't include the significant JST changes to Isaiah 29 identified in the Book of Mormon because the Scripture Publications Committee was instructed by the First Presidency to avoid duplicating material that appears elsewhere in scripture. Thus, changes in the JST

that also appear in places like the Book of Moses, Joseph Smith—Matthew, and the Book of Mormon were not included. Thomas E. Sherry and Jeffrey Marsh, "Precious Truths Restored: Joseph Smith Translation Changes Not Included in Our Bible," 64.

30. Oliver Cowdery, "To W. W. Phelps," 80.

31. Dean C. Jessee, comp. and ed., *The Personal Writings of Joseph Smith*, 14. See also Brant Gardner, *The Gift and Power*, 4–5, 121–22, 244–45.

32. See "Joseph Smith," Topical Guide, LDS Bible.

33. Parley P. Pratt, *Key to the Science of Theology*, 77; emphasis mine.

34. Joseph Fielding Smith, *Doctrines of Salvation: Compiled Sermons of Joseph Fielding Smith*, 3:11.

35. See, for example, W. Sibley Towner, "Malachi,"1432.

36. Ibid., 1428.

37. Mark D. Thomas, "A Mosaic for a Religious Counterculture: The Bible in the Book of Mormon," 55.

38. BYU Religion Professor Scott Esplin notes that the interpretation of Isaiah 11 as an allusion to Joseph Smith came in the wake of mounting doubts expressed regarding his calling. Hence the revelation "reveals that Joseph was not a fallen prophet, as his adversaries in Kirtland proclaimed." Scott C. Esplin, "The Fall of Kirtland: The Doctrine and Covenants' Role in Reaffirming Joseph," 19.

39. McConkie, *The Millennial Messiah*, 339–40; Keith H. Meservy, "God Is With Us (Isaiah 1–17)," 102. Hyrum L. Andrus, *Doctrines of the Kingdom*, 567 note 46.

40. Andrew F. Ehat and Lyndon W. Cook, *The Words of Joseph Smith*, 331.

41. Quinn, *The Mormon Hierarchy: Origins of Power*, 231.

42. Sidney B. Sperry, *Book of Mormon Compendium*, 222.

43. Joseph Smith apparently thought verses 2–5 were describing "the stem of Jesse" (D&C 113:1–2) instead of describing the rod or branch emanating from the stem.

44. Christopher R. Seitz, *Isaiah 1–39*, 107–108; House, *Old Testament Theology*, 280–81.

45. See, for example, McConkie, *The Millennial Messiah*, 602–11; Bruce R. McConkie, *A New Witness for the Articles of Faith*, 518; Robert L. Millet, "Life in the Millennium," 182; Kent P. Jackson, "The Lord Is There (Ezekiel 37–48)," 306–7.

46. See, for example, Bruce R. McConkie, *The Promised Messiah: The First Coming of Christ*, 192; Joseph Fielding McConkie and Robert L. Millet, *Doctrinal Commentary on the Book of Mormon*, 1: 281.

47. An early LDS example is cited in Terryl Givens, *By the Hand of Mormon: The American Scripture that Launched a New World Religion*, 13. For a current example, see Michael T. Griffith, *One Lord, One Faith: Writings of the Early Christian Fathers as Evidences of the Restoration*, 94. An editorial in *Times and Seasons* 2 (April 1, 1841): 359, had to correct "some who have lately embraced the faith of the 'Saints'; and who fancy that it [Moses's prophecy] applies to the prophet [Joseph Smith] whom God hath raised up in these last days."

48. Frank F. Judd, "Prophets 'Like unto Moses,'" 7.

49. See Ronald E. Clements, "Deuteronomy," 297.

50. *New American Bible*, 178 note 18, 15.

51. Ehat and Cook, *The Words of Joseph Smith*, 365–69; emphasis mine.

52. According to John Taylor, the first "marring" occurred "near the hill Cumorah, when Joseph Smith was knocked down with a handspike, and afterwards healed almost instantly! The second time he was marred . . . his flesh was scratched off, and he was tarred and feathered. He was again healed instantly, fulfilling the prophecy twice." He also interpreted this passage as a reference to Joseph Smith. John Taylor, "Reflections," 359.

53. James E. Talmage, *Jesus the Christ: A Study of the Messiah and His Mission According to Holy Scriptures Both Ancient and Modern*, 47; Gordon B. Hinckley, *Be Thou an Example*, 87.

54. See Bruce R. McConkie, *Mortal Messiah: From Bethlehem to Calvary*, 4:354.

55. Joseph Fielding McConkie, *Answers: Straightforward Answers to Tough Gospel Questions*, 125-26.

56. Though the authorship of Ephesians is disputed (together with certain other epistles traditionally attributed to Paul), a Pauline authorship is assumed here for simplicity sake.

57. LDS Bible Dictionary, s.v. "Dispensation," 657.

58. Ehat and Cook, *The Words of Joseph Smith*, 39.

59. Philip L. Barlow, *Mormons and the Bible: The Place of Latter-day Saints in American Religion*, 176.

60. Michael J. Vlach, "What Is Dispensationalism?"

61. Ehat and Cook, *The Words of Joseph Smith*, 370.

62. "Conference Minutes," *Times and Seasons* 2 (February 1841): 307.

63. LDS Bible Dictionary, s.v. "Dispensation," 657.

64. F. F. Bruce, ed., *Vine's Expository Dictionary of Old and New Testament Words*, 321.

65. Frank E. Gaebelein, ed., *The Expositor's Bible Commentary*, 11:26.

66. Herman N. Ridderbos, *Paul: An Outline of His Theology*, 487.

67. John A. Tvedtnes, "Review of Michael T. Griffith, *One Lord, One Faith: Writings of the Early Christian Fathers as Evidences of the Restoration*," 39.

68. Merrill J. Bateman, "A Pattern for All," 76.

69. Jan Shipps, *Sojourner in the Promised Land: Forty Years among the Mormons*, 229.

70. Some Bible commentators such as Adam Clarke suggest that Peter may be referring to the restoration of the kingdom of Israel since it was referred to earlier in Acts 1:6 and was a common theme of many Old Testament prophecies. Craig S. Keener, *The IVP Bible: Background Commentary*, 332. Scholars generally point out, however, that such an interpretation is too limiting, given the more universal scope implied by the phrase "all things."

71. Beverly Roberts Gaventa, "Acts," 2064.

72. Hosea Ballou, *A Treatise on Atonement*, 179.

73. Reprinted in *The Universalist Register: Containing the Statistics of the Church, with an Almanac for 1874*, 20–21. In the early 1800s, Protestants asserted that Universalism was "the prominent heresy of our times." Parson Cooke, "Review of 'Commendation and Reproof of Unitarians,'" 224. For an analysis of the pervasive anti-Universalist rhetoric in the Book of Mormon,

see Dan Vogel, "Anti-Universalist Rhetoric in the Book of Mormon," 21–52. For a response to Vogel, see Martin S. Tanner, "Is There Anti-Universalist Rhetoric in the Book of Mormon?" 21–52.

74. See, for example, G. W. J., "Essay on Future Punishment," 444.

75. "An attempt to explain several of the principal texts . . . ," *Connecticut Evangelical Magazine* 6 (September 1805): 83–84.

76. Ibid., 87.

77. Edwin Firmage Jr., "Historical Criticism and the Book of Mormon: A Personal Encounter," 61.

78. Cited in Grant Underwood, "Attempting to Situate Joseph Smith," 44.

79. Jessee, *Personal Writings of Joseph Smith*, 387.

80. Parley P. Pratt, *Voice of Warning and Instruction to All People . . .* , 93. In May 1841, Pratt wrote a letter to Queen Victoria in which he spoke of a complete "revolution" of the earth and society constituting "the restoration of all things." He further stated that Christ would come "at the times of restitution." Parley P. Pratt, *An Appeal to the Inhabitants of the State of New York . . .* , 10.

81. "The Millennium," *Times and Seasons* 3, no. 7 (February 1, 1842): 672.

82. See Adam Clarke, *Commentary on the Bible*, s.v. Matt. 17.

83. Joseph Fielding Smith asserts that this prophet named Elias was Noah. Joseph Fielding Smith, *Answers to Gospel Questions*, 3:138. Bruce R. McConkie speculates that "Elias" could have been Abraham himself, a prophet living at the time of Abraham, or simply a title for a restorer. McConkie, *The Millennial Messiah*, 103.

84. Ehat and Cook, *The Words of Joseph Smith*, 370. McConkie's later solution to all of these "apparently contradictory" identifications of Elias was to interpret Elias as a "composite personage" consisting of anyone who restored keys. Bruce R. McConkie, *Mormon Doctrine*, 221.

85. Ehat and Cook, *The Words of Joseph Smith*, 327.

86. As if Joseph was unaware or unconvinced that the name "Elias" in the New Testament was simply the Greek form of "Elijah," he revised Mark 9:4, which speaks of the appearance of Elias (i.e., Elijah) and Moses on the Mount of Transfiguration, to read "John the Baptist and Moses" (JST Mark 9:4). This substitution of John the Baptist for Elijah is generally either ignored in LDS commentary or explained as an addition, rather than a substitution, since it would be inconsistent with other scriptures that mention Elijah and Moses. See, e.g., the LDS Bible Dictionary, s.v. "Elias." Doctrine and Covenants 27:6–9, 110:12–13, and 138:45–46, also speak of Elias and Elijah as two separate prophets. For a recent discussion on Joseph's use of Elias, see Samuel M. Brown, "The Prophet Elias Puzzle," 1–17.

Joseph seems to have been similarly unaware that the name "Esaias" is simply the Greek form of "Isaiah" (which is how it appears in the New Testament) and therefore mysteriously proclaimed Esaias to be a prophet who "lived in the days of Abraham" many centuries before Isaiah (D&C 84:11–13). Doctrine and Covenants 76:100 explicitly distinguishes "Esaias" from "Isaiah."

87. Ehat and Cook, *The Words of Joseph Smith*, 42.

88. Ibid., 43.

89. Joseph Smith Jr., "The Elders of the Church in Kirtland, to their Brethren Abroad," *Evening and Morning Star* 2 (March 1834): 143.

90. Ehat and Cook, *The Words of Joseph Smith*, 43. Even though Joseph stated that it was the pre-Mosaic sacrificial offering performed by Melchizedek Priesthood authority that would be restored (ibid., 44), the authority to perform these sacrifices was part of the Aaronic Priesthood authority that was restored by John the Baptist (D&C 13). Joseph further taught that the 144,000 mentioned in Revelation 14:1 represented "the number of priests who should be appointed to administer in the daily sacrifice." Ibid., 170.

91. Ibid., 43.

92. Joseph Fielding Smith, *Doctrines of Salvation: Compiled Sermons of Joseph Fielding Smith*, 3:94.

93. McConkie, *Mormon Doctrine*, 666.

94. John A. Widtsoe, *Priesthood and Church Government*, 5 note.

95. *History of the Church*, 1:357–59; Ehat and Cook, *The Words of Joseph Smith*, 43.

~ 4 ~

The Restoration of the Priesthood and the Church

In LDS thought, the latter-day restoration consists first and foremost of the return of priesthood authority and the reestablishment of Christ's church on the earth. All blessings pertaining to salvation are administered by God's authorized servants in his restored church. This chapter examines the extent to which biblical writers appear to have anticipated the restoration of the priesthood and the Church, and how this idea developed in early Mormonism.

Restoration of the Priesthood

Latter-day Saints view the restoration of the priesthood by angelic messengers as being an essential prerequisite for reorganizing Christ's church in the latter days. According to the accounts of Joseph Smith and Oliver Cowdery, the Aaronic Priesthood was conferred on them by John the Baptist on May 15, 1829 (D&C 13). This was followed by the restoration of the Melchizedek Priesthood by Peter, James, and John either sometime before the end of June 1829 or sometime around July 1830.[1] Finally, on April 3, 1836, Elijah, Moses, and Elias restored their respective keys (i.e., authoritative privileges) in the Kirtland Temple (see D&C 110). On various other occasions, "divers angels, from Michael or Adam down to the present time" also visited the Prophet, "all declaring their dispensation, their rights, their keys, their honors, their majesty and glory, and the power of their priesthood" (D&C 128:21). According to traditional LDS narratives, this restoration of priesthood authority fulfills ancient prophecy.

Old Testament

The principal Old Testament prophecy[2] cited as a reference to the latter-day restoration of priesthood authority is Malachi 4:5–6:

> I will send you Elijah the prophet before the coming of the great and dreadful day of the Lord:
> And he shall turn the heart of the fathers to the children, and the heart of the children to their fathers, lest I come and smite the earth with a curse.

The basic LDS understanding of this passage, as expressed in the Church publication *Gospel Principles*, is that "Elijah would restore the sealing powers so families could be sealed together. He would also inspire people to be concerned about their ancestors and descendants."[3] Latter-day Saints view this prophecy as having been fulfilled with the coming of Elijah to the Kirtland Temple on April 3, 1836 (D&C 110:13–16). Elaborating on the nature of the sealing power of Elijah, Bruce R. McConkie writes, "Elijah came and restored the sealing power—the power that binds on earth and seals in heaven, the power by which all ordinances have efficacy beyond the grave, the power that turns the hearts of children to their fathers and fathers to their children. It is a power that operates for the living and the dead."[4] This understanding of Elijah's mission is the culmination of several successive interpretations of Malachi's prophecy given by the Prophet during his lifetime, which seem to reflect progressive stages in his theological understanding.

Malachi's prophecy, as it appears in the Old Testament, gives no indication that Elijah would restore priesthood keys or reveal sealing ordinances either for the living or the dead. The New English Bible (NEB) translation of Malachi 4:6 reads that Elijah will come to "reconcile fathers to sons and sons to fathers." The apocryphal Book of Ecclesiasticus, written about 200 B.C., similarly states that Elijah's mission was "to reconcile the heart of the father to the son, and to restore the tribes of Jacob" (Ecclus. 48:10).

The New Testament interprets Elijah's coming as having been fulfilled in John the Baptist who went before Jesus "in the spirit and power of Elias [i.e., Elijah], to turn the hearts of the fathers to the children, and the disobedient to the wisdom of the just; to make ready a people prepared for the Lord" (Luke. 1:17; see also discussion in Chapter 3). John's coming in the spirit of Elijah, therefore, was for the purpose of turning the affections of parents to their children and, in general, turning the disobedient to God. There is no mention of John exercising what Mormons traditionally understand as sealing powers, but then, according to LDS doctrine, he would have been unable to because he held only the Aaronic Priesthood.

In Chapter 3, we noted that Elijah's coming was seen by many of Joseph Smith's contemporaries as having a dual fulfillment: once with the coming of John the Baptist, and the other by a yet-to-be-identified latter-day Elijah, whom some believed to be Elijah himself.[5] It was generally understood that the turning of the hearts of fathers and children meant improving family relations and, in general, restoring obedience to God's laws.[6]

An 1832 LDS editorial in the *Evening and the Morning Star* echoed the belief that "an" Elijah would come twice. "Now the Savior said he [Elijah] is come already, but the Jews knew it not, so he did not turn the hearts of the fathers to the children." Consequently, Elijah "will yet come and restore the tribes of Jacob."[7] The notion was that because Elijah (in the person of John the Baptist) failed to turn the hearts of the fathers and children to each other at the time of Christ, he (or one like him) must yet come to accomplish this mission.

This popular Christian view of a future coming of Elijah was refuted by traditional Christian theologians of the day, who pointed to Christ's own explanation that Elijah had already come in the person of John the Baptist. In 1827, Presbyterian writer Josiah Priest wrote,

> Some Millenarians have imagined that Elijah the prophet is yet to come, as a forerunner of the Messiah's second advent. They disallow that John the Baptist was Elijah, because, say they, he did not do the work foretold of him by Malachi, 'which was to turn the heart of the fathers to the children, and the heart of the children to their fathers.' Mal. iv.6. This work is supposed by them . . . [to] be accomplished by the real Elijah, when he comes as a forerunner of the second advent of Christ. But that opinion has its refutation in the assertion of Christ, who well knew . . . [that] John the Baptist was Elias.[8]

Joseph Smith and his associates seem to have initially understood the promise of Elijah's return along the traditional lines of strengthening families and restoring the disobedient Jews to God. An LDS revelation given in 1833 urged Saints to

> seek diligently to turn the hearts of the children to their fathers, and the hearts of the fathers to the children;
> And again, the hearts of the Jews unto the prophets, and the prophets unto the Jews; lest I come and smite the whole earth with a curse. (D&C 98:16–17)

Significantly, in all versions of Malachi's prophecy revealed to Joseph Smith prior to 1838, there is no change in the wording from the KJV, nor is there any indication that Elijah would restore any sealing authority. This includes passages in the Book of Mormon (3 Ne. 25:5–6), the Doctrine and Covenants (D&C 27:9, 110:13–16), and even JST Malachi 4:4–5. On July 2, 1833 Joseph dictated the word "correct," which his scribe wrote at the head of the book of Malachi indicating his approval of the text as it stood. Even the account of Elijah's return to the Kirtland Temple in April 1836 states only that the keys he restored were intended "to turn the hearts of the fathers to the children, and the children to the fathers" (D&C 110:14). There is no mention of a conferral of "sealing" powers.

It was in May 1838 that Joseph first gave any indication of a different understanding of Elijah's mission, which is reflected in his rewording of Malachi's prophecy:

> Behold, I will reveal unto you the Priesthood, by the hand of Elijah the prophet. . . .
> And he shall plant in the hearts of the children the promises made to the fathers, and the hearts of the children shall turn to their fathers (JS–H 1:38–39; see also D&C 2:1–2).[9]

Elijah's mission is now to "reveal the priesthood" and "plant the promises made to the fathers" in the hearts of the children. To "reveal the priesthood" presumably meant making known the authority or blessings appertaining to the priesthood.[10] The "promises made to the fathers" appears to have reference to the promises made to the ancient patriarchal fathers: Abraham, Isaac, and Jacob. Joseph had frequently spoken of the promises made to these ancient fathers regarding the glories to be revealed in the last days and that "the children of the fathers have claim [on these promises] unto this day."[11] This is the first time, however, that the Prophet makes reference to these promises in connection with the coming of Elijah.

In July 1839, Joseph spoke of a more active sense in which these ancient fathers would turn to their children: "These men are in heaven, but their children are on earth. Their bowels yearn over us. . . . All these authoritative characters will come down & join hand in hand in bringing about this work."[12] In this same discourse, he said, "The hearts of the children will have to be turned to the fathers, & the fathers to the children living or dead to prepare them for the coming of the Son of Man."[13] Thus, righteous fathers who are in heaven are to "turn" to their children on earth by joining forces with them in building God's kingdom on earth. Absent, however, is any mention of Elijah restoring any sealing power, nor is his coming associated with the performance of saving ordinances for the dead—that development would not occur until 1842 (D&C 128:17–18), two years after vicarious work for the dead was introduced in the Church (see Chapter 16).

In October 1840, the Prophet first made clear that Elijah came to "restore the authority and deliver the keys of the priesthood." This is different from the earlier language of Doctrine and Covenants 110:13–16, which has him committing the keys, not of the priesthood *per se*, but "to turn the hearts of the fathers to the children, and the children to the fathers." As the Prophet now expresses it, Elijah restored the necessary authority so that "all the ordinances may be attended to in righteousness."[14] Joseph did not explain what significance this new interpretation had for the validity of ordinances performed prior to the coming of Elijah and if they were somehow *not* performed "in righteousness." Joseph Fielding Smith attempted to resolve this conundrum by suggesting that the Prophet had reference only to the higher ordinances of the temple.[15] This explanation is problematic, however, since temple ordinances had not yet been introduced and, furthermore, the Prophet spoke of "all the ordinances." Why Elijah's authority would have been needed to make any ordinance binding is unclear—since Peter, James, and John restored "the keys of the kingdom," which included the authority to "bind on earth" and "in heaven" (Matt. 16:19).

Two years later, in September 1842, the first explicit association was made between the coming of Elijah and salvation for the dead. After citing Malachi 4:5–6, Joseph Smith commented that "the earth will be smitten with a curse unless there is a welding link of some kind or other between the fathers and the children, upon some subject or other—and behold what is this subject? It is the baptism for the dead" (D&C 128:18). The Prophet saw baptism for the dead as a practice which connects dispensations; prophets (the fathers) from former dispensations restored keys to perform such baptisms, and saints (the children) in this dispensation are baptized for those of prior dispensations. This "welding together of dispensations" (D&C 128:18) is the "welding link" the prophet spoke of. It was not, as yet, used to denote a welding of family generations through sealings.

In August 1843, Joseph Smith began associating Elijah's coming with the power to seal individuals up to eternal life—even though elders had already been using their priesthood since 1831 (five years prior to Elijah's coming) to seal individuals and even entire congregations to eternal life[16] (see Chapter 15). Now couples would be sealed to eternal life when they entered into the new and everlasting covenant of marriage. This seal of eternal life was also believed to automatically secure their posterity to them for all time. The Prophet remarked, "When a seal [of eternal life] is put upon the father and mother it secures their posterity so that they cannot be lost but will be saved by virtue of the covenant of their father [and mother]."[17] A few months later in January 1844, he delivered a sermon in which he declared that the word "turn" in Malachi 4:5 "should be translated bind or seal."[18] Then in answer to the question, "How is it [i.e., Malachi's prophecy] to be fulfilled?" Joseph responded,

> By [the Saints] building thair temples erecting their baptismal fonts & going forth & receiving all the ordinances, baptisms, confirmations, washings anointings ordinations & sealing powers upon their heads in behalf of all our progenitors who are dead & redeem them that they may come forth in the first resurrection & be exalted to thrones of glory with us, & here in is the chain that binds the hearts of the fathers to the children, & the children to the fathers which fulfills the mission of Elijah.[19]

According to this explanation, Elijah restored the power to perform all of the saving ordinances on behalf of our dead progenitors, which included the practice of sealing the saints to eternal life. This sealing did not initially involve the ordinance of sealing children to parents but rather referred to the sealing ordinance by which an individual, living or dead is sealed up to eternal life (see Chapter 15). As yet, there was no mention of any ordinance in which children were sealed to parents either living or dead.

It wasn't until March 1844, eight years after Elijah's appearance in the Kirtland Temple, that Joseph Smith spoke of an actual sealing ordinance that directly joins children to parents. He stated that God "should send Elijah to seal the children to the fathers & fathers to the children," and explained that this sealing power includes "the power . . . to seal those [children] who dwell on earth to those [fathers] which dwell in heaven."[20] He therefore instructed the Saints, "Go & seal on earth your sons & daughters unto yourself, & yourself unto your fathers in eternal glory."[21]

A discernible progression is evident in Joseph's explications of Malachi's prophecy. Prior to 1838, he consistently spoke of Elijah's coming only in terms of turning the affections of living parents and children to each other. In May 1838, he spoke somewhat enigmatically of Elijah "revealing the priesthood" and planting the covenants revealed to the ancient patriarchs in the hearts of the children. By October 1840, Elijah was seen as actually restoring the priesthood keys necessary for all ordinances of the gospel to be performed with lasting validity. In September 1842, he saw Elijah's mission as turning the hearts of those in present and past dispensations to each other through the institution of baptism for the dead. In 1843, Elijah was seen as having restored the power to seal individuals, either living or dead, to eternal life. In March 1844, he finally expressed that Elijah restored the power to seal children to their parents, living or dead. It is of interest to note that, although he admonished the Saints to become "sealed" to their deceased parents, this practice wasn't put into full effect in the Church until 1894.[22] Joseph's older brother Alvin, who was baptized by proxy in 1840, wasn't sealed to his parents until August 1897.

New Testament

Like the Old Testament, the New Testament gives little indication that priesthood authority would be restored in the latter days. Latter-day Saints, however, frequently cite Matthew 17:11, in which Jesus states: "Elias truly shall first come, and restore all things" (Matt. 17:11), as proof that such a restoration was prophesied to occur. Bruce R. McConkie construed this Elias of the restoration to be a latter-day composite Elias—that is, Elias is viewed, not as a single individual, but rather as multiple individuals who came and restored priesthood keys in the latter days.[23] Most scholars would argue, however, that Matthew is simply alluding to Malachi's prophecy of the coming of Elijah (Mal. 4:5–6). As noted in the previous chapter, Matthew is citing the Greek Septuagint, which uses the word *Elias* when speaking of the coming of Elijah to "restore" the children to the fathers and the Jews to righteousness. The interpretation that Jesus himself gives of this prophecy is that the coming of Elias (i.e., Elijah) was fulfilled in the person of John the Baptist who had already come (Matt. 17:12–13).

Early Mormonism

The Book of Mormon says nothing regarding the restoration of priesthood authority or its importance in the latter-day work of the Lord. The first recorded reference to restorations of their respective priesthoods by John the Baptist and by Peter, James, and John wasn't until 1834, some five years after these events reportedly occurred.[24] The original sixty-five sections of the Doctrine and Covenants published as the *Book of Commandments* in 1833 make no mention at all of Aaronic and Melchizedek priesthoods, much less their restoration. Section 13, which references the "the priesthood of Aaron," wasn't recorded until Joseph Smith wrote his history in 1838 (JS-H 1:69). The references to John the Baptist and Peter, James, and John in section 27 of the current Doctrine and Covenants were added in 1835. David Whitmer and William E. McLellin, who at the time were close associates of the Prophet, later alleged that they knew nothing of any priesthood restoration taking place.[25] Their understanding was that Joseph and Oliver's authority to ordain each other, and others, to ministerial offices (e.g., elder, priest, teacher) was received by commandment, and not by angelic administration.[26] Initially, these offices had no connection to Aaronic or Melchizedek priesthoods.[27] Richard L. Bushman has observed that "the late appearance of these accounts [of the restoration of the priesthood] raises the possibility of later fabrication."[28] Joseph Smith gave his own explanation for this five-year silence regarding priesthood restoration: "We were forced to keep secret the circumstances of having received the Priesthood and our having been baptized, owing to a spirit of persecution in the neighborhood" (JS–H 1:74–75). Those who take the Prophet and his associate Oliver Cowdery at their word have no problem allowing for this silence on the priesthood restoration. Skeptics suggest instead that a later spirit of apostasy and challenge to authority caused Joseph and Oliver to produce accounts of angelic visitations to keep followers from defecting.[29] Ultimately, acceptance of these angelic ministrations becomes a matter of faith.

Establishment of the Church in the Latter Days

Mormonism teaches that the Church or kingdom of God has been intermittently on the earth since the time of Adam and that its establishment on the earth in modern times was foretold in the Bible. While there are, indeed, biblical prophecies regarding the establishment of God's "kingdom" in the last days, this kingdom is never explicitly equated with Christ's church. Here we examine what scripture seems to say about the latter-day restoration of Christ's church.

Old Testament

One Old Testament prophecy frequently cited as a reference to the restoration of the Church in the last days is King Nebuchadnezzar's dream (Dan. 2:31–45). In his dream, the king saw a giant statue or colossus made of different materials. The "head was of fine gold, his breast and his arms of silver, his belly and his thighs of brass, his legs of iron, his feet part of iron and part of clay" (vv. 32–33). He then saw "that a stone was cut out without hands, which smote the image upon his feet that were of iron and clay, and brake them to pieces" (v. 34). This stone "became a great mountain, and filled the whole earth" (v. 35).

Daniel interpreted the king's dream as a description of events that "shall be in the latter days" (Dan. 2:28) with the different body parts representing successive kingdoms that would succeed the Babylonian kingdom of which Nebuchadnezzar was king. Thus, Daniel told Nebuchadnezzar, "Thou art this head of gold" (v. 38). Daniel then described four subsequent kingdoms, the last being represented by feet of iron and clay (v. 42) which signified that "the kingdom would be partly strong, and partly broken" (v. 42). Daniel declared that "in the days of these kings shall the God of heaven set up a kingdom, which shall never be destroyed and the kingdom shall not be left to other people, but it shall break in pieces and consume all these kingdoms, and it shall stand for ever" (v. 44).

Daniel's interpretation of the king's dream is mentioned nowhere in the New Testament; however, there is evidence in Revelation 1:13 that early Christians anticipated its imminent fulfillment with the coming of Daniel's prophesied "Son of Man" (Dan. 7:13). Indeed, Christians came to view the fourth kingdom as being the Roman Empire with the stone being Christianity itself, which has rolled forth since the time of Christ. This interpretation has generally persisted in Christian thought as each successive generation anticipated that Christianity was about to fill the earth. For example, early nineteenth-century Bible commentator Adam Clarke wrote that the stone represents "the spiritual kingdom of the Lord Jesus, which is to last for ever, and diffuse itself over the whole earth."[30]

In Joseph Smith's day, Nebuchadnezzar's prophetic dream had also become a means of explaining God's hand in contemporary political events. The Prophet's grandfather, Asael Smith, like others at this time, considered one fulfillment of this prophecy to be the establishment of the sovereign United States after the Revolutionary War.[31] Whether the stone was perceived as political or spiritual, the mountain into which it would eventually grow was generally perceived as being the millennial kingdom of Christ.[32] Mormonism similarly came to see its own restoration as the stone that would expand into the millennial kingdom (D&C 109:72).

Joseph Smith's interpretation of Nebuchadnezzar's dream differed from that of mainstream Christianity in that he saw the stone cut out without hands as being the restored church instead of the first-century Christian church. Said he, "I calculate to be one of the instruments of setting up the kingdom of Daniel . . . and I intend to lay a foundation that will revolutionize the whole world."[33] In October 1831 Joseph received a revelation stating that the "gospel" or "kingdom of God" shall "roll forth unto the ends of the earth, as the stone which is cut out of the mountain without hands shall roll forth, until it has filled the whole earth" (D&C 65:2–6).

Critical Bible scholars see Daniel's prophesied kingdom differently from both traditional Christians and Latter-day Saints. According to Yale University Old Testament professor John Collins, "all but the most conservative scholars now accept the conclusion that the book of Daniel is not a product of the Babylonian era but reached its present form in the 2nd century B.C.E. Daniel is not a historical person but a figure of legend."[34] Scholars point to literary and historical evidence that indicates that at least this portion of the book of Daniel was actually written between 168 and 164 B.C.[35] and not in the sixth century B.C.—which also means it was written pseudonymously, like several other known works that have Daniel as the pretended author.[36]

These scholars further interpret the four kingdoms in Nebuchadnezzar's dream as kingdoms in antiquity, which were known to the writer. Biblical scholar Matthias Henze, writing in *The New Interpreter's Study Bible*, states that the four kingdoms are "easily identified as Babylon (Nebuchadnezzar), Media (Darius the Mede), Persia (Cyrus of Persia), and Greece (the 'prince of Greece' [Alexander the Great] in [Daniel] 10:20)."[37] The feet of iron and clay are seen as representing the partly strong and partly weak kingdoms created when the Hellenistic empire of Alexander the Great was divided up upon his death. One of these kingdoms became the Seleucid Empire which ruled Jerusalem at the time the book of Daniel was actually written.[38] According to L. Michael White, a professor of classics and religious studies at the University of Texas at Austin, "In Daniel's interpretation . . . these [different body parts] refer to the succession of kingdoms after the Babylonians, the very kingdoms that are in charge of the Jews, ending with the Seleucids, who are the feet of clay, whom the forces of God crumble, causing the statue to collapse and this gives rise to a new kingdom of Israel."[39]

Bible scholars explain that it was during the Jewish rebellion against the Seleucids, known as the Maccabean Revolt, that the book of Daniel was written. The Jews temporarily won their freedom, but the predictions in Daniel beyond this point, including the establishment of a new kingdom of Israel, failed to materialize. Seen from this perspective, the book of Daniel provided hope for captive Jews of the time by showing that God was about to set up a kingdom on earth where they could finally live in peace. However, since neither the times nor the names of the kingdoms (beyond the first) are explicitly identified in Daniel, Nebuchadnezzar's dream has served as a source of validation and hope for many Jewish and Christian movements ever since the time it was given.

Another prophetic image in the Old Testament traditionally viewed by Latter-day Saints as describing the setting up of God's church on earth in the last days is Isaiah's prophesied "ensign" or "standard" that is raised to summon the nations. In Mormon discourse this ensign is interpreted as the LDS Church to which all nations will flow. According to Isaiah 11:12, the Lord "shall set up an ensign for the nations, and shall assemble the outcasts of Israel, and gather together the dispersed of Judah from the four corners of the earth."

Interestingly, this prophecy is repeated in the Isaiah texts in the Book of Mormon (2 Ne. 21:11–12), only there it is used to prophesy the coming forth of the Book of Mormon in the latter days. Thus, the Book of Mormon depicts *itself* as the ensign or standard to be raised (2 Ne. 29:2), and prophesies that latter-day opposition would not be directed at the church, but toward the Book of Mormon: "Many of the Gentiles shall say: A Bible! A Bible! We have got a Bible, and there cannot be any more Bible" (2 Ne. 29:3).

It wasn't until March 1831 that the "standard" became more broadly equated in Mormon thought with the gospel (D&C 45:9); and in 1832, the first issue of the Church's newspaper, the *Evening and the Morning Star*, designated the Church as "an ensign to all nations."[40] Nearly six years later, a revelation received April 26, 1838 called upon "The Church of Jesus Christ of Latter-day Saints" as a body of members to become "a standard for the nations" (D&C 115:4–5). Currently, the ensign spoken of by Isaiah is typically viewed as being synonymous with the Church and, more broadly, Mormonism.[41]

Though Latter-day Saints tend to see the LDS Church in Isaiah's ensign imagery, non-LDS biblical scholars interpret Isaiah's gathering to the ensign (Isa. 11:12) as what was perceived at the time to be an imminent restoration of the house of Israel to the lands from which it had been displaced. In ancient Israel, an ensign was a tribal banner or national flag. In this passage, the ensign was a call for the Israelites to gather together physically as a people. The Lord "shall assemble the outcasts of Israel, and gather together the dispersed of Judah from the four corners of the earth" (v. 12). There is no implication of a *spiritual* gathering or rallying of any kind around a religious standard.

Isaiah actually speaks of the raised ensign or standard in several different contexts: sometimes it is as a call to battle and other times it is to summon the dispersed. In LDS discourse, however, virtually all such references are lumped together and viewed collectively as prophecies of the gathering of Israel to the Church in the last days.[42] For example, Isaiah 5:26–29 states that God "will lift up an ensign to the nations from far" who will "come with speed swiftly" like lions "and lay hold of the prey, and shall carry it away safe." The chapter heading of the LDS edition of the Bible states: "The Lord shall lift an ensign and gather Israel." It is clear from the context, however, that this ensign was originally meant to rally Israel's enemies to take up arms against the rebellious Israelites and lead them "away" into captivity (v. 29). J. J. M. Roberts, a professor of Old Testament at Princeton Theological Seminary, explains that the raising of the ensign here means that "God will summon the Assyrians as his agent to punish Israel (cf. 7:18-20; 8:7; 10:5-6)."[43] Contextually, it doesn't appear that Isaiah's ensign is meant to be an ensign lifted up to the Israelites, and it is certainly not lifted with the intent of gathering them.

Another popular Old Testament prophecy cited as evidence of a restoration of the Church and kingdom in the latter days is Isaiah 29:14, which states: "I will proceed to do a marvellous work among this people, even a marvellous work and a wonder." Joseph Fielding Smith commented, "This marvelous work is the restoration of the Church and the Gospel with all the power and authority, keys and blessings which pertain to this great work for the salvation of the children of men."[44]

Prior to the organization of the Church in 1830, Isaiah's "marvelous work and a wonder" was understood by Mormons in a slightly different light than it is today. In the Book of Mormon, for instance, the "marvelous work and a wonder" wasn't the restoration of the Church and gospel, but the temporal and spiritual gatherings of Israel in the last days, mainly through the instrumentality of the Book of Mormon (1 Ne. 14:7; 2 Ne. 25:17–18; 29:1, 7). Similarly, early revelations in the Doctrine and Covenants exclusively reference the "marvelous work and a wonder" as the gathering of the righteous as they hear and accept the gospel contained in the Book of Mormon (D&C 4:1; 6:1; 11:1; 12:1; 14:1; 18:44). Once the translation of the Book of Mormon was completed, almost a year before the Church was founded, scriptural references to a "marvelous work and a wonder" ceased.

When read in context, the "marvelous work and a wonder" (NRSV = "things . . . shocking and amazing") in Isaiah appears to refer to God's work of vengeance on the ungodly, not his blessing of the righteous. The Lord declares, "Forasmuch as this people . . . have removed their heart far from me . . . I will proceed to do a marvellous work among this people, even a marvellous work and a wonder for the wisdom of their wise men shall perish, and the understanding of their prudent men shall be hid" (Isa. 29:13–14). It will be a wonder "for" (i.e., because) the wisdom of the wise shall perish. God's wonderful and marvelous works are not always positive in nature (see, for example, the "wonderful" plagues described in Deut. 28:59).[45] This may explain why the very next verse reads, "Woe unto them that seek deep to hide their counsel from the Lord" (Isa. 29:15).

New Testament

Several New Testament passages referring to the establishment of God's kingdom through Christ's first advent are viewed by many Latter-day Saints as referring to the Church's restoration in modern times. As discussed in Chapter 2, Joseph Smith recast several of the parables in Matthew 13, such as the parable of the wheat and the tares and the parable of the mustard seed, as references to the establishment of the LDS Church in the latter days. Most Bible scholars, however, see these parables as simply alluding to the way God's kingdom would start small with Jesus's inauguration and gradually expand. Indeed, there is no indication in the parables of a much later "restored" church or kingdom.

Many New Testament scholars question whether Jesus established or even intended to establish a formal church organization. The word "church" appears in the Gospels only in Matthew (16:18; 18:17)—which many scholars see as reflecting a later perspective some thirty to forty years after Christ's crucifixion when Matthew was written. These scholars note that Jesus and his disciples anticipated an imminent advent of the kingdom of heaven, which would have precluded the need for an institutionalized church. Paul Avis, writing in *The Encyclopedia of Christianity*, observes:

> Scholars are virtually unanimous that Jesus did not consciously intend the church as we know it [i.e., as an institutional organization] and did not foresee it. Jesus believed that his mission was the harbinger of the end-time *eschaton*. Divine judgment would supervene and through cataclysmic events God would make a new beginning. He therefore did not expect his cause to be carried forward through history in institutional form.[46]

Scholars explain that it was only after expectations for the end time began to wane and local congregations began to multiply that a clear church organization started to emerge.

Early Mormonism

While dozens of references to the kingdom of God appear in the Book of Mormon, they are always either in the context of Christ coming to set up his kingdom among the Nephites after his resurrection or of a heavenly place of rest for the righteous in the hereafter. This is similar to the traditional Christian understanding of the kingdom taught in the New Testament. In the Book of Mormon, there is no mention of a church or kingdom of God being "restored" to the earth in the last days.

It is true that the Book of Mormon speaks of two churches in the latter days: "the church of the Lamb of God" and "the church of the devil" (1 Ne. 14:10). However, as BYU religion professor Stephen Robinson observes, these churches are not spoken of in an institutional sense, but rather as two "apocalyptic categories" or ideological camps, and are used to distinguish between "those, both LDS and non-LDS, who fight against the Lamb" and "those, both LDS and non-LDS, who worship Christ and seek to do his will."[47] The Book of Mormon speaks of everyone in the latter days as belonging to one camp or the other, for "whoso belongeth not to the church of the Lamb of God belongeth to that great church [of the devil]" (1 Ne. 14:10). Rather than prophesying of a universal apostasy from the New Testament church, the Book of Mormon instead proclaims that the already existing "holy church of God" would be largely polluted by the proud with "none save a few only" being recognized by the Lord because of their humility (Mormon 8:36). A whole different picture of how the Book of Mormon views the latter-day church of Christ comes into focus when one reads Book of Mormon references to Christ's church in the latter days without automatically assuming they refer to a "restored" church.

It isn't clear exactly when the Prophet understood that his mission would involve restoring an actual church organization. He appears to have initially viewed himself more as a reformer than a restorer. A revelation received March 1829, a year prior to the organization of the Church, speaks of the Lord performing "a reformation" among the people.[48] In the summer of 1828, nearly two years before Joseph Smith organized the church, the Lord explained that he would bring his people the gospel as contained in the Book of Mormon:

> Behold, I do not bring it to destroy that which they have received, but to build it up [i.e., strengthen what they already have].
>
> And for this cause have I said: If this generation harden not their hearts, I will establish [cause to be firmly rooted (see Mosiah 27:13; Alma 4:4)] my church among them.
>
> Now I do not say this to destroy my church [i.e., humble souls who already follow Christ's teachings], but I say this to build up my church [i.e., strengthen those who are already Christ's disciples];
>
> Therefore, whosoever belongeth [in 1828] to my church need not fear, for such shall inherit the kingdom of heaven (D&C 10:52–55).

So two years before the organization of the Church, the Lord here tells those who already belong to his church that they "need not fear" because he intends not to destroy his church, but to build it up. He goes on to say that only those who have built up churches "unto themselves to get gain" will he cause to "tremble and shake" (D&C 10:56). Christ's church is thus equated here with the humble and penitent, not with any particular organization. The revelation concludes by emphasizing that "whosoever repenteth and cometh unto me, the same is my church" (D&C 10:67). That repentance and discipleship appear to be the sole requirements for membership in Christ's church is evident by the very next verse: "Whosoever declareth more or less than this, the same is not of me, but is against me; therefore he is not of my church" (D&C 10:68).

What this revelation seems to be alluding to is the historical Protestant notion of the "invisible" church. Many Protestants during the Reformation, while claiming that the original apostolic church (i.e., the "visible" church) had been taken from the earth, held that the "invisible" church, consisting of the humble followers of Christ, was still very much alive upon the earth.[49] An 1826 Universalist publication explained, "There may be many who are outwardly connected with the different visible churches which are remonstrating against each other, who possess the spirit of Christ and are connected to his true invisible church by a spiritual communion."[50] During the Reformation, Christ's true church was identified by its being built on Christ's gospel, not on any particular organizational framework.[51] Such was also the case in the Book of Mormon (2 Ne. 28:3–5; Mosiah 25:22; 26:22; 3 Ne. 27:8–11). It isn't until after the Church was organized in 1830 that one starts to see biblical passages being cited as prophecies of the restoration of Christ's church and priesthood.

Notes

1. There was no recorded date for the restoration of the Melchizedek priesthood. Larry Porter, "Dating the Melchizedek Priesthood," 5–10, cites circumstantial evidence to support the June 1829 date. Michael Quinn notes that "no mention of angelic ordinations can be found in original documents until 1834–1835" and that "thereafter accounts of the visit of Peter, James, and John by Cowdery and Smith remained vague and contradictory." D. Michael Quinn, *The Mormon Hierarchy: Origins of Power*, 15. Quinn also argues that the appearance of Peter, James, and John could not have occurred before July 1830 (p. 22). Richard Bushman also finds compelling evidence for a July 1830 restoration date. A summer 1830 dating means that the Church was organized without the Melchizedek Priesthood. This would imply what many LDS historians assert: that "priest" and "elder" were simply ordained offices in the infant church and were without the conferral of the Aaronic or Melchizedek priesthood. Richard L. Bushman, *Joseph Smith and the Beginnings of Mormonism*, 162–63, 240–41. See also Richard L. Bushman, *Joseph Smith: Rough Stone Rolling*, 158–59.

2. A lesser known prophecy, purported to have been given by Joseph of old, was revealed by Joseph Smith and refers to the restoration of the priesthood. As reported by Oliver Cowdery, this ancient patriarch prophesied of blessings that "should come upon the seer [i.e., Joseph Smith] of the last days and the scribe [i.e., Oliver Cowdery] that should sit with him, and that should

be ordained with him, by the hands of the angel in the bush, unto the lesser priesthood." Oliver Cowder, to Phineas Young, Tiffin, Ohio, March 23, 1846, quoted in Joseph Fielding Smith, *Doctrines of Salvation: Compiled Sermons of Joseph Fielding Smith*, 3:101. That Joseph and Oliver would have been the subjects of such an ancient prophecy (nearly 4,000 years old) is extraordinary in itself—not to mention the fact that the prophecy implies that Joseph of old had knowledge of the priesthood of Aaron, which wouldn't be introduced in Israel for another 400 years.

    3. *Gospel Principles* (2009), 254.

    4. Bruce R. McConkie, *The Millennial Messiah: The Second Coming of the Son of Man*, 119.

    5. Elias Boudinot, a statesman and devout Episcopalian, wrote in 1815, "John the Baptist came in the power and spirit of Elias, and was the harbinger of Christ's first coming, but he did not restore the heart of the fathers to the children; and the heart of the children to the fathers—this is reserved for the real Elijah, the great harbinger of Christ's second coming in glory." Elias Boudinot, *The Second Advent*, 35.

    6. As explained by Richard Brothers, this latter-day Elijah "will suppress war and violence, which sets the old against the young and the young against the old. He will command peace, and by the great power given him from heaven, enforce an obedience wherever he comes." Richard Brothers, *A Revealed Knowledge of the Prophecies and Times*, 56.

    7. "The Ten Tribes," *Evening and the Morning Star* 1 (October 1832): 34.

    8. Josiah Priest, *A View of the Expected Christian Millennium*, x.

    9. These words were recorded in 1838 although they were presumably spoken by Moroni in his visit to Joseph Smith in 1823. This causes one to wonder why, in all of the occurrences of Malachi 4:6 prior to 1838, the reading remains unchanged from the traditional KJV. This includes appearances in both the Book of Mormon and Joseph Smith's revision of the Bible. One would certainly expect the JST to reflect this correction that had already been made known to Joseph. Oliver Cowdery's lengthy and detailed 1835 account of Moroni's visit to Joseph Smith makes no mention of this passage even being cited. These facts suggest that the 1838 account likely reflects a later understanding of Malachi's prophecy.

    10. It isn't certain whether "revealing" the priesthood meant conferring the priesthood or simply making known the rights and privileges associated with the priesthood. Joseph used "reveal" in the sense of confer when explaining how Christ "had before revealed the priesthood to Moses." Andrew F. Ehat and Lyndon W. Cook, *The Words of Joseph Smith*, 158. Nearer to the time he wrote his history in 1838, Joseph recorded that "the priesthood was revealed" to Adam (Abr. Fac. 2, Fig. 3) in that he received "the grand Key-words of the Holy Priesthood" (see also Fac. 2, Fig. 7).

    11. Joseph Smith Jr., "To the Elders of the Church of the Latter Day Saints," *Latter Day Saints' Messenger and Advocate* 2 (November 1835): 210.

    12. Ehat and Cook, *The Words of Joseph Smith*, 10.

    13. Ibid., 11.

    14. Ibid., 43.

    15. Joseph Fielding Smith, *Elijah the Prophet and His Mission*, 13–14.

16. Lyndon W. Cook, *The Revelations of the Prophet Joseph Smith: A Historical and Biographical Commentary of the Doctrine and Covenants*, 186.
17. Ehat and Cook, *The Words of Joseph Smith*, 242.
18. Ibid., 318.
19. Ibid.
20. Ibid., 329.
21. Ibid., 331.
22. Gordon Irving, "Law of Adoption," 291–314.
23. Bruce R. McConkie, *Mormon Doctrine*, 221.
24. Kirtland Council Minutes, February 12, 1834, 27, reprinted in Dan Vogel, *Early Mormon Documents*, 1:32.
25. David Whitmer, one of the three witnesses of the gold plates, later claimed, "I never heard that an Angel had ordained Joseph and Oliver to the Aaronic Priesthood until the year 1834[,] [183]5. or [183]6—in Ohio. . . . I do not believe that John the Baptist ever ordained Joseph and Oliver . . . " Vogel, *Early Mormon Documents*, 5:137. William McLellin, one of the original twelve apostles of the restored Church, later reported, "In 1831 I heard Joseph tell his experience many times about angels visits, and about finding the plates, and their contents coming to light, but I never heard one word of John the baptist, or of Peter, James, and John's visit and ordination. Till I was told some years afterward in Ohio." Stan Larson and Samuel J. Passey, eds., *The William E. McLellin Papers: 1854–1880*, 392.
26. This was Joseph Smith's initial explanation. Dean C. Jessee, ed., *The Papers of Joseph Smith: Autobiographical and Historical Writings*, 1:299.
27. David Whitmer, one of the three witnesses to the Book of Mormon, reflected many years after leaving the church, "This matter of 'priesthood,' since the days of Sydney Rigdon, has been the great hobby and stumbling-block of the Latter Day Saints. . . . I do not think the word priesthood is mentioned in the New Covenant of the Book of Mormon. Authority is the word we used for the first two years in the church—until Sydney Rigdon's days in Ohio. This matter of two orders of priesthood in the Church of Christ . . . originated in the mind of Sydney Rigdon. . . . This is the way . . . the 'priesthood' as you have it, was introduced into the Church of Christ almost two years after its beginning—and after we had baptized and confirmed about two thousand souls into the church." David Whitmer, *An Address to All Believers in Christ*, 64.
28. Bushman, *Joseph Smith: Rough Stone Rolling*, 75.
29. Grant H. Palmer, *An Insider's View of Mormon Origins*, 228.
30. Clarke, *Commentary on the Bible*, s.v. Daniel 2.
31. Joseph Fielding Smith, *Life of Joseph F. Smith*, 22–23. For related early American sermons, see Ellis Sandoz, *Political Sermons of the American Founding Era: 1730–1805*.
32. Ethan Smith, *A Key to the Figurative Language Found in the Scriptures*, 96–97.
33. Ehat and Cook, *The Words of Joseph Smith*, 367.
34. John J. Collins, "Daniel, Book of," 2:30.
35. St. Jerome pointed out in the early fifth century that, as early as the third century, Porphyry of Tyros had insisted that the author of Daniel's prophecy was clearly relating events already in the past and that events that

were to follow the time of Antiochus Epiphanes were mere speculation. Saint Jerome, *Commentary on Daniel*.

36. For a list of writings falsely attributed to Daniel, including the Apocalypse of Daniel and several texts from Qumran, see Lorenzo Di Tommaso, *The Book of Daniel and the Apocryphal Daniel Literature*.

37. Matthias Henze, "Daniel," 1235.

38. Collins, "Daniel, Book of," 30.

39. Norman Cohn, "The Book of Daniel." This PBS special featured several noted biblical scholars, all of whom agreed that the book of Daniel was written as "prophecy after the fact."

40. "To the Church of Christ Abroad in the Earth," *Evening and the Morning Star* 1, no. 1 (June 1832): 6.

41. *Old Testament: Gospel Doctrine Teacher's Manual*, 177; McConkie, *Mormon Doctrine*, 228.

42. McConkie, *Mormon Doctrine*, 228.

43. J. J. M. Roberts, "Isaiah," 1022.

44. Joseph Fielding Smith, *Church History and Modern Revelation*, 1:35.

45. David P. Wright, "Joseph Smith's Interpretation of Isaiah in the Book of Mormon," 196–204.

46. Paul Avis, "Church," 233.

47. Craig L. Blomberg and Stephen E. Robinson, *How Wide the Divide? A Mormon and an Evangelical in Conversation,* 161.

48. *Book of Commandments* (1835) 4:5.

49. Menno Simmons, *Complete Writings*, 300. Simmons was a radical reformer who espoused this view.

50. "What Is Truth?" *The Candid Examiner* 2 (November 6, 1826): 87.

51. Alister E. McGrath, *Christian Theology: An Introduction*, 481.

≈ 5 ≈

Doctrinal Truths Restored

Latter-day Saints believe that, as part of the restoration of all things, all doctrinal truths that were revealed in previous gospel dispensations will be revealed anew. As doctrines were introduced in the early LDS Church, they were often presented as "restored" doctrines that were taught in ancient times. The restoration of lost doctrinal truths subsided dramatically with the death of Joseph Smith, although the Church continues to maintain that God "will yet reveal many great and important things pertaining to the Kingdom of God" (A of F 9). This chapter explores the degree to which the restoration of ancient truths was anticipated in the Bible and how latter-day scripture, particularly the Book of Mormon and the Pearl of Great Price, are seen as fulfilling ancient prophecy. This includes noncanonical works, such as Joseph Smith's Translation of the Bible and his various published sermons, which also contain doctrinal teachings that Joseph claimed had been lost from the earth.

To say that doctrines taught in the LDS Church today are restored doctrines implies that they were previously taught in biblical times before being lost. Few of the doctrines unique to Mormonism, however, are sufficiently elucidated in the Bible to be clearly recognizable. Among these are doctrines of the preexistence, eternal marriage, and salvation for the dead. Referring to these and other distinctive Mormon doctrines, LDS scholar Terryl Givens observed, "In none of these cases, or a dozen others that could be mentioned, could one make a reasonable theological defense of the Prophet's ampler enactment of these principles and practices on the basis of the few paltry biblical allusions that exist."[1] Subsequent chapters will explore the extent to which these doctrines appear to have been understood by biblical writers and how they developed to their current formulations.

Here we look only at how doctrinal truths were perceived as having been lost from the Bible and being in need of restoration.

The Coming Forth of the Book of Mormon

The work of the restoration was initially seen as a restoration of gospel truths that had been lost or removed from the Bible. This restoration began with the coming forth of the Book of Mormon, which itself states that it shall make known the "plain and precious parts of the gospel of the Lamb which have been kept back by that abominable church" (1 Ne. 13:34–36).

Mormonism teaches that the Book of Mormon came forth in fulfillment of biblical prophecies. Considering that there are no clear biblical prophecies predicting the eventual compilation and impact of the Bible on later world history, non-Latter-day Saints are skeptical of LDS claims that the Bible predicts the coming forth of the Book of Mormon. The Book of Mormon, for its part, speaks extensively of its own impact as well as that of the Bible on the modern world. As will be seen, the Prophet amended several biblical prophecies so as to refer to the presence and influence of both the Bible and the Book of Mormon in the latter days.

Old Testament

One Old Testament passage that Latter-day Saints frequently cite as a prophecy of the coming forth of the Book of Mormon in the latter days is Isaiah 29, which speaks of "the vision of all" becoming "as the words of a book that is sealed" (v. 11). The book is delivered to "one that is learned" and "one that is not learned" (vv. 11–12), neither of whom can read it. Latter-day Saints go beyond the traditionally accepted allegorical meaning of this passage and its fulfillment in ancient Israel to see a literal book that came to light in the latter days through the "unlearned" prophet Joseph Smith. "The vision of all" is spoken of in the Book of Mormon as a literal vision of all things—"a revelation from God, from the beginning of the world to the ending thereof" (2 Ne. 27:7)—that would be recorded in a sealed book (i.e., the sealed portion of the gold plates) to come forth in the latter days. The "learned" individual is interpreted as being Charles Anthon, a professor of Greek and Latin languages at Columbia College (later Columbia University), who reportedly said he could not read the book "for it is sealed" (2 Ne. 27:15–20; Isa. 29:11).[2]

As explained in Chapter 3, what seems to be overlooked in this interpretation is that Isaiah isn't talking about a literal book, much less one that would come forth in the future. The sealed book is a figure of speech used to describe Israel's spiritual blindness: their vision is "*as* the words of a book that is sealed" (v. 11). Isaiah had just described how God had "covered" (past tense) the eyes of the prophets and seers because of wickedness (vv. 9–10), and therefore the heavens are sealed just like a sealed book that no one can read.[3] LDS scholars who take the historical context of Isaiah 29 more seriously explain that the LDS interpretation may be better thought of as an application (see Chap. 3).

Another Old Testament passage traditionally cited as a reference to the Book of Mormon is Ezekiel 37:16–17:

> Moreover, thou son of man, take thee one stick, and write upon it, For Judah, and for the children of Israel his companions: then take another stick, and write upon it, For Joseph, the stick of Ephraim, and for all of the house of Israel his companions:
>
> And join them one to another into one stick; and they shall become one in thine hand.

The popular LDS interpretation of this passage is that the stick of Judah is the Bible while the stick of Joseph or Ephraim is the Book of Mormon (see Bible Dictionary, s.v. "Ephraim, Stick of"). When the 1979 LDS edition of the scriptures was published with footnotes and a topical guide that integrates all of the standard works, Elder Boyd K. Packer announced, "They are indeed one in our hands. Ezekiel's prophecy now stands fulfilled."[4]

Scholars point out that each of the sticks Ezekiel refers to is no more than a piece of wood (hence the term "stick"), on which he was to inscribe a short phrase. It doesn't appear to have been a scroll or writing board on which a lengthy record might be kept.[5] The Lord told Ezekiel to write "For Judah and all the Israelites associated with him" on one stick and "For Joseph and all the Israelites associated with him" on the other—short and simple. There is no mention of any other writing, nor is there any implication that Judah and Joseph or the fruit of their loins would do any writing. Any uncertainty regarding the intended meaning of this passage disappears in the next verse in which the people ask "Wilt thou not show us what thou meanest by these?" (v. 18). Ezekiel responds that the sticks represent the kingdoms of Judah and Joseph, and that the joining of the two sticks symbolizes the reuniting of the two kingdoms under one king (vv. 19–23). Many LDS scholars today concur with this contextual meaning and therefore see the traditional LDS interpretation as a "secondary," "revealed" meaning.[6]

There are also a couple poetic images used in the Old Testament that Latter-day Saints have traditionally taken as references to the Book of Mormon. In Genesis 49:22–26, Jacob blesses his son Joseph saying, "Joseph is a fruitful bough, even a fruitful bough by a well; whose branches run over the wall.... The blessings of thy father have prevailed above the blessings of my progenitors unto the utmost bound of the everlasting hills." The chapter heading of the 1979 LDS Bible identifies Joseph's "branches" as "the Nephites and the Lamanites." The "everlasting hills" are often interpreted as the Rocky Mountains.[7] Non-LDS Bible scholars see the "everlasting hills" as simply an image for a lasting source of blessings. Indeed, the NRSV, like other modern translations, reads, "The blessings of your father are stronger than the blessings of the eternal mountains, the bounties of the everlasting hills" (NRSV Gen. 49:26). Ancient Israelites were evidently impressed by the strength and bounties of the hills making them an apt symbol of sure and bounteous blessings. Moses similarly blessed the tribe of Joseph with "the chief things of the ancient mountains, and ... the precious things of the lasting hills" (Deut. 33:15). To interpret either of these blessings as a prophecy that Joseph's descendents would one day migrate to the Americas and inhabit the region of the Rocky Mountains seems to stretch the imagery. Notably, there is no indication that Book of Mormon people saw themselves as fulfilling this promise of Jacob when they migrated to America.

Another Old Testament image taken as a reference to the Book of Mormon is Psalms 85:11, which speaks of a time when "truth will spring forth out of the earth and righteousness shall look down from heaven." The chapter heading in the 1979 LDS Bible states that the truth springing from the earth is "the Book of Mormon." The book of Moses, revealed to Joseph Smith just months after the Book of Mormon's publication, implicitly corroborates this interpretation. In a prophecy to Enoch, the Lord states, "Truth will I send forth out of the earth, to bear testimony of mine Only Begotten" (Moses 7:62).

According to at least non-LDS Bible scholars, the intended meaning of Psalms 85:11 has little to do with the coming forth of gospel truths. The Hebrew word for "truth" here refers to truth of character in the sense of being true or faithful to God's laws. The NRSV renders this verse more precisely: "*Faithfulness* will spring up from the ground, and righteousness will look down from the sky" (emphasis mine). Scholars explain that this is a Hebrew parallelism conveying the idea that faithfulness or righteousness would bear sway on the earth when the kingdom of Israel is restored (Ps. 19:9, 40:10–12, 89:14–16, 96:13, 98:2–3, 119:142; Isa. 9:7, 11:3–5). In poetic imagery, righteousness is depicted as rising from the earth and spreading forth from the heavens so that the Lord's will is obeyed on earth and in heaven (Ps. 33:4–5, 57:3). The springing forth from the earth, therefore, is a figurative image of the flourishing of God's righteousness on earth and not the literal unearthing of gold plates.

New Testament

A New Testament passage believed to refer, not to the coming forth of the Book of Mormon per se, but to the people of the Book of Mormon, is John 10:16. Here the Savior tells his disciples, "And other sheep I have, which are not of this fold: them also I must bring, and they shall hear my voice; and there shall be one fold, and one shepherd." In the Savior's visit to the Nephites, he tells them, "Ye are they of whom I said: Other sheep I have which are not of this fold." He then explains that the Jews "understood me not, for they supposed it had been the Gentiles; for they understood not that the Gentiles should be converted through their preaching" (3 Ne. 15:11–24; see also D&C 10:59).

In retrospect, it seems odd that Jesus's disciples in Jerusalem would have thought that the other sheep that Christ was to bring into the fold were the gentiles when he expressly told them, "I am not sent but unto the lost sheep of the house of Israel" (Matt. 15:24) and had earlier forbidden the Twelve from preaching to the gentiles (Matt. 10:5). Peter, for one, would no sooner preach to a gentile than he would violate Jewish dietary laws (Acts 10). After the gospel was taken to the gentiles, many Christians did come to believe that the "other sheep" referred to gentiles, and that was the general belief at the time of Joseph Smith.[8]

Anticipating the Book of Mormon interpretation of Christ's "other sheep" as the inhabitants of the American continent, in 1697 influential Puritan magistrate Samuel Sewall argued that "the ten tribes are the [other] sheep" spoken of by John and that they were none other than the American Indians. He therefore declared that "America is the distinct fold" to be brought in.[9] Sewall believed that, when Christ comes to establish the New Jerusalem in America, Native American Indians who are of the tribe of Israel will hear his voice.[10]

The actual identity of the "other sheep" in John 10:16 is not expressly given in the Bible, so it could conceivably have reference to the ancient inhabitants of America. However, non-LDS commentators suggest that these sheep were not yet believers, since Jesus states that he must "bring" them into his fold. Jesus also states that these sheep will "hear" his voice, not in the sense of having the privilege of listening to him speak as indicated in 3 Nephi 15:23, but in the sense of *heeding* his word. Jesus had just characterized his sheep as being those who "hear" (i.e., heed) his voice (vv. 3–5; cf. 10:27, 18:37).

Another New Testament passage frequently cited as a reference to the coming forth of the Book of Mormon in the latter days is Revelation 14:6–7:

> And I saw another angel fly in the midst of heaven, having the everlasting gospel to preach unto them that dwell on the earth, and to every nation, and kindred, and tongue, and people,
>
> Saying with a loud voice, Fear God, and give glory to him; for the hour of his judgment is come: and worship him that made heaven, and earth, and the sea, and the fountains of waters.

Commenting on this passage in an LDS general conference in April 2006, President James E. Faust, second counselor in the First Presidency, remarked, "This prophecy has been fulfilled. That angel was Moroni, who appeared to the Prophet Joseph Smith."[11]

From the early days of the Church, Moroni has been identified, at least by implication, as the angel prophesied by John. In a revelation received November 1831, the Lord declared,

> I have sent forth mine angel flying through the midst of heaven, having the everlasting gospel, who hath appeared unto some and hath committed it unto man, who shall appear unto many that dwell on the earth. . . .
>
> And the servants of God shall go forth, saying with a loud voice: Fear God . . . for the hour of his judgment is come. (D&C 133:36–39)

The angel is depicted here as having only "committed" the gospel to man while it is man on earth who would do the actual preaching unto the inhabitants of the earth. So it is the ministers of the restored gospel who fulfill the role of the angel spoken of in Revelation. In this same way, the Prophet alluded to himself in 1844 as fulfilling the role of this angel. "John," he said, "saw the angel having the holy Priesthood. . . . God had an angel, a special messenger, ordained & prepared for that purpose in the last days—Woe! Woe! be to that man, or set of men, who lift up their hands against God and his witness in these last days."[12] George Laub quoted Joseph as saying, "The original translation reads thus, 'and I will send you another witness and he shall preach this gospel to all nations.'"[13] The preaching of the gospel predicted in Revelation 14:7, therefore, is something the Prophet evidently thought would be fulfilled primarily by mortals, not by the angel.

More than one evangelical group at the time of Joseph Smith claimed that their evangelizing efforts fulfilled the prophecy of the angelic proclamation in Revelation. Noted Methodist Bible scholar Richard Watson (1781–1833) explained that since "angel" means "messenger," Revelation 14:7 must be referring to "Christian ministers"; and therefore, it is "a prediction of a zealous ministry, to be raised up by God for the conversion of all nations, and that even now it is receiving its accomplishment."[14] In an account published October 22, 1823, in the Palmyra, New York, *Wayne Sentinel*, Asa Wild reported receiving a vision in which God told him that the millennium was only seven years away, that all the churches were corrupt, and that God "had raised up, and was now raising up, that class of persons signified by the Angel mentioned by the Revelator, xiv. 6, 7, which flew in the midst of heaven; having the everlasting gospel to preach."[15]

While Latter-day Saints today generally view this prophecy as having been fulfilled by the visitation of the angel Moroni, Bruce R. McConkie's interpretation of this passage is that the angel is actually a "composite angel" consisting of every angel who "restored the priesthood and keys."[16] This interpretation accommodates the multiple angels who are believed to have had a role in restoring the gospel, but it seems to read more into John's prophecy than what is implied in the text itself.

Non-LDS scholars see little indication of a gospel restoration in this passage. They point out that, as one of three angels John saw being sent to proclaim judgment on the wicked, this first angel came not to "preach" but, as most modern translations read, "proclaim" the good news that "the hour of his [God's] judgment is come" and that wickedness has therefore ended. Notably, the NRSV translates this passage as saying that the angel would proclaim "an" everlasting gospel or message, not "the" everlasting gospel. David Aune, Notre Dame professor of New Testament theology, explains that the angel proclaimed "an eternal gospel, not the saving message of Jesus's death and resurrection, but the message in 14:7 [i.e., that the hour of judgment is come]."[17] It is instructive to note that this proclamation isn't to occur until after the Lamb of God comes to Mount Zion with his redeemed (Rev. 14:1). The angel will then declare that "the hour has come" to pour out judgment upon the earth, implying that the time for preaching repentance is past.[18] Of course, John also believed that the fulfillment of this prophecy was imminent.

Restoring Biblical Truths

One of the main purposes of the Book of Mormon, as stated in the book itself, is to "make known the plain and precious things which have been taken away from [the Bible]" (1 Ne. 13:40). Many early American divines, including Jonathan Edwards, believed that God had imparted to the ancients essential gospel truths that were subsequently lost.[19] Several leading ministers even produced their own "corrective" versions of the Bible.[20]

Aside from the countless minor scribal errors, scholars maintain that, "in general, the Bible has been transmitted and translated remarkably well."[21] BYU religion professor Stephen Robinson notes that "informed Latter-day Saints" are in general agreement that, since the time of its compilation in the late second or third century, the Bible has been preserved with reasonably high fidelity and "the texts are essentially correct in their present form."[22]

This assessment of the integrity of the Bible is somewhat more favorable than that given in the Book of Mormon and by the Prophet Joseph Smith. The Book of Mormon states that "when it [i.e., the Bible] proceeded forth from the mouth of a Jew it contained the fulness of the gospel of the Lord" (1 Ne. 13:24), but "after the book hath gone forth through the hands of the great and abominable church, . . . many plain and precious things [are] taken away from the book" (1 Ne. 13:28). Since LDS scholars generally concur that the Bible as we now have it is an essentially faithful translation of the surviving manuscripts, some have chosen to interpret 1 Nephi 13:24 as meaning that these plain and precious truths were either removed from individual manuscripts before the Bible was compiled, or they were present in certain manuscripts that never found their way into the Bible.[23] Nephi specifically states, however, that it was "the book" itself that would go forth "from the Jews in purity unto the Gentiles" (1 Ne. 13:23–25), and only "after" that did he see "the formation of that great and abominable church, which . . . [has] taken away from the gospel of the Lamb many parts which are plain and most precious" (1 Ne. 13:26).

In Joseph Smith's day the Book of Mormon's assertion of biblical corruption was generally understood as meaning that the Catholic Church had corrupted the Bible—a perception widely held by Protestants of all persuasions.[24] A June 1832 editorial in the LDS *Evening and Morning Star* explains that, in fulfillment of Nephi's prophecy, "the most plain parts of the New Testament have been taken from it by the Mother of Harlots while it was confined in that Church,—say, from the year A.D. 460 to 1400."[25]

In 1832, Joseph Smith first publicly acknowledged that, in addition to teachings being "taken" from the Bible, teachings might have also been "lost before it was compiled."[26] This may have been what he had in mind when he revised Jesus's rebuke of the lawyers (i.e., scribes) saying: "Woe unto you, lawyers! For ye have taken away the key of knowledge, *the fulness of the scriptures*" (JST Luke 11:53; emphasis mine).

The Joseph Smith Translation of the Bible

As the prophet of the Restoration, Joseph considered one "branch of [his] calling"[27] to be the restoration of lost biblical scripture or "the key of knowledge" to the world by either expanding or altering Bible texts as he felt inspired. In December 1830, he received a revelation directing Sidney Rigdon to "write for him [Joseph Smith]; and the scriptures [i.e., the Bible] shall be given, even as they are in mine own bosom" (D&C 35:20). Joseph's work to restore the Bible began in June 1830—beginning with a revelation attributed to Moses predicting that a latter-day prophet (presumably Joseph Smith) would one day restore the lost truths of the Bible. In this prophecy, the Lord told Moses that "many" teachings would be taken from the Bible but that, in the last days, "I will raise up another like unto thee; and they shall be had again among the children of men" (Moses 1:41).

Although Joseph spoke of his revision of the Bible as a "translation," unlike traditional translations of the Bible, he did not actually work with ancient biblical manuscripts; rather, he simply read the KJV and made corrective changes and additions where he felt clarifications were needed. As he stated on one occasion, "There are many things in the Bible which do not, as they now stand, accord with the revelations of the Holy Ghost to me."[28] According to Philip Barlow, rather than being an actual restoration of ancient texts that had been lost, the JST "is better explained by Joseph Smith's effort to remove difficulties in the KJV—to harmonize scripture with itself, with 'common sense,' and with his own revelations."[29] In addition to making revisions even to his own revisions, he later discarded some of his revisions in favor of the original KJV reading. Several passages were even marked "correct" and then later revised. Barlow observes that "Joseph Smith clearly experimented with the Bible as he sought to bring its text in line with the insights of his revelations and understanding."[30]

The JST, though declared "finished" by the Prophet on July 2, 1833,[31] has never been published as a complete work by the LDS Church.[32] It is the least known scriptural production of Joseph Smith, yet it is perhaps the most doctrinally significant. Few doctrines were introduced in the Book of Mormon that weren't already in wide circulation at the time of Joseph Smith. In contrast, nearly all of the new doctrines he introduced during the Kirtland period came as a result of his work with the Bible. The United Order, priesthood offices beyond teacher and priest, preexistence, the degrees of glory, salvation for the dead, plural marriage, and patriarchal blessings were all tied in some way to the Prophet's interaction with the Bible.[33]

The Book of Abraham

Another Joseph Smith work that can be thought of as an effort to restore ancient scriptural truths is the book of Abraham, which the preface describes as containing "the writings of Abraham while he was in Egypt" as "written by his own hand, upon papyrus."[34] At least a portion of the papyri and facsimiles comprising the book of Abraham was recovered in 1966. Scholars have determined, however, that the discovered papyri contains common, early Christian-era Egyptian funeral writings that have little relationship to the message recorded in the book of Abraham. BYU Egyptologist Michael Rhodes acknowledges, "These Egyptian documents can be reliably dated to somewhere between 220 and 150 b.c.....They cannot possibly date to the period of Abraham—around 2000 to 1800 b.c. . . . Moreover, the writing on the surviving fragments can all be translated, and none of it mentions Abraham or seems to be related to the text of the book of Abraham."[35]

As might be expected, this discovery has further fanned the controversy regarding the authenticity of the book of Abraham. Although Mormon apologists claim that the book of Abraham contains certain material and teachings about the universe that were new and startling to the world, critics point to evidence that Joseph had ready access to this information from his own immediate environment.[36] Many critics further point to what they perceive as an obvious connection between the book of Abraham and Joseph's Hebrew study of Genesis and that the presence of ideas such as the plurality of Gods, creation from preexisting matter, and Hebrew terms such as "Raukeeyang," "kolob," and "kokaubeam" are best explained by the Prophet's growing fascination with Hebrew and exposure to rabbinical tradition as part of his Hebrew tutelage.[37] As one Hebrew scholar observed, the Prophet would often "theologize" with his Hebrew and used his Hebrew training, not to discover what the original author was trying to say, but "as a foundation for theological innovations."[38] Mormon apologists writing for FARMS counter that, despite criticisms, there is still ample evidence for the ancient origin of the book of Abraham. They present plausible alternative theories of how Joseph's translation can still be considered authentic.[39]

The conclusion one draws about the book of Abraham's authenticity is based largely on one's perspective of Joseph Smith. Those who accept him as a prophet in the traditional sense of speaking the pure word of God see a genuine restoration of Abraham's teachings in the book of Abraham. Those who reject Joseph Smith as a fraud look upon the book of Abraham as a hoax calculated to deceive and mislead. Others who accept him as inspired but not as a genuine translator see the papyri as a kind of catalyst for the creation of new scripture.

Joseph Smith's Sermons

Joseph Smith's public sermons also served as a convenient outlet for expressing many of his biblical corrections. During the course of a sermon, the Prophet would refer to a biblical passage and occasionally cite the original Hebrew or Greek, or even appeal to the German translation to support his interpretation. Usually, however, he would merely state what the correct interpretation should be, often attributing it to revelation from the Holy Ghost.[40]

The Prophet's sermons near the end of his life contain some of his most revolutionary theological ideas which he was careful to couch in what he perceived to be "correct" biblical readings. Subsequent chapters will show how he was thereby able to provide scriptural support for such radical teachings as the plurality of Gods and the prior mortality of God.

The Lost Legacy of Translation

Joseph Smith saw his mission initially as a restorer of lost truths through the translation of ancient records, particularly the Book of Mormon. The Book of Mormon contains a prophecy attributed to the Old Testament Joseph stating that Joseph Smith "shall do none other work" than to bring forth the Book of Mormon (2 Ne. 3:7–8). This was Joseph's gift and calling. A revelation dated March 1829 stated that "he shall pretend to no other gift, for I [the Lord] will grant him no other gift."[41] Shortly after the publication of the Book of Mormon in March 1830, David Whitmer said that Joseph told him "he was done through the work that God had given him the gift to perform, except to preach the gospel."[42]

Although Joseph's work was initially confined to the bringing forth of the Book of Mormon, his later work on the translation of the Bible necessitated the lifting of this restriction. Thus, when he translated the Bible, he included the Book of Mormon prophecy attributed to Joseph of old; but instead of saying that the latter-day seer "shall do none other work" (2 Ne. 3:7–8), the revised prophecy stated that he "shall do whatsoever work I shall command him" (JST Gen. 50:28). The 1829 revelation in the *Book of Commandments* commanding Joseph Smith to "pretend to no other gift"[43] was also later amended to read that he "should pretend to no other gift *until my purpose is fulfilled in this*" (D&C 5:4; emphasis mine).

After the Prophet finished translating the Book of Mormon, he felt that it would be his mission and the mission of his associates to bring many more ancient records to light. He informed Oliver Cowdery that he also had the gift to translate "records that contain much of [the] gospel . . . which have been hidden because of wickedness" (D&C 6:26; see also 8:1, 9:2). He promised Warren Parrish that he would "see much of [the Lord's] ancient records, and shall know of hidden things, and shall be endowed with a knowledge of hidden languages."[44] Such promises, however, never came to fruition. Even though Joseph's initial work concentrated heavily on bringing forth ancient scripture, and although his associates expected that he would continue in this vein, he virtually abandoned translation activities after 1836 and changed his vocation from a restorer of ancient records to a builder of God's kingdom on earth. The Church has yet to realize the vision the Prophet had for bringing additional lost scriptures to light; however, many have expressed a sense of partial fulfillment of that vision in LDS academic involvement with the Dead Sea scrolls—even though they do little to corroborate LDS teachings.[45]

Notes

1. Terryl Givens, *By the Hand of Mormon: The American Scripture that Launched a New World Religion*, 48.

2. The Charles Anthon/Martin Harris incident occurred in February 1828, prior to the dictation of the Isaiah prophecy in the Book of Mormon which references this incident. No Hebrew text supports the rendering of Isaiah 29:11 as it appears in 2 Nephi 27:15–20. Interestingly, in 1832 Joseph Smith related that, when Harris asked Anthon if he could translate the characters, Anthon said, "I cannot." Dean C. Jessee, ed., *The Papers of Joseph Smith: Autobiographical and Historical Writings*, 1:9. Later, in 1838, however, Joseph related that Anthon not only pronounced the characters genuine, but had certified that the "translation was correct, more so than any he had before seen translated from Egyptian" (JS–H 1:64).

3. See David P. Wright, "Joseph Smith's Interpretation of Isaiah in the Book of Mormon," 196–204. Many scholars interpret the "vision" as the prophetic vision of Isaiah himself that the people whom he is addressing are unable to comprehend because of their spiritual blindness. This is the sense of NRSV Isaiah 29:11, which reads: "The vision of all this [i.e., what Isaiah has been trying to describe] has become for you [i.e., the Jews to whom he is speaking] like the words of a sealed document."

4. Boyd K. Packer, "Scriptures," 53.

5. Keith Meservy and Kevin L. Barney explain that "stick" in Ezekiel refers to a Babylonian writing board. Keith H. Meservy, "Ezekiel's Sticks and the Gathering of Israel," 4–13; and Kevin L. Barney, "A Seemingly Strange Story Illuminated," 8 note 24. Brian E. Keck maintains that Ezekiel was referring to a small piece of ordinary wood on which only a few words could fit. In either case, the allusion is to some medium on which a short phrase could be written, not a complete history. Brian E. Keck, "Ezekiel 37, Sticks, and Babylonian Writing Boards: A Critical Reappraisal," 126–38

6. Kent P. Jackson, "The Lord Is There (Ezekiel 37–48)," 302–303. Interestingly, Doctrine and Covenants 27:5 doesn't refer to the Book of Mormon as the stick of Ephraim but as "the record of the stick of Ephraim," thus possibly intending to use the metaphor of a stick in the same way Ezekiel uses it—to refer to the tribe of Ephraim.

7. Hoyt W. Brewster, *Doctrine and Covenants Encyclopedia*, 164.

8. See, for example, John Wesley, "John Wesley's Notes on the Bible," s.v. John 10. Andreas J. Kostenberger notes that it is "the broad scholarly consensus that John 10:16 refers to the Gentile mission." Andreas J. Kostenberger, "Jesus the Good Shepherd Who Will Also Bring Other Sheep (John 10:16): The Old Testament Background of a Familiar Metaphor," 72 note 19. He further notes (71–72) that, although the earlier-written synoptic Gospels steer clear of any intimation that the gospel is to be preached to the Gentiles, the Gospel of John was written "when the outreach to the Gentile world had already progressed to a significant extent," so that it served to validate this proselytizing effort. According to Kostenberger (71), the statement in John 10:16 is one of several sayings by Jesus recorded in John "that clearly refer to the future mission of the exalted Lord [to the Gentiles] through his disciples (see 4:34–38; 14:12; 17:20; 20:21–23; 21:15–19)." For a passage many believe to be related to John 10:16, see John 11:52.

9. Samuel Sewall, *Phaenomena Quaedam Phaenomena quaedam Apocalyptica ad aspectum Novi Orbis configurata. Or, some few lines towards a description of the New Heaven*, 41–42.

10. Ibid., 1–2, 42.

11. James E. Faust, "The Restoration of All Things," 67.

12. Andrew F. Ehat and Lyndon W. Cook, eds., *The Words of Joseph Smith*, 366–67.

13. Ibid., 369–70; see also 371.

14. Richard Watson, *The Works of the Rev. Richard Watson*, 4:155, 161.

15. Quoted in Elden J. Watson, "The 'Prognostication' of Asa Wild," 229.

16. Bruce R. McConkie, *Mormon Doctrine*, 635.

17. David E. Aune, "Revelation," 2326.

18. Joseph Smith considered the "hour of His judgment" to have commenced with the restoration of the gospel, which would continue until the second coming. Ehat and Cook, *The Words of Joseph Smith*, 180.

19. See Terryl Givens, "Joseph Smith: Prophecy, Process, and Plenitude," 63.

20. At least ten translations of the New Testament were produced between 1823 and 1833, including those of Alexander Campbell (1826), Alexander Greaves (1828), John Palfrey (1828), Noah Webster (1833), and Rodolphus Dickinson (1833). John V. Madison, "English Versions of the New Testament," 273–75.

21. Richard Y. Duerden, "Review of David Daniell, *The Bible in English: Its History and Influence*," 144.

22. Craig L. Blomberg and Stephen E. Robinson, *How Wide the Divide? A Mormon and an Evangelical in Conversation* 63, 75.

23. Ibid. See also Kent P. Jackson, *From Apostasy to Restoration*, 21.

24. See Philip L. Barlow, *Mormons and the Bible: The Place of Latter-day Saints in American Religion*, 5–10.

25. "Selected," *Evening and Mormon Star* 1, no. 1 (June 1832): 3.

26. *History of the Church of Jesus Christ of Latter-day Saints*, 1:245.

27. B. H. Roberts, *A Comprehensive History of the Church of Jesus Christ of Latter-day Saints*, 1:238.

28. *History of the Church*, 5:425.
29. Barlow, *Mormons and the Bible*, 55.
30. Ibid., 50.
31. *History of the Church*, 1:368.
32. Robert J. Matthews, "The 'New Translation' of the Bible, 1830–1833: Doctrinal Development during the Kirtland Era," 400–422. Matthews explains that Joseph considered his work finished in July 1833 and that afterwards his attention was only on getting it printed. Robert J. Matthews, "Joseph Smith's Efforts to Publish His Bible 'Translation.'" 57–64. The book of Moses and the 24th chapter of Matthew (JS–M), contained in the Pearl of Great Price, are actual excerpts from the JST. Many excerpts from the JST are also included in footnotes and the appendix in the LDS edition of the KJV. The Community of Christ church has always held the JST as sacred canon and still keeps it in print.
33. Matthews, "The 'New Translation' of the Bible." See also Brant A. Gardner, *The Gift and Power: Translating the Book of Mormon*, 206–15.
34. *History of the Church*, 2:235, 236, 348–51. Though LDS apologists have argued that Joseph Smith never stated that the papyri contained the actual writings of Abraham, several of the Prophet's close associates reported hearing him say that the papyri were a record written by the hand of Abraham. H. Michael Marquardt, "The Book of Abraham Revisited."
35. Michael D. Rhodes, "Teaching the Book of Abraham Facsimiles," 116.
36. Grant H Palmer, *An Insider's View of Mormon Origins*, 19.
37. Louis C. Zucker, "Joseph Smith as a Student of Hebrew," 41–55; Michael T. Walton, "Professor Seixas, the Hebrew Bible, and the Book of Abraham," 41–43; Karl C. Sandberg, "Knowing Brother Joseph Again: The Book of Abraham and Joseph Smith as Translator," 31–32.
38. Zucker, "Joseph Smith as a Student of Hebrew," 53.
39. For a list of relevant FARMS publications, visit the Maxwell Institute Website, http://maxwellinstitute.byu.edu/publications/bookofabraham.php (accessed September 19, 2007).
40. Ehat and Cook, *The Words of Joseph Smith*, 345, 351, 360.
41. *Book of Commandments*, 4:2.
42. David Whitmer, *An Address to All Believers in Christ*, 32.
43. *Book of Commandments*, 4:2.
44. Jessee, *The Papers of Joseph Smith*, 2:79.
45. Discussions have been ongoing regarding the extent to which the Dead Sea scrolls support Mormon doctrine. FARMS has published LDS research on the Dead Sea Scrolls which explores possible parallels but cautions against reading more into the scrolls than what is actually warranted. In answer to the question, "Is the plan of salvation attested in the Dead Sea Scrolls?" Dana Pike states, "From a Latter-day Saint perspective the answer is a definite no." Pike, "Is the Plan of Salvation Attested," 74; Donald W. Parry and Stephen C. Ricks note that "there are actually far more differences between the Qumramites and the Latter-day Saints than there are similarities." Donald W. Parry and Stephen C. Ricks, *The Dead Sea Scrolls: Questions and Responses for Latter-day Saints*, xii

≈ 6 ≈

The Godhead and Plurality of Gods

The term "godhead" in LDS discourse denotes "the supreme governing council in the heavens" consisting of the Father, Son, and Holy Ghost.[1] According to Joseph Smith, "these 3 constit[ute] 3 distinct personages & 3 Gods."[2] In addition to the three Gods comprising the godhead, traditional LDS teachings assert that an infinite number of Gods exists, even above the God we worship.

Nature of the Godhead

The term "godhead" is Middle English and means deity or godhood, which is the state or quality of being divine, and that is its meaning in the KJV where it appears three times (Acts 17:29, Rom. 1:20, Col. 2:9). The underlying Greek in each instance also means deity or godhood. In Paul's teachings, Christ was not in the godhead, but the godhead (i.e., godhood) was in Christ. He wrote to the Colossians, "For in him dwelleth all the fulness of the Godhead [NRSV = "Deity"] bodily" (Col. 2:9). The qualitative meaning of the word "godhead" has faded with time to where the term is now used in many circles (including Mormonism) as a collective noun denoting the Father, Son, and Holy Ghost.

Old Testament

Although the traditional Mormon doctrine of a three-member godhead is not explicitly taught in the Old Testament, the Hebrew scriptures do contain evidence of a belief in a broader heavenly council that carried out Yahweh's commands. An allusion to this council can be seen in the creation story of Genesis which has God saying, "Let *us* make man in *our* image" (Gen. 1:26; emphasis mine). Though the plural *us* has been interpreted in various ways, including a plurality of majesty and, in Christian tradition, the Trinity, Theodore Hiebert writing in *The New Interpreter's Study Bible* states that "here, as elsewhere in Genesis (e.g., 11:7), God is addressing the divine council, the assembly of heavenly beings believed to assist God in governing the world and communicating with the human race (Gen. 1:16; 16:7; 1 Kgs. 22:19–23; Job 1:1–7; Jer. 23:18, 22)."[3] According to Old Testament scholar G. Ernest Wright, "There is a large amount of evidence in the Old Testament for the heavenly assembly or council, presided over by God and composed of Divine attendants, heralds, and administrators."[4] This heavenly council has been compared to an earthly monarchy, with God sitting as king and the council members surrounding him as his advisors.

> Just as earthly monarchs have a court and a government, the King of kings had his court of advisors. . . . The God of the Bible is surrounded by myriads of heavenly beings, for whom the Hebrew language has a rich terminology. Thus, we encounter such designations as "the sons of God," "the divine council"; and the "divine assembly."[5]

This notion of a heavenly council, however, is not the same as the LDS doctrine of the godhead since it does not depict a supreme three-member body. Moreover, members of this heavenly council are inferior and subordinate to the Most High God. There is no clearly designated Christ figure in the Old Testament, and the Holy Ghost (called the Spirit of the Lord in the Old Testament) is never referred to as an agent or personal entity existing on its own.

In LDS discourse, the term "Elohim" is used to designate God the Father while "Jehovah" is considered to be the name of the premortal Christ. "Elohim" and "Jehovah" are used frequently in the Old Testament, but often interchangeably and with no clear evidence that they referred to two different individuals belonging to a godhead. The closest Old Testament tradition resembling a Father-Son relationship among the gods comes from an ancient Israelite belief in a high God (El Elyon), who had numerous sons, among whom was Yahweh, who was given Lordship over the House of Israel.[6] This model resembles the neighboring Canaanite tradition that El was the high god and Baal, his son, was a virile young warrior who succeeded his father as divine king. Just as Baal had his divine consort, Anath, so did Yahweh: the goddess variously known in the Old Testament as Asherah, Ashtoreth, the Queen of Heaven, Eve, and Wisdom.[7]

Scholars also note that later Old Testament writings appearing during the Jewish captivity show a strong monotheistic understanding of deity which would challenge the early Christian elevation of Christ and the Holy Ghost to the status of God. An examination of this shift to monotheism is provided later in this chapter.

New Testament

At the time of Christ the Jewish community from which the first Christians came was predominantly monotheistic (see John 4:32). Jesus spoke of himself as being sent from the "only true God" (John 17:3), and Paul declared that there is "one God, the Father . . . and one Lord, Jesus Christ" (1 Cor. 8:6; see also Eph. 4:6; 1 Tim. 2:5). Although Paul professes a single God, he acknowledges Jesus as "Lord" in the sense of God's agent in both creation and salvation.[8] Thus, in New Testament theology, there is a single God, often referred to as the Father, whose Son acts as his delegate on earth. Nowhere does the New Testament speak of Gods (plural) reigning in a godhead. In a few New Testament writings, Christ is identified with God (John 1:1, 18; 20:28; Heb. 1:8; Titus 2:13; 2 Pet. 1:1)—but never as *a* God or *another* God.

Like the Old Testament, the New Testament speaks of the Holy Ghost as a power or influence. Unlike the former, however, the latter refers to the Spirit as an agent separate from God—though still not as a personage with human form. The New Testament refers to the Spirit in a non-possessive sense—*the* Spirit—rather than strictly as the *Lord's* Spirit as in the Old Testament (see chapter 9). The Spirit operates on believers to sanctify them and confer spiritual gifts. Thus, the New Testament depicts Christ and the Holy Ghost participating as expressions of the divine activity, but not as individual gods.

Most theologians agree that there is no definitive doctrine of the godhead or trinity in the New Testament.[9] Though not explicitly taught in the New Testament, trinitarianism seemed to early Patristic theologians to be the most logical (though not the only) way, based on Greek metaphysics, of reconciling New Testament references to the divinity of Christ with the strong monotheism evidenced in the Old and New Testaments. Nearly all of the doctrinal variations of the godhead that have continued to the present day emerged from similar efforts to resolve this dichotomy.

Early Nineteenth-Century Christianity

There were two principal views of the godhead espoused by clerics at the time of Joseph Smith: trinitarianism, which held that there were three persons in the godhead, and unitarianism, which held that only a single person was God and that Christ, though God's son, was not deity. Heated debates took place between trinitarians and unitarians which "peaked between 1815 and 1833 in New England, where Joseph Smith spent his early years."[10] Whether Christ himself was divine and coeternal with the Father (the trinitarian view) or whether he was created and therefore ontologically (in substance or being) separate from and inferior to God (the unitarian view) was the primary issue in this controversy. Since the earliest LDS perception of God was strikingly similar to trinitarianism (the Book of Mormon was decidedly anti-unitarian), this view merits further exploration.

Trinitarianism is the belief that, although there are three persons in the godhead, these persons comprise one God or divine substance. As stated in the Athanasian Creed: "We worship one God in trinity [i.e., one divine substance in three persons], and trinity in unity [i.e., three persons composed of one divine substance], neither confounding the persons nor dividing the substance. For the person of the Father is one; of the Son, another; of the Holy Spirit, another. But the divinity of the Father and of the Son and of the Holy Spirit is one." Orthodox trinitarianism walks a fine line between modal trinitarianism (or modalism) on one side, which is the belief in one God manifest in three modes or offices (not strictly persons), and tritheism on the other, which is the belief in three persons who are three Gods. According to trinitarians, modalism commits the error of "confounding the persons" while tritheism errs by "dividing the substance."[11]

Modalism was a popular alternative to orthodox trinitarianism at the time of Joseph Smith and differed from orthodox trinitarianism in ways that were subtle and lost on most laypersons. They both maintained that the Father, Son, and Holy Ghost were "one God"; however, modalism saw them as three modes rather than three persons. In 1818, David Millard, a preacher in the Christian Connexion, explained that modalists are "trinitarians . . . [who] reject the term *person*, and instead of this, use the term *mode*, or *office*: and hold that the Trinity consists in one God, acting in three distinct *offices*: that the three distinct *offices* are those of the Father, Son, and Holy Ghost."[12] Modalists, therefore, made no essential distinction between persons in the godhead, holding that the Father not only begat the Son but also became the Son. Thus, the person of Jesus could appropriately be called the Father *and* the Son.

In 1826, Methodist minister Elijah Bailey wrote a treatise criticizing modalists for maintaining "that Jesus Christ is the Eternal Father, and that the Father and the Son are without distinction."[13] Where orthodox trinitarians held that the second person of the Trinity (i.e., God the Son) came to earth in the flesh, modalists believed that God the Father *became* the Son through incarnation, thus becoming the Father *and* the Son. For modalists, the titles "Father" and "Son," when applied to Christ, were intended to differentiate between his role as the eternal God (i.e., the Father) and his role as the incarnate God (i.e., the Son).

Early Mormonism

The earliest LDS teachings portray the godhead in recognizably trinitarian terms. The trademark trinitarian expression of the Father, Son, and Holy Ghost being "one God" is given emphasis in the Book of Mormon (2 Ne. 31:21; Mosiah 15:4–5; Morm. 7:7) and in the 1830 testimony of the three witnesses, which concludes: "And the honor be to the Father, and to the Son, and to the Holy Ghost, which is one God" (front matter of Book of Mormon). This same classical trinitarian expression also appears in the 1830 articles and covenants of the Church which declares that the "Father, Son, and Holy Ghost are one God" (D&C 20:28).

This Book of Mormon (and classical trinitarian) enunciation of a three-in-one God is not found in the Bible.[14] It emerged as a later creedal formulation first articulated by Tertullian ca. A.D. 200. In the Bible, the expression "one God" is used only in reference to God the Father. Christ declared that he and his Father were "one," but not one God. Paul was unequivocal in his designation of the Father as the one and only true God, with Jesus being the only Mediator between God and man (1 Cor. 8:6; 1 Tim. 2:5). The Book of Mormon declaration of a three-in-one God, therefore, resembles most nearly post-biblical trinitarianism.

The Book of Mormon understanding of the godhead has been characterized as a lay trinitarianism with elements of both orthodox and modal trinitarianism using language that is mixed and sometimes inconsistent.[15] Evidence of modalism in the Book of Mormon can be seen in language that depicts Christ as being both the Father and the Son. Abinadi calls the Son "the very Eternal Father" (Mosiah 16:15). In answer to Zeezrom's question: "Is the Son of God the very Eternal Father?" Amulek responds: "Yea, he is the very Eternal Father of heaven and of earth, and all things which in them are" (Alma 38:39). Today, Latter-day Saints understand this verse to mean that Christ is the Father, but only in the limited sense of being the creator under the direction of God the Father, who is the Father of our spirits, including Christ's.[16] In the Book of Mormon, however, there is no notion of spirit birth and therefore no higher expression of fatherhood than that of being the creator of "all things" or source of all existence. To say that Christ is "the *very* Eternal Father" seems to be synonymous with saying that he *is* God the Father. As the prophet Abinidi explained, "the Father and Son . . . are one God, yea, the very Eternal Father of heaven and of earth" (Mosiah 15:4). This is much like the way modalists would say they are one and the same God and Father of all things.

The Book of Mormon assignation of Christ as "the very Eternal Father" makes it difficult to determine whether "the Eternal Father" refers to the Father or the Son in any particular instance, or if even such a distinction is intended. Book of Mormon passages speak of Christ as both "the Father and the Son" in an ordinary modalistic fashion (see Mosiah 15:2; Morm. 9:12; Ether 3:14)—a sense that orthodox trinitarians would consider as a confusion of the persons.

The explanation of how Christ is both the Father and the Son is also modalistic. Abinadi states that Christ is

> the Father, because he was conceived by the power of God; and the Son, because of the flesh; thus becoming the Father and the Son—
> And they are one God, yea, the very Eternal Father of heaven and of earth. (Mosiah 15:3–4)

Christ is designated as the "Father" because he possesses God's power or "Spirit" (Mosiah 15:5), while he is the "Son" because he became "flesh"—that is, because he "dwelt in the flesh" (v. 2) and was made "flesh and blood," bearing "the image of man" (Mosiah 7:27). This notion of the Father and the Son being combined in the person of Jesus in this fashion appears modalistic and is not the way orthodox trinitarians or even modern Latter-day Saints would normally express the relationship between the Father and the Son. In current LDS discourse, Christ isn't characteristically referred to as "the Eternal Father," a title generally restricted to God the Father (see D&C 20:77, 79). Furthermore, Christ is currently referred to as the Son because he was begotten of God in the flesh, not because he was literally God in the flesh as the Book of Mormon has it. In summary, the Father and the Son are often combined in one person in the Book of Mormon in a typical modalistic fashion.

It is true that certain Book of Mormon passages speak of the Father and the Son as separate entities, such as when Christ prays to the Father in 3 Nephi, which sounds incongruous with modalism. Mormon critic Dan Vogel points out, however, that this is no different than New Testament distinctions between the Father and the Son which were still seen by modalists as different modes of God and not separate persons united as God. Consequently, he argues that one cannot simply assume that such distinctions indicate an anti-modalist perspective. According to Vogel:

Passages which speak of the Father sending the Son (Alma 14:5; 3 Ne. 27:13–14; 26:5) do not necessarily support a trinitarian [non-modalistic] view and should be understood in light of Ether 4:12: "He that will not believe me will not believe the Father who sent me. For behold, I am the Father." In other words, Jesus as the Father sent himself into the world to redeem his people. Nor do passages which speak of the Son being prepared from before the foundation of the earth (Mosiah 18:13) necessarily imply two persons existing before the incarnation. Consider the following: "I am he who was prepared from the foundation of the world to redeem my people. Behold, I am Jesus Christ. I am the Father and the Son" (Ether 3:14). The Book of Mormon therefore violates a major tenet of trinitarianism by confusing the persons of the Father and Son and by referring to Jesus as the Father.[17]

Notably, several Book of Mormon passages which now refer to Christ as "the Son of the Eternal Father" (1 Ne. 11:21, 11:32, 13:40) actually referred to him as "the Eternal Father" in the original 1830 edition. This first edition also had Mary as the "mother of God" (1 Ne. 11:18), which changed in the 1837 edition to the "mother of the Son of God." These changes may, in part, reflect Joseph's later tendency to more clearly differentiate between the Father and the Son in his teachings.

It appears that the dual identity of Christ as both the Father and the Son occurs only in the earliest teachings of Joseph Smith, including his early revisions to the Bible. A passage in Luke states, "No man knoweth who the Son is, but the Father; and who the Father is, but the Son, and he to whom the Son will reveal him" (Luke 10:22). Joseph revised this passage to read, "No man knoweth that the Son *is* the Father, and the Father *is* the Son, but him to whom the Son will reveal it" (JST Luke 10:22; emphasis mine). By melding the identities of the Father and the Son, Joseph Smith effectively interjected a dose of modalism into the New Testament.

Conservative LDS scholars who maintain that Mormon doctrine did not evolve contend that the Book of Mormon doctrine of the godhead is completely consistent with what is taught today. Indeed, most LDS doctrinal expositions on the godhead assume a unity of teachings on the subject in the Bible, Book of Mormon, and other latter-day scripture.[18] BYU religion professor Robert Millet asserts that "the doctrine of the godhead in the Book of Mormon is actually deeper and more penetrating than that found in any other book of scripture" and that "the Book of Mormon theology was not a part of a line-upon-line unfolding of doctrine in this dispensation."[19] The Book of Mormon doctrine of the godhead may indeed sound more abstruse than many later teachings of Joseph Smith, but one wonders if this is because it is "deeper and more penetrating," or if it is because its language was shaped by now unfamiliar, early nineteenth-century trinitarian discourse.

From a current LDS perspective, early LDS teachings seem a bit vague and indiscriminant in referring to both Christ and the Father as "God" rather than as two distinct gods. In writing of this early period of doctrinal formulation, LDS historian Thomas G. Alexander comments, "There is little evidence that [early] Church doctrine . . . specifically differentiated between Christ and God. Indeed, this distinction was probably considered unnecessary since the early discussions also supported trinitarian doctrine"[20]

Kirtland Period

The teaching that God and Christ are "one God" begins to diminish in LDS writings during 1830 as the Prophet began differentiating more clearly between the Father and the Son. Although a March 1830 revelation designated Christ as "God, the greatest of all" (D&C 19:18), a revelation given in June 1830 has the Father acknowledging Christ as his Son and then declaring, "but there is no other God beside me [i.e., God the Father]" (Moses 1:6). No longer are the Father, Son, and Holy Ghost routinely called "one God;" instead, they are now understood as three members of one god*head*.

The 1834–35 *Lectures on Faith* explicitly differentiates between the Father and the Son in the godhead: "There are two personages who constitute the great, matchless, governing, and supreme, power over all things. . . . They are the Father and the Son . . . [both] possessing the same mind . . . which mind is the Holy Spirit . . . and these three constitute the godhead, and are one."[21] It should be noted, that at this stage in the development of Mormon thought, only the Father and the Son are designated as actual "personages" while the Holy Ghost is depicted as the indwelling "mind" or power they share in common. This mid–1830s perception of the godhead has been characterized as binitarian since it acknowledges only two *persons* in the godhead.[22] In response to the question, "How many personages are there in the godhead?" the unequivocal answer given in the *Lectures* is "Two: the Father and Son."[23]

Some theologians define binitarianism as "the belief that there are only two persons in the godhead instead of the three of the Trinity, thus involving the denial of the deity of the Holy Spirit."[24] The *Lectures* aren't binitarian in this sense, since they also acknowledge that all "three constitute the godhead;" it is just that only two are considered personages. The *Lectures* give little support for the personality—but full support for the deity—of the Holy Ghost. This position differs from traditional trinitarianism which sees the Holy Ghost as an actual person—not necessarily in the sense of having human form, but in the sense of being a center of consciousness separate from the Father and the Son. Many primitivists of the early 1800s held the belief that the godhead consisted of only two persons and that the Holy Ghost was, in primitivist David Millard's words, "a divine emanation of God."[25] Noted nineteenth-century Baptist preacher Charles Spurgeon observed that, in the early nineteenth century, even traditional trinitarians had "acquired the habit of regarding the Holy Ghost as an emanation flowing from the Father and the Son, but not as being actually a person himself."[26]

Nauvoo Period

The Nauvoo period brought an increased distinction between members of the godhead, as well as recognition of the Holy Ghost as a personage. In February 1841, Joseph drew on a popular caricature of orthodox trinitarianism when he argued that "the godhead . . . was Not as many imagined—three Heads & but one body." Rather, said Joseph, "the three were separate bod[ies]."[27] Joseph now appears to be leaning toward social trinitarianism, which considers members of the godhead to be distinct individuals who are one only in purpose, and not in substance.

In May 1841, Joseph reaffirmed that the godhead consisted of "three personages" and differentiated their roles stating, "[An] Everlasting covenant was made between three personages before the organization of this earth and relates to their dispensation of things to men on the earth. These personages according to Abraham's record are called God the first, the Creator; God the second, the Redeemer; and God the third, the witness or Testator."[28] While this idea of members of the godhead entering into a covenant before the creation and agreeing to their respective roles in the salvation of man is non-biblical, it was an integral part of Reformed or covenant theology of the early nineteenth century. According to an 1823 Calvinist creed, "God from eternity made a gracious covenant or plan . . . for the salvation of men. The parties to this covenant are . . . the Father, Son, and the Holy Ghost." As a result of this everlasting covenant, "distinctive operations are ascribed to each Person: creation and election to the Father, redemption to the Son, sanctifying and sealing to the Holy Ghost."[29] That Joseph Smith would later enunciate an almost identical covenant, even to the attributing of the role of creator to the Father instead of the Son, suggests a possible Protestant influence on his thinking in this matter.

In March 1839, Joseph first hinted that there may be more than "one God" (D&C 121:28); however, it wasn't until 1842 that he specifically referred to the godhead as consisting of three separate beings who were also "three Gods."[30] He seems to now consider them to be one only in the sense that they "agree as one."[31] In his last public discourse, given June 16, 1844, Joseph repudiated the trinitarian notion of a three-in-one God. "Men say there is one God—the Fa[the]r, Son & the H.G. are only 1 God—It is a strange God anyhow 3 in one & 1 in 3."[32] On this occasion, he definitively stated that the godhead consists of "3 distinct personages & 3 Gods."[33]

Joseph's teachings regarding the members of the godhead appear to have progressed from essentially a trinitarian three-in-one God with a modalistic flavor, to a godhead consisting of "two personages" united by the indwelling Holy Spirit, to a godhead consisting of "three personages," and finally to a godhead consisting of "three Gods."

Contemporary Mormonism

The current LDS understanding of the godhead is primarily based on Joseph Smith's later tritheistic teachings, although, according to Alexander, tritheism wasn't uniformly taught in the Church until the early 1900s.[34] Until that time, a variety of teachings were in circulation. Modern LDS doctrinal expositors have had the task of reconciling the current tritheistic doctrine of the godhead with earlier LDS trinitarian teachings of the Book of Mormon and the pronounced monotheism of the Bible. Early LDS references to the Father and Christ being "one God" are now interpreted as meaning they are one god*head*.[35]

Plurality of Gods

One of the most distinctive doctrines of Mormonism is the belief in a plurality of Gods.[36] This is generally understood to mean that there are innumerable Gods besides (and above) the God that we worship, all of whom are creators of worlds and objects of worship. Furthermore, these Gods were all once human, and just as they attained Godhood, so can we. This view goes beyond the traditional Christian doctrine of human divinization or theosis in which the righteous are partakers of the nature of God through the indwelling of God's Spirit.

Much of Joseph Smith's developed thinking on the plurality of Gods seems to be linked to his interaction with the text of Genesis while studying Hebrew in late 1835 and early 1836, particularly under the tutelage of Hebrew professor Joshua Seixas. Having learned that the Hebrew term *Elohim* was actually the plural form of

God (*El*), he translated the book of Abraham to read that the "Gods" created the heavens and the earth. On March 20, 1839, the Prophet told the Saints that the Lord would reveal to them "whether there be one God or many Gods" (D&C 121:28). He also spoke of a "Council of the Eternal God of all other gods" that convened "before this world was" (D&C 121:32).

It isn't clear whether Joseph initially saw these "other gods" as gods in the full sense or in a lesser sense than the "Eternal God." When the book of Abraham speaks of "the Gods" who "organized and formed the heavens and the earth" (Abr. 4:1; see also 4:2–29), it is generally understood that it is referring to preexistent noble spirits rather than to resurrected exalted beings (though this is not required by the text). These beings may have been the individuals who, according to Joseph Smith, "exalt[ed] themselves to be Gods even from bef[ore] the foundation of the world & are the only Gods I have a reverence for."[37] Abraham speaks of intelligences existing one above another, culminating with God who is "more intelligent than they all" (Abr. 3:19). The notion of intelligences of varying degrees existing beneath God was widely held at Joseph Smith's time. For example, Charles Buck's *Theological Dictionary*, a popular 1830 reference records: "The existence of intelligences of a higher order than man, though infinitely below the Deity, appears extremely probable."[38]

Blake Ostler notes that the plurality of Gods as taught in the book of Abraham mirrors references in the Old Testament to gods in a heavenly council in which "God is . . . the sovereign Lord who summons emissaries of the divine council and sends them as agents."[39] Theologians refer to this concept as monolatrism, which is the belief in a plurality of minor gods that are subject to the supreme God whom all worship. This appears to be the concept portrayed in the book of Abraham.

During the late Nauvoo period, the Prophet acknowledged the existence of even higher gods and reportedly taught that "intelligences exist one above anot[he]r [so] that there is no end to it."[40] This implies that there are intelligences even higher than God the Father. Indeed, by June of 1844 it was reported that Joseph was teaching that there are "innumerable Gods as much above the God that presides over this universe, as he is above us."[41] According to Joseph, "God the Father of Jesus Christ had a Father," and we "may suppose that He had a Fa[the]r also—where was ther[e] ever a Son with[ou]t a Fa[the]r."[42] These teachings gave rise to the belief in an endless hierarchy of Gods with each presiding over an ever-expanding dominion of creations.

Old Testament

While the Old Testament is traditionally seen as monotheistic, traces of polytheism can be found in early Old Testament passages. Most scholars now agree that "the earliest Hebrew conception of God was pluralistic" and only later "evolved toward universal monotheism."[43] Mark S. Smith, a scholar of Near Eastern religions, notes that early Israelite religion was not unlike other Canaanite belief systems and that "the number of deities in Israel was relatively typical for the region."[44] In particular, "Baal was an accepted Israelite god," and renunciation of his cult began only in the eighth or ninth century B.C.[45]

According to Near Eastern archeologist William Dever, "Virtually all mainstream scholars (and even a few conservatives) acknowledge that true monotheism emerged only in the period of the exile in Babylon in the 6th century B.C.E., as the canon of the Hebrew Bible was taking shape."[46] The first clear biblical evidence of monotheism is in Isaiah 45:5, 21 where the Lord declares: "I am the Lord, and there is none else . . . . There is no God else beside me; a just God and a Saviour; there is none beside me."[47] This one and only true God was savior, lawgiver, lord, and king. God, not the godhead nor one of several individuals in the godhead, created, sustained, saved, and judged the nations.

Polytheistic passages in the Old Testament are believed to have been altered with time to bring them into harmony with later monotheism. For example, Deuteronomy 32:8 speaks of a time "when the most High divided to the nations their inheritance, when he separated the sons of Adam, he set the bounds of the people according to the number of the children of Israel." An early rendering of this passage preserved in the Greek (Septuagint) and the Dead Sea Scrolls reads "the sons of God" rather than "the children of Israel" (this reading has been restored in the RSV). In the Ras Shamra tablets dating to 1400 B.C., *El* or God is said to have had seventy sons, and in the Hebrew tradition there were seventy nations (Gen. 10). In Deuteronomy 32:8, "the most High" (*El*) divides the nations and gives *Yahweh*, one of the seventy sons of El, Israel as "the Lord's [*Yahweh's*] portion" (Deut. 32:9).[48] A similar revision was made to Psalms 96:7 which currently reads: "Give unto the Lord, O ye kindreds of the people, give unto the Lord glory and strength." The original manuscript read, "Ascribe to the Lord, *O divine beings*, ascribe to the Lord glory and strength."[49] Thus, the command was issued to other "divine beings," not necessarily to mortals.

A passage sometimes cited by Latter-day Saints as a reference to a plurality of Gods is Psalms 82:6 in which the seer Asaph declares, "I have said, Ye are gods; and all of you are children of the most High." While it may be tempting to read this passage as meaning that we are all children of God and, therefore, potentially gods, it would be a mis-

THE GODHEAD AND PLURALITY OF GODS 117

reading. Prior to this verse, Asaph acknowledges that God "judgeth among the gods" (v. 1), who have dealt unjustly with the fatherless and the needy; and therefore, even though they are gods, they "shall die like men, and fall like one of the princes." Scholars note that there are at least two possible meanings of the word "gods" in this passage: the divine assembly of gods (described earlier) or human judges who ruled under God's authority.[50] In either case, it refers to beings currently bearing the title "gods" with whom God is displeased and therefore pronounces judgment upon them. In the Old Testament, "god" is a title that could apply to men, angels, or other beings God established as his rulers or ministers. In Exodus 7:1, for example, Moses is made "a god to Pharaoh." However, there is never a mention of Gods in the LDS sense of beings once human ruling over worlds of their own.

Interestingly, Jesus cites Psalms 82:6 to justify his divine Sonship, arguing that if the individuals in this passage merited the title "gods," then it should not be blasphemy to calls himself "the Son of God" (John 10:34–36). Scholars (LDS and non-LDS) generally agree that Jesus was most likely interpreting Psalms 82:6 as referring to mortals acting as God's representatives rather than heavenly gods.[51]

New Testament

Based on their writings, New Testament Christians seem to have inherited the monotheism taught in the late Old Testament period. As we have seen, Paul was emphatic in proclaiming the one and only true God. In spite of the clear monotheistic teachings of the New Testament, during the Nauvoo period Joseph Smith drew upon several New Testament passages to support a plurality of Gods. Ironically, one of the passages he cited is from Paul:

> As concerning therefore the eating of those things that are offered in sacrifice unto idols, we know that an idol is nothing in the world, and that there is none other God but one.
>
> For though there be that are called gods, whether in heaven or in earth, (as there be gods many, and lords many,)
>
> But to us there is but one God, the Father. (1 Cor. 8:4–6)

Commenting on this passage, Joseph stated, "Paul says there are Gods many etc . . . [which] makes a plurality of Gods."[52] Joseph explained that Paul's assertion "to us there is but one God" means "pertaining to us,"[53] thus allowing for other Gods pertaining to other worlds.

Non-LDS scholars universally maintain that the gods to whom Paul referred were heathen gods and that he was contrasting those heathen who offer sacrifices to idols "that are *called* gods" (v. 5)[54] with "us," the Christians, who know that there is only one God (v. 6). This view is consistent with Paul's assertion in verse 5 that "there is none other God but one." Notwithstanding the implied meaning that "gods" refers to heathen gods, Joseph was bold enough to declare, "I have a witness of the H.G. & a test[imony] that Paul had no allusion to the Heathen G[ods] in the text."[55] It is ironic that a passage in which Paul seemingly argues *against* a plurality of Gods was appropriated by the Prophet to argue *for* a plurality of Gods.

Another New Testament proof-text for the plurality of Gods is Revelation 1:6 in which John proclaims that Christ "hath made us kings and priests unto God and his Father." In June 1844, the Prophet approved this verse as "altog[ethe]r correct in the translation" and interpreted "his Father" to mean God the Father's father (i.e., Christ's grandfather).[56] While the expression "God and his Father" may sound like two separate individuals, a common convention in the New Testament is to refer to God as the "God and Father" of Jesus Christ (2 Cor. 11:31; Eph. 1:3; Col. 1:3; 1 Pet. 1:3). Modern translations avoid the ambiguity of the KJV by rendering the expression as "unto *his* [i.e., Christ's] God and Father," indicating that "God" and "Father" both refer to God, the Father of Jesus Christ.

Joseph's apparent misreading of this verse is not altogether surprising given the ambiguous wording in the KJV, even though such a reading seems inconsistent with New Testament theology. It is noteworthy that, when the Prophet earlier came upon this passage while translating the Bible (sometime between February 1832 and February 1833), he changed "God and his father" to read "God, his father," thus making "his father" merely an appositive for "God," similar to modern translations. This is one of several examples of how the Prophet read monotheism into ambiguous Bible passages early in his career and then, as though undergoing a shift in his theology, began reading a plurality of Gods into them.

Early Mormonism

The early works of Joseph Smith show a clear monotheistic leaning. When a Book of Mormon prophet was asked whether there was more than one God, the answer was a resounding "no" (Alma 11:28–29). The Book of Mormon repeatedly emphasizes that there is "one God" (see, for example, 2 Ne. 31:21; Mosiah 15:4–5; Morm. 7:7). After the publication of the Book of Mormon, Joseph began revising the Bible and seems to have "consciously attempted to remove all references to a plurality of Gods."[57] In JST Genesis, for example, he removed any possibility of "God" being plural, despite the presence of the Hebrew plural *Elohim*, by changing virtually all occurrences of "God" to the first person, singular: "I" or "I, God . . . ." He further made it clear that the reference to "us" in the creation story refers specifically to the Father and the preexistent Jesus Christ (see Moses 2:26–27), which was a common trinitarian reading. The *Lectures on Faith* similarly state that "it [was] by the Father and the Son that all things were created."[58] Only after embracing a plurality of Gods (sometime after 1838) do we have record of his interpreting "us" as "the Gods" (Abr. 4:26–27).[59] The JST changed the word "god" to "prophet" in the passage referring to Moses being "a god" to pharaoh (JST Ex. 7:1). Moses 1:6 has God declaring the divine Sonship of Christ and then quickly clarifying, "but there is no other God beside me." In sum, Joseph's early teachings evidence a tendency to emphasize the singularity of God.

Similarly, monotheism appears to be the underlying theology in the revelations of the Doctrine and Covenants until at least 1839. Although Doctrine and Covenants 76, given in 1832, refers to heirs of the celestial kingdom as "gods, even the sons of God" (D&C 76:58), this expression (borrowed from Psalms 82:6), which could possibly be referring to gods in the full sense of God the Father, is more likely only intended to convey the notion that heirs of the celestial kingdom receive the fulness of the glory of God. Christians had for centuries embraced the doctrine of divinization to the extent that the righteous would become gods by participating in the fullness of God's glory as joint heirs with Christ. It is also the scholarly consensus that biblical references to humans becoming gods were never intended to imply that they would be Gods (capital "G") in the same absolute sense that God the Father is God,[60] especially in light of Paul's insistence that there is only "one God, the Father, of whom are all things" (1 Cor. 8:6). Even Adam and Eve became "as gods" after partaking of the forbidden fruit, but only in the sense that they obtained a divine knowledge of good and evil (Gen. 3:5). In short, it seems unlikely that Doctrine and Covenants 76:58 was either given or initially understood as a pronouncement that human beings would become gods in the absolute sense of becoming creators of worlds.[61] It would be another decade before this kind of godhood would be ascribed to exalted humans.

The literalistic thinking of many early converts soon led to a literal understanding of the godhood of humankind. In the spring of 1840, while discussing the scriptures with an acquaintance, Lorenzo Snow, a future Church president, received what he considered to be a revelation showing "the pathway of God and man." As a result he penned the couplet "As man now is, God once was: As God now is, man may be."[62]

Ironically, just as Joseph earlier seemed to rid the Bible of references to a plurality of Gods, later in life he read a plurality of Gods back into the Bible. For example, on June 16, 1844, he proclaimed that the Hebrew term *Elohim* "ought to be in the plural all the way thro[ugh the Bible]—Gods."[63] Where he earlier removed the ambiguity in Revelation 1:6 so that it spoke only of God the Father, in 1844, in support of the developing doctrine of a plurality of Gods, he called the original KJV reading of Revelation 1:6 "altogether correct" and interpreted it as a reference to both God the Father and to God the Father's father. It is unclear what Joseph meant when later remarking, "I have always—& in all congregat[ion]s when I have preached it has been the plurality of Gods."[64] This comment may have been spoken retroflectively as no record can be found during most of the first decade of the Church in which Joseph Smith or any of his associates explicitly taught a plurality of Gods.[65]

Contemporary Mormonism

In current LDS thought, the idea of human beings becoming like God is sometimes marginalized, especially in interfaith dialogues where it continues to be a controversial issue. In his Mormon-evangelical exchange, Mormon co-author Stephen Robinson gives this explanation: "What do Latter-day Saints mean by 'gods'? Latter-day Saints do not, or at least should not believe that they will ever be independent in all eternity from their Father in heaven or from their Savior or from the Holy Spirit. Those who are exalted by his grace will always be 'gods' (always with a small 'g', even in the Doctrine and Covenants) by grace, by an extension of 'his' power, and will always be subordinate to the Godhead."[66] BYU religion professor Roger Keller conceded at a multi-denominational conference in 2002 that "there will always be a qualitative difference between the Father, the Son, and us."[67] Thus, although the doctrine of becoming like God is still acknowledged in the Church, there seems to be a growing tendency to explain it in a more traditional Christian sense rather than in an absolute sense.

Notes

1. Joseph Fielding Smith, *Doctrines of Salvation: Compiled Sermons of Joseph Fielding Smith*, 1:1.
2. Andrew F. Ehat and Lydon W. Cook, *The Words of Joseph Smith*, 378.
3. Theodore Hiebert, "Genesis," 8.
4. G. Ernest Wright, *The Old Testament against Its Environment*, 32–33, see also 30–41. For a discussion of the divine council as a parallel to the LDS concept of a council of gods, see Roger D. Cook, "Hebrew, Early Judaic, and Early Christian Thought."
5. Frederick H. Cryer, *In Search of God*, 133; see also 134–35.

6. For a fascinating study of the El-Yaweh relationship in Israel, see Margaret Barker, *The Great Angel: A Study of Israel's Second God*. For an LDS approach to this relationship, see Blake T. Ostler, *Exploring Mormon Thought: Of God and Gods*, 32–120.

7. Daniel C. Peterson, "Nephi and His Asherah," 16–25.

8. Gerald O'Collins, *Christology: A Biblical, Historical, and Systematic Study of Jesus*, 138.

9. Edmund J. Fortman, *The Triune God: A Historical Study of the Doctrine of the Trinity*, 32, 35; Paul J. Achtemier, *Harper's Bible Dictionary*, 1099.

10. Van Hale, "Defining the Contemporary Mormon Concept of God," 11.

11. Kevin Giles, *Jesus and the Father: Modern Evangelicals Reinvent the Doctrine of the Trinity*, 158.

12. David Millard, *The True Messiah Exalted, or Jesus Christ Really Is the Son of God . . .* , 8; emphasis his; quoted in Dan Vogel, "The Earliest Mormon Concept of God," 18.

13. Elijah Bailey, *America in Primitive Trinitarianism Examined and Defended*, 24.

14. A New Testament passage having a vague semblance to the trinitarian formula of Father, Son, and Holy Ghost as one God is 1 John 5:7 which states that "the Father, the Word, and the Holy Ghost . . . are one" (but not necessarily one "God"). Even this passage, however, is widely acknowledged by biblical scholars as a later trinitarian insertion (probably sometime after the second century) since it appears in none of the oldest manuscripts. George Arthur Buttrick, et al., *The Interpreters Bible*, 12:293–94. Brant Gardner, *Second Witness*, 2:447, argues that the trinitarian formula in the Book of Mormon "is probably a contribution of Joseph Smith's vocabulary."

15. Vogel, "The Earliest Mormon Concept of God," 24; Melodie Moench Charles, "The Book of Mormon Christology," 100–101. Both of these writers acknowledge that, though strongly modalistic, the Book of Mormon also contains passages that evidence a more orthodox trinitarian perspective.

16. James E. Talmage, *Articles of Faith*, 421.

17. Vogel, "The Earliest Mormon Concept of God," 22.

18. See, for example, Talmage, *Articles of Faith*, 26–44 . For a rebuttal of the notion that the LDS doctrine of the Godhead evolved from Modalism, see Ari D. Bruening and David L. Paulsen, "The Development of the Mormon Understanding of God: Early Mormon Modalism and Other Myths," 109–69.

19. Robert L. Millet, *Selected Writings of Robert L. Millet*, 112.

20. Thomas G. Alexander, "The Reconstruction of Mormon Doctrine: From Joseph Smith to Progressive Theology," 25.

21. *Lectures on Faith*, 5:2. Although the authorship of the *Lectures* has long been debated, it has traditionally been the consensus that Joseph Smith ultimately endorsed their contents and sanctioned their publication. See, for example, Larry E. Dahl and Charles D. Tate, *The Lectures on Faith in Historical Perspective*, 10. BYU professor of political science Noel Reynolds has more recently argued, however, that not only was Joseph Smith not the author, but that he had little influence on its content and publication. Noel B. Reynolds, "The Case for Sidney Rigdon as Author of the Lectures on Faith," 1–41. Interestingly, this particular lecture (no. 5) has been largely attributed

in wordprint studies to W. W. Phelps, who remarked in May 1835 that, even prior to joining Mormonism he considered himself to be "a believer in God, and the Son of God, as two distinct characters [note the exclusion of the Holy Ghost as a character], and a believer in sacred scripture." William W. Phelps, "To Oliver Cowdery, Esq.," *Latter Day Saints' Messenger and Advocate* 1 (May 19, 1835): 115.

22. See, for example, Kurt Widmer, *Mormonism and the Nature of God: A Theological Evolution, 1830–1915*, 6; Hale, "Defining the Contemporary Mormon Concept of God," 11; and Vogel, "Earliest Mormon Concept of God," 17–33. The confusion created by the binitarian teachings in the *Lectures*—in light of the later tritheistic Godhead—was a major factor in the removal of the *Lectures* from the Doctrine and Covenants. Richard S. Van Wagoner, Steve C. Walker, and Allen D. Roberts, "The 'Lectures on Faith': A Case Study in Decanonization," 71–77.

23. *Lectures on Faith*, 5:1.

24. Frank L. Cross and Elizabeth A. Livingstone, *The Oxford Dictionary of the Christian Church*, s.v. "binitarianism."

25. David Millard, quoted in Vogel, "The Earliest Mormon Concept of God," 18.

26. Charles H. Spurgeon, *Sermons of C. H. Spurgeon of London*, 46.

27. Ehat and Cook, *The Words of Joseph Smith*, 63. Similarly, Emanuel Swedenborg, a contemporary of Joseph Smith, wrote that people trying to describe the classical doctrine of the Trinity "cannot present it . . . otherwise than as a man of three heads upon one body." Emanuel Swedenborg, *The True Christian Religion: Containing the Universal Theology of the New Church Foretold by the Lord . . .* , 145.

28. Ehat and Cook, *The Words of Joseph Smith*, 87–88. Ehat and Cook note that the May 1841 dating of this remark is only an estimate as the William Clayton's report is undated. The expression "God the first . . . God the second . . . and God the third" is not the same as saying there are three gods. The widely adopted and familiar Westminster Confession of Faith of 1647, for example, also spoke of "God the Father, God the Son, and God the Holy Ghost." See "Westminster Confession of Faith," chapter 2. This confession was written in 1646 and approved in 1647.

29. See "Confessions of Faith of the Calvinistic Methodists or the Presbyterians of Wales."

30. "A Visit to Joe Smith," *Times and Seasons* 3 (September 15, 1842): 926. This article is extracted from an exchange paper related by a clergyman in Illinois.

31. Ehat and Cook, *The Words of Joseph Smith*, 63.

32. Ibid., 380.

33. Ibid., 378. See also Greg Kofford, "The First Vision: Doctrinal Developments and Analysis."

34. Alexander, "The Reconstruction of Mormon Doctrine," 27–31. See also Thomas G. Alexander, *Mormonism in Transition: A History of the Latter-day Saints, 1890–1930*, Chapter 14.

35. Joseph Fielding Smith, *Answers to Gospel Questions*, 1:2.

36. Though Latter-day Saints prefer to speak of a "plurality" of Gods, non-Mormons consider Mormons thoroughgoing polytheists. Technically speaking, polytheism is the belief in and worship of many gods. Instead of

worshipping multiple gods who all rule within the same realm, as did the ancient Greeks and Romans, Mormons understand themselves to be worshipping only one God, while acknowledging the existence of other divine beings. In this sense Mormonism is perhaps better understood as being henotheistic.

37. Ehat and Cook, *The Words of Joseph Smith*, 381.

38. Charles S. Buck, *Theological Dictionary*, 123. Joseph Smith would have been well aware of this dictionary since it was referenced in the *Lectures on Faith* as well as in articles published in the LDS *Times and Seasons* prior to 1844.

39. Blake T. Ostler, "Re-vision-ing the Mormon Concept of Deity."

40. Ehat and Cook, *The Words of Joseph Smith*, 380. Ostler refutes the idea that Joseph taught an infinite regress of Gods as it would be inconsistent with his earlier teachings of a "head God." Blake T. Ostler, *Exploring Mormon Thought: The Attributes of God*, 442–47.

41. "Preamble," *Nauvoo Expositor* 1, no. 1 (June 7, 1844): 2. The statement attributed to Joseph Smith was apparently voiced by the editors, William Law, Wilson Law, Jane Law, and Robert D. Foster.

42. Ehat and Cook, *The Words of Joseph Smith*, 380. Orson Pratt describes the generation of Gods: "The person of our Father in Heaven was begotten on a previous heavenly world by His Father; and again, He was begotten by a still more ancient Father; and so on, from generation to generation, from one heavenly world to another still more ancient, until our minds are wearied and lost in the multiplicity of generations and successive worlds." Orson Pratt, "The Pre-Existence of Man," *The Seer* 1, no. 9 (September 1853): 132.

43. Kevin L. Barney, "Examining Six Key Concepts in Joseph Smith's Understanding of Genesis 1:1," 112.

44. Mark S. Smith, *The Early History of God: Yahweh and the Other Deities in Ancient Israel*, 64.

45. Ibid., 75.

46. William G. Dever, *Did God Have a Wife? Archeology and Folk Religion in Ancient Israel,* 294–95. Biblical scholar Richard Hooker notes that "while the Hebrews are enjoined to worship no deity but Yahweh, there is no evidence that the earliest Mosaic religion denied the existence of other gods. In fact, the account of the migration contains numerous references by the historical characters to other gods, and the first law of the Decalogue is, after all, that no gods be put before Yahweh, not that no other gods exist. While controversial among many people, most scholars have concluded that the initial Mosaic religion for about two hundred years was a monolatrous [i.e., many gods with one supreme god] religion." Richard Hooker, "Monolatry ~1300–1000 BC."

47. For ease in reading, I have standardized the all-capitalized KJV "Lord" in this chapter.

48. For a summary of scholarly explanations of this passage, see Kerry A. Sheets, "The 'Adat El, 'Council of the Gods' and Bene Elohim, 'Sons of God': Ancient Near Eastern Concepts in the Book of Abraham." Deuteronomy 32:7–8 has received interesting Mormon interpretations. Phelps interpreted it to simply mean that Adam had twelve sons. William W. Phelps, "Despise Not Prophesyings," 299. Talmage, however, interpreted it to mean that God chose spirits who were faithful in the preexistence to be born into the house of

Israel. Talmage, *Articles of Faith*, 175. See also, Harold B. Lee, *Teachings of Harold B. Lee*, 24–25.

49. Emanuel Tov, *Textual Criticism of the Hebrew Bible*, 269; emphasis mine.

50. See Daniel C. Peterson, "Ye Are Gods: Psalm 82 and John 10 as Witnesses to the Divine Nature of Humankind," 471–594.

51. See David E. Bokovoy, "'Ye Really *Are* Gods': A Response to Michael Heiser Concerning the LDS Use of Psalm 82 and the Gospel of John," 304–8.

52. Ehat and Cook, *The Words of Joseph Smith*, 379.

53. Ibid., 378. In modern Bible translations, the phrase "to us" is translated "for us," meaning "for us [Christians] there is only one God."

54. Modern translations such as the NIV and NASB read "even if there are so-called gods," making it unmistakably clear that the reference is to heathen gods.

55. Ehat and Cook, *The Words of Joseph Smith*, 379.

56. Ibid., 378.

57. Boyd Kirkland, "The Development of the Mormon Doctrine of God," 36. See, for examples, Exodus 7:1, 22:28; 1 Samuel 28:13, and Revelation 1:6.

58. *Lectures on Faith*, 5:3.

59. In light of the later development of the concept of Heavenly Mother, "us" is now sometimes interpreted as referring to Heavenly Father and Mother, since both male and female were created after their image. Elaine Anderson Cannon, "Mother in Heaven," 2:961.

60. Michael J. Christensen, "The Problem, Promise, and Process of Theosis," 23–25.

61. In June 1844 as part of his defense of a plurality of Gods, Joseph cited different ways in which individuals are referred to as "gods" in the scriptures and referred to Doctrine and Covenants 76:58 stating that "every man who reigns is a God." He didn't explain, however, the sense in which they would be Gods. Ehat and Cook, *The Words of Joseph Smith*, 381.

62. Eliza R. Snow, *Biography and Family Record of Lorenzo Snow*, 46–47. In January 1843, Lorenzo Snow related his revelation to Joseph Smith who responded, "Brother Snow, that is a true gospel doctrine, and it is a revelation from God to you." Quoted in LeRoi C. Snow, "Devotion to a Divine Inspiration," 656.

63. Ehat and Cook, *The Words of Joseph Smith*, 379. Scholars note that there are clearly places in the Old Testament where Elohim is joined with singular verbs or adjectives, making it a singular noun.

64. Ibid., 378.

65. See also, , "The First Vision."

66. Craig L. Blomberg and Stephen E. Robinson, *How Wide the Divide? A Mormon and an Evangelical in Conversation*, 86.

67. Roger R. Keller, "Jesus Christ: Priest, King, and Prophet," 355.

7

God the Father

In traditional Mormon theology God the Father, whose exalted name-title is Elohim, is literally the Father of our spirits and was himself once a man who went through the same stages of progression that humans go through. As an exalted man, God now knows all things, is all powerful, and permeates all of His creations through his immanent Spirit.

To most Latter-day Saints there is no difference between the God of the Old Testament and the God of Mormonism. Critical Bible scholars, however, view the God of ancient Israel as the fusion of a number of gods whom this nomadic nation had encountered in its wanderings. Moreover, God was described, not as some transcendent being, but rather in light of Israel's customs and experiences. The God of the Old Testament was a tribal God who thought and behaved according to the tribal customs of the children of Israel. According to *The Anchor Bible*, "It was customary in biblical times to assume that God functioned according to the customs and practices that were common to Near Eastern society."[1]

For example, the Canaanites were a people of war and, coincidentally, Yahweh reveals himself as a war-god, the Lord of hosts (i.e., armies), who commands Israel to slaughter men, women, and children (Num. 31:16-18; 1 Sam. 15:3). It was the custom of ancient Near Easterners to back up their promises by swearing with an oath. God similarly makes promises accompanied by oaths (Gen. 22:16). Just as Canaanite clans each perceived themselves as specially favored by Deity, God singles out Abraham and his posterity as his chosen people (Deut. 14:2). The ancient Near East was dominated by patriarchal rule with women having few privileges. In ancient Israel, God operated through and even reinforced customary patriarchal governance. In short, this ancient tribal God is seen by many scholars as far removed from the universal God that begins to emerge in later Old Testament times. This chapter looks at changing ideas about God in ancient and modern times.

An Absolute Versus a Finite God

Traditional Christianity has come to view God in absolute terms—i.e., he is absolutely transcendent and perfect in every aspect of his being. According to the absolutist view, God is:

- the only uncreated, self-existent being
- omnipotent, omniscient and omnipresent
- the same unchangeable God from everlasting to everlasting
- the source of everything (time, space, matter, laws, etc.) that exists.

Bible

Although the earliest Old Testament writings depict a tribal God with human-like characteristics of uncertainty, misjudgment, and even regret (see, for example, Gen. 6:6–7, 22:10–12; Job 1:7; 1 Sam. 15:11), later writings seem to support a more absolutist view of God who is described as being "from everlasting to everlasting"—evincing what seems to be a belief in a God that is uncreated and unevolved (Ps. 90:2, 93:2; Mal. 3:6; Deut. 33:27). Psalm 147:4–5 declares God's omniscience saying his "understanding is infinite." He is all powerful (Jer. 32:17) and fills the universe (1 Kgs. 8:7). In the New Testament, God is depicted as the cause, through Christ, of "all things" that exist (John 1:3; 1 Cor. 8:6; Col. 1:16). Whether it was intended that these depictions of God were to be taken literally or figuratively, at face value or with qualification, is not always clear.

Early Mormonism

Virtually all Christian denominations held an absolutist view of God at the time of Joseph Smith, and early Mormonism was no exception. Boyd Kirkland notes, "Joseph Smith's earliest statements and scriptural writings describe God as an absolute, infinite, self-existent, spiritual being, perfect in all his attributes and alone in his supremacy."[2] Indeed, early LDS literature contains many of the same descriptions of God that can be found in other contemporary Christian literature.

One of the absolutist beliefs about God pertains to his eternal godhood. Eighteenth-century clergyman Samuel Clarke, similar to others of his day, preached that God is "Lord . . . from Eternity to

Eternity" and possesses an "infinity of fullness."³ LDS scripture also depicts God as possessing an "infinity of fullness from all eternity to all eternity" (D&C 109:77). This idea of God's *eternal* possession of infinite fulness seems to indicate a belief in an eternally unchanging God. In the Book of Mormon, God is not "a changeable being; but he is unchangeable from all eternity to all eternity" (Moro. 8:18). Similarly, an early revelation by Joseph Smith refers to him as "the same God yesterday, today, and forever" (D&C 20:12), noting that "from everlasting to everlasting [he is] the same unchangeable God" (v. 17). The *Lectures on Faith* also state that God "is the same from everlasting to everlasting, being the same yesterday, today, and for ever."⁴ These expressions are similar to Protestant declarations that God is "unchangeable [and] the same from everlasting to everlasting."⁵ In sum, early LDS scripture and teachings consistently present God as having continued uninterruptedly as God from all eternity.

Later Mormonism

During the Nauvoo period, this absolutist view began giving way to a finitist view in which God was seen as existing in time and having progressed to his status as God. In his famous King Follett discourse (June 1844), Joseph repudiated the traditional belief in God's eternality stating, "We suppos[e] that God was God from eternity. I will refute that idea."⁶ The Prophet then declared, "God himself the father of us all dwelt on an earth [the] same as J[esu]s himself did & I will show it from the Bible."⁷ He continued: "The Scriptures inform us that Jesus said, As the Father hath power in Himself, even so hath the Son power—to do what? Why, what the Father did. The answer is obvious—in a manner to lay down His body and take it up again. Jesus, what are you going to do? To lay down my life as my Father did, and take it up again."⁸

This scriptural inference deserves closer examination. The Prophet is combining two passages, John 5:26 and John 10:17–18,⁹ and taking considerable liberty with the text. These verses, as they stand, provide little support for a belief that the Father laid down his life and took it up again. John 5:26 merely states, "For as the Father hath life in himself; so hath he given to the Son to have life in himself." Regarding Jesus's power to lay down his life and take it again, John 10:17 has Jesus saying, "I have power to lay it down, and I have power to take it again. This commandment have I received of my Father." These passages seem to merely indicate that God imbued Jesus with power over death and commanded him to use this power. Nothing in the passage suggests that God himself used these powers on his own behalf in some past eon of time.

The second passage that Joseph cited as proof, by inference, that God was once mortal is John 5:19: "The Son can do nothing of himself, but what he seeth the Father do: for what things soever he doeth, these also doeth the Son likewise." Giving his own version of this passage, the Prophet stated, "What did Jesus do[?] Why I do the things that I saw the father do when worlds came into existence. I saw the father work out a kingdom with fear and trembling and I can do the same."[10] Though John 5:19 does not state clearly the sense in which Jesus "seeth" the works of the Father, the present tense of the verbs (he *does* what he *sees* the Father *do*) suggests that the Son's actions were simultaneous with the Father's. That is, Jesus's only desire was to carry out the will of his Father, thus making him the Father's instrument. Jesus's remark, "The Father that dwelleth in me, he doeth the works" (John 14:9), captures the essence of this idea. Thus, this passage seems only to imply that Jesus and his Father were one in their work, not that Jesus walked in the footsteps that his Father had previously walked.

With respect to God's eternality, several explanations have been given to reconcile earlier biblical and LDS teachings that God has always been God with the later Nauvoo doctrine that there was a time when God was not God. When Mormons today read passages proclaiming that God is "from everlasting to everlasting" (Moro. 7:22), one interpretation given is that God had an eternal existence as an intelligence and eventually became a human being and then a God. But this doesn't really address the several scriptures cited above that clearly suggest that God was *God* from all eternity. Some LDS doctrinal expositors have expressed the view that God has been eternally God only in a relative sense or from our finite point of view.[11] Others explain that, in the Bible, eternity means "an age" which has a beginning and an end, so he is God from an age past to an age to come.[12] Eternity has also been interpreted to mean "that existence gained by exalted beings,"[13] rather than duration of existence. Thus, "from eternity to eternity" is an expression that can be applied to any being who "has joined the ranks of eternal [i.e., exalted] beings."[14] Another explanation redefines God to mean the entire endless genealogy of Gods. B.H. Roberts, for example, suggested that one should think of God as "the harmonized community of Divine Intelligences of the Universe."[15] Thus, it is this endless collection of Gods that has always existed. Orson Pratt defined God abstractly as a "fulness of truth," and wherever this truth exists, there is God.[16] According to this definition, it is the principle of divine truth and light that has always existed, not any particular embodiment of this truth. One wonders if any of these explanations was necessary for the original audience of the scriptures who seemed to be comfortable taking the eternality of God at face value.

One of the earliest LDS finitist conceptions regarding God relates to his dependency on faith and is based on a peculiar reading of Hebrews 11:3 which states, "Through faith we understand that the worlds were framed by the word of God." This verse was turned around in the *Lectures on Faith* to read, "We understand that through faith the worlds were framed." So essentially "all things in heaven, on earth, or under the earth, exist by reason of faith as it existed in HIM."[17] As Joseph himself declared, "By faith the worlds were made."[18] Scholars, however, take Hebrews 11:3 to be saying that it is through faith that *we understand* God's creative acts. For example, the *Phillips Modern English Bible* translates this passage: "It is only by faith that our minds accept as fact that the whole universe was formed by God's command." The idea that seems to be expressed throughout Hebrews 11 is that human beings must rely on faith because they are unable to see the things of God (v. 1). It isn't *God*, therefore, that has the faith spoken of in Hebrews, but rather humans, who can understand the mysterious acts of God only through faith. This doesn't mean that God doesn't operate by faith, only that faith doesn't appear to be attributed to him anywhere in the Bible.

The *Lectures on Faith* described God as absolute in terms of having "a knowledge of all things . . . from the beginning to the end."[19] Brigham Young, however, later taught that God does not know all things[20] but is still progressing in knowledge.[21] He publicly reprimanded Apostle Orson Pratt for teaching that God had achieved a fullness of knowledge and power. President Young declared, "It is not true."[22] The doctrine that God continues to progress in both knowledge and power was widely taught by Church leaders beginning with Brigham Young and continuing until at least the turn of the twentieth century.[23]

In more recent times, the doctrine that God progresses in knowledge has been repudiated by Church leaders. As president of the Church, Joseph Fielding Smith remarked in 1971, "I am grateful that we know that he [God] is an infinite and eternal being who knows all things and has all power and whose progression consists not in gaining more knowledge or power, not in furthering his godly attributes, but in the increase and multiplying of his kingdoms."[24] Bruce R. McConkie subsequently labeled the doctrine a "deadly heresy," saying, "There are those who say that God is progressing in knowledge. . . . This is false—utterly, totally, and completely. There is not one sliver of truth in it."[25]

So even though a God of finite knowledge and power was commonly taught in Mormonism through much of the second half of the nineteenth century, by the start of the twentieth century the Mormon doctrine of Deity began to return to one that was more absolutist.[26] At present, both absolutist and finitist views coexist in Mormonism. In 1965, Sterling McMurrin pointed out that, while it is common to "sermonize with a language" of absolutism, the traditional Mormon view is that God is "a temporal being with a past, present, and future, a being genuinely involved in the processes of the world."[27]

The coexistence of these two opposing traditions about God has led to conflicting views and confusing dialogue when discussing the nature of God. Whether one's particular theological leaning is finitist or absolutist seems to determine the interpretive sources one chooses to emphasize. At times the perspective chosen seems to be dependent on the purposes of the discussion. To appear more conforming to mainstream Christianity, Latter-day Saints have often minimized finitist statements about God by presenting the absolutist view as if it is the only view.[28] At the other extreme are those who draw upon finitist statements about God because they explain difficult philosophical issues, such as human suffering[29]—God somehow appears less culpable for human suffering if he is not absolutely all-powerful. He can also be excused from responsibility for our actions since he is not the ultimate source of our being. While some point to Joseph's pronouncement that "the past, the present, and the future were and are with him [God] one eternal Now"[30] as evidence that God has absolute foreknowledge,[31] others see philosophical problems with an omniscient God and find intimations in Joseph's teachings that suggest God is limited in his knowledge of the future.[32]

The Corporeal Nature of God

Divine corporeal embodiment, or the teaching that God possesses a body of flesh and bones, is rather unique today to LDS theology. According to the LDS Church lesson manual *Gospel Principles*, "Our bodies are like His body. His eternal spirit is housed in a tangible body of flesh and bones (see D&C 130:22)."[33] This is in contrast to the traditional Christian belief that God is a spirit.

Old Testament

The Old Testament speaks of God in human terms as having bodily features and human passions. Such anthropomorphisms paralleled those of other Near Eastern religions. The Old Testament is not always consistent, however, in portraying God anthropomorphically. Passages depicting God as having human form need to be weighed against less anthropomorphic descriptions such as God's question to Jeremiah, "Do not I fill heaven and earth?" (Jer. 23:24).

For the most part, critical Bible scholars see the God of the early Old Testament as a person in human form, noting that it is only later, when Judaism collided with the Hellenistic world, that certain Jews, such as Philo, became consciously uncomfortable with the idea of God possessing a physical body.[34] Many critical scholars attribute Old Testament depictions of God possessing a human form to the fact that ancient Israel had reworked and adapted the anthropomorphic ideas of their neighbors.[35] Some see the God (or gods) of early Israel as not only corporeal, but of super-human size. Indeed, God was perceived by ancients as a warrior God who, after the flood, set his giant bow in the sky (Gen. 9:31). According to 1 Kings 6:23–28, the throne built for God in Solomon's temple was approximately 15 by 15 feet.[36]

It has long been debated whether Genesis 1:26, which speaks of man being created in the "image of God," was intended to be taken literally or figuratively. A sizable number of scholars concede that ancient Israelites would have likely taken the word "image" quite literally to include all aspects of God's being. According to Old Testament scholar Von Rad, the words "image" and "likeness" in Genesis 1:26 "refer to the whole of man and do not relate solely to his spiritual and intellectual being: they relate equally, if not first and foremost, to the splendor of his bodily form."[37]

Latter-day Saints share the scholarly view that the God of the Old Testament was corporeal, pointing to the many Old Testament passages in which God manifests himself in human form (a quick glance at the LDS Topical Guide under "God, Body of—Corporeal Nature" illustrates this view). Often overlooked, however, is the fact that Saints have been instructed to read these same passages as descriptions of the premortal, unembodied Christ and not of God the Father. According to Joseph Fielding Smith, "All revelation since the fall has come through Jesus Christ, who is the Jehovah of the Old Testament. . . . The Father has never dealt with man directly and personally since the fall, and he has never appeared except to introduce and bear record of the Son."[38] Consequently, the account of Moses speaking to God "face to face, as a man speaketh unto his friend" (Ex. 33:11) is generally understood in Mormonism as a conversation with Christ's premortal spirit, not with God the Father. Thus, strictly speaking, Old Testament anthropomorphisms cannot be taken by Latter-day Saints as evidence in themselves that God has a body of flesh and bones. Given the LDS understanding of Christ as God of the Old Testament, BYU religion professor Stephen Robinson acknowledges that the doctrine of the corporeality of the Father is not explicitly taught in the Bible.[39]

New Testament

The underlying mindset of New Testament writers most likely reflected their Jewish heritage resulting in an anthropomorphic concept of God. This didn't necessarily mean, however, that they viewed

God's body as consisting of flesh and bones. In his survey of rabbinic literature covering the first few centuries of the Christian era, Alon Gottstein observes that "there is not a single statement that denies that God has body or form," and that the only question remaining unanswered was "What kind of body does God have?"[40] According to first-century Jewish historian Josephus, Jewish teachings "represented God as unbegotten, and immutable, through all eternity, superior to all mortal conceptions in pulchritude: and, though known to us by his power, yet unknown to us as to his essence."[41]

Latter-day Saints and traditional Christians disagree in their interpretation of New Testament passages bearing on the corporeality of God. Many New Testament scholars maintain that New Testament teachings are simply inconclusive on the matter.

A New Testament passage many Christians interpret as teaching that God is incorporeal is John 4:24 in which a Samaritan woman asks Jesus about the appropriate place to worship God. Jesus tells her that, since "God is a Spirit,"[42] it doesn't really matter where one worships as long as it is "in spirit and truth." Though this passage is generally taken by Christians to indicate that God is *only* a spirit, Latter-day Saints argue that God's being a spirit doesn't necessarily preclude him from also having a body. So the passage doesn't prove conclusively that God is *only* a spirit.

Hebrews 1:3 describes Christ as "the express image of his [God's] person." Latter-day Saints often cite this passage as proof that God has a physical body, reasoning that, if Christ is in the image of God and Christ has a physical body, then God must also have a body. Saints often take it one step further, claiming that Christ is, in Bruce R. McConkie's words, "identical in appearance" to the Father, since he is in the "express" image of God.[43] This LDS understanding goes back as early as March 1842 when Joseph Smith, recounting his vision of the Father and the Son in the spring of 1820, stated that they "exactly resembled each other in features and likeness."[44]

This passage in Hebrews actually does little to bolster the argument for a corporeal God since the Greek word for "image" here is *character*, which is used elsewhere in the New Testament to convey a spiritual or divine likeness (Col. 1:15; Rom. 8:29). The thrust of Hebrews 1–2 is to extol the excellence of Christ by showing how he started out with a nature and status less than the angels, but then surpassed them through his resurrection and exaltation: "We see Jesus, who was made a little lower than the angels . . . [now] crowned with glory and honour" (Heb. 2:9). So it isn't Christ's physical resemblance to God that is being emphasized in Hebrews 1:3, but rather his similitude to God in "glory and honor." The NRSV translation captures this sense, stating that Christ "reflects the glory of God and bears the very stamp of his nature." Other modern translations similarly communicate "image" here as a divine likeness rather than a physical semblance.

Interestingly, in the *Lectures on Faith*, which were prepared in 1835 before Mormon theology developed the concept of a corporeal God, Hebrews 1:3 is interpreted as a divine likeness, rather than a physical likeness. The *Lectures* explain that, in contrast to being a personage of tabernacle like Christ, God the Father "is a personage of spirit, glory and power."[45] Christ is described as being "in the express image and likeness of the Father," but only in the sense that he is "filled with the fullness of the mind of the Father; or, in other words, the Spirit of the Father."[46] In a similar way, the *Lectures* explain that the faithful will become "joint heirs with Jesus Christ; possessing the same mind, being transformed into the same image or likeness, even the express image of him who fills all in all."[47] Christ's disciples, therefore, are to be transformed into the express image of Christ just as he bears the express image of the Father—by possessing the same "Spirit" or "mind" as the Father.

Early Nineteenth-Century Christianity

The trinitarian Christian view in the early nineteenth century was that God is a shapeless spirit. The 1647 Westminster Confession states, "There is but one only living and true God, who is infinite in being and perfection, a most pure spirit, invisible, without body, parts, or passions."[48] As one of the persons in the trinity, God the Father is one manifestation of this pure spiritual essence.

With this perception of God as a formless spirit, many Christians came to see man as having been created in *Christ's* image rather than the image of God the Father. The belief was that the "image of God" in Genesis 1:26 referred to what was called the "human soul" of Christ. According to Charles Buck's 1830 *Theological Dictionary*, "Adam was made in the likeness of the human soul of Christ."[49] The understanding was that Christ's premortal form was human in imitation of the physical body he would have on earth. Using Christ's "human soul" as the pattern for creating human beings allowed for a more literal interpretation of "image" in the absence of a corporeal concept of God. The idea that human beings were created in the image of Christ's human soul traces back to Osiander (1498-1552) who maintained that Adam was created in the likeness of the physical body that Christ would later assume and, therefore, Adam served as a model or type of Christ's future incarnation.[50] As will be shown, a similar idea seems to be intimated in the Book of Mormon as well.

In contrast to traditional trinitarianism, which viewed God as a formless, immaterial spirit, certain primitivist groups (Campbellites, Hicksites, etc.) held that God the Father was a spirit in the form of a man.[51] In 1829, primitivist preacher William Kinkade criticized the trinitarian view of God pointing out that, given all the anthropomorphic descriptions of God in the Old Testament, "if God is shapeless, without body, parts, or passions, with his centre every where, and his circumference no where, all the inspired writers have misrepresented him."[52] Kinkade advocated a literal interpretation of "image" in Genesis 1:26 stating, "Some suppose that being created in the image of God, only means that man was made holy; but I think we should not restrict the word to the quality, it certainly extends to the personal appearance of the man; because in scripture the words *image* and *likeness*, are most generally used to represent the bodily appearance."[53] This assertion that Adam was created in the image of God's "bodily appearance" wasn't meant to suggest that God had a body of flesh and bones, but only that he was a spirit with human form.

Early Mormonism

References to God in the Book of Mormon employ trinitarian language and seem to have in mind the same being who would later become incarnate as Jesus Christ. According to LDS historian Thomas Alexander, "The Book of Mormon tended to define God as an absolute personage of spirit who, clothed in flesh, revealed himself in Jesus."[54] The wayward Zoramites worshipped saying, "Holy, holy God; we believe that thou art God, and we believe that thou art holy, and that thou wast a spirit, and that thou art a spirit, and that thou wilt be a spirit forever" (Alma 31:15; see also Alma 18:4–5, 26–29; 22:8–11). Their belief was that God would never take upon himself flesh and blood as the Nephite Christians believed (Mosiah 7:27). Note that the falsehood Alma attacks in these teachings is not that God is a spirit, but that he will always be a spirit—in other words, that he will never be incarnated as Christ (see Alma 31:15–17, 28–30). Of course modern Latter-day Saints would argue that since Christ was the God of the Book of Mormon, he was, at that time, still a spirit. But this reading imposes a later theology on the Book of Mormon than what is evident in the book itself—namely, that Christ was both the Father and the Son and, therefore, the coming of Christ was the coming of the Father himself (see Chapter 8).

The Book of Mormon seems to espouse the Protestant notion that man was formed physically in the image of the human-shaped spirit of Christ. It prophesies that Christ would "take upon him the image of man, and it should be the image after which man was created in the beginning" (Mosiah 7:27). After the brother of Jared learned that everyone was created "after Christ's own image" (Ether 3:15), the Savior appeared to him and explained somewhat enigmatically, "This body, which ye now behold, is the body of my spirit; and man have I created after the body of my spirit; and even as I appear unto thee to be in the spirit will I appear unto my people in the flesh" (v. 16). Therefore the Book of Mormon doesn't depict man as being created in the image of God the Father's physical body (which is how Latter-day Saints today generally understand "image"), but rather in the image of Christ's spiritual body which was in the form Christ would assume in mortality.

There are indications that, during the early years of the Church, the Saints understood humans as having also been created in the image of God the Father's spiritual body. Moses 6:9, revealed sometime prior to March 1831, states that man was created "in the image of his [God's] own body." While one might be tempted to interpret God's "body" here as his physical body, as noted above, it was common among primitivists to view humans as being created in the image of God's spiritual body. Notably, the book of Moses also speaks of man being created in the image of Christ (Moses 2:27), who was considered to be a spirit prior to his incarnation.

It would have been almost inconceivable to the earliest Mormon converts that God would have flesh and bones, a characteristic universally associated with mortality and denigrated for its corruption and imperfection. Indeed, as late as 1840, Mormon elder Samuel Bennett argued that "God is a Spirit" with "body and parts . . . however small the tenuity may be."[55] In an 1840 reply to a Pennsylvania man who accused Mormonism of corporealizing God, Elder Erastus Snow corrected the antagonist stating, "What Mormon, understanding our doctrines, ever said that God the Father had flesh and bones?" Quoting from the *Lectures on Faith* where God the Father is described as "a personage of spirit, glory and power," Snow challenged, "Does it necessarily follow that because God is a spirit, possessing universal knowledge, *that* spirit has no form, shape, or bodily appearance as you would have it?"[56] In the same year (1840) Apostle Parley P. Pratt commented, "Whoever reads our books, or hears us preach, knows that we believe in the Father, Son, and Holy Ghost as one God. That the Son has flesh and bones, and the Father is a spirit. . . . [A] personage of Spirit has its organized formation, its body and parts, its individual identity, its eyes, mouth, ears, &c., and that it is in the image or likeness of the temporal body, although not composed of such gross materials as flesh and bones."[57] The idea of a human body being created after the image of God the Father's *physical* body doesn't explicitly appear in LDS teachings until 1841 when Joseph began teaching that God the Father has a physical body.

Many Latter-day Saints today assume that Joseph's First Vision provided ample evidence to early Saints that God is a personage of flesh and bones;[58] the Prophet's 1832 account, however, related only that he "saw the Lord." It wasn't until 1838 that he provided more detail to include the Father and the Son, and even then, there is no indication that Joseph thought of them both as having bodies of flesh and bones.

Nauvoo Period

"By 1841," observes LDS historian Richard L. Bushman, Joseph "had moved from a traditional Christian belief in God as pure spirit to a belief in his corporeality."[59] It appears that the Prophet first ascribed corporeality to God in 1841 when he declared, "That which is without body or parts is nothing. There is no other God in heaven but that God who has flesh and bones."[60] On April 2, 1843 he reaffirmed, "The Father has a body of flesh and bones as tangible as man's" (D&C 130:22). This bold new doctrine would fit in nicely with Joseph's subsequent teachings on God's progression through mortality and resurrection as well as the human potential to become like God after a physical resurrection.

Has Any Mortal Seen God?

Related to the concept of a corporeal God is the issue of whether human beings have seen, or are even capable of seeing, God. Biblical teachings equivocate about whether any human has ever seen God. Several passages directly state that mortals have not and cannot see God—or at least, see him and live (Ex. 33:20; John 1:18; 1 Tim. 1:17, 6:15–16; 1 Jn. 4:12). These passages stand in contrast to other passages, especially in the Old Testament, which declare that prophets saw God with human eyes "face to face" (Ex. 24:9–10; see also Gen. 18:1, 32:30; Ex. 33:11; Isa. 6:1).

Many scholars explain that conflicting biblical teachings regarding whether one can see God are due to differences in perspective among Old Testament writers.[61] The Priestly writer, designated as "P,"

> had an exalted and sophisticated view of Yahweh. He did not believe, for example, that anybody could actually *see* God in the way that J [a writer living in the southern kingdom of Judah] had suggested. . . . In P's story of Moses on Sinai, Moses begs for a vision of Yahweh, who replies: "You cannot see my face, for no man can see me and live." Instead, Moses must shield himself from the divine impact in a crevice of the rock, where he would catch a glimpse of Yahweh as he departed, in a kind of hindsight. P had introduced an idea that would become extremely important

in the history of God. Men and women can see only an afterglow of the divine presence, which he calls "the glory (*kavod*) of Yahweh," a manifestation of his presence, which is not to be confused with God himself.[62]

Certain New Testament writers appear to have been partial to the view that no one has seen nor can see God. John 1:18 reads, "No man hath seen God at any time; the only begotten Son, which is in the bosom of the Father, he hath declared him" (or, as modern translations read, "he has made him known"). In other words, though no one has seen God before, now that Christ has come as a manifestation of God, speaking his words and doing his works, one can effectively see God by seeing Christ. As Jesus informed Phillip, "he that hath seen me hath seen the Father" (John 14:9; see also John 12:45).

At the time of Joseph Smith, the idea of seeing God with one's spiritual eyes or through the eyes of faith was not only deemed possible, but encouraged of Christians. Nearly half a century prior to the Prophet's birth, John Wesley qualified John 1:18 stating, "No man hath seen God—With bodily eyes: yet believers see him with the eye of faith."[63] Many pre-1820 clerical teachings claimed that genuine visions of deity were possible, but only through the "spiritual" and not the "natural" eye.[64]

As Joseph Smith made revisions to the Bible, he similarly made allowance for the righteous to be able to see God through spiritual eyes. Where Exodus 33:20 states, "for there shall no man see me, and live," the JST reads, "*no sinful man . . .* shall see my face and live" (JST Ex. 33:20; emphasis mine). Joseph modified New Testament assertions that no one has seen God by appending various exceptions to them: "except he hath borne record of the Son" (JST John 1:19), "except them who believe" (JST 1 Jn. 4:12), and "only he who hath the light and the hope of immortality dwelling in him" (JST 1 Tim. 6:15–16). Concurrent with these textual changes, Joseph brought to light a theophany received by Moses which has him exclaiming, "But now mine own eyes have beheld God; but not my natural, but my spiritual eyes, for my natural eyes could not have beheld; for I should have withered and died in his presence; but his glory was upon me; and I beheld his face, for I was transfigured before him" (Moses 1:11). Thus, seeing God requires not only personal purity but also spiritual, rather than physical, eyesight.

In September 1832, the Prophet extended the requirements for seeing God to include the Melchizedek Priesthood and its ordinances stating, "Without the ordinances thereof, and the authority of the priesthood . . . no man can see the face of God, even the Father, and live" (D&C 84:21–22). Notably, this stipulation doesn't appear in his modifications to the Bible. Of course this new requirement raises the question of how Joseph saw the Father and the Son in 1820, nearly a decade before he received the priesthood or any of its ordinances.[65]

God as Elohim

Latter-day Saints consider Elohim to be a name title specifically reserved for God the Father.[66] The word *Elohim* is the Hebrew plural of the Canaanite *El* or the Hebrew *Eloah*; consequently, its literal meaning is "Gods." In the Hebrew Old Testament it isn't used as a name, but rather as a common noun for "God" or "the Gods." The KJV translates it as God. Many Mormons do not see the use of Elohim in the Old Testament as necessarily referrring to God the Father, because it is also a tenet of LDS theology that it is the premortal Christ who is the God of the Old Testament (see Chap. 8).

Use of *Elohim* as a transliteration from the Hebrew doesn't occur anywhere in the KJV, neither is it found in any LDS literature until the latter part of the Nauvoo period. After learning this term through his study of Hebrew, the Prophet first used it in a public discourse delivered in July 1843: "We believe in the Great Eloheim who sits enthroned in yonder heavens," he declared. "So do the Presbyterians."[67] Even here it wasn't used as God's personal name, but rather as a synonym for God.

It wasn't until a considerable length of time after the Prophet's death that Latter-day Saints came to consider "Elohim" as a special name reserved only for God the Father. As noted, the Prophet first used the term as simply a synonym for God, not as God's name. In his last public discourse he taught that the Hebrew *Elohim* means "the Gods," stating, "[Elohim] ought to be in the plural all the way thro[ugh the Bible]—Gods."[68] For the next three decades, in conjunction with Brigham Young's Adam-God doctrine, Church leaders used "Elohim" to refer to the head god who was also ambiguously identified as God, God's father, and even God's grandfather.[69] It wasn't until 1916 that a doctrinal exposition by the First Presidency and Twelve under President Joseph F. Smith officially declared that "God the Eternal Father" is the being "whom we designate by the exalted name-title 'Elohim.'"[70]

God as the Father of Our Spirits

The doctrine that God, through a procreative act involving a heavenly mother, is the literal father of our spirits expresses the most fundamental and important relationship between God and humankind in LDS theology.[71] Surprisingly, however, nowhere is this doctrine explicitly taught in any of the standard works, neither is it found in any of Joseph Smith's recorded teachings. Indeed, his later teachings stressed the idea that spirits are eternal, with no birth stage mentioned, and that God merely provided a plan for these uncreated and unrelated spirits to come to earth to receive physical bodies (see Chapter 11). The few references Joseph makes to God's fatherhood appear to have been figurative, mirroring contemporary Christian usage. The 1828 *Webster's Dictionary* reflects the common view of God's fatherhood, giving as one definition of *father:* "He who creates." It further states, "God as creator is the father of all men."[72]

Old Testament

The earliest Old Testament Hebrew refers to God as *Elohim* or *Yahweh* with no mention of any role as "father" of humankind or of the human spirit. The first mention of God as a father occurs in 2 Samuel 7:14 where it describes a covenant relationship between God and the king: "I will be his father, and he shall be my son." While God is thereafter occasionally depicted as a father, this title is used figuratively to denote God's covenant relationship with his anointed kings or with Israel as his chosen people (Jer. 31:9). There is no evidence of any understanding in the Old Testament that God is the literal father of our spirits.

New Testament

The New Testament redefines the requirements for entering into this covenant father-son relationship by commanding all persons everywhere to repent and follow Christ, "that ye may be the children of your Father which is in heaven" (Matt. 5:45). Thus, individuals could *become* the children of God through discipleship. When speaking to his disciples, Jesus referred to God as "My Father, and your Father (John 20:17)," which describes a relationship they attained in this life, not in the preexistence. Jesus distinguished between the faithful who were children of God and the disobedient whose father was Satan. "If God were your Father, ye would love me," he told the disbelieving Jews, but "ye are of your father the devil" (John 8:42, 44).

The two New Testament verses footnoted in the LDS hymnbook for "O My Father," a hymn that highlights the LDS doctrine of spirit birth, are Acts 17:28 and Romans 8:16. In Acts 17:28, Paul denounces the idol worship of the Athenians and notes that even certain of their own poets (Aratus) acknowledged, "We are his [Zeus's] offspring."[73] Paul reasons that, since God created us as intelligent beings and continues to sustain our existence, "we ought not to think that the Godhead is like unto gold, or silver, or stone, graven by art and man's device" (v. 29).

The two questions to be answered for this passage are (1) whether Paul was referring to creation in a premortal context, and (2) whether "offspring" meant *direct* offspring. That Paul was most likely referring to earthly creation is evidenced from the preceding verses where he had been explaining how God "giveth to all life, and breath" (v. 25) and "hath made of one blood all nations of men" (v. 26). It is in this context of granting physical life that he appeals to Aratus's teaching that we are God's offspring. As to whether God *directly* sired the nations of the earth, some of the many Greek myths have the gods giving birth to the first race of humans while in other myths the gods form the first humans.[74] In none of these myths, however, were *spirits* mentioned as being begotten of God, nor was everyone *directly* begotten of God in the flesh. It appears that Paul was merely drawing on a source familiar to his Greek audience—to the Greeks, Paul became a Greek (1 Cor. 9:19)—to demonstrate that we are the workmanship of God's hands and not vice versa. Notably, in 1842 Joseph Smith, like Paul, stated that God views the human family "as his offspring," but only in the sense that God is "the great parent of the universe [i.e., of all creation]."[75]

The second New Testament passage used to support the idea that God is the literal father of our spirits is Romans 8:16: "The Spirit itself beareth witness with our spirit, that we are the children of God." Read in context, it becomes apparent that Paul is referring to the principle of "adoption" (v. 15) by which believers are adopted into God's spiritual family, thus becoming his children. It is what Christians (including Latter-day Saints) refer to as spiritual rebirth. Commenting on this and other New Testament passages referring to God as our father, even Bruce R. McConkie acknowledges, "[They] have no reference to our birth in preexistence as the children of Elohim."[76] Paul frequently referred to the special father-son relationship with God that believers achieve by putting on Christ through baptism, but never in the context of a premortal spirit birth.

Another New Testament passage often cited as support for God's literal fatherhood of the spirits of humankind is Hebrews 12:9, which refers to God as "the Father of spirits." It should be noted that this passage doesn't say that God is the Father of "our" spirits, which may be significant given that the same verse refers to the fathers of "our" flesh. Scholars suggest that the word "spirits" is most likely used here in the common Jewish sense of "the angels," the same sense in which it is used in Hebrews 1:14.[77] It is also the scholarly consensus that only a figurative fatherhood is implied, with God being the creator and sustainer of these spirits. In a similar way, God is referred to as the "Father of lights" (James 1:17; cf. Gen. 1:14), the "Father of mercies" (2 Cor. 1:3) and the "Father of glory" (Eph. 1:17). Presumptively, none of these ascriptions of fatherhood denotes a literal begetting.

Early Mormonism

In the Book of Mormon, references to God's fatherhood pertain either to his role as the spiritual head of his disciples, just as in the New Testament, or to his role as creator of heaven and earth. The Book of Mormon calls God "the very Eternal Father of heaven and earth" (Mosiah 15:4), but nowhere is there mention of God being the father of our spirits.

In the book of Moses, which Joseph began preparing in June 1830, God calls Moses his "son" (Moses 1:13, 16), which is commonly understood by Latter-day Saints to mean that Moses is literally begotten of God in the spirit.[78] There is no indication in Moses, however, that such a relationship is implied by the term "son of God." What is expressed about this term is that individuals "*become* the sons of God" through discipleship (Moses 7:1; emphasis mine). In Moses 8:13, Noah and his sons hearkened to the Lord and were therefore "called the sons of God." In contrast, Moses 5:54–55 labels the wicked as the "sons of men." Eventually, an unholy union would take place between the daughters of the "sons of God" and the "sons of men" (Moses 8:14). The only definition of "son of God" given in Moses as it applies to humans, therefore, is essentially the same definition found in traditional Christianity, which derives from New Testament usage where all who receive Christ *become* "sons of God" (John 1:12).[79]

The Doctrine and Covenants similarly makes no reference to God being the literal father of our spirits. Doctrine and Covenants 76:24, which speaks of individuals being "begotten sons and daughters unto God," is often used as a proof-text for premortal spirit birth,[80] but read in its entirety, the verse rather implies that it is "by," "through," and "of" *Christ* that individuals are begotten "unto" God. The preposition "unto" makes God the recipient of those who are begotten, not the source.[81] In other words, the faithful are spiritually begotten "unto" God "through" the atonement of Christ. This also happens to be the interpretation given by Joseph Smith,[82] by an official First Presidency declaration under Joseph F. Smith,[83] and by the section heading of the current edition of the Doctrine and Covenants.[84]

Later Mormonism

The first clear allusion to the doctrine of spirit birth in LDS literature appeared in Orson Pratt's *Prophetic Almanac*, which was in press in June 1844 and went on sale August 3, 1844. Pratt explained that human mortal existence was preceded by a spiritual state. In answer to the question of how humans began that state, Pratt wrote, "He was begotten and born of God."[85] The next public mention of spirit birth was at the dedication of the Nauvoo Seventies Hall in December 1844 where Brigham Young, John Taylor and W. W. Phelps all alluded to it.[86] Phelps specifically referred to "our Father in heaven, and Mother, the Queen."[87] The following year the doctrine of premortal spirit birth appeared frequently in church publications, finding its most memorable expression in Eliza R. Snow's poem, "O My Father" published in October 1845.[88] The doctrine of spirit birth remains central to LDS theology and is reaffirmed in the 1995 proclamation on the family which states that each human being is literally a "spirit son or daughter of heavenly parents."[89]

The Adam-God Doctrine

The Adam-God doctrine, which according to available evidence was introduced in Mormonism by President Brigham Young, is the belief that Adam is literally God the Father—the father of our spirits and of Jesus Christ in the flesh. Despite President Young's affirmation that this was a doctrine "which God revealed to me,"[90] it is no longer countenanced by the Church and, in fact, has been labeled by Bruce R. McConkie as a "deadly heresy" inspired of the devil.[91]

Brigham Young first preached this Adam-God doctrine in an April 1852 sermon in which he stated, "[Adam] is our FATHER and our GOD, and the only God with whom WE have to do. . . . When the Virgin Mary conceived the child Jesus, the Father had begotten him in his own likeness. He was not begotten by the Holy Ghost. And who is the Father? He is the first of the human family."[92] At the end of his sermon Brigham stated, "Now, let all who may hear these doctrines, pause before they make light of them, or treat them with indifference, for they will prove their salvation or damnation."[93]

Unlike doctrines which appear to have been based on a particular interpretation of scripture, the Adam-God doctrine seems to have been tied to a peculiar interpretation of Joseph Smith's teachings. Brigham Young apparently got the idea of Adam-God from the ever progressive teachings of the Prophet Joseph Smith on the Godhead, the plurality of Gods, and origin of Adam and Eve. Although some have attributed the Adam-God doctrine to Joseph Smith himself, there is no record or evidence of the doctrine being taught prior to its introduction by Brigham Young in 1852. From the reaction of leading brethren present at President Young's sermon, it also appears to have been their first exposure to the doctrine. LDS scholar David Buerger notes, "The complete absence of any hint that Adam-God was taught before 1852 is further substantiated by a literature search of over 1,000 doctrinal books, epistles, broadsides, hymnals, 'anti-Mormon' texts, speeches, etc. published between 1826 and 1852, which failed to turn up any evidence."[94]

Joseph consistently differentiated between God the Father and Adam, treating them as separate individuals. To be sure, many of Young's associates resisted this doctrine, arguing that it conflicted with earlier revelations. Later LDS commentators would minimize the significance of Brigham Young's Adam-God teachings, explaining that he was either misunderstood or was merely theorizing. However one chooses to interpret the historical record, President Young discontinued teaching the doctrine publicly after 1861 and, following his death, the doctrine gradually fell into disfavor and is now regarded as heretical.[95]

Notes

1. George Wesley Buchanan, *To the Hebrews: Translation, Comment and Conclusions*, 115.
2. Boyd Kirkland, "The Development of the Mormon Doctrine of God," 35.
3. John Clarke, ed., *The Works of Samuel Clarke, D. D., Late Rector of St. James's Westminster*, 2:175, 540. See also William Law, *A Practical Treatise on Christian Perfection*, 274.
4. *Lectures on Faith*, 3:15.
5. Richard Wright, *The Anti-Satisfactionist: or, the Salvation of Sinners by the Free Grace of God*, 72.
6. Andrew F. Ehat and Lyndon W. Cook, *The Words of Joseph Smith: The Contemporary Accounts of the Nauvoo Discourses of the Prophet Joseph Smith*, 344.
7. Ibid., 350.
8. Ibid., 346.
9. Ibid., 285 note 18. Ehat and Cook note that the Prophet reportedly sometimes substituted "power" for "life" when paraphrasing John 5:26 as he did here.
10. Ibid., 358. From the Prophet's interpretation that Christ did only what he saw his father do, one could infer that the Father was also a savior of worlds and that he was born into a world as his own father's only begotten son, just as Jesus was so born. Blake T. Ostler, *Exploring Mormon Thought: The Attributes of God*, 79.
11. Robert L. Millet, *The Mormon Faith: A New Look at Christianity*, 169, explains, "Because he has held his exalted status for a longer period than any of us can conceive, he is able to speak in terms of eternity and can state that he is from everlasting to everlasting."
12. Craig L. Blomberg and Stephen E. Robinson, *How Wide the Divide? A Mormon and an Evangelical in Conversation*, 57.
13. Bruce R. McConkie, *The Promised Messiah: The First Coming of Christ*, 166.
14. Ibid.
15. B. H. Roberts, *A Comprehensive History of the Church of Jesus Christ*

of Latter-day Saints, 2:401. For a more recent argument for this position, see Ostler, *Exploring Mormon Thought: The Attributes of God*, 79–81, 467.

16. Orson Pratt, February 18, 1855, *Journal of Discourses*, 2:342–43; see also his article, "The Pre-Existence of Man," *The Seer* 1, no. 9 (September 1853): 132–33.

17. *Lectures on Faith*, 1:15; capitalization in original.

18. *History of the Church*, 5:218.

19. *Lectures on Faith*, 4:11.

20. Brigham Young, June 13, 1852, *Journal of Discourses*, 1:93.

21. All these Brigham Young addresses on this point are in the *Journal of Discourses*: July 10, 1853, 1:349; February 7, 1856, 3:202; March 4, 1860, 8:10; April 20, 1863, 10:221; January 13, 1867, 11:286.

22. Brigham Young, "Hearken, O Ye Latter-day Saints," 2:234–35.

23. The following General Authorities all taught, like Brigham Young, that God progresses in knowledge: Wilford Woodruff, December 6, 1857, *Journal of Discourses*, 6:120; Lorenzo Snow, *Conference Report*, April 1901, 2; George Q. Cannon in Jerreld L. Newquist, comp. and ed., *Gospel Truth: Discourses and Writings of President George Q. Cannon*, 1:118; and B. H. Roberts, *Mormon Doctrine of Deity*, 69–70.

24. Joseph Fielding Smith, "The Most Important Knowledge," 3.

25. Bruce R. McConkie, "The Seven Deadly Heresies," 75.

26. Thomas G. Alexander, "The Reconstruction of Mormon Doctrine: From Joseph Smith to Progressive Theology," 24–33.

27. Sterling M. McMurrin, *The Theological Foundations of the Mormon Religion*, 13.

28. Blomberg and Robinson, *How Wide the Divide?*, 77–78.

29. David L. Paulsen, "Joseph Smith and the Problem of Evil."

30. *History of the Church*, 4:597. This was a common way of expressing God's absolute omniscience and foreknowledge in Joseph Smith's day. Methodist theologian Adam Clarke (1760–1832) wrote, "God who dwells in every point of eternity; with whom all that is past, and all that is present, and all that is future to man, exists in one infinite, indivisible, and eternal NOW." Clarke, *Commentary on the Bible*, s.v. Acts 2.

31. Neal A. Maxwell, *All These Things Shall Give Thee Experience*, 7–8.

32. Ostler, *Exploring Mormon Thought: The Attributes of God*, 150–52. LDS philosophers have taken a keen interest in the thriving area of process theology which emphasizes the finiteness of God and his continuing progression in knowledge and power, and open theology which emphasizes a limit to God's foreknowledge to allow libertarian free-will.

33. *Gospel Principles* (2009), 6.

34. Alon Gottstein, "The Body as Image of God in Rabbic Literature," 176.

35. Paul R. House, *Old Testament Theology*, 61.

36. For a discussion of Yahweh's superhuman size, see Mark S. Smith, *The Origins of Biblical Monotheism: Israel's Polytheistic Background and the Ugaritic Texts*, 84–86.

37. Gerhard Von Rad, *Old Testament Theology*, 144.

38. Joseph Fielding Smith, *Doctrines of Salvation: Compiled Sermons of Joseph Fielding Smith*, 1:26–27. The next chapter discusses how early Latter-

day Saints understood the Jehovah of the Old Testament to be God the Father and hence took passages regarding Jehovah's corporeality more literally.

39. Blomberg and Robinson, *How Wide the Divide?*, 78.

40. Gottstein, "The Body as Image of God," 172.

41. Josephus, *The Works of Flavius Josephus in Four Volumes*, 4:219.

42. Because Greek has no indefinite articles (e.g., "a"), translators must decide when such an article is appropriate. The literal reading of John 4:24 is "God is Spirit." This verse is substantively changed in the JST to read "God has promised his Spirit" (JST John 4:26).

43. Bruce R. McConkie, *Doctrinal New Testament Commentary*, 3:138.

44. *History of the Church*, 4:536.

45. *Lectures on Faith*, 5:2. This now outmoded doctrine of God as a spirit was one of the major reasons why the *Lectures on Faith* were decanonized and removed from the Doctrine and Covenants. Richard S. Van Wagoner, Steve C. Walker, and Allen D. Roberts, "The 'Lectures on Faith': A Case Study in Decanonization," 71–77.

46. *Lectures on Faith*, 5:2. Reconciling this statement with later LDS theology, Bruce R. McConkie, *Doctrinal New Testament Commentary*, 2:160, argues that the statement, the Father is "a personage of spirit," means that "he has a spiritual body which by revealed definition is a resurrected body of flesh and bones (1 Cor. 15:44–45; D&C 88:27)." This interpretation misses the essential distinction being made in the text, which is that the Father is a personage of spirit while the Son is a personage of tabernacle.

47. *Lectures on Faith*, 5:2.

48. See "Westminster Confession of Faith."

49. Charles S. Buck, *A Theological Dictionary*, 481.

50. John Calvin refuted Osiander's teaching that Adam was created in the image of Christ's future human body. John Calvin *Institutes of the Christian Religion*, 1.15.3.

51. Several examples are cited in Grant Underwood, "A 'Communities of Discourse' Approach to Early LDS Thought," 29.

52. William Kinkade, *The Bible Doctrine of God, Jesus Christ, the Holy Spirit, Atonement, Faith and Election*, 169.

53. Ibid., 161. For Kinkade, the bodily image of God meant "the shape of his person" (ibid.), not the physicality of his person.

54. Alexander, "The Reconstruction of Mormon Doctrine," 25.

55. Samuel Bennett, *A Few Remarks by Way of Reply to an Anonymous Scribbler . . .* , 4–5.

56. Erastus E. Snow, *E. Snow's reply to the Self-Styled Philanthropist, of Chester County*, 6; emphasis in original.

57. Parley P. Pratt, *An Answer to Mr. William Hewitt's Tract against the Latter-day Saints*, 9.

58. The First Vision is currently used extensively to support the belief that the Father and Son are individual personages of flesh and bones. Joseph Fielding Smith states, for example, "The vision of Joseph Smith made it clear that the Father and the Son are separate personages, having bodies as tangible as the body of man." Smith, *Doctrines of Salvation*, 1:2. In the April 2005 general conference, President Gordon B. Hinckley stated that Joseph learned

from the First Vision that God "was in form like a man, a being of substance." Gordon B. Hinckley, "The Great Things Which God Has Revealed," 81.

59. Richard L. Bushman, *Joseph Smith: Rough Stone Rolling*, 420.

60. Ehat and Cook, *The Words of Joseph Smith*, 60; see also page 64 for a later statement to the same effect.

61. The attribution of the first five books of the Old Testament, the Pentateuch, to multiple authors is called the "documentary hypothesis" and, while accepted by critical scholars, has had mixed acceptance by Latter-day Saints. Kevin L. Barney, "Reflections on the Documentary Hypothesis," 57–99.

62. Karen Armstrong, *A History of God: The 4000-Year Quest of Judaism, Christianity, and Islam*, 62–63.

63. John Wesley, "John Wesley's Notes on the Bible," 1.24.1.

64. Susan Juster, *Doomsayers: Anglo-American Prophecies in the Age of Revolution*, 114–17.

65. Explanations about how Joseph could have seen God before being ordained to the Melchizedek Priesthood or having received its ordinances have been varied. Early Mormon brethren who confronted this issue concluded that Joseph did hold the priesthood having, in some sense, brought it with him from the preexistence. See, for example, Orson Pratt, October 10, 1880, *Journal of Discourses* 22:30; B. H. Roberts, "Seventies Council Table," 558; Orson F. Whitney, *Gospel Themes*, 78. According to Joseph Fielding Smith, since the priesthood wasn't yet on the earth, young Joseph was exempt from this requirement. Smith, *Doctrines of Salvation*, 1:4

66. James E. Talmage, *Articles of Faith*, 466.

67. Ehat and Cook, *The Words of Joseph Smith*, 229.

68. Ibid., 379.

69. Kirkland, "The Development of the Mormon Doctrine of God," 38–44.

70. Quoted in Talmage, *Articles of Faith*, 421.

71. *Gospel Principles* (2009), 10.

72. *Webster's First Edition (1828) of An American Dictionary*, s.v. "father."

73. The phrase "we are his offspring" occurs literally in the poems *Phaenomena* by Aratus (ca. 315–240 B.C) and *Hymn to Zeus* by Cleanthes (ca. 331–233 B.C.). Greg Herrick, "Is the Bible the Only Revelation from God?"

74. H. J. Rose, *A Handbook of Greek Mythology*, 15–28.

75. Joseph Smith Jr., "Baptism for the Dead," 759.

76. McConkie, *The Promised Messiah*, 351–52.

77. This interpretation is supported by the parallel idea found in Numbers 16:22, 27:16, where God is called "the God of spirits and of all flesh" (See also 2 Macc. 3:24).

78. Ronald A. Rasband, "'Moses, My Son,'" 43–44.

79. The fact that Moses challenges Satan's identity by essentially saying, "I am a son of God; who are you?" hardly makes sense if he is talking about being a spirit son of God, for Satan is also a spirit son of God according to Mormon doctrine. For a discussion of how Moses was considered to be a "son of God, in the similitude of his [God's] only Begotten" (Moses 1:13), as well as its seeming linkage to the gospel of John (see Chapter 8).

80. Using Doctrine and Covenants 76:24 as a proof-text for spirit birth to counter the theory of evolution, Joseph Fielding Smith wrote, "It was made

known through the Prophet Joseph Smith and Sidney Rigdon . . . that the inhabitants of this earth and other worlds are begotten sons and daughters unto God. That ought to put an end—so far as Latter-day Saints are concerned—to all this nonsense prevailing in the world regarding the origin of man." Smith, *Doctrines of Salvation*, 1:63.

81. For similar use of the preposition "unto" to express the begetting of children for the benefit of others, see Isaiah 9:6 ("unto us a child is born"), Matthew 22:24 ("his brother shall . . . raise up seed unto his brother"), and Jacob 2:30 ("if I will, saith the Lord of Hosts, raise up seed unto me . . . "). It wasn't until 1852 that Orson Pratt made use of Doctrine and Covenants 76:24 as a proof-text for spirit birth; but even then, he continued to acknowledge the indirect nature of this "birth." "Notice," states Pratt, "this does not say that God, whom we serve and worship, was actually the Father himself, in His own person, of all these sons and daughters of the different worlds, but they are begotten sons and daughters unto God; that is, begotten by those who are made like him. . . . [T]hey begat sons and daughters, and begat them unto God, to inhabit these different worlds." Orson Pratt, August 29, 1852, *Journal of Discourses*, 1:57.

82. Joseph Smith Jr., "The Answer," 85. Despite the traditional attribution to Joseph Smith, it may have been written by W. W. Phelps. Michael Hicks, "Joseph Smith, W. W. Phelps and the Poetic Paraphrase of 'The Vision,'" 63–84.

83. The First Presidency and the Twelve, headed by Joseph F. Smith, announced in 1916: "By the new birth—that of water and the Spirit—mankind may become children of Jesus Christ, being through the means by Him provided 'begotten sons and daughters unto God' (D.&C. 76:24)." Quoted in Talmage, *Articles of Faith*, 470.

84. Bruce R. McConkie is the author of these headnotes. "Elder Bruce R. McConkie: 'Preacher of Righteousness,'" 15–22. See also his *Mormon Doctrine*, 130.

85. Orson Pratt, *Prophetic Almanac for 1845*, 7–8.

86. See Charles R. Harrell, "The Development of the Doctrine of Preexistence: 1830–1844," 88–89.

87. William W. Phelps, "A Voice from the Prophet: 'Come to Me,'" 783.

88. Eliza R. Snow, "My Father in Heaven," 1039.

89. "The Family: A Proclamation to the World," 102.

90. Brigham Young, "Discourse," *Deseret News*, June 18, 1873, 308.

91. McConkie, "The Seven Deadly Heresies," 78. While many LDS apologists have denied that Brigham Young ever taught that Adam is God, in a letter to BYU English professor Eugene England, Elder McConkie acknowledged that "Brigham Young did teach that Adam was the father of our spirits," but that he was uninspired because the teaching is "out of harmony with the gospel." McConkie, Letter to Eugene England, February 19, 1981.

92. Brigham Young, April 9, 1852, *Journal of Discourses*, 1:50–51.

93. Ibid., 1:51.

94. David John Buerger, "The Adam-God Doctrine," 51 note 49.

95. Ibid., 55–56.

~ 8 ~

Jesus Christ

In LDS theology, Jesus Christ is the second member of the Godhead and the creator and redeemer of the world. According to a January 2000 declaration by the First Presidency and Quorum of the Twelve under President Gordon B. Hinckley, "He was the Great Jehovah of the Old Testament, the Messiah of the New. Under the direction of His Father, He was the creator of the earth.... He was the Firstborn of the Father, the Only Begotten Son in the flesh, the Redeemer of the world.... He is the light, the life, and the hope of the world."[1] Mormons, with the rest of Christianity, regard Jesus Christ as the source of all that is of lasting value in life. According to the Book of Mormon, "All things which are good cometh of Christ; otherwise men were fallen, and there could no good thing come unto them" (Moro. 7:24).

Mormons, like traditional Christians, see numerous references to Christ in the Old Testament. Christian fundamentalists have identified more than 300 such references.[2] Critical Bible scholars, on the other hand, see no direct references at all and contend that any allusion to Christ must be read into Old Testament narratives—as was the case with New Testament writers. Catholic New Testament scholar Raymond Brown notes that, while Old Testament writers "sometimes preached a 'messianic' deliverance (i.e., deliverance through one anointed as God's representative, thus a reigning king or even a priest), there is no evidence that they foresaw with precision even a single detail in the life of Jesus of Nazareth."[3] Even many LDS scholars acknowledge the absence of unambiguous references to Christ in the Old Testament. BYU religion professor Kent Jackson observed, "From the time of Moses to the end of the Old Testament, there are no clear and explicit references to Jesus Christ and His gospel."[4] According to critical Bible scholarship, all that one can defensibly show is that the Old Testament *foreshadows* Christ. In other words, the life of Christ parallels many of the events of the Old Testament—such as Israel's exodus from Egypt, finding the Promised Land, and offering sacrifices. Whether Israel's plight in the Old Testament intentionally foreshadows the life and sufferings of Christ or whether its symbolism just happens to be universal enough to fit this and a variety of similar situations is a conclusion left to faith.

Writers of the New Testament proclaimed that all Old Testament prophets prophesied of Christ (Acts 3:18, 10:43), and that "the spirit of prophecy" itself is "the testimony of Jesus" (Rev. 19:10). The Gospel of John asserts that Abraham "saw" the day of Christ "and was glad" (John 8:56).[5] Paul believed that references to Christ in the Old Testament are veiled from the spiritually hardened but that this "vail is done away in Christ" (2 Cor. 3:14). Since New Testament times, Christians have maintained that reading the Old Testament through Christ-colored spectacles is the only way it can be correctly understood.

The notion that Christ has played an active role in the salvation of humankind ever since the Fall was pronounced in Reformation thought. Martin Luther wrote:

> [T]he faith of the fathers was grounded on Christ which was to come, as ours is on Christ which is now come. . . . Therefore the diversity of times never changeth faith. . . . For there hath been, is, and ever shall be, one mind, one judgment and understanding, concerning Christ, as well in the ancient fathers, as in the faithful which are at this day, and shall come hereafter. So we have as well Christ to come, and believe in him, as the fathers in the Old Testament had.[6]

This same Christological view of the Old Testament is expressed in early LDS scriptures. The Book of Mormon presents itself as a tangible witness that righteous people living before Christ, in both the eastern and western hemispheres, were well acquainted with the Savior and plan of redemption.[7] Book of Mormon prophets identified what they considered to be unmistakable references to Christ in numerous Old Testament passages. The Book of Mormon also reinforces many New Testament and traditional Christian interpretations of Old Testament prophecies. Like the New Testament, it proclaims that all prophets testified of Christ (Jacob 4:4, 7:11; Mosiah 13:33; see also D&C 20:26).

To bolster the assertion that Christ was present in Old Testament history, the Book of Mormon rewords certain Old Testament passages using familiar Christian phraseology. For example, the Old Testament term "Sun of righteousness" (Mal. 4:2), which is a metaphor for the Lord God (see Ps. 84:11), is rendered "Son of Righteousness" in 3 Nephi 25:2, thus making it an explicit reference to Christ. Indeed, the appellation "Son of Righteousness" was commonly used in reference to Christ in Joseph Smith's day.[8] Unfortunately, this Christian pun on the word "sun" doesn't actually work in the original Hebrew of Malachi 4:2.

Where many Protestants saw no more than hints and shadows of Christ in the Old Testament, others insisted that these allusions were more than typological and had direct reference to Christ. Joseph Smith's teachings remove all doubt on this issue for Latter-day Saints by inserting explicit references to Christ into his inspired revision of the Bible. The first chapter of JST Genesis alone has three references to the "Only Begotten" of the Father (JST Gen. 1:2, 27, 29), which is three more than the entire KJV Old Testament.

In the Book of Mormon, prophetic precision goes well beyond that found in the Old Testament. Book of Mormon prophets knew the precise details of where Jesus would be born, the name of his mother, and even the exact year of his birth. Curiously, foreknowledge of his birth year corresponds more closely to the sequence in which Joseph Smith dictated the Book of Mormon than with Book of Mormon chronology. LDS scholars generally agree that after Martin Harris lost the first 116 pages of Book of Mormon manuscript, Joseph resumed translation beginning with Mosiah and later went back to redo the lost portion, this time translating from "the small plates of Nephi" which were handed down from generation to generation with the rest of the plates. It is in these early pages that Lehi (1 Ne. 10:4), an angel (1 Ne. 19:8), and "the prophets" (2 Ne. 25:19) all predict that Jesus would be born precisely 600 years from the time Lehi left Jerusalem. Later prophets in the Book of Mormon, however, seem to be unaware of these predictions and speak of his birth with much less precision, using only such vague terms as "soon at hand" (Mosiah 3:5; Alma 5:28, 50; 7:7; 9:26; 13:21). Alma, for example, expressed the desire that "it might be in my day," but confessed that "we know not how soon" it will be (Alma 13:25). One wonders how later prophets could have failed to pick up this important fact from the written and oral teachings passed down or why the Lord chose to withhold it from them.

Relying largely on Doctrine and Covenants 20:1 which speaks of "the rise of the Church of Christ in these last days, being one thousand eight hundred and thirty years since the coming of our Lord and Savior Jesus Christ in the flesh," Latter-day Saints have traditionally held that Jesus was born on April 6 in the year 1 B.C.[9] Based on historical evidence, however, most non-LDS and even many LDS scholars place Jesus's birth between 4 and 7 B.C.[10] Paul Maier, a professor of ancient history at Western Michigan University, explains, "Since the chronologies of the Herods, the Roman emperors and the governors within the time frames of the Gospels are firm, Jesus's birth can reliably be placed between June and December of 5 B.C. The date of His crucifixion is even more precise, with a balance of scholarship now inclining to April 3, A.D. 33."[11] This dating would mean that Christ lived to be thirty-six years of age, which conflicts with the traditional LDS view that Jesus was born on April 6, 1 B.C. and lived for only thirty-three years (3 Ne. 2:8, 8:5).[12] One is left to wonder whether these discrepancies are due to human error in the creation of scripture, human misunderstanding in the interpretation of scripture, or inaccuracy in the dates proposed by scholars.

Jesus Christ

"Jesus Christ" is considered by many Christians (including Latter-day Saints) to be Christ's given name, even though the angel told Joseph that his name would be simply "JESUS: for he shall save his people from their sins" (Matt 1:21). The name Jesus is the anglicized version of the Greek form of the Hebrew *Yehoshua* (or its shortened form, *Yeshua*), meaning "Yahweh is salvation." In Greek, it became *Iesous*, thence *Iesus* in Latin and *Jesus* in English. At the time and place Jesus was born, surnames were uncommon, so a person received only one name. To distinguish an individual from others having the same name, the person's father or grandfather was mentioned. Jesus, therefore, would have been known among his contemporaries as *Yeshua ben* (son of) *Yoseph* in Hebrew or *Yeshua Bar Yoseph* in Aramaic. In villages outside his hometown, he was referred to as Jesus of Nazareth.[13]

The term "Christ" was a title and not a name Jesus went by during his lifetime. It comes from *Christos*, the Greek word for the Hebrew *Messiah* meaning "the anointed one." The New Testament witness was that Jesus is the Christ or Messiah spoken of in the Old Testament. As BYU religion professor Thomas Wayment explains, "The name Jesus Christ is a later development when the title [Christ] was widely accepted and recognized as referring to Jesus of Nazareth."[14]

Even though the name "Jesus Christ" came to be applied to Jesus only after his resurrection, prophecies in the Book of Mormon seem to indicate that it would be his given name. In approximately 550 B.C., an angel revealed to the Nephite prophet Jacob that "Christ . . . should be his name" (2 Ne. 10:3).[15] Curiously, Joseph Smith repeatedly interjected the name "Jesus Christ" in his revised account of Genesis as "the only name which shall be given under heaven, whereby salvation shall come unto the children of men" (JST Gen. 6:53, 60; 7:57; see also

Moses 6:52, 57; 7:50). The JST explains that baptisms were performed by ancient patriarchs "in the name of Jesus Christ" (JST Gen. 8:11; see also Moses 8:24). LDS revelations and teachings since 1830 routinely refer to Jesus of Nazareth as Jesus Christ as though that were his actual name.

Jesus as Messiah

Christians take Jesus to be the Messiah or "anointed one" spoken of in the Old Testament. Jesus himself announced his Messiahship in his first public sermon, reading aloud in the synagogue the words of Isaiah, "The Spirit of the Lord is upon me, because the Lord has anointed me" (Isa. 61:1–2). After the reading he sat down and proclaimed, "This day is this scripture fulfilled in your ears" (Luke 4:21). According to most scholars, Isaiah uttered this passage in reference to his own anointing with no intended messianic reference. Even conservative Methodist Bible commentator Adam Clarke expressed the view that, although Isaiah 61:1–2 can be seen as a "shadow" of Christ's mission of salvation, "it primarily refers to Isaiah preaching the glad tidings of deliverance to the Jews."[16] Jesus, however, appropriated the passage to support his proclamation as the Messiah. James Sanders, a professor of intertestamental and biblical studies at the Claremont School of Theology, notes that Isaiah 61:1-2 became a messianic prooftext during the post-exilic period, and the New Testament followed suit. So "what originally was an exilic text referring to an historical situation [i.e., the liberation of the Jews in captivity] ... became ... an eschatological reference [i.e., the end-time salvation from sin]."[17]

Critical scholars question the legitimacy of claims that this and other Old Testament messianic prophecies were alluding to Christ. They see nothing in Old Testament writings that would connect messianic prophecies with a redeemer of the world who would establish a spiritual kingdom and in whom all must put their faith or perish. To them, the Messiah spoken of in the Old Testament was a near-term or even present figure who would usher in an earthly kingdom.[18] J. J. M. Roberts, a professor of Old Testament at Princeton Theological Seminary, notes that, of the thirty-nine occurrences of the Hebrew word for *messiah* in the Hebrew Bible, "not one of [them] ... refers to an expected figure of the future whose coming will coincide with the inauguration of an era of salvation."[19] According to Roberts, every reference to a messiah or anointed one in the Old Testament pertains to a past or present political or religious leader who is appointed by God, and not an expected future figure.[20]

Most Bible scholars see Jewish expectations of a Messiah as a later development in Judaism occurring during the first century or two prior to the Christian era. Old Testament scholar J. Becker states categorically that "there was not even such a thing as messianic expectation until the last two centuries B.C."[21] Messianic thinking at the time of Christ was the result of years of suffering in war and hope for deliverance. Biblical scholar James H. Charlesworth notes, "Jewish messianology developed out of the crisis and hope of the non-messianic Maccabean wars of the second century B.C. Palestinian Jews yearned for salvation from their pagan oppressors. For an indeterminable number of Jews the yearning centered on the future saving acts by a divinely appointed, and anointed supernatural man: the Messiah."[22] Thus, late Judaism anticipated that the Messiah would be a liberator from temporal oppression.

These Jewish messianic traditions were reinterpreted by the first Christians as having fulfillment in Christ. Jesuit theologian Gerald O'Collins explains, "Both he [Christ] and his followers massively reinterpreted the messianic figure. Behaving in an unregal and unwarlike fashion (see Mark 10:42–44; Luke 22:24–27), Jesus never promised, let alone tried, to free the people from foreign domination. Nor did he announce the imminent lordship of Israel over all nations (see Isa. 2:2–3; 25:6–9; Micah 4:1–2)."[23] This New Testament conception of Christ as a spiritual Messiah, together with the early Christian perception of Christ as the fulfillment of the suffering-servant hymn of Isaiah 53, formed the basis for future Christian messianic traditions, as well as the Christian belief that Jews had looked beyond the mark in anticipating only a regal messiah.

The Son of God

Jesus is universally recognized by Christians as the Son of God, a title which refers to his divine Sonship as the Only Begotten of the Father. The LDS understanding of this title is that Jesus is the only begotten Son of God "in the flesh." That is, God was literally the biological father of Jesus. Latter-day Saints also assert that Christ's spirit was literally begotten of God in the preexistence; but since Mormonism teaches that we are all literally the spirit offspring of God in the preexistence, the title "Son of God" is more generally used in LDS discourse to denote Christ's biological relationship to the Father in the flesh.

Old Testament

In the Old Testament, "son of God" was a title given to individuals who entered into a special or favored relationship with God. As O'Collins notes, "In the Old Testament divine sonship was attributed to . . . angelic beings, the chosen people, and their king."[24] Angels are designated "sons of God" in several Old Testament passages (Job 1:6, 2:1, 38:7; Ps. 29:1; Dan. 3:25). Applied to humans, the title conveyed the idea of "belonging to God."[25] The Israelites were called God's "children" (Deut. 32:5) or God's "sons" (Isa. 45:11) because God delivered them from Egypt and made them his own covenant people. Hosea 11:1 records, "When Israel was a child, I loved him, and out of Egypt I called my son."

Many Old Testament passages that speak of God's "son" are in reference to the coronation of Israel's king. Each king was God's recognized son or representative on earth. Only later in the New Testament were these same passages applied to Christ. Psalms 2:7 states, "Thou art my Son; this day have I begotten thee." This was a ceremonial proclamation made whenever a king was crowned (2 Sam. 7:14; Ps. 89:26–27). Raymond Brown notes: "At the moment of coronation a prophetic oracle explained to the people what God in heaven was saying of the king: 'You are my son; today I have begotten you.'"[26] As part of the coronation declaration, other kings and judges of the earth were commanded to "serve the Lord" (Ps. 2:11) and "kiss the Son" (Ps. 2:12), both of which referred to making obeisance to the new king. This coronation passage, therefore, referred to the currently reigning king with no explicit allusion to a future messianic king. Neither this nor any other passage in the Old Testament containing the expression "son of God" appears to have had Christ or a Messiah figure in mind. According to O'Collins, "'Son of God' hardly entered messianic expectations and was not an Old Testament messianic title."[27]

Many scholars see the New Testament application of the royal, coronation psalms to Christ as an example of proof-texting to legitimize the claim that Jesus is the Messiah. After explaining the setting and purpose of the royal psalms, Methodist scholar Knut Heim writes, "Not one royal psalm originated as a prediction of a future savior king; all of them originally referred to the king actually reigning at the time. A messianic meaning was given to them only after the disappearance of the Davidic dynasty. In particular, it arose from the contrast between Nathan's promise of an everlasting rule for David's house and the fact that the dynasty had ceased to be a political reality, the situation reflected in Psalm 89."[28]

A related coronation passage that was interpreted in the New Testament as a reference to Christ is Psalms 110:4: "The LORD said to my Lord, sit thou at my right hand until I make thine enemies my footstool." Matthew 22:44 records Jesus citing this psalm to proclaim that he was David's Lord.[29] Although the actual Psalm has God speaking to his newly anointed king on earth, the New Testament interpretation is that "the LORD [meaning the Father] said unto my Lord [meaning

Christ], sit thou at my right hand [etc.]." The original intended meaning of this Psalm becomes clear when it is realized that, in the Old Testament "LORD" (uppercased in the KJV) refers to Yahweh or Jehovah (the God of the Old Testament) while "Lord" (in upper- and lower-case letters) often refers to the reigning king. As king, Saul was David's Lord while God was Saul's LORD (1 Sam. 22:12, 17; 25:26, 30). David refers to Saul as "my Lord" and Jehovah (God) as "the LORD" (1 Sam. 24:10). So although Psalms 110:4 may be taken as a shadow of Christ, the actual meaning is: "The LORD [God] said unto my Lord [the reigning king], sit thou at my right hand [etc.]."[30]

To summarize, the predominant scholarly view is that none of the coronation Psalms predicts a future regal figure, much less the coming of a Messiah. They were all originally intended for the currently reigning king. A messianic meaning was given to them only after the rule of David's house ended.

A curious Old Testament passage that has been interpreted as a reference to Christ's divine Sonship is Isaiah 53:8, which asks regarding the unidentified suffering servant, "Who shall declare his generation?" According to McConkie, the servant is Christ, and Isaiah is asking "Who will give his genesis? Who will reveal his genealogy? Who will give the source from whence he sprang? Who will announce the divinity of the mortal Messiah?"[31] Traditional Christianity has also understood this passage as an allusion to Christ's divine birth. In contrast, the Book of Mormon, while interpreting the servant as Christ, interprets "generation" as Christ's offspring through spiritual rebirth (Mosiah 15:10–13). This view of Isaiah 53:8 happens to correspond to an interpretation popular at Joseph Smith's time. Congregationalist minister Ethan Smith wrote in 1824, "The generation of Christ, in this passage, does not relate to the generation of his person, or nature, divine nor human. . . . The word generation is often used . . . to denote a progeny, or family [i.e., children of Christ]."[32]

Scholars acknowledge that the actual meaning of Isaiah 53:8 is difficult to ascertain as the Hebrew itself is obscure. Given that the context is the ill fate of the suffering servant—"he was cut off out of the land of the living" (Isa. 53:8)—scholars suggest that the meaning is an expression of pity rather than a pronouncement of either noble birth or privileged offspring. The NRSV translation of Isaiah 53:8 reads: "Who could have imagined his [ill-fated] future?"

Another occurrence of the "Son of God" in the Old Testament that some Latter-day Saints regard as a reference to Christ is Daniel 3:25 in which Shadrach, Meshach, and Abed-nego are bound and cast into a fiery furnace to suffer death as punishment for refusing to worship Nebuchadnezzar's image. Suddenly, a fourth person appears in the furnace who, according to Nebuchadnezzar, has a form "like the Son of

God" (Dan. 3:25). The chapter heading in the LDS Bible identifies this person as literally "the Son of God," meaning Christ.

Early nineteenth-century Bible commentator Adam Clarke pointed out the absurdity of presuming that Nebuchadnezzar, an idolatrous king, would have thought that this fourth personage was Christ.[33] The phrase "like the Son of God" in this passage is rendered in most modern translations as "like a son of the gods" and, as many scholars agree, was Nebuchadnezzar's way of describing a divine intermediary like an angel. Indeed, in verse 28 the king states: "Blessed be the God of Shadrach, Meshach, and Abed-nego, who hath sent his angel, and delivered his servants that trusted in him." LDS Old Testament scholar Kent Jackson explains,

> The translators of the KJV identified the one "like the Son of God" (Dan. 3:25) with Christ, as shown by the capital letter on "Son" (Hebrew and Aramaic have no capital letters). More likely, it was an angel, because the Aramaic term, *bar-'elahin*, was used commonly in ancient literature for subordinate gods, angelic beings, members of the heavenly council, etc.[34]

Thus, it has been in the tradition of modern Christian proof-texting that many Latter-day Saints have viewed this and other Old Testament passages as expressly referring to Christ as the Son of God.

New Testament

Coming into New Testament times, Jews were predominantly monotheistic and, according to many scholars, wouldn't have anticipated the Messiah's arrival as a fully divine Son of God. Religious historian Karen Armstrong asserts: "Nobody since the return from Babylon had imagined that Yahweh actually had a son, like the abominable deities of the *goyim* [Gentiles]."[35] Though perhaps foreign to Jewish tradition, by New Testament times a custom had become established in the Roman Empire of attributing divine sonship to their emperors. Caesar Augustus, who was emperor when Christ was born, was hailed as the "son of god" (*divi filius*) and was proclaimed "Lord" and "Savior of the whole world." His birthday was looked upon as "good news for the world," and he inaugurated what was hoped to be a lasting reign of peace (*Pax Augusta*).[36] Andrew Lincoln, professor of New Testament at the University of Gloucestershire, England, notes that "Luke's story [of Jesus's birth] both echoes and challenges the imperial propaganda about Augustus."[37]

Though Christ is referred to as the Son of God over thirty times in the New Testament, in only a few instances does this title pertain to his biological birth. In the majority of cases, the title carries other meanings. The earliest New Testament writers drew on the coronation proclamation "thou art my Son" (Ps. 2:7) to extol Christ's Sonship. Interestingly, however, it was not through birth that Christ was viewed as having attained this Sonship, but by adoption at the time of his resurrection and glorification (Acts 2:30, 13:32–33; Heb. 1:3–5, 13). New Testament scholar James Dunn notes, "The use of Ps. 2:7 in [the epistle to the] Hebrews . . . reflects an association with Jesus's exaltation, with Ps. 2:7 being taken as an allusion to Jesus's appointment to high-priestly status consequent upon his suffering (1:3–5; 5:5–10; 7:28)."[38] Dunn further states, "On the basis of Rom. 1:4 and Acts 13:33 we may conclude . . . that the first Christians thought of Jesus's divine sonship principally as a role and status he had entered upon, being appointed to at his resurrection."[39]

The attribution of divine Sonship to Christ through death and resurrection may seem a little peculiar to Latter-day Saints who generally think of him as becoming the Son of God through his birth. Nonetheless, in antiquity it was a common practice to deify kings and emperors upon their death. It has been suggested that, in referring to Christ as the Son of God through his resurrection (Rom. 1:4), Paul "is probably alluding to the death of the emperor Claudius on 13 October 54 [the Epistle to Romans was written about 56] and his divinization after death. Claudius came from the Julian-Claudian house and (like other emperors) was only elevated to *divus* after his death."[40] The implication is that Paul may have ascribed deity to Christ upon his death and resurrection as a response to the deification proclaimed by the Roman senate of their recently deceased emperor.

Over time, Psalms 2:7 became applied to other phases of Christ's ministry. According to Raymond Brown, "This type of coronation psalm reference is applied verbatim to the resurrection of Jesus in Acts 13:32–33. . . . When the christological declaration of divine sonship was moved to the beginning of the ministry and to the baptism, the coronation language was also moved."[41] According to Luke 3:22, a voice was heard at Jesus's baptism proclaiming, "Thou art my beloved Son" as though Christ was already God's son prior to his baptism. New Testament scholar Bart Ehrman notes, however, that the oldest New Testament manuscripts contain the added clause "today I have begotten you,"[42] indicating that Christ *became* God's Son through baptism in an adoptionistic sense. Adoptionism, which was widely held before it was first declared a heresy at the end of the second century, was the belief that Jesus was born as a mere human and became divine through adoption at his baptism or resurrection. Ehrman suggests that the phrase in Luke was likely removed by trinitarians who opposed adoptionism.

The Gospel of John seems to give another sense in which Christ was the Son of God, pointing to his glorified status with God from before creation. John states that Christ was "in the beginning with God" (John 1:2) and that God subsequently "sent . . . his son into the world" (John 3:17). John further explains that Christ's Sonship is evident from his being "full of grace and truth" (John 1:14), and that all who "believe on his [Christ's] name" partake of his grace and truth, thereby becoming also empowered "to become the sons [Greek *tekna* = children] of God" (John 1:12). Jesus's designation as the Son of God in this context appears to be the result of his partaking of the glory of God from before the foundation of the world.

Though Paul and John give different meanings to Christ's divine Sonship, neither writer speaks of Christ becoming the Son of God through biological birth. Birth enters into Christ's divine Sonship only in the writings of Matthew and Luke, believed to have been written in the late 70s or 80s (several decades after Paul and with a different Christology than John). In Luke, Gabriel tells Mary: "The power of the Highest shall overshadow thee: therefore also that holy thing which shall be born of thee shall be called the Son of God" (Luke 1:35). Significantly, the gospel of Mark, which is believed to be the earliest gospel, shows no knowledge of Christ's divine birth. Andrew Lincoln points out that

> this is not simply an argument from silence, since . . . the evangelist is quite clear about the attitude of Jesus' mother and brothers towards Jesus; it is one of alienation and unbelief [see Mark 3:20–35; 6:1–6]. This makes it highly improbable that Mark was aware of a tradition that Jesus' birth was an extraordinary occurrence about which his parents had received some special revelation.[43]

Of course, this does not disprove that Christ was the Son of God in the flesh; but as Lincoln notes, "This tradition is unlikely to have originated very early or to have been widespread."[44]

Early Nineteenth-Century Christianity

At the time of Joseph Smith, evangelicals viewed Christ's divine Sonship in several ways based on New Testament teachings as interpreted in light of traditional trinitarianism. One sense in which many nineteenth-century trinitarians considered Christ to be the Son was because of his human nature.[45] The notion was that Christ had both a divine nature and a human nature that were effectively two wills, one of the Father and one of the Son. Writing on the nature of Christ in 1791, Congregationalist trinitarian Caleb Alexander asserted,

> Christ's highest capacity and character is, not the Son, but, the Everlasting Father, the Mighty God, the Almighty, the Creator of all things, the Possessor of heaven and earth. His lowest capacity and character is the *Son*, the *Righteous Servant*. The term *son*, whether *son of man* or *Son of God*, is ever, when applied to Christ, expressive of his humanity. . . . The term Son, consequently, when applied to him, has, always, an especial reference to his *human* nature.[46]

Variations on this two-nature doctrine of Christ can be traced back to the Patristic era (100–451) when a debate arose over whether Christ had only a single nature (*monophysitism*), which was considered to be divine, or whether he possessed two natures (*dyophysitism*), a divine nature and a human nature. In the two-nature view, which became the orthodox Christian view, Jesus's human nature bowed to the will of his divine nature in effecting the atonement. In spite of scholarly consensus that this doctrine is nowhere expressly found in the New Testament,[47] it has persisted and was popular at the time of Joseph Smith.

In addition to Christ's designation as the Son of God because of his human nature, he was also sometimes depicted as the Son because of his divine, pre-existent nature, similar to the idea of Christ's divine Sonship expressed in the Gospel of John. In August 1825, *The Methodist Magazine* published a sermon titled "Divinity" by the Reverend Jacob Moore in which he delineated two distinct ways that Jesus was the Son of God: (1) "Christ is God's Son as it respects his human nature,"[48] (already discussed above) and (2) "He is the Father's Son as it respects his divine and pre-existent nature."[49] It should be observed that these two modes of Sonship have to do with Christ's *nature* rather than the manner of his generation or birth. Regarding his human nature, Moore explains that "Christ's human nature is . . . the Son of God, because it is the shrine of him who was divinely and essentially the Son of God."[50] In other words, Christ's flesh was the earthly tabernacle of his divine essence and therefore warranted the designation Son of God. Regarding his divine and preexistent nature, Moore states, "The Son of God is the same in glory, duration and essence, with the Father."[51]

As explained in Chapter 6, modalists also considered Christ to be the Son of God because of his flesh, but in a different sense than traditional trinitarians. For modalists, God is a single being who was the Father in Old Testament times and became the Son of God through his incarnation or appearance in the flesh. The Father is to the Son what the soul is to the body, being two aspects of the same individual.

Early Mormonism

Early LDS teachings expressed Christ's divine Sonship much along the same line as contemporaneous trinitarians, which tended to emphasize either his human nature or his divine, preexistent nature. Notably, nowhere in LDS scripture is Christ expressly referred to as the Son of God because he was *begotten* of God either in the spirit or in the flesh.

The earliest LDS teachings seem to refer to Christ as the Son of God to denote his human nature. In this sense, Book of Mormon Christology is reminiscent of orthodox trinitarianism in its espousal of a two-nature view of Christ. Christ was "the Father and the Son" (Mosiah 15:2), possessing a divine will and a human will or a will of "the Spirit" and a will of "the flesh" (Mosiah 15:5). Thus, Christ is called the Son "because of the flesh" (Mosiah 15:3; 3 Ne. 1:14), i.e., because he had a human body, and the Father "because he was conceived by the power of God" (Mosiah 15:3), and, consequently, was filled with the Spirit. Today Latter-day Saints would say that his conception in the flesh by God's power is why he is called the Son, not the Father. In the Book of Mormon, however, Christ is the Son because he took "upon him the image of man" or in other words "flesh and blood" (Mosiah 7:27). Thus, he is "the Son because of [his] flesh" (3 Ne. 1:14), not because God was his biological father. (In the Book of Mormon Christ was conceived "of the Holy Ghost" [Alma 7:10].)

It is interesting that in the Book of Mormon, Christ is generally referred to as God or the Father prior to his birth, but then called the Son of God after he is born in the flesh. Kurt Widmer, an instructor in religious studies at the University of Lethbridge, notes, "The theology of the *Book of Mormon* refers to the preincarnate Jesus as: 'the Father,' 'the Eternal God,' 'the everlasting God,' 'the Father of heaven and earth,' 'the Father and the Son,' and 'the Father of all things.' . . . In the 1830 *Book of Mormon*, 'the Son' is used only to refer to the incarnate Jesus."[52] This language, of course, is consonant with modalist explanations.

Doctrine and Covenants 93 similarly refers to Christ as the Son "because he was in the world and made flesh [his] tabernacle, and dwelt among the sons of men" (D&C 93:4). The revelation further states that Christ "was called the Son of God, because he received not of the fulness [of God's glory] at first" (D&C 93:12). Thus, the title "Son of God" denotes Christ's earthly, finite existence prior to his glorification. In the Gospel of John, which is the source of much of the language of Doctrine and Covenants 93, Christ was called the "Son of God" because he possessed a fulness of the glory of the Father, i.e., he was "full of grace and truth" (John 1:14). Doctrine and Covenants 93, however, has him being the "Son of God, because he received not of the fulness at the first" (D&C 93:14). John 1:16 explains that it is man who must receive "grace for grace" while Doctrine and Covenants 93:12 has Christ himself growing "grace for grace." In sum, early Mormonism designates Christ as the Son because he took on the finite characteristics of humans, not because he was God's biological son. Even the *Lectures on Faith* affirm that Christ was "called the Son because of the flesh,"[53] that is, because he took upon himself flesh and mortality.

Another sense in which Christ was designated as the Son of God after 1830 was in connection with his being "in the bosom of the Father, even from the beginning" (D&C 76:13, 25). This sense resembles the traditional Christian understanding of John's teachings in the New Testament of the way Christ was considered to be the Son from eternity. Joseph Smith referred to Christ as "the anointed Son of God [not anointed *to become* the Son of God], from before the foundation of the world."[54] While more will be said about this unique relationship between the Father and the Son, we can here observe that Joseph Smith never referred to Christ as God's begotten Son in either the spirit or the flesh in any of his recorded teachings.[55] The title "Son of God" was used to designate either his humanity during his earthly ministry or his premortal divine affinity with God. The expressions "Son of God" and "Only Begotten Son" don't appear to have been used to signify Christ's birth in the flesh until at least the Nauvoo period,[56] in part, perhaps, because God wasn't perceived as being corporeal until then. Today in LDS discourse, this meaning is almost the exclusive understanding of the title "Son of God" when applied to Christ.

Only Begotten Son

In current LDS theology, Jesus's title of "Only Begotten Son" has essentially the same meaning as "Son of God" and refers to his unique and literal Sonship of the Father in the flesh. According to Joseph Fielding Smith, "All through the ministry of our Savior he acknowledged the fact that he is the Only Begotten Son of God *in the flesh*."[57] Such an assertion is a bit of an overstatement, however, as the few references in the New Testament to Christ being God's "only begotten son" appear to be in the sense of his being God's only son from eternity who subsequently dwelt in the flesh. Significantly, none of the standard works ever explicitly refers to Jesus as the Only Begotten Son of God *in the flesh*.

Jesus's designation as the "Only Begotten Son" appears in the Bible only in the writings of John (John 1:14, 18; 3:16, 18; 1 Jn. 4:9), although the Prophet felt inspired to interject this Johanine ascription into the writings of Paul as well (JST 1 Tim. 2:4). Linguists note that the New Testament (KJV) expression "Only Begotten" may not be the best translation of the Greek *monogenes* which is a combination of two words: *monos* meaning "only" or "alone," and *genos* meaning "of the same nature, kind, sort, species."[58] The Greek word *genos* is only distantly related to the verb *gennan* which means "to beget." Hence, several modern translations drop the word "begotten." Even the NASB, which retains the phrase "only begotten" in the text, has a footnote stating that the literal translation is "unique, only one of His kind." The implication is that Christ is God's uniquely special Son, but not necessarily his literally *begotten* son.

In the New Testament, John's designation of Jesus as God's "Only Begotten Son," or God's "uniquely special son," is never suggestive of Christ's birth in the flesh. Rather John seems to call Christ the unique, only-one-of-a-kind Son of God because he was the only being who actually "proceeded forth [not necessarily begotten] and came from God" (John 8:42). Thus, he was "in the bosom of the Father" (John 1:18) from the beginning. John contrasts the existence of Christ with the existence of all other humans stating that Christ was in the beginning with God (John 1:2) while everyone else's existence begins on earth (John 1:13, 30). He is the only one who comes "from above" and so is preeminent among all men: "Ye are from beneath; I am from above" (John 8:23), Jesus said, and "He that cometh from above is above all" (John 3:31). John, therefore, spoke of Christ being "the Only Begotten Son" evidently because of his coexistence with God from the beginning; not because he later *became* the Only Begotten Son by being born of God in the flesh. Accordingly, John wrote that God "sent his Only Begotten Son into the world" (1 Jn. 4:9, 3:16–17), which, according to biblical linguist W. E. Vine, "must not be taken to mean that Christ became the Only Begotten Son by Incarnation. The value and the greatness of the gift lay in the Sonship of Him who was given. His Sonship was not the effect of His being given."[59] This interpretation is certainly consistent with the general message of John that Christ alone proceeded from the Father and was therefore in the beginning with God as His unique, one-of-a-kind Son.

The religious discourse in Joseph Smith's day revived an ongoing debate since early Christianity of whether Jesus was called the Only Begotten Son because he proceeded eternally from God (called eternal generation) or because he was created by God at some definite point in eternity past. In either case, this ascription pertained to a relationship Christ had with the Father from before the creation. In the third century, Origen advocated the doctrine of eternal generation—that Christ proceeded eternally from the Father and was not created. In the fourth century, Jerome championed Origen's view in opposition to the growing Arian view that Jesus was not with God from all eternity. In suppressing Arianism as a heresy, the Council of Nicaea in 325 made the doctrine of the Son's eternal generation a pillar of the doctrine of the Trinity.

As the Reformation got underway, the Nicene Creed had a marked influence on the formulation of Reformation theology. The popular *Book of Common Prayer* published in the sixteenth century reads: "I believe . . . in one Lord Jesus Christ, the only-begotten Son of God, begotten of the Father before all worlds; God of God, Light of Light, very God of very God; begotten, not made, being of one substance with the Father, by whom all things were made."[60] Here Christ is called "the only-begotten Son of God," not in the flesh as in Mormon theology, but in the sense of being the one and only "begotten of [i.e., derived from] the Father *before all worlds*."

Similar to traditional Christian usage, the title "Only Begotten" in the Book of Mormon also seems to refer to Christ's unique divine affinity with the Father from before the foundation of the world. Book of Mormon passages speak of the Only Begotten Son who *would come* into the world—not who would *become* the Only Begotten Son by coming into the world. According to 2 Nephi 25:12, "The Only Begotten of the Father . . . shall manifest himself . . . in the flesh." Alma 5:48 likewise states, "The Only Begotten of the Father, full of grace, and mercy, and truth . . . cometh to take away the sins of the world" (see also Alma 9:26). Nowhere does the Book of Mormon refer to Christ *becoming* the Only Begotten Son of God through being born of God in the flesh.

Christ's designation as the Only Begotten Son of God turns up again in the Prophet's revision of the Bible, particularly in the creation story canonized in the book of Moses. This account contains numerous references to Christ's divine Sonship using language akin to that found in the New Testament writings of John. The book of Moses identifies (an astonishing twenty-five times) the preexistent Christ (not the mortal Christ) as God's "Only Begotten." Once again, these references seem to allude to Christ's special relationship with the Father from the beginning (Moses 1:6, 32; 5:7; 6:52; 7:59). This relationship may explain Satan's attempt to pass himself off to Moses as God's chosen one saying, "I am [present tense] the Only Begotten" (Moses 1:19). God revealed to Moses that he was in the similitude of the "Only Begotten" (Moses 1:6), which seems to refer to Moses's spiritual rebirth, thus becoming "a son of God, in the similitude of his [God's] Only Begotten" (Moses 1:13). That others could spiritually become sons of God, even though Christ was the only begotten son of God *from eternity,* was a common Christian concept and is expressed most succinctly in John Mannock's 1815 *Poor Man's Catechism*: "As Christ is by nature the eternal son of God, a Christian by grace is the adopted son of God ; and so receives, in some proportion, by a spiritual regeneration, what the Son of God received by his eternal generation."[61]

Regarding the use of the term "Only Begotten Son" in the Book of Mormon and book of Moses to designate the premortal Christ, BYU professor of religion Rodney Turner observed:

> Prior to his mortal advent, the Only Begotten is repeatedly referred to in the present tense in the Book of Mormon and in Moses.... While it may be argued that this simply means that he was appointed to become so, I believe that the tenor of the relevant passages in both of these scriptures is that he was functioning as the Only Begotten from the beginning.[62]

Of course, referring to the premortal Christ as the Only Begotten from the beginning would have made perfect sense to trinitarians.

Early revelations in the Doctrine and Covenants also suggest that Christ was the Only Begotten Son in glory from the beginning (D&C 29:46; 49:5; 76:13, 23, 25; 93:11; 124:123), again with the promise that those who come unto him may likewise become God's sons and daughters (D&C 76:23–24). As Rodney Turner explains, "Jesus was the first and *only* spirit begotten into the Father's fulness in pre-mortality. All others are spiritually begotten *through* the Son (D&C 93:22). Therefore, ... Jesus *is* ... the Only Begotten of the Father into the fulness of immortal glory."[63] In none of these occurrences of the title "Only Begotten Son" is it implied that Christ is the Only Begotten Son of God "in the flesh," nor is it stated that he became the Only Begotten Son of God upon being born in the flesh. All occurrences of the expression "Only Begotten Son" in the Doctrine and Covenants, as also in the Book of Mormon and Pearl of Great Price, seem to reflect the traditional Christian understanding of Christ's glorified status with the Father before the world was.

As if unable to reconcile how others can become sons of God when Christ was designated as God's *only* begotten son, on September 9, 1835, W. W. Phelps, Joseph's scribe and associate, wrote a letter to his wife Sally explaining "that by obeying the laws and commandments of his Creator, he [i.e., man] might be rewarded with honor and glory in eternity; that he might become a Son of the Lord Jesus, for Jesus was the Only Begotten of the Father."[64] The implication is that humans become sons of Christ, not God, in their endowment of "glory," since Christ is the Only Begotten Son of God in glory.

The current LDS view that the expression "Only Begotten Son" means the Only Begotten Son "in the flesh" has been further understood by many Church authorities to mean that Mary was literally impregnated by God the Father.[65] Bruce R. McConkie explained that the title "Only Begotten Son" means "the only Son of the Father in the flesh" and "is to be understood literally. . . . [that] Christ was begotten by an Immortal Father in the same way that mortal men are begotten by mortal fathers."[66] Of course, to keep God's sexual intimacy with Mary within the proper bounds of matrimony, it is stated that Mary was legally and lawfully wedded to God the Father. A First Presidency Message under the administration of Joseph F. Smith states, "The Christian denominations believe that Christ was begotten not of God but of the spirit that overshadowed his mother. This is nonsense. . . . We must come down to the simple fact that God Almighty was the Father of His Son Jesus Christ. Mary, the virgin girl, who had never known mortal man, was his mother. . . . Mary was married to Joseph for time. No man could take her for eternity because she belonged to the Father of her divine Son."[67]

Biblical scholars maintain that, even though there is precedent for the idea of sexual intercourse between gods and humans in Jewish and Greek mythology, there is no scriptural support for the notion that God had a sexual relationship with Mary. When the angel tells Mary, "The Holy Ghost shall come upon thee, and the power of the highest shall overshadow thee" (Luke. 1:35), the angel uses parallel expressions, where the second phrase simply repeats the first. Thus, scholars see the power of the Highest being the Holy Ghost—not God, as taught in some LDS commentaries.[68] Raymond Brown dismisses any idea that "the divine begetting of Jesus" was "a sexual begetting. The Holy Spirit [feminine in Hebrew and neuter in Greek] is the agency of God's creative power, not a male partner in a marriage between a deity and a woman (*hieros gamos*)."[69] According to Matthew 1:18, after Mary was "found with child *of the Holy Ghost*," an angel counseled Joseph not to dissolve their betrothal "for that which is conceived in her is *of the Holy Ghost*." The idea of Christ being literally conceived by God appears nowhere in early LDS scriptures, which all follow the New Testament notion of conception by the Holy Ghost and seem to be based on a theology in which God is incorporeal. The Book of Mormon, for example, states that "Mary . . . shall be overshadowed and conceive by the power of the Holy Ghost" (Alma 7:10). There is no mention of Christ being literally begotten of God.

Virgin Birth

Related to the LDS doctrine of Christ being the Only Begotten Son of God in the flesh is the doctrine of the virgin birth or, the more technically accurate, virginal conception. Latter-day Saints proclaim with the rest of Christianity that Christ was born of the virgin Mary. Eleanor Colton, writing in the *Encyclopedia of Mormonism*, states that "Mary, mother of Jesus Christ, was a virgin at the time of Jesus's birth."[70] The Book of Mormon confirms the traditional story of the virgin birth identifying Mary by name and calling her "a virgin, most beautiful and fair above all other virgins" (1 Ne.11:15).

An Old Testament passage cited in support of the belief in a virgin birth is Isaiah 7:14: "Therefore the Lord himself shall give you a sign; Behold, a virgin shall conceive, and bear a son, and shall call his name Immanuel." This verse was applied to Christ's birth in Matthew 1:23. The Hebrew (Masoretic) text of Isaiah 7:14 reads that a "young girl" (Hebrew *alma*) shall conceive. The Septuagint or Greek translation from which the KJV was taken reads *parthenos* or "virgin." This difference "has given rise to some of the most famous debates in the history of exegesis,"[71] starting at least as early as the second century. The KJV follows the Septuagint, while modern translations, such as the NRSV, follow the Hebrew. These translations have been assailed by Latter-day Saints and actually burned by Christian fundamentalists because they were viewed as denying the virgin birth.[72]

Scholars contend that the literal meaning of Isaiah 7:14 is readily discernable from its historical context. Raymond Brown notes that it was directed "to the wicked King Ahaz (ca. 735–715 B.C.).... It was intended as a sign to this disbelieving monarch during the Syro-Ephraimite war of 734 and must refer to something that took place during that year or shortly thereafter."[73] The NRSV actually speaks of the young woman that Ahaz saw as *already* being with child and soon to be delivered. Thus, the passage was an announcement of a near-term sign to King Ahaz. "The sign offered by the prophet was the imminent birth of a child, probably Davidic, but naturally conceived, who would illustrate God's providential care for his people. The child would help to preserve the House of David and would thus signify that god was still 'with us.'"[74] Many conservative Christian scholars are willing to accede this historical meaning, but also see a typological reference to the birth of Christ.

Of course, for Latter-day Saints who hold the belief that Christ was literally conceived by God the Father, the idea of a virgin birth becomes a bit problematic as it would presumably change Mary's status as a virgin. Bruce R. McConkie gives his resolution to this conundrum by redefining "virgin" to mean a woman who has not known a *mortal* man: "She conceived and brought forth her Firstborn Son while yet a virgin because the Father of that child was an immortal personage."[75]

The Firstborn

A distinctive LDS doctrine is that Christ was not only the offspring of God as a spirit in the preexistence, like all of God's other children, but he was also the firstborn spirit "to whom all others are juniors."[76] Orson Pratt observed, "How long ago since . . . the Savior's birth took place is not revealed; it might have been unnumbered millions of years for aught we know. But we do know that he was born and was the oldest of the family of spirits."[77] Thus, Christ is often referred to by Mormons as "our elder brother."

Although the title "firstborn" as it relates to the law of primogeniture was well known in Old Testament times, it often had reference to the preferred status of individuals and nations in God's sight, not to their birth order. The nations of Israel (Ex. 4:22) and Ephraim (Jer. 31:9), for example, were both designated as God's "firstborn." Speaking of David and his royal dynasty, Psalm 89:27 declares: "I will make him my firstborn, higher than the kings of the earth." In this passage, the emphasis is clearly on the king's preeminence and superiority, but not through a literal birth process. He would be *made* or appointed as the firstborn, not begotten.

The New Testament contains several references to Christ as the firstborn of God in letters attributed to Paul that some Latter-day Saints understand to mean the "firstborn of all of God's spirit children."[78] But when examined carefully, Paul's teachings show little evidence of a belief that Christ was the firstborn spirit in the preexistence. The word "firstborn" is translated from the Greek *prototokos* and, depending on the context, means first in sequence of birth or, figuratively, first in rank, preeminent.[79] New Testament scholar George Ladd explains, "'Firstborn' (prototokos) can have two meanings; temporal priority, or sovereignty of position. David, the youngest of eight sons, was to be made the firstborn, the highest of the kings of the earth (Ps. 89:27)."[80] In the New Testament, the term "firstborn" is applied to Christ's preeminent status in several different ways.

One instance of Christ's designation as the firstborn is in Romans 8:29: "For whom he did foreknow, he also did predestinate to be conformed to the image of his Son, that he might be the firstborn among many brethren." President Joseph F. Smith interpreted this passage as meaning that "the spirits who were juniors to Christ were predestined to be born in the spirit in the image of their Elder Brother."[81] According to scholars, however, Paul is not referring to premortal spirit birth, but to Christ becoming the firstborn in attaining God's glory, a status which would subsequently be attained by "many brethren" (i.e., disciples). These brethren were predestined "to be conformed [not born] to the image of his Son" (v. 29), meaning that they would become sons of God in the same adoptive sense in which Christ was seen by Paul as God's son (see Rom. 8:19). Here the emphasis seems to be on Jesus as the forerunner of salvation,[82] not on his order of premortal birth.

Another New Testament instance of Christ being called the firstborn is Hebrews 1:6: "And again, when he bringeth in the firstbegotten into the world, he saith, And let all the angels of God worship him." This doesn't expressly state that Christ is the "firstbegotten" in the sense of being the first born spirit of God. Notably, this passage is actually adapted from a text that had reference to Adam's physical creation and had no reference at all to Christ. LDS scholar John Tvedtnes explains: "The original story, found in a number of early pseudepigraphic works, makes Adam, not Christ, the firstbegotten whom God commanded the angels to worship. Here as elsewhere, the author of Hebrews, in typical Jewish fashion, borrows a passage unrelated to his current topic as a 'proof-text.'"[83]

Several places in the New Testament where Christ is designated as the "firstborn" have unmistakable reference to his preeminence in the resurrection from the dead. In Colossians 1:18 Christ is referred to as "the firstborn from the dead." Revelation 1:5 also calls Jesus "the first begotten of the dead," or, as many versions read, "the first begotten *from* the dead."

A final New Testament passage that Latter-day Saints often construe as a reference to Christ being literally the firstborn of God in the spirit is Colossians 1:15, which refers to him as "the firstborn of every creature." The next verse, however, explains: "For by him were all things created." Eduard Lohse, professor of New Testament theology at the University of Göttingen, explains that the ascription of firstborn to Christ in this passage "is not intended to mean that he was created first and thereby began the succession of created beings. Rather, it refers instead to his uniqueness, by which he is distinguished from all creation (cf. Heb 1:6)."[84] In other words, Christ, as the creative agent of "all things," is given the preeminent designation "firstborn."[85]

For Jesus to be the firstborn spirit would imply that other spirits would have been subsequently born; but for Paul, there are no subsequent spirit births because "all things" (everyone and everything) are the creation of Christ. So once again the term "firstborn" signifies preeminence as "he is before all things, and in him all things consist" (v. 17). Significantly, the NIV translates Colossians 1:15 to read that Christ is "the firstborn *over* all creation," thus removing any sense of "firstborn" being a reference to order of birth, much less spirit birth.

To summarize, in the New Testament Christ is the firstborn in the sense of (1) being prior to and the source of all creation; (2) being the first to receive exaltation and glory; and (3) being the first to rise from the dead, "that in all things he might have the preeminence" (Col. 1:18). With respect to Christ being the firstborn spirit son of God in the preexistence, LDS scholar John Tvedtnes acknowledges that "the Bible itself is hardly proof of this. From the Bible, one can only conclude that Jesus is the first person resurrected from the dead."[86]

Neither the Book of Mormon nor the Pearl of Great Price refers to Christ as the Firstborn. The only express mention of Christ being the Firstborn in any latter-day scripture is in Doctrine and Covenants 93:21 where Christ declares, "And now, verily I say unto you, I was in the beginning with the Father, and am the Firstborn." Notably, this verse doesn't say he was the firstborn *spirit* in the preexistence but simply that he *is* the firstborn—seemingly indicating his current favored status with God, not unlike the way Israel was anciently referred to as God's firstborn (Ex. 4:22). Moreover, those who are spiritually born again through Christ share the same glory or favored status as the firstborn. Thus, Doctrine and Covenants 93:22 reads, "And all those who are begotten through me are partakers of the glory of the same, and are the church of the Firstborn." Earlier revelations also spoke of the "glory . . . of the church of the Firstborn" (D&C 88:5; see also 76:71) prepared for those who inherit the same glory as Christ. One should not automatically assume, therefore, that the designation of Christ as the Firstborn in Doctrine and Covenants 93 is an affirmation of his status as the firstborn spirit child of God in the preexistence. Indeed, the Mormon concept of spirit birth wouldn't be articulated in any recognizable way for at least another decade.

The concept seemingly expressed in Doctrine and Covenants 93 also finds its way into Joseph's revision of Romans 8:28–29. As noted above, scholars generally interpret this passage as a declaration that Christ was the "firstborn" in receiving God's glory and those who become his disciples inherit the same glory, thus making Christ "the firstborn among many brethren" (v. 29). The JST reinforces this interpretation: "For him [Jesus] whom he [the Father] did foreknow, he [the Father] also did predestinate to be conformed to his [the Father's] own image, that he [Jesus] might be the firstborn among many brethren" (JST Rom. 8:29). The image to which Christ was made to conform was God's glorious image.

The doctrine that Christ was the firstborn spirit child of God doesn't appear in LDS teachings until after Joseph Smith and was part of the larger doctrine of spirit birth that was beginning to take shape in the latter part of 1844 (see Chapter 7). The first documented public reference to spirit birth, which also alludes to Christ as "our Brother," comes from Orson Pratt's *Prophetic Almanac* for 1845. Under a section entitled "The Mormon Creed," Pratt declares, "What is man? The offspring of God. What is God? The father of man. Who is

Jesus Christ? He is our Brother."[87] The actual designation of Christ as the firstborn spirit initially appeared publicly at the dedication of the Seventies Hall on December 26, 1844, some six months after Joseph Smith's death. George Laub reported that Brigham Young delivered a sermon at the dedication in which he taught: "Christ is our head and Elder Brother. For we were once organized before God, and Jesus was the firstborn or begotten of the Father."[88] The day before the dedication, W. W. Phelps wrote a letter published in the *Times and Seasons* which referred to Jesus Christ as "our eldest brother" who "kept his first estate . . . and [was] crowned in the midst of brothers and sisters, while his mother stood with approving virtue."[89] As the emphasis on Christ being the firstborn spirit offspring of God grew from this point, scriptural references to the Firstborn were reinterpreted to provide supporting proof-texts for this doctrine.

Son of Man

Another title from the scriptures that Latter-day Saints generally understand as referring to Christ is "Son of Man," usually equating with "Son of God." According to Joseph Fielding Smith, "Son of Man" is derived from God's title "Man of Holiness" recorded in the Pearl of Great Price (Moses 6:57); thus, "the Son of Man" is an abbreviation for "the Son of Man of Holiness or in other words, the Son of God."[90]

In the Old Testament, "son of man" appears in several places (for example, Job 25:6; Ps. 146:3; Isa. 51:12) but never as a title for Christ. It was an expression used to designate a human being. "Son of x" was a Semitic idiom for something having the characteristics of x. Thus, a son of man has the characteristics of man—i.e., he is human.

Many Christians, including Latter-day Saints, argue that the occurrence of "son of man" in Daniel 7:13 is an exception. Former LDS Apostle James E. Talmage stated: "The distinctive title 'The Son of Man' as applied to Jesus Christ occurs only once in the Old Testament. It is in the seventh chapter of Daniel."[91] Daniel 7 describes a vision in which "one like the son of man came with the clouds of heaven, and came to the Ancient of Days." The chapter headnote in the 1979 LDS edition of the Bible identifies the "one like the son of man" as "the Son of Man (Christ)." If Daniel was actually referring to Christ, one wonders why he didn't simply call him "the" son of man instead of "one like" the son of man.

Significantly, in modern translations and scholarly commentaries, this phrase in Daniel is rendered "one like *a* son of man," (NRSV = "one like a human being") signifying a man-like figure,[92] in contrast to the strange, beast-like figures that Daniel had been shown. Matthias Henze, writing in *The New Interpreter's Study Bible*, notes that the imagery of the beasts represents "the historical sequence of Gentile kingdoms" up through the divided Greek empire of Alexander the Great.[93] Though "the traditional interpretation is that the *Son of Man* is the Messiah," observes Henze, "modern scholars understand the Son of Man to refer either to the faithful Jews, or . . . an angelic being."[94] After the fulfillment of the prophesied judgment pronounced on the Greeks, who were currently persecuting the Jews when the book of Daniel is believed to have been written, the kingdoms of the world would be given to the Jews or to the unidentified, human-like angel himself who would reign for all time (Dan. 7:14).

Modern scholars contend, therefore, that Daniel's expression, "one like *a* son of man," had no messianic import to Jews at the time. According to James Dunn, "There is no evidence that there existed prior to Christianity a belief in a heavenly Son of Man who would appear from heaven as Israel's Messiah; so far as we can tell it was Christianity (Jesus or the first Christians) who made the first identification of the 'son of man' in Daniel's vision as a particular individual."[95]

Many references in the New Testament designating Christ as the "Son of Man" (Mark 2:10, 28; 14:61–62; Rev. 1:13) appear to be linked to Daniel's prophecy. According to New Testament scholar F. F. Bruce, "when Jesus spoke of the Son of man, he meant 'the one like a son of man' to whom was given 'dominion and glory and kingdom, that all peoples, nations, and languages should serve him.'"[96] Thus, what was a reference in the Old Testament to "one like a son of man" or to a human-looking being, likely symbolizing God's kingdom, was applied in the New Testament to Christ, signifying the role he was perceived to have had in setting up this kingdom in the last days.[97]

One interesting Old Testament reference to "the son of man" that was applied to Christ in the New Testament is Psalms 8:4–5: "What is man, that thou art mindful of him? and the son of man, that thou visitest him? For thou hast made him a little lower than the angels, and hast crowned him with glory and honour." This is a Hebrew parallelism in which "man" and "son of man" are used synonymously. The passage is generally considered to be referring to the fact that humans are created with a status just below the angels and are crowned with glory and honor. This is also at least one LDS interpretation of the passage, as evidenced by the footnote in the 1979 LDS edition of the Bible, which points to "man, potential to become like Heavenly Father" in the LDS Topical Guide.[98] What makes this passage interesting is that it is cited in the New Testament (Heb. 2:6–10) as though the "son of man" were an explicit reference to Christ.

The title "Son of Man" appears nowhere in the Book of Mormon. In the book of Moses, which is the earliest place it appears in latter-day scripture, it seems to allude to the eternal relationship Christ has with the Father, much like the title "Only Begotten Son" (see Moses 7:47, 54–56, 65). A half century later, third LDS Church President John Taylor saw the title more in the traditional sense of referring to Christ's kinship with mortals. According to Taylor, "As the Son of Man, He endured all that it was possible for flesh and blood to endure; as the Son of God He triumphed over all, and forever ascended to the right hand of God."[99]

Subsequently, as the Son of Man became interpreted more in terms of the Son of God, some authorities expressed concern that equating man with God may elicit controversy outside the Church. In the early twentieth century, Anthon H. Lund, then a counselor to Joseph F. Smith, reviewed a manuscript by James E. Talmage who "[made] the statement that the Son of God is called the 'Son of Man' because God is a man and He is the father of Jesus! The President felt the effect that it would have on the work to emphasize the fact that God has been passing through man's estate, that the cry would be raised that we worship a man." When Lund transmitted this message to Talmage the next day, Talmage, a future apostle, "believed he was right in his conception of the Son of Man, but was willing to cut that out of his discourse."[100] By the end of the twentieth century, this view was more openly avowed. Bruce R. McConkie declared, "The sectarian world has falsely assumed that the more than 70 New Testament references to Christ as the Son of Man have a similar meaning, that is, that they convey the thought of his manhood rather than of his Divinity."[101]

Christ as Jehovah

Latter-day Saints consider "Jehovah" to be Christ's eternal name, especially the name by which he was known in his preexistent state. According to Bruce R. McConkie, "Christ is Jehovah; they are one and the same Person."[102] Thus, Saints generally assume that all occurrences of "Jehovah" in the scriptures are references to Christ. This perspective, however, is not shared by many LDS scholars. BYU Old Testament professor Keith Meservy, for example, wrote in the June 2002 *Ensign* that "in at least three Old Testament passages it appears that LORD [i.e., Jehovah] applies to Heavenly Father, not Jesus Christ: Ps. 2:7, 110:1; Isa. 53:10."[103]

In the Old Testament, the Hebrew *Jehovah* or *Yahweh* is the name-title applied to God, meaning "self-existing one." In Hebrew, this name is spelled with four letters, called the Divine Tetragrammaton, which are usually represented in English as YHWH or JHVH, as ancient written Hebrew had no vowels. In the KJV, Old Testament, "Jehovah" is usually translated "LORD" (upper-cased), and was used interchangeably with Elohim or God. Deuteronomy 6:4

reads, "Hear, O Israel: The LORD [*Jehovah*] our God [*Elohim*] is one LORD [*Jehovah*]." This declaration, known as the *shema*, was and is an important Jewish affirmation of faith. On the other hand, in Greek YHWH is rendered with the generic *kurios* ("Lord") out of a sense of reverence for the divine name. "Jehovah" therefore does not appear in the English New Testament which was translated from Greek.

Among Christian preachers and theologians at the time of Joseph Smith, "Jehovah" was generally understood as just another name for God, which, from a trinitarian perspective, consisted of the Father, Son, and Holy Ghost. Thus, noted Methodist theologian Richard Watson explained that any one of them can appropriately be referred to as Jehovah—just as each can be thought of as God.[104] It is in this sense that certain trinitarians believed that it was actually Christ who appeared to prophets in the Old Testament under the assumed name of Jehovah or the Lord God.

In early Mormon scripture, "Jehovah" was also used as a generic reference to God. LDS scholar Boyd Kirkland explains:

> With the interchangeability of the roles of the Father and the Son in earliest Mormon theology, it is impossible to identify specifically Joseph's first few Jehovah references as either the Father or the Son. However, after the identities of the Father and the Son were more carefully differentiated in Mormon theology around 1835, Joseph clearly began to use the divine name Jehovah to refer to the Father. Significantly, he apparently never specifically identified Jehovah as Jesus, nor Jehovah as the Son of Elohim.[105]

The Book of Mormon has only two occurrences of "Jehovah," both of which appear to refer to God rather than specifically to Christ (2 Ne. 22:2; Moro. 10:34). The first time "Jehovah" appears in the Doctrine and Covenants is at the dedicatory prayer of the Kirtland Temple in March 1836 (D&C 109:34, 42, 56, 68). In this prayer to the "Holy Father, in the name of Jesus Christ" (v. 4), Joseph pleads, "O Jehovah, have mercy on this people" (v. 34). And again, "Deliver thou, O Jehovah, we beseech thee" (v. 42). Although it seems clear that these petitions to Jehovah are directed to the Father, McConkie, in conformity with the Christ-as-Jehovah paradigm, explains that these petitions are actually "accolades of praise" given to Christ and are cloaked "in the language of prayer."[106]

Kirkland notes that, after Joseph Smith studied Hebrew in 1835–36, he began using "Elohim" to designate the Supreme Being and "also began to use Jehovah more often . . . . [and] used them interchangeably as epithets for God the Father."[107] A prayer Joseph Smith recorded in 1842 illustrates this: "O Thou . . . eternal, omnipotent, omniscient, and omnipresent Jehovah—God—Thou Elohim, that sittest, as saith the Psalmist, 'enthroned in heaven,' look down upon Thy servant Joseph at this time; and let faith on the name of Thy Son Jesus Christ . . . be conferred upon him."[108] Thus, "Jehovah" was simply another name for God.

Surprisingly, the first recorded instance of "Jehovah" being applied uniquely to Christ doesn't occur until 1885.[109] It has since become recognized in Mormonism as Christ's premortal name and the name by which he was known in the Old Testament.

Concerning the identity of Jehovah in the Old Testament, Mormon scholar Lowell Bennion mused: "When Christ was on the earth he taught his disciples to worship the Father. It doesn't seem logical to me that Christ would ask in the Old Testament to be worshipped, and not have the Father worshipped as in other scriptures, in other dispensations. . . . [The] Jews and their Old Testament ancestors considered Elohim and Jehovah to be two names for God which both refer to a single deity."[110] The modern use of "Jehovah" as an exclusive designation for the premortal Christ is a convention made official through a doctrinal exposition, "Christ as the Father and the Son," published by the First Presidency in 1916.[111] This use, however, is a twentieth-century development that did not exist in early Mormonism, neither is it evident in LDS scripture.

Christ as the Father

In LDS theology, "Father" is applied to Christ in three distinctive ways enumerated in the 1916 First Presidency statement:

1. Father of heaven and earth in the sense of the creator (Ether 4:7; Alma 11:38; Mosiah 15:4).

2. Father of eternal life or spiritual rebirth (Mosiah 5:7).

3. Father by divine investiture of authority; "so far as power, authority, and Godship are concerned, His words and acts were and are those of the Father" (D&C 29:1, 42, 46; Moses 1:1–6).[112]

The only Old Testament occurrence of "Father" that Christians (including Latter-day Saints) view as a reference to Christ is Isaiah 9:6, "Unto us a child is born . . . and his name shall be called . . . the everlasting Father." Although some 250 references to Isaiah can be found in the New Testament to support Christian themes, this passage is never once cited in spite of its wide recognition today among Christians as a prophecy fulfilled in Christ.[113] Neither is "Father" ever applied to Christ in the New Testament. Instead, Jesus referred to God as "my Father, and your Father" (John 20:17). It is not until the post-

Apostolic era that Christ was called "Father," and it is this single passage in Isaiah that apparently became the justification for its use.[114]

Like many biblical scholars, J. J. M. Roberts, professor of Old Testament literature at Princeton Theological Seminary, sees Isaiah 9:6 as "an oracle for the coronation of a Judean king, probably Hezekiah."[115] According to Roberts, this passage uses the same divine-sonship language found in Psalms 2:7 to announce the coronation of the king. The epithets bestowed on the king in Isaiah 9:6 (Wonderful, Counselor, The mighty God, The everlasting Father) are "coronation names like those given Egyptian kings at their accession."[116]

At the time of Joseph Smith, trinitarians used "Everlasting Father" or "Eternal Father" to signify Christ's identity with the Father in the sense of Jesus's possessing the same nature as the Father. A debated issue ever since the patristic era was whether Christ, being God's own Son, participated in God's eternal nature and substance and was therefore completely—ontologically and functionally—one with the Father, or whether he was created and therefore ontologically different from God and thus a finite mediator. For Methodists, Christ partook of the Father's nature and was therefore, in his divine nature, identical with the Father. As one Methodist elder wrote in 1826, "Jesus Christ in his divine nature is the Eternal Father."[117]

In the Book of Mormon, Christ is called "the Father and the Son" (Mosiah 15:3; Morm. 9:12; Ether 3:14) in a sense that seems to be referring to two different aspects of his nature—that of his divine nature and that of his human nature. As to his divine nature, the Book of Mormon states that Christ is called "the Father, because he was conceived by the power of God" (Mosiah 15:3). Today, Latter-day Saints would say that his conception "by the power of God" is why he is called the Son, not the Father. This is different from any of the three ways explained in the First Presidency exposition cited above. It is noteworthy that, after May 1833, perhaps as the result of the Father and Son becoming more differentiated in LDS thought, Joseph Smith ceased using the term "Father" when referring to Christ.[118]

The Book of Mormon additionally refers to Christ as the Father in the sense of being the creator of heaven and earth (2 Ne. 25:12; Mosiah 3:8, 7:27, 15:4; Alma 11:38–39; Hel. 14:12, 16:18; Ether 4:7). This title, however, is not attributed to Christ separately and distinctly from God the Father. The Book of Mormon speaks of a single God with Christ as merely the embodied manifestation of the one Eternal God. In Mosiah 15:4, for example, Jesus Christ and God the Father are identified as "one God, yea, the very Eternal Father of heaven and of earth." Thus, to say that Christ is the Father of heaven and earth is the same as saying he is the one and only "Lord omnipotent" (Mosiah 3:21). John Wesley and other evangelicals similarly taught that, since Christ was the creator of all things under the Father, he can appropriately be considered identical to the "Everlasting Father."[119]

To summarize, references to Christ as the Father appear nowhere in the Bible. Early LDS use of "Father" in reference to Christ seems to have drawn upon contemporary trinitarianism which saw Christ as being the Father because the Father dwelt in him. Significantly, after May 1833 when the Father and Son became more differentiated in LDS thought, the Prophet never again used the term "Father" when speaking of Christ. Thereafter, "Father" was a term he reserved only for God the Father. It was nearly a century later that "Father" became a term having application to Christ in the three ways noted in the First Presidency exposition cited above. This doctrinal exposition seems to have been necessitated by references to Christ as Father in the Book of Mormon—references which would otherwise appear to reflect a modalistic concept of God.

Christ as God of the Old Testament

Current LDS teachings are emphatic in declaring Christ to be the God of the Old Testament. Bruce R. McConkie deemed it a "fact that Jehovah-Christ is the God of Israel" and "that he and not the Father spoke to all the ancient prophets."[120]

As pointed out in Chapter 6, with the two exceptions of the earliest Hebrew belief in a pantheon of gods and the ancient tradition that Yahweh was the Son of the Most High God *El*, there is little indication after the exile that the Israelites understood the God they worshipped to actually be the Son of God. For them, there was one God above all and before whom there were to be no other gods.

Even the New Testament speaks of God the Father, not Christ, as the God of the Old Testament. Christ referred to his Father as "my God, and your God" (John 20:17). The apostle Peter equated the God of ancient Israel with God the Father stating, "The God of Abraham, and of Isaac, and of Jacob, the God of our fathers, hath glorified his Son Jesus" (Acts 3:13). Similarly, Hebrews 1:1–2 starts out, "God, who at sundry times and in divers manners spake in time past unto the fathers by the prophets, hath in these last days spoken unto us by his Son." If Christ was the Son of the God of the Old Testament, it would be incongruous to speak of him as also the God of the Old Testament.

One of the distinctive features of the Gospel of John, in comparison to the other gospels, is its high Christology in which Christ is elevated to deity. In one of the earliest commentaries on John (ca. 240), Origen makes the point that, while the other gospels describe Jesus's great works, "none of them clearly spoke of his divinity, as John does."[121] Christ is depicted in John 1:1–4 as being in the beginning with God as the creator of all things. In this Gospel, Jesus states: "I and my Father are one" (John 10:30). When Thomas touched the resurrected Jesus, John records that he exclaimed: "My Lord and my God" (John 20:28). In John, Jesus boldly proclaims to the Jews that he was before Abraham as the "I am" (John 8:58). These declarations don't necessarily imply that John saw Christ as being fully God since John also recorded statements of Jesus that seem to indicate his inferiority to the Father, such as, "The Father is greater than I (John 14:28)," and the Father is "the only true God" (John 17:3).

Given the strong, Jewish, monotheistic background of New Testament writers, scholars question whether any of them perceived Christ to be fully God. Many scholars view New Testament expressions of Christ's divinity as metaphorical. LDS scholar John Tvedtnes points out that even "Emmanuel" (God [*El*] is with us), ascribed to Jesus in Matthew 1:23, should not necessarily be taken literally because "a number of Old Testament personalities bore theophoric names but were also not God."[122] Consider some of the many other Old Testament names containing *El* (God): Samu*el*, Gabri*el*, Micha*el*, Jo*el*, *El*izabeth, *El*ijah, *El*isha, Isra*el*, Ezeki*el*, and Nathani*el*. Even John's pronouncement of "the Word" being in the beginning with God may not have been intended to mean that Jesus himself was God from the beginning. According to Colin Brown, general editor of *The New International Dictionary of New Testament Theology*, "It is a common but patent misreading of the opening of John's Gospel to read it as if it said: 'In the beginning was the *Son* . . . and the *Son* was God' (John 1:1)."[123]

At the time of Joseph Smith, opinions differed about whether the God of the Old Testament was Christ or God the Father. Many leading trinitarians maintained that it was the person of Christ who appeared as God in Old Testament times (see, for example, Gen. 3:8; 17:1; 28:12–13; 32:24; Ex. 3:2).[124] Unitarians, on the other hand, opposed this view, insisting that it was God the Father who was the God of the Old Testament. Because they rejected the idea that Christ was anything more than a man, they could not believe that he preexisted as the Israelite God.

Modern Mormon scriptures are somewhat ambivalent about the identity of the God of the Old Testament, speaking at times as though it is God the Father and at other times as though it is Christ. This equivocation may be partially due to the early LDS modalistic perspective of the Godhead which makes no essential distinction between the Father and the Son.[125] In the Book of Mormon, Jesus isn't *a* God or even ontologically distinct from God, but instead is the "very God" (Morm. 3:21). The Book of Mormon was written as a witness "that JESUS is the CHRIST, the ETERNAL GOD" (title page).

As Mormons began to embrace tritheism after 1843, they increasingly spoke of God the Father as the God of the Old Testament. This tradition can be seen particularly in the teachings of Brigham Young.[126] It wasn't until after the turn of the twentieth century that the role of Christ as God of the Old Testament became so strongly affirmed. Apostle James E. Talmage helped solidify this view in his 1915 *Jesus the Christ*: "We claim scriptural authority for the assertion that Jesus Christ was . . . the God of the Old Testament."[127] All scripture, both ancient and modern, that has God dealing with man prior to the birth of Jesus is now interpreted as Christ speaking with "divine investiture of authority."[128] So when "the Lord God Almighty" appears to Moses (Moses 1:3) and tells him all about his "Only Begotten Son" (Moses 1:6–33), we are to understand that it is actually Christ speaking as though he is the Father. According to Joseph Fielding Smith, God the Father has never spoken to man since the fall except to introduce his Son.[129]

Notes

1. "The Living Christ: The Testimony of the Apostles, The Church of Jesus Christ of Latter-day Saints," 2–3.

2. Josh McDowell, *The New Evidence that Demands a Verdict*, contains a detailed list of what he considers to be Old Testament allusions to Christ.

3. Raymond E. Brown, *The Birth of the Messiah*, 146.

4. Kent P. Jackson, "I Have a Question," 66.

5. Joseph Smith inserted this New Testament understanding (that Abraham saw Christ) back into the Old Testament account itself (JST Gen. 15:12).

6. Martin. Luther, *A Commentary on St. Paul's Epistle to the Galatians*, 157–58.

7. Pseudepigraphic works written within the first few centuries after Christ also claim that Adam and other ancients knew of the details of Christ's life. John A. Tvedtnes, "Knowledge of Christ to Come," 159–60.

8. Brent Lee Metcalfe, "The Priority of Mosiah: A Prelude to Book of Mormon Exegesis," 426; George Whitefield, *The Works of the Reverend George Whitefield M. A.*, 50; see also the Christmas carol, "Hark! The Herald Angels Sing." Brant Gardner, Second Witness, 5:565, argues that the substitution of "Son" for "Sun" in 3 Nephi could have been a scribal error because they are homophones. That it was left this way in future versions and even appears in two other places (Ether 9:22; 2 Ne. 26:9) suggests, however, that the spelling was intentional.

9. For references to Christ's birth date, see Harold B. Lee, *Conference Report*, April 1973, 4; Spencer W. Kimball, *Conference Report*, April 1975, 4. This traditional LDS dating of Christ's birth has been challenged by LDS biblical scholars who concur with the dating given by secular scholars. S. Kent

Brown, C. Wilfred Griggs, and H. Kimball Hansen, "Review of *April Sixth* by John C. Lefgren," 375–83.

10. Historical records show that Herod the Great died in 4 B.C., so if Christ was born during Herod's reign, he couldn't have been born later than 4 B.C. This fact was even acknowledged by Bruce R. McConkie, *The Mortal Messiah: From Bethlehem to Calvary*, 1:350.

11. Paul L. Maier, "The Times and Places of Jesus."

12. According to Joseph F. Smith, "We would scarcely think the Lord would make any mistake about dates. Least of all he who was born on that day, and on that day thirty-three years later was crucified." B. H. Roberts, *Outlines of Ecclesiastical History*, 17.

13. Brown, *The Birth of the Messiah*, 65.

14. Thomas A. Wayment, *To Teach as Jesus Taught*, 166 note 2.

15. Prior to Jacob's time, Jesus was known in the Book of Mormon only as the Messiah, although an anachronistic reference to "Christ" appeared in the 1830 first edition (1 Ne. 12:13; modern versification). In subsequent editions, this term was changed to "Messiah." Obviously, if Jacob was the first Book of Mormon prophet to have the name "Christ" revealed to him, Nephi's use of the name "Christ" in his record would be problematic because he wrote prior to Jacob.

16. Adam Clarke, *Commentary on the Bible*, s.v. Isaiah 61.

17. James A. Sanders, "From Isaiah 61 to Luke 4," 54.

18. Phillip P. Jenson notes that "when we do find a royal figure portrayed in various texts, it often appears to be a short-term prediction, referring to someone shortly to be born. Specifically, the term 'messiah' is never used to describe a future saviour figure in the Old Testament." Phillip P. Jenson, "Models of Prophetic Prediction and Matthew's Quotation of Micah 5:2," 205

19. J. J. M. Roberts, *The Bible and the Ancient Near East*, 376.

20. Ibid.

21. Joachim Becker, *Messianic Expectation in the Old Testament*, 93.

22. Quoted in Stephen E. Thompson, "Messiah in Context," 76.

23. O'Collins, *Christology: A Biblical, Historical, and Systematic Study of Jesus*, 28. Catholic theologian Hans Küng asserts that "even more conservative exegetes conclude that Jesus himself did not assume any title implying Messianic identity: not 'Messiah,' nor 'Son of David,' nor 'Son,' nor 'Son of God.'" Such titles were conferred upon him by his disciples after his death and resurrection. Hans Küng, *On Being a Christian*, 289.

24. Gerald O'Collins, *Christology*, 117.

25. Alister E. McGrath, *Christian Theology: An Introduction*, 352.

26. Brown, *The Birth of the Messiah*, 136.

27. O'Collins, *Christology*, 117.

28. Heim, "The Perfect King," 224.

29. What makes this passage interesting is that, according to scholars, it appears to be an admission by Christ that he was not of Davidic descent. It is an example of a haggada or apparent contradiction within scriptures since most New Testament evidence points to Christ as a descendent of David. Brown, *The Birth of the Messiah*, 509–11.

30. Ibid., 509; Num. 36:2.

31. Bruce R. McConkie, "Who Shall Declare His Generation?" 554.

32. Ethan Smith, *View of the Trinity: A Treatise on the Character of*

Jesus Christ, and on the Trinity in Unity of the Godhead . . . , 27. According to Smith, "The sense of the passage we learn from a parallel passage, Psalm 22:30" which states that "a seed shall serve him and it shall be accounted to the Lord for a generation." For a Mesoamerican context see Brant Gardner, *Second Witness*, 3:303.

33. Clarke, *Commentary on the Bible*, s.v. Daniel 3.
34. Jackson, "I Have a Question," 66.
35. Karen Armstrong, *A History of God: The 4000-Year Quest of Judaism, Christianity, and Islam*, 80.
36. Andrew T. Lincoln, "'Born of the Virgin Mary': Creedal Affirmation and Critical Reading," 89.
37. Ibid.
38. James D. G. Dunn, *Christology in the Making*, 36.
39. Ibid., 36. Dunn adds: "Whether they thought of him as already God's son during his earthly ministry we cannot say. But even if they did recall his 'abba relationship' with God while on earth, they nevertheless regarded Jesus's resurrection as introducing him into a relationship with God decisively new, eschatologically distinct, perhaps we should even say qualitatively different from what he had enjoyed before."
40. Gerd Theissen, *A Theory of Primitive Christian Religion*, 52. An exception to this tradition was the emperor Domitian, who was proclaimed a god while still reigning.
41. Brown, *The Birth of the Messiah*, 137.
42. Bart Ehrman, *Lost Christianities: The Battle for Scripture and the Faiths We Never Knew*, 222.
43. Lincoln, "Born of the Virgin Mary," 92.
44. Ibid., 93.
45. Elijah Bailey, *America in Primitive Trinitarianism Examined and Defended*, 92.
46. Caleb Alexander, *An Essay on the Real Deity of Jesus Christ* . . . , 41.
47. McGrath, *Christian Theology*, 382.
48. Jacob Moore, "Divinity," 291.
49. Ibid., 290.
50. Ibid., 291–92.
51. Ibid., 291.
52. Kurt Widmer, *Mormonism and the Nature of God: A Theological Evolution, 1830–1915*, 36.
53. *Lectures on Faith*, 5:2.
54. Joseph Smith Jr., "Baptism," *Times and Seasons* 3 (September 1, 1842): 905.
55. The reference in *History of the Church,* 5:556 to Jesus as "the only begotten of the Father according to the flesh" is a later insertion and doesn't appear in any of the original accounts. See Andrew F. Ehat and Lyndon W. Cook, *The Words of Joseph Smith*, 243–47.
56. As late as 1840, certain Mormon elders were preaching an adoptionistic view of Christ's sonship stating that, in the New Testament, "Jesus Christ was never acknowledged to be the Son of God, till after his baptism," making it a covenant relationship with God. Defending this position, Elder Samuel Bennett argued that Luke 1:35 states only that Jesus "*shall* [i.e., not necessar-

ily at birth] be called the Son of God." Samuel Bennett, *A Few Remarks by Way of Reply to an Anonymous Scribbler* . . . , 6; emphasis in original.

57. Joseph Fielding Smith, *Answers to Gospel Questions*, 5:33.

58. Joseph Henry Thayer, *A Greek-English Lexicon*, s.v. "monogenes."

59. W. E. Vine, *Vine's Expository Dictionary*, 3:140–41.

60. *The Book of Common Prayer and Other Rites and Ceremonies of the Church* . . . , 43.

61. John Mannock, *The Poor Man's Catechism; or, the Christian Doctrine Explained*, 3. For a discussion of the meaning of Moses's designation as "son of God" in the book of Moses, see Chapter 7.

62. Rodney Turner, "The Doctrine of the Firstborn and Only Begotten," 117 note 37.

63. Ibid., 109–110.

64. Quoted in "Letters from W. W. Phelps to his wife, Sally Phelps."

65. See, for example, James E. Talmage, *Jesus the Christ: A Study of the Messiah and His Mission According to Holy Scriptures Both Ancient and Modern*, 38; Joseph Fielding Smith, *Doctrines of Salvation: Compiled Sermons of Joseph Fielding Smith*, 1:18; Brigham Young, July 8, 1860, *Journal of Discourses*, 8:115; Ezra Taft Benson, *The Teachings of Ezra Taft Benson*, 7; Bruce R. McConkie, *The Promised Messiah: The First Coming of Christ*, 468.

66. Bruce R. McConkie, *Mormon Doctrine*, 546.

67. James R. Clark, *Messages of the First Presidency*, 4:327–30. A minority voice cautioned against inferring a sexual relationship between God and Mary. Harold B. Lee, *Teachings of Harold B. Lee*, 14

68. See, for example, McConkie, *The Mortal Messiah*, 1:319; Andrew C. Skinner, "Birth of Jesus Christ," 2:729.

69. Brown, *The Birth of the Messiah*, 137.

70. Eleanor Colton, "Virgin Birth," 4:1510.

71. Brown, *The Birth of the Messiah*, 145.

72. Apostle Marion G. Romney commented, "When Isaiah used the word virgin, he was saying that a woman who had not known a man should bear a son. The modern translators say, 'Behold a young woman etc. . .' (Revised Standard Version). You see, they do not believe that Christ was divine." Marion G. Romney, *Look to God and Live*, 39.

73. Brown, *The Birth of the Messiah*, 147.

74. Ibid., 148. According to Susan Ackerman, scholars generally understand the "young woman" to be King Ahaz's wife or perhaps even Isaiah's. Susan Ackerman, "Isaiah," 968

75. Bruce R. McConkie, *Doctrinal New Testament Commentary*, 1:82.

76. Joseph F. Smith, *Gospel Doctrine: Selections from the Sermons and Writings of Joseph F. Smith*, 70.

77. Orson Pratt, November 12, 1876, *Journal of Discourses*, 18:290.

78. Brent L. Top, *The Life Before*, 28.

79. G. Kittel and G. Friedrich, *Theological Dictionary of the New Testament*, 6:876–81.

80. George E. Ladd, *A Theology of the New Testament*, 459. For a similar explanation see Clark, "Words Relating to the Lord Jesus Christ," 84.

81. Joseph F. Smith, quoted in James E. Talmage, *Articles of Faith*, 472.

82. James D. Tabor, "The Message and Mission of Paul."

83. John A. Tvedtnes, "Review of Michael T. Griffith, *One Lord, One Faith: Writings of the Early Christian Fathers as Evidences of the Restoration*, 37. Regarding the profuse use of proof-texts in Hebrews, biblical scholar George Wesley Buchanan states: "In the first two chapters alone, the author of Hebrews understood Jesus, the Messiah, to be the subject of statements originally made about some unknown Jewish or Israelite king being enthroned, the children of Israel, Solomon, a warrior king, God, and man." George Wesley Buchanan, *To the Hebrews: Translation, Comment and Conclusions*, 30:xxii.

84. Eduard Lohse, *Colossians and Philemon*, 48–49.

85. Kittel and Friedrich, *Theological Dictionary of the New Testament*, 6:879. Colin Brown similarly states that *prototokos* here is "a title for the mediator of creation." Colin Brown, *The New International Dictionary of New Testament Theology*, 668.

86. John A. Tvedtnes, "A Much Needed Book that Needs Much," 37.

87. Orson Pratt, *Prophetic Almanac for 1845*, 7–8.

88. Eugene England, ed., "George Laub's Nauvoo Journal," 178.

89. William W. Phelps, "The Answer," 758.

90. Joseph Fielding Smith, *Answers to Gospel Questions*, 1:9.

91. James E. Talmage, *Conference Report*, April 1915, 122. Of course, Psalms 8:4–5 is another Old Testament reference to the "Son of Man" that was used as proof-text for Christ in Hebrews 2:6–10.

92. F. F. Bruce, *New Testament History*, 130.

93. Matthias Henze, "Daniel," 1243–44.

94. Ibid., 1244.

95. Dunn, *Christology in the Making*, 252.

96. F. F. Bruce, *Paul: Apostle of the Heart Set Free*, 57. Of course, if the "one like a son of man" is not Christ, then is the "Ancient of days" in the same passage really Adam (see D&C 27:11)? Scholars interpret the "Ancient of days," who gave dominion and glory to the one like a son of man, as God.

97. See Craig A. Evans, "Jesus' Self-Designation: 'The Son of Man' and the Recognition of His Divinity," 29–47.

98. Latter-day Saints further point out that the correct translation of the Hebrew should be "gods" instead of "angels" (see footnote to this verse, 1979 LDS edition of the Bible). In the New Testament application of this passage to Christ, the Greek Old Testament (i.e., the Septuagint) is used which translates the Hebrew "gods" as "angels" and builds a whole sermon around Christ's relationship to the angels.

99. John Taylor, *The Mediation and Atonement*, 151–52.

100. Lund diary, May 5–6, 1915, in John P. Hatch, ed., *Anthon H. Lund, Danish Apostle: Diaries of Anthon H. Lund, 1890–1921*, 577.

101. McConkie, *Mormon Doctrine*, 742. Contrary to McConkie's assertion, most non-LDS scholars actually do see a reference to Christ's divinity in New Testament uses of the title "Son of Man."

102. Ibid., 392.

103. Keith H. Meservy, "Lord = Jehovah," 29 note 3.

104. Richard Watson, *Theological Institutes; or A View of the Evidences, Doctrines, Morals, and Institutions of Christianity*, 1:466–75.

105. Boyd Kirkland, "The Development of the Mormon Doctrine of God," 37. D&C 110:3 refers to Christ's voice being "as the sound of the rushing of great waters, even the voice of Jehovah," but this rare association of Christ with Jehovah doesn't necessarily mean that Jehovah is Christ's name. Jehovah seems to be used to emphasize the magnitude of Christ's voice as the voice of Almighty God.

106. McConkie, *The Promised Messiah*, 337.

107. Kirkland, "The Development of the Mormon Doctrine of God," 37.

108. *History of the Church*, 5:127.

109. Kirkland, "The Development of the Mormon Doctrine of God," 41. He quotes a sermon by Franklin D. Richards in August 30, 1885: "His [Jesus's] name when he was a spiritual being, during the first half of the existence of the earth, before he was made flesh and blood, was Jehovah."

110. Lowell L. Bennion, "The Mormon Christianizing of the Old Testament: A Response," 40.

111. Quoted in Talmage, *Articles of Faith*, 465–73.

112. Ibid.

113. John Sawyer, *The Fifth Gospel: Isaiah in the History of Christianity*, 21, 31.

114. Ibid., 31.

115. J. J. M. Roberts, "Isaiah," 1025. See also Daniel Schibler, "Isaiah 1–12 and 28–33," 100–101.

116. Roberts, "Isaiah," 1026.

117. Bailey, *America in Primitive Trinitarianism*, 117.

118. Dan Vogel, "The Earliest Mormon Concept of God," 26. See also Kirkland, "The Development of the Mormon Doctrine of God," 36.

119. Bailey, *America in Primitive Trinitarianism*, 127.

120. McConkie, *The Promised Messiah*, 122.

121. Origen, quoted in Elaine Pagels, *Beyond Belief: The Secret Gospel of Thomas*, 37.

122. Tvedtnes, "A Much Needed Book," 41.

123. Colin Brown, "Trinity and Incarnation: In Search of Contemporary Orthodoxy," 89.

124. This was the view of famed Protestant pastors, Isaac Watts, Philip Doddridge, and many other religionists of the time. Hannah Adams, *A Dictionary of All Religions and Religious Denominations*, 227–29.

125. See Melodie Moench Charles, "The Book of Mormon Christology," 99.

126. Kirkland, "The Development of the Mormon Doctrine of God," 50 note 15; See, for example, the *Journal of Discourses* for these Brigham Young addresses: July 24, 1853, 1:238; April 6, 1853, 2:30; October 21, 1860, 8:228; March 2, 1862, 9:240; February 23, 1862, 286; February 10, 1867, 11:327; November 17, 1867, 12:99; February 20, 1870, 13:236; May 8, 1870, 14:41.

127. Talmage, *Jesus the Christ*, 32.

128. Talmage, *Articles of Faith*, 424.

129. Joseph Fielding Smith, *Doctrines of Salvation*, 1:26–27.

9

The Holy Ghost

The Holy Ghost is the third member of the godhead in both Latter-day Saint and traditional Christian theology. As discussed in Chapter 6, conceptions regarding this member of the Godhead have evolved gradually since Old Testament times. In the Old Testament, the Spirit was at work in the creation of the world and in prophecy. This Spirit was God's influence and the manifestation of God's power in the earth. In the New Testament, the Holy Ghost was still mainly an influence but was also spoken of as God's agent in bestowing gifts and sanctifying powers on believers. It is not until after New Testament times that the Holy Ghost comes to be generally seen as a person. What distinguishes the LDS doctrine of the Holy Ghost from that of traditional Christianity is the belief that the Holy Ghost is both a begotten human spirit "that has the form and likeness of a man"[1] and "a God in his own right."[2]

Old Testament

The Old Testament doesn't use the term "Holy Ghost," but instead uses "the Spirit of the Lord," which, according to scholars, is spoken of as an influence rather than a personage or conscious entity. The term is feminine in Hebrew (*ruah*) and neuter in Greek (*pneuma*),[3] and denotes wind, the breath of life, or the divine inspiration that comes upon prophets. Gerald O'Collins notes that "the 'spirit' was a way of articulating the divine activity and revelation in the world."[4] L. A. Bushinski, writing in the *New Catholic Encyclopedia*, concurs: "The Old Testament clearly does not envisage God's spirit as a person. . . . God's spirit is simply God's power. If it is sometimes represented as being distinct from God, it is because the breath of Yahweh acts exteriorly."[5]

Unlike the New Testament, nowhere does the Old Testament speak of gifts of the Spirit or of receiving a testimony or witness of eternal truths through the power of this Spirit. The most visual manifestation of the Spirit in humans is in connection with prophetic utterances. A prophet's credentials rested upon an endowment of the Spirit (Isa. 61:1, Ezek. 2:1–2, Micah 3:8, Zech. 7:12) causing his words to be "God-breathed."

New Testament

This concept of the Holy Ghost as God's influence rather than an individual entity persisted until at least New Testament times. James D. G. Dunn notes, "At the time of Jesus, the divine 'spirit' or 'Spirit' was not yet thought of in Judaism even as a semi-independent divine agent."[6] The New Testament introduced a new way of thinking about the Holy Ghost, referring to it as a sort of proxy for God that was sent to renew and strengthen the Saints with its attendant gifts (Luke 24:49, Acts 2:33). Even then, the Spirit doesn't appear to have been viewed as a person. Bushinski in the *New Catholic Encyclopedia* continues: "The majority of New Testament texts reveal God's spirit as some*thing*, not some*one*; this is especially seen in the parallelism between the spirit and the power of God."[7]

It is only in the Gospel of John, one of the last-written books of the New Testament, that the Holy Ghost begins to be depicted in more personal terms. Here, the Comforter is spoken of using the pronoun "he" (John 14:16–17; 15:26; 16:8, 13–16). What is lost in translation, however, is the fact that the masculine pronoun in these instances is necessitated because the Greek word *paraclete*, which is usually translated as "Comforter," happens to be a masculine noun.[8] Thus, it is the *word* "Comforter" that is masculine, and not necessarily the Holy Ghost itself. Interestingly, the word translated "spirit" (as in the Holy Spirit) is the gender-neutral *pneuma*, which is referenced in the New Testament with the neutral pronoun "it." Given the non-personal way that the Holy Ghost appears in New Testament writings, one gets the impression that it wasn't generally regarded as a person.[9]

Early Nineteenth-Century Christianity

At the time of Joseph Smith, Christians usually spoke of the Holy Ghost in a manner similar to that of the New Testament—as a divine influence or agent that inspires and vitalizes. While centuries of creedal development had also institutionalized the belief that the Holy Ghost is a person, this designation did not mean that the Holy

Ghost has a human form. It merely denoted a conscious center of intelligence, will, and action.

While traditional trinitarians believed that the Holy Ghost is a person, binitarians and Unitarians saw the Spirit as merely a manifestation of God's power. Unitarian minister Noah Worcester explained in 1812 that if "God is represented by the metaphor of the natural sun . . . then the rays . . . which emanate or proceed from the sun, are an emblem of the Holy Spirit, which proceedeth from the Father. Like the rays of the sun, these Divine emanations . . . illuminate, quicken, invigorate and fructify."[10] Primitivist binitarian David Millard also called the Holy Ghost "a divine emanation of God."[11] As noted in Chapter 6, in the early 1800s even trinitarians had "acquired the habit of regarding the Holy Ghost as an emanation flowing from the Father and the Son, but not as being actually a person [i.e., a conscious entity] himself."[12]

Early Mormonism

The earliest LDS revelations and teachings speak of the Holy Ghost using traditional Christian terminology emphasizing its illuminating and quickening nature rather than traits that would identify it as a person. The Book of Mormon refers to the Holy Ghost as "it," not "he" (2 Ne. 32:5; Alma 34:38, 39:6), and early revelations in the Doctrine and Covenants similarly speak of the Holy Ghost as "it" in the sense of an influence (D&C 76:35, 88:3).

Some LDS commentators have pointed to a passage in 1 Nephi which speaks of the "Spirit of the Lord" appearing in "the form of a man" as evidence that early LDS scripture depicts the Holy Ghost as having a human form (1 Ne. 11:11).[13] This reading, however, is problematic because the same text speaks of the Holy Ghost as having "the form of a dove" just a few verses later (1 Ne. 11:27). If one assumes that Nephi's Spirit of the Lord was the Holy Ghost, then it seems that the Holy Ghost is not inherently just a personage in the form of a man, but can also be in the form of a dove, or perhaps whatever form it chooses.

Early LDS scriptures, in fact, indicate that the Holy Ghost assumed the form of a dove when it rested on the Savior at his baptism. This is in contrast to the current LDS teaching which asserts that the Holy Ghost descended *like* a dove—meaning that its descent was "calm, serene, and peaceful,"—but not that it had the actual "form" of a dove.[14] The Book of Mormon, however, states that the Spirit descended and abode on Christ "in the form of a dove" (1 Ne. 11:27, 2 Ne. 31:8). Similarly, a revelation given in 1833 confirms that the Holy Ghost appeared "in the form of a dove, and sat upon him" (D&C 93:15). This depiction is actually congruent with the account in

Luke 3:21–22, which has the Holy Ghost descending on Christ "in a bodily shape like a dove," or, as rendered less ambiguously in the J. B. Phillips's version, "in the bodily form of a dove." This portrayal of the Holy Ghost descending in the shape of a dove may reflect what scholars note as a more literalist tendency of Luke over his co-Gospel writers.

The evidence suggests that early Latter-day Saints understood the Holy Ghost to be a spiritual power or influence, not a personage. While Latter-day Saints now distinguish between the Holy Ghost, the influence of the Holy Ghost, and the light of Christ, such differentiation was unknown and unnecessary to the early Saints. The *Lectures on Faith* published in 1835 defined the Holy Ghost as the "mind" of God, noting that only the Father and the Son are "personages."[15] Today the "mind" of God would be equated with the light of Christ or influence of the Holy Spirit; not with the Holy Ghost itself.[16]

Nauvoo Period

The LDS doctrine of the Holy Ghost being an actual personage appears to have been first suggested by the Prophet in February 1841, when he spoke of the godhead saying that "the three were separate bod[ies]."[17] In March 1841, he differentiated between the Holy Ghost and the Father and Son saying, "The Son had a tabernicle & so had the father but the Holly [sic] Ghost is a personage of spirit without tabernicle."[18] Then, in January 1843, he pointedly stated that "the Holy Ghost is a personage in the form of a personage."[19] Again, in April 1843, as recorded by William Clayton, Joseph taught, "The Holy Ghost is a personage, and a person cannot have the personage of the H. G. in his heart. A man [may] receive the gifts of the H. G., and the H. G. may descend upon a man but not to tarry with him."[20]

This last statement is interesting because it explicitly declares that the personage of the Holy Ghost cannot dwell in a person's heart. When this statement was published much later as Doctrine and Covenants 130:22–23, it was reworded to give just the opposite meaning, so that the very reason why the Holy Ghost is a spirit is so that he *can* dwell in our hearts. According to Andrew F. Ehat and Lyndon W. Cook, "Neither the William Clayton Diary, the Joseph Smith Diary . . . , nor the *draft* Manuscript History of the Church . . . implies the phrasing of D&C 130:22: 'Were it not so [that the Holy Ghost is a spirit], the Holy Ghost could not dwell in us.' Originally the wording in the Manuscript History of the Church entry for this date was the same as in the original draft, but in the 1850s the Church historians reworded it to read the way it appears in the Doctrine and Covenants."[21] In current doctrinal discourse, this change makes little difference as it is generally taught that the Holy Ghost can only be in one place at one time, and that his influence is felt in one's heart through the medium of the light of Christ. However, if the Holy Ghost cannot or does not dwell personally in a person's heart—but only exerts his influence on the heart—, it is unclear why the Holy Ghost would need to be a spirit at all. The implication is that an embodied spirit is unable to make his influence felt in one's heart as effectively as an unembodied one.

Evidently, the teaching that the Holy Ghost is a personage wasn't widely disseminated prior to 1856, as it does not appear to have been common knowledge among the Saints. Indeed, the material comprising D&C 130:22–23 wasn't published until 1856 and wasn't included in the Doctrine and Covenants until the 1876 edition.[22] As late as 1855, Orson Pratt delivered a sermon saying that he knew of no revelation clarifying whether the Holy Ghost was "a person" and concluded, "We are left to form our own conclusions on the subject."[23] The later canonization of the doctrine of the Holy Ghost as a personage caused earlier contrary teachings to be revisited. In 1915, Charles Penrose, a member of the First Presidency, revised Parley P. Pratt's 1855 definitive theological treatise *Key to the Science of Theology*, removing Pratt's descriptions of the Holy Ghost as a "spiritual fluid" pervading the universe. The similar non-personal description of the Holy Ghost in the *Lectures* undoubtedly contributed to its removal from the Doctrine and Covenants in 1921.

While earlier LDS revelations follow New Testament depictions of the Holy Ghost appearing in the form of a dove at Jesus's baptism, during the Nauvoo period Joseph gave a different view, averring that the dove was only a "sign" of the presence of the Holy Ghost and that "the Holy Ghost cannot be transformed into a dove."[24] This later notion of the dove as merely a "sign" of the Holy Ghost appears also in the Book of Abraham (Fac 2: item 7), which was written during the same period. With this change in perception of the nature of the Holy Ghost, earlier passages referring to the Holy Ghost's appearance in the *form* of a dove are now interpreted to harmonize with this later understanding.

The LDS teaching that the possession of a physical body is essential for exaltation (D&C 93:33–34, 131:2–4), coupled with Joseph's Nauvoo teachings related to the corporeality of God, inevitably led to speculation concerning whether or not the Holy Ghost would ever receive a body. In a Sunday address given in August 1843, the Prophet remarked that "the Holy Ghost is now in a state of probation which if he should perform in righteousness he may pass through the same or a similar course of things that the Son has."[25] Joseph didn't elaborate on the nature of this "probation" or clarify whether the Holy Ghost is destined to become a savior himself at some time in the future. George Laub reported a June 1844 discourse of the Prophet in which he taught that "the Holy Ghost is yet a Spiritual body and waiting to take to himself a body, as the Savior did or as God did, or the gods before them took bodies."[26]

Interestingly, in the Prophet's discussion of the Holy Ghost being a spirit and waiting to take a body and pass through a probationary state, he compares the Holy Ghost to the Father and the Son, but never identifies him as one of God's spirit offspring. It wasn't until late 1844 that the doctrine of spirit birth began to emerge, and only then did it start to become natural for Saints to think of the Holy Ghost, like all other human-shaped beings, as a spirit child of God. In 1857, Heber C. Kimball, counselor to President Brigham Young, stated as a matter of fact: "The Holy Ghost is a man; he is one of the sons of our Father and our God."[27]

Contemporary Mormonism

Following the death of Joseph Smith, speculations began cropping up regarding the identity of Holy Ghost, including the notion that Joseph himself was the Holy Ghost.[28] Church leaders have generally been successful in quelling such speculations, even though the question of his identity inevitably still surfaces in gospel discussions.

The currently accepted LDS doctrine is that the Holy Ghost is a personage of spirit in human form that is incapable of appearing in any other shape. It is not his person but his influence that fills the universe. This concept has forced a reinterpretation of scriptures which speak of the Holy Ghost itself as though it were an influence, especially an influence that emanates from God. Bruce R. McConkie instructed Church members that, when reading the scriptures, "sometimes the designation Holy Ghost is used to mean, not the Individual or Person who is a member of the Godhead, but the power or gift of that Personage."[29] Furthermore, LDS scriptures using the term "Spirit" are now viewed as referring to either the light of Christ, the Spirit of the Lord, the Holy Ghost or to Christ himself (D&C 93:9, 26) depending on the context. This multifaceted understanding of the word "Spirit" prompted McConkie to state, "To gain a sound gospel understanding, the truth seeker must determine in each scriptural passage what is meant by such titles as *Spirit, Holy Spirit, Spirit of the Lord, Spirit of God, Spirit of truth.*"[30] For early Saints these titles were interchangeable and such a differentiation would have likely been perceived as artificial.

Notes

1. *Gospel Principles* (1997), 37. This description of the Holy Ghost having "the form and likeness of a man" was removed in the 2009 edition of *Gospel Principles*, perhaps to avoid going beyond what is explicit in the scriptures.

2. Bruce R. McConkie, *A New Witness for the Articles of Faith*, 254.

3. Raymond E. Brown, *The Birth of the Messiah*, 124.

4. Gerald O'Collins, *Christology: A Biblical, Historical, and Systematic Study of Jesus*, 148.

5. L. A. Bushinski, "Spirit of God," 13:426.

6. James D. G. Dunn, *Christology in the Making*, 132–36.

7. Bushinski, "Spirit of God," 13:428.

8. Raymond E. Brown, "The Holy Ghost as Paraclete: The Gift of John's Gospel."

9. The personhood of the Holy Ghost didn't become official church dogma until the Council of Constantinople in 381. Stanley J. Grenz, *Theology for the Community of God*, 374.

10. Noah Worcester, *Bible News, or Sacred Truths Relating to the Living God, His Only Son, and Holy Spirit*, 192.

11. David Millard, quoted in Dan Vogel, "The Earliest Mormon Concept of God," 18.

12. Charles H. Spurgeon, *Sermons of C. H. Spurgeon of London*, 46.

13. See, for example, James E. Talmage, *Articles of Faith*, 164–65. Bruce R. McConkie expressed his opinion that the "Spirit of the Lord" in 1 Nephi 11:11 refers to "the Spirit Christ ministering to Nephi much as he did to the Brother of Jared." Bruce R. McConkie, *Mormon Doctrine*, 712.

14. McConkie, *Mormon Doctrine*, 712.

15. *Lectures on Faith*, 5:1–2.

16. Joseph F. Smith, *Gospel Doctrine: Selections from the Sermons and Writings of Joseph F. Smith*, 61.

17. Andrew F. Ehat and Lyndon W. Cook, *The Words of Joseph Smith: The Contemporary Accounts of the Nauvoo Discourses of the Prophet Joseph Smith*, 63.

18. Ibid., 64.

19. Ibid., 160.

20. Ibid., 170; see also 173.

21. Ibid., 268–69.

22. Lyndon W. Cook, *The Revelations of the Prophet Joseph Smith: A Historical and Biographical Commentary of the Doctrine and Covenants*, 291.

23. Orson Pratt, February 18, 1855, *Journal of Discourses* 2:337–38. Pratt was able to rationalize his notion of the Holy Ghost as "an inexhaustible substance" with scriptural references to the Holy Ghost appearing as a dove, as cloven tongues, and as a man by explaining that "different portions of the Holy Ghost can assume different shapes at different times." Orson Pratt, "Questions for the Latter-day Saints. By the Rev. F. Austin, A Roman Catholic Minister," 239.

24. Ehat and Cook, *The Words of Joseph Smith*, 163.

25. Ibid., 245.
26. Ibid., 305, note 26.
27. Heber C. Kimball, August 23, 1857, *Journal of Discourses* 5:179.
28. See Vern G. Swanson, "The Development of the Concept of a Holy Ghost in Mormon Theology," 97.
29. McConkie, *Mormon Doctrine*, 359.
30. Ibid., 752.

≈ 10 ≈

Satan

Satan is viewed by the Christian world and in Mormonism as a fallen angel and God's nemesis. He is known by various names including Lucifer, Beelzebub, and "that old serpent . . . the Devil" (Rev. 12:9). For Latter-day Saints, Satan is further believed to be "a spirit son of God who was born in the morning of the pre-existence."[1] However, in consequence of his open rebellion against God in the pre-existence, he was cast down to the earth to lie and tempt mortals to sin so "that all men might be miserable like unto himself" (2 Ne. 2:27).

Aside from the LDS view that Satan is a literal spirit-born son of God, there is little difference between the LDS and the traditional Christian concept of Satan. Christians also hold the tradition that Satan was a son of God (i.e., an angel of authority) who was cast out of heaven for excessive ambition (see Chapter 11) and who will be conquered in the end.

Old Testament

Critical scholars maintain that the concept of Satan in Old Testament narratives differs markedly from what would develop in later Christianity. For example, Christians, including Latter-day Saints, identify the serpent in the Garden of Eden as Satan. The account in Genesis, however, makes no such connection; neither is there any such linkage made elsewhere in the Old Testament. It isn't even Satan speaking through the serpent, for the serpent on its own "was more subtle than any beast of the field which the Lord God had made" (Gen. 3:1). God cursed the serpent "above all the other animals" (Gen. 3:14) and then declared, "I will put enmity between thee and the woman, *and between thy seed and her seed*" (Gen 3:15; emphasis mine; see also Moses 4:21).[2] Thus, it isn't Satan, but the serpent—which is just another creature that God had made after its kind—and the serpent's offspring (i.e., all future serpents) that are cursed and destined to afflict humans.[3] Old Testament scholar Theodore Hiebert notes that it was only later that "Jewish and Christian interpreters of Gen. 3:15 understood this verse as a reference to the Messiah's coming victory over Satan."[4]

Aside from an apocryphal reference in the Book of Wisdom 2:24 (written in the first or second century B.C.), the Bible makes only a veiled reference to the serpent as Satan in Romans 16:20. The book of Revelation speaks of "that old serpent, called the Devil" (Rev. 12:9; see also 20:2), but this serpent is not explicitly linked to the serpent that tempted Eve in the Garden of Eden. Scholars note that the description of Satan here as a cosmic dragon or serpent may be a reference to the legendary primordial leviathan or sea serpent found in Near Eastern mythology (see Isa. 27:1).[5] The only explicit New Testament reference to the serpent in the Garden of Eden comes from Paul who makes no express connection between the serpent and Satan, though it could be inferred: "The serpent beguiled Eve through his subtilty" (2 Cor. 11:3).

In the Old Testament, there is no evil force or influence such as Satan operating in opposition to God. Instead, the Old Testament is much more monistic than dualistic, with God being the source of both good and evil.[6] In most explanations for trouble and evil-doing in the Old Testament, Yahweh himself is the cause (see, for example, Ex. 4:11; 7:2–3; Deut. 32:39; Job 2:10; Ps. 105:25; Isa. 45:5–7; 63:17; Lam. 3:37–38). According to *The New Interpreter's Study Bible*, "Ancient Israel . . . claimed that God is the source of everything in the world, both good and bad (cf. Job 1:21, 2:10). The concept of another supernatural power, beyond God's control, causing evil, was not conceived in their belief system."[7] When the Spirit of the Lord departed from Saul, "an evil spirit *from the Lord* troubled him" (1 Sam. 16:14; emphasis mine). And it was the Lord that "hardened Pharaoh's heart" so that he repeatedly refused to release the Israelites (Ex. 7:13; 9:12; 10:1, 20; 11:10; 14:8).[8] The idea is succinctly expressed in Isaiah 45:7, "I make peace, and create evil; I the Lord do all these things." In his book, *A History of the Devil*, Gerald Messadie summarizes the Old Testament notion of Satan: "The essential thing is that until the third or second century B.C., the image of Satan as God's declared enemy is absent from Judaism. Satan and the demons—who do not seem to have a master-servant relationship, the former being nowhere referred to as the chief of the latter—are the servants of God. As troubling as this might seem, the texts are there to prove it."[9]

The Hebrew term translated as "Satan" is *ha'satan* and literally means "the satan" or "the accuser" in the sense of being an office or role (Job 1:6, 12, 2:1; Zech. 2:1). The satan, therefore, is not the name of any particular, let alone evil, character.[10] The *HarperCollins Study Bible* explains, "The use of the article before the word *satan* in Hebrew makes clear that this is a title and not a proper name. The satan is a member of the divine council whose task it is to discover and indict malefactors (see Job 1:6-12). . . . The picture of the divine council given in 1 Kings 22.19-23 shows spirits performing various functions in God's court, including that of testing and provoking sinners."[11] Interestingly, in Job 1:6 the satan appears to be numbered among "the sons of God."

Christians, including Latter-day Saints, have inherited certain conceptions of Satan through a later interpretation of Isaiah 14:12–16, which speaks of an individual referred to as "Lucifer" who sought to "exalt [his] throne above the stars of God" to become "like the most High." Having "fallen from heaven" he was "brought down to hell [i.e., *sheol* or the grave], to the sides of the pit." Though this may sound like the traditional Satan, verse 4 explicitly states that this statement was spoken as a "proverb against the king of Babylon"; and verse 20 states that the king would not be joined with the other kings in burial "because thou hast destroyed thy land, and slain thy people." It wasn't uncommon in Jewish literature for kings to be compared to deity; and accordingly, the king of Babylon is here depicted as falling from his glorious reign as though he were falling from heaven.

Most conservative Christian scholars concede that Isaiah 14 has at least primary reference to the king of Babylon but argue that it also alludes to the traditional view of Lucifer or Satan. This is, in fact, the explanation given in the footnote of the LDS Bible. The historical meaning seems to reveal something different. The Hebrew expression translated "Lucifer" in the KJV is *helel ben shachar*, which literally means "shining one, son of dawn." The gods of Near Eastern religions were often identified with different stars and planets. For example, the planet Venus was called Helel, son of the moon god Shahar. According to ancient Near Eastern mythology, Helel was banished from heaven for trying to usurp the throne of the Most High God of the assembly of gods. It is Helel whom Isaiah gives as a metaphor for Nebuchadnezzar who, it is prophesied, would fall for seeking to rise above his station and become king of all the earth.[12] Thus, *helel ben shachar* was a reference to a non-Israelite astral god, and not to Satan.

It was Jerome who, at the turn of the fifth century, translated *helel* in the Latin Vulgate as *lucifer* (i.e., light bearing), which was a common Latin term for Venus. Even then it wasn't intended as a synonym for Satan. However, because many Christians, including Jerome, saw this passage in Isaiah as an allusion to the fall of Satan in addition to the fall of the king of Babylon, Lucifer eventually became popularized as being another name for Satan. Theology professors T. J. Wray and Gregory Mobley write that "Postbiblical writers are responsible for connecting the dots between 'Day Star'/Lucifer and Satan, an identification that was never made in the Hebrew Bible."[13] The New Testament mention of Satan's "fall from heaven" like lightning (Luke 10:18) unwarrantedly contributed to the development of this idea. According to biblical scholar William Kent, writing in the *Catholic Encyclopedia*, "Modern commentators take this text [Luke 10:18] in a different sense, and refer it not to the original fall of Satan, but his overthrow by the faith of the disciples, who cast out devils in the name of their Master."[14]

Nineteenth-century Methodist Bible commentator Adam Clarke was bewildered that post-apostolic Christians would even consider linking Lucifer (a morning star) with Satan (prince of darkness). He explained that "the text speaks nothing at all concerning Satan nor his fall, nor the occasion of that fall, which many divines have with great confidence deduced from this text."[15] Congruent with the Christian understanding of Isaiah 14 that eventually evolved, the Book of Mormon describes Satan as having "fallen from heaven" (2 Ne. 2:17–18). So while Isaiah 14:12–16 could certainly be interpreted as a *symbolic* reference to Satan, this reference has become viewed as more explicit in Mormonism.

New Testament

It isn't until the New Testament that Satan begins to be depicted as an evil, sinister being who tempts mortals to sin (1 Thess. 2:18; Matt. 4:1–11). How this transition occurred is not clear; it seems that somewhere between the Old and New Testaments, Satan morphed from an office to a distinct personality, and from an accuser (though not necessarily evil) to a deceiver and tempter. R. H. Charles, an expert on the influence of apocryphal texts on the New Testament, traces the early stages of this transformation back to apocryphal texts of the second and third century B.C., such as Enoch.[16] Scholars suggest that the influence of Persian demonology during the Diaspora likely helped solidify the Jewish concept of Satan as an evil spirit.[17]

The view of Satan as a specific person who is both a liar and archenemy of God has its most complete expression in the book of Revelation. Beliefs about Satan held by Christians today, including Mormons, are largely based on Revelation's description of Satan waging war in heaven (Rev. 12:7), drawing a third of the stars of heaven and casting them to earth (Rev. 12:4), engaging in works of blasphemy and deceit (Rev. 13:1–14), and becoming locked in the bottomless pit (Rev. 20:3). It has been commonly believed that Satan's expulsion to the earth explains the source of evil influences in the world since the time of Adam and Eve. Most biblical scholars, however, see the expulsion spoken of in Revelation as having an end-time fulfillment, which John seems to have believed was then in progress. (See Chap. 11).

Early Nineteenth-Century Christianity

By the 1800s, an essentially uniform doctrine of Satan had emerged in traditional Christian writings and creeds. Many of these ideas can be traced to the teachings of St. Augustine (A.D. 354–430) who considered Satan to be a fallen angel that was originally created good like all the other angels. However, this particular angel sought to become like God and assume supreme authority. As a result of his rebellion Satan was cast out of heaven with a third of the host thereof, and thus began the spread of his rebellion on the earth.[18]

Universalists, in contrast to traditional Christians, rejected the idea of Satan altogether along with a belief in hell. They came under the increasing contempt of early nineteenth-century orthodox Christians who chided them for deluding themselves. Likewise, the Book of Mormon calls attention to the delusional nature of these beliefs, prophesying of a latter-day people whom Satan "flattereth away, and telleth them there is no hell; and he saith unto them: I am no devil, for there is none" (2 Ne. 28:22).

Mormonism

Early LDS descriptions of Satan are not unlike those that emerged in classical Christianity. He is described as "an angel of God" who became a devil, "having sought that which was evil before God" (2 Ne. 2:17; D&C 76:25). Although Satan himself is mentioned nowhere in the Garden of Eden story of Genesis, in the Book of Mormon (2 Ne. 2:18) and early revelations (D&C 29:40; Moses 4:1–3, 6–7) he is depicted as playing a pivotal role in the fall of Adam and Eve.

Neither the standard works nor any other recorded Church teachings during the lifetime of Joseph Smith ever refer to Satan or his angels as fallen spirit children of God. In the Bible, all angels were created by God (Ps. 148:2–5) including Satan (Col. 1:16). This was the general Christian understanding of Satan's origin at the time of Joseph Smith, and the early Saints' understanding appears to have been no different. The notion of Satan and his angels being God's literal offspring didn't emerge in LDS thought until after the Prophet's death,[19] but it has since become an accepted LDS tenet.

Notes

1. Bruce R. McConkie, *Mormon Doctrine*, 192.

2. The current LDS endowment ceremony has God placing enmity between only the serpent (not its seed) and the woman's seed so that it better fits the Christian tradition that the enmity is between Satan and humans.

3. Joel W. Rosenberg, "Genesis," 8–9. According to Rosenberg, snakes were represented as sly creatures in antiquity as illustrated by the snake who steals a plant possessing the power of immortality in the *Epic of Gilgamesh*.

4. Theodore Hiebert, "Genesis,"12.

5. See, for example, Howard Wallace, "Leviathan and the Beast in Revelation," 67.

6. Robert P. Carroll, *Wolf in the Sheepfold: The Bible as Problem for Christianity*, 45.

7. Lisa Davison, "Job," 747.

8. Joseph Smith, changes these passages in the JST to have Pharaoh hardening his own heart.

9. Gerald Messadie, *A History of the Devil*, 240.

10. Elaine Pagels, *The Origin of Satan*, 39.

11. W. Sibley Towner, "Zechariah," 1415.

12. See Richley H. Crapo, "An Anthropologist Looks at the Judeo-Christian Scriptures."

13. T. J. Wray and Gregory Mobley, *The Birth of Satan: Tracing the Devil's Biblical Roots*, 110.

14. W. H. Kent, "Devil," 764. Joseph A. Fitzmyer, *The Gospel According to Luke*, 860.

15. Adam Clarke, *Commentary on the Bible*, s.v. Isaiah 14.

16. R. H. Charles, *A Critical and Exegetical Commentary on the Revelation of St. John . . .* , 1:326..

17. W. F. Barnett, "Satan," 12:698–99.

18. Alister E. McGrath, *Christian Theology: An Introduction*, 293–94.

19. In a letter to William Smith December 25, 1844, W. W. Phelps wrote that "Lucifer, son of the morning, [was] the next heir to Jesus Christ, our eldest brother," but he lost his first estate "by offering to save men in their sins on the honor of a God, or on his father's honor." William W. Phelps, "The Answer," 758. See also Brent L. Top, "War in Heaven," 4:1546–47.

11

The Preexistence

The LDS doctrine of the preexistence is one of the most distinctive teachings in Mormonism and pertains to our spiritual existence prior to being born into mortality. According to sixth Church President Joseph F. Smith, "All men and women are . . . literally the sons and daughters of Deity. . . . Man, as a spirit, was begotten and born of heavenly parents, and reared to maturity in the eternal mansions of the Father, prior to coming upon the earth in a temporal [physical] body."[1] The LDS Church publication *Gospel Principles* explains that we were not all equal there, but "we possessed different talents and abilities,"[2] which we developed to varying levels. Because there were limits on how far we could progress as spirits, the Father provided a plan whereby we could become like him by obtaining physical bodies and passing tests of obedience.

Knowing that we would all sin in mortality if given our agency, a savior was chosen who would redeem us if we would repent and obey the gospel. Satan presented a counterproposal saying, "I will redeem all mankind, that one soul shall not be lost, and surely I will do it; wherefore give me thine honor" (Moses 4:1). Satan's plan would have destroyed human agency by forcing everyone to be obedient.[3] Because God chose Jesus to be the Savior, Satan rebelled and a war ensued in which he and a third of Heavenly Father's children who followed him were cast out of heaven and denied the opportunity of further progress.[4]

Nature of the Soul

Before examining biblical and modern teachings on the preexistence of the soul, it is helpful to have some idea of just what this soul was believed to be. Judeo-Christian teachings concerning the nature of the soul have developed gradually over several millennia. The earliest writings of the Old Testament seem to give no indication at all of a soul or spirit separate from the body. Everett Ferguson, professor of early church history at Abilene Christian University, indicates that "the familiar dichotomy in Western thought between body and soul is a product of the Platonic tradition," and that "from the biblical perspective . . . [they] never should have been separated."[5] This position starkly contrasts with the LDS perception of the soul, which not only has an existence independent of the body, but is also a material being of sorts.

Old Testament

Ancient Hebrews evidently didn't think of themselves as dual beings composed of both body and spirit, but merely as bodies animated by the breath of life. The Old Testament concept of life was simple: living things breathe; dead things don't. The Genesis creation story clearly depicts the animating power of breath. God, after having fashioned Adam from the dust, breathes into him the breath of life so that he can become "a living soul" (Gen. 2:7).[6] Similarly, in Ezekiel's vision of the valley of dry bones (Ezek. 37:1–14), the dead bones return to life when breath enters them. Regarding this Old Testament understanding, the *New Catholic Encyclopedia* explains, "Since God is the life-giver, life breath comes from Him and man lives as long as God's breath remains in him (Job 27:3; Isa. 42:5; Zech. 12:1)."[7] Thus, there was no spirit as a distinct entity coexisting with the body, but simply the breath of life. For ancient Hebrews, breath *was* life.

During the late Old Testament period and into the New Testament era, the idea of spirits or ghosts is believed to have become more commonplace in Jewish thought, and a distinction began to be made between the soul and the body. This changing perception of the soul is thought to have been influenced by the Persians and Greeks, who believed in the independence and immortality of the soul.[8] According to Kaufmann Kohler, Isaac Broyde, and Ludwig Blau, writing in the *Jewish Encyclopedia*: "Only through the contact of the Jews with Persian and Greek thought did the idea of a disembodied soul, having its own individuality, take root in Judaism and find its expression in the later Biblical books, as, for instance, in the following passages: 'The spirit of man is the candle of the Lord' (Prov. 20:27); 'There is a spirit in man' (Job 32:8); 'The spirit shall return unto God who gave it' (Eccl. 12:7)."[9] Even in these isolated verses it isn't entirely clear what a spirit consists of and whether it has meaningful existence independent of the body.

New Testament

The New Testament continues to speak of the soul in this later Jewish sense with no clear anthropological explanation of its essence or mode of existence. Dutch theologian G. C. Berkouwer notes that there is "a fairly general consensus of opinion . . . among theologians" that "no part of man is emphasized [in the Bible] as independent of other parts; not because the various parts are not important, but because the Word of God is concerned precisely with the whole man in his relation to God."[10] Accordingly, there is no clear and concise delineation of the basic components of human existence in the New Testament, which seems to use terms such as *heart, mind, soul,* and *spirit* often indiscriminately with little or no precision in meaning. One can only wonder, for example what is meant to divide one's "soul and spirit" (Heb. 4:12) or to have one's "spirit and soul and body preserved" (1 Thess. 5:23). The distinction made between the soul and spirit in these verses strains modern Christian (including LDS) categories.

Early Nineteenth-Century Christianity

At the time of Joseph Smith, Christians generally regarded the soul as being capable of existing independent of the body. With respect to the physical composition of the soul, however, there were essentially two schools of thought. One was the classical Christian view that espoused the immateriality of the soul. Buck's *Theological Dictionary*, published in 1832, defined spirit as "that vital, immaterial, active substance, or principle, in man, whereby he perceives, remembers, reasons and wills. It is rather to be described to its operations, than to be defined as to its essence."[11] Rationalists of the Enlightenment repudiated the classical Christian notion that spirits are immaterial calling it unscientific and irrational. In his influential *Leviathan* (1651), philosopher Thomas Hobbes argued that any speech referring to "immaterial substances . . . [is] without meaning" and that "to say an angel or spirit is . . . an incorporeal substance is to say, in effect, there is no angel nor spirit at all."[12]

Many Christians accommodated the postulates of rationalist thinking by conceding that spirit is indeed material, but of a refined nature. As Puritan writer Richard Baxter observed in 1650: "The soul is a substance; for that which is nothing can do nothing. . . . It is not bones and flesh that understand, but a purer substance, as all acknowledge."[13] Similarly, almost thirty years before the birth of Joseph Smith, the British scientist and Unitarian theologian Joseph Priestley wrote, "The original, and still prevailing idea concerning a soul or spirit, is that of a kind of attenuated aerial substance, of a more subtle nature than gross bodies."[14]

Mormonism

The classical Christian view of spirits as immaterial is the only view expressed in early LDS literature.[15] A revelation received in May 1833 draws a distinction between "spirit," which is defined as "intelligence or the light of truth," and "element," which comprises the physical tabernacle of the spirit (D&C 93:29, 33). Two years later, in March 1835, LDS correspondent Warren Cowdery affirmed that "if there be intelligence there must be spirit or mind for matter is inert and abstract from mind has neither intelligence or mind."[16] At this time in Mormon thought, spirit was seen as being essentially the antithesis of matter.

In April 1842, the Prophet first publicly voiced the more Enlightenment view of spirit, proclaiming that "the spirit is a substance; that it is material, but that it is more pure, elastic and refined matter than the body."[17] In May 1843, he corrected a Methodist minister stating, "There is no such thing as immaterial matter. All spirit is matter but it is more fine or pure, and can only be discerned by purer eyes" (D&C 131:7). Thus, where earlier LDS literature differentiated between spirit and element, spirit was now seen as a refined form of element.

Preexistence of Souls

The Bible provides little insight into the origin of the human spirit besides its creation by God. Most Bible scholars maintain that there is no unambiguous teaching of the preexistence of souls in the Bible. J. I. Marais, writing for the *International Standard Bible Encyclopedia*, goes so far as to say, "[Nowhere] does Scripture teach the pre-existence of the soul."[18] Congregational theologian Edward Beecher (1803–95), who was an avowed believer of preexistence himself, acknowledged that "even those serious theologians who assert the doctrine of preexistence do not claim any express scriptural evidence for it, only that it nowhere expressly refutes it."[19] This is not to say that, in the Bible, God has no *fore*knowledge of individuals before they were created, for he knows "the end from the beginning, and from ancient times the things that are not yet done" (Isa. 46:10). The existence of individuals in God's mind before they had actual existence is referred to by theologians as "ideal" preexistence. While there is ample biblical evidence of *ideal* preexistence, scholars see little convincing biblical support for the belief in *actual* preexistence. Not until Joseph Smith began his translation of the Bible in 1830 would actual preexistence become explicit in LDS scripture.

Old Testament

An Old Testament passage commonly cited by Latter-day Saints today as evidence for the preexistence of souls is Jeremiah 1:5: "Before I [God] formed thee in the belly I knew thee; and before thou camest forth out of the womb I sanctified thee, and I ordained thee a prophet unto the nations." Latter-day Saints adduce that, since God "knew" and "ordained" Jeremiah before he was born, he therefore must have existed before his birth. However, most biblical scholars interpret this passage as having reference to only *ideal* preexistence.[20] LDS scholar Lowell L. Bennion concurs, averring that Jeremiah 1:5, as well as other biblical passages which Mormons interpret as referring to man's preexistence, "may be interpreted also as meaning God's foreknowledge rather than man's preexistence." He further observes that "a pre-earth life for man . . . cannot be clearly and indubitably established by the Bible."[21]

Latter-day Saints frequently cite Job 38:7 to show that, "when the plan for our salvation was presented to us in the premortal spirit world, we were so happy that we shouted for joy."[22] In Job 38:4–7, the Lord asks Job: "Where wast thou when I laid the foundation of the earth . . . when the morning stars sang together, and all the sons of God shouted for joy?" Joseph Smith used this passage as "evidence that Job was in existence somewhere at that time."[23] Otherwise, he reasoned, why would God ask where Job was? Most biblical scholars, however, see God's question as rhetorical and intended to highlight the fact that Job was nowhere around during the creation. The whole tenor of the Lord's query, when read in context with the entire chapter, is to emphasize the insignificance and fleeting nature of human existence. The Lord does tell Job, however, that the "sons of God" were there and "shouted for joy" (Job 38:7), but there is no indication that Job was numbered among them. In the book of Job, according to scholarly commentaries, the "sons of God" refer to angelic counselors in God's court; not to preexistent human spirits. Old Testament scholar Brendan Byrne explains that the designation "sons of God" in Job 38:7 "does not imply actual progeny of God . . . but reflects the common Semitic use of 'son' (Heb *ben*) to denote membership of a class or group. 'Sons of the gods,' then, designates beings belonging to the heavenly or divine sphere . . . forming his [God's] heavenly court or council."[24] Note that it is these same "sons of God" who "present themselves before the Lord" to consider Job's current mortal situation in Job 1:6.

It is interesting that the Prophet referred to this passage as proof of preexistence because of Job's presumed existence at the foundation of the world but gave no indication that the "sons of God" were preexistent spirits. This is likely because he didn't view them as spirit children of God. Parley P. Pratt interpreted "sons of God" in this passage in 1838 as referring to resurrected beings from bygone worlds, and not to preexistent spirits.[25] The idea of spirit offspring had not yet been introduced in LDS teachings, so "sons of God" was understood in a traditional Christian sense of saved beings (John 1:12). There is no evidence of an understanding during the Prophet's lifetime that "sons of God" in this passage referred to preexistent spirits.

While the Old Testament itself provides little evidence of a belief in preexistence, apocryphal writings dating from the end of the Jewish exile to the time of Christ indicate a late Jewish belief in the doctrine. The Slavonic Book of Enoch 23:5 states, "All souls are prepared before the foundation of the world." No mention is made of what souls did in this preexistent state, only that they were held in reserve for mortality. The Syriac Apocalypse of Baruch 30:2–3 refers to "the storehouses in which the foreordained number of souls is kept." Biblical scholars suggest that this late Jewish belief in preexistence was acquired through extensive association with Persian and Greek cultures during the exile. Pythagoreans and Platonists had been advocating the preexistence of the human soul since at least the fourth century B.C. Calling it an "importation into Jewish theology through Plato and Philo," Marais explains that "this doctrine was well known to Jewish writers, and was taught in Talmud and Kabbalah."[26]

New Testament

Like the Old Testament, the New Testament seems to depict human existence as beginning in this life with no explicit mention of a pre-earth life. Nowhere are callings, activities, or outcomes in this life attributed by New Testament writers to a preexistent state. This, however, doesn't mean that belief in the preexistence of souls was non-existent in the early Church. As noted above, it was adopted by certain of the Jews who comprised the first Christians.

A New Testament passage often cited by Latter-day Saints in support of preexistence describes Jesus passing by "a man which was blind from his birth. And his disciples asked him, saying, Master, who did sin, this man, or his parents, that he was born blind?" (John 9:2). A common LDS interpretation is that the very fact that the disciples asked the question presupposes a belief in the preexistence of spirits. This, however, is not the only reasonable interpretation of this passage. According to New Testament scholar Raymond Brown, this reference to sinning before birth may have been an allusion to contemporary rabbinic teachings regarding infants who sin while still in the womb.[27] Nineteenth-century Christian scholar Thomas Thayer notes that it could also reflect the popular Hellenistic belief in the transmigration of souls (i.e., reincarnation), which included the belief in "retribution beyond death," thereby impacting how one comes back in the next life cycle.[28] He further notes that transmigration appears in Jewish apocryphal writings and that Josephus claims that the Pharisees believed it.[29] Some see possible evidence of a cultural belief in transmigration in Matthew's account that some perceived Jesus to be "John the Baptist: some, Elias [i.e., Elijah]; and others, Jeremias, or one of the prophets" (Matt. 16:14). In sum, there were several beliefs regarding ways an individual might commit sin prior to birth making it difficult to state with certainty what the underlying supposition was of Jesus's inquirers. Even if Jesus's inquirers did have in mind sins committed in the preexistence, there is no evidence that Jesus himself sanctioned the belief. The only explanation he gave for the man's blindness was so "the works of God should be made manifest in him" (John 9:3).

The only explicit teachings of preexistence in the New Testament are in relation to Christ. Paul explains that after a heavenly existence "in the form of God," Jesus took on himself "the likeness of men" (Phil. 2:6–8). John identifies preexistence as one of the principal differences between Christ and the rest of humankind. In testifying of Christ's preexistence, John the Baptist, who was six months older than Christ (Luke 1:24–26), declared, "He existed before I was born!" (Phillips Version John 1:30). John alludes twice to Christ's uniqueness in coming down from heaven in contrast to man who originated on earth (John 3:13, 31).[30]

Belief in a preexistence of the human soul doesn't explicitly appear in Christianity until the post-apostolic church; however, it was never universally held and eventually lost favor. Marais notes that "the doctrine with some modifications passed into the Christian church, was accepted by Justin Martyr, Theodoretus, Origen and others of the church Fathers, but became obsolete by the latter part of the 4th century. . . . It was formally condemned by a synod held at Constantinople in the 6th century."[31] Origen of Alexandria (185–254) taught that spirits preexisted and had agency; but unlike Mormonism, he believed that being sent to earth was a punishment for disobedient spirits.[32] Latter-day Saints often consider these isolated expressions of belief in preexistence to be vestiges of an earlier, purer theology.[33] Non-LDS Bible scholars, as noted, see them as essentially Greek and Hellenized Jewish ideas that were absorbed into the early Christian church.

Early Nineteenth-Century Christianity

The predominant Christian view regarding the origin of spirits at the time of Joseph Smith was that each human spirit was created *ex nihilo* (i.e., out of nothing) through a fiat act of God (i.e., God simply spoke and spirits came into being) either at the time of conception or at birth. Characterizing this prevalent creationist view, Orson Pratt explained in 1852,

> It is believed, by the religious world that man, both body and spirit, begins to live about the time that he is born into this world, or a little before; that then is the beginning of life. . . . How was the spirit formed? Why says one, we suppose it was made by a direct act of creation, by the Almighty Himself; that He moulded the spirit of man, formed and finished it in a proper likeness to inhabit the tabernacle He had made out of the dust.[34]

A variation of creationism is *traducianism*. This is the belief, held by some, that every human spirit was seminally created in Adam and then individually and naturally propagated through mortal parentage.[35] Neither of these entail the preexistence of conscious souls.

Though creationism and traducianism were widely held at the time of Joseph Smith, a variation of creationism was also entertained which taught that God created the spirits of all humans *before* they were born. These "preexistencists," as they were called, believed that "at the beginning of the world, God created the souls of all men, which, however, are not united to the body till the individuals for whom they are destined are begotten or born into the world."[36] Refuting the traditional view that spirits are created at the time of birth, Lorenzo Dow, a Methodist preacher, wrote in 1804, "I deny it, for the bible says, Gen. [2:1–3], that God finished the heavens (that is the starry heavens) and earth and all the HOST of them, and then God rested from the works of creation on the seventh day—he hath not been at work in creating new souls ever since."[37] Echoing ancient apocryphal teachings, Dow believed that spirits "were laid up in a store house in Heaven" in a state of happiness until their mortal bodies were prepared.[38]

Regardless of the timing—at the time of birth or at the beginning of the world—most Christians saw the human spirit as a product of special creation. This didn't preclude many evangelicals, however, from viewing God as our Father more than in the sense of being just our creator. Indeed, many nineteenth-century Christians came to view God as our Father in the sense of his endowing each human spirit with a portion of his divinity. In 1824, for example, the *Christian Magazine*, a publication of the Congregationalist Church, declared that man's soul possesses "a spark of his [i.e., God's] intelligence, and continues to be in a high and peculiar sense 'his offspring.' Hence the nature of the soul, and its relation and resemblance to the divinity, proclaim its worth."[39] Even the Heavenly Mother and Father concept of later Mormonism was to be found in the esoteric teachings of the Kabbalah, which intrigued Christian mystics at the time of Joseph Smith. According to this tradition, the soul is "born into this world in which we live, through the union of the King and Queen who are, as regards the generation of the soul, like the human species in the generation of the body."[40] While Latter-day Saints initially acknowledged, along with other Christians, God's figurative Fatherhood, they soon began regarding it more literally (see Chapter 7).

Early Mormonism

The first intimation of preexistence in modern revelation is generally believed to be found in the Book of Mormon. It is doubtful, however, that many of the first converts would have initially perceived the idea of preexistence in this book of scripture. In reflecting back on his own initiation to the doctrine of preexistence, Orson Pratt, who was one of the most theologically astute of the early Saints, observed that, had it not been for revelations subsequent to the Book of Mormon, "I do not think that I should have ever discerned it in that book."[41] Modern Saints commonly point to Alma 13 as evidence of preexistence in the Book of Mormon. Alma 13:3 states that anciently, priests were "called and prepared from the foundation of the world according to the foreknowledge of God, on account of their exceeding faith and good works; in the first place being left to choose good or evil; therefore they having chosen good, and exercising exceeding great faith, are called with a holy calling." This verse is generally interpreted to mean that these priests existed as spirits before they were born and exercised "faith and good works" in their preexistent state.[42]

When read without the filter of current LDS theology, this passage seems to imply only that their *calling* was before the foundation of the world and that it was predicated on God's foreknowledge of their *future* faith and good works. Early Latter-day Saints would have been no more disposed to read preexistence into this passage than they would in similar New Testament passages that describe how the elect are "afore prepared" (Rom. 9:23) and "chosen . . . before the foundation of the world" (Eph. 1:4) "according to the foreknowledge of God" (1 Pet. 1:2). Traditionally, Christians have seen no evidence of actual preexistence in these passages, only ideal preexistence (i.e., existence in God's prescient mind). The language of Alma 13 evokes the early nineteenth-century Free Will Baptist idea that individual election is "from all eternity" according to "the foreknowledge of God . . . [of] the future faith and good works of the elect."[43]

The earliest explicit teachings on preexistence come from the book of Moses and early sections of the Doctrine and Covenants. These revelations present a simple concept of preexistence that resembled the contemporary notion of preexistencism in that the spirits of all human beings are depicted as having been created before the world was made. The first seven chapters of the revised account of the creation (recorded in June 1830) and now published as the book of Moses make repeated reference to man's spiritual creation as well as the creation of all other things spiritually before they existed naturally upon the earth (Moses 3:1–7; 5:24; 6:36, 51, 63). Several revelations during the next two years appear to reinforce this premortal spiritual creation of "all things" (D&C 29:30–32, 49:17, 77:2). Mysteriously, after this initial flurry of references to a spiritual creation, Joseph makes no further mention of it in any later revelations or teachings.

Kirtland Period

In May 1833, a shift occurred in the Prophet's teachings regarding the origin of spirits when he received a revelation indicating that every spirit of man was in the beginning with God as intelligence (not to be confused with *an* intelligence, a doctrine later taught in Nauvoo), and that this "intelligence or the light of truth was not created or made, neither indeed can be" (D&C 93:29). This intelligence is also equated with the "Spirit of truth" (v. 23) which is the same principle identified as the light or glory of God (v. 36). Elaborating on this spirit or intelligence, Parley P. Pratt wrote in 1842, "*The Spirit of Truth, proceeding from the Father and the Son . . . is the light, life, and spirit of all things.*"[44] Thus, the spirit of human beings was seen as a portion of the divine Spirit.

This concept of spirits being created from eternal, divine intelligence is similar to the ancient Gnostic doctrine of emanation and is not unlike that taught in Hosea Ballou's popular book *A Treatise on Atonement* (1805). Ballou, a Universalist, "blurred the distinction between the human and the divine by contending that human beings embodied a divine principle, having been created from the 'fulness' of God rather than from nothing."[45]

It isn't clear whether section 93 was understood as teaching that intelligence became individual spirits prior to the time of mortal birth or whether a portion of it becomes a spirit each time a human fetus is created. Verse 38 explains that "every spirit of man was innocent in the beginning," suggesting a premortal individuation. On the other hand, Thomas Ward, editor of the LDS *Millennial Star*, remarked in

1843 that "what the church of Jesus Christ understood by salvation . . . was this, that intelligence [not *an* intelligence], or the light of truth being connected with elementary matter [i.e., the physical body], which constituted our existence, had become, through the fall as Gods, knowing good and evil."[46] In either case a portion of this divine intelligence becomes "independent in the sphere in which God has placed it, to act for itself" (D&C 93:30).

Nauvoo Period

After the brief mention of uncreated intelligence in Doctrine and Covenants 93, the Prophet remained silent on the subject of the origin of spirits for the next six years. Then, in 1839, he revived the topic with another shift to a doctrine of eternally existing intelligence*s* (now plural). His public teachings in this regard correspond to teachings he was concurrently bringing to light in the book of Abraham. Abraham 3 describes eternally existing intelligences, stating that "spirits" or "intelligences have no beginning; they existed before, they shall have no end, they shall exist after, for they are gnolaum, or eternal" (Abr. 3:18). Notably, the idea of spirits being uncreated appears in all of the Prophet's pronouncements on the origin of spirits after 1833:

> *ca. August 1839:* The Spirit of Man is not a created being; it existed from Eternity and will exist to eternity.[47]
> *February 1840:* I believe that the *soul* is eternal; and had no beginning.[48]
> *January 1841:* If the soul of man had a beginning it will surely have an end. . . . Spirits are eternal.[49]
> *March 1841:* The spirit or the intelligence of men are [sic] self Existant principles.[50]
> *April 1842:* The spirits of men are eternal.[51]
> *April 1844:* "I wish to speak of . . . the soul—the immortal spirit—the mind of man. Where did it come from? All doctors of divinity say that God created it in the beginning; but it is not so . . . Is it logical to say that a spirit is immortal and yet have a beginning? Because if a spirit of man had a beginning it will have an end. . . . God never had power to create the spirit of man at all! . . . Intelligence is eternal and exists upon a self-existent principle. It is a spirit from age to age, and there is no creation about it. All the minds and spirits that God ever sent into the world are susceptible of enlargement.[52]

The book of Abraham further states that these intelligences "were organized before the world was" (Abr. 3:22), which later LDS commentators have assumed to be referring to their spirit birth. It would seem, however, that from an examination of all the Prophet's related teachings during the same period, the organization spoken of in Abraham 3 refers to a social organization of eternally existing intelligences and not a material organization of intelligence into intelligent entities through some process such as spirit birth.[53] The following quotations represent the extent of the Prophet's recorded usage of the term *organization* when referring to spirits:

> *ca. August 1839:* The Father called all spirits before him at the creation of man, and *organized* them.[54]
>
> *January 1841:* At the first *organization* in heaven we were all present and saw the Savior chosen and appointed, and the plan of salvation made and we sanctioned it.[55]
>
> *April 1842:* The spirits of men are eternal. . . . They are *organized* according to that Priesthood which is everlasting.[56]
>
> *May 1843:* He who rules in the heavens when he has a certain work to do calls the Spirits before him to *organize* them.[57]
>
> *October 1843:* The *organization* of . . . spiritual and heavenly beings, was agreeably to the most perfect order and harmony—that their limits and bounds were fixed irrevocably, and voluntarily subscribed to by themselves.[58]

The only organization of intelligences envisioned by the Prophet in these statements is a social organization and not an organization of intelligence into spirits.

Joseph taught that "God Himself found Himself in the midst of spirits and glory. Because He was greater He saw proper to institute laws whereby the rest, who were less in intelligence, could have a privilege to advance like Himself. . . . So He took in hand to save the world of spirits."[59] According to this, it seems that God's plan for saving spirits resulted from the happenstance of a benevolent, superior intelligence finding himself in the midst of unorganized, inferior intelligences. As the Prophet declared in March 1841, "God is good and all his acts is for the benifit of infereir inteligences—God saw that those inteligences had Not power to Defend themselves against those that had a tabernicle therefore the Lord Calls them togather in Counsel [organizes them?] and agrees to form them tabernicles."[60]

It wasn't until after the Prophet's death that the idea of a spirit birth began to appear in LDS sermons and writings (see Chapter 7). From 1839 to his martyrdom, Joseph used "intelligences," "minds," "spirits," and "souls" interchangeably to refer to the eternal, uncreated, and unmodified human spirit. His recorded teachings, therefore, seem incompatible with the doctrine of spirit birth. LDS scholar Van Hale observes, "Either the Mormon spirit birth doctrine was the result of Smith's early followers misunderstanding the prophet's doctrinal statements, or they taught unrecorded doctrine taught by Smith privately in Nauvoo, however much in conflict with Smith's earlier teachings."[61] Yale University professor Harold Bloom similarly notes: "Smith's passionate belief (wholly Gnostic) that our spirit or intelligence is as old as God and the gods, and so need never have been begotten, is rather clearly at variance with the doctrine of spirits being engendered for the unborn. We have the anomaly of a doctrine of Spirit Birth that not only has no sanction in the scriptures that Smith composed, but that also seems to violate one of his most basic principles."[62]

Contemporary Mormonism

Modern expositors of LDS doctrine are left with the task of reconciling the many disparate teachings of the Prophet and his successors on preexistence. Were spirits created? Were they begotten? Have they always existed? The position taken relative to each of these questions requires that conflicting scriptures be reinterpreted if scriptural unity is to be maintained. For example, the current position, as taught in the Church publication *Gospel Principles*, is that spirits "are literally the sons and daughters of God."[63] Therefore, Joseph Fielding Smith and Bruce R. McConkie both maintained that the account of the spiritual creation spoken of in early LDS revelations doesn't refer to the spirit creation or the creation of the human spirit, but rather to the creation of Adam's spiritual-physical (i.e., paradisiacal) body in the Garden of Eden (see Chapter 12.)

Today, the predominant LDS view of the human spirit includes the belief that we existed prior to our spirit birth as some form of intelligence. There is a difference of opinion, however, as to whether we always existed as individual intelligences or were part of a pool of intelligence that became individuated through spirit birth.[64] There are also differences of opinion as to whether our eternal intelligence existed independently of spirit matter, was a property of spirit matter, or was synonymous with spirit matter. Joseph Fielding Smith taught that intelligence exists independently of spirit element and that "intelligence combined with the spirit constitutes a spiritual identity or individual."[65] Orson Pratt earlier taught that intelligence was an attribute of spirit matter and that, prior to spirit birth, "each particle [of spirit matter] was an intelligent, living being of itself."[66] Parley P. Pratt also taught that spirit "is a substance endowed with the attributes of intelligence."[67] For Bruce R. McConkie, "intelligence or light and truth, is . . . a synonym for spirit element," making intelligence and spirit element one and the same.[68]

A distinctive LDS teaching today regarding preexistence is that all living things—humans, animals, plant life, and even the earth itself—had a preexistence as spirits.[69] The idea that the trillions upon trillions of insects and noxious weeds have spirits that existed for aeons prior to their fleeting and seemingly insignificant existence on earth is a curious thought. Even more astounding is the notion that they will be resurrected to immortal glory at some unspecified time in the future. (See Chapter 20.)

Foreordination

Associated with the doctrine of preexistence is the LDS belief that certain spirits were foreordained in pre-earth life to receive special blessings and callings in this life. According to current LDS thought, God's foreordination of individuals in the preexistence is based largely on how valiant they were in that first estate.

Biblical Teachings

Latter-day Saints cite several biblical passages to support the idea of an *actual* foreordination of spirits in the preexistence. However, close scrutiny shows that actual foreordination proves difficult to establish as a biblical doctrine. For one thing, foreordination in and of itself does not necessarily imply or require the prior existence of the one foreordained. We have already noted that Jeremiah's "foreordination" (Jer. 1:5) is generally seen by Old Testament scholars as an ideal foreordination (i.e., in God's prescient mind).

An Old Testament passage frequently used in Mormon discourse as evidence of the foreordination of faithful spirits in the preexistence to be born into the house of Israel is Deuteronomy 32:7–8:

> Remember the days of old, consider the years of many generations ask thy father, and he will shew thee; thy elders, and they will tell thee.
> When the most High divided to the nations their inheritance, when he separated the sons of Adam, he set the bounds of the people according to the number of the children of Israel. [70]

The scholarly understanding of this passage (see also Chap. 6) is that God is here depicted assigning different deities to different nations with Yahweh being designated as Israel's God. The text describes the separation of the "sons of Adam" (implying a post-Fall separation), and not the separation of the spirit children of God. There is no implication here of a preexistent foreordination of individuals.

In the New Testament, Acts records Paul stating that God "hath made of one blood all nations of men for to dwell on all the face of the earth, and hath determined the times before appointed, and the bounds of their habitation" (Acts 17:26). Some LDS authors and leaders interpret this passage to mean that premortal worthiness determines where and when one comes to earth.[71] Once again, however, there is no requirement of human preexistence for God to determine the times and places into which individuals are born. Incidentally, the "appointment" spoken of in Acts 17:26 pertains to the bounds and habitations of "nations," not individuals.

Early Nineteenth-Century Christianity

In Protestantism, two rival doctrines had developed with respect to the receipt of callings and blessings in this life. Calvinists or predestinationists held that callings and appointments in this life are the result of God's sovereign will from eternity, not of any individual acts of worthiness. By 1800 many Protestants were abandoning belief in traditional predestination in favor of the doctrine of foreordination based on God's foreknowledge of how one will choose to act in this life. Those who believed that free will played a role in callings and appointments were known as Arminians, after the early free-will advocate Jacob Arminius (1560–1609).[72]

The difference between Calvinists and Arminians stems largely from differences in interpretation of New Testament passages that speak of God's foreordination and foreknowledge of Christ, of Israel, and of believers in general. The New Testament states that Christ "was foreordained before the foundation of the world" (1 Pet. 1:20) and was slain according to "the determinate counsel and foreknowledge of God" (Acts 2:23). As pertaining to Israel, Paul states that God "foreknew" them (Rom. 11:2), and preserved a remnant "according to the election of grace" (Rom. 11:5). Regarding believers who obtain eternal life, Paul said, "For whom he did foreknow, he also did predestinate to be conformed to the image of his Son" (Rom. 8:29) and to be "justified" and "glorified" (v. 30). Peter called these the "elect according to the foreknowledge of God" (1 Pet. 1:2). The common factor in all of these divine appointments is God's foreknowledge, a concept that was understood differently by Calvinists and Arminians.

Calvinists, who represented more traditional Protestant Christian thought, maintained that God's foreknowledge is a *result* of his foreordination of people and events. In other words, God foreknows because he determines in advance whom he chooses to bless. Calvinists argued that nowhere in the Bible is God's foreknowledge of human beings' voluntary works designated as the basis of God's foreordination, instead pointing to scriptures which state that election comes "according to his [God's] purpose" (Rom. 8:38; see also Eph. 1:11), "according to the good pleasure of his will" (Eph. 1:5), and "according . . . to grace" (Rom. 11:5). Paul taught that God "hath saved us, and called us with an holy calling, not according to our works, but according to his own purpose and grace" (2 Tim. 1:9; see also Rom. 9:11). Calvinists perceived there to be ample scriptural support, at least in Paul's writings, for the belief that it is God's sovereign will, rather than his foreknowledge of the exercise of human free will, that determines callings.

Arminians, on the other hand, felt justified in reading voluntary human righteousness into these same passages since free will is implied elsewhere in the New Testament. They contended that God foreordained individuals to blessings and callings in this life as a result of his absolute foreknowledge of the choices people would make in this life. Arminian Methodist John Wesley, for example, taught that God "fore-appoint[ed] obedient believers to salvation, not without, but 'according to his foreknowledge' of all their works from the foundation of the world."[73] This appointment, as noted earlier, is not dependent on their preexistence. Wesley states, "[God] calleth men 'elected from the foundation of the world,' though not elected till they were men in the flesh. Yet it is all so before God, who, knowing all things from eternity, 'calleth things that are not as though they were.'"[74] Arminians, therefore, held that God foresaw who would be obedient through their own free will and foreordained them to salvation accordingly.

Early Mormonism

It was the spreading Arminian belief in foreordination based on "the foreknowledge of God . . . from all eternity . . . [of] the future faith and good works of the elect"[75] that resonates in early Mormon teachings. Alma 13, for example, speaks of ancient priests being "called and prepared from the foundation of the world according to the foreknowledge of God, on account of their exceeding faith and good works" (Alma 13:3–4). In 1841, approximately one year prior to the publication of the book of Abraham in which foreordination based on premortal works was introduced, Brigham Young and Willard Richards, cite Alma 13 and state, "God chose, elected, or ordained Jesus Christ, His Son, to be the creator, governor, savior, and judge of the world; and Abraham to be the father of the faithful, on account of His foreknowledge of their obedience to His will and commandments."[76] They make no mention of faithfulness in the preexistence, only foreknowledge of faithfulness in mortality.

Just as Mormons joined with Arminians in attributing individual election and foreordination to God's foreknowledge of one's future voluntary works in mortality, they also used the same rationale as Arminians to explain seeming biblical references to predestination. According to Arminians, it was the *terms* of salvation that were predestined or ordained from the foundation of the world, not individual salvation itself. Thus, predestination for Arminians meant that "God has predestined that a specific group of people will be saved—namely, those who believe in Jesus Christ. By believing, individuals fulfilled the predestined condition of salvation."[77] Joseph Smith likewise repudiated the Calvinist concept of predestination, stating in a sermon on May 16, 1841, that "unconditional election of individuals to eternal life was not taught by the apostles."[78] Echoing the Arminian predestination of the terms of salvation, he declared that "God did elect or predestinate, that all those who would be saved, should be saved in Christ Jesus, and through obedience to the gospel."[79]

Nauvoo Period

In the book of Abraham, the basis of foreordination shifts from God's foreknowledge of a person's future righteousness in mortality to a knowledge of that person's premortal righteousness. Here, Abraham sees a gathering of preexistent spirits: "And among all these were many of the noble and great ones." He then records God saying, "These I will make my rulers . . . . Abraham, thou art one of them; thou wast chosen before thou wast born" (Abr. 3:22–23). Thus, foreordination is explained as being based on premortal nobility, without a mention of God's foreknowledge of one's future righteousness—although such foreknowledge is certainly not precluded.

Contemporary Mormonism

Today, Mormons generally follow Joseph Smith's later teaching that the foreordination of prophets and other individuals called to fill special missions is based on premortal worthiness.[80] Latter-day Saints who acknowledge the role of God's foreknowledge in the foreordination and election of individuals don't all agree as to whether God's foreknowledge is absolute, as Arminians would claim, or whether it is just an incredibly accurate prediction based on his past intimate acquaintance with individuals, a concept that emerged from the LDS doctrine of a finite or limited God. Reflecting this latter view, Apostle James E. Talmage taught that God "has a full knowledge of the nature and disposition of each of His children, a knowledge gained by long observation and experience in the past eternity of our primeval childhood" and that elections are made "by reason of that surpassing knowledge."[81] Thus, according to Talmage, foreordination isn't based on absolute foreknowledge, but on predictive foreknowledge using inductive logic, similar to a weather forecast. Expressing a contrary, absolutist view, Apostle Neal A. Maxwell wrote, "God's omniscience is not solely a function of prolonged and discerning familiarity with us—but of the stunning reality that the past and present and future are part of an 'eternal now' with God!"[82]

The book of Abraham's doctrine of foreordination based on premortal righteousness colors the way earlier passages are currently understood. Alma's teaching that the foreordination of priests is based on God's foreknowledge of their works in this life, for example, is sometimes viewed as foreordination based on premortal worthiness, thus making it consistent with teachings in Abraham 3:22–23. The Church publication *Gospel Principles* cites Alma 13:1–3 as teaching that "the prophets prepared themselves to become leaders on earth while they were still spirits in Heaven." Consequently, "God foreordained (chose) them to be his leaders on earth."[83] Alma 13, however, was not initially understood as entailing human preexistence much less varying levels of personal preparation in the preexistence.

Even scriptures with no apparent reference to foreordination are read as though foreordination is implied in one way (premortal righteousness) or the other (divine foreknowledge). An example of this is Jesus's statement, "My sheep hear my voice" (John 10:27). According to Bruce R. McConkie, people are "chosen" to become Christ's sheep in the preexistence "because of their pre-existent training, election, and foreordination."[84] Apostle Neal A. Maxwell, whose theology tends to draw upon earlier LDS teachings that were more in harmony with Arminian thinking, taught that those whom Christ calls his sheep are so designated from preexistence because of God's "divine foreknowledge concerning all mortals and their response to the gospel."[85] However, when read in context, Christ seems to be simply saying that those who hear his voice in this life thereby qualify to become his sheep. There is no implication of any foreordination (John 7:17, 8:32–33, 18:37). This also seems to be the sense of similar expressions found in the Book of Mormon (Mosiah 26:21, 3 Ne. 18:31).

In some interpretations of LDS theology, the doctrine of foreordination to callings and elections in this life includes the belief that being born into a particular lineage and race is determined by one's righteousness in the preexistence. Those who were valiant in the preexistence were foreordained to be born into the chosen lineage of Israel. Bruce R. McConkie states that righteous spirits "were chosen, before they were born, to come to earth as members of the house of Israel. . . . They are foreordained to be baptized, to join the Church, to receive the priesthood, to enter the ordinance of celestial marriage, and to be sealed up unto eternal life."[86] The implication, of course, is that those who are not of the house of Israel were seen by God as being less likely to be saved. If foreordination to salvation is based on God's absolute foreknowledge of what one will do in this life, one has to ask if it is even possible for one to be saved who isn't thus foreordained. Of course, the whole practice since New Testament times of taking the gospel to the gentiles is predicated on their potential for embracing the gospel.

The War in Heaven

In Mormon theology, the war in heaven refers to an ideological confrontation that occurred in the preexistence in which Satan or Lucifer and one third of the spirits that followed him were cast down to earth because of their rebelliousness. The contention was over the role played by moral free agency in the salvation of mortal human beings. The Father's plan called for individual accountability, with his firstborn son to be offered as a sacrifice for those who would repent. Satan proposed to save all of humanity by denying them agency. The Father rejected Satan's plan and cast him down to earth with all his followers. It is believed that this war continues to be waged on earth and can be seen in various ideologies (socialism, totalitarianism, etc.) that threaten moral free agency.[87]

Old Testament

Before looking at biblical passages cited by Latter-day Saints as references to the war in heaven, it is instructive to note that ancient Hebrews developed a number of creation stories that paralleled those of their Near Eastern neighbors. Many of these involved some type of combat among the gods at the time of the creation. Isaiah alludes to this combat when he says of God: "Art thou not it that hath cut Rahab, and wounded the dragon?" (Isa. 51:9). Rahab, the dragon, refers to a primeval sea monster, God's opponent in mythic portrayals of the creation battle.[88] This seems to be the only primordial war alluded to in the Old Testament.

As discussed in Chapter 10, scholars don't see Old Testament writers as having viewed Satan as a rebellious spirit who was cast out from the presence of God, but rather as a respectable member of God's court who bargained with and even received challenges from God (see Job 1:6–12, 2:1–6). One of the initial tales of Satan being cast out of heaven is a late Jewish tradition in which Satan was commanded to pay homage to Adam who was made in the image of God. Satan refused saying, "'I will exalt my throne above the stars of God, I will be like the Most High!' At once God flung Satan and his host out of heaven, down to the earth, and from that moment dates the enmity between Satan and man."[89] Later Christian thought moved Satan's ejection to an earlier (primordial) time and a different set of circumstances.

New Testament

By New Testament times, a Jewish tradition had developed which saw Satan and his angels as outcasts from heaven. Jude 1:6 states that those "angels which kept not their first estate but left their own habitation, he hath reserved in everlasting chains under darkness unto the judgment of the great day." In Mormon theology, keeping one's "first estate" means being faithful in one's premortal existence (Abr. 3:26). Biblical scholars, however, generally understand it as referring to a station of authority. Thus, the NIV reads that these angels "did not keep their positions of authority but abandoned their own home." Other modern translations give a similar rendering. The footnote in the Jerusalem Bible states that these renegade angels are those "sons of God" briefly mentioned in Genesis 6:1–2, but elaborated on in the Book of Enoch. As interpreted in 1 Enoch 6–19, these angels left heaven to mate with mortal women. Jude is familiar with the Book of Enoch and refers to it in Jude 1:14.

According to the Genesis account:

> The sons of God saw the daughters of men that they were fair; and they took them wives of all which they chose. . . .
> There were giants in the earth in those days; and also after that, when the sons of God came in unto the daughters of men, and they bare children to them, the same became mighty men which were of old, men of renown. (Gen. 6:2, 4)

Scholars explain that this account refers to angels who descended from heaven and married humans. Their offspring were called "Nephilim," or giants; and they were great antagonists in the land of Canaan (Num. 13:33; Deut. 2:10–11, 20–21, 3:11; Josh. 12:4, 17:15).[90] First-century Jewish historian Josephus explains, "Many angels of God, accompanied with women, and begat sons that proved unjust, and despisers of all that was good, on account of the confidence they had in their own strength, for the tradition is that these men did what resembled the acts of those whom the Grecians call giants."[91] According to Josephus, it was a Jewish "tradition" that fallen angels were, in some sense, the fathers of the giants of old.[92]

In an apparent effort to make sense out of this passage in Genesis, and since the sons of God were understood in early Mormonism as righteous mortals who embraced the gospel (D&C 11:30, 34:3, 35:2), Joseph Smith altered this passage to read that it was the daughters of these righteous sons of God (rather than the sons of God themselves) who apostatized by marrying non-believing men (see Moses 8:13–15). Interestingly, later in life he adopted Josephus's interpretation of this Genesis passage, telling the Saints in a sermon on April 13, 1843: "The history of Josephus in Speaking of angels [who] came down and took themselves wives of the daughters of men . . . . These ware resurrected Bodies, [who] Violated the Celestial laws."[93] The LDS interpretation of this passage today is that the sons of God were mortal male members of the Church who married women outside the faith. According to Bruce R. McConkie, "Men were marrying out of the Church because they preferred a lewd and lascivious way of life rather than the one decreed in proper matrimony."[94] Thus, McConkie points to mortal men who were rebellious rather than women (as originally taught by Joseph Smith) or angels (as taught by Josephus and in Joseph Smith's later sermons).

Returning to the passage in Jude, it is noteworthy that the angels alluded to were not cast down to earth to tempt humans (as in Mormon theology), but were shackled with chains and confined to darkness (Jude 1:6). Jude's description thus corresponds to 2 Peter 2:4, which states that God consigned these "angels that sinned . . . to hell, and delivered them into chains of darkness, to be reserved unto judgment." Both views are consistent with the revelation of John in which he saw an angel who was given "the key of the bottomless pit" (Rev. 9:1). The footnote to this verse in the Jerusalem Bible specifies that this pit or abyss was believed to be the place "where fallen angels are imprisoned, to be released only to their final punishment." The pseudepigraphic book of 1 Enoch, an apocalyptic work composed in the third century B.C., contributed to this idea of wicked angels falling and being locked up till the last days. They were to be bound "hand and foot" and "cast into darkness" (1 Enoch 10:6), and "in the great day of judgment," they were to be "cast into the fire" (1 Enoch 10:9).

In Jude 1:6 these angels were not punished because of their protest against God's plan but because they "left their own habitation" (i.e., they physically went where they shouldn't have gone). Their subsequent bondage "in everlasting chains" was neither the result of any kind of war or debate, nor was their punishment to be cast down to earth.

The only biblical passage that mentions anything about an actual conflict or war in heaven involving Satan and his angels is found in Revelation. Prior to this time, there doesn't appear to be any notion of such a conflict. Catholic New Testament scholar David Aune states, "Nowhere else in Jewish or early Christian literature is a heavenly battle depicted."[95] Nor does the heavenly war in Revelation seem to refer to a *premortal* war among God's spirit children.

Though Revelation speaks of a heavenly battle, there is no indication that it was a premortal battle. In this conflict, Satan, who is portrayed as "a great red dragon" (Rev. 12:3), "drew the third part of the stars of heaven, and did cast them to the earth" (Rev. 12:4). Mormons typically understand this as a reference to a third of the hosts of heaven who followed Satan in the preexistence.[96] Though not equating Satan's hosts with God's premortal offspring, many Christians prior to the Restoration also understood the banishment of Satan's followers from heaven as occurring at the creation of the world. This is most dramatically depicted in Milton's seventeenth-century epic poem, *Paradise Lost*. Biblical scholars point out, however, that the text itself has this ejection from heaven taking place after mortals were already inhabiting the earth: "Woe to the inhabiters of the earth and of the sea! for the devil is come down unto you" (Rev. 12:12).[97] John further places Satan's banishment to earth some time after the woman or the church[98] brings forth the man child (Rev. 12:13). Thus, this event would have coincided with the persecution of the Christian church. John's revelation was about "things which must shortly come to pass" (Rev. 1:1). As an explanation for Revelation's supposed reference to a premortal war in heaven following the description of the early Christian persecution, Bruce R. McConkie suggested that it was a "parenthetical interpolation" and was not intended to be a sequential narrative.[99]

This reference to a war in heaven is generally understood by scholars as being a depiction of the persecution of the early Christian church and having nothing to do with a premortal conflict.[100] M. Eugene Boring, writing in *The New Interpreter's Study Bible*, states, "The conflict in heaven in which the dragon is defeated is the result of the birth and exaltation of the Messiah. This conflict is not an explanation of the origin of Satan as a 'fallen angel' who rebelled prior to the creation of the world (as in Milton's *Paradise Lost*)."[101] Given that the war with the dragon in heaven is presented in the context of the persecution of the early Christian church, scholars believe that the imagery was simply a way of conveying the cosmic nature of the forces of evil that had combined against the church. This was also the view shared by the third-century Christian historian Victorinus.[103] For John, it appears to have been an eschatological battle signaling the end time, which he believed to be imminently approaching.

Early Mormonism

By the time of Joseph Smith, the New Testament view of the devil and his angels being cast out of heaven had been combined with a literal reading of Isaiah in which Lucifer falls from heaven because of his arrogance in vaunting himself above God. The Book of Mormon, however, uses only the Isaiah imagery, stating that "an angel of God . . . had fallen from heaven . . . having sought that which was evil before God" and thus became the devil (2 Ne. 2:17). Notice that, as yet, no war or strife over agency is mentioned. Satan is simply depicted as seeking to do evil and consequently falling from heaven.

In the Summer of 1830, shortly after the publication of the Book of Mormon, the Prophet received two revelations explaining more precisely that Satan "rebelled" against God and "sought to destroy the agency of man." Borrowing language from Revelation 12, these revelations state that Satan and "a third part of the host of heaven" were consequently "cast down" to the earth (D&C 29:36; Moses 4:3–4). Interestingly, modern LDS scripture never uses the term "war" or any of its synonyms to describe Satan's premortal rebellion. While Doctrine and Covenants 76:28–29 speaks of Satan being cast out of heaven and consequently "mak[ing] war with the saints of God," this war occurs after being ejected from heaven. The only place in scripture that refers to a "war in heaven" is Revelation 12:7, however this is presented as a premillennial rather than a premortal war.

Significantly, in July 1832, Joseph Smith revised Revelation 12, clearly showing his understanding that the war in heaven was a premillennial war (see JST Rev. 12:5–8). He then received a revelation in September 1832 describing the postmillennial battle in Revelation 20, but with Michael as commander. In this conflict, the "devil shall gather together his armies . . . and shall come up to battle against Michael and his armies" (D&C 88:113; cf. Rev. 12:7). Satan and his hosts will be defeated and "cast away" (D&C 88:114; cf. Rev. 20:10).

Nauvoo Period

It wasn't until Joseph began his work on the book of Abraham that one can see a clear teaching that the contention in heaven involved premortal spirits. Until then, the participants of this heavenly rebellion were referred to in a rather classical Christian sense as "the devil and his angels" (D&C 29:37). Abraham 3, which Joseph prepared for publication in March 1842, relates that when God asked whom he should send into the world (presumably to redeem mankind), two spirits volunteered. God chose the first (presumably Christ) and therefore "the second [presumably Satan] was angry, and kept not his first estate; and, at that day, many followed after him" (Abr. 3:28). In May 1843, Joseph taught that Satan "drew many away with him & the greatness of his punishment is that he shall not have a tabernacle."[103] Again in May 1843, Joseph explained that those spirits that followed Satan are "like the devil" in the sense that they have "no bodies" and "kept not their first estate."[104] In these remarks, Joseph is now clearly referring to Satan and his followers as premortal spirits, though this rebellion still isn't referred to as a "war in heaven," neither is Michael mentioned as playing any major role.

Later Mormonism

In April 1853, Orson Pratt provided the first recorded LDS interpretation that the war in heaven alluded to in Revelation 12 took place in "the first estate," with "Michael . . . head[ing] the armies in heaven against the Devil's forces."[105] The combatants in this war were also now generally considered to have been spirit children begotten of God, but not necessarily all destined for *this* earth. In June 1856, Brigham Young asked, "Do you suppose that one third part of all the beings that existed in eternity came with him? No, but one third part of the spirits that were begotten and organized and brought forth to become tenants of fleshly bodies to dwell upon this earth."[106] Of course, this raises the question of whether other worlds populated by Heavenly Father's children would also have evil spirits led by a Satan.

As a final note, the scriptures never explain how Satan would "destroy the agency of man" (Moses 4:3). In current LDS thought, Satan's plan is generally understood as destroying human agency by coercing obedience.[107] During the first several decades of the Church, however, Satan was seen more as a Universalist whose plan for destroying agency was to remove human accountability. In other words, Satan would save people *in* their sins. "An agency was given to all intelligent beings," wrote Orson Pratt, "and . . . Satan sought to destroy this . . . and to redeem them all in their sins."[108] In a letter to William Smith dated December 25, 1844, and published in the *Times and Seasons*, W. W. Phelps wrote, "Lucifer lost his [first estate] by offering to save men in their sins."[109] The fact that Moses 4:1 has Satan proposing to "redeem" all mankind seems to imply that souls would sin. In a Nauvoo sermon reported by George Laub, Joseph Smith taught that Satan "boasted of himself Saying Send me I can save all Even those who Sined against the Holy Ghost."[110] Thus, Satan's plan would have even saved those who commit the unpardonable sin. This early LDS notion of destroying human agency by removing the consequences of sin is rarely presented in current LDS discourse.

Notes

1. Joseph F. Smith, "The Origin of Man," 78, 80.
2. *Gospel Principles* (2009), 10.
3. Ibid., 13–15.
4. Ibid., 16.
5. Everett Ferguson, *Backgrounds of Early Christianity*, 334–35.
6. The Hebrew and Greek words in the King James Version that are translated as *soul* or *spirit* are words that literally mean "breath" or "wind." For example, the Hebrew word *neshamah* that is rendered as *spirit* or *soul* literally means "breath." The Greek word rendered *ghost* or *spirit* in the New Testament is *pneuma* which, again, literally means "breath." Even in English, *spirit*, generally a synonym for *soul*, comes from the Latin *spiritus* and originally meant "breath." (The English words *spiritual* and *respiratory* both derive from the same root.) One of Joseph Smith's early translations utilized a later Judeo-Christian understanding of the soul by providing a modified account of the creation which includes the merging of a spirit being with the body (Abr. 5:7).
7. L. A. Bushinski, "Spirit (in the Bible)," 13:424.
8. Ibid., 13:425.
9. Kaufmann Kohler, Isaac Broyde, and Ludwig Blau, "Soul," 472.
10. G. C. Berkouwer, *Man: The Image of God*, 200.
11. Charles A. Buck, *A Theological Dictionary*, 2:438.
12. Thomas Hobbes, *Leviathan or the Matter, Forme, & Power of a Commonwealth: Ecclesiasticall and Civill*, 28, 249.
13. Leonard Bacon, *Baxtor's Works*, 2:28.
14. Joseph Priestley, *Disquisitions Relating to Matter and Spirit*, 52.
15. For references to early LDS teachings espousing the immateriality of the soul, see Charles R. Harrell, "The Development of the Doctrine of Preexistence: 1830–1844," 82.
16. Warren Cowdery, letter, *Latter Day Saints' Messenger and Advocate* 1 (April 1835): 97
17. *History of the Church*, 4:575.
18. J. I. Marais, "Psychology," 4:2495.
19. Edward Beecher, *The Conflict of the Ages*, 563.
20. Marais, "Psychology," 4:2495; Leo G. Perdue, "Jeremiah," 1113.
21. Lowell L. Bennion, *An Introduction to the Gospel*, 50.
22. *Gospel Principles* (2009), 13
23. Andrew F. Ehat and Lyndon W. Cook, *The Words of Joseph Smith*, 68.
24. Brendan Byrne, "Sons of God," 6:156. See also Marvin Pope, *Job*, 9, 292–93.
25. Parker Pratt Robinson, ed., *Writings of Parley P. Pratt*, 65, 216.
26. Marais, "Psychology," 4:2495. See also Terryl Givens, *When Souls Had Wings: Pre-Mortal Existence in Western Thought*, 26–29.
27. Raymond E. Brown, *The Gospel according to John*, 371.
28. Thomas B. Thayer, *The Origin and History of the Doctrine of Endless Punishment*, 105.

29. Ibid., 106.

30. In some ways, Doctrine and Covenants 93 is an expansion on ideas found in the Gospel of John and ascribes to all individuals what was originally ascribed uniquely to Christ. In John, only Christ was "in the beginning with God" (John 1:2); in Doctrine and Covenants 93, "man was also in the beginning with God" (v. 29). In John, only Christ was uncreated and "all things were made by him" (v. 3). In Doctrine and Covenants 93, neither Christ nor man "was created or made" (v. 29).

31. Marais, "Psychology," 4:2495.

32. Origen, *De Principiis*, 262–64, 286–89, 349–82.

33. See, for example, Joseph Fielding McConkie, "Premortal Existence, Foreordinations, and Heavenly Councils," 174.

34. Orson Pratt, August 29, 1852, *Journal of Discourses*, 1:54.

35. John Newton Brown, "Pre-existiani," 964.

36. Ibid. An 1825 Presbyterian magazine stated, "If we must speculate and form a theory on this subject, the safest and most rational is, to suppose that all souls were created at the beginning of the world; that they remain in a quiescent state, till the bodies which they are to inhabit are formed." "Lectures on the Shorter Catechism of the Westminster Assembly of the Divines," 530.

37. Lorenzo Dow, *The Opinion of Dow; or, Lorenzo's Thoughts, On Different Subjects . . .* , 108.

38. Ibid., 110.

39. Theophilus, "On the Value of the Soul," 107.

40. As paraphrased by Isaac Myer, *Qabbalah*, 273.

41. Orson Pratt, December 15, 1872, *Journal of Discourses*, 15:249.

42. See, for example, Bruce R. McConkie, *Mormon Doctrine*, 290. Brant Gardner, *Second Witness*, 4:214, agrees that the passage does not concern the preexistence and argues that it instead "positions the priests at the 'foundation' of the world, thus locating them somewhere in the Garden of Eden framework, although they were not personally present in the garden."

43. H. N. "Sermon," *The Hopkinsian Magazine* 3 (Nov. 1828): 242.

44. Parley P. Pratt, "The True God and His Worship Contrasted with Idolatry," 187; emphasis his.

45. E. Brooks Holifield, *Theology in America: Christian Thought from the Age of Puritans to the Civil War*, 229.

46. Thomas Ward, "General Conference," 33.

47. Ehat and Cook, *The Words of Joseph Smith*, 9.

48. Ibid., 33.

49. Ibid., 60.

50. Ibid., 68.

51. Joseph Smith Jr., "Try the Spirits," 745.

52. Stan Larsen, "The King Follett Discourse: A Newly Amalgamated Text," 203–4. Larsen's amalgamated version of the King Follett discourse is particularly significant here in that it preserves the wording of the original firsthand accounts, which read that "a spirit" is uncreated. Joseph Fielding Smith altered the wording to read "the intelligence of spirits" in his collection of the Prophet's teachings, which is frequently quoted as proof that the Prophet had in mind the intelligence of spirits, not spirits themselves, when he spoke of

spirits as being uncreated. Joseph Fielding Smith, *Teachings of the Prophet Joseph Smith,* 353.

53. For examples of Abr. 3:22 being interpreted as referring to spirit birth, see McConkie, *Mormon Doctrine,* 442; James E. Talmage, *The Vitality of Mormonism,* 240. It is noteworthy that Joseph Fielding Smith also used "organize" to describe the social or ecclesiastical organization of preexistent spirits. From Abraham's teaching that there were many intelligences (spirits of men), and that they were organized before the world was formed, he concludes: "Men were organized in some such way as we are organized here in the kingdom of God. Among the spirits of men there were superior intelligences chosen to act in authority." Joseph Fielding Smith, *The Way to Perfection,* 27–28.

54. Ehat and Cook, *The Words of Joseph Smith,* 9; emphasis mine.

55. Ibid., 60; emphasis mine.

56. Smith, "Try the Spirits," 745; emphasis mine.

57. Ehat and Cook, *The Words of Joseph Smith,* 207; emphasis mine.

58. Ibid., 253; emphasis mine.

59. Larsen, "The King Follett Discourse: A Newly Amalgamated Text," 204.

60. Ehat and Cook, *The Words of Joseph Smith,* 67–68 (original spelling).

61. Van Hale, "The Origin of the Human Spirit in Early Mormon Thought," 124.

62. Harold Bloom, *The American Religion: The Emergence of the Post-Christian Nation,* 124.

63. *Gospel Principles* (2009), 9.

64. Differing opinions on the nature of intelligence are described in Paul Nolan Hyde, "Intelligences," 2:692–93.

65. Joseph Fielding Smith, *The Progress of Man,* 11.

66. Orson Pratt, "The Pre-Existence of Man" *The Seer* 1, no. 7 (July 1853): 103.

67. Parley P. Pratt, *Key to the Science of Theology: Designed as an Introduction to the First Principles of Spiritual Philosophy, Religion, Law and Government . . . ,* 97. For a discussion of different LDS perspectives on intelligence, see Kenneth W. Godfrey, "The History of Intelligence in Latter-day Saint Thought," 235.

68. McConkie, *Mormon Doctrine,* 387.

69. Joseph Fielding Smith, *Doctrines of Salvation: Compiled Sermons of Joseph Fielding Smith,* 1:64.

70. Talmage, *Articles of Faith,* 175; Harold B. Lee, *Teachings of Harold B. Lee,* 24–25.

71. See, for example, Smith, *Way to Perfection,* 47; Harold B. Lee, *Conference Report,* October, 1973, 7.

72. Roger E. Olsen, *The Story of Christian Theology,* 454.

73. John Wesley, quoted in John L. Girardeau, *Calvinism and Evangelical Arminianism,* 21.

74. Ibid.

75. H. N. "Sermon," 242.

76. Brigham Young and Williard Richards, "Election and Reprobation," 218.

77. McGrath, *Christian Theology,* 470.

78. Ehat and Cook, *The Words of Joseph Smith,* 74, 189.

79. Ibid.

80. *Gospel Principles* (2009), 9–10.
81. James E. Talmage, *The Great Apostasy*, 20.
82. Neal A. Maxwell, *All These Things Shall Give Thee Experience*, 8.
83. *Gospel Principles* (2009), 9.
84. McConkie, *Mormon Doctrine*, 291; see also Bruce R. McConkie, *Doctrinal New Testament Commentary*, 1:490.
85. Neal A. Maxwell, *Things as They Really Are*, 25.
86. Bruce R. McConkie, *A New Witness for the Articles of Faith*, 512–13.
87. C. Terry Warner, "Agency," 1:26–27.
88. John Day, "Rahab," 5:610.
89. Louis Ginzberg, *The Legends of the Jews*, 1:64.
90. Joel W. Rosenberg, "Genesis," 2306.
91. Josephus, *The Antiquities of the Jews*, 28.
92. Ibid.
93. Quoted in Eugene E. England, "George Laub's Nauvoo Journal," 174 (original spelling).
94. Bruce R. McConkie, *The Millennial Messiah: The Second Coming of the Son of Man*, 360.
95. David E. Aune, "Revelation," 2324.
96. Top, "War in Heaven," 4:1547.
97. Aune, "Revelation," 2323.
98. Ibid.
99. McConkie, *Doctrinal New Testament Commentary*, 3:518.
100. L. Michael White, "The AntiChrist: A Historical Puzzle." M. Eugene Boring, "Revelation," 2229.
101. Boring, "Revelation," 2229.
102. Thomas W. Mackay, "Early Christian Millenarianist Interpretation of the Two Witnesses in John's Apocalypse 11:3–13," 1:268.
103. Ehat and Cook, *The Words of Joseph Smith*, 201.
104. Ibid., 205.
105. Orson Pratt, "The Pre-Existence of Man" *The Seer* 1, no. 4 (April 1853): 50–51. I am indebted to Mormon blogger Aquinas for pointing out this reference.
106. Brigham Young, June 22, 1856, *Journal of Discourses*, 3:369.
107. *Gospel Principles* (2009), 13–15.
108. Orson Pratt, July 18, 1880, *Journal of Discourses*, 21:288.
109. Phelps, "The Answer," 758.
110. England, "George Laub's Nauvoo Journal," 171. The allusion to Satan saving even sons of perdition is particularly noteworthy in light of a sermon the Prophet delivered on April 7, 1844, in which he taught: "God has wro[ugh]t out sal[vatio]n for all men unless they have com[mitte]d a cert[ai]n sin." He then explained that in the council in heaven, "J[esus] cont[ende]d that there wo[ul]d be cert[ai]n souls that wo[ul]d be condemned & the d[evi]l s[ai]d he co[ul]d save them all." Ehat and Cook, *The Words of Joseph Smith*, 353. The implication is that Satan wasn't proposing to save everyone in the celestial kingdom, but only from outer darkness.

≈ 12 ≈

The Creation

The LDS doctrine of the creation builds upon and expands the implicit teachings contained in the simple creation story in Genesis. It also addresses many of the outdated and unscientific assumptions underlying traditional Judeo-Christian views of the creation. Initial LDS creation concepts correspond to progressive cosmological views of the early nineteenth century. Just as Old Testament teachings on the creation reflected a primitive cosmology similar to that of neighboring civilizations of the period, LDS teachings reflected ideas that came into vogue during the Enlightenment but also reflected traditional Christian views favoring special creation and the absence of death prior to the Fall. Scriptures related to the creation are generally interpreted today in ways that accommodate modern science, even though some predominant scriptural teachings reflecting traditionalist ideas, such as special creation, have sometimes posed a challenge.

The Genesis Creation Story

The creation narrative in Genesis explains how life, the world, and the extended universe came to be. God created the earth and the heavens (i.e., everything outside the earth) "and all the hosts of them" (Gen. 2:1) by the power of his word. The earth was a flat disk surmounted by an immense hard dome or vault ("firmament") of the heavens (Gen. 1:7–8). The placement of the sun, moon, and stars at the ceiling of this dome in the sky reflected a primitive, geocentric (earth-centered) view of the universe. Thus, the entire universe was believed to fit compactly within the earth's atmosphere, with the earth being the center of that universe.[1] After creating man, God planted a garden "eastward in Eden" (Gen. 2:8)[2] where he placed the man whom he had formed. Everything was created in six Jewish days (a Jewish day is from sundown to sundown); thus, "the evening and morning were the first day" (Gen. 1:5).[3]

Mythical stories of the creation were numerous in the ancient world, and Hebrew cosmogony fit right into the genre of ancient Near Eastern creation mythology. The ancient Sumerians, Babylonians, and Hebrews had a rather limited view of the universe with mortal life existing between the solid firmament of earth below and the solid vault or firmament of heaven above. The overhead vault kept the waters above it from falling down and inundating the world. Small windows or sluice-gates in the vault allowed some of the waters to fall as rain, hence the phrase "opening the windows of heaven" (Gen. 7:11, 8:2; Mal. 3:10). The gods controlled the windows of heaven and mortals feared that if the gods forgot or chose not to close the windows, the earth would flood. The waters below the firmament were controlled by the spirits of the underworld.[4] Although there are some differences between the Hebrew account and neighboring mythological views, a common underlying ancient Near Eastern tradition is evident. According to Old Testament scholar Walter Brueggemann, both the creation and the flood stories as recorded in Genesis were "appropriated by Israel from older, well-developed cultures. In some cases, we have available parallel texts that are older and which evidence the antecedents to the biblical texts."[5]

In Hebrew thought, the universe consisted of three realms or parts. The first was the upper realm or vault of the heavens just described. The second realm was the solid ground or "dry land" which was viewed as a flat surface or disc set on immovable pillars or foundations, hence the question to Job: "Where wast thou when I laid the foundations of the earth?" (Job 38:4). Finally, below the earth was the underworld of the dead, which the Hebrews called *sheol*, and the waters of "the deep." The earth was believed to restrain the waters of the deep from rushing up through rivers or seas. When the earth was flooded, "all the foundations of the great deep burst forth, and the windows of the heavens were opened" (Gen. 7:11; see also Mal. 3:10).[6] The inhabitants of these three realms are succinctly described in Psalms: "The heavens are Yahweh's heavens, but the earth he has given to the sons of men. The dead do not praise Yahweh, nor do any that go down into silence" (RSV Ps. 115:16–18).

In more modern times, the awareness of a universe beyond the atmospheric heavens together with the mounting evidence that life evolved over millions of years has resulted in new ways of interpreting the traditional creation story. Accommodation has been made for the scientific view of the sidereal heavens and their seemingly endless expanse. Literal interpretations of the creation, such as the length of a day in the creation being a twenty-four-hour period and man being formed from dust and woman from his rib, have been increasingly losing favor among modern Christians.

Agent and Method of Creation

In the Old Testament, it is God who creates the heavens and the earth and all things therein. When it came to the creation of man, however, "God said, Let *us* make man in *our* image" (Gen. 1:26; see also 3:22). This curious reference to the plural "us" has been interpreted in numerous ways. Traditional Jewish and Christian scholars have interpreted it in a monotheistic light and view the "us" as depicting a plurality of majesty (the "royal we"), and not a plurality of persons.[7] As noted in Chapter 6, an increasing number of biblical scholars have come to view the "us" as referring to the members of the divine council that assisted in the creation (Judg. 5:2; Isa. 35:3–4, 40:1–8), which also parallels ancient Mesopotamian creation myths. Since many Christians have traditionally seen Christ as playing a prominent role in the creation, a common understanding in Joseph Smith's day was that the "us" refers to the persons in the Trinity, with the Holy Spirit being present as it "moved upon the face of the waters" (Gen. 1:2). In 1825, an article appearing in a Presbyterian periodical explained, "When the world was formed and completely furnished for his [i.e., man's] residence, a council of the Godhead [i.e., the Father, Son and Holy Ghost] is held on the creation of man—'Let us make man' [etc.]."[8]

According to later Old Testament writings, the creation was accomplished by God alone: "I am the LORD that maketh all things; that stretcheth forth the heavens alone; that spreadeth abroad the earth by myself" (Isa. 44:24). No involvement by agents or intermediaries is ever implied in the writings of the prophets.

In the Old Testament, the entire creation was effected verbally (*creatio per verbum*): "God *said*, Let there be light" (Gen. 1:4), etc. Thus, God's word alone brought the universe into existence. Psalm 33:6, 9 declares: "By the word of the Lord were the heavens made; and all the host of them by the breath of his mouth. . . . he spake, and it was done." The same view appears in 2 Esdras 6:38 (NRSV), an apocryphal book: "I said, O Lord, you spoke at the beginning of creation, and said on the first day, 'Let heaven and earth be made,' and your word accomplished the work."

The New Testament adds little to the Old Testament creation narrative besides the declaration that it was Christ, rather than God the Father, who was the direct agent in the creation of the world and, indeed, of "all things" including humankind (John 1:3; Eph. 3:9; Col. 1:16).

Nineteenth-century Christians, as well as early Mormons, largely adhered to the New Testament view that it was Christ, as God's agent, who acted as the creator. The Book of Mormon echoed this traditional Christian belief stating that "Jesus Christ . . . created . . . all things" (Mosiah 4:2; cf. 3 Ne. 9:15) including "man" (Ether 3:15–16; cf. 2 Ne. 11:7; Mosiah 7:27, 26:23; Alma 5:15). Similar to trinitarianism, however, the Book of Mormon makes no essential distinction between the Father and the Son in the act of creation (see Mosiah 4:9) since they are one God.

The Book of Mormon also affirms the biblical and traditional Christian teaching that creation was a verbal act: "By the power of his word man came upon the face of the earth, which earth was created by the power of his word. Wherefore, God . . . [was] able to speak and the world was, and to speak and man was created" (Jacob 4:9). The Book of Mormon further affirms the biblical view of man's creation from the dust stating: "By the power of his word man was created of the dust of the earth" (Morm. 9:17; see also Mosiah 2:25).

The book of Moses account of the creation, revealed in June 1830, builds on ideas contained in the Book of Mormon, while continuing to identify Christ as the creative agent of all things, including Adam and Eve. God reveals: "By the word of my power, have I created them, which is mine Only Begotten Son" (Moses 1:32; cf. 1:33, 2:1). A revelation received by the Prophet near the same time introduces the role of the Spirit in the creative process saying, "By the power of my Spirit created I them; yea, all things both spiritual and temporal" (D&C 29:31). Doctrine and Covenants 88:66, revealed in 1832, equates "Spirit" with Christ's voice, thus maintaining the process of Christ speaking and calling all things into being. Early revelations in the Doctrine and Covenants are univocal, like the Book of Mormon and book of Moses, in teaching that Christ spoke and that, by the power of his word alone, everything temporal and spiritual, including man (D&C 45:1, 76:42, 93:10), was created.

The 1835 *Lectures on Faith* reinforces this verbal mode of creation saying, "It is by words, instead of exerting his physical powers" that God created the world.[9] "God spake, chaos heard, and worlds came into order."[10] Thus, early LDS teachings generally support a traditional view of the creation in which Christ, as God, spoke and heaven and earth came into existence. He similarly spoke and man was created from the dust of the earth.

Teachings during the Nauvoo period expanded the number of agents involved in the creation to include many of the great and noble preexistent spirits. The book of Abraham has the Lord telling these intelligences, "We will go down, for there is space there, and we will take of these materials, and we will make an earth whereon these [presumably the rest of the organized intelligences] may dwell" (Abr. 3:24). This new scripture also has these Gods creating man: "And the Gods took counsel among themselves and said: Let us go down and form man in our image" (Abr. 4:26–27). It is unclear exactly what role these intelligences were understood to have played in the creation since, in the Bible and early LDS revelations, God merely spoke and the elements responded. Notably, there is no mention of a spirit creation in the book of Abraham—perhaps because intelligences at this stage of the Prophet's teachings are considered to be "gnolaum, or eternal" (Abr. 3:18). (See Chapter 11.)

During the later Nauvoo period, the Prophet reportedly taught that Adam "came here from another planet, an immortalized Being, and brought his wife Eve with him, and by eating of the fruit of this earth, became subject to death and decay."[11] From Brigham Young onward, many Church authorities have taught that Adam was begotten, not created.[12] Thus, Bruce R. McConkie qualified Christ's exclusive leadership role in the creation stating that, with the help of other great and noble children of God, he created all things "save only man."[13] In this view, Adam and Eve are understood to have been begotten by God the Father and one of his celestial wives.[14]

Those who hold the view that God the Father, rather than Christ, created Adam and Eve tend to minimize the significance of scriptures that depict Christ as the creator of humankind. Scriptures attributing the creation of humanity to Christ are thus explained by invoking the doctrine of "divine investiture of authority,"[15] which states that Christ was speaking, not as himself, but as though he were the Father. This explanation is problematic, however, in light of passages containing references to both the Father and the Son and specifically stating that the Father created man "by" Jesus Christ (D&C 76:42, 93:10). Such passages don't allow the substitution of God (the Father) for Christ since it isn't a matter of someone speaking in the first person for someone else. What these scriptures explicitly state is that Christ, not God the Father, made human beings. Reconciling the view that Adam was physically begotten of the Father with the teaching in Abraham that the Gods, rather than specifically God the Father, "formed" the first humans (Abr. 4:27) is equally challenging.

Meaning of "Create"

For Latter-day Saints, the creation signifies the organization of all things from existing matter (*ex materia*) as opposed to the traditional Christian view of bringing everything into existence from nothing (*ex nihilo*). The LDS view is based on the belief that matter is eternal and can neither be created nor destroyed. This doctrine, however, is not found in the earliest LDS teachings, nor is it something explicitly stated in the Bible—though it is not inconsistent with ancient Hebrew thought.

It was common in the ancient Near East to speak of creation as being effected *ex materia*. Of significance in this regard is the fact that ancient non-Hebrew accounts of creation "most frequently" presuppose prior existing matter.[16] LDS scholar Kevin Barney argues persuasively that the account in Genesis suggests that God worked with preexisting chaotic materials in the creation.[17] According to E. Loveley and H. J. Sorenson, writing in the *New Catholic Encyclopedia*, "Few modern scholars hold that creation 'out of nothing' is taught in the Old Testament. The abstract notion of nothing does not seem to have been reached by the Israelite mind at that time."[18] Of course, Old Testament support for the doctrine of creation *ex materia* does not necessarily imply that the preexisting material used in the creation was itself uncreated. The Bible simply doesn't address the issue of the origin or eternal nature of matter.

The apocryphal book of 2 Maccabees, written about 100 B.C., contains what scholars generally accept as the first explicit statement of creation *ex nihilo* in canonical or deuterocanonical writings.[19] The passage reads, "I implore you, my child, observe heaven and earth, consider all that is in them, and acknowledge that God made them out of what did not exist, and that mankind comes into being the same way" (2 Macc. 7:28).

Leander Keck, professor of biblical theology at Yale Divinity School, observes that, coming into New Testament times, "the belief that God created out of nothing (*creatio ex nihilo*) was common in Hellenistic Judaism."[20] Scholars are doubtful, therefore, that New Testament writers would have held, or at least universally held, a belief in creation *ex materia*. According to Keck, there are several indications suggesting an early Christian understanding of creation *ex nihilo*.[21] For example, Paul told the Romans that God "calls into existence the things that do not exist" (NRSV Rom. 4:17). The New Testament also attributes the existence of all things to Christ, who, besides God, was the only uncreated form of existence (John 1:3, Eph. 3:9, Col. 1:16).

Whatever the beliefs of New Testament Christians, theological historian Alister McGrath notes that the doctrine of creation *ex nihilo* was widely held by early church fathers and continued through the Middle Ages and the Reformation.[22] The Westminister Confession of Faith (1647) asserts: "It pleased God . . . in the beginning, to create or make of nothing the world, and all things therein."[23]

Initial Mormon views were consistent with the traditional Christian doctrine of *ex nihilo* creation. This is evident from teachings presented in early LDS scriptures as well as in Church periodicals. As already discussed, the Book of Mormon portrays God as bringing the world into existence by merely speaking (Jacob 4:9). Even the 1830 JST account of the creation in Moses says nothing about preexisting matter in the creation of the world. Consistent with this understanding, an article by an unidentified author in the LDS *Evening and the Morning Star* in 1832 portrays human souls as tenuous, stating that the creator "gave [them] existence" and "can either eternally preserve them or absolutely annihilate them."[24]

While *ex nihilo* creation was the traditional Christian view, Enlightenment thinkers saw matter as being eternal and thus favored creation *ex materia*. LDS scientist David Grant explains that, by the time of Joseph Smith, "the view that matter was created from nothing (*ex nihilo*) . . . [had] lost the support of modern science."[25] Theologian and scientist Joseph Priestley noted in 1777, "The ancients . . . supposed that two distinct things, or principles, had been from eternity, viz. matter and Spirit."[26] Priestley reports that these two uncreated principles were, in his day, widely considered as the bases of all existence. This Enlightenment view of matter spilled over into popular religious thought at the time of Joseph Smith. An editorial in an 1826 Universalist publication declared, "we are not bound to believe that all things were created out of nothing lest this should presuppose that all will return to nothing again in the final end, as we may safely believe that any thing which has a beginning of existence . . . can never have eternity connected with it."[27]

The idea of eternally existing matter and spirit first appears in LDS literature in a revelation recorded in 1833. Doctrine and Covenants 93:23 and 33 speak of "element" (i.e., matter) and "Spirit" being "eternal." In July 1839, Parley P. Pratt affirmed, like Priestly, that "matter and Spirit are the two great principles of all existence. Everything animate and inanimate is composed of one or the other, or both of these eternal principles."[28] The use of "Spirit" (with a capital 'S') implies that it is divine Spirit or God's Spirit from which everything spiritual derives. (See Chapter 11.)

In 1842, Joseph Smith introduced the doctrine that all spirit is simply refined matter.[29] Spirit would thus come to be viewed in Mormonism as having similar properties to physical matter, including an existence apart from God.[30]

With this new emphasis on the eternal duration of matter, the word "create" in Genesis and the book of Moses becomes "organized" in the book of Abraham (Abr. 4:1). In January 1841 Joseph argued that even the Genesis account should have used the word "formed or organized" rather than "created."[31] Speaking of the physical world, he stated, "The elements are eternal. That which has a beginning will surely have an end."[32]

Biological Evolution

Mormonism, much like conservative evangelicalism, has traditionally voiced opposition to theories of biological evolution, particularly as they apply to the evolution of man from lower life forms. The reaffirmation of the Genesis account of the creation in early LDS teachings gives little leeway for accommodating evolutionist ideas. The later LDS doctrine of Adam as God's literal physical offspring further precludes any allowance for evolution in the creation of Adam and Eve.

Both the Bible and early LDS scriptures indicate that Adam was formed from the dust of the earth and that the entire creation was completed in six Hebrew days. Further, the Book of Mormon emphasizes that there was no death prior to the fall and that, had Adam and Eve not transgressed, "all things which were created must have remained in the same state in which they were after they were created; and they must have remained forever, and had no end" (2 Ne. 2:22). This passage, if taken in its most straightforward sense, poses a challenge to Latter-day Saints who find compelling geological evidence that death had been occurring for millions of years before the traditional dating of Adam's fall.

Like the Book of Mormon, Joseph Smith's revised account of the creation in the book of Moses emphasizes Adam's position as the "first man" upon the earth, as well as being the "first flesh." This would seem to preclude Adam from having any biological ancestors. Bruce R. McConkie states categorically, "There were no pre-Adamites" and that "any assumption to the contrary runs counter to the whole plan and scheme of the Almighty in creating and peopling this earth."[33] As for the absence of death prior to the fall, the LDS Bible Dictionary under "death" states unequivocally, "Latter-day revelation teaches that there was no death on this earth for any forms of life before the fall of Adam."

Attempts to reconcile evidence of pre-Adamic life with this LDS creationist position have proved to be challenging. Some Latter-day Saints have invoked a statement of Joseph Smith recorded by his private secretary that "this earth was organized or formed out of other planets which were broke up and remodelled and made into the one on which we live."[34] Scientists generally refute this claim as unsupported by the geological record. According to LDS biologist Duane Jeffery, "No scientific evidence whatsoever exists to support such a model, and massive amounts of data indicate that our planet has, from its beginning, been a single dynamic but integrated entity—with continued accretions of space dust and meteorites of course."[35] This recycling theory is also inconsistent with the teachings of other LDS leaders who taught that the worlds which have once been inhabited have already "passed away to their exaltation and glory."[36] Echoing a popular fundamentalist explanation for dinosaurs, Joseph Fielding Smith affirmed the notion that dinosaurs and other forms of prehistoric life did not predate Adam, but were killed in the flood at the time of Noah.[37] Of course, such an assertion is incompatible with modern scientific understanding. Elder Marion G. Romney taught that, while there were no pre-Adamites "in the line of Adam," this would not preclude the possibility of humans living and dying before Adam who were unrelated to him.[38] The difficulty with this theory is that it appears to violate both the first-flesh and the first-death doctrines taught in LDS scripture. Furthermore, the book of Moses states that Adam was "the first man *of all men*" (Moses 1:34; emphasis mine). Other theories have also been advanced, but they all appear to conflict with one or more criteria imposed by scripture.[39]

Many Christians have dealt with the difficulties of creationism by embracing theistic evolution, which postulates that God created humankind using the process of evolution. A variation of this idea is that evolution was used to create all life forms except Adam, who came by special creation. In commenting on this and related theories, Bruce R. McConkie states categorically, "These false notions, together with whatever variations of them happen to be in vogue at any given time, are simply an attempt, on the part of those whose faith falls short of the divine standard, to harmonize the specious theories of men with the revelations of the Lord."[40]

Church teachings today generally run counter to evolutionary claims. The Church publication *Gospel Principles*, which enunciates basic LDS doctrines, states, "Adam and Eve were chosen to be the first people to live on the earth (see Moses 1:34; 4:26). Their part in our Father's plan was to bring mortality into the world."[41] Notwithstanding the denunciation of the theory of biological evolution by more conservative Church authorities—especially as it applies to human beings—other authorities have been more tolerant of evolutionary ideas, which has prevented the Church from taking any "official" position on the matter.[42]

Length of a "Day"

As mentioned earlier, Genesis speaks of the "days" of the creation in a very literal Hebrew sense (sundown to sundown). Belief that the universe was literally created in six days had always been met with some skepticism, but the Enlightenment thinking of the seventeenth and eighteenth centuries raised this skepticism to new levels. By the time of Joseph Smith, it was widely recognized that science and scripture were at odds regarding the length of a day in the creation. One way in which many Bible believers reconciled science and scripture was to apply a figurative interpretation to the days of creation. Thus, a day was interpreted to mean some indeterminate length of time or, according to what many believed to be God's reckoning of time, a thousand years (2 Pet. 3:8). Such explanations, however, seem to stretch the plain meaning of the Genesis record which speaks of ordinary Jewish evening-to-morning periods. In 1832, Andover Theological Seminary's Moses Stuart, a leading biblical scholar at the time, contended that to interpret the "days" of Genesis as long, indefinite periods of time was a perverse attempt to wrest the plain meaning of the scripture to bow to the pressures of modern science. "I am unable to see," he wrote, "how the discoveries of modern science . . . can determine the meaning of Moses's words."[43] More recently, James Barr, professor of Hebrew at Oxford University, confirmed that the words used in Genesis 1 refer to "a series of six days which were the same as the days of 24 hours we now experience." He further noted that he knew of no professor of Hebrew at any leading university who would claim otherwise.[44]

Joseph Smith's 1830 translation of the Genesis creation story speaks of the days of the creation in the ordinary Genesis (and Hebrew) sense of "sundown to sundown" (Moses 2:4–31). In 1832, he drew a comparison between the periods of the creation of the earth and the periods of the earth's temporal existence noting that they both consisted of "seven" time periods. The only difference, he pointed out, was that the creation took seven "days," whereas the earth's temporal existence took seven "thousand years" (D&C 77:6, 12). As Joseph became more acutely aware of scientific repudiations of the view that twenty-four hour days were used in the creation, his later Nauvoo production of the book of Abraham redefined "day" to be a thousand years with the explanation that the earth was on the same clock as Kolob (Abr. 5:13) and that "one day in Kolob is equal to a thousand years according to the measurement of this earth" (Abr. Facsimile 2, Fig. 1). According to this view, days on earth were reckoned to be a thousand earth years in length until the fall of Adam. More literalist LDS doctrinal expositors such as Hyrum L. Andrus,[45] Joseph Fielding Smith[46] and, initially, Bruce R. McConkie[47] accepted these passages at face value, deeming each of the days of creation in the book of Abraham to be a thousand years in length.

As noted above, equating one day of the Lord with a thousand earth years was one of the interpretations given by Christians in Joseph Smith's day and is believed to have been based on a literal interpretation of 2 Peter 3:8 that "one day is with the Lord as a thousand years, and a thousand years as one day." This expression in 2 Peter, however, is regarded by scholars as figurative (note the word "as"), having its basis in Psalms 90:4: "For a thousand years in thy sight are but as yesterday when it is past, and as a watch in the night." In modern translations, the figurative nature of the "thousand years" spoken of in 2 Peter 3:8 is more explicit. *Today's English Version* reads, "There is no difference in the Lord's sight between one day and a thousand years; to him the two are the same." It is in this same figurative vein that Alma 40:8 declares, "All is as one day with God, and time only is measured unto man." Not until the Nauvoo period would the expression in 2 Peter come to be taken literally in LDS literature and applied to the days of the creation.

Even though the book of Abraham makes it quite clear that the length of a "day" or "time" in the creation was a thousand years, since the time of Joseph Smith there have been Saints who have suggested that the creation "day" may actually represent some indeterminate period of time of whatever duration was needed to accomplish the work.[48] Undoubtedly persuaded by the preponderance of scientific evidence indicating that the earth is approximately 4.5 billion years old, most modern LDS commentators have similarly argued that a creation "day" is not necessarily to be interpreted as a thousand years. According to them, the term "time" also appears in the creation account of Abraham and could refer to a period of any duration.[49] This argument, while more accommodating of the geological record, seems to ignore the fact that Abraham specifically designates "time" to be equivalent to one day of the Lord's time which, by definition, is a thousand years. When Abraham speaks of events that occurred during the second "time," the explanation is given that "this was the second time that they called night and day" (Abr. 4:8). LDS scholars F. Kent Nielsen and Steven D. Ricks note that, even though "time" is a "permissible alternative" to "day" in describing the periods of creation, "it is explicitly pointed out that the 'time' [spoken of in Abraham] . . . 'was after the Lord's time, which was after the time of Kolob [a great star that Abraham had seen nearest to the throne of God, whose revolution, one thousand years by our reckoning, is a day unto the Lord]; for as yet the Gods had not appointed unto Adam his reckoning' (Abr. 5:13, 3:2–4)."[50]

Interestingly, in a 1982 *Ensign* article McConkie retreated from his earlier position that a creation day equals a thousand years thereby giving license to those who prefer to view a day as an indefinite period of time. According to his later view, a "day" is a non-specific term and means only "a specified time period; it is an age, an eon, a division of eternity; it is the time between two identifiable events." He further declared that "there is no revealed recitation specifying that each of the 'six days' involved in the Creation was of the same duration."[51] Conveniently, this understanding allows a day to be whatever length is necessary to accommodate the seemingly ever-increasing age attributed to the earth by science. The current Old Testament teaching manual published by the Church states non-definitively: "The length of time required for the Creation is not known."[52] Thus, where earlier interpretations of "days" of creation were more literal and had little regard for the claims of science, more recent interpretations liberally accommodate scientific evidence.

Plurality of Inhabited Worlds

One of the reputedly distinctive ideas in Joseph's revelations is that God created "worlds without number" (Moses 1:33), each with "inhabitants on the face thereof" (Moses 1:29). In a general conference address, Apostle Neal A. Maxwell declared that Joseph Smith gave us "a description of a universe far, far exceeding the astrophysics of the 1830s."[53] What many modern Latter-day Saints are unaware of is that popular textbooks and even reputable scientists of the early 1800s were espousing views about the universe very similar to those Joseph brought to light: an infinite expanse populated by countless inhabited worlds all collectively orbiting an enormous star or star cluster where God resides–which was also the grand governing center of the universe.[54] Of course, compared to the primitive, geocentric cosmology of the Bible, and the Book of Mormon's single clarifying explanation that the earth revolves around the sun (Hel. 12:15), it is natural to be somewhat astonished at the expansive view presented in the book of Moses of a countless number of inhabited worlds as well as the book of Abraham's teaching of God ruling the vast universe from his throne near a grand governing star called Kolob (see Abr. 3:2, 9).

In defense of the antiquity of the cosmological teachings expressed in the Pearl of Great Price, the idea of innumerable inhabitable worlds was in circulation from pre-Socratic times and was espoused by Democritus in the fifth century B.C. who averred that worlds were constantly coming into and going out of existence. Certain ancient Greeks also surmised that the sun was the center of our planetary system. It was during the Age of Enlightenment, however, that the idea of innumerable inhabited worlds became particularly popular.[55] Scientific historian Erich Robert Paul notes that "the cosmologies of Descartes and Newton in the seventeenth century both adopted the view that the universe was full of planetary systems."[56] One of the most widely read and discussed works near the end of the eighteenth century was Thomas Paine's *The Age of Reason* (1794) which speaks of the "immensity of space" that is "filled with systems of worlds" such that "no part of space lies at waste."[57] Similar ideas were later expressed in the Doctrine and Covenants which also speaks of the "immensity of space" and there being "no space in the which there is no kingdom [i.e., world]" (D&C 88:12, 37). Paine also alluded to the age-old concept of "fixed stars," such as our sun, which were believed to be stationary and about which planets revolve. Eighteenth-century Puritan Jonathan Edwards spoke of the throne of God being located on a "fixed abode" at the center of the universe that is not a "moveable globe" like the earth.[58] This same understanding of the cosmos appears in the book of Abraham (Facsimile 2, figure 5) where Kolob, as well as our own sun, falls under the category of "fixed planets or stars."

Facsimile 2 in the book of Abraham also refers to the sun as a "governing planet," an astrological term in Joseph Smith's day.[59] A two-volume work by Thomas Taylor published in 1816 contains several astronomical concepts that would later appear in Abraham 3 and Facsimile no. 2: "fixed stars and planets," identification of certain planets as "governors," and a "grand key." Taylor also refers to the sun as a planet that receives its light and power from a higher sphere (compare Fac. 2, fig. 5).[60] At the time of Joseph Smith, scientists were unaware that the sun generated its energy through hydrogen-helium fusion, so its energy source was a subject of speculation.

Not only was a plurality of worlds a popular view in the late 1700s and early 1800s, but so was the belief that these worlds (which for many included the sun, moon and stars) were inhabited, like our earth. For example, in 1784, Ethan Allen, a rational Deist, spoke of God's creations as "infinite" and stated that "it is altogether reasonable to conclude that the heavenly bodies ... throughout immensity, are each and every one of them possessed or inhabited by some intelligent agents or other."[61] In 1819, Methodist theologian Daniel Isaac wrote matter-of-factly: "There is a plurality of inhabited worlds."[62]

A common justification given for the belief in the inhabitation of the innumerable spheres throughout the universe was the belief that God surely would have created them only for the purpose of supporting his intelligent creations. At Harvard, professors of divinity taught that "all planets in the solar system, not just the earth, are inhabited; otherwise, they argued, these planets would have been created in vain, which God, of course would not do."[63] In 1811, Methodist scholar Adam Clarke remarked, "we are led to infer that all the planets and their satellites, or attendant moons, are inhabited, for matter seems only to exist for the sake of intelligent beings."[64] In 1826, natural and religious philosopher Thomas Dick wrote, "Since ... the Creator made nothing in vain; it is a conclusion to which we are necessarily led, that the planetary globes are inhabited by various orders of intellectual beings, who ... celebrate the glory of their Creator."[65]

Secular books at the time of Joseph Smith also referred to God's infinite and endless work in the creation and population of worlds when offering explanations of the universe. An 1824 textbook of geography and history asserted that God filled the universe with endless inhabited worlds.[66] Thomas Dick's popular work, *Philosophy of a Future State* (1829), promoted, like his earlier 1827 work, the idea of multiple inhabited worlds and is of particular interest since it is known that the Prophet actually owned a copy.[67] Dick observed that the universe is made up of innumerable worlds inhabited by "organized and intelligent beings."[68] He also believed there was fairly conclusive evidence that "all the systems of the universe revolve around a common centre" of enormous size, which he asserted to be the location of "the throne of God."[69] He further suggested that it is from this "central body" that "motion of every kind originates, to produce the order and harmony of the universe,... in order to preserve the balance of the universal system."[70] With the widespread circulation of works such as Dick's, Erich Robert Paul concludes: "We can posit with reasonable confidence that Joseph first heard of the plurality idea during the revivalistic meetings of his youth."[71]

In addition to the belief that other planets were inhabited, another prevalent belief during this time was the notion that the sun and moon were also inhabited.[72] William Herschel, who discovered the planet Uranus, declared in 1795 that the sun "is most probably also inhabited, like the rest of the planets, by beings whose organs are adapted to the peculiar circumstances of that vast globe.... I think myself authorized, *upon astronomical principles*, to propose the sun as an inhabitable world."[73] Regarding habitation on the moon, Methodist theologian Adam Clarke wrote in 1811: "There is scarcely any doubt now remaining in the philosophical world that the moon is a habitable globe. The most accurate observations that have been made with the most powerful telescopes have confirmed the opinion."[74]

This popular lore of an inhabited sun and moon apparently intrigued Joseph Smith who reportedly stated in 1837 that "the moon was inhabited by men and women the same as this earth, and that they lived ... to near the age of 1000 years." Additionally, the men were "near six feet in height, ... dressing quite uniformly in something near the Quaker style."[75] Brigham Young shared a similar belief of an inhabited moon as well as an inhabited sun, stating decisively that there is "no question of it."[76] Even in the twentieth century, Joseph Fielding Smith expressed his "judgment and belief that the sun is a celestial body" and "is inhabited." He also spurned scientific assertions regarding the eventual energy loss of the sun, stating, "That energy is not diminishing and will endure forever."[77]

Today the astronomical and cosmological views expressed in the book of Abraham, which reflected a Newtonian world concept, are viewed by some as being largely outdated. Modern scientific views of the universe introduced by Einstein and others are vastly different from those in vogue during the early nineteenth century. In light of these new theories and discoveries, LDS scholar Keith Norman observes, "This new scientific cosmology pose[s] a serious challenge to the Mormon version of the universe."[78]

In Michael Crowe's survey of Enlightenment beliefs regarding the cosmos, he notes that the notion of a heavily inhabited universe subsided in the wake of scientific developments of the early twentieth century. He states that by 1917, "the confidence prevalent a century earlier that the universe teems with life had seriously diminished."[79] In spite of continued failure to find signs of intelligent life in the universe, even as scientists probe farther into deep space, Latter-day Saints continue to hold to the doctrine of a heavily—though not a densely—inhabited universe. Non-LDS Christians, however, have become much more conservative in this regard—though scientists and theologians haven't totally abandoned the possibility, and even high probability, that extraterrestrial life exists elsewhere in the universe.[80]

The Spiritual Creation

Joseph's revision of the Genesis account of the creation, which he began in June 1830, states that God "created all things . . . spiritually, before they were naturally upon the face of the earth" (Moses 3:5). This concept of a spiritual creation preceding the physical creation appears repeatedly in the book of Moses (Moses 3:1–7; 5:24; 6:36, 51, 63). A revelation given concurrently with the development of the book of Moses affirmed this same two-step process of creation: "For by the power of my Spirit created I them; yea, all things both temporal and spiritual. First spiritual, secondly temporal" (D&C 29:31–32).

In Joseph Smith's day, positing a two-stage creation was one way to reconcile what scholars say are actually two different accounts of the physical creation in Genesis. The first account ends at Genesis 2:3 and the second begins at Genesis 2:4.[81] Scholars who affirm this view point to both a difference in style and vocabulary as well as factual differences in the narratives themselves. The first account, for instance, has plants and animals being created before Adam; in the second account this sequence is reversed. Universalist preacher Hosea Ballou in his popular 1805 work, *A Treatise on the Atonement*, reconciles these two accounts by suggesting that Adam was first created as a spirit and then later physically from dust of the earth. Commenting on the Genesis creation narrative, Ballou wrote,

> After God had finished his work of creation, consecrated the seventh day, and rested from his labor, we are informed that there was not a man to till the ground. This information is reasonable, and authorizes me to say, that as man stood in his *created* character, which is Christ, the heavenly man, he was not, at that time, formed of the dust of the ground, was not of the earth earthly, and was therefore not a tiller of the ground. We are then informed, by the sacred text, that God *formed* (not created) man of the dust of the ground, breathed into his nostrils the breath of life, whereby man became a living soul, or creature. Man is now a partaker of flesh.[82]

Like Ballou, the book of Moses also deals with this disjointed narrative by shaping it into a spiritual creation followed by a physical creation. To fit both of these creations within the same seven-day period, the book of Moses reports that all things were created spiritually during the first six days, with the entire physical creation occurring on the seventh day. A revelation in March 1832 similarly affirmed that "on the seventh day [God] finished his work, and sanctified it, and also formed man out of the dust of the earth" (D&C 77:12).

In Nauvoo, Joseph began expressing the doctrine that spirits or intelligences were eternal and had no creation. Because humans were no longer portrayed as having a spiritual creation, it was necessary to take a different approach to resolve the conflicting creation stories in Genesis. In the book of Abraham, the creation story has its beginning in a council in heaven where the spirits or intelligences of all human beings already exist. The spiritual creation preceding the physical creation in the book of Moses appears to be recast in Abraham as merely a planning or preparatory phase for the physical creation (see Abr. 4–5).

Partially to reconcile the account of the spiritual creation in Moses 2 with the book of Abraham's lack of such an account, it is now commonly asserted that Moses 2 is an account of a paradisiacal-physical creation that is spiritual only in the sense that the bodies of Adam, Eve, and all animal life were "quickened by spirit and not by blood."[83] The second creation account, depicted in Moses 3 as a physical creation, is now viewed as a *temporal* creation or transformation to mortality resulting from the Fall. Joseph Fielding Smith and Bruce R. McConkie both maintained that there is no actual account of the *spirit* creation and that the explanation in Moses 3:5–9 is an "explanatory interpolation" or an aside intended only to indicate that such a spirit creation had occurred.[84] Joseph Smith's associates, Brigham Young and Orson Pratt, however, took Moses 3:5–9 to mean that Moses 2 is an account of the spirit creation.[85]

First Flesh

Interpreting Moses 2 as a physical creation rather than a spiritual creation poses an inconsistency, for the text has the animals being created before Adam in Moses 2; but then in Moses 3, Adam is created first and becomes "the first flesh upon the earth, the first man also" (Moses 3:7). The designation of Adam as the "first flesh," which doesn't appear in the KJV, seems to have been added specifically as a clarification that Adam preceded the animals in the sequence of physical creation, the first creation having only been spiritual. Given the current teaching that Moses 2 is an account of the physical creation, the designation of Adam as the "first flesh" has come to be interpreted to mean that he was the first to enter into a mortal state, which was the consequence of partaking of the forbidden fruit.[86] The LDS Bible Dictionary (s.v. "flesh") states, "Since flesh often means mortality, Adam is spoken of as the 'first flesh' upon the earth, meaning he was the first mortal on the earth, all things being created in a nonmortal condition, and becoming mortal through the fall of Adam."

The current tendency to view the term "first flesh" as referring to Adam being the first mortal—as opposed to being the first life form created that has flesh—is also necessary in order to maintain harmony with the temple endowment which reverses the sequence of creation from Moses 3 and Abraham 5 by having Adam being created *after* the animals. Thus, according to the creation sequence portrayed in the temple endowment, Adam can't be the first living flesh created on earth. In short, not only is the first creation spoken of in Moses 2 now seen as the physical creation in the Garden of Eden instead of a spirit creation, but "first flesh" is now considered to be a reference to Adam's becoming the first mortal rather than being the first life form created having flesh.

This later shift in understanding of the phrase "first flesh" in the book of Moses is problematic for a number of reasons. To begin with, the record clearly states: "I, the Lord God, formed man from the dust of the ground, and breathed into his nostrils the breath of life; and man became a living soul, the first flesh upon the earth" (Moses 3:7). The mention here of Adam being the "first flesh" seems to be an obvious reference to the pronouncement that "there was not yet flesh upon the earth" just two verses earlier in Moses 3:5. Until that time, there were no physically embodied creatures because everything had been created "spiritually . . . in heaven" (Moses 3:5). The account later explains that when Eve was created from Adam's side, she became "flesh of my [Adam's] flesh" (Moses 3:23), seemingly signifying that she was taken from his physical body, which was non-mortal. Harking back to the spiritual creation, Moses 6:51 states that God "made . . .

men [the plural "men" implies more than just Adam—hence, a spirit creation] before they were in the flesh [i.e., before they were created physically]." BYU religion professor Hyrum Andrus has identified additional problems with interpreting "first flesh" as the first mortal being rather than the first physically created being.[87]

Adam, the Son of God

As noted earlier in this chapter, it is often taught in LDS discussions that, instead of being the product of special creation like the plants and animals, Adam was begotten like everyone else who obtains a physical body.[88] Of course, in Genesis man is "formed" out of the earth, which, according to Old Testament scholar Ronald Hendel, "suggests an act of physical molding, as a potter forms clay."[89] Indeed, this is the way the creation of man was typically described in Mesopotamian and Egyptian creation myths.[90] In Hebrew thought, man is a creature like everything else, being created from the dust of the earth.

The New Testament, when giving Christ's genealogy back to Adam, states that Adam was "the son of God" (Luke 3:38). This appellation has been traditionally viewed as a figurative sonship and therefore consistent with Adam's being formed out of clay. The Prophet himself revised this passage to read that Adam was "formed of God," thus aligning with the traditional view of special creation, which was apparently his understanding at least until 1833.[91]

With the post-1843 view that Adam was born rather than being the product of special creation, Luke's statement that Adam was "the son of God" began to be taken literally. A 1912 letter from the First Presidency (Joseph F. Smith was president) reinforced Brigham Young's teaching that Adam was not fashioned from earth like an adobe, but was begotten by God and states as proof: "Adam is called in the Bible 'the son of God' (Luke 3:38)."[92] Bruce R. McConkie notes that "this statement [in Luke], found also in Moses 6:22, has a deep and profound significance and also means what it says."[93] In reconciling God's siring of Adam with the doctrine that Jesus is the "only begotten" of the Father, McConkie explains, "Jesus, on the other hand, was the Only Begotten in the flesh, meaning into a world of mortality where death already reigned."[94] The LDS Bible dictionary (s.v. "flesh") corroborates this interpretation: "Jesus is the 'Only Begotten of the Father' in the flesh, meaning he is the only one begotten of the Father into mortality (Moses 3:7)." Moses 3:7, which speaks of Adam being the "first flesh," is then cited as a proof-text that "flesh" means mortal. However, as previously noted, there are difficulties in interpreting "flesh" in this verse as being mortal as opposed to simply being in possession of a physical body.

Purpose of the Creation

In LDS thought, humankind was created to have eternal joy. Joseph Smith taught: "Happiness is the object and design of our existence; and will be the end thereof, if we pursue the path that leads to it."[95] This is quite different from the purposes of creation expressed in most of the Old Testament which is lacking in teachings of an afterlife. In the Old Testament, God creates the righteous for the sole purpose of glorifying His name and creates the wicked to show forth his power and might. According to Isaiah, God speaks to His people saying, "Every one that is called by my name I have created him for my glory" (Isa. 43:7). On the other hand, with no express provocation, God hardens Pharoah's heart (Ex. 9:12) saying, "For this cause have I raised thee up, for to shew in thee my power; and that my name may be declared throughout all the earth" (Ex. 9:16).[96]

Certain New Testament passages seem to reaffirm the Old Testament idea that God creates both "vessels of wrath" and "vessels of mercy" as he capriciously chooses (Rom. 9:22–23; cf. Isa. 49:5). In New Testament writings, where belief in a hereafter finally comes into full view, God's purpose in creation becomes one of blessing the righteous with His eternal presence and glory. Thus, while the Old Testament viewed the creation of man solely in light of God's own interests, the New Testament at least has man sharing in that interest and becoming "glorified together" as "heirs of God" (Rom. 8:17).

At the time of Joseph Smith, Calvinists and Arminians held conflicting views regarding the purpose of creation. Calvinists maintained that God's own glory was the overriding purpose in human creation while Arminians touted human happiness as the principal end. In 1819, Calvinist minister John Brown issued a refutation against the Arminian position writing, "If rendering men happy to the uttermost was his [God's] principal or sole end, how can he, consistent with his infinite power, wisdom, and goodness, permit them ever to be, in the least, miserable?" Brown concluded, therefore, that, rather than "advancing their happiness, . . . manifesting the glory of his own perfections, must have been his chief end in making . . . men, and . . . every other creature."[97] Calvinists held that some souls were *predestined* to damnation, which would be incongruous for a God whose primary goal is to make everyone happy. For Calvinists, even those who are damned bring glory to God by showing his absolute sovereignty to act according to his own will and pleasure. Criticizing the Calvinistic view of God's purpose in the creation, an article in the *Methodist Magazine* charged, "Their grand principle is, that God made all things for his own glory" and that "God had no other view in creating men . . . than his own interest."[98] The article reasoned that, while God created man for His own glory, God's glory consists of blessing His creations with joy and happiness. Thus, "God created men for their own happiness."⁹⁹

The notion that God created human beings so they could have eternal joy and happiness was a concept espoused from early on in Mormonism as well. The Book of Mormon proclaims that "men are, that they might have joy" (2 Ne. 2:25). Happiness, as the end of human existence, was extended in 1832 to include the entire animal kingdom. In the resurrection, all animals will enter "their destined order or sphere of creation, in the enjoyment of their eternal felicity" (D&C 77:3).

Notes

1. Ronald Hendel, "Genesis," 4; Paul H. Seely, "The Firmament and the Water Above," 227–40.

2. Genesis situates the garden near the Tigris and Euphrates rivers (Gen. 2:10–14), which flow through modern-day Turkey, Syria, and Iraq. The Prophet's 1830 revised account of Genesis also mentions the location of the Garden near these same rivers (Moses 3:10–14). Notably, however, he later taught that the Garden of Eden was located in Jackson County, Missouri (D&C 117:8). Conforming to this later view, the account of the creation which appeared in the book of Abraham refers only to rivers without mentioning their names (Abr. 5:10).

3. Gerhard F. Hasel, a professor of Old Testament and biblical theology at Andrews University, notes that it is the conclusion of "numerous scholars and commentators . . . that the creation 'days' cannot be anything but literal 24-hour days." He further observes that "the most widely recognized Hebrew lexicons and dictionaries of the Hebrew language published in the twentieth century affirm that the designation 'day' in Genesis 1 is meant to communicate a 24-hour day." Gerhard F. Hasel, "The 'Days' of Creation in Genesis 1: Literal 'Days' or Figurative 'Periods/Epochs' of Time," 22.

4. Douglas A. Knight, "Cosmology," 175.

5. Walter Brueggemann, *An Introduction to the Old Testament: The Canon and Christian Imagination*, 29.

6. According to the biblical account, there was evidently no rain until the flood as "the Lord God had not caused it to rain upon the earth . . . but there went up a mist from the earth, and watered the face of the whole ground" (Gen. 2:5–6). Therefore, it wasn't until after the flood that the first rainbow appeared (Gen. 9:13).

7. See the new Jewish Publication Society translation of the Pentateuch, the Torah. The *Anchor Bible* also renders this verse in the singular: "Thus God said, I will make man in my image after my likeness." In opposition to this interpretation, Jon Levenson, a professor of Jewish studies at Harvard Divinity School, stated that "the 'royal we' was not part of the vocabulary of

kings or individual gods in the ancient Near East." Jon E. Levenson, *Creation and the Persistence of Evil,* 158 note 14.

8. "Lectures on the Shorter Catechism," 49. This non-biblical notion of a creation "council" would show up in Joseph Smith's teachings as well. See Andrew F. Ehat and Lyndon W. Cook, *The Words of Joseph Smith,* 341; see also D&C 121:32.

9. *Lectures on Faith,* 7:3.

10. Ibid., 1:22.

11. Anson Call reported to John M. Whitaker that he heard Joseph give this explanation. Perry L. Porter, "Anson Call: Excerpts from His Autobiography."

12. Brigham Young, April 20, 1856, *Journal of Discourses,* 3:319; see also Joseph F. Smith, John R. Winder, and Anthon H. Lund, "The Origin of Man,"1:95.

13. Bruce R. McConkie, "Christ and the Creation," 15. The *Gospel Principles* lesson manual, which tends to simplify Mormon doctrines, teaches that Christ created "everything" in this world. see *Gospel Principles* (2009), 23.

14. Bruce R. McConkie told Reed C. Durham that "it was a true doctrine that God the Father, Eloheim, a divine resurrected being came down to this earth after its creation, with a wife and produced in the natural way of sexual intercourse, a child who grew up and became known as ADAM. They did the same and brought forth a girl who grew up and became EVE. They had bodies of flesh and bone etc., but were not mortal (not till they fell). They (Adam and Eve) were not resurrected and not translated beings. God really did create their bodies on this earth. They were not transported here (only their spirits). He then said that his father-in-law [Joseph Fielding Smith] told him that was a true doctrine; that it had been taught a great deal by President J. F. Smith (6th president). He also added that President Joseph Fielding Smith said it was too deep now for most saints—that's the reason for saying about the creation of Adam and Eve in the temple, 'It's only figurative . . .'" Reed C. Durham quoted in Elden Watson, "Different Thoughts—#7: Adam-God." Several of the Prophet's associates, such as Brigham Young and Parley P. Pratt, went so far as to assert that all plants and animals were the products of natural reproduction rather than special creation, having been transplanted to earth from another world. See Brigham Young, April 20, 1856, *Journal of Discourses,* 3:319; Pratt, *Key to the Science of Theology,* 48-49. This would effectively leave only the organization of inert matter to the work of special creation.

15. Bruce R. McConkie, *Doctrinal New Testament Commentary,* 22.

16. G. Sanders, "Cosmology," 4:283.

17. Kevin L. Barney, "Examining Six Key Concepts in Joseph Smith's Understanding of Genesis 1:1," 108–12.

18. E. Loveley and H. J. Sorenson, "Creation," 4:341–42.

19. Everett Ferguson, *Backgrounds of Early Christianity,* 448.

20. Leander E. Keck, "Romans," 2121.

21. Ibid., 2121–22.

22. Alister E. McGrath, *A Scientific Theology. Vol. 1: Nature,* 159–65.

23. See "The Westminster Confession of Faith."

24. "Comparison between Heathenism and Christianity," *Evening and the Morning Star* 1 (October 1832): 36.

25. David M. Grant, "Creation," 1:868.

26. Joseph Priestley, *Disquisitions Relating to Matter and Spirit*, 177.

27. "What is Truth?," *The Candid Examiner* 2 (November 6, 1826): 86.

28. Parker Pratt Robinson, *Writings of Parley P. Pratt*, 63–64.

29. *History of the Church*, 4:575; D&C 131:7.

30. Grant, "Creation," 1:868.

31. Ehat and Cook, *The Words of Joseph Smith*, 60.

32. Ibid., 60.

33. Bruce R. McConkie, *Mormon Doctrine*, 254.

34. Ehat and Cook, *The Words of Joseph Smith*, 60.

35. Duane E. Jeffery, "Noah's Flood: Modern Scholarship and Mormon Traditions," 37.

36. Joseph Fielding Smith, *Doctrines of Salvation: Compiled Sermons of Joseph Fielding Smith*, 1:62.

37. Joseph Fielding Smith, Letter to Thales A. Derrick, September 25, 1961; photocopy in author's possession. McConkie, *Mormon Doctrine*, 208, speaks of dinosaurs living prior to the flood.

38. Marion G. Romney, "Records of Great Worth," 5.

39. Few Church leaders toed the scriptural line in fending off evolutionist claims as much as Joseph Fielding Smith, even to the point of sternly resisting attempted accommodations of evolution by fellow Church leaders. See Richard Sherlock, "'We Can See No Advantage to a Continuation of the Discussion': The Roberts/Smith/Talmage Affair," 63–78.

40. Bruce R. McConkie, *A New Witness for the Articles of Faith*, 99.

41. *Gospel Principles* (2009), 27.

42. See R. Gary Shapiro, "Book Review of *Mormonism and Evolution: The Authoritative Statements* by William E. Evenson and Duane E. Jeffery."

43. Moses Stuart, quoted in Philip L. Barlow, *Mormons and the Bible: The Place of Latter-day Saints in American Religion*, 90. Stuart's Hebrew Grammar was one of the texts used at the Kirtland Hebrew School.

44. James Barr, Letter to David C. C. Watson, April 23, 1984.

45. Hyrum L. Andrus, *God, Man, and the Universe*, 317.

46. Smith, *Doctrines of Salvation*, 1:80.

47. McConkie, *Mormon Doctrine*, 180.

48. F. Kent Nielsen and Stephen D. Ricks, "Creation, Creation Accounts," 1:342.

49. Elder Russell M. Nelson, in the April 2000 general conference, remarked, "Whether termed a day, a time, or an age, each phase was a period between two identifiable events—a division of eternity." Nelson, "The Creation," 85.

50. Nielsen and Ricks, "Creation, Creation Accounts," 1:341.

51. McConkie, "Christ and the Creation," 11.

52. *Old Testament: Gospel Doctrine Teacher's Manual*, 11.

53. Neal A. Maxwell, "How Choice a Seer!" 99.

54. Michael J. Crowe, *The Extraterrestrial Life Debate, 1750–1900: The Idea of a Plurality of Worlds from Kant to Lowell*, 241–46.

55. For a review of these ideas, see Douglas F. Salmon, "Parallelomania and the Study of Latter-day Scripture: Confirmation, Coincidence, or the Collective Unconscious?" 140–42.

56. Erich Robert Paul, *Science, Religion, and Mormon Cosmology*, 194.

57. Thomas Paine, *Age of Reason: In Two Parts*, 52. According to Joseph's mother, her father-in-law, Asael Smith, angrily tossed *Age of Reason* at her husband telling him to "read it until he believed it." Lavina Fielding Anderson, ed., *Lucy's Book: A Critical Edition of Lucy Smith's Family Memoir*, 291.

58. Jonathan Edwards, *The Works of Jonathan Edwards: With an Essay On His Genius by Henry Rogers and Memoir by Sereno E. Dwight*, 2:630–32. The ancient Greeks also had a notion of "fixed stars" but in the sense that they are fixed relative to each other. It was anciently the common belief that even these fixed stars revolved around the earth.

59. D. Michael Quinn, *Early Mormonism and the Magic World View*, 58.

60. Thomas Taylor, *The Six Books of Proclus: The Platonic Successor, on the Theology of Plato*, 1:361; 2:130, 136, 142.

61. Ethan Allen, *Reason: The Only Oracle of Man; or a Compendius System of Natural Religion*, 18.

62. Daniel Isaac, *The Doctrine of Universal Restoration Examined and Refuted*, 52.

63. Quoted in Paul, *Science, Religion, and Mormon Cosmology*, 51.

64. Adam Clarke, *Commentary on the Bible*, s.v. Genesis 1:16.

65. Thomas Dick, *The Christian Philosopher*, 225.

66. Abraham T. Lowe, *The Columbian Class Book, Consisting of Geographical, Historical and Biographical Extracts . . .* , 351.

67. Kenneth W. Godfrey, "A Note on the Nauvoo Library and Literature Institute," 387.

68. Thomas Dick, *The Philosophy of a Future State*, 211.

69. Ibid., 242.

70. Ibid., 244.

71. Paul, *Science, Religion, and Mormon Cosmology*, 82.

72. For a sampling of Enlightenment claims that the sun and moon are inhabited, see Timothy Harley, *Moon Lore*, 160–78.

73. William Herschel, "On the Nature and Construction of the Sun and Fixed Stars," 63.

74. Clarke, *Commentary on the Bible*, 1:36.

75. Oliver B. Huntington, "Our Sunday Chapter: The Inhabitants of the Moon," 263.

76. Brigham Young, July 24, 1870, *Journal of Discourses*, 13:271.

77. Joseph Fielding Smith Jr. and John J. Stewart, *The Life of Joseph Fielding Smith*, 295–96.

78. Keith E. Norman, "Mormon Cosmology: Can It Survive the Big Bang?" 19–23.

79. Michael J. Crowe, "A History of the Extraterrestrial Life Debate," 159.

80. Evangelical Reverend Billy Graham once stated, "I firmly believe there are intelligent beings like us far away in space who worship God, but we would have nothing to fear from these people. Like us, they are God's creation." Quoted in Ted Peters, *Science, Theology, and Ethics*, 126.

81. The view that Genesis contains two different creation accounts written by different people at different times is part of the broader "documentary hypothesis," which holds that the Torah, or first five books of the Old Testament, represents a combination of documents from at least four different authors or editors. For an introduction to this hypothesis, see Richard E. Friedman, *Who Wrote The Bible?*.

82. Hosea Ballou, *A Treatise on Atonement*, 30.

83. Smith, *Doctrines of Salvation*, 1:76–77.

84. Ibid., 1:72–78; McConkie, *Mormon Doctrine*, 170.

85. See these *Journal of Discourses* addresses by Brigham Young, April 9, 1852, 1:50; February 8, 1857, 4:218; February 17, 1861, 9:125; June 23, 1874, 18:243; October 8, 1876, 257; and Orson Pratt, November 12, 1879, 21:199–200.

86. Smith, *Doctrines of Salvation*, 1:77–78; 92; 107–20; McConkie, "Christ and the Creation," 9–15.

87. Andrus, *God, Man, and the Universe*, 359–60.

88. A statement by the First Presidency under Joseph F. Smith states that all who come to earth, including Adam, have received their body "in like manner." Joseph Fielding Smith, *Man: His Origin and Destiny*, 354.

89. Hendel, "Genesis," 8.

90. David Adams Leeming and Margaret Adams Leeming, *Encyclopedia of Creation Myths*, 60.

91. Joseph likely made this revision to Luke just before February 1833, since by then he was already revising the Gospel of John (see D&C 76:15).

92. James R. Clark, ed., *Messages of the First Presidency*, 4:266.

93. McConkie, *Doctrinal New Testament Commentary*, 1:95; see also 3:392.

94. Ibid., 1:95.

95. *History of the Church*, 5:134.

96. Joseph Smith revised this and other passages to read that Pharoah hardened his own heart (JST Ex. 9:12).

97. John Brown, *A Compendious View of Natural and Revealed Religion*, 38.

98. "New and Old Calvinism," *Methodist Magazine and Quarterly Review (1830–1840)* 13 (January 1831): 225.

99. Ibid.

≈ 13 ≈

The Fall and Nature of Humanity

The crowning act of the creation was the formation of a man and woman to whom the Lord gave dominion "over all the earth" (Gen. 1:26). Prior to their fall, Adam and Eve resided for an unspecified period in the paradisiacal Garden of Eden where they partook of spontaneously growing fruit; their lives free from pain and discomfort. The Lord gave them complete autonomy and freedom with the one stipulation that they not eat of the tree of the knowledge of good and evil, the penalty being certain death: "for in the day that thou eatest thereof thou shalt surely die" (Gen. 2:16–17).

The biblical account of Adam and Eve's transgression and consequent banishment from paradise is short and simple. Having been persuaded by the serpent that knowledge is good and the threat of death a lie, Adam and Eve partook of the forbidden fruit and were cast out of the garden to suffer pain and sorrow, eventually to be overcome by death. To prevent Adam and Eve from partaking of the tree of life and living forever—which would have voided God's word—the Lord "placed at the east of the garden of Eden Cherubims[1] and a flaming sword which turned every way, to keep the way of the tree of life" (Gen. 3:24).

Use of the term "fall" to denote Adam and Eve's transgression and banishment from the Garden is nonbiblical and didn't appear in the way it is commonly understood in much of Christianity (including Mormonism) today until post-New Testament times.[2] Like the account of the creation, the story of the Fall has been interpreted over the centuries both literally and figuratively. Speculations abound regarding the nature of Adam and Eve's transgression and the precise sense in which they "fell."

The doctrine of the fall of Adam is important to Christians, including Latter-day Saints, for a number of reasons, not the least of which is its perceived impact on Adam's posterity. Most Christians believe that, in some mysterious way, the fall affected not only Adam and Eve, but also their posterity, causing them to die both physically and spiritually.

Adam and Eve's "Transgression"

There are differing opinions, even among Latter-day Saints, as to whether Adam and Eve literally partook of forbidden fruit (the common LDS view) or whether this story is only symbolic of some other act they committed. The issue of interest from a doctrinal standpoint, however, is not so much *how* they violated God's command but what the moral implications of their act were. LDS teachings are rather unique in depicting Adam and Eve's transgression not only as a wise and noble act, but one performed with full cognizance that they were furthering God's purposes in the salvation of humankind. Apostle Dallin H. Oaks praised the "wisdom and courage [of Adam and Eve] in the great episode called the Fall."[3]

Historically, Adam and Eve have not been afforded such commendation. In Genesis, Adam and Eve's indulgence in partaking of the forbidden fruit is depicted as a sinful act in which they succumbed to the serpent's enticement and violated God's mandate to abstain from eating the fruit of the tree of the knowledge of good and evil (Gen. 3:4–6). When confronted by the Lord, Adam was ashamed and blamed Eve who, in turn, accused the serpent of trickery. The Old Testament gives no indication that their act was in some sense justifiable or that it was in any way part of God's overall plan for mankind.

The New Testament provides little additional illumination on the nature of Adam and Eve's transgression beyond what can be gleaned from the teachings of Paul, which refer to it in terms similar to the way it is described in Genesis. Though Paul states that it was Eve who was the one "deceived" into partaking of the forbidden fruit (1 Tim. 2:14), he doesn't let Adam off the hook, stating that it was on account of his "disobedience" that sin entered the world (Rom. 5:19). Thus, the fall is portrayed as a sinful act without justification and with no apparent awareness that it was fulfilling a higher law.

Later Christianity continued to uphold the view that Adam and Eve yielded to the serpent's temptation, with the serpent being seen as representing Satan. This same perspective is reflected in early LDS scripture, which uses language such as Satan "entice[d] our first parents to partake of the forbidden fruit" (Hel. 6:26), "the serpent beguiled [them]" (Moses 4:19), and "the devil tempted Adam, and he . . . transgressed the commandment, wherein he became subject to the will of the devil, because he yielded unto temptation" (D&C 29:40). Being enticed, tempted, beguiled, and then yielding to temptation and transgressing are all the hallmarks of sin. The Book of Mormon attributes Adam and Eve's transgression entirely to their weakness in succumbing to "the devil . . . that did beguile our first parents, which was the cause of their fall" (Mosiah 16:3).

Part of the justification for the current LDS teaching that Adam and Eve's transgression was not really a sin is the belief that they had no knowledge of right and wrong while in the garden and were therefore *incapable* of sinning.[4] This belief was expressed by others at the time of Joseph Smith[5] and is not unlike the Quaker perspective given in 1826 that Adam and Eve were "in a state of mere innocency" while in the Garden because "where there is no law there can be no transgression."[6] In contrast, traditional Christianity generally affirmed that Adam and Eve had full moral capacity while in the garden and were innocent only because they had not yet sinned. Thus, their transgression constituted a genuine moral sin rather than just an error in judgment.

The scriptures themselves are somewhat ambivalent in this regard. Though they consistently speak of their transgression as succumbing to temptation and meriting punishment—which would lead one to conclude that they were morally culpable—on the other hand, the Genesis explanation that it wasn't until after their transgression that they became aware of good and evil (Gen. 3:5, 22) suggests that perhaps they were morally incompetent and therefore incapable of committing sin while in the Garden. These conflicting teachings have contributed to the contrary views found today regarding Adam and Eve's moral culpability.

In Mormonism, it is the Book of Mormon that explicitly attributes Adam and Eve's moral "innocence" in the garden to the fact that they could do "no good, for they knew no sin" (2 Ne. 2:23). Presumably, this means that they couldn't sin because they had no knowledge of good and evil. Despite the presumptively innocent nature of their transgression, the Book of Mormon reverts to traditional Christian language to express the complete displeasure of God it incurred. Alma refers to their transgression as a "provocation" of the Lord causing him to "send down his wrath" upon them just as he does upon anyone who commits sin (Alma 12:36).

In LDS thought, Adam and Eve's decision to transgress gradually came to be regarded even more favorably than an innocent error in judgment. It is now seen as a wise and righteous decision made with God's full commendation. At the outset, though LDS teachings portrayed Adam's transgression as evoking the wrath of God, they also depicted it as fulfilling the purposes of the Lord, a perception also found in other contemporary Christian teachings. Based largely on Paul's teachings that Adam's disobedience put into effect God's remedial gift of grace through Christ (Rom. 5), many Christians at the time of Joseph Smith believed that the fall was actually part of God's plan for the salvation of humankind. Eighteenth-century Methodist founder John Wesley wrote that, rather than berating Adam for effecting the Fall, "we [should] bless him from the ground of the heart, for therein laying the grand scheme of man's redemption."[7] This perspective of the fall as a blessed event was known as *felix culpa* (literally, "happy fault") or "fortunate fall." Those who held this view maintained that if it wasn't for the fall of Adam, "humankind could not have experienced the unsurpassable joy of redemption."[8]

Like many Christian sermons in Joseph Smith's day, early LDS scripture depicts the fall as having furthered the purposes of God in the salvation of humankind. The Book of Mormon explains that "if Adam [and Eve] had not transgressed . . . they would have had no children . . . [and] no joy" (2 Ne 2:22–23). The book of Moses records that Eve rejoiced upon learning that "were it not for our transgression we never should have had seed, and never should have known good and evil, and the joy of our redemption" (Moses 5:11).

In February 1840, Joseph proclaimed what many clerics had been advocating—that "it was foreordained he [Adam] should fall."[9] One year later, he invoked Adam's foreordination as grounds for exonerating Adam stating, "Adam did not commit sin in eating the fruits, for God had decreed that he should eat and fall."[10] Joseph's rationale, which was not uncommon, was that it wouldn't make sense for God to condemn Adam for something that he himself decreed should happen.

Additional explanations for why Adam and Eve's transgression wasn't a sin were advanced by later Church authorities, including the idea that they didn't really *succumb* to temptation and that the fruit wasn't actually forbidden.[11] Joseph Fielding Smith stated, "I think the Lord has made it clear that it was not forbidden. He merely said to Adam, if you want to stay here [in the garden] this is the situation. If so, don't eat it."[12] How this is "made clear" given the Lord's express prohibition—"I forbid it"—in Moses 3:17 is rather unclear.

In current LDS discourse, Adam and Eve's transgression is generally justified on the premise that Adam and Eve's innocence in the garden meant that they were incapable of sinning, and not that they merely had not yet sinned. They are also excused in light of the Mormon understanding that partaking of the forbidden fruit was the only way they could fulfill the first commandment to multiply and replenish the earth. According to LDS teachings, the commandment given to Adam and Eve to be fruitful and multiply was impossible to fulfill without partaking of the tree of knowledge of good and evil.[13] Since this first commandment was considered more important than the commandment not to eat of the forbidden fruit, partaking of the forbidden fruit was the right thing to do. James E. Talmage explains,

"Adam found himself in a position that made it impossible for him to obey both of the specific commandments given by the Lord. . . . He deliberately and wisely decided to stand by the first and greater commandment."[14] Adam's display of wisdom in choosing to partake of the forbidden fruit is also emphasized in the LDS temple endowment ceremony, which portrays Adam as partaking to fulfill what he understood to be the higher command to multiply and replenish the earth.

This later teaching—that Adam partook of the forbidden fruit knowing that it would enable him to fulfill a higher law—has influenced the way the Book of Mormon passage, "Adam fell that man might be" (2 Ne. 2:25), is now interpreted. Today it is generally taken as an explanation of Adam's motive for partaking of the fruit.[15] It isn't clear how this explanation is reconciled with the preceding verse which states, "All things have been done in the wisdom of him who knoweth all things" (2 Ne. 2:24).[16] The implication seems to be that the expression "Adam fell that man might be" is a declaration of God's divine purpose in allowing the fall.

In summary, the Old and New Testaments depict Adam and Eve's disobedience as a sinful act bringing about only dire consequences. Later Christians continued to view their disobedience as sinful, but many also believed it to be part of God's eternal plan for bringing about the salvation of humankind. Mormonism initially shared this perspective of a "fortunate fall" but then went one step further by claiming that the fall was not only providential, but wisely enacted by Adam and Eve, who were confident they were doing the right thing. Thus, the fall became seen in Mormonism as the prudent violation of a lesser law in order to comply with a higher law.

Physical Consequences of the Fall

In Genesis, the effects of the fall are entirely negative and physical in nature—"for in the day that thou eatest thereof thou shalt surely die" (Gen. 2:17). Adam and Eve were physically driven out of Eden and subjected to a life of toil, hardship and pain, eventually ending in death.[17] They were consigned to work the earth "in sorrow . . . all the days of [their lives]" (Gen. 3:17). Scholars note that the story of Adam and Eve's disobedience and consequent punishment served as an etiology or explanation to people of the ancient world for why they suffer various hardships in life—laborious toil, thorns and thistles, affliction by snakes, pain in childbearing, and ultimately death.[18]

In spite of the baneful physical consequences of the fall depicted in Genesis, many Latter-day Saints find indications of positive physical outcomes as well. The cursing of the ground "for [their] sake" (Gen. 3:17), for example, is often taken to mean "for their benefit" rather than "because of their doing,"[19] thus turning what scholars perceive as a cursing into a presumptive blessing. Adam and Eve are also seen as obtaining the power of procreation through the fall, which, in Mormon doctrine, they could not have had while in the garden.

Physical Death

According to the Genesis account, Adam and Eve were immune to death while in the garden. Whether this was because they were innately immortal or because they regularly ate from the tree of life is not specified. The implication, however, is that Adam and Eve had unrestricted access to the tree of life (Gen. 2:9, 16), which was the source of their immortality and from which they were subsequently barred after partaking of the forbidden fruit. There is no indication that Adam and Eve were *innately* immortal and that the fall caused them to become mortal. Old Testament scholar Theodore Hiebert, writing for *The New Interpreter's Study Bible*, states that the Genesis account suggests that "they were created mortal from the earth at the beginning (2:7; 3:19) and were later kept from gaining immortality when they were expelled from the garden and denied the fruit of the tree of life (3:22)."[20]

Turning to the New Testament, Paul seems to have assumed that Adam and Eve were immune to death as long as they were in the Garden. Whether Paul believed they were innately immortal or dependent upon access to the tree of life is not specified. He did indicate, however, that Adam *introduced* death into the world by his transgression. To the Romans he wrote, "By one man sin entered into the world, and death by sin" (Rom. 5:12). This should not necessarily be taken to mean that all die *because* of Adam's sin, but only that as a result of his sin, "death by sin" entered the world; and according to Paul, because we are all sinners, we all die. The full verse reads: "Wherefore, as by one man sin entered into the world, and death by sin; and so death passed upon all men, for that all have sinned."

At the time of Joseph Smith, Christians generally held that the fall brought mortality upon all flesh. This was assumed to include the mortality of the entire animal kingdom. In 1823, Timothy Merritt, writing in the *Methodist Magazine*, proclaimed that, through the fall, "pain and death took hold on all animals."[21]

The Book of Mormon echoes this common Christian view stating that the fall brought "death . . . upon all men" (2 Ne. 9:6), and that "if Adam had not transgressed . . . all things which were created [presumably including even animal and plant life] must have remained in the same state in which they were after they were created; and they must have remained forever, and had no end" (2 Ne. 2:22). Adam's transgression was thus perceived as bringing mortality upon all living things.

Later LDS doctrinal expositors have attempted to explain the actual physical transformation that took place in Adam and Eve's body to bring about their mortality. In the mid-twentieth century, Bruce R. McConkie, following the lead of Joseph Fielding Smith, asserted that "Adam . . . was first placed on earth as an immortal being," and that "blood did not flow in Adam's veins."[22] The notion of Adam and Eve being innately immortal makes one wonder what function the tree of life served, or any fruit of the garden, unless it gave them sensory pleasure—which would also be problematic, given that the Book of Mormon states that they knew neither pleasure nor pain (2 Ne. 2:23). According to Joseph Fielding Smith, "the forbidden fruit had the power to create blood and change his [Adam's] nature and mortality took the place of immortality."[23] This explanation is reaffirmed in the LDS Bible dictionary (s.v. "Fall of Adam") which states, "Before the fall, Adam and Eve had physical bodies but no blood. . . . With the eating of the 'forbidden fruit,' Adam and Eve became mortal . . . [and] blood formed in their bodies." Joseph Fielding Smith further taught that, not only Adam and Eve underwent a physiological change, but "all [living] things, partaking of the change, became mortal."[24]

Power of Procreation

In LDS thought, Adam and Eve's transgression gave them the ability to reproduce.[25] Going back to the simple creation story in Genesis, there is no indication that Adam and Eve were unable to comply with any of the commandments they were given while in the garden or that any of them were conflicting. Rather, the implicit expectation seems to have been that they would obey all of them, including the injunction to multiply and replenish the earth.[26] In the second-century B.C. Book of Jubilees (3:6)—also called Little Genesis—Adam and Eve have sexual relations as soon as God introduces them.

The New Testament likewise makes no mention of Adam and Eve's inability to procreate while in the garden. Neither does it teach that it was the fall that endowed them with procreative powers.

For centuries Christians have speculated regarding Adam and Eve's sexual activity prior to the fall. Most Christians and Jews have traditionally assumed that Adam and Eve were sexually active and would have reproduced as commanded if they had not been cast out so abruptly. The traditional perception is that God's purpose in creating the world was for Adam, Eve, and their descendants to enjoy a happy life in the Garden of Eden, but this plan was frustrated when Adam and Eve succumbed to temptation and partook of the forbidden fruit. There were, however, Christian writers since the days of Augustine who believed that Adam and Eve did not have sexual activity until after the fall. In the influential *Paradise Lost*, Milton repudiated such a view and asserted that Adam and Eve undoubtedly had sexual intercourse in the garden, though it was devoid of lust and produced no offspring.[27]

Early LDS scripture gives no indication whether Adam and Eve had sexual relations prior to the fall, noting only that they were incapable of reproduction before the fall (2 Ne. 2:23; Moses 5:11). Through the fall they gained the means of conceiving offspring (2 Ne. 2:25; Moses 6:48). This continues to be the LDS view, which, by implication, is generally assumed to apply to all other life forms as well.

Physical Banishment

In Mormon theology, both the earth and all living things thereon were physically banished from the presence of God as a result of the fall. This separation from God is referred to in Mormonism as spiritual death. With respect to Adam and Eve, the Church publication *Gospel Principles* states, "Adam and Eve . . . suffered spiritual death. This meant they and their children could not walk and talk face to face with God."[28]

In Genesis, Adam and Eve are expelled from the garden, but there is no mention of being shut off from the presence of God who continues conversing with them (Gen. 4:6, 9, 15). It isn't until Cain slew Abel that Cain "went out from the presence of the Lord" (Gen. 4:16; cf. 4:14). The idea that Adam and Eve were cut off from God's presence as a result of the fall appears nowhere in the Old or New Testament. Rather, it was a later Christian development[29] that would also be echoed in the Book of Mormon. In the words of the prophet Alma, "Our first parents were cut off both temporally [i.e., physically] and spiritually from the presence of the Lord" (Alma 42:7). The book of Moses similarly states that Adam and Eve "were shut out from his presence" as a result of the fall (Moses 5:4).

Removal of the Earth

From both the Bible and early LDS scripture, the impression one gets is that, when the earth was created, it was positioned in its current location in relation to the sun and moon, which gave it light during the day and night respectively. In the standard works, the earth is cursed as a result of Adam's transgression, but only to the extent that it would no longer bring forth fruit spontaneously. Nauvoo period teachings suggest, however, that when Adam fell, the earth also fell from its original orbit near Kolob, which is "nigh unto the throne of God" (Abr. 3:19). Echoing teachings given only a few months earlier by Joseph Smith, in May 1841, Elder Benjamin Winchester wrote, "The earth no longer retained its standing in the presence of Jehovah, but was hurled into the immensity of space."[30] Brigham Young later taught the same doctrine, observing that "when man fell, the earth fell into space, and took up its abode in this planetary system, and the sun became our light."[31] As a result of the earth's removal from its original position in space, its reckoning of time presumably changed from Kolob time to solar time (see Abr. 5:13).

Spiritual Consequences of the Fall

Mormonism, like traditional Christianity, sees spiritual consequences resulting from the Fall in addition to physical ones. For most Christians this means inheriting a nature that is degenerate and sinful, bereft of even the will to do good. For many Latter-day Saints, however, it means only separation from God and subjection to a world of sin and corruption.

Spiritual Death

As noted in the discussion above on the physical consequences of the fall, Mormonism holds that Adam and Eve suffered a "spiritual death," which is often simply defined as their separation from the presence of God. Many Latter-day Saints would agree, however, that spiritual death entails more than just a physical separation from God, since those who are spiritually dead are cut off, at least in large measure, from the influence of God's spirit as well. It is in this sense of spiritual depravity that spiritual death will be examined here.

In the Genesis account of the Fall, there are no spiritual consequences mentioned. Neither Adam nor Eve became spiritually desensitized because of the Fall; nor did they pass on a sinful nature to their posterity. The only punishment mentioned is that they would suffer physical pain and sorrow (Gen. 3:16–19), and ultimately return to the dust, "for dust thou art, and unto dust shalt thou return" (Gen. 3:19).

The LDS concept of spiritual death appears to have closer ties to the classical Christian doctrine of original sin and total depravity than to any doctrine articulated in the Bible. Though later Christianity came to attribute humanity's sinful nature to the effects of the Fall, there is little indication that early Israelites made such a connection. This is not to say that there was no acknowledgment in the Old Testament of a human disposition to do evil. The Old

Testament portrays human beings as inclined to evil but capable of responding to instruction and discipline. After nearly all of humankind was swept from the earth in the Flood, the Lord observed, almost as a law of human nature, that "the imagination of man's heart is evil from his youth" (Gen. 8:21). Other Old Testament passages also attest to the human propensity for evil (Ps. 51:5; Jer. 17:9). Nowhere in the Old Testament, however, is this sinful human nature linked to the Fall, nor is it regarded as something that can't be overcome through conscientious effort. Significantly, many of the traditional Christian ideas about the fall bringing some sort of spiritual death or depravity on Adam's posterity have never been adopted by Judaism and Islam, both of which recognize only Old Testament explanations of the Fall.

The one Old Testament passage traditionally cited by Christians to support the idea that humans inherit a sinful nature at birth is Psalms 51:5: "Behold, I was shapen in iniquity; and in sin did my mother conceive me." Biblical scholars fail to see any indication of infants being born with a sinful nature from this verse, noting that there are more plausible interpretations. For instance, it may have been spoken from the perspective of the child conceived by the sinful union of David and Bathsheba (2 Sam. 11:5). It may also simply refer to the sinful world into which all infants are born. Alternatively, David may have been merely using hyperbole to express his own frustration with sin and indicating that it is *as though* he had been born to commit it. The Old Testament teaches that evil arises in one's heart at the time of "youth," not at the point of one's conception or birth (Gen. 8:21).

Though the term "spiritual death" is found nowhere in the Bible, there are several places where death is used in a spiritual or, at least, metaphorical sense (see Ezek. 37:4–14, Rom. 7:10; 8:6)–though it is always the result of individual disobedience. For example, Paul reminded the saints at Ephesus they were once "dead in trespasses and sins" (Eph. 2:1) indicating that it was their own sins that brought this figurative death upon them.

So how did later Christians adduce from the scriptures that humankind became spiritually dead through the fall of Adam? It is largely from Paul's declaration: "By one man's [Adam's] disobedience many were made sinners" (Rom. 5:19), that later Christianity concluded that spiritual depravity resulted from the Fall. This passage has been interpreted in several different ways since the second century with no consensus on either the sense in which "many were made sinners," nor whether it was Adam's fall that *caused* them to sin. Donald McKim, author and editor of numerous books on Christian theology, notes that many early Christians, such as church apologist Justin Martyr (died A.D. 165) "did not draw a link between the sin of Adam and that of later persons." According to McKim, "Justin and the other apologists believed that [the] origin of evil in humanity was with evil demons who infected the race and put it under a curse. . . . In the more developed explanation of Tatian and Theophilus, the sin of Adam is seen as the point of entrance for sin into the world but as nothing more than a prototype or model of the sin that all humanity chooses."[32]

A survey of patristic literature from the second century to the time of Augustine (A.D. 354–430) reveals over time an increasing belief that Adam's sin somehow weakened him and his posterity, causing them to inevitably sin.[33] Even so, there is no indication of a belief in total depravity where humans were bereft of even the will to be good. Shirley Guthrie, a professor of religion at Columbia Theological Seminary, notes that, although some believed that one's "moral powers . . . [were] enfeebled by the Fall, . . . with one voice, up to the time of Augustine, the teachers of the Church declared they were not lost."[34]

Scholars credit Augustine with making the case that the Fall caused all of humanity to be totally depraved. This idea resurged in reformed theology, and by the time of Joseph Smith, Christians widely held that humans are naturally carnal because of Adam and can do no good without divine assistance. According to the Articles of Religion adopted by the Protestant Episcopal Church in 1801, and published in *The Book of Common Prayer*, "The condition of Man after the fall of Adam is such, that he cannot turn and prepare himself, by his own natural strength and good works, to faith. . . . Wherefore we have no power to do good works pleasant and acceptable to God, without the grace of God by Christ."[35] Evangelicals at this same time spoke of man's depraved condition as "man in a state of nature," "the natural man," or being in a "lost and fallen state by nature" —language which also would appear in the Book of Mormon.[36]

In the mid-eighteenth century, John Wesley invoked similar language, preaching that Adam's transgression resulted not only in "temporal death," but also in "spiritual death." He further explained, "The body dies when it is separated from the soul; the soul, when it is separated from God." According to Wesley, because Adam and Eve were separated from God, they and their posterity no longer had access to the influence of the Spirit and thus became slaves to their own "self-will" having now an "earthly, sensual, devilish mind."[37]

Early Mormon scriptures speak of a similar spiritual death resulting from the Fall. The Book of Mormon states, "The fall had brought upon all mankind a spiritual death as well as a temporal, that is, they were cut off from the presence of the Lord" (Alma 42:9). It further states that because they were "cut off . . . from the presence of the Lord . . . they became subjects to follow after their own will" (Alma

42:7); therefore, "they had become carnal, sensual, and devilish, by nature" (Alma 42:10; cf. Mosiah 16:1–4; Moses 5:13; 6:49; D&C 20:20). In the Book of Mormon, as in classical Christianity, spiritual death isn't just banishment from the presence of God; it is severance from all things spiritual; "for all mankind, by the fall of Adam being cut off from the presence of the Lord, are considered as dead, both as to things temporal and to things spiritual" (Hel. 14:16). Because they are cut off from things spiritual, "they are cut off . . . as to things pertaining to righteousness" (Hel. 14:18). Thus "all men . . . were lost, because of the transgression of their parents" (2 Ne. 2:21).

The Book of Mormon's attribution of man's sinful nature to the Fall is not too dissimilar from the view of depravity espoused by Methodists, who were paradoxically also among the most ardent advocates of human agency. The seventh article of the Methodist Church adopted in 1784 states, "Original . . . sin is the corruption of the nature of every man, that naturally is engendered of the offspring of Adam, whereby man is . . . of his own nature inclined to evil, and that continually."[38] The Book of Mormon expresses a similar view of man proclaiming that "because of the fall our natures have become evil continually" (Ether 3:2). Puritans in the seventeenth and eighteenth centuries spoke frequently of the "natural man" being "an enemy to God" (cf. Mosiah 3:19).[39] Similar to popular evangelical sentiment in Joseph Smith's day, the Book of Mormon states that "their [Adam and Eve's] fall . . . was the cause of all mankind becoming carnal, sensual, devilish, knowing evil from good, subjecting themselves to the devil" (Mosiah 16:3).

In his translation of the Bible, Joseph Smith interposed a similar doctrine of spiritual depravity in the Genesis narration of the Fall. Moses 6:55 reads, "And the Lord spake unto Adam, saying: Inasmuch as thy children are conceived in sin, even so when they begin to grow up, sin conceiveth in their hearts, and they taste the bitter, that they may know to prize the good." The expression "conceived in sin" as applied to Adam and Eve's posterity is the way original sin was often described by Protestants and is the expression used in the 1689 Baptist Confession of Faith which states that because "all their posterity . . . [are] conceived in sin, . . . [they are] by nature . . . the servants of sin."[40]

Later LDS teachings during the Nauvoo period continued to reaffirm the doctrine of spiritual depravity. Elder Benjamin Winchester, editor of the Mormon *Gospel Reflector*, wrote in 1841: "The spiritual death, or fall before mentioned, has rendered the human family depraved, subject to vice, folly, wickedness, and temptations, and when we yield to any of these propensities, and transgress a known law of God, we commit sin."[41]

As will be discussed more fully below and in Chapter 15, LDS scripture indicates that the spiritual depravity that befell Adam and his posterity wasn't a total depravity as in Calvinism, for it was mitigated in great measure by the atonement of Christ. First, little children are spiritually preserved in Christ until they reach the age of accountability. Additionally, all are endowed with the light of Christ to lead them into the greater light of the gospel. These were ideas also held by Arminian evangelicals who, along with Latter-day Saints, held to more of a doctrine of hypothetical depravity, which is the belief that humankind would have been totally depraved had it not been for the atonement of Christ and endowment of prevenient (i.e., preliminary) grace[42] which, in Mormonism, is the light of Christ.

Original Guilt

In addition to inferring from Paul's teachings that the sinful nature of humans is a result of the Fall, Christians came to believe that Paul also taught that humans are culpable for Adam's sin. Scholars note that the classical Christian doctrine of "original sin," a term coined by Tertullian (ca. A.D. 155–230), was originally used to designate the human inclination to sin that all inherit from Adam and Eve. Beginning primarily with Augustine, however, it took on the added meaning that humankind also inherits the guilt of Adam and Eve.[43] Augustine's belief in the imputation of Adam's guilt to humankind was based, in part, on a poorly translated Latin text of Romans 5:12. In the original Greek (Augustine couldn't read Greek), Romans 5:12 states that death passed to all human beings "inasmuch as all sinned." The Latin translators mistranslated the passage to read, *in quo omnes peccaverunt*, or "in whom [that is, Adam] all sinned." Thus, Augustine believed that all humankind sinned when Adam sinned.

Christianity on through the time of the Reformation largely adopted this doctrine of original guilt. As the Puritans of the seventeenth century phrased it, "In Adam's fall we sinned all." Belief in the transmission of both the guilt and sinful nature of Adam and Eve to their posterity was spelled out again in the 1647 Westminster Confession: "They [Adam and Eve] being the root, and by God's appointment, standing in the room and stead of all mankind, *the guilt of the sin was imputed*, and *corrupted nature conveyed*, to all their posterity descending from them by ordinary generation."[44]

Although in Reformed theology, original sin implied that both a corrupt human nature *and* the guilt of Adam were passed on to Adam's offspring, in Joseph Smith's day, many evangelicals saw original sin as consisting of only an inherited corrupt nature and believed that humankind was free of the guilt of Adam's transgression. A distinction was therefore often made between original *sin*, which is the depraved nature that all inherit, and original *guilt*, which is the culpability for Adam's sin.

In early nineteenth-century New England, the belief that an individual begins life with a clean slate, free of the guilt of Adam's sin, was becoming increasingly popular.[45] Nathaniel W. Taylor, the first professor of the Yale Divinity School, established in 1822, refuted the traditional claim that humans are guilty of Adam's sin. Taylor's views "gained entry into the Presbyterian Church . . . [and] Charles G. Finney . . . basically adopted Taylor's theology for his program of mass evangelism."[46] One of Taylor's students, Albert Barnes, became a Presbyterian minister and in 1829 delivered a controversial sermon, "The Way of Salvation," in which he, like his mentor, denounced the doctrine of original guilt. In direct opposition to the Westminster standard, Barnes declared that the Bible did not say "that the sinner is held to be personally answerable for the transgressions of Adam. . . . Such a charge, and such a requirement, would be most clearly unjust."[47] In a similar fashion, in 1826, Quaker preacher Elias Hicks delivered a sermon in which he strenuously argued that it is wrong to presume "that we are to stand accountable for Adam's sin."[48]

For evangelicals, rejection of the doctrine of original guilt didn't necessarily mean that humankind was *naturally* born free of the guilt of Adam, but rather that the atonement of Christ redeemed humankind from that guilt. That is to say, Christ atoned for original guilt, thus lifting the accountability for Adam's sin from his posterity. As John Wesley explained, "By the merits of Christ, all men are cleared from the guilt of Adam's actual sin."[49] Thus, just as many believed in a hypothetical depravity, many also believed in a hypothetical guilt for Adam's transgression (i.e., Adam's posterity *would* have been guilty of his transgression had Christ not atoned for that guilt).

Early LDS scriptural teachings similarly saw original guilt as having been absolved by the redemption of Christ. In the Prophet's restoration of the scriptures, he interjected this doctrine into the Genesis narrative, "The Son of God hath atoned for original guilt, wherein the sins of the parents cannot be answered upon the heads of the children" (Moses 6:54). This redemption of Adam's posterity from Adam's guilt is reaffirmed in an 1833 revelation which states, "Every spirit of man was innocent in the beginning; and God having redeemed man from the Fall, men became again, in their infant state, innocent before God" (D&C 93:38).[50] Accordingly, the atonement remits the original guilt that comes upon humankind as a result of Adam's transgression, so all are innocent at birth.

In LDS thought, like contemporary evangelicalism, Christ's redemption of humankind from the guilt of Adam's sin did not rid them of the sinful disposition inherited from Adam. This is what most evangelicals in Joseph Smith's day understood as original sin. Joseph's declaration in the Second Article of Faith, that "men will be punished for their own sins, and not for Adam's transgression," was not a denunciation of original *sin*, therefore, but only of original *guilt*. In laying out the principal beliefs of Mormonism—which Joseph Smith would later draw upon to develop the now canonized thirteen Articles of Faith—Orson Pratt elaborated on this very idea, stating, "We believe that all mankind, by the transgression of their first parents, and not by their own sins, were brought under the curse and penalty of that transgression."[51] Therefore, according to Pratt, all men *are* temporarily punished for the transgression of Adam, but "through the sufferings, death, and atonement of Jesus Christ, all mankind, without one exception, are to be completely, and fully redeemed, both body and spirit, from the endless banishment and curse, to which they were consigned, by Adam's transgression."[52]

Age of Accountability

Although Mormon scripture teaches that all are born into the world with a fallen and sinful nature, special allowance for misbehavior is given to little children who are kept "alive in Christ" until they reach the age of accountability. Many Christians had for centuries maintained that little children are not accountable for their actions until they develop the moral awareness of sin, or, as many Protestants described, until they become "moral agents."[53] Few ventured to assign a specific age when children become personally accountable for sin; only that it doesn't occur until they are able to discern between right and wrong, which was regarded as being different from child to child.[54] The Prophet's teachings were likewise initially non-specific regarding the age when children become accountable. The Book of Mormon emphasizes that "all little children are alive in Christ" (Moro. 8:22; see also vv. 8, 12, 19–20), but gives no indication of when they become accountable. A revelation in September 1830 simply stated that "power is not given unto Satan to tempt little children, until they begin to become accountable before me" (D&C 29:47). A subsequent revelation in November 1831, however, essentially set the age of accountability at "eight years" (D&C 68:27). The Prophet believed that this age was known in ancient times and was intended to correspond to the same number of days (eight) that circumcision was to be performed on male infants (JST Gen. 17:11).

The Dual Nature of Man

Mormonism espouses a dual nature of humans in which the pure spirit that dwelt with God is merged with the corrupt mortal flesh, thereby setting up a tension between the good and evil that are in them.

There doesn't appear to be any notion in Semitic thought of a person having a dual nature where one "part" is good and another "part" is evil. In the Old Testament, "a human being is a totality of being, not a combination of various parts and impulses."[55] Adam was simply created from the dust of the earth and given life through the breath of God. As noted in Chapter 11, the idea of a person consisting of both a body and a spirit is believed by scholars to be a Platonic rather than a Hebrew tradition. Even when the notion of a human spirit begins to appear in biblical writings, it isn't portrayed as having a nature contrary to the flesh. G. C. Berkouwer, chair of dogmatics at Free University in Amsterdam, observes that a "fairly general consensus of opinion has arisen among theologians" in support of Hebrew holism throughout the Bible rather than Greek dualism.[56] "It appears clearly," he notes "that Scripture [Old and New Testaments] never pictures man as a dualistic, or pluralistic being."[57]

Some have attributed the idea of a righteous spirit inhabiting a depraved body to Paul. Although Paul lamented that in his flesh "dwelleth no good thing" (Rom. 7:18) and spoke of the warfare that existed between the "members" of his flesh and "the law of [his] mind" (Rom. 7:23), he never suggested that the spirit is good while the flesh is evil. Describing Paul's use of the word "flesh," James Dunn writes:

> Translations like "unspiritual nature" and "sinful nature" give a misleading and falsely dual overtone to Paul's usage. Flesh for Paul was neither unspiritual nor sinful. The term simply indicated and characterized the weakness of a humanity constituted as flesh and always vulnerable to the manipulation of its desires and needs as flesh.[58]

Theological historian Roger Olson observed that "nowhere does the Bible teach that the soul or spirit is the rational part of the human person or that the body is 'the lower nature.'"[59]

Though Christianity would acquire the tradition of viewing humans as composed of both body and spirit, it has largely viewed humans as having a single rather than a divided nature. The general Christian tradition holds that when Adam fell, his entire being fell subject to evil, both body and spirit. This is evident in the many published sermons on depravity and the nature of humankind that were being circulated in Joseph Smith's day.

Early LDS literature, like contemporary evangelical publications, depicts human nature in monistic terms, in which humans possess only a single nature that is evil without the intervening grace of Christ. LDS scholar Thomas Alexander notes that the Book of Mormon and Joseph Smith's pre-1835 writings cast human nature pessimistically, as "less than the dust of the earth" (Mosiah 4:2; Hel. 12:7) and as "unworthy creatures" (Mosiah 4:11). In the Prophet's later teachings, however, he emphasized the divine nature and potential of humankind, minimizing its worthlessness.[60]

Protestants of the nineteenth century generally interpreted man's creation in God's image (Gen. 1:26) to mean that humans were created in the *moral* image of God—holy and pure. Though we lost much if not all of this image through the Fall, it was believed that we could regain that image again through sanctification of the Spirit. According to sixteenth-century Protestant Reformer John Calvin, "as the image of God . . . shone in Adam before his defection, but was afterwards so corrupted, and almost obliterated, that nothing remains from the ruin, but what is confused, mutilated, and defiled—it is now partly visible in the elect, inasmuch as they are regenerated by the Spirit."[61] This same concept seems to underlie the question posed by Book of Mormon prophet Alma when asking converts in his day, "Have ye received his [God's] image in your countenance?" (Alma 5:14). The Book of Mormon presents humans as having a single nature that is "an enemy to God" if left to themselves, but capable of becoming "saint[s] through the atonement of Christ" by "yield[ing] to the enticings of the Holy Spirit" (Mosiah 3:19). Like many of their Protestant contemporaries, early Latter-day Saints evidently held that God's moral image was only partially expunged from Adam and his posterity after the Fall. An 1832 article in the LDS *Evening and the Morning Star* explained that, as a result of the Fall, "the image of the Creator is partly erased from our hearts."[62] In 1843, Joseph would give a more optimistic assessment of human nature stating, "When man fell he did not lose his image but his character still retain[ed] the image of his maker."[63]

This later, more positive outlook on human nature became even more pronounced with the teaching that humans spirits are begotten of God. Openly challenging the teachings of the apostle Paul, Brigham Young remarked: It is "universally received by professors of religion as a Scriptural doctrine that man is naturally opposed to God. This is not so. Paul says, in his Epistle to the Corinthians, 'But the natural man receiveth not the things of God,' but I say it is the unnatural 'man that receiveth not the things of God.' . . . The natural man is of God."[64] John Taylor, third president of the Church, similarly taught that "it is not natural for men to be evil."[65]

This positive assessment of human nature was not to say that the flesh is morally good, but rather that man is a dual being with a divinely begotten spirit that is inherently good. According to Brigham Young, "The spirit which inhabits these tabernacles naturally loves truth . . . but being so closely united with the flesh . . . the spirit is indeed subject to be influenced by the sin that is in the mortal body, and to be overcome by it and by the power of the devil, unless it is constantly enlightened by that spirit which enlighteneth every man that cometh into the world, and by the power of the Holy Ghost which is imparted through the Gospel."[66]

To summarize, the Old Testament depicts a unity of human nature with humans having only a single disposition which is mischievous by nature—though not attributed to the Fall—and capable of correction. The New Testament continues to present humankind as largely monistic beings who are not only inclined to sin, but are now dependent on God's grace through Christ for righteousness. By the time of Joseph Smith, evangelicals were describing human nature as thoroughly depraved without God's grace. In early LDS thought, especially before the introduction of the concept of a premortal spirit, human beings, both body and spirit, were also viewed as being "carnal, sensual and devilish" by nature. In later LDS teachings, the duality of human nature was emphasized, with the divinely begotten spirit being in tension with the flesh. The spirit is by nature pure but, unaided by the Holy Ghost, is unable to overcome the flesh.

Notes

1. Cherubim were winged, sphinx-like creatures who guarded sacred artifacts such as royal thrones and the ark of the covenant. See William Foxwell Albright, "What Were the Cherubim?" 95–97.
2. James D. G. Dunn, *The Theology of Paul the Apostle*, 81, note 7.
3. Dallin H. Oaks, "The Great Plan of Happiness," 73.
4. See, for example, Bruce R. McConkie, *Mormon Doctrine*, 735.
5. J. K., "The Origin of Sin," 10.
6. Elias Hicks, "Sermon by Elias Hicks, Delivered at Darby, November 15, 1826," 2.
7. John Wesley, *Sermons on Several Occasions*, 93.
8. Victor Yelverton Haines, "Felix Culpa," 274.
9. Andrew F. Ehat and Lyndon W. Cook, *The Words of Joseph Smith*, 33.
10. Ibid., 63.
11. Joseph Fielding Smith, *Answers to Gospel Questions*, 2:214.

12. Joseph Fielding Smith, quoted in Robert J. Matthews, *A Bible! A Bible!*, 185–86.

13. Bruce R. McConkie, *A New Witness for the Articles of Faith*, 91.

14. James E. Talmage, *Articles of Faith*, 59.

15. See, for example, *Doctrines of the Gospel Student Manual*, 20.

16. The assertion in 2 Nephi 2:24 that the Fall was foreknown to God echoes the early 1800 Arminian perspective that the fall of Adam was foreknown to God, but not predestined as the Calvinists claimed. "Miltoniana," *The Baptist Magazine* 17 (November 1825): 464.

17. Anthony Hutchinson notes that the phrase "in the day thou eatest thereof thou shalt surely die" (Gen. 2:17) was intended to mean "at the moment you eat from it you will most certainly die." Anthony Hutchinson, "A Mormon Midrash? LDS Creation Narratives Reconsidered," 25. A Jewish tradition is that God took pity on Adam and Eve and, rather than follow through with a punishment of death on the spot, banished them from the garden and consigned them to a life of toil and pain until their natural return to dust. The book of Abraham resolves the problem of why Adam and Eve didn't die in "the day" they partook of the forbidden fruit by redefining the length of a day to mean one thousand years. Joseph Smith taught that the day the Lord had reference to was according to the Lord's time which was a thousand years. Ehat and Cook, *The Words of Joseph Smith*, 64–65. Though Genesis 5:5 has Adam dying at the age of 930 (Gen. 5:5), Joseph has him dying at age one thousand. Kent P. Jackson, *The Book of Moses and the Joseph Smith Translation Manuscripts*, 103. Joseph Smith reportedly informed Edward Stevenson that Adam lived within about 6 months of being a thousand years old. See Robert J. Matthews, *"A Plainer Translation": Joseph Smith's Translation of the Bible, a History and Commentary*, 84–85.

18. Theodore Hiebert, "Genesis," 12.

19. See, for example, Joseph Fielding McConkie and Robert L. Millet, *Doctrinal Commentary on the Book of Mormon*, 4:212; William B. Smart, *Messages for a Happier Life*, 4. Bible translators indicate, however, that "For thy sake" means "because of your doing" (Gen. 8:21 note) or "on your account" (Matt. 5:11 note). For similar uses, see Gen. 20:11; Deut. 1:37; 1 Sam. 23:10; Jac. 2:29.

20. Hiebert, "Genesis," 11. For further discussion of the evidence pointing to the mortality of Adam and Eve in the Garden, see Hutchinson, "A Mormon Midrash?" 25.

21. Timothy Merritt, "Divinity," *Methodist Magazine* 6 (September 1823): 322.

22. Bruce R. McConkie, *Mormon Doctrine*, 286. See also Smith, *Answers to Gospel Questions*, 1:179.

23. Joseph Fielding Smith, *Doctrines of Salvation: Compiled Sermons of Joseph Fielding Smith*, 1:77.

24. Ibid. Belief that the Fall brought death on all life forms seems to be suggested in *Gospel Principles*, which states, "[Adam and Eve's] part in our Father's plan was to bring mortality into the world." *Gospel Principles* (2009), 27.

25. Ibid., 29.

26. For a list of considerations as to whether the Genesis account weighs for or against sexuality in the garden, see David P. Wright, "Sex and Death in the Garden of Eden," 33–39. David Wright, an ancient Near Eastern scholar, states that the evidence and textual implications "lead decisively to the conclusion that the man and woman [were] sexually active in the garden" (38).

27. John Milton, *Paradise Lost, Illustrated with Texts of Scripture*, 4.741–43.

28. *Gospel Principles* (2009), 29.

29. See "The Westminster Confession of Faith."

30. Benjamin Winchester, "The Millennium," 248. This idea was likely obtained from Joseph Smith who, in January 1841, instructed the Saints that when the earth is redeemed, it "will be rolled back into the presence of God and crowned with celestial glory." Ehat and Cook, *The Words of Joseph Smith*, 60.

31. Brigham Young, July 19, 1874, *Journal of Discourses*, 17:143.

32. Donald K. McKim, *Theological Turning Points: Major Issues in Christian Thought*, 66.

33. Bernard Ramm, *Offense to Reason: A Theology of Sin*, 52.

34. Shirley C. Guthrie, *Christian Doctrine*, 307.

35. *The Book of Common Prayer and Other Rites and Ceremonies of the Church . . .* , 378.

36. Mark D. Thomas, *Digging in Cumorah: Reclaiming Book of Mormon Narratives*, 128.

37. Wesley, *Sermons on Several Occasions*, 1:403.

38. Philip Scharff, *The Creeds of the Evangelical Protestant Churches*, 808.

39. See, for examples, Thomas Goodwin, *The Works of Thomas Goodwin*, 2:10; Jonathan Edwards, *The Works of Jonathan Edwards: With an Essay on His Genius . . .* , 2:81, 131, 138. For similar expressions by Joseph Smith's contemporaries, see Thomas, *Digging in Cumorah*, 128.

40. See "The Baptist Confession of Faith," chap. 6.

41. Benjamin Winchester, "The Divinity of Christ—The object of His mission—The kingdom of God . . . ," 37. Brigham Young similarly taught, "Mankind are revengeful, passionate, hateful, and devilish in their dispositions. This we inherit through the Fall, and the grace of God is designed to enable us to overcome it." Brigham Young, September 2, 1860, *Journal of Discourses*, 8:160. Today there seems to be a reticence among Latter-day Saint expositors to interpret the Book of Mormon as teaching that natural man is in any way depraved due to the Fall. For example, the entry on "Natural Man" in the *Encyclopedia of Mormonism* reads, "The phrase 'natural man' is understood by Latter-day Saints to be an unrepentant person [i.e., one who has sinned and remains in sin]; it does not imply that mortals are by nature depraved or evil, but only that they are in a fallen condition." R. J. Snow, "Natural Man," 3:985.

42. Roger E. Olsen, *Arminian Theology: Myths and Realities*, 155.

43. Shirley C. Guthrie, *Christian Doctrine*, 306–7.

44. See "The Westminster Confession of Faith"; emphasis added.

45. Nathaniel W. Taylor, *Essays, Lectures, Etc. upon Selected Topics in Revealed Theology*, 165–67; and E. Brooks Holifield, *Theology in America: Christian Thought from the Age of Puritans to the Civil War*, 350–51.

46. D. G. Hart and John R. Muether, "Turning Points in American Presbyterian History—Part 5: The Plan of Union, 1801."

47. Albert Barnes, quoted in ibid.

48. Elias Hicks, "Sermon by Elias Hicks, Delivered in Wilmington, Del. Sunday Morning, December 3, 1826," 183.

49. John Wesley, quoted in John L. Peters, *Christian Perfection & American Methodism*, 42.

50. This verse has been interpreted to mean that Christ atoned for sins that spirits commit in the preexistence. Joseph Fielding Smith, *Take Heed to Yourselves*, 261–62. Such an interpretation, however, presupposes that spirits had agency and capacity for sin in the preexistence, a notion that had not yet appeared in LDS thought. Note that the verse doesn't say that Christ redeemed spirits from sins they committed in the preexistence, but rather that he redeemed them "from the fall" so they would be untainted by Adam's sin at mortal birth. Orson Pratt captures this sense in his explaination that, "the atonement restored all mankind, in their infant state, from spiritual death to spiritual life. As in Adam all died spiritually; even so in Christ all, in their infancy, are made alive spiritually." Orson Pratt, "The Fall and Atonement," 609.

51. Orson Pratt, *An Interesting Account of Several Remarkable Visions*, 24.

52. Ibid., 25.

53. For statements by Christian writers, see Taylor, *Essays, Lectures, Etc.*, 216.

54. "The Christian Education of Children," 345.

55. Barry Stricker, "Anthropology," 61.

56. G. C. Berkouwer, *Man: The Image of God*, 200.

57. Ibid., 203.

58. Dunn, *The Theology of Paul the Apostle*, 70.

59. Roger E. Olsen, *The Story of Christian Theology*, 89.

60. Thomas G. Alexander, "The Reconstruction of Mormon Doctrine: From Joseph Smith to Progressive Theology," 24–33.

61. John Calvin, *Institutes of the Christian Religion*, 1.15.4; 176–77.

62. "Comparison between Heathenism and Christianity," 35. In 1818 a New England pastor of the First Church of Christ wrote, "By many it is contended, that by the fall, man but partly lost the moral image of God; and that all his posterity have sustained the same mixed character; being deeply corrupted in heart, being partly, but not totally depraved. Others maintain the opinion, that the immediate, and the abiding consequence of the first transgression, was total sinfulness and depravity of heart." Jacob Catlin, *A Compendium of the System of Divine Truth*, 98.

63. Ehat and Cook, *The Words of Joseph Smith*, 231.

64. Brigham Young, June 15, 1862, *Journal of Discourses*, 9:305.

65. John Taylor, May 18, 1862, *Journal of Discourses*, 10:50.

66. Brigham Young, June 3, 1866, *Journal of Discourses*, 11:238. Traditional Christians who, since the time of Tertullian (died A.D. 165), believed that man had both a spirit and a body, deemed that the spirit inherited a sinful nature along with the body. McKim, *Theological Turning Points*, 66.

~ 14 ~

The Atonement

The atonement of Jesus Christ is viewed by traditional Christians and Mormons alike as the ultimate manifestation of God's love for his children and the basis of all hope for the hereafter. According to Mormon theology, the atonement of Jesus Christ redeems all humankind from the consequences of the fall of Adam and saves those who repent from the effects of personal sin. It thus forms the central core of the gospel, giving substance and significance to all that is taught. Concerning the Atonement, Joseph Smith declared: "All other things which pertain to our religion are only appendages to it."[1]

The Atonement in Historical Perspective

Traditional LDS theology teaches that the Atonement was preached, predicted, and prefigured in the Old Testament. Mormonism, like traditional Christianity, maintains that prophets have been preaching and prophesying both directly and indirectly of Christ's atonement since the beginning of the world. For instance, though the Bible makes no mention of Adam and Eve offering sacrifices, modern LDS scripture has them offering sacrifices soon after their ejection from the Garden of Eden, with the instruction given them that "this thing is a similitude of the sacrifice of the Only Begotten of the Father" (Moses 5:7). Many of Joseph's contemporaries had a similar understanding. For example, an 1825 article in a Presbyterian publication suggested that "the beasts with whose skins Adam and Eve were clothed . . . had been offered in sacrifice" and "thus early was typified, that great atoning sacrifice of the Son of God."[2] Though Mormons and other Christians see numerous images of the Atonement in Old Testament writings, it is not at all clear that the writers themselves had Christ's atonement in mind. Notably, Jews and Muslims, who also accept the Old Testament, find no imagery that to them prefigures Christ's atonement.

Old Testament

The concept of atonement has its roots in the Hebrew practice of sacrifice, which played a prominent role in Israelite worship. The Old Testament Hebrew word for atonement is *kapar* which means "propitiate, appease."[3] In the Old Testament, animal and grain sacrifices were initially offered up as gifts to God by Adam and Eve's offspring with no apparent connection to the sacrifice of Christ. Abel brought the firstlings of the sheep and goats of his flock, together with their fat, and offered them as a "gift" (*minchah*) to God (Gen. 4:4). Cain similarly brought his offering of "the fruit of the ground" (Gen. 4:3), which was also a "gift" (*minchah*) to God—a gift that God did "not respect" (Gen. 4:5).[4] These offerings were burnt offerings in which the animal or plant ascended in smoke to God. They were offered in thanksgiving for one's flocks and harvest of crops, similar to meal-gift offerings in other ancient Near Eastern and Egyptian cultures. Emphasis is given in Genesis 4:4 to the fact that Abel especially offered up the fat, which was seen as the choicest part of the animals. This, rather than a mentioning of the blood, suggests that those who performed these early sacrifices had no understanding that animal and grain sacrifices typified the shedding of Christ's blood for a remission of sins.

Scholars explain that it likely wasn't until the Babylonian captivity of Israel that sacrifice took on more of an atoning function.[5] The *Theological Dictionary of the Old Testament* explains, "During the period of the monarchy [David to the Babylonian exile], most sacrifices were probably offered in connection with thanksgiving, vows, or adoration. Atonement sacrifice probably did not become customary until the time of the Second Temple; when the exile was interpreted as a judgment upon the sins of the people, a ritual was developed for sin and guilt offerings."[6]

The presence of this ritual in the law of Moses is seen as a back-projection introduced by the priestly writer of Leviticus who lived during this period. The law of Moses specified that God could be appeased for sins committed by offering sacrifices in which animals without blemish were killed and butchered. The blood was sprinkled upon the altar through a priestly ritual, and the flesh was burned on the altar as an offering to God. There were even provisions made for substituting a grain offering if a person could not afford an animal (Lev. 5:11–13). These offerings were all offered to God in ceremonial sacrifices described in great detail by God himself (Lev. 1–7).

The law of Moses spells out several types of sacrifice, including gift offerings (to express homage and thanksgiving), burnt offerings (usually on behalf of the community as a whole), and sin and guilt offerings (to deal with unintentional offenses against God for which the worshipper sought pardon). Except for rare circumstances, sin offerings secured forgiveness only for trivial, unintended transgressions (Lev. 4:1–35). They appear to have been ineffectual in atoning for intentional transgressions. The brazen sinner was barred from the sanctuary and had to bear his own iniquity, sometimes being stoned to death, because of his willful rebellion against God (Num. 15:27–31).

There is little, if any, indication in the Bible that ancient Israelites saw an antitype in the sacrifices they offered. Sacrifices appear to have been viewed as having inherent redemptive merit; in other words, the sacrifices themselves appeased God and brought forgiveness of sins. The instructions in Leviticus on sacrifices are clearly spelled out: If a person inadvertently sins, he is to bring a sacrificial animal to the priest who kills and offers it as a sacrifice for sin. God is thereby appeased, and the person's offense against God is forgiven. In the Old Testament, God shows mercy because he is merciful and is moved by the prayers and offerings of the penitent (Ex. 34:6–7). There is no clear attribution of his mercy to the merits of a future messianic sacrifice.

Old Testament prophecies that Christians believe to be references to Christ's atonement have been lumped together with what are known as messianic prophecies. According to critical biblical scholars, however, the Old Testament never refers to the Messiah as one who would redeem humankind from sin and death. As discussed in Chapter 8, the identity of the promised Messiah in the Old Testament is ambiguous, and the role he would play in the salvation of Israel is equally unclear. Some Old Testament writers spoke of him as a prophet, others as a Davidic king, and still others as God himself. Although the acts and achievements of Jesus seem to fit several of the roles described for this Messiah, his suffering and death for the sins of humankind don't appear to fit any of them. Christian biblical scholar Eduard Lohse has noted that, common to all messianic beliefs,

> was the conviction that the one anointed by God would appear as a ruler and judge, would exalt the lowliness of Israel, drive out the heathen, and establish the kingdom of glory. But nowhere do they speak of a suffering Messiah who because of the sins of the people would take upon himself humiliation and death. Where the relationship of man to God is determined entirely by the Law, where people seek after righteousness under the Law and know no other way to salvation outside the Law, there can be no place for a suffering Messiah who takes upon himself the guilt of others.[7]

Additionally, one is at a loss to find any messianic prophecies portending an individual who triumphs over death to bring about the resurrection of humankind. Belief in the redemption of humankind from Adam's transgression and from individual sin is fundamental to the exercise of faith in Christ, yet there appears to be little indication in the Old Testament of any such awareness.

Christians often point to Genesis 3:15, traditionally referred to as the Protoevangelium or "first gospel," as the earliest allusion to Christ and the Atonement. It speaks of the serpent (presumed to be Satan) bruising the heel of man, and the woman's seed (presumed to be Christ) crushing the serpent's head. Critical biblical scholars, however, see no intended reference to Christ in this passage, viewing it as simply a Hebrew description of the enmity that exists between snakes and humans. According to Sigmund Mowinckel, professor of Old Testament studies at the University of Oslo, "It is now generally admitted by those who adopt the historical approach to theology that there is no allusion here to the Devil or to Christ as 'born of woman,' but that it is a quite general statement about mankind, and serpents, and the struggle between them which continues as long as the earth exists."[8] The association of the serpent with Satan and the woman's seed with Christ appears to have been a later Christian allegorical reading (see Chapter 10).

An Old Testament passage presumed by most Christians to be a prophecy of the passion or agony of Christ is Psalm 22, which begins: "My God, my God, why hast thou forsaken me?" (v. 1). This was the reported utterance of Jesus on the cross (Matt. 27:46), which many scholars interpret as his way of signaling that he had fulfilled this particular psalm.[9] Allusions to Psalm 22 can be found in several New Testament passages in connection with Christ's crucifixion (Matt. 27:39//Ps. 22:7; Matt. 27:43//Ps: 22:8; John 19:28//Ps. 22:15; John 19:23//Ps. 22:18). Was Psalm 22 written with Christ in mind? Or could the Psalmist have been inspired to use the wording he did so that it could later be applied to Christ's crucifixion? Scholars answer "no" to the first question, and the answer to the second depends on one's perspective of the inspiration of the scriptures.

Scholars largely agree that Psalm 22 is neither messianic nor prophetic. In his commentary on Psalms, H. J. Kraus states that New Testament writers "permitted themselves to conclude that Psalm 22 belongs to the 'messianic prophecies.' But this interpretation has proved to be inappropriate. Psalm 22 does not deal with the 'Messiah' (in the sense of an end-time king of salvation), nor is it a 'prophecy.'"[10] Herman Gunkel, a Protestant Old Testament scholar, observes that "the messianic interpretation . . . has conclusively been dropped since it was recognized that the psalm actually contains no prophecy and, what is more, that the idea of a suffering Messiah is foreign to the Old Testament."[11] According to Rabbi Abraham Cohen, a Jewish Talmudic scholar, "A Christological intention has long been read into this Psalm, but modern Christian exegetes are agreed that it describes a situation then existing and does not anticipate an event of the future."[12]

What, then, should be made of Psalm 22? Scholars suggest that, like many other Psalms, it is a prayer psalm, a song of distress in which the petitioner is weighed down with a variety of afflictions and is crying to God for help. Though some have thought that it had direct application to David, other scholars agree that it is not necessarily reflecting the experiences of any specific individual. Old Testament scholar James Mays states,

> Psalm 22 shares words and motifs with other prayers for help as well as structural features. Like the other psalms of its genre, Psalm 22 was composed for liturgical use. What one hears through it is not the voice of a particular historical person at a certain time, but one individual case of the typical. Its language was designed to give individuals a poetic and liturgical location, to provide a prayer that is paradigmatic for particular suffering and needs.[13]

As a model prayer for anyone suffering comparable afflictions, the psalm certainly may be applied to Christ's passion, which might explain its use by the first Christians. According to Mays, "In the intellectual world of Judaism, one of the most important ways of understanding the meaning of present experience was to make sense of the contemporary by perceiving and describing it in terms of an established tradition. That seems to be happening in the connection between psalm and passion Story."[14]

Another Old Testament passage that some Latter-day Saints see as a reference to Christ's crucifixion is Isaiah 22:23: "And I will fasten him as a nail in a sure place; and he shall be for a glorious throne to his father's house." Bruce R. McConkie interprets this as a "reference to the nails driven in the Crucified One."[15] However, read in context, this passage contains no direct allusion to Christ's crucifixion. According to scholars the metaphor is that of a hook or "peg" (RSV) fastened securely so that valuables may be suspended from it like a coat hook. Isaiah prophesies that Eliakim is to replace Shebna as the leader of the king's court—a position similar to a present-day secretary of state. Eliakim is to be established firmly like a nail in a sure place, and all of his family's hopes will hang on him. Isaiah warns, however, that Eliakim will be removed from his position as the "nail that is fastened in the sure place [shall] be removed" (v. 25) and his family will fall with him. Even a symbolic association of this passage with the Messiah is awkward,[16] as Eliakim failed in his calling, causing those who depended on him to also come to ruin.

An Old Testament prophecy that most Christians read as both messianic and an unmistakable reference to Christ is Isaiah 53 which speaks of God's "righteous servant" (v. 11) who "is despised and rejected of men; a man of sorrows, and acquainted with grief" (v. 3). The servant's hardships are associated with vicarious suffering for sin and healing of the people:

> Surely he hath borne our griefs, and carried our sorrows. . . .
> He was wounded for our transgressions, he was bruised for our iniquities . . . and with his stripes we are healed.
> All we like sheep have gone astray . . . and the Lord hath laid on him the iniquity of us all. (vv. 4–6)

For obvious reasons this passage has come to be called the song of the suffering servant. This unidentified servant "bare the sin of many, and made intercession for the transgressors" (Isa. 53:12).

Christians since New Testament times have traditionally held that Isaiah 53 is a direct reference to Christ's suffering. Scholars, however, are less sanguine, noting that it is not altogether clear whether the servant even refers to an individual since the nation of Israel as a whole is often referred to as God's servant in Isaiah's writings (Isa. 41:8–9, 44:1–2, 21; 45:4; 48:20; 49:3).[17] Jesuit professor of Christology, Gerald O'Collins, observes, "The identity of the servant in these songs is by no means clear: the nation of Israel, an individual, or both."[18] Scholars who argue that the servant is an individual are generally of the opinion that it was likely Isaiah himself or at least a contemporary of Isaiah.[19] It is noteworthy that much of the song of the suffering servant is written in the past tense and therefore appears to be referring to hardships already suffered.

Scholars reject the idea that Jews at the time would have connected the servant in Isaiah with the idea of a coming Messiah who would atone for sins. As discussed in Chapter 8, the Jewish conception of the Messiah was primarily that of a political ruler who would conquer their enemies—an image inconsistent with that of a suffering servant. According to O'Collins, "Jewish messianic expectations hardly show a hint of envisaging a suffering and martyred Messiah, who would be the persecuted and vindicated 'servant' of God (Acts 3:13, 26; 4:27,30)." He further notes that "a crucified (and resurrected) Christ was even more alien to Jewish messianic expectations."[20] Baptist scholar H. H. Rowley states, "There is no serious evidence of the bringing together of the concepts of the Suffering Servant and the Davidic Messiah before the Christian era."[21] Anglican theologian N. T. Wright similarly observes, "It seems very unlikely . . . that there was a well-known pre-Christian Jewish belief, based on Isaiah 53, in a coming redeemer who would die for the sins of Israel and/or the world."[22]

New Testament writers saw a clear match between Jesus and the suffering servant in Isaiah. O'Collins notes that "eventually the New Testament was to include ten literal quotations from this poem and around thirty allusions to it."[23] In Acts 8:32–34, for example, Philip converses with a eunuch who was reading from this passage in Isaiah. In response to the eunuch's question regarding the identity of the suffering servant, "Philip opened his mouth, and began at the same scripture, and preached unto him Jesus" (v. 35). Bible scholar Walter Brueggemann writes, "Although it is clear that this poetry does not in any first instance have Jesus on its horizon, it is equally clear that the church, from the outset, has found the poetry a poignant and generative way to consider Jesus, wherein humiliation equals crucifixion and exaltation equals resurrection and ascension."[24]

In the Book of Mormon, the pre-Christian prophet Abinadi affirms the traditional Christian view that Isaiah 53 is Messianic. For Abinidi, however, it is not God's servant who would be sent, but God himself coming as the servant. Indeed, Abinadi prefaces his recitation of Isaiah 53 stating "that God himself should come down among the children of men. . . . and that he, himself, should be oppressed and afflicted" (Mosiah 13:34–35). After reciting Isaiah 53 he again emphasizes "that God himself shall come down among the children of men" (Mosiah 15:1). True to Book of Mormon (and trinitarian) theology which equates Christ with God, the suffering servant is depicted, not as the servant of the Lord in a subservient sense as portrayed by Isaiah, but as the Lord God himself in a condescending sense.

Incidentally, the fact that the suffering servant song in Mosiah begins with Isaiah 53:1 is a bit puzzling given that the natural starting point is actually Isaiah 52:13, three verses earlier.[25] Old Testament manuscripts weren't divided into chapters. Modern chapter divisions were created in 1205 by Stephen Langton, a professor of theology in Paris and later Archbishop of Canterbury. Unfortunately, these divisions don't always follow the natural narrative.[26] BYU law professor John Welch surmised that the Book of Mormon recitation of the suffering servant song skips the first three verses because "the ancient Nephites understood that a poetical unit began at Isaiah 53:1."[27] Critics, on the other hand, argue that the fact that Mosiah breaks into the suffering servant passage precisely at Isaiah 53:1 indicates an apparent reliance on this much later (and inaccurate) chapter division.

It is interesting to compare how the New Testament and Book of Mormon make sense of Isaiah's phrase "he hath borne our griefs, and carried our sorrows" (Isa. 53:4). In the New Testament, it is interpreted as a description of Christ's healing ministry. Matthew records that many were brought to Christ with infirmities and he "healed all that were sick: that it might be fulfilled which was spoken by Esaias [i.e., Isaiah] the prophet, saying . . . [He] took our infirmities, and bare our sicknesses" (Matt. 8:17). Note that the "griefs" and "sorrows," spoken of in Isaiah, which Christians often equate with sins, become "infirmities" and "sicknesses" in Matthew.[28] Furthermore, Matthew has Christ taking away these infirmities in the sense of lifting them from the afflicted (i.e., healing them), and not suffering vicariously for them. The Book of Mormon has Christ taking upon himself "the pains and sicknesses of his people" (Alma 7:11), not by vicariously suffering for them as in Isaiah, nor by removing them as he does in Matthew, but in the sense of subjecting himself to the pains and sicknesses common to all human beings. Using language also found in Hebrews 2:18, which has Christ "being tempted" so that he may "be able to succour them that are tempted," the Book of Mormon has Christ suffering infirmities so "that he may know according to the flesh how to succor his people according to their infirmities" (Alma 7:12). Thus, he suffers pain and sicknesses to have greater empathy for human suffering. Perhaps because the idea of Christ taking upon himself human infirmities sounds like taking upon himself human sins, recent LDS expositors have interpreted this Book of Mormon passage to mean that Christ bore our infirmities in a substitutionary sense, just as he bore our sins.[29]

The Book of Mormon assertion that Christ suffered the infirmities common to man is noteworthy considering there is no mention of Jesus ever being afflicted with illnesses or diseases of any kind in the New Testament. From the earliest New Testament commentators to the time of the Reformation, it was widely held that Christ was immune to human sicknesses.[30] By the time of Joseph Smith, however, the idea that Christ suffered common human infirmities had become embraced by many. The influential 1647 Westminster Confession of Faith, for example, asserts that Christ did "take upon him . . . the . . . common infirmities [of mortality]."[31] Thus, the Book of Mormon doesn't follow Matthew's understanding of Christ taking on himself people's infirmities through healing the sick, but follows the Westminster Confession by having him personally suffer human infirmities so that he can be more compassionate towards the sick.

An Old Testament prophecy often cited by Latter-day Saints as providing a graphic image of Christ's atonement is Isaiah 63, which speaks of the Lord coming "with dyed garments" (Isa. 63:1) having trodden the winepress of the fierceness of the wrath of God saying, "I have trodden the winepress alone" (Isa. 63:3). LDS Apostle Neal A. Maxwell interpreted this passage as a prophecy of Christ's sacrifice in which he would take upon himself the blood or sins of the world in "awful aloneness."[32] While the imagery is striking, in the original context it has nothing to do with the Lord's suffering by atoning for sin, but rather with his vengeful trampling of the wicked (vv. 1–6). The Lord's "aloneness" spoken of in Isaiah is not the solitary suffering of Christ in Gethsemane,[33] but an allusion to God's single-handed thrashing of the wicked. His garments are stained red, not from his own blood, nor from the blood of the repentant sinner, but from the blood of evil doers when he tramples them in his fury. The Lord says of the evil oppressors of Israel: "For I will tread them in mine anger, and trample them in my fury; and their blood shall be sprinkled upon my garments, and I will stain all my raiment" (v. 3). The entire passage describes a "day of vengeance" (v. 4), not the Savior's suffering in atonement.

The book of Revelation uses the same winepress imagery with the same meaning as the Old Testament, only now Christ is the Lord who "treadeth the winepress of the fierceness and wrath of Almighty God" (Rev. 19:13–15; cf. 14:18–20). Early LDS revelations echo this same sense of Christ treading upon the wicked (D&C 76:106–7; D&C 133:38–50).[34] It seems to be only much later that LDS commentators began appropriating Isaiah 63 as a proof-text for Christ's atonement.

New Testament

The New Testament record portrays Jesus as shedding his blood and giving his body for our sins (Luke 22:19–20). Peter wrote that he "bare our sins in his own body on the tree" (1 Pet. 2:24). According to Paul's teachings, "the blood of his cross . . . reconcile[d] all things unto himself" (Col. 1:20; cf. Eph. 2:16). The essential testimony of the New Testament is "that Christ died for our sins . . . that he was buried, and that he rose again the third day" (1 Cor. 15:3–4). Theologians note that there is no complete or consistent explanation in the New Testament of how Christ's atonement actually works (various theories would follow in the post-apostolic era), but somehow his suffering and bloodshed paid the price of sin (Eph. 1:7; Col. 1:14; 1 Pet. 3:18; Rev. 1:5).

The conquering of physical death is also a major theme in the New Testament, especially in the writings of Paul who taught, "Now is Christ risen from the dead, and become the firstfruits of them that slept" (1 Cor. 15:20). Thus, in New Testament theology, Christ both "gave himself for our sins" (Gal. 1:4) and brought about "the resurrection of the dead" (1 Cor. 15:21).

It is commonly taught in Mormon discourse that Christ had inherent power over death and thus raised himself from the dead. Much of the New Testament, however, especially the writings of Paul, emphasizes that it was God who raised Jesus from the dead so that Christ was *made* alive (Rom. 4:24–25, 6:4, 7:4, 8:11, 10:9; 1 Cor. 6:14, 15:15; 2 Cor. 4:14; Gal. 1:1; Eph. 1:20; Heb. 13:20; Col. 2:12; 1 Thess. 1:10; 1 Pet. 1:21). It seems that Paul held a traditional Jewish view of one God and spoke of Christ as having become God's son, not by birth, but by being raised by God from the dead. Only then was Christ given power over death. It would be the later Gospel of John that would portray Jesus as having power to take up his own life (John 10:18). John's high Christology seems to promote the rather unique view that Christ was divine at birth and, therefore, possessed inherent power over death. Catholic biblical scholar Hans Küng observes, "Today we speak perhaps too glibly of 'resurrection' in the sense simply of Jesus' action by his own power. In the New Testament, however, 'resurrection' is rightly identified as 'raising by God.' It is essentially a work of God on Jesus, the one crucified, dead and buried. Jesus' 'raising' (passive) is probably therefore more original in the New Testament and certainly more universal than Jesus' resurrection (active)."[35]

Early Nineteenth-Century Christianity

Christian theologians from the second century have developed various theories to explain how the Atonement works. A theory that came to full expression in the eleventh century in the writings of St. Anselm, Archbishop of Canterbury, is called the "satisfaction theory," which holds that Christ's atonement satisfied an eternal "debt" to justice. According to this view, even God's mercy can't rob justice, but takes effect only because Christ satisfied the demands of justice. The satisfaction theory was popular among evangelicals at the time of Joseph Smith. In 1822, Timothy Merritt, a Methodist minister, stated that "if we incur the penalty of the law by transgression, that penalty must be executed either on us or on our substitute. If on us, then no favour is shown us; but if on our substitute, the way is opened, and mercy may be extended to us." Thus, "the atonement was . . . made . . . to satisfy the claims which his [i.e., God's] justice had against us as transgressors, and open the way by which he might extend mercy to us consistently with his character as Lawgiver and Judge."[36]

Mormonism

When it comes to teachings on the Atonement, the Book of Mormon adopts the same terminology to articulate the same views held by early nineteenth-century evangelicals. For example, phrases such as "according to the law and justice," "the demands of justice," "endless happiness," "endless misery," "infinite atonement," "plan of mercy," "plan of salvation," and "this fallen state" appear both in the Book of Mormon and in preceding works of Union College president Jonathan Edwards Jr. (1745–1801).[37] The Book of Mormon prophet Alma, like Edwards, distinguishes between justice and mercy in the same way Paul distinguishes between the law of Moses and grace (Rom. 4–5). As Mormon critic Ted Chandler points out, "Like Edwards, Alma recasts Paul's argument about the law and grace into a discussion of the quite different terms of justice and mercy. Both Edwards and Alma are talking about attributes of God, rather than about Mosaic law."[38] Methodist preacher and Bible scholar Adam Clarke (1762–1832) also declared that "the salvation of the human soul" ultimately concerns God's attributes of "justice" and "mercy." He noted that "these attributes appear to have very opposite claims; nevertheless, in the scheme of salvation laid down in the gospel, these claims are harmonized."[39] The Book of Mormon also reduces the plan of salvation largely to a harmonizing of these claims (see, for example, Alma 42:21–31). Concepts and expressions such as these which are used to teach the Atonement in the Book of Mormon are foreign to the Old and New Testaments, but were part of the idiom of early nineteenth-century evangelicalism.[40]

Current LDS teachings on the Atonement draw heavily from Book of Mormon language, although different meanings are sometimes given than what appear to have been originally intended. For example, Book of Mormon teachings follow New Testament writings that attribute the power of Christ's resurrection to God rather than to Christ himself (3 Ne. 20:26; Morm. 7:5). Modern Mormonism, however, tends to follow the Gospel of John in attributing the power of the resurrection to Christ himself.[41] As discussed in more detail below, the "infinite atonement" spoken of in the Book of Mormon has also undergone a change in the way it has been generally understood in the Church.

The Infinite Atonement

The "infinite atonement" is a Book of Mormon expression that appears in neither the Old or New Testament. It was, however, an integral part of St. Anselm's satisfaction theory of the Atonment, and refers to the idea that because God is infinite, all of his attributes—particularly his justice—are also infinite. Thus, any violation of God's laws is infinitely offensive to the infinite justice of God and requires a sacrifice of infinite merit to make amends. Such a sacrifice can only be made by an infinite being, i.e., by God himself.[42] As expounded by Methodist theologian Adam Clarke in 1815, the Atonement is infinite because it is "infinitely meritorious" or of "infinite worth," and "no being of limited and finite powers, can perform acts of infinite worth." Therefore it "requires *unlimited* [i.e., infinite] *powers* in the *agent*."[43] Clarke further remarked that Jesus came to earth as "*God*, that the suffering [in his atonement] might be stamped with an infinite value; and thus . . . might be a sufficient sacrifice and atonement for the sin of the world."[44]

At the time of Joseph Smith, the doctrine of an infinite atonement was a point of contention between Universalists and trinitarians. Universalists rejected the need for a redeemer and believed that, although sinners may suffer punishment for their sins, this punishment is of finite duration and all would be saved in the end. In 1805, Universalist Hosea Ballou repudiated the trinitarian view "that sin is infinite, and that it deserves an infinite punishment; that the law transgressed is infinite, and inflicts an infinite penalty; and that the great Jehovah took on himself a natural body of flesh and blood, and actually suffered death on a cross, to satisfy his infinite justice, and thereby save his creatures from endless misery."[45] In spite of such repudiations by Universalists, trinitarians remained firm in their insistence that sin has infinite consequences and therefore requires an infinite sacrifice to reclaim its victims.

The Book of Mormon echoes this popular trinitarian notion of the Atonement asserting that "save it should be an infinite atonement . . . the first judgment which came upon man must needs have remained to an endless duration" (2 Ne. 9:7). The Book of Mormon also makes clear that, for the Atonement to be infinite, the sacrifice offered must also be infinite. The prophet Amulek states that "there is not any man that can sacrifice his own blood which will atone for the sins of another" (Alma 34:11); therefore, "it is expedient that there should be . . . a sacrifice [not] of man, neither of beast, neither of any manner of fowl; for it shall not be a human sacrifice; but it must be an infinite and eternal sacrifice" (Alma 34:10). Thus, according to Amulek, "that great and last sacrifice will be the Son of God, yea, infinite and eternal" (Alma 34:14). It should be noted that "Infinite" and "Eternal" were common Christian descriptors of God in Joseph Smith's day. An early LDS revelation also calls God "infinite and eternal" (D&C 20:17, 28). Commenting on Book of Mormon teachings regarding the infinite atonement, Orson Pratt states that they are essentially saying that "the voluntary sufferings of an infinite eternal Being [i.e., God incarnate as Christ], satisfied the demands of an infinite law which had been broken. The penalty being infinite in duration could only be satisfied by an infinite sacrifice."[46]

In the Book of Mormon, the fact that the Atonement was effected by God himself is repeatedly emphasized. The prophet Abinadi declared,

"God himself should come down among the children of men" (Mosiah 13:34; cf. 17:8) and "shall make [atonement] for the sins and iniquities of his people" (Mosiah 13:28). Amulek likewise stated, "God himself atoneth for the sins of the world . . . to appease the demands of justice" (Alma 42:15). 1 Nephi 11 speaks of the "condescension of God"—a common trinitarian expression used to denote the incarnation of God in Christ—again with the idea that it is God who would come to earth in a body to suffer and die.[47]

In the Book of Mormon the atonement has infinite merit not only so it can offset the endless duration of punishment, but also so that its redemptive reach can extend to the sins of the entire world. One of the divisions between Arminians and Calvinists during the eighteenth and nineteenth centuries was in regard to the extent of the Atonement's reach. Calvinists advocated a limited atonement contending that Christ died only for those predestined for salvation.[48] For Arminians, however, the Atonement had infinite value and was therefore not limited in its potential reach. Thus, Methodist preacher Adam Clarke asserted, "Nothing less than a sacrifice of infinite merit, can atone for the offences of the whole world."[49] The Book of Mormon echoes this Arminian perspective proclaiming that "there can be nothing which is short of an infinite atonement which will suffice for the sins of the world" (Alma 34:12).

The concept of the Atonement being infinite essentially in the sense of being effected by an infinite or divine being and therefore having infinite merit is found in the teachings of several early Church leaders. Brigham Young explained, "Our first parents transgressed the law that was given them in the garden; their eyes were opened. This created the debt. What is the nature of this debt? It is a divine debt. What will pay it? I ask, Is there anything short of a divine sacrifice that can pay this debt? No; there is not."[50] In answer to the question, "Why did it need an infinite atonement?" John Taylor responded, "For the simple reason that a stream can never rise higher than its fountain. . . . A man, as a man, could arrive at all the dignity that a man was capable of obtaining or receiving; but it needed a God to raise him to the dignity of a God."[51] Thus, in early Mormonism, the term "infinite" when applied to the Atonement was understood primarily as being indicative of the infinite nature of the being that was offered.

Instead of viewing the Atonement as being infinite in the sense of having been wrought by an infinite being and, therefore, having infinite value, the current LDS tendency is to speak of the Atonement as being infinite in terms of the infinite extent of its impact. According to Bruce R. McConkie, "When the prophets speak of an infinite atonement, they mean just that. Its effects cover all men, the earth itself and all forms of life thereon, and reach out into the endless expanses of eternity."[52] Jeffrey R. Holland, writing for the *Encyclopedia of Mormonism*, similarly states, "The Atonement is . . . infinite in the sense that its impact and efficacy in making redemption possible for all reach back in one direction to the beginning of time and forward in the other direction throughout all eternity."[53] This interpretation, though certainly not inconsistent with the view of the Atonement being infinite in the sense that it was God himself that was sacrificed, goes beyond Book of Mormon theology, which confines its scope of influence to the "sins of [this] world" (Alma 34:8, 12). In the Book of Mormon, the Atonement is "infinite for all mankind" (2 Ne 25:16), but not necessarily for an infinitude of humankind. The current interpretive tendency relies on the post-Book of Mormon doctrine that Christ's redemption extends to worlds without number (D&C 76:24).

A somewhat unique interpretation of Christ's infinite atonement has been advanced by LDS theologian Blake Ostler. While affirming the popular view that the Atonement is infinite "because it is universal in scope for all persons for all times,"[54] Ostler further argues that "the Atonement is infinite in the sense that Christ's atonement [i.e., his suffering for sin] is endless or unlimited both in duration through time and in magnitude of pain for all sins."[55] This notion of an "unlimited duration" to Christ's suffering seems to suggest that he still continues to suffer incomprehensibly for human sin. As Ostler states, "The Atonement is infinite because only a capacity to endure pains for an endless duration and for all people for all times can suffice."[56] In addition to this intriguing slant on Christ's infinite atonement, Ostler emphatically refutes that any form of satisfaction theory of the Atonement is taught in the Book of Mormon and insists that it should not be viewed "as analogous to an economic transaction where Christ satisfies a debt that we cannot pay."[57] Ostler's views are representative of some of the ways atonement theory is being reassessed in LDS intellectual circles.

Retroactive Redemption

A question that theologians have grappled with since New Testament times is how the faithful who lived prior to Christ could have been sanctified through the Atonement before its historical enactment. The traditional Christian response is that the effects of the Atonement are retroactive and, therefore, efficacious from the foundation of the world. The 1742 Philadelphia Confession of Faith of the Baptist Church explains: "Although the price of redemption was not actually paid by Christ till after his incarnation, yet the virtue, efficacy, and benefit thereof were communicated to the elect in all ages." In answer to the question, "How . . . were those saved who . . . died before he [i.e., Christ] came into the world, and made the atonement?"

Presbyterian minister Josiah Priest replied, "They were saved in the same way souls are saved now; only with this difference; men are saved now by a Saviour already *come,* and they were saved by a Saviour who *was* to come, our faith going back and theirs reaching forward."[58]

Though the doctrine of a retroactively efficacious atonement is congruent with the notion of a just and merciful God, there is no indication in the Old Testament of an understanding that remission of sins came through the future atonement of a redeemer. New Testament scholars point out that the traditional justification for the belief in retroactive redemption is based largely on a misplaced prepositional phrase in Revelation 13:8, which states that Christ was "slain before the foundation of the world." Newer translations such as the NRSV and the *New American Standard Bible* (NASB) recognize the prepositional phrase "from the foundation of the world" as describing "those whose names are written in the book of life," not Christ's sacrifice. Thus, the NASB translates Revelation 13:8 to refer to "everyone whose name has not been written from the foundation of the world in the book of life of the Lamb who has been slain." This is actually more consistent with the subsequent reference in Revelation 17:8 to those "whose names were not written in the book of life from the foundation of the world."

The idea that the benefits of the Atonement were available to the ancients, even before its actualization, became a major point of emphasis in early Mormonism. The Book of Mormon repeatedly attests to the sanctification and redemption of those living before Christ through his future atonement (1 Ne. 10:18; Mosiah 4:6, 7; 15:19; 18:13; Alma 12:25, 30; 13:5, 18:39; 22:13; Ether 3:14; see also Moses 5:57). Moses 7:47 even echoes the disputed KJV wording of Revelation–"the Lamb is slain from the foundation of the world"—to claim that pre-Christian era Saints could and did come unto the Father "through faith" in Christ's future atonement.

Since the middle of the nineteenth century, LDS expositors have suggested that the atonement was operative even back in the preexistence.[59] As noted in Chapters 11 and 13, several scriptural proof-texts (e.g., Alma 13:2-12; D&C 93:38) have been employed to support this idea. Though the idea of sinning in the sense of rebelling in the preexistence is evident in the LDS teaching that Satan and his followers rebelled and were cast out, there is no clear scriptural teaching that Christ's atonement paid for sins committed in a preexistent state.

Universal Effects of the Atonement

The doctrine of a retroactive atonement is particularly crucial to the LDS belief that Christ's atonement pertained not only to this world, but to worlds that have previously passed on to glory. As discussed in Chapter 12, it was widely held at the time of Joseph Smith that the universe consisted of innumerable inhabited worlds, all created by Christ. It was also believed that the Earth's inhabitants are more wicked than those of other worlds (cf. Moses 7:36)[60] and that Christ came to this lowliest of worlds to die for all of God's creatures throughout the vast universe. In the 1820s, renowned Christian apologist Thomas Chalmers popularized the idea that the Atonement's power extends throughout the universe.[61] Thus, by the time Joseph began his work, the notion of Christ atoning for the sins of the inhabitants of worlds without number had gained broad appeal.

Within a few years after recording an 1830 revelation stating that Christ was the creator of innumerable worlds (Moses 1:33), the Prophet received another revelation declaring Christ to also be the redeemer of these worlds (D&C 76:24). Thus, Christ's atonement was declared in Mormonism, as in many Christian circles, to be applicable to worlds without end.

Traditionally, Christians have understood all redemption in worlds throughout eternity to be effected by only a single redeemer.[62] With Joseph Smith's introduction during the Nauvoo period of an endless hierarchy of Gods, the distinctive LDS idea of multiple saviors emerged as a logical extension. In 1870, Brigham Young went so far as to declare that "every earth has its redeemer, and every earth has its tempter."[63] Orthodox Christianity rejects the notion of multiple Gods and redeemers and, therefore, asserts that Christ's creative and redemptive works are exhaustive of all creation.[64]

Notes

1. *History of the Church*, 3:30.
2. "Lectures on the Shorter Catechism of the Westminster Assembly of the Divines—Addressed to Youth," 54.
3. B. Lang, "Kipper," 291. Lang notes that the traditional definition "to cover" is likely incorrect. For a more traditional LDS interpretation of the Hebrew *kaphar*, see Blake T. Ostler, *Exploring Mormon Thought: The Problems of Theism and the Love of God*, 246–47.
4. Supposing these gift offerings to be sacrificial offerings, Joseph Smith taught that God rejected Cain's sacrifice because it wasn't a blood sacrifice, and "without the shedding of blood was no remission." *History of the Church*, 2:16. John Taylor taught that the rejection was "because the Lord knew that Cain had departed from him, and that he was not sincere in his offering." August 28, 1881, *Journal of Discourses*, 22:301. The Book of Jasher 1:16 indicates that God rejected Cain's sacrifice because "he had brought from the infe-

rior fruit of the ground." Indeed, Genesis 4:3 states that Cain offered of "the fruit of the ground," but not necessarily the first fruit as Abel did the "firstling" of the flock.

5. H. Wheeler Robinson, *The Religious Ideas of the Old Testament*, 147–48.
6. J. Bergman, H. Ringren, and W. Dommershausen, "Kohen," 70.
7. Eduard Lohse, *The New Testament Environments*, 192.
8. Sigmund Mowinckel, *He That Cometh*, 11.
9. "Citing the first words of a text was, in the tradition of the time, a way of identifying an entire passage." Mays, "Prayer and Christology," 322.
10. Kraus, *Psalms 1–59*, 300–301.
11. Herman Gunkel, quoted in ibid., 301.
12. Cohen, *The Psalms*, 61.
13. James L. Mays, "Prayer and Christology: Psalm 22 as Perspective on the Passion," 323.
14. Ibid.
15. Bruce R. McConkie, *The Promised Messiah: The First Coming of Christ*, 529.
16. This appears to be the understanding expressed in the footnote for Isaiah 22:20 in the LDS Bible, which reads: "Eliakim . . . becomes representative of the Messiah, the Savior, especially v. 23–25."
17. Biblical scholar James M. Ward observes that most scholarly Jewish and Christian commentaries today interpret the servant of Isaiah 53 to be Israel. "Jewish interpreters once considered him [the servant] to be the messiah," he notes, "but his identification with Israel, collectively, has been the dominant Jewish view since the Middle Ages. The collective interpretation is also the most popular among Christian scholars today, though a few continue to think of the servant primarily in relation to Jesus." James M. Ward, *Thus Says the Lord: The Message of the Prophets*, 90.
18. Gerald O'Collins, *Christology*, 29.
19. Donald J. Goergen, *The Death and Resurrection of Jesus*, 43–45.
20. O'Collins, *Christology*, 27–29.
21. H. H. Rowley, quoted in ibid., 29.
22. N. T. Wright, quoted in ibid.
23. Ibid., 78.
24. Walter Brueggemann, *Isaiah 40–66*, 143.
25. See, for example, Ronald Bergey, "The Rhetorical Role of Reiteration in the Suffering Servant Poem (Isa. 52:13–53:12)," 177–88.
26. Emanuel Tov, *Textual Criticism of the Hebrew Bible*, 52.
27. John W. Welch, "Isaiah 53, Mosiah 14, and the Book of Mormon," 295.
28. Matthew's reference to "infirmities" and "sicknesses" follows the Hebrew (Masoretic text) of Isaiah 53 rather than the Greek (Septuagint) from which Matthew more frequently quoted. Scholars explain that in the Old Testament God afflicted the sinner with physical pain and sickness which, in Isaiah 53, were born vicariously by God's servant.
29. According to Neal A. Maxwell, "the Atonement involved bearing our pains, infirmities, and sicknesses, as well as our sins." Neal A. Maxwell, *"Not My Will, but Thine,"* 51. Jeffrey R. Holland similarly commented, "Alma said the Atonement would remedy pain, affliction, sickness, sorrow, temptation,

and infirmities of every kind." Jeffrey R. Holland, *Christ and the New Covenant: The Messianic Message of the Book of Mormon*, 113. See also, Ostler, *Exploring Mormon Thought: The Problems of Theism and the Love of God*, 211–13.

30. Walter Drum, "Incarnation," 7:715.

31. See "Westminster Confession of Faith."

32. Neal A. Maxwell, "Testifying of the Great and Glorious Atonement," 14. This is an interpretation that became popularized in medieval Christianity. John Sawyer, *The Fifth Gospel: Isaiah in the History of Christianity*, 95–97.

33. Maxwell construes this clear reference to the Lord's wrath as an allusion to his suffering, saying, "His agony was all the more astonishing in that He trod 'the winepress alone' (D&C 133:50)." Neal A. Maxwell, "Plow in Hope," 60.

34. A poetic paraphrase of Doctrine and Covenants 76:106–7, equates treading the winepress with treading "all enemies down." This poem was first published as "The Answer," and though it has been traditionally attributed to Joseph Smith, it was likely written by W. W. Phelps. Michael Hicks, "Joseph Smith, W. W. Phelps, and the Poetic Paraphrase,'" 63–84.

35. Hans Küng, *On Being a Christian*, 349.

36. Timothy Merritt, "Divinity," 244–45.

37. See Thomas E. Donofrio, "Early American Influences on the Book of Mormon." In addition to the dozens of Book of Mormon expressions identified by Donofrio that have antecedents in Edwards's teachings, Edwards taught that the atonement "answer[s] the . . . ends of . . . the law" [cf. 2 Ne. 2:7] so that "the way is prepared" [cf. 1 Ne. 10:18] and "justice [is] . . . satisfied" [cf. 2 Ne. 9:26; Mosiah 15:9]. Jonathan Edwards, "The Necessity of the Atonement, and the Consistency Between That and Free Grace, in Forgiveness," 334, 378.

38. Ted Chandler, "Alma 42 and the Atonement." Though many writers view Alma's teachings on the Atonement as congruent with traditional satisfaction theory, Ostler argues against any such similarity. See Ostler, *Exploring Mormon Thought: The Problems of Theism and the Love of God*, 203–4.

39. Adam Clarke, *A Collection of Discourses*, 69.

40. For other expressions and symbols, such as hell being a "monster," see Mark D. Thomas, *Digging in Cumorah: Reclaiming Book of Mormon Narratives*, 130–35.

41. *Gospel Principles* (2009), 57, 61.

42. Olsen, *The Story of Christian Theology*, 322–25.

43. Clarke, *A Collection of Discourses*, 49; italics in original.

44. Ibid., 102.

45. Hosea Ballou, *A Treatise on Atonement*, iv.

46. Orson Pratt, "The Fall and Atonement," 596.

47. For example, this expression, as found in the Council of Trent in 1564, states, "God condescended to assume the lowliness and frailty of our flesh." *The Catechism of the Council of Trent*, 42.

48. Jacob Catlin, *A Compendium of the System of Divine Truth*, 118.

49. Clarke, *A Collection of Discourses*, 108.

50. Brigham Young, July 10, 1870, *Journal of Discourses*, 14:71.

51. John Taylor, *The Mediation and Atonement*, 145–46.

52. Bruce R. McConkie, *Mormon Doctrine*, 64. Of course, there are other LDS scholars who acknowledge the Book of Mormon meaning of "infinite atonement." Joseph Fielding Smith explained, for example, "By infinite atonement we mean an atonement made by one who was infinite or eternal." Joseph Fielding Smith, *Answers to Gospel Questions*, 1:187.

53. Jeffrey R. Holland, "Atonement of Jesus Christ," 1:84.

54. Ostler, *Exploring Mormon Thought: The Problems of Theism and the Love of God*, 217.

55. Ibid., 216. Ostler refutes any interpretation of the Atonement being infinite in the sense of Christ, as God, being offered as a sacrifice to satisfy the demands of justice. Ibid., 230–31. According to Ostler, "God can forgive us without requiring that Christ must innocently suffer as our substitute."

56. Ibid., 218.

57. Ibid., 204.

58. Josiah Priest, *The Anti-Universalist: or Fallen Angels of the Scriptures; Proofs of the Being of Satan and of Evil Spirits*, 82.

59. See, for example, Orson Pratt, "The Pre-existence of Man," *The Seer* 1, no. 4 (April 1853): 54. For a more recent example, see Harold B. Lee, *Ye Are the Light of the World*, 94.

60. Daniel Isaac, *The Doctrine of Universal Restoration Examined and Refuted*, 52. Isaac's argument for Earth being the most wicked is a concession to Universalists that, in the grand scheme of things, the vast majority of God's creations will be redeemed, just not a vast majority of those who live on this world.

61. Thomas Chalmers, quoted in Erich Robert Paul, *Science, Religion, and Mormon Cosmology*, 80. For an excellent summary of prevailing views during the early nineteenth century, see Cynthia Ann Miller Smith, "Shadows of Things to Come: The Theological Implications of Intelligent Life on Other Worlds."

62. In 1837, Josiah Priest emphasized that, while redemption has occurred and will continue to occur on worlds throughout the vast immensity of space, "there can be but one Son of God, but one Lord Jesus Christ" by whom this redemption is made. Priest, *The Anti-Universalist*, 81.

63. Brigham Young, July 10, 1870, *Journal of Discourses*, 14:71–72. This, of course, does not say that every Earth has a different redeemer, but the idea of multiple redeemers seems to be implied. BYU religion professor Rodney Turner noted: "Other, unpublished, remarks of Brigham Young support the view that he believed that there was more than one savior pertaining to all worlds." Rodney Turner, "The Doctrine of the Firstborn and Only Begotten," 118, note 27.

64. See Thomas F. O'Meara, "Christian Theology and Extraterrestrial Intelligent Life," 3–30.

15

The Gospel Plan

In Mormonism, "the gospel of Jesus Christ comprises fundamental principles and ordinances that must be followed to obtain a fulness of salvation. The first steps are faith in the Lord Jesus Christ, repentance, baptism by immersion for the remission of sins, and the laying on of hands by one who is in authority for the gift of the Holy Ghost. Additional ordinances are administered in the temple."[1] This gospel plan was prepared from the foundation of the world and contains provisions for people of every time and circumstance, including little children who die in infancy and adults who die in ignorance of the plan.

Though Mormonism has traditionally taught that the gospel, when it has been on earth in its fulness, has always been essentially the same, the scriptural record as it has been passed down gives a different picture. Here we look at biblical and traditional Christian teachings regarding the gospel plan and how the LDS concept of the gospel seems to have developed.

The Everlasting Gospel

In the traditional LDS view, the gospel plan taught in the Church today is the same gospel that was preached to Adam and has existed, except for times of apostasy, essentially unchanged throughout history. According to the LDS Bible Dictionary (s.v. "dispensations"), "The plan of salvation, which is older than the earth, has been revealed and taught in every dispensation beginning with Adam and is the same in every age of the world." Joseph Smith likewise taught that "all things pertaining to . . . [the present] dispensation should be conducted precisely in accordance with the preceding dispensations."[2] Among other things, Joseph believed that gospel ordinances should remain unchanged, for God "set the ordinances to be the same forever and ever."[3] They were "instituted in heaven before the foundation of the world" and "are not to be altered [or] changed. All must be saved upon the same principle[s]."[4] Joseph further taught that, regardless of when individuals lived on the earth, they must receive the same ordinances as "there is no other way beneath the heavens whereby God hath ordained for man to come to Him to be saved."[5]

Allusions to the gospel's antiquity can be found in the New Testament (Gal. 3:8; Heb. 4:1–2), which identifies several gospel images in Old Testament stories—for example, the baptism of Israel "in the cloud and in the sea" (1 Cor. 10:2). Hebrews 4:6 states that the gospel "was first preached" to the children of Israel. According to Paul, God's promise to Abraham that "in thee shall all nations be blessed" (Gal. 3:8) signifies that the gospel was preached even to Abraham. While New Testament authors may have believed that their ancient predecessors had received the same Christian ordinances and gospel, the authors of the Old Testament do not give any indication that such was the case.

It was post-apostolic Christianity that fully articulated the view that the gospel was literally on the earth from the time of the Fall. Eusebius (c. 260–339), a bishop and the first historian of the Christian church, asserted that Christianity was not just a 300-year-old religion, but the "first, most ancient, and most primitive of all religions."[6] In the fifth century, Augustine wrote, "What is now called Christian religion has existed among the ancients, and was not absent from the beginning of the human race."[7] Many had the sense that if the gospel is truly the *everlasting* plan of salvation, it must have been in force since the beginning.

In the early 1800s there was a perception among many Christians that the gospel plan was eternal and was embraced by Adam and Eve after the Fall. In a January 1824 article published in the Congregationalist's *Christian Magazine* entitled "The Everlasting Gospel," the writer states that "the gospel was devised from eternity" and that "the scheme of redemption is . . . the eternal purpose of God and his ultimate design in the work of creation."[8] Quaker preacher Elias Hicks wrote in 1828 that the gospel "was preached to our first parents in the garden, when they transgressed."[9]

Belief that the gospel was revealed to Adam after the Fall is expressed in the Westminster Confession of Faith of 1647, which identifies two plans or covenants given to humankind since the creation: "The first covenant made with man was a covenant of works, wherein life was promised to Adam; and in him to his posterity, upon condition of perfect and personal obedience. Man, by his fall, having made himself incapable of life by that covenant, the Lord was pleased to make a second, commonly called the covenant of grace; wherein he freely offereth unto sinners life and salvation by Jesus Christ."[10] In 1767,

Calvinist theologian John Gill wrote that the covenant or "law" that was first given to Adam "contained a promise; which was a promise of life, of natural life to Adam, and of a continuation of it so long as he should observe the condition of it." Thus, this first law impacted Adam's temporal life. Gill further observed that the second law or "covenant of grace" offered "eternal life . . . through Christ as the Mediator of the covenant of grace." In other words, the second law or covenant of grace pertained to Adam's spiritual life.[11]

This idea of a covenant or law of works preceding the fall, followed by a covenant of grace introduced after the fall, is a reformed theological innovation and doesn't appear explicitly in the Bible. A similar concept does, however, show up in the Book of Mormon which, like the Westminster Confession, speaks of a "temporal law" (2 Ne. 2:5) given to Adam before the fall with the penalty for disobedience being "temporal death" (Alma 12:24), and a "spiritual law" (2 Ne. 2:5) being given after the fall with the penalty for disobedience being "everlasting death" (Alma 12:32). According to the Book of Mormon, after Adam and Eve "transgressed the first commandments as to things which were temporal" (Alma 12:31), which constituted a covenant of works aimed at testing their obedience, God gave them a set of "second commandments" (Alma 12:32, 37) based on the gospel of Jesus Christ (i.e., a covenant of grace), which pertained to spiritual blessings.

To suppose that the ancients had no knowledge of Christ or the plan of salvation was inconceivable to Joseph Smith who believed that "all that were ever saved, were saved through the power of this great plan of redemption, as much before the coming of Christ as since."[12] The Prophet even changed John 1:1 from "in the beginning was the Word" to "in the beginning was the gospel preached through the Son" (JST John 1:1). From the beginning of this dispensation, it was made clear that the gospel restored in these latter days was the same gospel that had been preached since the Fall (see D&C 20:26; Moses 5:59).

Of course, a stated purpose of the Book of Mormon in this regard is to bear witness that the gospel was known even to the ancient inhabitants of the American continent. The Book of Mormon prophet Jacob states, "For this intent have we written these things, that they [i.e., future readers] may know that we knew of Christ, and we had a hope of his glory many hundred years before his coming" (Jacob 4:4). Though the LDS claim that ancient American natives were Christians may seem rather bold, certain contemporaries of Joseph Smith actually already held such a view. For example, five years before the publication of the Book of Mormon, Congregationalist minister Ethan Smith wrote that "the gospel had in very remote times, been already preached in America."[13]

The First Principles and Ordinances of the Gospel

In Mormon theology, the gospel plan consists first of a set of principles and ordinances which entitle one to membership in the church and admittance in the hereafter to the celestial kingdom. According to the current fourth Article of Faith, "the first principles and ordinances of the Gospel are: first, Faith in the Lord Jesus Christ; second, Repentance; third, Baptism by immersion for the remission of sins; fourth, Laying on of hands for the gift of the Holy Ghost" (A of F 4).

When considering what scripture has to say about gospel ordinances, it should be noted that, in the Bible and in all LDS scripture until 1832, the term "ordinances" encompassed all of God's statutes and regulations and was not used specifically to designate priesthood rites such as baptism. In this regard, it is interesting that even the original 1842 wording of the fourth Article of Faith (see above) excludes the word "principles," and instead lumps faith and repentance together with baptism and confirmation as gospel "ordinances."[14] There wasn't an umbrella term in either the Old or New Testament for what Latter-day Saints currently call ordinances and what traditional Christianity calls sacraments.[15] Gospel ordinances were simply referred to by their individual names, e.g., sacrifice, baptism, etc.

Old Testament

What Latter-day Saints currently consider as the saving ordinances of the gospel are found nowhere in the Old Testament, even though it describes many other rites and practices in great detail. The religious practices of the Israelites closely resembled those of their Near Eastern neighbors. Virtually every facet of Israelite worship had a precedent in neighboring Near Eastern religions, including circumcision,[16] priestly sacrifice, and ceremonial washing. J. J. M. Roberts, an Old Testament professor at Princeton Theological Seminary, identified six different ancient Near Eastern law codes preceding the law of Moses and noted:

> Not only are these collections of cuneiform law older than the legal collections in the OT, comparative study shows that they constitute particular embodiments of a common law tradition that, for all its local and temporal variations, was basically shared throughout the region of Mesopotamia, Syria, and Palestine.[17]

Moreover, Israel's neighbors conducted cultic ceremonies in temples resembling the later temple of Solomon. The blueprints for these temples were revealed by their gods, just as the temple of Solomon was revealed by Yahweh (1 Chr. 28:11–19).[18]

Salvation in the hereafter was never a stated objective in the Old Testament. Whenever the word "save" or "salvation" appears in the Old Testament, it refers to salvation from hardship and oppression in this life—most often from human hostility. Just as Christ's atonement is nowhere explicitly mentioned in the Old Testament (see Chapter 14), the gospel message of faith in Christ and adherence to what are currently considered to be the gospel's saving ordinances are likewise missing. Though Israelites were admonished to trust in the Lord, they appear to have had no conception of faith as a belief in the redemptive power of a Messiah or Christ as in the New Testament. Jesuit theologian Avery Dulles writes, "The Old Testament has no single term exactly corresponding to the New Testament term *pistis* [the Greek term for faith] and its cognates. The term *he'emin*, the hiphil of the verb *'mn*, is used to mean: he believed, he trusted, he relied on.... The Hebrew noun *'emunah*, which one would expect to be used to designate belief, trust, and the like, is rarely, if ever so used in the Old Testament."[19] Dulles points to Isaiah 26:2 as one possible exception, but notes that "even here, the word ... *'emunah* means rather truth, honesty, loyalty."[20]

According to Mormon theology, the fulness of the gospel, which presumably included all of the ordinances of exaltation performed in LDS temples today, was upon the earth from Adam until the time of Moses, but then was taken away from the children of Israel when they rebelled against God in the wilderness (D&C 84:25). The book of Moses, however, which was revealed to Joseph Smith before temple ordinances were introduced in Mormonism, speaks only of the first principles and ordinances of the gospel being extant prior to Moses (Moses 6:64–66; 7:11; 8:23–24).

A revelation given in September 1832 explains that, from the time of Moses to the time of John the Baptist, the children of Israel practiced "the gospel of repentance and of baptism" (D&C 84:27; see also vv. 17–26; JST Ex. 34:1–2). The Old Testament, however, gives no indication that baptisms were ever performed during this time. LDS commentators have suggested that either the laver, a large bronze basin in Solomon's temple located between the altar and the sanctuary entrance (Ex. 30:19–21), or the molten sea (1 Kgs. 7:23) was used for baptisms.[21] According to the Bible, however, these wash basins were intended only for the priests to wash their own hands and feet before entering and exiting the holy place (Ex. 30:18–20; 2 Chr. 4:2–6).

Common Israelites practiced ritual purification to remove the contamination of death, sexual activity, and disease; however, no ceremonial washing served as a sin-removing rite or functioned as a means of entering into the covenant community. Furthermore, none of the rites practiced in the Old Testament is presented as relevant to salvation in the next life. These ceremonies are depicted solely as a means of pleasing God and gaining acceptance as his holy and peculiar people on earth.

Kaufmann Kohler and Samuel Kraus, writing in the *Jewish Encyclopedia*, indicate that the practice of baptism doesn't appear in Jewish history until near the time of Christ and then only in certain Jewish sects "first as a means of penitence" and then "to receive the spirit of God, or to be permitted to stand in the presence of God."[22] One New Testament scholar notes that, during the first century A.D., it became customary to admit proselytes to Judaism, not only with circumcision, but also with immersion (often self-administered) to wash away the impurities associated with being a gentile.[23] LDS biblical scholar Kevin Barney observes, "Although modern scripture asserts that baptism for the remission of sins dates back to Adam (Moses 6:64–68), it had no role in Mosaic religion. The Law does, however, prescribe various ritual washings, and by John's day baptism with more-or-less its full significance was not unknown."[24]

The Israelites don't appear to have viewed the law of Moses as an inferior or interim law, but as the principal law that God intended for his chosen people for all time.[25] Just as Latter-day Saints currently believe that the gospel of Christ has been in effect from eternity, Jews believe that the law of Moses was eternally in force, having been instituted from before the foundation of the world. According to Jewish tradition, even God studies the Torah.[26] Nowhere in the Old Testament does the Lord tell his people that the law was temporary or that he will one day send a Messiah into the world to fulfill the law. On the contrary, Yahweh set a list of curses at the end of his covenant to ensure that his law would be obeyed forever: "All these curses shall come upon you . . . [if you will not] obey the Lord your God, by observing the commandments and decrees that He commanded you. They shall be among you and your descendants as a sign of portent *forever*" (NRSV Deut. 28:45–46; emphasis mine). Even the offering of sacrifices instituted under Moses was to be "an ordinance *for ever* to Israel" (2 Chr. 2:4; emphasis mine). The Old Testament makes it clear that the law was to stand "forever" as an "everlasting" or "perpetual covenant" and was to remain in effect "throughout generations" (Ex. 12:14, 17, 24; Lev. 3:17; 16:34; 17:7).

The only explicit mention of a "new" covenant in the Old Testament is Jeremiah 31:31–33 where the Lord speaks of a future day when he will make "a new covenant with the house of Israel" (v. 31). The book of Hebrews, whose authorship is unknown, interprets this new covenant as the gospel covenant mediated by Christ through his atonement (Heb. 8:8–13), and this has been the traditional understanding of Christians ever since. The footnote for Jeremiah 31:31 in the LDS Bible references the "new and everlasting covenant" and "restoration of the gospel" in the latter days, giving it more of a Restoration fulfillment.

Critical scholars note that, in Jeremiah, the newness of the covenant pertains to the way it would be enacted, not in what it would comprise. The Lord states, "I will put my law [i.e., the Torah] in their inward parts, and write it in their hearts" (v. 32). Thus, instead of the law being written on stone tablets (Deut. 5:22), it will be written upon the hearts of the children of Israel. It is enacted anew because Israel had broken the old covenant (Jer. 31:31). Harold Attridge, dean of Yale Divinity School, explains, "Jeremiah envisioned a renewal of the Sinai covenant, but the author of Hebrews envisions its replacement."[27] According to University of Exeter theology professor David Rhymer, this passage in Jeremiah is "often (mis)appropriated by Christian commentators" who fail to recognize that it is no more than "a prophetic imagining of a post-exilic community where knowledge of God (through the 'internalized' Torah) is shared by all."[28] It would appear, therefore, that this prophecy was uttered with neither New Testament Christianity nor the later restored gospel in mind.

New Testament

The New Testament introduced a new covenant of salvation based on the gospel of Jesus Christ. In this gospel or "good news," salvation now meant dwelling with God and Christ in the coming kingdom. The requirements for salvation in the New Testament are not entirely clear, and it isn't certain whether the law of Moses was to stay or to go. The Jewish Gospel of Matthew records Jesus as teaching that he came to "fulfill" the law (Matt. 5:17), not in the sense of bringing it to a conclusion, but in the sense of strictly obeying it and reinforcing the fact that it was to remain in force "till heaven and earth pass" (v. 18). Jesus further condemns any who "shall break one of these least commandments, and shall teach men so" (v. 19). This condemnation was not limited only to the violation of the Ten Commandments, for he forbids violating even one "jot or one tittle" of the law (Matt. 5:18). New Testament scholar James Dunn observes that, in Matthew, Jesus "is not to be understood as superseding it [i.e., the Law], or leaving it behind. On the contrary, 'fulfillment' is defined as the antithesis with 'destroy': Jesus came not to abolish . . . but . . . to realize or complete the law and thus establish it, set it on a firmer basis."[29] The book of Acts reveals that as late as A.D. 40, ceremonial circumcision and adherence to the law of Moses were still practiced in the church, even among the leading brethren (Acts 15:1–5, 24).

In Paul's writings, which are more accommodating of gentiles, Christ came to destroy the law so that it was completely "abolished" by his death on the cross (Eph. 2:14–15). Paul taught that Christ "took it [the law] out of the way, nailing it to his cross" (Col. 2:13–14). That the law here referenced appears to include not only the ceremonial law, but also the Ten Commandments, is evident by the reference to the tenth commandment in Romans 7:7 (cf. Ex. 20:17).

While Calvinists (e.g., Presbyterians) as well as Latter-day Saints view the Ten Commandments as still in force, most evangelicals, together with most New Testament scholars, believe Paul viewed them as having been superseded by the law of Christ, which is love (Rom. 13:8–10).[30] F. F. Bruce explains, "It is sometimes said that Christ is the end of the ceremonial law (including not only the sacrificial cultus but circumcision and the observance of the sacred calendar) but not of the moral law [i.e., the Ten Commandments]. . . . This is a perfectly valid, and to some extent an obvious, theological and ethical distinction; but it has no place in Pauline exegesis. It has to be read into Paul, for it is not a distinction that Paul himself makes."[31] In Mormonism, the Ten Commandments are considered integral to the gospel and are enumerated as such in Doctrine and Covenants 42:18–28. As explained by Bruce R. McConkie, "The Ten Commandments . . . being eternal in their nature, are part of the fulness of the everlasting gospel; they have always been in force in all dispensations. They are part of 'the law of Christ' (D&C 88:21)."[32] Thus, in Mormon theology the Ten Commandments are not considered part of the law of Moses to be superseded by the gospel; rather, they are an integral part of the gospel itself.

New Testament passages indicating that the law was to be done away are unclear about what, exactly, was to go and what was to stay. None of the death penalties spelled out in Mosaic law (Ex. 21:12–17; Deut. 13) was ever explicitly rescinded in the New Testament. Nor is it clear why certain ordinances practiced prior to the law of Moses, such as circumcision and sacrifice, were abolished when they predated the law.

The New Testament repeatedly emphasizes the importance of faith, repentance, baptism and the gift of the Holy Ghost (see, for example, John 3:3–5;[33] Acts 2:38; 3:19). It is not entirely clear, however, that New Testament writers were in agreement on the necessity of baptism and the laying on of hands for the gift of the Holy Ghost, nor is it clear that they were to be performed in the same way as practiced by Mormons today.

Scholars note that baptism was initially performed by John the Baptist and Jesus's disciples as a cleansing rite to prepare them for the coming kingdom of God, which was perceptually distinct from the

Church. Kevin Barney explains, "Its *full* significance as a rite marking formal initiation into the Church is a later Christian innovation."[34]

There is evidence that, in earliest Christianity, baptisms were performed in the name of Jesus and not in the name of the Father, Son, and Holy Ghost. As Gerald O'Collins notes, "Christians began baptizing 'in the name of Jesus' (Acts 2:38, 10:48; Rom. 6:3; 1 Cor. 1:13, 15; 6:11). Then at some point they introduced the tripartite formula which has remained normative ever since."[35] The trinitarian baptismal formula in Matthew 28:19 to baptize "in the name of the Father, and of the Son, and of the Holy Ghost," is considered by scholars to be a later (second or third century) scribal addition to Matthew.[36]

A single, uniform prescription for bestowing the Holy Ghost is also difficult to find in the New Testament. John the Baptist told his followers that, although he baptized with water, only Christ could baptize "with the Holy Ghost, and with fire" (Matt. 3:11). Followers of John the Baptist were to look to Jesus to receive the Holy Ghost, but there is no mention of an accompanying rite, such as the laying on of hands. After his resurrection, Jesus assured his disciples that this baptism of the Holy Ghost would transpire "not many days hence" (Acts 1:5). This promise was fulfilled on the day of Pentecost, again with no indication that hands were laid on anyone.

Christ himself received the Holy Ghost as he came up out of the waters of baptism (Matt. 3:16). The only action coming close to an ordinance of conferring the gift of the Holy Ghost in the Gospels is when the resurrected Christ "breathed"[37] collectively on his apostles saying, "Receive ye [plural] the Holy Ghost" (John 20:22). It wasn't until several years after the day of Pentecost that the laying on of hands begins to appear in accounts of individuals receiving the Holy Ghost (Acts 8:12–17, 19:1–7).

Early Nineteenth-Century Christianity

At the time of Joseph Smith, Christian Primitivists were advocating a return to the gospel of the New Testament, appealing to Acts 2:38, which calls for faith in Jesus Christ, repentance of sins, baptism for the remission of sins, and the gift of the Holy Ghost. To this sequence was often appended the call to endure to the end. Walter Scott, an early leader of the Disciples of Christ, pressed for this standard in 1827 stating: "The great elements of the gospel assumed the following definite, rational, and scriptural order: (1) Faith; (2) Repentance; (3) Baptism; (4) Remission of sins; (5) The Holy Spirit; (6) Eternal life, through a patient continuance in well doing."[38]

In addition to following certain prescribed principles and ordinances, most Christians believed that humankind was in need of divine grace in order to overcome their depraved nature and be saved. They were divided, however, in their understanding of how that grace was to be obtained. Calvinists believed that individuals received grace through no choice or individual effort of their own, hence the doctrine of irresistible grace or predestination. In contrast, evangelical Methodists advocated an Arminian, free-will approach to grace with God endowing every person born into the world with a preliminary or "prevenient" grace, which enlightens and empowers individuals sufficiently to choose between good and evil.[39] Those who choose good and repent are brought to the greater light and sanctifying influence of the Holy Ghost. According to John Wesley, this light "would shine more and more to the perfect day" (cf. D&C 50:24).[40] Those who persistently rebelled against God lost this light until it was said of them, "[their] day of grace is passed, and . . . the Holy Spirit has left [them] to ripen for destruction [cf. Morm. 2:15]."[41]

The manifestation of the Spirit in evangelical converts during the Second Great Awakening of the early nineteenth century was often dramatic. Accounts speak of penitent souls experiencing a mighty change of heart and collapsing from being overcome by the Spirit—a phenomenon referred to as the "falling exercise." Mark D. Thomas explains:

> [A] common manifestation of those under conviction [of sin] is the falling exercise, or falling "under the power of God" . . . . The falling exercise itself took several forms. Sometimes those who fell simply lost the use of their limbs but were still conscious and would "cry for mercy." At other times, they apparently stopped breathing and were described "as if they were dead," or "as if they were dying." . . . The falling exercise could be a manifestation of joy as well as conviction.[42]

American political and religious historian Charles Johnson described the ecstasy of those reviving from the falling exercise: "When the 'fallers' . . . recovered, they often arose shouting, 'Praise God!' . . . . Some had seen visions, heard unspeakable words . . . and had 'a delightful singing in the breast.'"[43] This singing was popularly referred to by evangelicals as "the song of redeeming love."[44]

When revivalist preachers sermonized on the plan of salvation the typical approach was to lay out the fall of humanity, their consequent carnal and depraved nature, the atonement of Christ, and their redemption through spiritual rebirth. Characterizing what he called "the principle [sic] doctrines of the gospel" that were so often preached in camp meetings in upstate New York, Methodist minister Buel Goodsell wrote in 1825, "The fall of man, his consequent depravity and helplessness, the divinity of Christ, the atonement, the influence of the Holy Spirit, and the necessity of faith in Christ to procure pardon and holiness: these are the truths which were repeatedly explained."[45] This pattern of gospel preaching, which begins with the fall of Adam to establish humanity's fallen and depraved state and their consequent need for redemption and the sanctifying influence of the Holy Ghost through the power of the atonement, is not found in the Bible *per se*, but developed in the patristic era and had become the hallmark of Reformation preaching in Joseph Smith's day. One Christian writer observed in 1827 that "the whole fabric of the Reformation was reared on the doctrines of the fall of man and the entire corruption of his nature; and of his recovery by the one meritorious sacrifice of the death of Christ, and by the sanctifying operations of the Holy Ghost."[46]

Early Mormonism

The preaching of the gospel in the Book of Mormon is reminiscent of early nineteenth-century frontier camp meetings. In presenting the gospel message to a Lamanite king, for example, the Book of Mormon states that the Lord's servant Aaron

> expound[ed] unto him the scriptures from the creation of Adam, laying the fall of man before him, and their carnal state and also the plan of redemption . . . through Christ, for all whosoever would believe on his name. And since man had fallen he could not merit anything of himself; but the sufferings and death of Christ atone for their sins, through faith and repentance, and so forth. (Alma 22:13–14).

Joseph Fielding McConkie has correctly noted that "the Book of Mormon has no scriptural peer in teaching the doctrines of the fall, the atonement, and the need for a Redeemer."[47] However, while no peer may exist in biblical scripture, a close parallel can be seen in the sermons of early nineteenth-century Protestant revivalists.

The Book of Mormon is, according to BYU religion professor Stephen Robinson, "thoroughly Arminian" in the way salvation is proclaimed.[48] Though all are fallen, "through the great Mediator of all men," all have freedom to choose between good and evil (2 Ne. 2:27). But unless one "yields to the enticings of the Holy Spirit," he remains "an enemy to God" (Mosiah 3:19; cf. 16:1–4; 26:4). Thus, all persons are given prevenient grace through the atonement of Christ. They, however, must respond of their own free will to the influence of the Spirit in order to receive the full blessings of the atonement. The Book of Mormon expresses contempt for the Calvinistic doctrine of predestined salvation and damnation (see Alma 31:16–18). In a 1999 FARMS apologia, LDS scholar Blake Ostler wrote that, not only do "Mormon scriptures show influences of nineteenth-century Arminianism," but also, "given Joseph Smith's Methodist leanings and the interpretation inherent in translation, that is what one would expect."[49]

Prior to Christ's visit to the Nephites, the Book of Mormon faithful had already embraced the gospel of Christ, but at the same time they continued to comply fully with the law of Moses. Description of the rites they practiced under the law of Moses are sketchy, however, with only a passing comment that the people observed "to keep the judgments, and the statutes, and the commandments of the Lord in all things according to the law of Moses" (2 Ne. 5:10). The difference, as Book of Mormon prophets were careful to point out, between the way they practiced the law of Moses and the way Jews in Palestine practiced it, was that the Nephites understood the purpose for which it was given, which was to point souls to Christ (Jacob 4:5).

In contrast to the Sermon on the Mount in Jerusalem, where Jesus explains that the law of Moses is to be scrupulously followed even "till heaven and earth pass away" (Matt. 5:18), Christ's sermon at the temple, delivered to the Nephites after his resurrection, presents the law of Moses as having been done away in Christ: "For verily I say unto you, one jot nor one tittle hath not passed away from the law, but *in me it hath all been fulfilled*" (3 Ne. 12:17–18; emphasis mine; cf. Matt. 5:17–18). In the JST, the Prophet similarly revised the text of Matthew 5:21 to read that the law of Moses must be obeyed only "until it be fulfilled." Joseph Smith also marginalized the importance of the law of Moses in other changes he made to the New Testament. Romans 7:12, for example, extols the law of Moses saying "the law is holy"; however, Joseph modified earlier verses in the chapter so that the "law" referred to "the commandment of Christ" (vv. 9–10). This brings the passage more in harmony with the traditional Christian understanding of Paul's teachings regarding the inferiority of the law of Moses.

Surprisingly, nowhere does the Book of Mormon acknowledge the distinct advantage Book of Mormon people would have had over the Jews in Palestine in possessing "the Melchizedek Priesthood" and "the fulness of the gospel" (cf. D&C 20:9; 27:5; 42:12; 135:3).[50] Presumably this would entitle them not only to the gift of the Holy Ghost, but to all of the ordinances of exaltation currently performed in LDS temples. According to Joseph Fielding Smith, "By fulness of the gospel is meant all the ordinances and principles that pertain to exaltation in the celestial kingdom."[51] What one finds, however, is that the Book of Mormon makes no mention of any of the higher ordinances of exaltation performed in temples today. Bruce R. McConkie accounted for this absence by suggesting that the Book of Mormon contains the fulness of the gospel only "in the sense that the Book of Mormon is a record of God's dealings with a people who had the fulness of the gospel."[52] This interpretation, however, seems to overlook the passages listed above which expressly state that the book itself contains the fulness of the gospel. Another common, though not entirely satisfactory, explanation of how the Book of Mormon contains the fulness of the gospel is "that it contains the fulness of all truths essential in placing one on that path which, if followed, leads to eternal life."[53] Thus, the Book of Mormon contains the initial principles and ordinances needed to get one on the path to receiving the fulness of the gospel and eventually eternal life. The higher ordinances of eternal life are presumably to be found further along on the path.

The Book of Mormon and other early LDS revelations give a different explanation of what was meant at the time by "the fulness of the gospel." The Book of Mormon informs that the gospel in its entirety consists of faith, repentance, baptism, and the gift of the Holy Ghost, and "whoso shall declare more or less than this, and establish it for my doctrine, the same cometh of evil" (3 Ne. 11:40). This definitive scope is again reiterated in Doctrine and Covenants 10:67–68. It seems evident that early revelations declaring that the Book of Mormon contains the fulness of the gospel were based on what was understood at the time as the sum total of the saving ordinances of the gospel. It is of interest to note that the original version of the fourth Article of Faith omitted the word "first" when referring to the principles and ordinances of the gospel, thus implying that faith, repentance, baptism and gift of the Holy Ghost were alone the only requirements of salvation.[54]

Conversion in the Book of Mormon often goes beyond the simple change of heart described in the New Testament. Converts in the Book of Mormon fell to the ground "as though dead" at the preaching of the word (Alma 18:42; 19:17–18) and experienced a "mighty change" of heart (Mosiah 5:2; Alma 5:12). They were also "brought before the altar of God, to call on his name and confess their sins before him" (Alma 17:4). These are identical to experiences and practices found in early nineteenth-century frontier camp meetings.[55] Expressions used by ancient Book of Mormon people to describe their conversion experience include being "encircled about eternally in the arms of his love" (2 Ne. 1:15; see also Alma 26:15), being "spiritually born of God" (Alma 5:14), "sing[ing] redeeming love" (Alma 5:9; see also Alma 5:26, 26:13), having "his arm of mercy . . . extended towards you" (Jacob 6:5; see also Mosiah 16:12, 29:20; Alma 5:33; 3 Ne. 9:14), and being "awakened . . . to a sense of your nothingness, and your worthless and fallen state" (Mosiah 4:5). Again, such expressions were all part of the revival vernacular of Joseph Smith's day.[56]

In the Book of Mormon conversion is often, but not always, accompanied by baptism. There are no instances, however, of converts receiving the laying on of hands for the gift of the Holy Ghost. The Holy Ghost was a blessing promised to those who repented and sought it through prayer, but with no mention of the need of a human intermediary or ordinance. When manifesting itself in connection with baptism, it came as a direct outpouring from God (2 Ne. 31:13–14, 17–18; 32:5; Mosiah 18:10, 12, 14, 16). In contrast to the detailed instructions given by the Savior at his appearance on the manner in which baptisms were to be performed and the sacrament administered, there is no prescription given on how the gift of the Holy Ghost was to be conferred. It is only as a postscript to Mormon's abridgment that Moroni interjects that Christ had, in fact, prescribed the laying on of hands to his disciples as the manner in which the Holy Ghost should be conferred (Moro. 2:1–3).

Just as the New Testament reads baptism back into the Old Testament, 1 Nephi 20:1 introduces baptism into the text of Isaiah 48:1, which refers to Israel coming forth "out of the waters of Judah," adding that they also came "out of the waters of baptism." This reference to baptism, putatively by Isaiah, wasn't added, however, until the 1840 edition of the Book of Mormon, which seems to point to an ongoing propensity to interject gospel references into Old Testament narratives.

Brent Lee Metcalfe has observed that the Book of Mormon shows an understanding of the gospel that evolved, not chronologically (beginning with 1 Nephi), but according to the sequence of dictation (beginning with Mosiah).[57] He notes that the book of Mosiah shows a rather primitive understanding of the gospel with repentance and spiritual rebirth being identified as the only necessary requirements for salvation (Mosiah 4:5–8). According to Metcalfe, "Baptism in the Book of Mosiah is portrayed as a novelty," which is a bit surprising given that over 400 years earlier—though later than Mosiah in sequence of translation—a "Christocentric baptismal covenant" is fully articulated (2 Nephi 31:11).[58] The most complete expression of the gospel is found, not after the Savior's visit in 3 Nephi, but in 2 Nephi 31 which is at the beginning of the Book of Mormon chronology, but near the end of the dictation sequence.[59]

In the Book of Mormon and early revelations of the Church, the gospel or "doctrine of Christ" consisted of coming to Christ through faith, repentance, and baptism with the promise of receiving the gift of the Holy Ghost (2 Ne. 31:17–21; 32:1–6; 3 Ne. 11:31–39). Bestowal of the Holy Ghost through the laying on of hands hadn't become formally adopted until the organization of the Church on April 6, 1830. After Joseph Smith and Oliver Cowdery administered the sacrament to members of the newly formed church, Joseph reports, "We then laid our hands on each individual member of the Church present, that they might receive the gift of the Holy Ghost, and be confirmed members of the Church of Christ."[60]

It is interesting to note that, although the Bible speaks of the imposition of hands for the gift of the Holy Ghost (Acts 8:14–17, 19:1–6), nowhere is there any specific mention of confirmation, an ordinance that developed later in the Roman Catholic Church. The *Catholic Encyclopedia* explains, "Confirmation is a striking instance of the development of doctrine and ritual in the Church." It adds that "the word *confirmation* is not used to designate this sacrament [of conferring the Holy Ghost] during the first four centuries."[61] It was even later when confirmation came to include conferral of Church membership.

Soon after the first principles and ordinances of the gospel were established in the Church, "higher" ordinances were added, including ordination to the Melchizedek Priesthood for men and, beginning in 1842, temple ordinances. These higher ordinances would come to be considered as ordinances of exaltation. Essential temple ordinances currently consist of a washing and anointing, an endowment ceremony, and a (non-polygamous) marriage ceremony.

Melchizedek Priesthood Ordination

Although obtaining the Melchizedek Priesthood is currently regarded as essential for attaining exaltation, the origin and development of this requirement is a bit obscure. In the Bible and Book of Mormon, ministerial callings were conferred on only a select few to administer the laws and ordinances of the gospel to others. There is no mention that ordination to the priesthood itself was essential for obtaining exaltation in either the Bible, Book of Mormon, Pearl of Great Price, or the Doctrine and Covenants prior to the September 1832 revelation in section 84. It is true that Doctrine and Covenants 76, revealed February 16, 1832, states that those who inherit the celestial kingdom "inherit all things," thereby becoming "priests," "kings," and "gods" (D&C 76:55–59); but these appear to be exalted titles bestowed in the resurrection. The only requirements spelled out before section 84 for reigning as priests in the hereafter are baptism, the gift of the Holy Ghost, and faithfulness to the end (D&C 76:51–53).

The primary scriptural basis for the LDS belief that ordination to the Melchizedek Priesthood is essential to obtaining eternal life is Doctrine and Covenants 84:33–44, which is commonly referred to as "the oath and covenant of the priesthood." The revelation states that "all they who receive this priesthood . . . receiveth my Father's kingdom" (vv. 35–38), and "this is according to the oath and covenant which belongeth to the priesthood" (v. 39). This passage has come to be interpreted to mean that one must *obtain* the Melchizedek Priesthood in order to obtain exaltation—which, since given prior to Doctrine and Covenants 131 when the ordinance of celestial marriage was revealed, doesn't make any provision for women. It isn't clear, however, that this passage is really an injunction to *obtain* the priesthood. The phrase "receive this priesthood" (v. 35) is ambiguously used throughout the section and, in verse 35, can just as easily be read to mean *obey* or *follow* those who hold the priesthood. The word "receive" occurs seven times before verse 35, all with the meaning of *obtain* or *have conferred upon*. Of the nine times it appears in conditional clauses after verse 35, eight of them clearly mean *follow* or *obey*. The meaning in the remaining instance (v. 40) is ambiguous and depends on the way verse 35 is interpreted. The idea of receiving the priesthood seems to shift in meaning in verse 35 from *obtaining* the priesthood to *obeying* to the priesthood. The phrase "receive the priesthood" in verse 35 is, in fact, clarified in the very next verse which explains, "*For* he that receiveth my servants receiveth me." Receiving the priesthood is thus equated with receiving, i.e., hearkening to, the Lord's servants. Similarly, verse 42 speaks of "coming unto" the priesthood, which also seems to refer to obeying the priesthood and not obtaining the priesthood—just as the scriptural phrase "coming unto Christ" means obeying Christ (see D&C 18:11, 19:41, 20:59).

Although there is no contemporaneous commentary on Doctrine and Covenants 84:35–38 that would indicate whether this passage was understood one way or the other, the earliest commentaries that do appear generally interpret *receiving* the priesthood in the sense of *following* or *obeying* the priesthood. Orson Pratt remarked in 1876: "He [Joseph Smith] said all they that receive this priesthood, *that is, those who receive the testimony of the servants of God*, receive me."[62] Understood this way, saying that "all those who receive the priesthood, receive this oath and covenant of my Father" (v. 40) would mean that those who receive (i.e., obey) the laws and ordinances of the priesthood receive, by oath and covenant, the blessings appertaining thereto. Apostle George Q. Cannon gave a similar explanation in 1884 saying, "When an Elder lays his hands upon the head of a man or a woman who has been . . . baptized and says unto that individual, 'receive ye the Holy Ghost,' God in heaven, bound by the oath and the covenant that He has made, bound by all the conditions that pertain to the everlasting Priesthood, will cause the Holy Ghost to descend upon that soul, and he or she will be filled therewith."[63] In 1881, Wilford Woodruff interpreted Doctrine and Covenants 84:35–40 as applying to all faithful saints who come unto (i.e., obey) the priesthood, that "by obeying the celestial law [as administered by the priesthood], all that our Father has shall be given unto us."[64] In 1882, he commented again on this passage saying, "If we abide the laws of the priesthood [not *obtain* the priesthood] we shall become heirs of God and joint-heirs with Jesus Christ."[65] In 1894, and then as Church president in 1898, Lorenzo Snow gave a similar interpretation in sermons he delivered to the Saints.[66]

It is interesting to note that when the Melchizedek Priesthood is conferred on individuals, there is no explicit promise or covenant of eternal life that is uttered by the recipient or pronounced by the officiator as in other higher ordinances of the priesthood such as the endowment or marriage. Although early LDS literature most often explained Doctrine and Covenants 84:33-41 in terms of receiving eternal life through obedience to the law of the priesthood, Latter-day Saints today commonly understand this passage as teaching that this covenantal promise can only be obtained through priesthood ordination itself.[67] Even if obtaining the priesthood may not have been intended in section 84 as a requirement for exaltation, we shall see that it later became a prerequisite for exaltation as part of what would become known as "the fulness of the priesthood" received through the sealing ordinance of the temple (see Chapter 17).

The Temple Endowment

According to fourteenth Church President Howard W. Hunter, the temple endowment "consists of two parts: first, a series of instructions, and second, promises or covenants that the person receiving the endowment makes—promises to live righteously and comply with the requirements of the gospel of Jesus Christ."[68] The development of the endowment to its current form is a good example of the evolutionary nature of prophetic vision.[69]

Old Testament

In LDS teachings, the temple endowment was revealed to Adam and continued to be practiced in ancient Israel until the time of Moses, when the priesthood and higher ordinances of the gospel were taken away due to disobedience (D&C 84:25).[70] The Old Testament, however, gives no indication that temple endowments were received by God's people anciently, even prior to the time of Moses when the Melchizedek priesthood was presumably on the earth.

New Testament

The New Testament alludes to a number of ordinances, none of which corresponds to the higher ordinances of the gospel currently performed in LDS temples. According to the teachings of some LDS leaders, the reinstatement of the Melchizedek Priesthood at the time of Christ opened the way for the temple endowment and eternal marriage. Joseph Fielding Smith taught that Peter, James, and John received their endowments on the Mount of Transfiguration and that afterwards "they could, and most likely did, give endowments to the other apostles and many others in some secluded spot or on some mountain."[71] Rather than viewing the endowment on the day of Pentecost as an outpouring of the Holy Ghost as described in Acts, some LDS commentators superimpose a temple motif, so that the Pentecostal endowment is perceived as being the same endowment received in LDS temples today. Bruce R. McConkie, for example, writes that the endowment in Acts consisted of "knowledge, powers and special blessings, normally given only in the Lord's temple."[72]

The New Testament itself is devoid of any references to temple ordinances being performed in the early Christian church. The whole concept of the temple tends to be spiritualized in New Testament teachings. Paul speaks of church members as collectively comprising a "holy temple in the Lord" (Eph. 2:21) with God dwelling in them through his Spirit. Hebrews 4:14–16, 9:24 refers to Jesus as a high priest ministering from "heaven itself" rather than in an inferior earthly temple. LDS apologists point to certain secret, mystical rites in Christian era Jewish and Gnostic sects that bear some resemblance to those practiced in LDS temples today (e.g., ceremonial washings, anointings, etc.),[73] but whether these practices have an actual temple linkage has been a debated issue.

Early Mormonism

According to LDS teachings, the inhabitants of ancient America had the fulness of the gospel and, presumably, the Melchizedek Priesthood, yet there is no indication that they performed temple ordinances like those performed in LDS temples today. Though they built temples after the manner of Solomon's temple (2 Ne. 5:16), which was used for priestly rites under the law of Moses, the Book of Mormon is silent as to any other purpose these temples served other than being a place for preaching the gospel (see Jacob 1:17; Mosiah 7:17; Alma 16:13). When Jesus appeared at the temple in the land Bountiful after his resurrection, he carefully instructed his disciples on the administration of the sacrament and procedure for baptism, but there is no indication that he gave them any instruction regarding the temple or that it had any significance in the plan of salvation.[74]

Revelations prior to 1831, including the book of Moses which reveals the fulness of the gospel as given to Adam and the ancient patriarchs, give no indication that an endowment ceremony was considered to be a part of the plan of salvation. It was in 1831 in Kirtland that Joseph Smith introduced the concept of the endowment, which would not take on its current meaning or become a requirement for exaltation until 1842.[75]

Initially, the endowment was understood in Mormonism as simply an outpouring of the Holy Ghost similar to what occurred on the day of Pentecost. On January 2, 1831, three days after the Saints were commanded to "assemble together at . . . Ohio" (D&C 37:3), the Lord revealed, "there you shall be endowed with power from on high" (D&C 38:32; see also 39:15). The phrase "endowed with power from on high" echoes Jesus's instruction to his disciples: "Tarry ye in the city of Jerusalem, until ye be endued with power from on high" (Luke 24:49). On the day of Pentecost, this endowment came as "they were all filled with the Holy Ghost" (Acts 2:4), thereby receiving "power" to preach the gospel (Acts 1:8). Latter-day Saint elders were to receive a similar spiritual endowment to empower them to preach the gospel. In February 1831, a revelation was given pertaining to "the elders of my church" (D&C 44:1) in which the Lord declared: "I will pour out my Spirit upon them in the day that they assemble themselves together. And it shall come to pass that they shall go forth into the regions round about, and preach repentance unto the people" (D&C 44:2–3). This endowment was received on June 3, 1831, during a conference held in Kirtland, Ohio, where a number of these elders were ordained to the High Priesthood which was accompanied by spiritual manifestations. What they experienced "consisted [of] the endowment—it being a new order—and bestowed authority."[76]

A similar endowment of "power from on high" (D&C 95:8) was to be received by elders participating in the School of the Prophets (January 1833 to March 1835), only this time it was accompanied by the ordinance of foot washing—patterned after Jesus's washing of his disciples' feet following the Last Supper.

In June 1834, a revelation was received instructing the elders of the Church that the Lord had "prepared a great endowment . . . to be poured out upon them" (D&C 105:12) such that they were to be "endowed with power from on high" (D&C 104:11). Then, in fall 1835, Joseph told members of the Quorum of the Twelve that they were to organize a school of the elders, repeating the same procedure followed in organizing the initial School of the Prophets in 1833—with the same promise of an outpouring of power from on high in connection with a solemn assembly and ordinance of foot washing. This plan, however, was changed before it was implemented. "Instead, JS organized the Elders School on 1 November 1835 without a solemn assembly, and the foot-washing ordinance was performed during a solemn assembly in the House of the Lord at the conclusion of a set of newly instituted ordinances."[77]

The Kirtland "House of God" (it wasn't referred to as a temple until several years after its completion[78]) was dedicated on March 27 1836, and incorporated these newly instituted ordinances to prepare participants (still limited to only males) for the endowment. This endowment or spiritual outpouring was like the 1831 endowment; however, it was preceded by the candidate's bathing and perfuming himself (or being bathed and perfumed) and then being anointed with oil (on the head)—a ceremony which, as LDS historian Richard Bushman notes, Joseph adapted from Old Testament descriptions pertaining to the washing and anointing of the priests of Aaron (see Ex. 30:22–30; 40:12–15).[79] This was followed by the receipt of a personal blessing which was sealed with uplifted hands. At this point candidates were often reported to have experienced spiritual manifestations. After this initial ceremony, the brethren met in the solemn assembly room to receive the ordinance of washing of feet, which was then followed with the sacrament. Of course, this is not the endowment one receives in LDS temples today, which consists of signs, tokens, pledges, and the repetition of a creation narrative. A primary objective of the Kirtland Temple endowment, as indicated in the dedicatory prayer (see D&C 109), was for elders to be taught and ceremonially cleansed to merit an endowment of the Spirit, "that . . . [they] may go forth from this house armed with [God's] power" (v. 22) to build the kingdom and preach the gospel.

LDS scholar Greg Prince points out that the sudden show of interest beginning in January 1831 to have the elders receive an endowment of the Spirit to empower them for the ministry seems to have been linked to the influence of former Campbellite minister Sidney Rigdon.[80] Rigdon joined up with Joseph Smith in December 1830 and immediately became his confidant and personal scribe. He believed the message of the early Mormon elders who converted him, but thought they lacked the power that the New Testament apostles exhibited—a lack which the endowment was intended to remedy.

Nauvoo Period

It wasn't until May 1842 in Nauvoo that a ceremonial endowment having signs and tokens—much like the current LDS endowment—was presented to a few select men in the upper room of Joseph Smith's red brick store. (Women didn't begin receiving the endowment until September 1843, with Emma Smith being the first.) Not coincidentally, this new endowment came just two months after Joseph was initiated into the Masonic order.[81] It was on March 15, 1842, that Joseph

Smith and Sidney Rigdon were initiated into the Masonic order, and on the following day both were made Master Masons. In a public discourse just four days later, Joseph spoke for the first time of "certain key words & signs belonging to the priesthood which must be observed in order to obtain the blessings."[82] "Keywords" and "signs" (as well as "tokens" and "penalties") were terms of significance in Masonic rituals.[83] In May 1842, Joseph instituted a new endowment called "the Holy Order," which was altogether different from the Kirtland endowment and incorporated numerous Masonic tokens and signs, including various Masonic pledges of secrecy.[84]

Though different in certain respects, many similarities can be seen between this new temple endowment and Freemasonry ceremonies. For example, the endowment incorporated the same five points of fellowship (since 1990 it has no longer been used in the Mormon endowment),[85] the same kinds of gruesome penalties (also discontinued in 1990), and the same compass and square symbols.[86] The Masonic ritual included a rehearsal of the "periods of creation"[87] as initiates representing Adam progressed through stages according to their "sincere desire to make advances in knowledge and virtue."[88] Initiates to Freemasonry also wore ceremonial regalia (aprons, robes, etc.) with instructions that they were "never to be forgotten or laid aside."[89] BYU humanities professor George S. Tate notes that prayer circles were also conducted by "Freemasons of the period [who] arranged themselves in circular formation around an altar, repeating in unison the received Masonic signs."[90]

These and other striking similarities between the endowment ceremony and Freemasonry rites prompted Bushman to assert that "the endowment ceremonies . . . instituted in Nauvoo [were] inspired by the rituals of freemasonry to which Smith had recently been exposed."[91] For many Latter-day Saints, both the LDS endowment and Freemasonry are presumed to have a common origin in antiquity. This perception is based, in part, on a comment made by Joseph Smith recorded by Heber C. Kimball in June 1842: "Thare is a similarity of preast Hood in masonry. Bro Joseph ses masonary was taken from preasthood but has become degenrated. but menny things are perfect."[92]

Modern scholarship rejects the claim that Freemasonry originated in antiquity, especially the claim that the particular elements adopted by Mormonism date back to antiquity. Scholars see little evidence of most modern Freemasonry practices going back further than the trade guilds of the Middle Ages.[93] This is not to say that there weren't certain rituals in ancient Christianity and Judaism that bear some correspondence to elements in the endowment ceremony.[94] It does suggest, however, that Joseph likely drew upon elements from his environment, including Freemasonry, when composing the details of the endowment.

To Mormon critics, the fact that Joseph appears to have leveraged ritual forms he encountered in Freemasonry to formulate the endowment ceremony proves that he was a fraud. An alternative explanation, however, is that the essential elements of the endowment are covenants that relate to sacrifice, obedience, chastity, and consecration, which are all inspired principles found in ancient scripture. So it may have been only the outward administration of these covenants that was left largely to the creative initiative of Joseph Smith and his successors. On February 8, 1877, Brigham Young related in the presence of St. George Temple recorder L. John Nuttall that Joseph had not finalized the endowment ceremony and therefore instructed Brigham in May 1842 to "organize and systematize all these ceremonies."[95] The removal and modification of elements of the endowment ceremony over the years to accommodate modern views and sensibilities is further evidence that the Church perceives the covenants to be a more essential and enduring part of the endowment. As one LDS apologist intimately acquainted with Freemasonry explains:

> When Joseph was first trying to communicate the truths of the endowment he used a ritual form familiar to the Saints of his day. That ritual form was, in some respects, Masonic in nature. As the Saints lost their connection to Masonry the symbolic meaning of the penalties and other Masonic elements was lost as well. They became meaningless to all but a few Latter-day Saint Freemasons. So the penalties were removed along with other elements both Masonic and non-Masonic which no longer served the purpose of communicating the truths of the endowment.[96]

Notably, as work began on building the Nauvoo temple, the Prophet seemed to have envisioned that it would effectively operate in much the same way as the Kirtland temple: providing instruction and getting elders and leaders spiritually cleansed and prepared to preach the gospel and build the kingdom. Though some LDS commentators have suggested that the Kirtland temple was intended as a kind of preparatory temple to the Nauvoo temple, the Prophet seemed to have initially envisioned the same activities occurring in both temples. Indeed, the floor plan of the Nauvoo temple was essentially the same as the Kirtland temple, both consisting of a basement, a main floor assembly hall, a second floor assembly hall, and an attic for offices. Prince writes that "the Nauvoo temple was designed like the Kirtland House of the Lord for the simple reason that as late as April 1842 no differences between the Kirtland and Nauvoo endowments were anticipated."[97] It wasn't until October 1841 that a decision was made to include a baptistry in the basement, and then in March 1842 to provide makeshift accommodations in the attic for the new endowment ceremony.

The introduction of signs, tokens, covenants, and ceremonial role playing in the Nauvoo endowment seems to have drawn some of the focus away from the customary view of the endowment as a spiritual outpouring. Where the Kirtland endowment was seen primarily as an outpouring of the Spirit, in the Nauvoo endowment the ceremony itself became a prominent part of the endowment. Mormon historian Lyndon Cook explains, "In Nauvoo the temple ordinances (wherein the Saints performed washings, and anointings and received signs and tokens of the Holy Priesthood), were known as the 'ancient order of the Priesthood' or simply as the 'endowment,' there being no particular attempt to distinguish between the ceremony and the spiritual outpouring."[98]

Later Mormonism

Eventually it became customary to refer only to the many temple ordinances as comprising the endowment. In 1853, Brigham Young taught, "Your endowment is, to receive all those ordinances in the house of the Lord, which are necessary for you . . . [to] gain your eternal exaltation."[99] Current LDS use of the term "endowment" is generally restricted further to the ceremonial session where individuals assume the roles of Adam and Eve and figuratively journey through the creation, the fall, and mortality, followed by receiving the signs, tokens, and robes of the priesthood prior to figuratively entering the celestial kingdom.[100]

Eternal Marriage

In LDS theology, eternal marriage is the union of a couple in a temple ceremony for time and all eternity. The covenant of eternal marriage appears to be a modern doctrinal development that isn't specifically mentioned in any of the standard works prior to 1843 (see D&C 132).

Old Testament

Marriage is depicted in the Old Testament as a culturally important practice, but there is no mention of its continuation beyond the grave. Doctrine and Covenants 132:30 refers to Abraham being married for eternity citing as evidence the Lord's promise to him that "his seed" would be "as innumerable as the stars; or . . . the sand upon the seashore." The rationale seems to be that the promise to Abraham of *innumerable* seed can make sense only if it is fulfilled in the hereafter, thereby confirming an eternal marriage relationship. In the Old Testament account, however, it wasn't Abraham's immediate seed that would be innumerable, but his extended posterity. (Modern translations use the word "descendants.") Moreover, the expression "sand of the sea" or "stars of heaven" didn't mean countless in number, but was simply Near Eastern hyperbole meaning "a whole lot"[101] (see Josh. 11:4; Judg. 7:12; 1 Sam. 13:5; 2 Sam. 17:11; 1 Kgs. 4:20; Nahum 3:16). In fact, one wonders if the biblical writer might have seen God's promise as having been fulfilled when Israel entered the Promised Land and Moses proclaimed, "The Lord your God hath multiplied you, and, behold, ye are this day as the stars of heaven for multitude" (Deut. 1:10; see also 10:22; 28:62; Neh. 9:23; 1 Kgs. 4:20).

New Testament

In the New Testament, marriage is not only excluded as a practice having any saving merit, but at times it is even denigrated. Though he opposed divorce, Jesus never went on record as proclaiming the sanctity of marriage and family and, in fact, stated that he had come to set family members against one another (Matt. 10:35–37).[102] He urged his followers to put the kingdom of God above family saying, "Verily I say unto you, There is no man that hath left house . . . . or wife, or children, for the kingdom of God's sake, who shall not receive manifold more" (Luke 18:29–30). Jesus commended those who, choosing not to marry, "have made themselves eunuchs [i.e., celibates] for the kingdom of heaven's sake" (Matt. 19:9–12). The only marriage extolled in the New Testament is the spiritual marriage of the believer to Christ (2 Cor. 11:2; Rev. 21:2).

According to non-LDS biblical scholars, Jesus didn't see marriage as something that would extend into the next life. They cite as evidence Mark 12:18–25 where the Sadducees, seeking to discredit belief in the resurrection, pose to Jesus the hypothetical situation of a woman marrying and becoming a widow seven times in succession and then ask of him which of all the seven men the woman will be married to in the resurrection. Jesus reprimands them for their lack of understanding and explains that "when they shall rise from the dead, they neither marry, nor are given in marriage; but are as the angels which are in heaven" (Mark 12:25). The non-LDS explanation of this passage is that Christ is pointing out the absurdity of their own inquisition, stating that such a hypothetical situation as this doesn't disprove the resurrection because life in the hereafter is not going to be like earth life; there is no marriage, but rather all become as the angels.[103] According to Rabbinical teachings dating back to the time of Christ, "In the world to come there is neither eating, nor drinking, nor procreation, nor strife; but the righteous sit encrowned and enjoy the splendor of the Shekinah [i.e., 'of God']."[104]

Christ's response to the Sadducees was left unmodified in the JST, although Doctrine and Covenants 132:15–16 adds the proviso that it is only those who are not married for all eternity by the proper priesthood authority that will become as angels and remain single. All others become gods and their marriage continues. In light of the LDS doctrine of eternal marriage, several explanations of Christ's response to the Sadducees have subsequently been proffered. James E. Talmage commented in 1899, "The Lord's meaning was clear . . . since all except the first had married her for the duration of mortal life only," she naturally belonged to the first.[105] Joseph F. Smith explained Christ's response in 1912: "Christ understood the principle [of eternal marriage], but he did not cast his pearls before the swine that tempted him."[106] Thus, Christ refused to give the Sadducees a real answer. A few decades later, Joseph Fielding Smith turned the Sadducees' question around to make it an inquiry expressly related to eternal marriage rather than a hypothetical question to disprove the resurrection. He contended that the Sadducees were fully aware that Christ preached eternal marriage, "otherwise they never would have presented the question to the Savior."[107] These various interpretations all achieve reconciliation between Christ's response to the Sadducees and the LDS doctrine of eternal marriage, though it is uncertain whether any one of them reflects the original intent of the passage.

A New Testament passage Latter-day Saints often cite as teaching eternal marriage is 1 Corinthians 11. Here Paul gives a lengthy sermon on why women should have their heads covered when they prophesy and pray, basically explaining that it symbolizes woman's subordination to man (1 Cor. 11:1–10). To ensure that the Corinthian saints don't take this to mean that men are superior to women, Paul immediately follows with: "Nevertheless neither is the man without the woman, neither the woman without the man, in the Lord" (v. 11). Latter-day Saints have traditionally interpreted this last verse to mean that man and woman must be eternally joined in marriage to stand approved before the Lord.[108] There is no express mention, however, of marriage in Paul's exposition as the context of his remarks is male and female relationships and customs in the church (1 Cor. 11:3–10). Thomas Schreiner, professor of New Testament interpretation at the Southern Baptist Theological Seminary, explains, "First Corinthians 11:3–10 is a sustained argument in favor of male headship and female submission, yet with full participation in worship for women. . . . Verses 11–12 function as a qualification so that the Corinthians will not misunderstand Paul's argument. Woman and man stand in interdependence in the Lord (11:11)."[109] That is, men and women who are "in the Lord" (i.e., Christ's disciples) are equally dependent on each other for their well-being—whether in or out of marriage—and men should not assume superiority just because they are the designated leaders. There is no indication that Paul was looking to the hereafter or proclaiming marriage to be a requirement for obtaining eternal life.

Though Paul himself may at one time have been married,[110] in his writings he expressed a determination to remain single (1 Cor. 7:7) and openly dissuaded fellow disciples from marrying (1 Cor. 7:1–9). At the same time, however, he condemned those who absolutely forbade marriage (1 Tim. 4:1–4).[111] His writings simply suggest a belief that marriage was less important than the work of the ministry. He wrote, "He that is unmarried careth for the things that belong to the Lord, how he may please the Lord: but he that is married careth for the things that are of the world, how he may please his wife" (1 Cor. 7:32–33).[112] With his apocalyptic perspective of an imminent return of Christ, Paul considered it imprudent to marry. To the saints in Corinth he wrote, "In view of the impending crisis, it is well for you to remain as you are [i.e., either married or single]" (NRSV 1 Cor. 7:26). To the single brethren he expressly instructed, "Do not seek a wife" (v. 27). Paul even seems to indicate that, at the Lord's coming, marriage would pass away with all other earthly relationships saying, "The appointed time [of Christ's second coming] has grown short; from now on, let even those who have wives be as though they had none. . . . For the present form of this world is passing away" (NRSV 1 Cor. 7:29).[113]

Nauvoo Period

As previously noted, the concept of eternal marriage isn't found anywhere in the Book of Mormon or other Latter-day scripture prior to 1843. It was in Nauvoo, in the summer of 1843, that Joseph Smith formally introduced the "new and everlasting covenant of marriage" (D&C 132), which initially entailed plural marriage. As to its connection to plural marriage, the revelation itself came in direct answer to Joseph's question as to why many of the Old Testament leaders had more than one wife (D&C 132:1). According to BYU religion professor Robert J. Matthews, a specialist on the Joseph Smith Translation, "It is likely that the question regarding the plurality of wives of Abraham, Isaac, and Jacob [in Doctrine and Covenants 132] could have arisen during the translation of the book of Genesis, which took place in 1830 and 1831."[114] Joseph taught that this practice was essential for exaltation (D&C 131:1–4)[115] and that whoever rejects this covenant is "damned, for no one can reject this covenant and be permitted to enter into my glory" (D&C 132:4).

Joseph took the first of his at least thirty-three documented plural wives (Fanny Alger) as early as 1836. Notably, nine out of the first eleven wives Joseph married were already married and cohabiting with their husbands, most of whom were faithful Mormons. This means polygamy initially allowed for polyandry, or the marriage of a woman to multiple husbands (though only one for eternity).[116]

Later Mormonism

Many Saints in Nauvoo resisted plural marriage, but the conviction that it was a command from God and essential to one's exaltation persuaded the more faithful to comply. As to the perceived necessity of entering into plural marriage in order to gain exaltation, early LDS leader William Clayton testified, "From him [i.e., Joseph Smith], I learned that the doctrine of plural and celestial marriage is the most holy and important doctrine ever revealed to man on the earth, and that without obedience to that principle no man can ever attain to the fulness of exaltation in Celestial glory."[117] Brigham Young declared in 1866, "The only men who become Gods, even the Sons of God, are those who enter into polygamy."[118] Joseph F. Smith, while an apostle, was adamant on this point and stated in 1878, "Some people have supposed that the doctrine of plural marriage was a sort of superfluity, or nonessential, to the salvation or exaltation of mankind. . . . I want here to enter my solemn protest against this idea, for I know it is false. . . . [W]hoever has imagined that he could obtain the fullness of the blessings pertaining to this celestial law, by complying with only a portion of its conditions, has deceived himself. He cannot do it."[119] Thus, it was firmly held and fervently taught through much of the latter-half of the nineteenth century that plural marriage, at least when in force, was essential to exaltation. Marriage to only one wife was widely regarded by church leaders as being insufficient to qualify a man for the highest kingdom in the celestial world.

On November 24, 1889, in the wake of mounting pressure by the U.S. government to discontinue polygamy, President Wilford W. Woodruff assured the Saints that "the Lord will never give a revelation to abandon plural marriage."[120] A year later, however, with federal pressure intensifying, he issued his Manifesto withdrawing support for new plural marriages and thereby opening the way for Utah statehood.

Contemporary Mormonism

Today the doctrine of plural marriage is seldom discussed in Church publications, and its significance and practice in early LDS history are sometimes marginalized.[121] Church authorities no longer maintain that plural marriage is required for exaltation, but instead assert that a husband can be exalted with only a single wife.[122] Although Bruce R. McConkie wrote in *Mormon Doctrine* that polygamy would "obviously . . . commence again after the Second Coming of the Son of Man and the ushering in of the millennium,"[123] LDS commentators today generally refrain from speculating on the future practice of polygamy.[124] Interestingly, polygamy is still practiced in the Church for the afterlife. A man who remarries after being widowed, for example, is permitted to be sealed to his new wife in the temple and is therefore married for all eternity to both wives.

Calling and Election Made Sure

The ultimate attainment to which Latter-day Saints aspire is to have their calling and election made sure, which is the unconditional promise of eternal life. Joseph Smith taught that a man may receive this promise in mortality "when the Lord has thoroughly proved him & finds that the man is determined to serve him at all hazard[s]."[125]

During much of the LDS Church's first century, this promise was commonly administered through an ordinance performed in the temple called the "second anointing." This second anointing was considered an essential ordinance for exaltation until Heber J. Grant initiated an official Church policy stating that it was no longer a requirement. It is the current teaching of the Church that only the routine temple ordinances are needed for exaltation.[126]

Biblical Teachings

The Old Testament mentions no guarantees of one's salvation, since the whole notion of salvation in a hereafter is not a developed concept. In New Testament times, although no guarantees were expressed, Saints were admonished to make their "calling and election sure" (2 Pet. 1:10). All Saints were considered called "unto his [God's] eternal glory" and "elected" in Christ (1 Pet. 5:10, 13). Peter seems to have been concerned, however, that those who didn't continue in the Christian life would forget that they had been forgiven and lose their calling and election (2 Pet. 1:1–9). It is in this context that he admonished them to strive to make their calling and election sure. There is no indication that he was referring to the performance of some rite, such as a second anointing, that would provide an unconditional guarantee of salvation that believers could receive while in mortality. Peter simply tells them that, by persisting in following righteousness, they will "never fall" (2 Pet. 1:10) but will ultimately gain "entrance . . . into the everlasting kingdom of our Lord" (2 Pet. 1:11). Nowhere in the New

Testament is an unconditional guarantee of salvation promised to believers while in mortality. Rather they were always commanded to remain faithful and steadfast unto the end (Matt. 10:22, 24:13; 1 Cor. 1:8; Heb. 3:6, 14, 6:11; Rev. 2:26).

2 Peter 1:19 speaks of having "the more sure word of prophecy," which, according to Joseph Smith's later teachings, "means a man's knowing that he is sealed up unto eternal life, by revelation and the spirit of prophecy through the power of the Holy Priesthood" (D&C 131:5). The full verse of 2 Peter 1:19 reads, "We have also a more sure word of prophecy; whereunto ye do well that ye take heed, as unto a light that shineth in a dark place, until the day dawn, and the day star arise in your hearts." Notice that, unlike the exhortation earlier to "give diligence to make your calling and election sure" (v. 10), obtaining this "more sure word of prophecy" is not presented as a mandate, as though it were a requirement or even a goal. When read in context (esp. 2 Pet. 1:16, 20–21; 3:1–4, 12–14), the "more sure word of prophecy" refers to Old Testament prophecy, which is to be taken as reliable and to which the Saints were commanded to "take heed" (v. 19). This is clear from the next verse (v. 20) which speaks specifically of "prophecy of the scripture."

According to most New Testament scholars, Peter was referring to what he perceived to be prophecies of Christ's second coming. It is "more sure" or reliable because "prophecy came not in old time by the will of man: but holy men of God spake as they were moved by the Holy Ghost" (v. 21). After giving a detailed analysis of the Greek text of 2 Peter 2:19, Daniel Wallace, professor of New Testament studies at Dallas Theological Seminary, paraphrases Peter as saying, "We have a very reliable authority, the Old Testament, as a witness to Christ's return."[127]

Interestingly, the JST version of this passage in Peter, completed sometime between 1832 and 1833, reads: "We have a more sure knowledge of the prophecy," which corroborates the general non-LDS understanding that Peter was referring to prophecy contained in the scriptures and not a personal promise of eternal life. It is only later (May 1843), to support the developing concept of making one's calling and election sure, that Joseph reinterpreted this passage.

Joseph also saw Ephesians 1:13 as a reference to making one's calling and election sure. Here the apostle Paul refers to Saints being "sealed with that holy Spirit of promise" (cf. Eph. 4:30). Instructing the Saints in June 1839, the Prophet explained that this was a promise of eternal life and was to be received "by this sealing power [of the priesthood] & the other Comforter spoken of [i.e., the personal presence of Jesus Christ] which will be manifest by revelation."[128] When read at face value, Paul seems to be simply indicating that the Lord's Spirit is a reassurance to the Saints of the promises of eternal life. This assurance is given to all Saints by virtue of their discipleship, since Ephesians 1:13 states, "*After that ye believed*, ye were sealed by the Holy Spirit of promise" (emphasis mine). Belief, therefore, is the only stated prerequisite for being sealed by the Holy Spirit of promise—a sealing which was not depicted as a priesthood ordinance, neither did it entail the presence of any comforter other than the Holy Ghost.

The Holy Spirit of promise is described in Ephesians 1:14 as "the earnest of our inheritance until the redemption of the purchased possession" (Eph. 1:14). Thus, the Holy Ghost is God's "earnest" (i.e., down payment or pledge of commitment) that the believer will ultimately receive what God has promised (cf. 2 Cor. 1:22, 5:5). This sealing, however, is never presented in the New Testament as a priesthood ordinance, nor as a witness one receives, as Joseph Smith taught, "after the Lord has thoroughly proved him." It is spoken of merely as an assurance, foretaste, or witness of the eventual blessings given to all the Saints contingent upon their continued faithfulness.

Joseph Smith also turned to John's teachings regarding "another comforter" (John 14:16) as a proof-text for making one's calling and election sure. In a revelation received December 1832, an assembly of elders was given "another Comforter . . . even the Holy Spirit of Promise which is the same that I [God] promised unto my disciples, as is recorded in the testimony of John. This Comforter is the promise of eternal life" (D&C 88:3–4). Evidently, at this point in his understanding, Joseph perceived the other Comforter of which John spoke to be the promise of eternal life, not the presence of the Father or the Son as is currently taught. It wasn't until June 1839 that the Prophet referred to the other Comforter in John 14 as "the Lord Jesus Christ himself." According to this later teaching, "When any man obtains this last Comforter, he will have the personage of Jesus Christ to attend him, or appear unto him from time to time, and even He will manifest the Father unto him, and they will take up their abode with him."[129]

Regarding this later understanding of John 14, it seems odd that the "other" Comforter Jesus promised his disciples, that would replace him, would be *himself*. Most New Testament exegetes interpret the other Comforter spoken of in John 14:26 as the Holy Ghost, which seems like the most straightforward interpretation. Consider the text: "But the Comforter, which is the Holy Ghost, whom the Father will send in my name, he shall teach you all things, and bring all things to your remembrance, whatsoever I have said unto you." The identity of this Comforter as someone other than Jesus is also implied in John 15:7–8: "Nevertheless I tell you the truth; It is expedient for you that I go away: for if I go not away, the Comforter will not come unto you; but if I depart, I will send him unto you."

The Prophet may have surmised that John was referring to a personal appearance of the Father and the Son from a couple of suggestive verses in John 14. After promising to send the Spirit to his disciples, Jesus tells them, "I will not leave you comfortless: *I will come to you*" (John 14:18; emphasis mine). He further states that both he and his Father would make their abode with the faithful (vv. 22–23). The question is whether this was to be a personal and visible visitation, or a manifestation of the Father and the Son through the Holy Spirit. According to James Dunn, "the clear implication of John 14:15–26 is that the coming of the Spirit fulfills the promise of Jesus to come again and dwell with his disciples (cf. 7:38f., 15:26; 19:30; 20:22)."[130] Jesus taught that when the Holy Ghost comes "he shall not speak of himself," but rather "he shall receive of mine, and shall shew it unto you" (John 16:13–14). It appears that Jesus would dwell with his disciples through the Holy Spirit, though a personal appearance is certainly not precluded.

As previously noted, the Prophet's later teachings show a more literal interpretation of the scriptures, and his interpretation of the Father and the Son making their abode with the Saints is another case in point. In correcting an address delivered by Elder Orson Hyde in April 1843, Joseph Smith declared that "the appearing of the Father and the Son" in John 14:23 (John actually uses the term *abide with*; not *appear to*) "is a personal appearance; and the idea that the Father and the Son dwell in a man's heart is an old sectarian notion, and is false" (D&C 130:3). Joseph's rejection of the idea of the Father and the Son dwelling in the human heart seems unsympathetic toward New Testament teachings referring to Christ and God abiding in the hearts of the righteous (Rom. 8:9–10; Eph. 2:22). The Book of Mormon likewise declares, "In the hearts of the righteous doth he [the Lord] dwell" (Alma 34:36).

Early Mormonism

Turning to modern scriptural teachings on being sealed to eternal life, little evidence of such can be found in the Book of Mormon, which presents a very simplistic concept of salvation. The promise is essentially: if you do what is right, in the end the Lord will "seal you his" (Mosiah 5:15); otherwise, the devil "doth seal you his" (Alma 34:35). In the Book of Mormon, sealing seems to be a direct act of the party—God or Satan—doing the sealing. It is not portrayed anywhere as a priesthood ordinance. The single example in the Book of Mormon of someone receiving a promise (not necessarily unconditional) of eternal life occurred when God blessed Alma saying, "I covenant with thee that thou shalt have eternal life" (Mosiah 26:20).

Beginning in 1831, individuals as well as entire congregations were sealed up to eternal life through the power of the priesthood.[131] Though no group sealings are documented after 1833, individual priesthood sealings continued to be common. Elders who were admitted to the School of the Prophets, which ran from 1833 to 1837, had their feet washed and were "sealed up to eternal life."[132]

It is currently taught that the *real* sealing power wasn't restored until Elijah's appearance in 1836, some five years after the first sealings occurred. Regarding the relationship between the sealing power restored by Elijah and the sealing power exercised prior to the coming of Elijah, LDS scholar Greg Prince observes:

> The power to seal was bestowed upon the elders in 1831, five years before the vision of Elijah, and while forms embodied by the concept of sealing evolved throughout the rest of Smith's ministry, all later forms were in continuity with the earliest form, and there is no point along the continuum where one can detect the influence of angelic ministration. Furthermore, no contemporary account of the 1836 vision of Elijah used the term "seal" with reference to his mission. Indeed, Smith himself made no explicit connection between Elijah and sealing until 1843—seven years after the vision—and the connotation of sealing most commonly used today by LDS did not develop until 1844.[133]

Thus, priesthood sealings weren't initially considered to be dependent on Elijah's coming, since they were performed prior to his coming. In fact, even for a seven-year period after he came, there was no discernible connection made between his coming and the restoration of sealing power (see Chapter 4).

The fact that individuals and congregations were sealed up to eternal life through the power of the priesthood prior to Elijah's coming raises the question of what purpose Elijah's visitation served. Were these earlier sealings not really valid or in some sense incomplete? Whatever the explanation, since 1843 it has been taught that the power to seal individuals to eternal life was restored by Elijah. Perhaps more significant for Latter-day Saints today is the question of why this once-common ordinance of making people's calling and election sure has all but disappeared from the Church, together with the ordinance of the washing of feet which accompanied it.[134]

Regarding foot washing, there is no indication in the Bible that it was ever practiced as a gospel ordinance, though it became such in later Catholic and Protestant traditions. Anciently, it was a Near Eastern custom to cleanse travelers' feet from the dusty roads. Paul speaks of widows being hospitable and washing the saints' feet (1 Tim. 5:10). As the washing of feet was a symbol of hospitality in the ancient world, the "shaking off the dust" from one's feet was an act performed against those who were detestable (Luke 10:10–12). Curiously, in JST John 13:10 Joseph linked the washing of feet to the law of Moses adding, "Now this was the custom of the Jews under their law; wherefore, Jesus did this that the law might be fulfilled." This is in spite of the fact that there is no mention of such a Mosaic ritual in either the Old Testament or the Book of Mormon. Assuming that it *was* part of the law of Moses, one is left to wonder why Joseph would state that it was fulfilled in Christ and then turn around and institute it again as an important gospel ordinance in the latter days (see D&C 88:139).

Nauvoo Period

By 1842 the sealing of individuals to eternal life started becoming dissociated with the endowment as it became part of the developing covenant of celestial marriage.[135] In July 1842, Joseph Smith was married for time and eternity to Sarah Ann Whitney, by one count his sixteenth plural wife. The wording of the ceremony, which was given by revelation, concluded with the promise: "Let immortality and eternal life henceforth be sealed upon your heads forever and ever."[136] It is noteworthy that the word "seal," when used in the marriage ceremony, didn't designate the joining of husband and wife, but rather signified that one's calling and election was made sure. Accordingly, the sealing spoken of in Doctrine and Covenants 132 (dated July 12, 1843) is not the sealing of wives to husbands, but rather the sealing or ratification of the promise of eternal life whereby "their exaltation . . . [is] sealed upon their heads" (D&C 132:19). In Orson Pratt's 1853 published account of the temple wedding ceremony, the word "seal" is used three times, all in reference to the sealing of the blessings of exaltation upon the couple's heads.[137]

In Doctrine and Covenants 132, this seal is unconditional and guarantees a couple's exaltation in spite of any and all subsequently committed sins except for the shedding of innocent blood. The promise is that if they "commit no murder wherein they shed innocent blood, yet they shall come forth in the first resurrection, and enter into their exaltation" (D&C 132:26). Two months prior to this revelation (May 16, 1843) Joseph informed a few of his associates that "those who are married by the power and authority of the priesthood in this life, and continue without committing the sin against the Holy Ghost, will continue to increase and have children in the celestial glory."[138] This is not to say that they will escape punishment for subsequent sins committed, only that in the end they will inherit the highest glory of the celestial kingdom.

Though the ordinance of sealing individuals to eternal life was subsumed under the marriage covenant, within a few months it reemerged as a distinct ordinance called the second anointing. The second anointing ordinance was instituted September 28, 1843, and over the next five months was received by twenty men and their wives.[139]

Contemporary Mormonism

Shifting the sealing from the marriage covenant to the second anointing has created a bit of confusion, since the sealing language of the marriage covenant has remained unchanged (D&C 132:19, 26–27). Today it is not clear whether couples should assume that their calling and election has been made sure as a result being righteously joined together in the temple, or if they should look forward to a second anointing or some other signal guaranteeing their eternal life. According to Bruce R. McConkie, "As with baptism, so with celestial marriage; after the glorious promise of eternal life that is part of each of these covenants, we must press forward in righteousness until our calling and election is made sure."[140] Thus, "after" celestial marriage, which itself "seals" every promised blessing on a couple through their continued faithfulness, an additional sealing of some kind appears necessary. Since the second anointing is no longer a customary practice, Saints are faced with the uncertainty of knowing when and whether their calling and election has been made sure.

Securing Children through the Sealing of Parents

During the year preceding the fall of 1843, not only was it taught that couples could be sealed up to eternal life through celestial marriage, but also that this sealing would automatically extend to their children. In August 1843, Joseph Smith taught that "when a seal [of eternal life] is put upon the father and mother, it secures their posterity so that they cannot be lost but will be saved by virtue of the covenant of their father [and mother]."[141] This teaching made an indelible impression on later Apostle Orson F. Whitney (a grandson of Heber C. Kimball) who commented in 1929,

> The Prophet Joseph Smith declared—and he never taught a more comforting doctrine—that the eternal sealings of faithful parents and the divine promises made to them for valiant service in the Cause of Truth, would save not only themselves, but likewise their posterity. Though some of the sheep may wander, the eye of the Shepherd is upon them, and sooner or later they will feel the tentacles of Divine Providence reaching out after them and draw-

ing them back to the fold. Either in this life or the life to come, they will return.[142]

Brigham Young similarly remarked that the children of righteous parents may stray, but "they are bound up to their parents by an everlasting tie, and no power on earth or hell can separate them from their parents in eternity; they will return again to the fountain from whence they sprang."[143] In an October 1893 general conference, Lorenzo Snow promised parents whose children had strayed that they would eventually "get all [their] sons and daughters in the path of exaltation and glory. This is just as sure as that the sun rose this morning over yonder mountains."[144]

Near the middle of the twentieth century Joseph Fielding Smith gave a more tempered explanation of this teaching: "All children born under the covenant belong to their parents in eternity, but that does not mean that they, because of that birthright, will inherit celestial glory. The faith and faithfulness of fathers and mothers will not save disobedient children. Salvation is an individual matter."[145] More recently, President James E. Faust put a few cuffs on Orson F. Whitney's divine "tentacles" saying that, in order for wayward children who have been sealed to their parents to be saved, they "must fully repent" and their salvation "must be fully earned."[146] The implication of these later teachings is that the salvation of sealed children is now seen as being essentially up to the individual and is not guaranteed by virtue of the covenant of the parents as in earlier teachings.

Perfectionism and Rise to Godhood

In LDS thought, humans have the potential to attain absolute perfection and become like God—a creator of worlds with the same glory and power. Joseph Fielding Smith said, "We have to pass through mortality and receive the resurrection and then go on to perfection just as our Father did before us."[147]

Old Testament

In the Old Testament, perfection was synonymous with living a God-fearing life. It was never described as a state one attained in the hereafter. (The Old Testament gives little notion of a hereafter.) God charged Abraham and later all Israel to "be perfect" (Gen. 17:1; Deut. 18:13). Noah was described as "a just man and perfect in his generations" (Gen. 6:9). Job was also perfect in that he was "upright . . . feared God, and eschewed evil" (Job 1:1). Perfection was thus viewed as a state of righteousness in this life, not an absolute state of being that one realizes in the hereafter.

New Testament

The personal perfection mandated in the New Testament appears to have been much like the God-fearing life enjoined in the Old Testament. In the Sermon on the Mount, just after his instruction to his disciples to love even their enemies, Jesus issued the charge: "Be ye therefore perfect, even as your Father which is in heaven is perfect" (Matt. 5:48). Some LDS expositors interpret this passage as having a view to the afterlife when one receives a resurrected, glorified body. Bruce R. McConkie states unequivocally that "when our Lord told the Jews, 'Be ye therefore perfect' . . . he was speaking of ultimate eternal perfection in his Father's kingdom."[148] This injunction, however, is regarded by most scholars (including some noted LDS biblical scholars) as simply the New Testament equivalent of the Old Testament command to be holy as God is holy (Lev. 19:2; see also 1 Peter 1:16).[149] Jesus is contrasting the "perfect" (Greek = complete) life of the disciple with the pretentious perfection of the scribes and Pharisees who "shall in no case enter into the kingdom of heaven" (Matt. 5:20).

In the New Testament, every disciple of Christ was expected to be perfect in conduct while yet in this life. Paul admonished the Saints in Corinth saying, "Be perfect . . . and the God of love and peace shall be with you" (2 Cor. 13:11). The epistle to the Hebrews also urged Saints to "go on unto perfection" (Heb. 6:1). There is no implication in New Testament writings that perfection was an absolute condition to be achieved in the hereafter.

Early Nineteenth-Century Christianity

The quest to achieve perfection while still in mortality through God's grace was a daily pursuit of Christians at the time of Joseph Smith. "Let us strongly and explicitly exhort all believers to go on to perfection,"[150] urged the 1784 *Methodist Book of Discipline*. One historian wrote of the early nineteenth-century revival period: "The diaries and letters of evangelical ministers repeatedly illustrate an overwhelming concern with perfectionism. Sanctification was a constant topic for sermons stressing the life after conversion."[151] The perfection sought was not of an absolute kind, but was a relative perfection believed to be within human reach while in mortality. In 1764, John Wesley declared: "Absolute perfection belongs not to man, nor to angels, but to God alone."[152] Methodists believed that the perfection Jesus commanded was wholly attainable in this life and simply meant becoming a sanctified disciple of Christ. It was not a condition an individual attained through his or her own works alone. "Perfection," wrote Methodist commentator Adams Clarke in 1828, was attainable only "in Christ" and through "the grace of God."[153]

Early Mormonism

The Book of Mormon teaches the same kind of perfectionism that was espoused by Methodists and uses the same language to emphasize its attainability in Christ through the grace of God. The concluding chapter of the Book of Mormon exhorts its latter-day readers to "come unto Christ, and be perfected in him . . . by the grace of God" (Moro. 10:32). It further equates perfection, as did Methodists, with sanctification (v. 33), which was attainable in mortality through God's grace. It wouldn't be until the Nauvoo period that the idea of human beings achieving absolute perfection in the hereafter would develop; and then it would incorporate the concept of progression beyond the grave.

Many Latter-day Saints today view Christ's injunction in the Book of Mormon to be perfect "even as I, or your Father who is in heaven is perfect" (3 Ne. 12:48) as an indication that the perfection prescribed is of an absolute kind since only now, after his resurrection, is Christ included with the Father as a model of perfection.[154] It should be noted, however, that in his preceding remarks leading up to this command, Jesus doesn't call attention to his glorified, resurrected body as the model for the Nephites to emulate, but rather emphasizes the Christian life of obedience and service. Even here, therefore, it seems more likely that he intended a kind of perfection that could be achieved in this life through the sanctification of the Spirit. Christ subsequently sent forth his disciples, commanding them to be (during their mortal ministry) "even as I am" (3 Ne. 27:27), a perfect model of righteousness.

Revelations subsequent to the Book of Mormon also emphasize the importance of achieving moral perfection while in mortality through sanctification (D&C 67:13, 76:69, 129:3). In the *Lectures on Faith*, delivered in 1835 (before God's corporeality was taught), Matthew 5:48, which contains Jesus's mandate to be perfect, is lumped together with scriptural injunctions to be "holy" (Lev. 19:2; 1 Pet. 1:15–16). The point is then made that the Saints must achieve this perfection and holiness prior to the Lord's coming, "that when he (the Lord) shall appear, the saints will be like him [see 1 Jn. 3:2–3]; and if they are not holy, as he is holy, and perfect, as he is perfect, they cannot be like him; for no being can enjoy his glory without possessing his perfections and holiness, no more than they could reign in his kingdom without his power."[155] To illustrate that such perfection was attainable in this life, the *Lectures* call attention to the fact that

Christ "kept the law of God, and remained without sin, showing thereby that it is in the power of man to keep the law and remain also without sin."[156]

An article entitled "Perfection," which appeared in the LDS *Messenger and Advocate* in May 1836, similarly emphasized the relative nature of perfection, explaining that being perfect as God is perfect means being perfect within our scope of capability just as God is perfect in his; it is to be perfect in everything one's "nature is capable of."[157]

Nauvoo Period

Although a primary focus of evangelicals was achieving perfection in this life, Protestant writers in the early 1800s also spoke of continuing progression in knowledge, holiness, and happiness in the next life. Reflecting a widespread spirit of optimism, numerous clergymen writing prior to the Restoration espoused a doctrine of eternal progression beyond the grave, though never to achieve God's level of perfection. In 1825, for example, *The Churchman's Magazine*, an Episcopalian periodical, noted that the redeemed will undergo "an infinite progression towards perfection" in the hereafter resulting in "an eternal advancement in happiness."[158] Reverend Edward D. Griffen, a contemporary Congregationalist minister, also spoke of "eternal progress" where the inhabitants of heaven "will eternally grow in capacity, knowledge, holiness, and happiness."[159] This progression, though eternal, ever falls short of the ultimate attainment of Godhood. *The Churchman's Magazine* article stated, "We may, to all eternity, approach [God] in perfection; yet leave an infinite distance between the creature and the Creator."[160]

Later teachings of Joseph Smith would also espouse the idea of progression in the hereafter, but with the goal of achieving absolute perfection. At the April 1844 conference, the Prophet spoke of God being once a man who progressed to become the God we worship.[161] He then compared our own ascent to Godhood to climbing a ladder, noting that we will continue "to learn salvation beyond the grave & it is not all to be com[prehended] in this world."[162] It is this idea of progression beyond the grave—together with the teaching that God is an exalted man—that eventually gave rise to the current doctrine that perfection means progressing to become just like God in the full and complete sense. (For more on the LDS doctrine of deification, see Chapter 6.)

Later Mormonism

Interestingly, the concept of absolute perfection was rarely spoken of in LDS literature of the nineteenth century, as it was seen as conflicting with the growing finitist view which rejected God's absolute perfection. In 1852, Brigham Young taught that the perfection of both God and man is forever relative saying, "We are now, or may be, as perfect in our sphere as God and Angels are in theirs, but the greatest intelligence in existence can continually ascend to greater heights of perfection."[163] Indeed, it was perceived as inconceivable that a being whose knowledge was stagnate could possibly continue to have joy. Today, God is generally viewed in more absolute terms, so the commandment in Matthew 5:48 to "be ye therefore perfect" tends to be interpreted as an injunction to reach the absolute pinnacle of perfection just like the Father and the Son—a state attainable only after the resurrection.[164]

The Salvation of Little Children

The Old Testament, which has little notion of a plan of salvation or life in the hereafter, provides no information concerning the status of little children who die in infancy. In revising the Old Testament, however, Joseph Smith interjected several Christian-era concepts into the text including the idea that children don't sin until they reach the age of accountability (JST Gen. 17:11). He even inserted a reference to a certain apostate group living in the days of Abraham whom the Lord censures saying, "[They] have turned from the commandment, and taken unto themselves the washing of children ... and have not known wherein they are accountable before me" (JST Gen. 17:6–7). Thus, the innocence of small children, which is never raised as an issue elsewhere in the Old Testament, emerges as a controversial issue in JST Genesis. It even becomes the basis for the Old Testament practice of circumcision (JST Gen. 17:11). This is in contrast to the KJV where circumcision is simply "a token of the covenant" that the Lord made with Abraham and his posterity to be his chosen people, having no association at all with the innocence of children (Gen. 17:11).

The salvation of little children doesn't enter biblical writings until the New Testament, which speaks optimistically regarding their fate.[165] Jesus said, "Suffer the little children to come unto me, and forbid them not: for of such is the kingdom of God" (Mark 10:14). Paul taught that "where no law is, there is no transgression" (Rom. 4:15), thus leaving the door open to excusing little children from sin.

Several different views on the status of little children can be found in post-New Testament Christianity. Since the time of Augustine (A.D. 354–430), many Christians have believed that the souls of unbaptized infants go to a place called limbo, which is not heaven because they are tainted by original sin. This belief was challenged by new religious movements at the time of Joseph Smith, almost all promoting the belief that little children go directly to heaven in the afterlife.[166] In contrast to the traditional doctrine of original sin, evangelical Protestants—especially those who held the doctrine of prevenient grace—believed that children are free from any accountability for Adam's transgression through the atonement of Christ and are therefore automatically saved (see Chapter 12). Methodists, for example, considered all infants to be innocent in Christ until they reach the age of accountability. In 1837, the president of Wesleyan University wrote, "To such as never come to a personally responsible age, this salvation was secured unconditionally by Christ."[167]

With respect to infant baptism, traditional Christianity held that it was necessary in order to remit the guilt inherited from Adam. Ironically, the innocence of little children has also been used as justification for why they *should* be baptized.[168] Martin Luther contended that since children are innocent, the only way to "suffer the little children to come unto [Christ]" (Mark 10:14) is by baptizing them. Under the Puritan system, children of baptized parents were considered to be "born in the covenant" and therefore rightful heirs to God's grace (a concept related to the later LDS concept by the same name). These children were baptized to symbolize the "seal of the covenant of grace" into which they were born by virtue of their parents' faith.[169]

More than a decade before the Book of Mormon was written, Ethan Smith, a leading Congregationalist, stated that to oppose infant baptism was to "mock God" and deny scripture.[170] A book on infant baptism published in 1810 cautioned, however, that those who provide no subsequent guidance to baptized infants also "solemnly mock God."[171] Ironically, the Book of Mormon would derogate infant baptism altogether as being a "solemn mockery before God" and a practice that "den[ies] the mercies of Christ" (Moro. 8:6, 9, 19). Most Christians favoring infant baptism believed that it was the New Testament replacement for the Old Testament practice of circumcision and that, since circumcision was performed on male infants, baptism should likewise be a ceremony for infants (of both sexes). [172]

Book of Mormon teachings on the status of little children conform to the common nineteenth-century conception that the atonement of Christ redeems little children from the guilt of Adam's transgression (see Chapter 13). The Book of Mormon also indicates that the atonement absolves little children from any personal responsibility for their actions. While the New Testament teaches that there is no sin without knowledge of the law (Rom. 4:15), the Book of Mormon, like much of Protestantism, considers ignorant misbehavior to be covered by the atonement (Mosiah 3:11). According to the Book of Mormon's namesake, "all little children are alive in Christ, and also all they that are without the law. For the power of redemption cometh on all them that have no law" (Moro. 8:22; see also vv. 8, 12, 19–20). Thus, the same principle of absolution applies to both the ignorant and little children. As the Book of Mormon states, "The blood of Christ atoneth for their sins" (Mosiah 3:16; see also v. 11). Doctrine and Covenants 74:7 similarly affirms that "little children are holy, being sanctified through the atonement of Jesus Christ."

Although the Book of Mormon says nothing about children being exempt from Satan's temptations, in a September 1830 revelation the Lord states, "Power is not given unto Satan to tempt little children, until they begin to become accountable before me" (D&C 29:47). Children who die before reaching the age of accountability have since been declared exempt from Satan's influence even in the next life. Speaking at the funeral of Heber J. and Emily Grant's child in 1895, Joseph F. Smith stated: "Little children who are taken away in infancy . . . are not capable of committing sin . . . and Satan has no power over them."[173] In the mid-twentieth century, Joseph Fielding Smith wrote to a correspondent: "Satan cannot tempt little children in this life, nor in the spirit world, nor after their resurrection."[174] This notion of perpetual immunity from temptation and sin comes, in part, from an 1836 revelation that states categorically, "All children who die before they arrive at the years of accountability are saved in the celestial kingdom of heaven" (D&C 137:10). Since roughly half of the earth's inhabitants who have ever been born have died in infancy, more souls will presumably be exalted in the celestial kingdom than those who inhabit any other degree of glory.

In Mormon thought, not only are little children guaranteed salvation in the celestial kingdom, but they are immediately much better off by being spared the hardships and trials of mortality. The Prophet stated in a discourse delivered in Nauvoo on March 20, 1842, "The only difference between the old & young dying is one lives longer in heaven & Eternal light & glory than the other & was freed a little sooner from this miserable wicked world."[175] Joseph Smith further taught that children who die will be reunited with their parents in the resurrection.[176] According to later LDS teachings, these children will have the privilege of being raised to adulthood by their parents[177] and even have the opportunity to enjoy all the blessings of marriage in the highest degree of the celestial kingdom.[178] Thus, unlike those who grow to mortal adulthood, they experience none of the trials while having all of the enjoyments of having a physical body.

So what actually determines whether certain individuals die before reaching the age of accountability? Is it circumstantial coincidence or providential prearrangement? Bruce R. McConkie taught, "We must assume that the Lord knows and arranges beforehand who shall be taken in infancy and who shall remain on earth to undergo whatever tests are needed in their cases."[179] It has been suggested that those who die in infancy have already proven themselves in premortality.[180] It is not uncommon to hear a statement by Joseph Smith used as a proof-text in support of this view: "The Lord takes many away even in infancy that they may escape the envy of man [and] the sorrows & evils of this present world & they were two pure & to lov[e]ly to live on Earth."[181] The Prophet isn't saying that they were too pure *in the preexistence.* He rather seems only to be implying that because they were such pure and lovely infants *on earth,* exposing them as they grow older to the hardships and crassness of the world would be cruel. Although the Church doesn't officially teach that those who die in infancy were more valiant in the preexistence, superior valiancy there seems to some to be the best explanation that fits the logic of LDS theology.

Notes

1. Alma P. Burton, "Salvation," 4:1257.

2. Andrew F. Ehat and Lyndon W. Cook, *The Words of Joseph Smith: The Contemporary Accounts of the Nauvoo Discourses of the Prophet Joseph Smith,* 39.

3. Ibid.

4. Ibid., 210.

5. Ibid., 108.

6. Eusebius of Caesarea, *The History of the Church from Christ to Constantine,* 14–16.

7. St. Augustine, *Retractions* 1:13.3, quoted in Joseph Keating, "Christianity," 3:712..

8. Judah, "The Everlasting Gospel," 2.

9. Elias Hicks, "Sermon by Elias Hicks, Delivered at Darby, November 15, 1826," 1.

10. See "Westminster Confession of Faith."

11. John Gill, *Gill's Complete Body of Doctrinal Divinity: Being a System of Evangelical Truths, Deduced from the Ancient Scriptures,* 222.

12. *History of the Church,* 2:17.

13. Ethan Smith, *View of the Hebrews: 1825 Second Edition Complete Text,* 187.

14. Joseph Smith Jr., "Church History," 709.

15. Another meaning of ordinances in early LDS literature and scripture, which was common in Joseph Smith's day, is that of ministerial callings (see Alma 13:8, 16; D&C 21:11; 77:13; 124:134; Moses 5:59). Charles Buck designates the calling to public or gospel ministry as an "ordinance." Charles S. Buck, *A Theological Dictionary,* s.v. "ordinance," and "Ministry, gospel."

Parley P. Pratt wrote that on the 6th of June 1831, he received the High Priesthood, being "ordained to this holy ordinance and calling by President Smith." Parely P. Pratt, *Autobiography of Parley P. Pratt*, 53. Joseph Smith recorded in 1832 that through "reception of the high priesthood" he received "power and ordinence [sic] from on high to preach the gospel." Dean C. Jessee, comp. and ed., *The Personal Writings of Joseph Smith*, 4. In explaining how the Lord called men to different priesthood positions for the perfecting of the saints, an early LDS publication states, "He bestowed offices and ordinances, with order, for the benefit of the whole church." "The Church of Christ," *Evening and Morning Star* 1 (March 1833): 73.

16. In the Old Testament, circumcision was first instituted at the time of Abraham and symbolized God's everlasting covenant with Israel (Gen. 17:7–12). The LDS Bible Dictionary (s.v. "circumcision") points out, however, that this rite didn't originate with the Hebrews, but was practiced long before by neighboring countries such as Egypt. In Genesis, circumcision is described as an "everlasting covenant" (Gen. 17:13), which was to be kept perpetually by Abraham's seed "in their generations" (Gen. 17:9).

The New Testament Church didn't know quite what to do with circumcision; and after "much disputing," Christ's apostles determined that circumcision was no longer necessary in light of their witness of God's manifest grace upon the gentiles who were uncircumcised (Acts 15:5–11). Circumcision thereafter appears to have become meaningful only as a figurative term used to symbolize putting off the sins of the flesh (Col. 2:11).

Many Protestants of the Reformation believed that circumcision was a sign of the old covenant and was replaced by the ordinance of baptism at the time of Christ. Of course, in LDS scripture, baptism predates and also overlaps the practice of circumcision, which precludes the possibility of its replacing circumcision. Regarding the discontinuation of circumcision, the Book of Mormon simply explains that "the law of circumcision is done away in [Christ]" (Moro. 8:8). In his revision of the Bible, Joseph modified the purpose given for circumcision so it was not just the token of the Abrahamic covenant, but was also a sign "that children are not accountable before me until they are eight years old" (JST Gen. 17:11). One is left to wonder why this symbol of a child's innocence would need to be "done away" (Moro. 8:8) when Christ came.

17. J. J. M. Roberts, *The Bible and the Ancient Near East*, 45.

18. Ibid., 53.

19. Avery Dulles, *The Assurance of Things Hoped For: A Theology of Christian Faith*, 7.

20. Ibid. Although Christian faith is not an Old Testament concept, the New Testament book of Hebrews extols the faith of many Old Testament prophets who were willing to put their trust in the Lord. Still, there is no mention that they had faith that, though the atonement of Christ, they could be saved in any eschatological sense.

21. Joseph Fielding McConkie notes that the laver was "used for cleansing rituals by the priests and obviously for baptisms." Joseph Fielding McConkie, *Gospel Symbolism*, 265. His father, Bruce R. McConkie writes, "It is clear that the molten sea was for baptisms and that the laver was for ritualistic washings." Bruce R. McConkie, *The Mortal Messiah: From Bethlehem to Calvary*, 1:105

22. Kaufmann Kohler and Samuel Krauss, "Baptism," 2:499.
23. Eduard Lohse, *The New Testament Environments*, 125.
24. Kevin L. Barney, "Introduction to Luke's Gospel," 27.
25. Interestingly, many liberal Protestants and even many U.S. Catholic bishops recognize Judaism as a religion sanctioned eternally by God and no longer believe that Jews need to convert to Christianity to be saved. Edward Kessler, *An Introduction to Jewish-Christian Relations*, 9–10, 172–75.
26. Dow Edgerton, "The Exegesis of Tears," 24.
27. Harold W. Attridge, "Hebrews," 2043.
28. David Rhymer, "Between Text & Sermon," 294.
29. James D. G. Dunn, *Unity and Diversity in the New Testament: An Inquiry into the Character of Earliest Christianity*, 265.
30. Ibid., xx.
31. F. F. Bruce, *Paul: Apostle of the Heart Set Free*, 192–93.
32. Bruce R. McConkie, *Mormon Doctrine*, 434.
33. Many biblical scholars see the birth by water in John 3:3–5 as a symbolic way of describing the purifying effects of being born of the Spirit and that water baptism was not intended. See D. A. Carson, *Exegetical Fallacies*, 42.
34. Barney, "Introduction to Luke's Gospel," 27.
35. Gerald O'Collins, *Christology*, 146.
36. Dale C. Allison Jr., "The Historians' Jesus and the Church," 87–88.
37. In his attempt to harmonize texts, Bruce R. McConkie expressed his opinion that Christ's breathing on the apostles "probably means that he laid his hands upon them." Bruce R. McConkie, *Doctrinal New Testament Commentary*, 1:856.
38. A. S. Hayden, *History of the Disciples in the Western Reserve, Ohio*, 71. Scott later, in 1827 or 1828, reduced the requirements from six to five so they could be named on the fingers of the hand. This became known as the famous "five-finger exercise": faith, repentance, baptism, remission of sins, and the gift of the Holy Ghost.
39. E. Brooks Holifield, *Theology in America: Christian Thought from the Age of Puritans to the Civil War*, 264.
40. John Wesley, "John Wesley's Notes on the Bible," 1.5.2.
41. Biblos, "On Despair of the Divine Mercy," 620.
42. Mark D. Thomas, *Digging in Cumorah: Reclaiming Book of Mormon Narratives*, 131–32.
43. Charles A. Johnson, *The Frontier Camp Meeting*, 58.
44. Thomas, *Digging in Cumorah*, 134.
45. Buel Goodsell, "Campmeetings on the Champlain District," 484.
46. "Review of New Publications," *The Christian Observer* 27 (January 1827): 29.
47. Joseph Fielding McConkie, *Seeking the Spirit*, 73.
48. Craig L. Blomberg and Stephen E. Robinson, *How Wide the Divide? A Mormon and an Evangelical in Conversation*, 147.
49. Blake T. Ostler, "Bridging the Gulf," 125.
50. Bruce R. McConkie, *The Promised Messiah: The First Coming of Christ*, 421.
51. Joseph Fielding Smith, *Doctrines of Salvation: Compiled Sermons of Joseph Fielding Smith*, 1:160.

52. McConkie, *Mormon Doctrine*, 333.
53. Joseph Fielding McConkie and Robert L. Millet, *Doctrinal Commentary on the Book of Mormon*, 1:7.
54. Smith, "Church History," 709. When the adjective "first" was used in connection with these principles and ordinances, it was to stress the importance of "adding" to them the Godly attributes spelled out in 2 Peter 1:5–7 (virtue, knowledge, temperance, etc.). See Jessee, *Personal Writings of Joseph Smith*, 297.
55. Thomas, *Digging in Cumorah*, 123–43.
56. Ibid.
57. Brent Lee Metcalfe, "The Priority of Mosiah: A Prelude to Book of Mormon Exegesis," 420.
58. Ibid., 419–20.
59. Ibid., 420.
60. *History of the Church*, 1:78.
61. T. B. Scannell, "Confirmation," 217.
62. Orson Pratt, November 12, 1876, *Journal of Discourses* 18:293; emphasis mine.
63. George Q. Cannon, October 18, 1884, *Journal of Discourses* 26:248–49. It should be noted that two months earlier in August 1884, Cannon interpreted the oath and covenant in Doctrine and Covenants 84 as referring specifically to those who obtain the priesthood but saw the same oath and covenant as applying equally to the gospel. Commenting on this oath and covenant he stated, "Therefore to the Latter-day Saints this Gospel and this Priesthood come on the one hand, accompanied by great blessings and promises, and great power and exaltation, and, on the other hand, they come accompanied by dreadful penalties, by degradation and condemnation, greater than it would be possible for any being to reach unless he had had the opportunities which the Gospel and the Priesthood bring and afford." George Q. Cannon, August 1884, *Journal of Discourses*, 25:290.
64. Wilford Woodruff, January 9, 1881, *Journal of Discourses*, 22:209.
65. Wilford Woodruff, December 10, 1882, *Journal of Discourses*, 23:329–30.
66. Lorenzo Snow, "The Object of This Probation,"4:56; Lorenzo Snow, *Conference Report*, April 10, 1898, 61–64.
67. See, for example, Jae R. Ballif, "Melchizedek Priesthood," 2:883.
68. Howard W. Hunter, *The Teachings of Howard W. Hunter*, 236.
69. For a detailed history of the development of the endowment, see Gregory A. Prince, *Power from On High: The Development of Mormon Priesthood*, 115–48.
70. Robert J. Matthews, *A Bible! A Bible!*, 40. LDS scholar Hugh Nibley has assembled considerable inferential evidence to support the thesis that forms of LDS temple worship were practiced in the ancient world. See, for example, Hugh W. Nibley, "On the Sacred and the Symbolic," 535–622.
71. Smith, *Doctrines of Salvation*, 2:165.
72. McConkie, *Doctrinal New Testament Commentary*, 1:859; John W. Welch, *The Sermon at the Temple and the Sermon on the Mount: A Latter-day Saint Approach*, 24. For the linkage of this idea to Joseph Smith, see Ehat and Cook, *The Words of Joseph Smith*, 306.

73. See John A. Tvedtnes, "Early Christian and Jewish Rituals Related to Temple Practices."

74. John Welch argues that Christ's sermon at the temple has allusions to modern-day temple ordinances such as washing and anointing. Welch, *The Sermon at the Temple*, 66. In a FARMS review of his book, however, Todd Compton notes that such an inference is tenuous at best. Todd M. Compton, "The Sermon at the Temple and the Sermon on the Mount," 319.

75. Prince, *Power from On High*, 145.

76. John Corrill, *A Brief History of the Church of Christ of Latter Day Saints (Commonly Called Mormons;) Including An Account of Their Doctrine and Discipline . . .* , 18.

77. Dean C. Jessee, Mark Ashurst-McGee, and Richard L. Jensen, eds., *Journals, Volume 1: 1832–1839*, 60.

78. Prince, *Power from On High*, 121–122.

79. Richard L. Bushman, *Joseph Smith: Rough Stone Rolling*, 312.

80. Ibid., 15–18. With Rigdon acting as advisor and scribe, in February or early March 1831, Joseph Smith added sixteen new verses to Genesis 14 describing the powers that should accompany the priesthood. Ibid., 118.

81. According to Prince, this new endowment was initially sparked by an incident that occurred with John C. Bennett who joined the Church in October 1840 and six months later (April 1841) was appointed assistant Church president. As a result of alleged sexual promiscuity, Bennett was nearly excommunicated and, in retaliation, vowed to expose Joseph Smith's practice of polygamy. Joseph, who was concerned that secrets were getting out, turned to Freemasonry, which was known for its binding oaths to ensure the secrecy of its ceremonies. Prince, *Power from On High*, 133–34.

82. Ehat and Cook, *The Words of Joseph Smith*, 108.

83. Prince, *Power from On High*, 139.

84. Michael W. Homer, "Similarity of Priesthood in Masonry: The Relationship between Freemasonry and Mormonism," 92.

85. Brent Lee Metcalfe, "Whence and Whither the Five Points of Fellowship?"

86. No author or title (New Haven, Conn.: Lagg and Gray, Printers, 1819), 10, 66. Microfiche in BYU Harold B. Lee library 080 Sh64a no. 47753.

87. Ibid., 94.

88. Quoted in ibid., 94.

89. Quoted in Homer, "Similarity of Priesthood in Masonry," 93.

90. George S. Tate, "Prayer Circles," 3:1121. Tate notes that these prayer circles were also "common in 19th century Protestant revivals."

91. Richard L. Bushman, "Joseph Smith and the Creation of the Sacred," 104.

92. Quoted in Stanley B. Kimball, *Heber C. Kimball: Mormon Patriarch and Pioneer*, 85.

93. See Homer, "Similarity of Priesthood in Masonry," 103–4. Homer notes that it is actually the more recent (eighteenth-century) forms of Masonic ritual that the LDS endowment resembled, not the earlier forms. Ibid., 103; see also Prince, *Power from On High*, 147.

94. See, for example, Tvedtnes, "Early Christian and Jewish Rituals Related to Temple Practices."

95. Brigham Young, quoted in L. John Nuttall, Diary, February 7, 1877, as quoted in Andrew F. Ehat, "'They Might Have Known That He Was Not a Fallen Prophet': The Nauvoo Journal of Joseph Fielding," 159 note 77.

96. Greg Kearney, "Ask the Apologist." For a similar explanation, see Jeff Lindsay, "Questions about the LDS Temple Ceremony and Masonry."

97. Prince, *Power from On High*, 132.

98. Lyndon W. Cook, *The Revelations of the Prophet Joseph Smith: A Historical and Biographical Commentary on the Doctrine and Covenants*, 250.

99. Brigham Young, April 6, 1853, *Journal of Discourses*, 2:31.

100. James E. Talmage, *The House of the Lord*, 83; Franklin D. Richards, "Happiness and Joy in the Temple," 70.

101. E. W. Bullinger, *Figures of Speech used in the Bible*, 426–27.

102. Christians view this passage as describing a consequence of accepting the gospel message, not Christ's intent. The wording, however, seems somewhat harsh and causes one to wonder why only a pessimistic outcome is expressed regarding the impact of the gospel on familial relationships.

103. Anthony A. Hoekema, *The Bible and the Future*, 252.

104. Talmud, *Berakot* 17a, quoted in Kaufmann Kohler, "Kingdom of God," 503. LDS scholar John Tvedtness suggests an alternative explanation for Jesus's response to the Sadduccees noting that the situation posed by the Sadduccees matches precisely the situation related in a story told in the apocryphal Book of Tobit. In this story, a woman had been married and widowed seven times. Finally, she married Tobias, who was the one God ultimately intended for her. Tvedtness suggests that Jesus may have had this specific incident in mind when he said that the widow would be married to none of her seven husbands in the resurrection, since it was only Tobias that she was sealed to for eternity. Tvedtnes, "A Much Needed Book that Needs Much," 41.

105. James E. Talmage, *Jesus the Christ: A Study of the Messiah and His Mission According to Holy Scriptures Both Ancient and Modern*, 548.

106. Joseph F. Smith, *Gospel Doctrine: Selections from the Sermons and Writings of Joseph F. Smith*, 280.

107. Smith, *Doctrines of Salvation*, 2:72.

108. Ibid., 2:70; McConkie, *Mormon Doctrine*, 120; Steven C. Walker, "Mankind," 2:853.

109. Thomas Schreiner, "Head Coverings, Prophecies, and the Trinity," 138.

110. There is uncertainty whether Paul was ever married. Though he likely would have been married had he been a member of the Sanhedrin, it has been argued that it is unlikely that someone as young as Paul would have been a member of this council composed of Jewish elders. F. F. Bruce, *New Testament History*, 283.

111. The Pauline authorship of the epistles to Timothy has been disputed by some biblical scholars.

112. Based on modifications the Prophet made in the JST, Latter-day Saints contend that Paul was speaking only to those serving as missionaries at the time and that, like modern LDS missionaries, they could better serve singly. Clyde J. Williams, "The JST and the New Testament Epistles," 223. This understanding, however, doesn't change the fact that Paul nowhere extols marriage nor extends it into the hereafter. He expressly states, "For the

woman which hath an husband is bound by the law to her husband so long as he liveth" (Rom. 7:2).

113. Victor Paul Furnish, "1 Corinthians," 2150.

114. Robert J. Matthews, "The 'New Translation' of the Bible, 1830–1833: Doctrinal Development during the Kirtland Era," 416.

115. The principal explanation of why David and Solomon's possession of many wives and concubines was considered "abominable" in the Book of Mormon (see Jacob 2:24) but later "justified" in the D&C 132:1 is that, it was only David and Solomon's *later* taking of wives and concubines for selfish reasons that was abominable to the Lord. Initially, the Lord sanctioned their practice of plural marriage. Robert L. Millet, "A New and Everlasting Covenant (D&C 132)," 522. This reasoning also seems to be suggested in Doctrine and Covenants 132:38–39. See also Brant Gardner, *Second Witness*, 2:494–95.

116. For a thorough treatment of the early practice of polygamy, see Todd M. Compton, *In Sacred Lonliness: The Plural Wives of Joseph Smith*. For a defense of Joseph's polyandry, see Samuel Katich, "A Tale of Two Marriage Systems: Perspectives on Polyandry and Joseph Smith." See also Brian C. Hales, *Joseph Smith's Polygamy Volume 1: History* (Forthcoming, Greg Kofford Books).

117. Robert C. Fillerup, comp., "William Clayton's Nauvoo Diaries and Personal Writings."

118. Brigham Young, August 19, 1866, *Journal of Discourses*, 11:269.

119. Joseph F. Smith, July 7, 1878, *Journal of Discourses*, 20:29. Twenty-six years later as Church president, Smith issued the "Second Manifesto" on plural marriage that added ecclesiastical teeth to the Manifesto of 1890 by imposing excommunication on Saints who refused to relinquish their plural wives. Harvard S. Heath, "Smoot Hearings," 3:1363. See also Brian C. Hales, *Modern Polyamy and Mormon Fundamentalistm: The Generations after the Manifesto*, 61–65.

120. Wilford Woodruff, *Wilford Woodruff's Journal, 1833–1899*, 9:67–69.

121. The LDS Church has been criticized for omitting references to the plural wives of early Church presidents in modern publications reporting on the family life of early Church presidents. For example, see Jerald Tanner and Sandra Tanner, "Covering Up Mormon Polygamy."

122. McConkie, *Mormon Doctrine*, 578.

123. Ibid.

124. See, for example, Danel Bachman and Ronald K. Esplin, "Plural Marriage," 3:1095.

125. Ehat and Cook, *The Words of Joseph Smith*, 5.

126. David John Buerger, *The Mysteries of Godliness: A History of Mormon Temple Worship*, 162.

127. Daniel B. Wallace, "The Translation of 2 Peter 1:19a."

128. Ehat and Cook, *The Words of Joseph Smith*, 4.

129. Ibid., 150–51. In interpreting the second comforter as Jesus Christ, Joseph Smith notes particularly John 14:16–18, 21, and 23. Ibid., 5.

130. Dunn, *Unity and Diversity in the New Testament*, 213.

131. Hyrum L. Andrus relates several incidents in which Joseph Smith and other Church elders sealed groups of Saints up to eternal life. Hyrum L.

Andrus, *Doctrinal Commentary on the Pearl of Great Price.*

132. Cook, *The Revelations of the Prophet Joseph Smith*, 186.

133. Prince, *Power from On High*, 171.

134. Joseph Smith instituted the ordinance of washing feet for the purpose of declaring elders to be "clean from the blood of this generation" and was "to be administered . . . according to the pattern given in the thirteenth chapter of [John]" (D&C 88:139). It was an integral part of making one's calling and election sure. See Prince, *Power from On High*, 172. Later it became part of the second anointing and was performed by one's wife. Ibid., 174. It has been erroneously supposed to have been subsumed into the washing and anointing ordinance of the temple. McConkie, *Mormon Doctrine*, 831.

135. For a fuller discussion on the development of the sealing ordinance, see Prince, *Power from On High*, 151–91.

136. Unpublished revelation dated July 27, 1842, quoted in ibid., 166.

137. Orson Pratt, "Celestial Marriage," 31–32.

138. *History of the Church*, 5:391.

139. Ehat and Cook, *The Words of Joseph Smith*, 241.

140. McConkie, *Doctrinal New Testament Commentary*, 3:334.

141. Ehat and Cook, *The Words of Joseph Smith*, 242.

142. Orson F. Whitney, *Conference Report*, April 1929, 110.

143. Brigham Young, April 29, 1866, *Journal of Discourses*, 11:216.

144. Lorenzo Snow, "The Object of This Probation," in Brian H Stuy, ed., *Collected Discourses*, 3:364–65.

145. Smith, *Doctrines of Salvation*, 2:91.

146. James E. Faust, "Dear Are the Sheep That Have Wandered," 62.

147. Smith, *Doctrines of Salvation*, 1:12.

148. McConkie, *Mormon Doctrine*, 568.

149. LDS scholar John A. Tvedtnes remarked that any appeal to Matthew 5:48 as proof of man's divine potential was "a weak argument, since the context of Jesus' statement is not becoming like God, but loving our fellowman as God loves us." John A. Tvedtnes, "Review of Michael T. Griffith, *One Lord, One Faith: Writings of the Early Christian Fathers as Evidences of the Restoration*," 33–42. Keith E. Norman makes a similar case stating that Matthew 5:48 calls God perfect, "not in the sense of metaphysical speculation, but in terms of moral perfection." Keith E. Norman, "Deification: The Content of Athanasian Soteriology," 6.

150. Quoted in John B. Boles, *The Great Revival, 1787–1805*, 139.

151. Ibid., 140.

152. Quoted in John L. Peters, *Christian Perfection & American Methodism*, 35.

153. Adam Clarke, *Christian Theology*, 206.

154. See, for example, Robert L. Millet, *Within Reach*, 59.

155. *Lectures on Faith*, 7:10.

156. Ibid., 5:2.

157. "Perfection," *Latter Day Saints' Messenger and Advocate* 2 (May 1836): 310–11.

158. "Sermon on 1 Corinthians 15:41–42," 105.

159. Edward D. Griffin, *Sermons by the Late Edward D. Griffin*, 443–44.

160. "Sermon on 1 Corinthians 15:41–42," 105. For other clergymen's teachings of eternal progression though still eternally beneath the perfection level of God, see Scott Goodwin, "Joseph's Ladder: Principles of Eternal Progression in Three Theological Traditions," 101–9.

161. Ehat and Cook, *The Words of Joseph Smith*, 357.

162. Ibid., 350.

163. Brigham Young, June 13, 1852, *Journal of Discourses*, 1:93.

164. Russell M. Nelson, *Perfection Pending, and Other Favorite Discourses*, 5; Maxwell, *Even As I Am*, i.

165. Alleging that "the apostle John understood [the] doctrine" of the innocence of little children, LDS apostle LeGrand Richards referred to 1 John 2:12: "I write unto you, little children, because your sins are forgiven you for his name's sake." LeGrand Richards, *A Marvelous Work and a Wonder*, 99. The question, of course, is whether John's reference to little children was literal or figurative.

166. David J. Shepherd, *Village Enlightenment in America: Popular Religion and Science in the Nineteenth Century*, 96.

167. Wilbur Fisk, *Calvinist Controversy*, 46.

168. Alexander Campbell tells of a clergyman's letter "pleading the innocence of children as a reason why they should certainly be baptized." Alexander Campbell, *Christian Baptism: with Its Antecedents and Consequents*, 316.

169. Mark L. Shand, "A Presbyterian View of Covenant Children," 75.

170. Mark D. Thomas, "Listening to the Voice from the Dust: Moroni 8 as Rhetoric," 23–24.

171. Thomas Bradbury, *The Duty and Doctrine of Baptism*, 10.

172. Baptism as a replacement for circumcision can be traced back at least to the Heidelberg Catechism, written in 1562 as an expression of Reformed beliefs. The catechism explains that infants are to be baptized "as by a Sign of the Covenant and be distinguish'd by that means from the Children of Unbelievers; as it was practiced under the Old Covenant by Circumcision." *Heidelberg Catechism*, 18. Subsequently, this is how Presbyterians, Congregationalists, Methodists, and some other denominations have viewed baptism.

173. Smith, *Gospel Doctrine*, 452.

174. Smith, *Doctrines of Salvation*, 2:57.

175. Ehat and Cook, *The Words of Joseph Smith*, 106.

176. Ibid., 347, 354.

177. Smith, *Gospel Doctrine*, 575–76.

178. According to Joseph Fielding Smith, "Little children . . . will automatically inherit the celestial kingdom, but not the exaltation in that kingdom until they have complied with all the requirements of exaltation." Ibid., 2:54. Bruce R. McConkie apparently felt that this compliance would be a given saying, "They shall rise in immortal glory, grow to full maturity, and live forever in the highest heaven of the celestial kingdom." Bruce R. McConkie, "The Salvation of Little Children," 3

179. Joseph Fielding Smith, paraphrased in ibid., 6.

180. Monte S. Nyman, "Hope, Faith, and Charity," 299.

181. Ehat and Cook, *The Words of Joseph Smith*, 106.

≈ 16 ≈

Salvation for the Dead

In LDS theology, all who have reached the age of accountability must comply with the ordinances of the gospel to gain exaltation. This requirement even applies to those who have died without a knowledge of the gospel or the opportunity to receive these ordinances. Mormonism, however, teaches that all who die without having the opportunity to hear and accept the gospel in this life will have that opportunity in the spirit world. This doctrine of salvation for the dead consists of two parts: preaching the gospel to departed spirits, which theologians refer to as postmortem evangelization,[1] and the vicarious performance of the saving ordinances by the living on behalf of the dead.

Old Testament

The Old Testament has no concept of saving ordinances for securing salvation in the hereafter, so not unexpectedly it contains no provision for those who die without receiving saving ordinances. This doesn't surprise Mormons who believe that salvation for the dead wasn't inaugurated until Christ ministered to the spirits in prison after his crucifixion.[2] Mormons nevertheless affirm that Old Testament prophets were aware of the doctrine and that it is alluded to in several Old Testament prophecies.

An Old Testament passage that Mormons frequently cite[3] as a prophecy of Christ's ministry to departed spirits following his crucifixion is Isaiah 61:1–2, which speaks of proclaiming "liberty to the captives" (NRSV reads "oppressed") and "opening of the prison to them that are bound." The original setting of this passage is Israel's political captivity and refers to a time when the Lord will liberate them and execute vengeance upon their oppressors. Once liberated they will "raise up the former desolations, and they shall repair the waste cities" (Isa. 61:4). There is no indication that the text has reference to any kind of spiritual deliverance as suggested by Luke or a postmortem release from spirit prison as taught by Joseph Smith.

The New Testament gospel of Luke has Jesus reading this passage in the synagogue and declaring, "This day is this scripture fulfilled in your ears" (Luke 4:21). The implication is that Jesus saw this passage as an expression of the spiritual deliverance he would bring to those imprisoned by sin. Here, the scripture acquires a spiritual connotation but is still without any reference to salvation for the dead. Notably, early Latter-day Saints also saw this passage as referring to deliverance from sin—though they understood it to be through the proclamation of modern-day missionaries.[4] It isn't until after the doctrine of salvation for the dead began being taught that this passage was appropriated to support the idea of freeing spirits from spirit prison.

In a sermon Joseph Smith delivered on salvation for the dead on April 15, 1842, he used Isaiah 61:1–2 to show that Christ preached to the deceased who were in spirit prison in order "to deliver, or bring them out of the prison house."[5] Of course, in Mormonism, it is more than hearing the gospel that delivers spirits from spirit prison. In September 1842 the Prophet emphasized the importance of Saints being baptized for their dead ancestors to "redeem them out of their prison; for the prisoners shall go free" (D&C 128:22). Joseph taught that "as soon as [they are baptized] . . . here by their friends, who act as proxy for them, the Lord has administrators there to set them free."[6]

In 1918, Joseph F. Smith, sixth Church president, referred to Isaiah 61:1–2 as a "prophecy that the Redeemer was anointed . . . to proclaim liberty to the captives, and the opening of the prison to them that were bound" by physical death rather than by spiritual death (D&C 138:42). For Joseph F. Smith, the entire spirit world was a prison and "bondage" was the state of all spirits who were separated from their bodies (D&C 138:50; cf. D&C 45:17).[7] "While this vast multitude waited and conversed, rejoicing in the hour of their deliverance from the chains of death," he reported, "the Son of God appeared, declaring liberty to the captives who had been faithful" (D&C 138:18).

Thus, from the Old Testament to modern-day Mormonism, what was originally a passage referring to Israel being freed from political captivity became a proclamation of Christ's mission of salvation from sin, then a latter-day call to proclaim the gospel to the living, then a proclamation of liberation of spirits from spirit prison, and eventually a declaration to righteous disembodied spirits that the time of their resurrection had come. In current LDS discourse on salvation for the dead, Isaiah 61:1–2 is interpreted almost exclusively as having reference to the liberation of spirits from spirit prison, or hell, into paradise once the living perform saving ordinances on their behalf.[8] Although the changing meanings ascribed to this passage can be explained as adaptations rather than proof-texts, in nearly each case the meaning is presented as though it was Isaiah's original intent.

A second Old Testament prophecy frequently cited as a reference to salvation for the dead is Obadiah 1:21: "And saviours shall come up on mount Zion to judge the mount of Esau; and the kingdom shall be the LORD's." Latter-day Saints usually understand "saviors on mount Zion" as referring to those who perform saving ordinances for the dead in the last days. Biblical scholars, however, note that the original meaning of this passage had reference to ancient judgments against the descendants of Esau for their offenses against the children of Israel. According to Obadiah, "saviors" would come "to judge the mount of Esau" (i.e., bring judgment on Esau) and reclaim the land for Israel.[9]

In Joseph Smith's day it was not uncommon to interpret Obadiah's "saviours on mount Zion" as referring to Christ's apostles and later gospel preachers, as well as any others who labor for the salvation of souls.[10] Early nineteenth-century Bible commentator Adam Clarke observed: "Some think these saviors . . . mean the apostles of our Lord." However, he noted that this was not its "literal fulfillment" as it literally referred the Israelites "who were delivered from captivity."[11] John Wesley acknowledged its literal fulfillment in ancient Israel but suggested that it also refers "mystically" to "Christ and his apostles, and other preachers of the gospel."[12]

The first recorded reference to "saviors on mount Zion" in Joseph Smith's teachings was in the same sense as that of his contemporaries. In May 1841 he used it to refer to the promised seed of Abraham who, "in the last days," would be "ministers" of salvation.[13] Five months later, in conjunction with his developing treatment of salvation for the dead, he drew upon Obadiah 1:21 again, only now in reference to those who are baptized for the dead. In this sermon, delivered October 1841, he "presented 'Baptism for the Dead' as the only way that men can appear as saviors on mount Zion."[14] He would continue to assert that those who are baptized for the dead are "fulfilling the words of Obadiah [1:21], when speaking of the glory of the latter-day."[15]

Brigham Young also saw this passage as having import for the work of salvation for the dead; however, he saw it as referring to those ministering in the afterlife. According to Young, "In the spirit world those who have got the victory go on to prepare the way for those who live in the flesh, fulfilling the work of saviors on Mount Zion."[16] Today this expression in Obadiah is most often understood in the way that Joseph Smith used it, referring to the living who perform saving ordinances in behalf of the dead. Speaking in the October 1994 general conference, Elder Russell M. Nelson alluded to a statement by President Howard W. Hunter on the importance of temple work for the living and dead. He remarked, "President Hunter's classic statement emphasizes the importance of temple work for our own families and helps us to understand the Old Testament prophecy that 'saviours shall come up on mount Zion.'"[17]

A final passage in the Old Testament presumed to be a prophetic statement regarding the performance of saving ordinances for the dead is Malachi 4:5–6, which states that Elijah would come before the great day of the Lord to "turn the heart of the fathers to the children, and the heart of the children to their fathers."[18] In expounding the doctrine of baptism for the dead in September 1842, Joseph appealed to this passage asserting that Malachi "had his eye fixed on the restoration of the priesthood, the glories to be revealed in the last days, and in an especial manner this most glorious of all subjects belonging to the everlasting gospel, namely, the baptism for the dead" (D&C 128:17). The coming of Elijah, at this point in the Prophet's teachings, concerned the restoration of the priesthood and baptism for the dead, which Joseph Smith described as a "most glorious" principle. Furthermore, in January 1844, he associated the coming of Elijah with the restoration of the sealing power to perform "all the ordinances . . . in behalf of . . . [the] dead,"[19] even though, in the Old Testament, Elijah never performed such ordinances for either the living or the dead nor did he authorize others to do so. As discussed in Chapter 4, the context of Malachi 4:5–6 doesn't appear to have initially contemplated salvation for the dead. Joseph Smith himself had given several other interpretations of this passage—from improving family relations to obeying the words of the ancient patriarchs to restoring the binding power of the priesthood. It is only during the Nauvoo period—beginning in September 1842—that Elijah's mission was understood to be relevant to the doctrine of salvation for the dead.

New Testament

Before examining New Testament passages that Latter-day Saints see as referring to salvation for the dead, it is instructive to note that a surprising number of biblical scholars argue that a belief in an uninterrupted continuation of the spirit at death is not altogether evident from New Testament writings. According to Edmond Jacob, writing in the *Interpreters' Dictionary of the Bible*, "No biblical text authorizes the statement that the soul is separated from the body at the moment of death."[20]

Many scholars suggest that early Christians likely held the traditional beliefs of their Jewish ancestors that those who have died are inert and wholly dead. According to Gerrit Berkouwer, professor of systematic theology at the Free University in Amsterdam, the Greek body-spirit dualism is not part of New Testament theology[21] and "scripture never takes up a natural immortality of the soul because of its inherent nature, but always concerns itself with the relationship of the whole man to God."[22] That is to say, the spirit is never depicted as a separate, inherently immortal part of man that goes on living after the death of the body. In Germany, Lutheran scholar Paul Althaus declared, "The Christian faith knows nothing of an 'immortality of the soul.'"[23] F. F. Bruce explains,

> Paul evidently could not contemplate immortality apart from resurrection; for him a body of some kind was essential to personality. Our traditional thinking about the "never-dying soul," which owes so much to our Graeco-Roman heritage, makes it difficult for us to appreciate Paul's point of view. It is, no doubt, an over-simplification to say that while for the Greeks man was an embodied soul, for the Hebrews he was an animated body; yet there is sufficient substance in the statement for us to say that in this as in other respects Paul was "a Hebrew born and bred" (Philip. 3:5). . . . If Paul longed to be delivered from the mortality of this present earthly "dwelling," it was with a view to exchanging it for one that was immortal; to be without a body of any kind would be a form of spiritual nakedness or isolation from which his mind shrank.[24]

The New Testament uses "sleeping" to refer to the time one is in the grave (1 Cor. 11:30; 15:6, 18, 51; 1 Thess. 4:13–15; 2 Pet. 3:4), which many scholars see as a state of unconsciousness. Colleen McDannell, professor of religious studies at the University of Utah, and Bernhard Lang, a professor of Old Testament and religious studies at Germany's University of Paderborn, observe that "as a Pharisee-turned-Christian, Paul drew from a set of basic concepts concerning life after death. Along with many first-century Jews, Paul accepted the idea that at death the person 'sleeps,' presumably in the netherworld."[25]

While many New Testament passages seem to support a New Testament belief in "soul-sleeping," there are others that point to a continuation of at least some aspect of human life after death. Berkouwer himself concedes that the New Testament seems to allude to some kind of continued existence after death but points out that it is in terms of "being with Christ" or "dwelling with the Lord;" and it is not necessarily a spirit or soul that continues. After referring to commonly cited New Testament examples used as evidence of an intermediate state (e.g., Luke 16:22, 23, 26; 23:43), he remarks that, even if we do survive death in some sense, "in the New Testament . . . we never encounter an anthropological definition or analysis of what it is that remains after death."[26]

Though the New Testament perception of the nature of the "soul" may be indiscernable, one can easily argue that not all New Testament writings attest to the notion of soul sleeping. Many Christians, for example, find ample evidence from the story of Lazarus and the rich man that the soul or spirit has a conscious existence after death and that not all souls enjoy the same status in this spirit realm. In this story the beggar Lazarus dies and is "carried by the angels into Abraham's bosom" (Luke 16:22). The rich man also dies; however, he is tormented "in hell" (v. 23). While Jesus didn't necessarily intend this as a doctrinal statement on the intermediate state of the soul, it undoubtedly reflected contemporary thinking on the spirit realm.

A related passage seen by many scholars, as well as Mormons and most Christians, as a reference to the intermediate state of the soul is Luke 23:43 where the crucified Christ says to the thief on the cross next to him, "To day shalt thou be with me in paradise." Interestingly, in early LDS scripture, the term "paradise" is used to refer to the abode of only *righteous* spirits in the hereafter (see 2 Ne. 9:13; Alma 40:12–14; D&C 77:2, 5). This usage is similar to the general understanding of other Christians since at least the time of the Reformation.[27] Joseph Smith's 1842 teaching on baptism for the dead, which stipulated that individuals must fully repent and be baptized before they can qualify to live in paradise, appears inconsistent with the Savior's remark to the thief that he would be with him in paradise that very day. It may have been in recognition of this inconsistency that in June 1843, Joseph Smith repudiated the view that Jesus had "paradise" in mind when he spoke to the thief. He explained, "There is nothing in the original . . . language that signifies paradise, but it was 'This day I will be with thee in the world of spirits.'"[28] This assertion is somewhat puzzling as M. Catherine Thomas, writing in the *Encyclopedia of Mormonism*, confirms that the Greek word here (*paradeisos*) is correctly rendered "paradise."[29] In New Testament writings, "paradise" is synonymous with heaven or abode of the righteous in the afterlife (2 Cor. 12:4; Rev. 2:7). In his extensive analysis of the use of the term "paradise" in early Jewish and Christian writings, biblical scholar Andrew Lincoln explains that "the term [paradise] came to be used for the abode of the blessed whether after death or after the final judgment." Accordingly, he notes that Jesus's promise to the thief on the cross "has reference to this [intermediate realm] . . . of the departed righteous."[30]

The evidence is sparse yet persuasive that at least some New Testatment writers conceptualized an intermediate state of the soul. In this state conscious spirits either enjoy God's favor or are tormented in hell. With this sketchy New Testament picture of the intermediate state of the soul, we can begin to examine commonly cited New Testament passages used in LDS discourse on salvation for the dead.

One passage that some LDS commentators construe as teaching that the gospel was preached to the spirits of the departed after Christ's death is John 5:28, which has Jesus saying, "the hour is coming, in the which all that are in the graves shall hear his [i.e., the Son of Man's] voice." This may seem like (and is often interpreted as) a reference to preaching the gospel to the dead, but it should be read in light of the next verse which explains what happens when they hear his voice: "And [they] shall come forth; they that have done good, unto the resurrection of life; and they that have done evil, unto the resurrection of damnation" (John 5:29). Interestingly, Bruce R. McConkie referred to John 5:28 in a 1976 *Ensign* article as a "perfectly clear" reference to the preaching of the gospel in the spirit world.[31] A few years later, however, he paraphrased the same verse as saying: "I, Jesus, shall call forth all that are in their graves [etc.],"[32] which makes it a reference to his resurrecting the dead.

Another New Testament passage sometimes interpreted by Latter-day Saints as a reference to redeeming the dead is Matthew 16:18: "Thou art Peter, and upon this rock I will build my church; and the gates of hell shall not prevail against it." As noted in Chapter 2, scholars disagree about whether the antecedent of "it" is the church or the rock. Equally unclear is what is meant by the inability of the gates of hell to prevail against it. W. D. Davies and Dale C. Allison Jr. surveyed twelve conflicting scholarly opinions on the interpretation of "the gates of hell" in Matthew 16:18.[33] These interpretations can be essentially divided into two groups: those that take "gates" more figuratively as a metonym for the powers of Satan (by metonymy, the gates represent the whole city as in Genesis 22:17, 24:60), and those who view "gates" more literally as an actual barrier preventing entrance or exit.[34] Many Latter-day Saints take the latter view, with "hell" being seen as a place of suffering for disobedient spirits. M. Catherine Thomas, writing in the *Encyclopedia of Mormonism* states, "The Savior's reference to the 'gates of hell' . . . indicates, among other things, that God's priesthood power will penetrate hell and redeem the repentant spirits there."[35] Most scholars who take the latter view see "hell" as synonymous with the grave and note that the "gates of hell," a common Semitic term for the threshold of the realm of death (Job 38:17, Ps. 9:13, Rev. 1:18), would not hold back the dead from being resurrected.[36] More commonly, scholars take the first view seeing the "gates of hell" as simply a metonym for the powers of Satan which will not be able to stop the advance of Christ's church. Notably, this is the sense in which "the gates of hell" was understood in modern revelations prior to 1834, always with the idea that the Saints would not be defeated or overcome by Satan in this life if they continued faithful (D&C 10:69, 17:8, 18:5, 21:6, 33:13, 98:22).

Like many sayings of Jesus, there is always the gnawing question of whether Matthew 16:17–19 was even uttered by Jesus. According to Catholic scholar Hans Küng, the consensus taking shape "between leading scholars of different Churches [both Catholic and Protestant]" is that this passage "is a very ancient post-paschal [i.e., post-resurrection] construction by the Palestinian community or by Matthew, presupposing a church already institutionally consolidated."[37] Whatever the source of the saying, it is by no means conclusive from the text itself that freeing spirits from spirit prison was expressly intended.

A New Testament passage that Latter-day Saints see as showing that the gospel was preached to the spirits of the dead is 1 Peter 3:18–20 which states that Christ was "put to death in the flesh, but quickened by the Spirit: By which also he went and preached unto the spirits in prison; Which sometime were disobedient, when once the longsuffering of God waited in the days of Noah." According to the LDS interpretation, during the three days that Christ's body lay in the tomb, he went as a spirit to minister to departed righteous spirits and empower them to preach the gospel to disobedient spirits (D&C 138:28–30). Several elements in this passage pose problems with this interpretation. First, when the New Testament speaks elsewhere of Christ being "quickened by the Spirit" (uppercase "S"), it refers to his resurrection from the dead (see Rom. 8:11). Paul Achtemeier, professor of biblical interpretation at Union Theological Seminary in Richmond, Virginia, notes: "While there has been much discussion about . . . how and in what form Christ was made alive [i.e., quickened], the verb contained in the participle (*zoopoeo*) is used in NT tradition principally to refer to the resurrection, and the contrast between Christ dead and alive similarly refers to cross and resurrection. On that basis one ought here to see . . . a reference to Christ's resurrection."[38] If this passage is referring to Christ's physical resurrection, then it wasn't as a *spirit* that he visited the spirits in prison.

A second complication with the conventional LDS interpretation is that, in 1 Peter, it was Christ himself who preached to those who "were disobedient . . . in the days of Noah" (v. 20). This runs contrary to the current LDS view that Christ preached only to the righteous and didn't personally go among the wicked.[39]

Besides considering the question of whether Christ visited the spirits in prison as a spirit or with a resurrected body, in person or by representatives, a more fundamental question bearing on the issue of salvation for the dead is: "Who were these imprisoned 'spirits' and what was the message (1 Peter 3:18–20 doesn't say it was the *gospel*) that was 'preached' to them?" Most non-LDS scholars maintain that the "spirits" in this verse are not departed spirits of the dead but rather fallen angels who, according to popular legend, had rebelled against God and instigated the great wickedness at the time of Noah.[40] Scholars note that the story of these fallen angels was well known at the time and most likely provided the backdrop for Peter's remarks. New Testament scholar Raymond Brown comments:

> The reference to disobedience in the days of Noah suggests that these are the angels or sons of God who did evil by having relations with earthly women according to Gen 6:1–4, a wickedness that led God to send the great flood from which Noah was saved (6:5ff.). In pre-NT Jewish mythology the story of these wicked angels is greatly elaborated, e.g., God had the spirits rounded up and imprisoned in a great pit under the earth until the day when they would be judged (1 Enoch 10:11–12; Jubilees 5:6). 1 Peter 3:19 has the risen Christ go down there to proclaim his victory and crush the Satanic forces. . . . In my judgment this is the most plausible explanation of 3:19.[41]

According to this explanation, Christ didn't go as a spirit to preach the gospel to the spirits of the deceased, but rather he went as a resurrected being to proclaim his triumph over evil to the rebellious angels, which the New Testament also calls "spirits" (Heb. 1:7, 14), who committed sin at the time of Noah. The propriety of this interpretation finds support in 2 Peter 2:4–9, which recounts how God imprisoned certain angels for rebelliousness. Scholars note that the Greek verb *kerusso*, translated "preached" in KJV 1 Peter 3:19, is better translated "proclaimed" (see NRSV) and is different from *euagglizo*, the common New Testament verb for preaching *the gospel*. Thus, the NEB states that Christ "made his proclamation to the imprisoned spirits."

In defending the view that 1 Peter 3:19 has reference to Christ preaching the gospel, Latter-day Saints point to 1 Peter 4:6 which states, "For this cause was the gospel preached also to them that are dead, that they might be judged according to men in the flesh, but live according to God in the spirit." The assumption is that 1 Peter 4:6 ties back to 1 Peter 3:19. A footnote in the New American Bible acknowledges that the "dead" in 1 Peter 4:6 "may be the sinners of the flood generation who are possibly referred to in 1 Peter 3:19," but notes that "many scholars think that there is no connection between these two verses, and that the dead here are Christians who have died since hearing the preaching of the gospel."[42] As grounds for arguing that these passages are disconnected, scholars note that not only has the topic of discussion shifted, but the language also changes. 1 Peter 3:19 speaks of Christ making a "proclamation" (Greek *kerusso*) to "spirits," where 1 Peter 4:6 refers to the gospel being "preached" (Greek *euagglizo*) to the "dead."

Of course, even if 1 Peter 4:6 doesn't tie back to 1 Peter 3:18–20, one could argue that it could easily stand on its own as a declaration that the gospel was preached to departed spirits.[43] Joel B. Green, Methodist professor of New Testament Interpretation at Ashbury Theological Seminary, states, in fact, that "from the early second century on, Peter was widely regarded as referring to Christ's descent into Hades in order that he might . . . rescue the righteous dead, and/or proclaim salvation to the dead."[44] Other non-LDS scholars argue that the preaching was to those who are "now dead" (NIV), i.e., they died subsequent to having the gospel preached to them.[45] Both sides acknowledge that the text is difficult and neither interpretation is without problems.

The LDS view that 1 Peter 3:18–20 refers to the gospel being preached to departed spirits is certainly not without precedent. This understanding is also found in early Christian writings dating back to at least the second century.[46] In the third century, Origen referred to this passage as giving "hope" to the deceased but only to "those who were destroyed in the deluge."[47]

At the time of Joseph Smith it wasn't uncommon, especially among Shakers and Universalists, to view 1 Peter 3:18–20 as an allusion to Christ, as a spirit, preaching the gospel to departed spirits. A confessional Shaker work written in 1823 states, "Christ . . . preached the glad tidings of salvation, both in this world and in the world of spirits; and has also commissioned his ministers to do the same. Hence his faithful and true witnesses, after putting off this mortal body, will find a work to do in preaching the gospel to those benighted spirits who never heard its peaceful sound in this world."[48] Universalist Elhanan Winchester argued in 1800 that Christ would not have preached to the "spirits in prison" if there was no hope of salvation after death.[49] In contradistinction to these views, an article in the 1819 *Methodist Magazine* repudiated what it considered to be the misguided interpretation that "the soul of Christ went to hell, immediately after its separation from the body at his crucifixion, and that he remained in hell preaching to the spirits in prison, until the third day, when he arose from the dead."[50]

Joseph Smith's own teachings related to the spirit prison spoken of in 1 Peter 3:18–20 show a progression in understanding up through the end of his ministry. It should be noted that in the Book of Mormon, which was published in March 1830, there is no mention of a spirit "prison." Departed spirits dwell in either "paradise" or "outer darkness" (Alma 40:12–13), which was also the common understanding of early nineteenth-century Protestantism. It doesn't appear that the spirit "prison" concept spoken of in 1 Peter was addressed in the Book of Mormon.

The first LDS reference to a spirit prison occurs in the book of Moses, which the Prophet dictated between June 1830 and February 1831. As though informed by 1 Peter 3:18–20 (the only biblical reference to spirits in prison and, more specifically, the spirits who were disobedient in the days of Noah whom Christ would visit after being "quickened"), the book of Moses explains that the disobedient in the days of Noah would be consigned to a specially prepared "prison" after death, but that they would be redeemed at Christ's resurrection. In Moses 7:36, the Lord shows Enoch the great wickedness that would prevail in the days of Noah and states, "Among all the workmanship of mine hands there has not been so great wickedness as among thy brethren." The Lord is merciful to them, however, noting that their wickedness was due to the iniquities of their parents and, therefore, "their sins shall be upon the heads of their fathers" (Moses 7:37). Still, their recalcitrance isn't totally excused, for the Lord tells Enoch, "[They] shall perish in the floods; and behold, I will shut them up; a prison have I prepared for them" (Moses 7:38). This imprisonment, however, was to last only until the resurrection of Christ: "Inasmuch as they will repent in the day that my Chosen shall return unto me, and until that day they shall be in torment" (Moses 7:39).[51] Significantly, when Enoch is shown the future resurrection of the Savior, he observes that not only "the saints arose" (Moses 7:56), but also "as many of the spirits as were in prison came forth, and stood on the right hand of God; and the remainder [i.e., those who were neither saints nor in prison] were reserved in chains of darkness until the judgment of the great day" (Moses 7:57). Thus, the book of Moses goes one step beyond the paradise/outer-darkness bifurcation of the Book of Mormon by adding a third category of spirits in the spirit world— those who were wicked at the time of Noah and therefore shut up in "prison," but only until the resurrection of Christ. This initial peculiar perspective of spirit prison is generally ignored in later LDS discussions on the spirit world.

In February 1832, Joseph received a revelation giving a different understanding of 1 Peter 3:18–20. Describing those who inherit a terrestrial glory in the resurrection, Joseph states that they include "the spirits of men kept in prison, whom the Son visited, and preached the gospel unto them, that they might be judged according to men in the flesh; who received not the testimony of Jesus in the flesh, but afterwards received it" (D&C 76:73–74). So instead of preaching just to those who were disobedient in the days of Noah, as suggested in 1 Peter 3:18–20 and Moses 7:57, Jesus is depicted preaching to all those who had rejected his testimony while in mortality. Presumably, this would include those in the days of Noah who rejected the commandments of God (Moses 7:33). Unlike the book of Moses, which has the imprisoned spirits being resurrected with Christ and standing "on the right hand of God" (Moses 7:57), those who receive Christ's message in the spirit world are now depicted as coming forth at the second coming and receiving only the terrestrial kingdom, which is outside God's presence (D&C 76:77).

By February 1833, Joseph Smith had completed his translation of the New Testament which included minor changes to 1 Peter 3:18–20. Congruent with Doctrine and Covenants 76, which has the gospel being taught to all the disobedient who had departed this life and not just to the disobedient who lived in the days of Noah, the Prophet revised 1 Peter 3:20 to read that Christ preached to disobedient spirits, "*some of whom* were disobedient in the days of Noah" (JST 1 Pet. 3:20; emphasis mine). Additionally, it is interesting to note that Joseph seems to have understood Christ's being "quickened by the Spirit" as referring to his bodily resurrection. The JST reads that Christ was "put to death in the flesh, but quickened by the Spirit, that he might bring us [the living] to God. For which cause also, he went and preached unto the spirits in prison" (1 Pet. 3:18–19). Notably, there is no clear indication from Moses 7, Doctrine and Covenants 76, or here that Jesus visited the spirits in prison *as a spirit*. It wasn't until October 3, 1841 that the Prophet unambiguously declared, "Jesus Christ became a ministering spirit, while His body [was lying] in the sepulchre, to the spirits in prison."[52]

The Prophet once again referred to 1 Peter 3:18–20 in a sermon delivered in April 1842, stating, "Here then we have an account of our Savior preaching to the spirits in prison . . . [who] had been imprisoned from the days of Noah."[53] Interestingly, he here acknowledges that the text confines the Savior's preaching to those who had been imprisoned "from the days of Noah." He goes on, however, to justify the belief that spirits from other ages were there, too, by quoting Isaiah 24:20–22, which refers to the rebellious "kings of the earth" (v. 21) and the fact that "they shall be gathered together, as prisoners are gathered in the pit, and shall be shut up in the prison, and after many days shall they be visited" (v. 22). From this passage the Prophet concludes, "Thus we find that God will deal with all the human family equally; and that as the antediluvians had their day of visitation, so will those characters referred to by Isaiah, have their time of visitation and deliverance; after having been many days in prison."[54] It is questionable whether the imprisonment of these kings refers to *spirit* prison and whether their "visitation" is one of mercy and deliverance. The NRSV translates verse 22 as "after many days they will be *punished*" (emphasis mine). For Joseph, however, "those characters referred to by Isaiah will be visited by the priesthood, and come out of their prison upon the same principle as those who were disobedient in the days of Noah were visited by our Savior and had the Gospel preached to them by Him in prison."[55]

Turning to another New Testament passage believed to support salvation for the dead, 1 Corinthians 15:29 states: "Else what shall they do which are baptized for the dead, if the dead rise not at all? why are they then baptized for the dead?" Latter-day Saints find reassurance in the general scholarly consensus that this passage indeed has reference to baptisms performed during New Testament times on behalf of the dead. Krister Stendahl, dean of the Harvard School of Theology, wrote of this passage: "The text seems to speak plainly enough about a practice within the Church of vicarious baptism for the dead. This is the view of most contemporary exegetes." Stendahl notes, however, that vicarious baptism may not have been practiced in the Church at large, as Paul seems to be referring to "a distinct group within the Church." Furthermore, Paul is not endorsing the practice, though "at least he does not see fit to condemn it as heretical."[56] New Testament scholar James Dunn observes that Paul often tolerated diverse practices in the church and that he "accepts a diversity of beliefs about baptism."[57] He notes that Paul saw his mission as having less to do with baptism than with proclaiming the gospel of the cross (1 Cor. 1:17). So was baptism for the dead a legitimate ordinance of the Church, or was it just another instance of an isolated practice that had crept into the Corinthian church like that of being baptized in the name of Paul (1 Cor. 1:13)? It should be noted that the voice changes from "we" to "they" for this verse only: Else what shall "they" do? And why are "they" baptized for the dead? Then the shift is back to "we"—why stand "we" in jeopardy? Could Paul be alluding to a practice that only "they" (not "we") were participating in?

Historically, Paul's reference to vicarious baptism for the dead has been seen largely as a practice of only a few Christian converts, and some assert that it was likely an adaptation of Jewish and Roman traditions involving the performance of pious acts for the dead in hopes of providing some redemptive benefit to them.[58] The early Christian writer Tertullian (ca. 180) states, "His [Paul's] only aim in alluding to it [baptism for the dead] was that he might all the more firmly insist upon the resurrection of the body, in proportion as they who were vainly baptized for the dead resorted to the practice from their belief of such a resurrection."[59] Other early Church historians (e.g., Ambrose, Chrysostom) also identified the practice of vicarious baptism as being confined to a minor segment of the Church. Notably, in modern times the Ephrata Society, a Christian sect in Pennsylvania in the 1700s, took up the practice of vicarious baptism for the dead as a legitimate vicarious ordinance and continued it into the 1840s.[60]

Joseph Smith quoted Hebrews 11:40 as another passage supporting the doctrine of baptism for the dead. Hebrews 11 is an exposition on faith and relates how the righteous in Old Testament times "all died in faith, not having received the promises, but having seen them afar off" (Heb. 11:13). The chapter concludes: "And these all, having obtained a good report through faith, received not the promise: God having provided some better thing for us [i.e., first-century Christians], that they [i.e., the faithful in Old Testament times] without us should not be made perfect" (Heb. 11:39–40).

The Prophet advanced several different interpretations of this passage as his doctrinal understanding seemed to evolve. He first altered it sometime between February 1832 and February 1833 to read, "without *suffering* they could not be made perfect" (JST Heb. 11:40; emphasis mine). This change undoubtedly made sense to him in light of the relationship between suffering and perfection expressed in Hebrews 5:8–9, but it takes the passage in a different direction from where he would later go with it. In July 1839, he altered this passage to parallel changes he made to Malachi 4:5–6, corresponding to his developing understanding of the priesthood and sealing power (see Chapter 4). According to this new rendition, "we cannot be made perfect without them [i.e., the dead], nor they without us."[61] Here, the Prophet makes the dependency bidirectional, which he will continue to do in all subsequent interpretations, so that the living and dead somehow depend on each other for their perfection. Joseph understood this to mean that "authoritative characters [holding priesthood keys] will come down & join hand in hand [with the living] in bringing about this work."[62] The idea expressed by the Prophet at this point is that, while the saints living in the dispensation of the fulness of times are to bring in the glory to be enjoyed by the righteous of all ages, they are to be assisted by the righteous of the past.

In August 1840 the Prophet gave the first sermon on baptism for the dead;[63] and in September 1842, he referred to Hebrews 11:40 for the first time as an explanation for how baptism for the dead joined present and past dispensations, "for we without them cannot be made perfect; neither can they without us be made perfect. . . . For it is necessary . . . that a whole and complete and perfect union, and welding together of dispensations, and keys, and powers, and glories should take place" (D&C 128:18). The idea here is that the righteous dead restore their keys so the living can receive the saving ordinance of baptism. In turn, the Saints are baptized for the deceased who died without receiving this ordinance. Thus, both present and past dispensations contribute to each other's salvation.

In March 1844, Joseph Smith first linked Hebrews 11:40 to the sealing power of the priesthood stating that the subject of Hebrews

11:40 is "the spirit of Elijah" which is "that we rede[e]m our dead & connect ourselves with our fathers which are in heaven & seal up our dead to come forth in the first resurrection."[64] It is this interpretation of Hebrews 11:40 that has lingered in LDS teachings—children being sealed to parents, thus creating a patriarchal chain of families going back to Adam.[65] One month later the Prophet related this passage to individual sealings as well, stating, "Paul said we cannot be made perfect without us [them], for it is necessary that the seals are in our hands to seal our children & our dead for the fulness of the dispensation of times."[66]

From a scholarly perspective, Hebrews 11 is essentially a tribute to the valiant saints of the Old Testament who "all died in faith, not having received the promises, but having seen them afar off" (Heb. 11:13). These faithful souls wouldn't obtain perfection until Christ offered a sacrifice for sin, so that only together with first-century Saints would they "be made perfect" (Heb. 11:39–40). As Wayne G. McCown, professor of Bible and ministry at Northeastern Seminary, explains, "A perfection not attainable previously [through the law of Moses] has been inaugurated through the Person and work of Christ."[67] The implication is that those who had died in anticipation of entering a "heavenly" city (Heb. 11:16), would finally be rewarded by such an entrance *in company* with those living in the Christian era.[68] There is no dependency implied as though the ancients needed ordinances or other services performed in their behalf by Christian-era Saints. It is just that any admission to heaven was to be deferred until the Christian era. As the NEB states, "Only *in company with us* should they [i.e., the ancient faithful] reach perfection" (emphasis mine). It should be noted that many of the ancients identified in Hebrews 11 (e.g., Abel, Enoch, Noah, Abraham, Isaac, Jacob, and Joseph) would have already received all of the ordinances of salvation according to LDS teachings and would therefore not need vicarious work performed for them.

One last New Testament passage[69] quoted by the Prophet as a reference to salvation for the dead is Revelation 20:12 where John saw "books" that were to be opened at judgment day, "and the dead were judged out of those things which were written in the books, according to *their* works." In September 1842 Joseph Smith wrote, "The books spoken of must be the books which contained the record of their works, and refer to the records which are kept on the earth" (D&C 128:7). He added, "John was contemplating this very subject" (i.e., baptism for the dead) when he envisioned these books (D&C 128:6). Of course, there is no way to verify whether this is what John was actually contemplating. However, the passage alone gives no indication that the "works" recorded in these books are vicarious baptisms. John states that it is by *"their* works" (Rev. 20:12–13; emphasis mine) that they will be judged. Most modern translations render this passage along these lines: "The dead were judged according to *what they had done* as recorded in the books" (NIV Rev. 20:12; emphasis mine).

The view that the books John saw were records of personal deeds, good and evil, is not only the traditional Christian interpretation, but it is also the understanding first expressed in the Book of Mormon (3 Ne. 27:24–26), published more than a decade before Joseph taught baptism for the dead. Interestingly, later in the dictation sequence of the Book of Mormon, the books out of which the dead will be judged are equated with the scriptures inclusive of the Book of Mormon (2 Ne. 29:11–12), thus appropriating the expression in Revelation to give support to the Book of Mormon. So the judgment "books" were first interpreted in Joseph Smith's writings in the traditional sense as a log of individual works, then as scriptural books (esp. the Book of Mormon), and finally as a record of vicarious ordinance work.

Early Nineteenth-Century Christianity

At the time of Joseph Smith, the general Christian perception of the state of the soul after death was not unlike what would be espoused in the Book of Mormon. One professor of theology writes, "Since the time of Augustine (A. D. 354–430), Christians have been taught that between death and resurrection—a period known as 'the intermediate state'—the souls of the dead either enjoy the beatitude of Paradise or suffer the affliction of Purgatory or Hell."[70] The 1742 Philadelphia Confession of Faith, echoing earlier confessions, states that, when persons die, "their souls . . . immediately return to God who gave them: the souls of the righteous . . . are received into paradise, where they are with Christ, and behold the face of God, in light and glory, waiting for the full redemption of their bodies; and the souls of the wicked are cast into hell, where they remain in torment and utter darkness reserved to the judgment of the great day."[71] Thus, an interim sentencing to paradise or hell at death provided a foretaste of the final judgment at the resurrection. This concept is an extrapolation from New Testament teachings as it isn't an explicit New Testament doctrine.

At the time of Joseph Smith, it was popularly believed that one's fate throughout eternity depended on decisions made during this brief mortal sojourn or "probationary state" (a non-biblical expression that coincidentally appears in Alma 12:24; 42:4). In 1776 anti-Universalist John Cleveland declared, "The time of life here on earth is our only probation time for eternity." He further stated that "after death . . . while our bodies are in the grave our souls will be in a fixed state of happiness or misery, according to the state we were in when we gave up the ghost . . . and after the resurrection and final judgment the wicked will be in a state of punishment in soul and body forever and ever."[72] In 1823, Timothy Merritt, writing for the *Methodist Magazine*, proclaimed that "the present is a probationary state" and that "none can be saved in the future state who are not prepared for the kingdom of heaven in this [life]." Furthermore, "this [probationary] state will not always last. The night will come when no man can work."[73]

This popular notion that mortality is man's only probationary state was vigorously contested by Universalists who maintained that all are eventually (in this life or the next) reconciled to God. Prior to his investigation of Universalism in 1822, Adin Ballou stated that he "firmly held the opinion that man's earth-life was his only probation for eternity." He quickly changed his mind, however, when he was given the challenge by a Universalist minister to actually find this teaching in the Bible. "To my astonishment," he exclaimed, "the word 'probation' was not in the bible, nor a single passage evidently intended to teach the doctrine that this life is man's only probationary state."[74]

While many Christians in Joseph Smith's day believed that all will be damned who have not accepted Christ and his gospel, others realized that such a judgment contradicts the idea of a just God and therefore held that individuals will be judged only according to the law they have been given. Thus, many evangelicals in Joseph Smith's day believed that those who die in ignorance of God's plan are automatically saved. They quoted Romans 4:15 ("for where no law is, there is no transgression") as justification for this belief. In 1804, Lorenzo Dow wrote, "Some people suppose that all the heathens are damned; but for my own part I beg leave to dissent. . . . For I cannot believe any man will be damned for the sin of ignorance, which he could not possibly avoid."[75]

Advocates of unconditional salvation for the ignorant were not necessarily suggesting that it came at no cost. Just as many evangelicals believed that it was Christ's atonement that purchased salvation for children who die in infancy (see Chapter 15), they also attributed the salvation of those who die in complete ignorance of the gospel to the atonement. As one evangelical expositor wrote, "I believe, that, as *infants*, who are incapable of hearing and believing the gospel, are saved, not as being free from guilt and depravity, but through the atoning blood of Jesus Christ; so some of the heathen *may* be saved, by the application of the same precious blood."[76]

Many believed that salvation in God's kingdom still required acceptance of the gospel or at least a determination, by God, that the deceased would have accepted the gospel wholeheartedly had the opportunity been provided. Molinism, which held that God's omniscience allows him to determine who would have accepted the gospel had they been given the opportunity, had been around since the sixteenth century.[77] Thus, many held some form of belief that individuals would be judged according to the light they had or according to the desire of their heart.

Early Mormonism

The evangelical concept of returning to God's presence and then being consigned to either paradise or hell to await the resurrection appears in the Book of Mormon which teaches that "the spirits of all men, as soon as they are departed from this mortal body . . . are taken home to that God who gave them life" (Alma 40:11).[78] Then "the spirits of those who are righteous are received into a state of happiness, which is called paradise" (Alma 40:12) while the spirits of the wicked are "cast out into outer darkness [where] there shall be weeping, and wailing, and gnashing of teeth" (Alma 40:13). The wicked "remain in this state, as well as the righteous in paradise, until the time of their resurrection" (Alma 40:14). Note that they "remain" in either paradise or hell until the resurrection with no express opportunity for them to repent and change their status.

The Book of Mormon echoed contemporary evangelical sentiment which viewed post-mortality as the "night of darkness wherein there can be no labor performed" (Alma 34:33). In the Book of Mormon, repentance must occur in this life (see Chapter 21). Consequently, Adam and Eve weren't put to death as soon as they sinned; rather, "there was a time granted unto man to repent, yea, a probationary time, a time to repent and serve God" (Alma 42:4; cf. Alma 12:24; D&C 29:42).[79] Thus, "the days of the children of men were prolonged, according to the will of God, that they might repent *while in the flesh*; wherefore, their state became a state of probation, and their time was lengthened" (2 Ne. 2:21; emphasis mine).

The Book of Mormon reflects a common evangelical view regarding the salvation of those who had no opportunity to hear the gospel in this life stating, "Those who . . . have died . . . in their ignorance, not having salvation declared unto them . . . have eternal life, being redeemed by the Lord" (Mosiah 15:24). And again, "For behold . . . his blood atoneth for the sins of those . . . who have died not knowing the will of God concerning them, or who have ignorantly sinned" (Mosiah 3:11). Mormon writes to his son Moroni, "The power of redemption cometh on all them that have no law . . . and unto such baptism availeth nothing" (Moro. 8:22). He further declares that "it is mockery before God, denying the mercies of Christ," to suppose that they are in need of baptism (Moro. 8:23). In the Book of Mormon baptism is a covenant intended to be received only while in mortality (Mosiah 18:13), and those who die in ignorance of the gospel automatically inherit eternal life, without the need of baptism.

There is no indication in the Book of Mormon that Christ introduced the doctrine of salvation for the dead during his visit to the Nephites—even though, according to LDS doctrine, he had just visited the spirits in prison and opened the door for their salvation. On the contrary, the Book of Mormon people were taught not to worry about those who die without having heard the gospel in this life since they are redeemed automatically through the Atonement. The whole notion of vicarious work for the dead seems incongruous with Book of Mormon theology.

Later Mormonism

While the Book of Mormon teaches that those who die in ignorance automatically inherit eternal life, a February 1832 revelation seems to relegate them to the terrestrial kingdom (the middle of three levels of salvation): "Behold, these are they who died without law . . . who are the spirits of men kept in prison, whom the Son visited, and preached the gospel unto them, that they might be judged according to men in the flesh; who received not [i.e., rejected] the testimony of Jesus in the flesh, but afterwards received it" (D&C 76:72-74). The terrestrial kingdom therefore includes all those who die in ignorance as well as the rebellious who reject the gospel in this life but afterwards receive it. It is noteworthy that there is no mention here that the gospel would be preached to those who die in ignorance. It is instead only preached to the rebellious. A revelation ten months later conveyed a similar idea, stating that the gospel would be preached to those "who have received their part in that prison which is prepared for them, that they might receive the gospel, and be judged according to men in the flesh" (D&C 88:99). This preaching seems to be targeted again at only the rebellious while ignoring the innocent ignorant. It appears from his earlier vision that only the rebellious were consigned to spirit prison (D&C 76:73). As in section 76, section 88 also has the ignorant as well as the rebellious who repent come forth at the "second trump" signaling the resurrection of terrestrial candidates (D&C 88:98-99). There is no indication that they could attain a celestial glory through vicarious baptism. Neither revelation mentions vicarious baptismal work being performed for individuals who accept the gospel in the spirit world. Perhaps since theirs is only a terrestrial glory, baptism wasn't perceived as being of any benefit to them.

In 1836 Joseph Smith reported a vision he received in which he saw his deceased brother, Alvin, in the celestial kingdom. This caused Joseph to "marvel" since Alvin "had not been baptized for the remission of sins" (D&C 137:6), especially since Joseph taught four years earlier that one "can never see the celestial kingdom of God, without being born of water and the Spirit."[80] This vision of the celestial kingdom partially returns to the Book of Mormon's teaching that those who die in ignorance would inherit eternal life—however, it differs by having eternal life attainable only for those who had good intentions in this life. The vision gave Joseph understanding that all who die in ignorance of the gospel "who would have received it if they had been permitted to tarry, shall be heirs of the celestial kingdom" (D&C 137:7).

What is puzzling about this vision is that while Alvin's unbaptized status is specifically noted, there is no mention of any necessity or provision for this ordinance. Instead it states that God "will judge all men according to their works, according to the desire of their hearts" (v. 9). Indeed, there is no mention of even having the gospel preached to these candidates. The implication seems to be that God's appraisal of the intent of their heart is sufficient. This idea is not inconsistent with the wording in Doctrine and Covenants 76 and 88 that have the gospel being preached only to those who *reject* the gospel in mortality.

It undoubtedly occurred to the Saints that those who die in ignorance of the gospel, but would have accepted it if given a chance, must at some time be given that chance. Writings during the next year (1837) indicate just such an understanding.[81] In July 1838, Joseph Smith plainly stated, "All those who have not had an opportunity of hearing the Gospel, and being administered unto by an inspired man in the flesh, must have it hereafter, before they can be finally judged."[82]

Still, there is no mention of baptismal work being performed in their behalf. As late as June 1840, when apostle Parley P. Pratt was asked if "the thief on the cross [was] saved without baptism," he responded that the thief was "included in the same mercy as the heathens, who have never had the offer of the Gospel, and therefore, are under no condemnation for not obeying it."[83] Thus, for eight years after the revelation in Doctrine and Covenants alluding to the gospel being preached to departed spirits in 1832 (D&C 76:73–74), there was no mention of vicarious work being performed in their behalf. LDS scholar Gregory Prince notes that, "while it may be claimed that Smith referred obliquely to the performance of baptism and other ordinances in their behalf, nothing else in the historical record for this period supports such an interpretation."[84]

Joseph Smith first preached the doctrine of baptism for the dead at the funeral of Seymour Brunson on August 15, 1840. Then, in October 1840, the Prophet wrote a letter to the Twelve, saying, "The Saints have the privilege of being baptized for those of their relatives who are dead, whom they believe would have embraced the Gospel."[85]

Vicarious baptism, at this point however, is a privilege extended only to those who would have received the gospel if they had the chance.

Joseph Smith would call vicarious work for the dead "the burden of the scriptures,"[86] in spite of the fact that, aside from what appears to be a single reference to an unendorsed practice of baptism for the dead in the New Testament (1 Cor. 15:29), there is no mention of performing saving ordinances for the dead in any of the standard works prior to 1842. While the Book of Mormon taught that mortality alone was the time for individuals to come unto God or be forever damned, the Prophet would later teach, in reference to salvation for the dead, that "there is never a time when the spirit is too old to approach God."[87]

Wilford Woodruff found the work of redemption of the dead particularly engaging and was extremely optimistic in his estimate of how many would embrace the gospel in the spirit world. In an April 1894 general conference, as president of the Church, he encouraged Saints to perform the saving ordinances for their dead ancestors, promising that "there will be very few, if any, who will not accept the gospel."[88] The only exception President Woodruff made at the time was for known murderers; the rest he suggested would be fully redeemed. Apostle Lorenzo Snow expressed a similar sentiment just three days earlier: "Very, very few of those who die without the Gospel will reject it on the other side of the veil."[89]

The doctrine that all non-members will have the opportunity to hear the gospel and receive its saving ordinances, whether or not they had the opportunity in this life to do so, was canonized in 1975 as Doctrine and Covenants 138, which contained Joseph F. Smith's 1918 vision of the redemption of the dead. While pondering Peter's teachings regarding Christ's "preaching" to the spirits in prison (1 Pet. 3:18–20; 4:6), Smith wondered "how it was possible for him [Christ] to preach to those spirits and perform the necessary labor among them in so short a time" (D&C 138:28). While musing on this question, his "understanding [was] quickened" and he "perceived" (v. 29) that:

1. Christ visited only the spirits of those who were righteous on earth and had received the gospel and its ordinances.
2. Christ "could not" visit the wicked "because of their rebellion and transgression," so he called and trained missionaries from among the righteous to take the gospel to them.
3. When faithful elders depart from mortal life, they continue their labors preaching to the spirits of the wicked.

The last of these items he gleaned was by no means new information. Church leaders prior to Joseph F. Smith drew similar inferences from 1 Peter and taught that Christ set up his church while in the spirit world.[90] The idea of departed righteous elders preaching the gospel to the wicked spirits in prison had also been taught for nearly eighty years. As early as 1837, Zebedee Coltrin promised Wilford Woodruff that he would "Preach to the spirits in Prision."[91] The Prophet taught publicly in May 1844 that "all those [who] die in the faith goe to the prison of Spirits to preach to the ded in body."[92] Joseph F. Smith was evidently aware of this tradition as he himself had previously taught on several occasions that departed missionaries continue their labors in the spirit world.[93] It is noteworthy, in fact, that when Joseph F. Smith's son and apostle, Hyrum Mack Smith, died of appendicitis earlier the same year that President Smith had his vision, it devastated President Smith; and many of the speakers at Hyrum's funeral offered consolation by reassuring the congregation that Hyrum was needed on the other side to preach the gospel to those who died without having a knowledge of it.[94]

What seems to have surprised Joseph F. Smith was that Christ didn't go at all among the wicked during his three-day sojourn in the spirit world. While his bypassing of the wicked explains how Jesus managed to accomplish his mission in so short a time, the reason given for not visiting them is somewhat perplexing: "he could not go personally, because of their rebellion and transgression" (v. 37). Is this to suggest that their rebelliousness *prevented* Jesus from going among them? What about those in spirit prison who were not rebellious? One wonders why he wouldn't have at least made a token appearance to the millions of honorable spirits who died without the opportunity to hear the gospel in mortality. But Joseph F. Smith gives no indication that such a group of honorable spirits was in the spirit world; everyone is categorized as either among the righteous who are "the spirits of the just, who had been faithful in the testimony of Jesus while they lived in mortality" (v. 12), or among "the wicked," "the ungodly" and "the unrepentant" (v. 20).[95]

While the clarification that Christ did not go personally among "the wicked" may explain how he was able to accomplish his mission in only three days, it is a departure from previous LDS teachings in which Christ expressly visits the wicked in spirit prison. In fact, the Doctrine and Covenants speaks of Christ's visit solely in terms of his preaching to "the spirits of men kept in prison . . . who received not the testimony of Jesus in the flesh, but afterward received it" (D&C 76:73–74). Joseph Smith explicitly stated, "Those who were disobedient . . . were visited by our Savior," and "the Gospel [was] preached to them, by Him in prison."[96] Brigham Young was particular in making this point declaring that "as he [Christ] went to preach to them [the wicked], he certainly associated with them . . . precisely as our Elders associate with the wicked in the flesh, when they go to preach to them."⁹⁷ Either Joseph F. Smith received additional light on this matter or simply felt that confining Christ's preaching to the righteous provided a good explanation for why his visit to the spirit world was so brief. In any event, to accommodate this new explanation, he expanded the concept of "spirit prison" to include all those awaiting the resurrection (D&C 138:18–19, 49–50) and not just those held in confinement because of their wickedness. This makes it still possible to speak of Christ visiting the spirits in "spirit prison."

Perhaps the most significant contribution of President Joseph F. Smith's vision in terms of its impact on the doctrine of salvation for the dead is his teaching that all will have an opportunity to hear the gospel and accept or reject it in the spirit world, whether or not they had already heard the gospel in mortality. He states that Christ "appointed messengers . . . and commissioned them to go forth and carry the light of the gospel to them that were in darkness, even to all the spirits of men. . . . Thus was the gospel preached to those who had died in their sins, without a knowledge of the truth [i.e., the ignorant], or in transgression, having rejected the prophets [i.e., the rebellious]" (D&C 138:30, 32; see also v. 57). Furthermore, President Smith gives the impression that both the ignorant and the rebellious have the same opportunity to embrace the gospel and receive the saving ordinances thereof. Referring to both the ignorant and the rebellious he states, "[All] these were taught faith in God, repentance from sin, vicarious baptism for the remission of sins, [and] the gift of the Holy Ghost by the laying on of hands" (D&C 138:33). He further states, "The dead who repent will be redeemed, through obedience to the ordinances of the house of God" (D&C 138:58). This represents a significant departure from initial LDS teachings contained in the Book of Mormon where there is no postmortem evangelization, no chance for repentance after death, and no vicarious ordinances performed for departed spirits. In the Book of Mormon, the rebellious are damned from the moment they die and remain so on through the resurrection.

It should be noted that when Church leaders assembled to review the transcript of President Smith's vision, concerns were expressed regarding apparent inconsistencies it contained. Anthon H. Lund, first counselor to President Smith, reported in his diary that, on November 14, six weeks after the revelation was given, "the brethren" met in the temple and "discussed the Revelation given to Prest. [Joseph F.] Smith." Without elaborating, President Lund noted that "there were some contradictions in the mind of the brethren" with respect to elements of the revelation.⁹⁸ One seeming contradiction in President Smith's vision is that the very same spirits whom Christ trained to preach the gospel (v. 36) were presumably also among those to whom he gave power to rise with him in his resurrection. Indeed, it is generally held that "with Christ in his resurrection were . . . all the holy prophets . . . and . . . all the saints of all prior ages who had been true and faithful in all things—*all* came forth in glorious immortality when the Lord Jesus turned the key (D&C 133:54–56)."[99] If there were exceptions to those who were to be resurrected, it isn't made clear. It is also unclear why Jesus would have preached the gospel to the spirits of the righteous when presumably they had already heard and accepted the gospel, having been "faithful in the testimony of Jesus" when in the flesh (D&C 138:12). It is equally unclear why he would have needed to empower them to preach the gospel (v. 30), since righteous priesthood bearers presumably automatically continue their ministry in the spirit world (v. 57). Indeed, Joseph F. Smith taught that elders preach to departed spirits by virtue of the "authority conferred upon them in the flesh."[100] Finally, there is the unexplained oddity of seeing Moses and Elijah in the spirit world with no acknowledgment that they were translated beings and not spirits (D&C 138:49–50). The Prophet taught that the "habitation [of translated beings] is that of the terrestrial order"[101] and that their ministration is only "to embodied spirits."[102] The implication from the Prophet's teachings is that translated beings and disembodied spirits don't intermingle.[103] Incongruencies such as these, even if only apparent, can be puzzling to the reader.

Contemporary Mormonism

Several of the changing teachings in early Mormonism regarding who would have the opportunity to hear the gospel in the next life, have been brought together by Bruce R. McConkie with this explanation: "There is no such thing as a second chance to gain salvation by accepting the gospel in the spirit world after spurning, declining, or refusing to accept it in this life. It is true that there may be a second chance to hear and accept the gospel, but those who have thus procrastinated their acceptance of the saving truths will not gain salvation in the celestial kingdom of God."[104] Thus, those who reject the gospel in mortality "may" have the gospel preached to them in the spirit world but cannot be saved in the celestial kingdom and therefore don't benefit from saving ordinances performed in their behalf. The LDS Church publication *Gospel Principles* offers them no opportunity, stating, "Those who reject the gospel after it was preached to them . . . on earth . . . suffer in a condition known as hell. . . . After suffering for their sins, they will be allowed, through the Atonement of Jesus Christ, to inherit the lowest degree of glory, which is the telestial kingdom."[105] This absence of a second chance to hear and receive the gospel appears to be a step back from the teachings of Joseph F.

Smith, who taught that the rebellious will not only have an opportunity to accept the gospel, but also to obtain the full blessings that come through the saving ordinances vicariously performed for them.

Notes

1. John P. Sanders, *No Other Name: An Investigation into the Destiny of the Unevangelized*, 177–210.
2. Joseph Fielding Smith, *Doctrines of Salvation: Compiled Sermons of Joseph Fielding Smith*, 2:100–196.
3. Ibid., 158; Spencer J. Condie, "The Savior's Visit to the Spirit World," 32–36.
4. Joseph Smith Jr., "To the Saints Scattered Abroad," 138.; See also D&C 93:51.
5. Joseph Smith Jr., "Baptism for the Dead," 760.
6. Andrew F. Ehat and Lyndon W. Cook, *The Words of Joseph Smith*, 368.
7. Bruce R. McConkie states that in this vision, "it is clearly set forth that the whole spirit world, and not only that portion designated as hell, is considered to be a spirit prison." Bruce R. McConkie, "A New Commandment: Save Thyself and Thy Kindred!," 11.
8. See, for example, Bruce A. Van Orden, "Redeeming the Dead As Taught in the Old Testament," 268.
9. For a more detailed explanation of this context, see Robert E. Clark, "Baptism for the Dead and the Problematic of Pluralism," 111.
10. See, for example, Thomas Shillitoe, *An Address to Friends in Great Britain and Ireland*, 22.
11. Adam Clarke, *Commentary on the Bible*, s.v. Obadiah 1.
12. John Wesley, "John Wesley's Notes on the Bible," 2.12.2.
13. Ehat and Cook, *The Words of Joseph Smith*, 73–74. In January 1842, the Nauvoo High Council also counseled the Saints to be saviors on Mount Zion in the sense of watching out for each other's general welfare: "We feel to advise taking the word of God for our guide, and exhort you not to forget that you have come up as saviors upon Mount Zion, consequently to seek each other's good." *History of the Church*, 4:504.
14. Ehat and Cook, *The Words of Joseph Smith*, 77.
15. Ibid., 317, 320, 362, 370.
16. Brigham Young, June 22, 1856, *Journal of Discourses*, 3:372.
17. Russell M. Nelson, "The Spirit of Elijah," 84. For similar interpretations, see Gordon B. Hinckley, "Closing Remarks," 104; McConkie, "A New Commandment," 8.
18. Malachi's prophecy of the coming of Elijah is found in all four books of LDS scripture and five times in the Doctrine and Covenants alone. Only two of these occurrences, however, expressly allude to salvation for the dead (see D&C 128:17, 138:46–47). These two occurrences were also the only ones recorded after 1840 when Joseph Smith began teaching this doctrine.

19. Ehat and Cook, *The Words of Joseph Smith*, 318.
20. Edmond Jacob, "Death," 1:802.
21. G. C. Berkouwer, *Man: The Image of God*, 203.
22. Ibid., 270.
23. Quoted in ibid., 250.
24. F. F. Bruce, "Paul on Immortality," 469.
25. Colleen McDannell and Bernhard Lang, *Heaven: A History*, 33.
26. Berkouwer, *Man: The Image of God*, 264.
27. For a Christian commentary using this interpretation, see John Calvin, *Calvin's Bible Commentaries: Matthew, Mark, and Luke, Part III*, 287.
28. Ehat and Cook, *The Words of Joseph Smith*, 213.
29. M. Catherine Thomas, "Paradise," 3:1062.
30. Andrew T. Lincoln, *Paradise Now and Not Yet: Studies in the Role of the Heavenly Dimension in Paul's Thought with Special Reference to His Eschatology*, 80.
31. McConkie, "A New Commandment," 8.
32. Bruce R. McConkie, *The Mortal Messiah: From Bethlehem to Calvary*, 2:75.
33. W. D. Davies and A. C. Allison Jr., *A Critical and Exegetical Commentary on the Gospel According to St. Matthew*, 630–32.
34. Jack P. Lewis, "'The Gates of Hell Shall Not Prevail Against It' (Matt 16:18): A Study of the History of Interpretation," 349–67.
35. M. Catherine Thomas, "Hell," 2:585.
36. Donald Hagner, *Matthew 14–28*, 33b:471.
37. Hans Küng, *On Being a Christian*, 285.
38. Achtemeier, *I Peter*, 249.
39. *Gospel Principles* (2009), 243.
40. Joel B. Green, *1 Peter: Two Horizons New Testament Commentary*, 122. See also John P. Sanders, "Those Who Have Never Heard: A Survey of the Major Positions," 314.
41. Raymond E. Brown, *Introduction to the New Testament*, 716.
42. *New American Bible*, 1351–52.
43. David G. Horrell, "Who are 'The Dead' and When Was the Gospel Preached to Them?: The Interpretation of 1 Pet 4.6," 70.
44. Green, *1 Peter*, 128.
45. Victor Paul Furnish, "1 Corinthians," 2283.
46. Richard Trumbower, *Rescue for the Dead*, 33–34.
47. Origen, *De Principiis*, 2:5:3.
48. Calvin Green and Seth Youngs Wells, *A Summary View of the Millennial Church or United Society of Believers, (Commonly Called Shakers)*, 172.
49. Elhanan Winchester, *A Course of Lectures on the Prophecies*, 340–54.
50. "Thoughts on 1 Peter 3:19," *Methodist Magazine* 2 (October 1819): 376.
51. It may have been this passage that evoked the following comment from President Lorenzo Snow in an April 1901 general conference of the Church: "The antediluvians rejected the word of God; but they were the sons and daughters of God, and He did not reject them, only for a time. After twenty-five hundred years had passed away the Lord revealed Himself to them again and gave them another opportunity. Then they no doubt accepted, gen-

erally if not altogether, that which they refused in the days of Noah." Lorenzo Snow, "Opening Address," 5 April 1901 *Conference Report* (April 1901), 3.

52. Ehat and Cook, *The Words of Joseph Smith*, 77.
53. Smith, "Baptism for the Dead," 760.
54. Ibid.
55. Ibid., 760–61..
56. Krister Stendahl, "Baptism for the Dead, Ancient Sources," 1:97.
57. James D. G. Dunn, *Unity and Diversity in the New Testament: An Inquiry into the Character of Earliest Christianity*, 25.
58. Trumbower, *Rescue for the Dead*, 10–34.
59. Tertullian, quoted in *The Ante-Nicene Fathers*, 3:449.
60. John L. Brooke, *Refiner's Fire: The Making of Mormon Cosmology, 1644–1844*, 44.
61. Ehat and Cook, *The Words of Joseph Smith*, 10.
62. Ibid.
63. Ibid., 49.
64. Ibid., 331.
65. Smith, *Doctrines of Salvation*, 2:175.
66. Ehat and Cook, *The Words of Joseph Smith*, 346.
67. Wayne G. McCown, "Holiness in Hebrews," 58.
68. Although Latter-day Saints and many other Christians assume that people of the Old Testament had access to Christ's grace, neither Old nor New Testament texts support this reading. Bible commentator James Moffat states that "in handling the pre-Christian period of God's relations with Israel, ... he [Paul] never cites any Old Testament text for grace." He further observes, "It is not ... that Paul conceives of God as ungracious during the pre-Christian period; Israel had its religious benefits. But 'grace' is so distinctively the mark of the revelation of God in Jesus Christ that he reserves it exclusively for the experiences of Christian men. In other words, 'grace' belongs to the years A.D., not to B.C." James Moffat, *Grace in the New Testament*, 198, 209.
69. This doesn't mean that Joseph Smith didn't see references to vicarious work for the dead in more obscure passages. For example, according to the Prophet, the plural "baptisms" in Hebrews 6:2 signifies baptism for the living as well as for the dead. Joseph Smith, reported by Edward Stevenson in Joseph Grant Stevenson, *Stevenson Family History*, 1:83.
70. Samuele Bacchiocchi, "The Survival of the Soul: A Historical Glimpse of the Belief in the Survival of the Soul,"2.
71. *A Confession of Faith Put Forth by the Elders and Brethren of Many Congregations of Christians (Based Upon Profession of Their Faith,) in London and the Country*, 71.
72. John Cleveland, quoted in Dan Vogel, *Joseph Smith: The Making of a Prophet*, 245.
73. Timothy Merritt, "Divinity," 322.
74. Adin Ballou, *The Autobiography of Adin Ballou 1803–1890*, 79, 81.
75. Lorenzo Dow, *The Opinion of Dow; or, Lorenzo's Thoughts, On Different Subjects, in an Address to the People of New-England*, 134.
76. "Letters on the Atonement," 141.

77. Adams, "Middle Knowledge and the Problem of Evil," 109.

78. Brigham Young would later spiritualize this passage, arguing that there is no place "where God is not. Let me render this scripture a little plainer; when the spirits leave their bodies they are in the presence of our Father and God, they are prepared then to see, hear and understand spiritual things." Brigham Young, June 22, 1856, *Journal of Discourses*, 3:368.

79. Anthony Hutchinson notes that the phrase "in the day thou eatest thereof thou shalt surely die" (Gen. 2:17) was intended to mean "at the moment you eat from it you will most certainly die." Anthony A. Hutchinson, "A Mormon Midrash? LDS Creation Narratives Reconsidered," 25. A Jewish tradition is that God took pity on Adam and Eve and, rather than follow through with a punishment of death on the spot, banished them from the garden and consigned them to a life of toil and pain until their natural return to dust. The book of Abraham resolves the problem of why Adam and Eve didn't die in "the day" they partook of the forbidden fruit by redefining the length of a day to mean one thousand years (See Chapters 12 and 13). Joseph Smith changed the age at which Adam died from 930 to 1,000. Kent P. Jackson, *The Book of Moses and the Joseph Smith Translation Manuscripts*, 103. Joseph Smith informed Edward Stevenson that Adam lived within about six months of being 1,000 years old. Robert J. Matthews, *A "Plainer Translation": Joseph Smith's Translation of the Bible, a History and Commentary*, 84–85.

80. Joseph Smith Jr., "Present Age of the World," 22.

81. Gregory Prince, *Power from On High: The Development of Mormon Priesthood*, 143.

82. Smith, [no title], *Elders Journal*, 43.

83. Pratt, "The Gospel Illustrated in Questions and Answers," 27.

84. Prince, *Power from On High*, 144.

85. Ehat and Cook, *The Words of Joseph Smith*, 49; cf. *History of the Church*, 4:231.

86. Ehat and Cook, *The Words of Joseph Smith*, 193.

87. Ibid., 77.

88. Wilford Woodruff, in Brian H. Stuy, ed., *Collected Discourses*, 4:74. Woodruff made this remark to deter Mormons who wanted to be sealed to prominent Church leaders rather than to their own deceased parents, especially if those parents were non-Mormon. Before this, the Church actually prohibited Saints from being sealed to deceased non-Mormon parents. This all changed in 1894 when President Woodruff instructed Saints to be "sealed to their parents, and run this chain through as far as you can get it. When you get to the end, let the last man be adopted to Joseph Smith, who stands at the head of the dispensation. This is the will of the Lord to this people." (73). Of course, being sealed finally to Joseph Smith is no longer considered to be "the will of the Lord."

89. Ibid., 68.

90. See these *Journal of Discourses* citations: Heber C. Kimball, June 29, 1856, 4:4–5; John Taylor, April 8, 1875, 17:375; Taylor, October 10, 1875, 18:138–39; Wilford Woodruff, October 8, 1881, 22:333–34; Taylor, August 28, 1881, 22:308–9; Woodruff, January 27, 1883, 24:54–55.

91. Dean C. Jessee, ed., "The Kirtland Diary of Wilford Woodruff," 378. Just as Joseph understood early on that Christ would preach to the spirits in prison as a resurrected being, Woodruff was also to preach to the spirits in prison in the flesh, after he was caught up to heaven.

92. Ehat and Cook, *The Words of Joseph Smith*, 370.

93. Joseph F. Smith, *Gospel Doctrine: Selections from the Sermons and Writings of Joseph F. Smith*, 133, 430, 460.

94. John P., Hatch, *Anthon H. Lund, Danish Apostle: Diaries of Anthon H. Lund, 1890–1921*, 677 note 1. Several others who knew Hyrum, including doctors, did not agree with the the idea that Hyrum was taken in order to preach the gospel in the spirit world. His appendicitis had been diagnosed for several days and he had been warned in the strongest terms that he must have an operation, but he said God would take care of him because he observed the Word of Wisdom. Thus, by the time he finally gave in and had the operation, it was too late and doctors had little hope for him. Bishop Charles W. Nibley put things in perspective when he finally arose near the end of the funeral service and said, "Had it not been for the iron will of brother Hyrum M. Smith, he might have been with us here today."

95. It certainly adds more credibility to President Joseph F. Smith's assertion that Christ visited only those who were baptized Saints when the only other group he could have visited were the souls of the wicked who weren't worthy of his presence.

96. Smith, "Baptism for the Dead," 760–61.

97. Brigham Young, December 3, 1854, *Journal of Discourses*, 2:137.

98. Hatch, *Anthon H. Lund, Danish Apostle*, 713.

99. Bruce R. McConkie, *The Millennial Messiah: The Second Coming of the Son of Man*, 627; emphasis mine.

100. Smith, *Gospel Doctrine*, 133.

101. Ehat and Cook, *The Words of Joseph Smith*, 41.

102. Ibid., 77.

103. Hatch, *Anthon H. Lund, Danish Apostle*, 713.

104. Bruce R. McConkie, *Mormon Doctrine*, 685.

105. *Gospel Principles* (2009), 244.

~ 17 ~

The Priesthood

In Mormon theology priesthood is the "eternal power and authority of God" that, when delegated to men on earth, "enables them to act in God's name for the salvation of the human family. Through it, they can be authorized to preach the gospel, administer the ordinances of salvation, and govern God's kingdom on earth."[1] This authority or priesthood is conferred by the laying of hands upon worthy male members of the Church twelve years of age and older.

In biblical times, priesthood wasn't spoken of as an abstract principle independent of priests. Priesthood was simply the state or quality of being a priest. It wasn't receiving the priesthood that made one a priest, but rather being made a priest gave one priesthood—just as being dubbed a knight gives one knighthood. Mormonism, in contrast, considers priesthood to be more of an eternal principle than a quality. According to Joseph Smith, "The priesthood is an everlasting principle, and existed with God from eternity, and will to eternity, without beginning of days or end of years."[2] Thus, in Mormonism, priests "hold" the priesthood and are priests by virtue of their possession of that priesthood.

Nature of the Priesthood

In Mormon thought, priesthood is a power that has functioned intermittently on the earth in a consistent way since the beginning of the world. Joseph Smith taught that "the Priesthood was first given to Adam" who "obtained it in the Creation."[3] According to the book of Moses, "this same Priesthood, which was in the beginning, shall be in the end of the world also" (Moses 6:7). Because of this continuity in priesthood operation, Bruce R. McConkie states in *Mormon Doctrine* that, "basically, church organization is the same in all ages."[4] In his

1980 *The Church of the Old Testament,* LDS biblical scholar John Tvedtnes asserts that "the Church of God has in all ages been organized in essentially the same manner." His premise is that, since God is perfect, "it would be impossible to improve on the perfection of God's organization; thus, it must always be basically the same."[5]

Old Testament

In the Old Testament, priesthood is an institution that doesn't really come on the scene until the time of Moses. Prior to that time, God-fearing patriarchs offered sacrifices (Gen. 8:20, 12:7; Job 1:5) with no mention of priesthood. Indeed, it was a common practice among all nomadic peoples of the region for heads of families or tribal elders to offer sacrifices.[6] Joseph Smith, however, interjected several references to pre-Mosaic priesthood ordinations in his revision of the Bible. In the JST, "the Lord *ordained* Noah after his own order" (JST Gen. 8:7; emphasis mine). Enoch, Melchizedek, and other men were also "*ordained* after this order" (JST Gen. 14:30–33; emphasis mine). Similarly, the Pearl of Great Price has Abraham being "*ordained* to administer" the blessings of the fathers (Abr. 1:2; emphasis mine).

Modern LDS scriptures give a long genealogy of the priesthood from Adam to Moses (D&C 84:6–16, 107:41–53) indicating that the Melchizedek Priesthood was held throughout this period by righteous male adults as it was handed down from father to son (D&C 107:40). A revelation to Joseph Smith explained that because of Israel's hard heartedness at the time of Moses, God "took Moses out of their midst, and the Holy Priesthood also; and the lesser [i.e., Levitical] priesthood continued . . . with the house of Aaron among the children of Israel until John [the Baptist]" (D&C 84:25–27; see also JST Ex. 34:1).[7]

According to Mormon doctrine, this shift from a higher to a lesser priesthood did not mean that the higher or Melchizedek Priesthood was entirely removed from the earth. Joseph Smith declared, "All the prophets had the Melchizedek Priesthood and [were] ordained by God himself."[8] Just how God ordained these prophets—by the imposition of hands or merely by the word of his mouth—is unspecified. If by imposition of God's hands it would be inconsistent with the LDS teaching that the Father has never interacted with humans on earth except to introduce his Son. The Prophet's teaching that an ordination can be performed only by one having a physical body[9] also precludes the premortal, unembodied Christ from having conferred it.

At the time of Moses, the priesthood became a special duty of the tribe of Levi. Levites who descended through Aaron were consecrated priests (Num. 3:6–12). Aaron himself, and later his firstborn son, was to stand at the head of this priesthood as high priest. All other Levites not descended through Aaron were to act as assistants and servants.

The Lord commanded Moses to "anoint" Aaron and his sons (once and for all) to "be an everlasting priesthood throughout their generations" (Ex. 40:15). Catholic biblical scholar Joseph Pohle, writing in *The Catholic Encyclopedia*, explains, "This single consecration included that of all the future [male] descendants of the priests, so that the priesthood was fixed in the house of Aaron by mere descent, and was thus hereditary."[10] This anointing didn't necessarily imply an imposition of hands, since in the same place the Lord also commanded Moses to "anoint the tabernacle, and all that is therein" (Ex. 40:9).[11] After this one-time anointing of Aaron and his sons, subsequent descendants were initiated for service through a protracted and complex rite lasting more than a week which included various sacrificial offerings. The detailed description of this procedure mentions nothing of an ordination through the laying on of hands (see Lev. 8), even though the laying on of hands is expressly mentioned in other religious matters (see Num. 8:10, 12; 27:23).

The priesthood was for the purpose of performing religious ceremonies: sin offerings, burnt sacrifices, peace offerings, etc. These priests and Levites also looked after the sanctuary and were given charge over the vessels in the Lord's house. Though mentioned less frequently, priests were also given responsibility to "teach the children of Israel all the statutes which the LORD hath spoken unto them by the hand of Moses" (Lev. 10:11). Ezra was one such priest, charged to read the law to Israel (Ezra 8:1–8). The concept of priesthood as an empowerment to work miracles and heal the sick is not found in the Old Testament. In fact, nowhere in the Old Testament is priesthood expressly associated with imparting spiritual blessings of any kind, except, of course, the pardon from sin through sacrificial offerings.

In addition to priests and Levites was the office of high priest, of which there was only one at any given time.[12] Once each year, the high priest went into the "Holiest of all" (Heb. 9:3) to offer sacrifices for himself and for the people (Heb. 9:7). This high priestly office was not the same as the Melchizedek Priesthood office of high priest in Mormonism but was an appointment given to a descendant of Aaron, again with no express ordination.

Preaching repentance in ancient Israel seems to have been primarily the province of prophets. The Old Testament never explicitly mentions that these spiritual leaders had priesthood authority conferred on them—only that God verbally commissioned them to declare his word. This appointment to be the Lord's spokesperson was also given to prophetesses and kings (Ex. 15:20; Judg. 4:4; 2 Kgs. 22:14; Neh. 6:14). The calling came from God either directly as when "the angel of the Lord" spoke to Moses from the burning bush (Ex. 3:1–17), or through one of God's agents, as in the case of Elijah leaving his mantle with Elisha (2 Kgs. 2:13–14). Perhaps the closest thing resembling a modern priesthood ordination occurred when Moses was commanded to separate out Joshua and "put some of [his] honour upon him" (Num. 27:20). Moses therefore "laid his hands on him, and gave him a charge" (Num. 27:23) in front of all the people.

New Testament

The New Testament doesn't explicitly state that the priesthood was given to any of Christ's disciples. Priesthood appears to have been viewed in the Jewish sense of ministering Levitical priests, but who were now superseded by the ministry of Christ. The book of Hebrews explains that, in the Old Testament, a succession of priests had to be appointed by reason of their mortality, "but this man [i.e., Christ], because he continueth ever, hath an unchangeable priesthood" (Heb. 7:23–24). So while anciently each mediating priest was replaced by his successor, now and forevermore there was to be only "one mediator between God and men, the man Christ Jesus" (1 Tim. 2:5).

Hebrews speaks of Christ being a "priest after the order of Melchisedec" (Heb. 5:6–10), but gives no indication that any of Jesus's disciples possessed this priesthood. There is no concept in Hebrews of a general order of the priesthood called the Melchizedek Priesthood. Christ alone is extolled as a priest in the "similitude of Melchizedek" (Heb. 7:15). Drawing on contemporary speculations regarding the king-priest Melchizedek, the writer of Hebrews explains that Melchizedek, as a type of Christ, had "neither beginning of days, nor end of life; but made like unto the Son of God; abideth a priest continually" (Heb. 7:3).

Unlike the New Testament that singles out Christ and Melchizedek as alone becoming priests "continually" (Heb. 7:3), the Book of Mormon states, "There were many before [Melchizedek], and also there were many afterwards" (Alma 13:19) who, like Christ and Melchizedek, became priests "forever" (Alma 13:9). To correct this scriptural inconsistency, Joseph later modified Hebrews to read, "All those who are ordained unto this priesthood" become "like unto the Son of God; abiding a priest continually" (JST Heb. 7:3).

The only ministerial priests and high priests spoken of in New Testament narratives were Jewish leaders who persecuted the Christians. The ecclesiastical office of priest doesn't appear in the Christian church until the second century when it was instituted as an office to symbolize Christ and his sacrifice anew in the sacrament. Though ministerial priests appear to have been absent in the early church, in a figurative sense, all of Christ's disciples were "priests unto God" (Rev. 1:6). Thus, Peter told the Saints of his day, "Ye are a chosen generation, a royal priesthood, an holy nation" (1 Pet. 2:9). As spiritual priests, they were to offer "spiritual sacrifices" (1 Pet. 2:5). While Latter-day Saints today have developed what has been termed a "lay priesthood" (i.e., a priesthood that ordinary male members can hold), many Protestant churches subscribe to the New Testament "priesthood of the laity" (i.e., a priesthood that *all* members *do* hold).

The first ministerial officers introduced by Christ were twelve apostles chosen from among his disciples (Luke 6:13). Christ emphasized that they had not chosen him, but rather he had chosen them and "ordained" them (John 15:16). Whether this included the laying on of hands isn't specified. In the New Testament, the Greek word translated as "ordain" means "to appoint," hence most modern translations state that Jesus "appointed" the twelve. This appointment wasn't to the priesthood or to the apostleship *per se*, but simply "to bring forth fruit" (John 15:16).

In addition to commissioning twelve of his disciples to preach the gospel of the kingdom, Jesus "appointed other seventy also, and sent them two and two before his face into every city and place, whither he himself would come" (Luke 10:1). In LDS teachings, this appointment of seventy men is indicative of a priesthood office called "seventy."[13] The notion of "seventy" as a priesthood calling or office, however, doesn't appear in any early Christian writings.

After Christ's crucifixion, his apostles met to fill the vacancy in the twelve left by Judas, who had betrayed Jesus. As a result of casting lots, Matthias became "numbered with the eleven apostles" (Acts 1:26) with no mention of any ordination. This lone mention of one of the twelve being replaced is generally understood in Mormonism to be an indication that a body of twelve living apostles was to be maintained. Many scholars suggest, however, that this was a one-time occurrence to replace Judas who had transgressed and could no longer fulfill his role with the rest of the original twelve who were to be judges in the kingdom of God when it arrived (Matt. 19:28; Rev. 21:14), which was perceived as imminent. According to New Testament scholar Raymond Brown, "*The Twelve* were irreplaceable eschatological [end-time] figures, not part of church administrative structure."[14] Notably, Peter's explicit requirement for filling this vacancy was that it had to be someone who "companied with us all the time that the Lord Jesus went in and out among us, beginning from the baptism of John" (Acts 1:21–22). First-hand knowledge of Christ's ministry, from the time of his baptism, seemed crucial to qualify as one of the twelve.

Those referred to as apostles in the New Testament, besides the Twelve, may have only been so designated in a generic sense ("apostle" literally means "one who is sent"). This would include Paul (Rom. 1:1), Barnabas (1 Cor. 9:5–6), and James, the Lord's brother (Gal. 1:19). The LDS Bible dictionary (s.v. "apostle") notes: "The New Testament does not inform us whether these three brethren also served in the council of the Twelve as vacancies occurred therein, or whether they were apostles strictly in the sense of being special witnesses for the Lord Jesus Christ. Jesus is referred to as an apostle in Heb. 3:1–2, a designation meaning that he is the personal and select representative of the Father." The New Testament even makes reference to a female apostle named Junias (Rom. 16:7). The Twelve Apostles seem to have had a unique status in the history of the early Christian church, and there is little indication in any of the early Christian annals of an understanding that additional apostles would succeed them.

There is no early record indicating an understanding that the death of the apostles spelled the end of the church or of the ability to function for the salvation of Christian believers. The earliest Church Fathers, who had first-hand acquaintance with the Twelve Apostles and wrote after their passing, spoke of the ministration of bishops as the natural progression of the Church administration, which apparently functioned for a time without a central administration. Near the end of the first century, Clement, bishop of Rome, wrote a letter to the saints in Corinth detailing "the orderly way" in which God had arranged for the succession of authority in the Church. He explained that the apostles had "appointed . . . bishops and deacons" and "afterwards gave instructions [to the bishops], that when these [bishops and deacons] should fall asleep, other approved men should succeed them in their ministry."[15] He gave no indication that God had originally planned for a succession of apostles in the Church. Ignatius of Antioch, who lived in the first century and was believed to have been a student of John the Apostle, spoke of the church as being fully functional under the direction of the bishops and presbyters following the death of the apostles.[16] These early Church Fathers spoke of the bishops as simply carrying on the work the Twelve had begun.

Latter-day Saints assume that the church would have been no longer complete without twelve apostles and cite Ephesians 2:19–20, which states that the church is built on the foundation of "apostles and prophets." New Testament scholars explain, however, that "apostle" here doesn't refer to an office (anymore than "prophet" does). Rather, it is a generic term (Greek *apostolos* = "one who is sent") applying to anyone sent forth to preach the gospel.

As Christianity spread further from its original center in Jerusalem, bishops or presiding elders were appointed to shepherd local congregations. Acts 14:23 records that Paul and Barnabas appointed elders in every church. The concept of "elder" came to the church naturally from its Jewish roots. Anciently, elders were simply the oldest men of a tribe who were usually entrusted with tribal leadership.

The New Testament terms "elder," "presbyter," "overseer," "pastor," and "bishop" are all descriptive titles for the same function of overseer. In Acts 20:17 Paul sends for the "elders" (*presbuteros*) of the church and gives them charge to "watch over . . . the flock of which the Holy Spirit has made you overseers [*episkopos*]" (Acts 20:28). When Paul writes to Timothy about the appointment of church leaders he uses the term "bishop" (1 Tim. 3:1), a translation of the Greek *episkopos*, which literally means "overseer." Phillip Schaff, historian of early Christianity, writes, "The terms Presbyter (or Elder) and Bishop (or Overseer, Superintendent) denote in the New Testament one and the same office, with this difference only, that the first is borrowed from the Synagogue, the second from the Greek communities; and that one signifies the dignity, the other the duty."[17] New Testament scholar F. F. Bruce similarly states, "There was in apostolic times no distinction between elders (presbyters) and bishops such as we find in the second century onwards: the leaders of the Ephesian church are indiscriminately described as elders, bishops (i.e., superintendents) and shepherds (or pastors)."[18] Thus, it wasn't until the post-apostolic church that a distinction began to be made between elders and bishops.

In general, elders or bishops were to govern or direct the affairs of the local churches (1 Pet. 5:1–3) and have charge over the saints' spiritual welfare (1 Tim. 3:1–7; Titus 1:5–9). In the New Testament, there wasn't necessarily a single bishop over each congregation, but each congregation appears to have had an overseeing body of bishops or elders, analogous to the board of elders in the Jewish synagogue.[19]

In addition to apostles and elders (or presbyters) is the less frequently mentioned calling of deacon (Greek *diakonos* = servant) (1 Tim. 3:8–13). The deaconate was not given any association with the Aaronic Priesthood, nor was it an office conferred on pre-teens as it is today. Deacons were to be adults and "husbands of one wife" with a record of "ruling their children and their own houses well" (1 Tim. 3:12).

Many roles in the apostolic church that Latter-day Saints consider to be ordained priesthood callings were actually spoken of in the New Testament as gifts or callings of the Spirit. In enumerating these ministerial gifts, Paul states that Christ "gave some to be apostles, some to be prophets, some to be evangelists, some to be pastors and teachers" (NIV Eph. 4:11). An evangelist, incidentally, was simply a preacher; not, as Joseph Smith asserted, a patriarch or "the oldest man of the blood of Joseph or of the seed of Abraham."[20] Prophets appear to be ranked second to apostles on the list of persons gifted by the Spirit. NIV 1 Corinthians 12:28 states: "In the church God has appointed first of all apostles, second prophets, third teachers, then workers of miracles, also those having gifts of healing . . . and finally those speaking in different kinds of tongues (cf. Eph. 2:19–20)." New Testament authority James Dunn explains, "These ministries should not be thought of as established or official ministries, and they were certainly not ecclesiastical appointments or church offices. Indeed we are told specifically in the case of Stephanas and his household that 'they took upon themselves their ministry to the saints' (1 Cor. 16:15)."[21] Prophets were prophets because they had the spiritual gift of prophecy, not because they were ordained prophets. Teachers were those who had the gift of teaching. In Paul's "body" metaphor for the church, everyone has a different role to play based primarily on his or her particular spiritual gift, not on an ecclesiastical calling (Rom. 12:3–8, 1 Cor. 12:1–31).

There is occasional mention of those discerned as possessing "ministerial gifts" having this gift confirmed upon them by the laying of hands (1 Tim. 4:14, 2 Tim. 1:6), but once again, the word "priesthood" or "authority" is never used. It was "the Holy Spirit" that "made" one a minister in the church (Acts 20:28). Ministerial gifts were thus listed right along with the gift of tongues and the gift of healing. Such gifts are often omitted in LDS discourse on spiritual gifts.[22]

Early Nineteenth-Century Christianity

By the time of Joseph Smith, several distinct views had developed regarding the qualifications and procedure for being called to the ministry. Callings in most Protestant faiths were generally considered to be twofold: spiritual and ecclesiastical. A spiritual or divine call came when one sensed his or her (Baptists, Quakers, and Methodists all allowed women preachers) election from God to be a minister. This call was believed to come through the Holy Ghost as one of the gifts of the Spirit spoken of in the New Testament (Eph. 4:11). An ecclesiastical call occurred when an ordained minister laid his hands on the one called and set him (or her) apart for the ministry.

There were two predominant beliefs regarding ecclesiastical callings at the time of Joseph Smith. Episcopalians believed that the choice and call of a minister rested with the superior clergy. Evangelical Christians (Methodists, Baptists, Presbyterians, etc.) believed that it should rest with the vote of the people to whom he is to minister.[23] Alexander Campbell claimed ecclesiastical authority to ordain through the consent of his congregation. Early Mormonism likewise tended to be more democratic than autocratic and, following the pattern of most evangelical Christians, required a "vote" of the Church for individuals to be ordained to callings (D&C 20:65).

Many New Testament ecclesiastical titles can be found in early American Protestant religions including "deacon," "elder," and "bishop." One of the most common titles used in Protestant churches on the American frontier was "elder." Free Will Baptists used "elder" generically for any ordained preacher and it wasn't uncommon for congregations to have several elders.[24] In the Methodist Church, as would occur in early Mormonism, the office of elder or presbyter was the highest office in the church. The "duties" of Methodist elders were "to preach, to administer the ordinances, and to watch over the Church."[25] They were to "have the authority of government . . . [and] the power of ordaining to the ministry."[26] These duties and authority are essentially the same that would be spelled out for early Mormon elders (D&C 20:42–51). Several groups, including Shakers and Disciples of Christ, had elders ministering in spiritual affairs while confining deacons to the temporal duties of the church.[27]

While ministerial callings were generally for the purpose of governance, preaching, and performing ordinances, some restorationists extended the ministerial role to include the working of miracles just as those whom Christ called and sent forth (Luke 10:9, 17–20). As will be seen, this was the empowerment that LDS convert Sidney Rigdon insisted should be part of the newly restored church.

The Book of Mormon

The word "priesthood" appears in the Book of Mormon only in reference to the "office of the high priesthood" (Alma 13:18), which was synonymous with being a high priest—just as it would also be in the Doctrine and Covenants.[28] There is no mention of priesthood as an abstract principle of authority like the Aaronic or Melchizedek Priesthood. Like much of early nineteenth-century Protestantism, the Book of Mormon speaks only of ministerial callings or orders to which individuals were called, for purposes such as preaching, baptizing, and leading congregations. Nowhere in the Book of Mormon are priests found offering sacrifices or performing other priestly rites so characteristic of the law of Moses—ordinances which the Nephites were commanded to keep (Mosiah 13:27; see also 2 Ne. 5:10, 25:25; Alma 25:15).

Not even the performance of miracles or bestowal of spiritual blessings are tied to priesthood in the Book of Mormon. As LDS scholar Gregory Prince notes, "The Book of Mormon . . . did not link tangible power to priesthood."[29] Those who exercised spiritual power in the Book of Mormon did so through the power of the Holy Ghost, not through the priesthood. Similarly, Book of Mormon prophets don't condemn those in the latter days who reject the priesthood, but rather those who deny "the power of the Holy Ghost" (2 Ne. 28:26; 3 Ne. 29:6).

The Book of Mormon often mentions the laying on of hands when individuals are called to ministerial offices (Alma 6:1; Moro. 3:2–3), but whenever callings are given to leading prophets, the laying on of hands is not specifically mentioned. Jacob was "ordained" and "consecrated" by Nephi, but nowhere is Nephi's ordination mentioned. (In 1 Nephi 10:22, "the Holy Ghost giveth [Nephi] authority.") The prophet Alma received authorization to baptize through "the Spirit of the Lord" (Mosiah 18:13). Nephi, the son of Helaman, ordained men unto the "ministry" to baptize (3 Ne. 7:25), but Nephi's authority is unexplained. Nephi was also given power to seal on earth and in heaven, a power he received, not through ordination, but through the voice of God (Hel. 10:6–7).

Alma 13 refers to non-Levitical high priests living before the time of Moses and describes "the manner after which they were ordained" (Alma 13:3) with no mention of the laying on of hands. One gathers from the text that their calling was a calling of the Spirit only. While inferences drawn from silence are inconclusive, one should not simply assume that the Book of Mormon understanding of priesthood follows modern LDS teachings. For instance, in the case of Alma, it is assumed that he was ordained because he performed baptisms. By inference, it is also assumed that he was already baptized—even prior to his own self-baptism recorded in Mosiah 18:14. This assumption is based on the current LDS practice of being baptized before receiving the priesthood. Joseph Fielding Smith remarked, "If he [i.e., Alma] had authority to baptize that is evidence that he had been baptized."[30] Such a supposition, however, is nowhere supported in the Book of Mormon text itself.

In the Book of Mormon there are only three offices: apostles or elders (the twelve disciples Christ chose in America were never explicitly referred to as apostles), priests, and teachers. The Book of Mormon says nothing about deacons, bishops, seventies, or patriarchs. Priests and teachers in the Book of Mormon received their callings through ordination or consecration (the word "appointed" is occasionally used) and had essentially identical duties, including baptizing (Alma 15:13) and presiding over congregations (Alma 45:22–23). The single distinction made is that only priests, together with elders, could administer the sacrament (Moro. 4:1–2).

It is currently assumed that ministers in the Book of Mormon held the Melchizedek Priesthood since none of the tribe of Levi came to America.[31] This assumption, however, is problematic given the mention of offices in the Book of Mormon that are typically associated with the Aaronic Priesthood: priests and teachers. Joseph Fielding Smith explained that the consecration of Jacob and Joseph as "priests and teachers" was "a general assignment to teach, direct, and admonish the people" and not an actual ministerial calling.[32] This explanation seems inconsistent, however, with other places in the Book of Mormon where the consecration of priests and teachers was clearly a ministerial calling (Alma 6:1, 15:13).

Joseph Fielding Smith further taught that, while there was no Aaronic Priesthood in America prior to Christ, "when the Savior came to the Nephites . . . not only was the fulness of the Melchizedek Priesthood conferred, but also the Aaronic, just as we have it in the Church today."[33] This assertion of Aaronic Priesthood presence in the Nephite church seems to be based, however, on the assumption of uniformity with the modern LDS Church. The text itself gives no indication of the Aaronic Priesthood operating after Christ's coming.

Early Mormonism

Prior to the publication of the Book of Mormon and formation of the Church, revelations to Joseph Smith regarding requirements for ministering in the kingdom make no mention of the priesthood. Revelations given to individuals between February and June 1829 merely state, "If ye have desires to serve God ye are called to the work" (D&C 4:3; see also 6:4; 11:4; 12:4; 14:4). In the list of qualifications for the ministry (D&C 4:5–7), having priesthood authority was not one of them. In March 1829, a revelation on behalf of Martin Harris stated, "Wo shall come unto the inhabitants of the earth, if they will not hearken [unto] my words" (Book of Commandments IV:3). To this was added in the 1835 publication of the Doctrine and Covenants: "For hereafter you shall be ordained and go forth and deliver my words unto the children of men" (D&C 5:6). Later also added to this same revelation was the instruction: "You must wait yet a little while; for ye are not yet ordained" (D&C 5:17). Even the book of Moses, written mostly during the latter part of 1830, initially made no mention of "priesthood" during the generations of Adam and his posterity—only that preaching took place by the Holy Ghost (Moses 5:14, 58).[34]

When the Church organization began taking shape in April 1830, the first several offices defined were identical to those mentioned in the Book of Mormon and equally few in number consisting only of apostles or elders, priests, and teachers (Alma 4:7; D&C 20:38–64).[35] D. Michael Quinn notes that, at the first conference of the Church held June 9, 1830, there were only twelve officers: seven elders, three priests and two teachers.[36] The first mention of deacons occurs in October 25, 1831.[37] The offices of deacon, bishop, and high priest that now appear in section 20 of the Doctrine and Covenants were added in late 1831.[38]

Similar to other Protestant denominations and the Book of Mormon, LDS elders were presiding authorities, and thus Joseph Smith was called the "first elder" and Oliver Cowdery the "second elder" (D&C 20:2–3). Richard Bushman observes that they were just like the presiding elders in Congregational and Presbyterian churches and had similar duties.[39]

One key to understanding how the priesthood was initially perceived in the early LDS Church is to recognize that, in the Book of Mormon and other LDS literature prior to 1832, there was no concept of priesthood apart from one's calling. Authority was understood as inherent in what are now termed offices.[40] People were called to ministerial offices with no mention of priesthood being conferred.

Moroni 2–6 and Doctrine and Covenants 20 (as it was first published) are nearly identical in outlining the organization and procedures to be followed in Christ's church. Oliver Cowdery initially composed this set of "procedural regulations" in Doctrine and Covenants 20, relying on the Book of Mormon for more than 50 percent of its content.[41] This consisted of only three ministerial offices (teacher, priest and elder), with no mention of Aaronic or Melchizedek Priesthood, and only a few simple ordinances and doctrines. The instruction for baptizing included only the requirement that "the person . . . is called of God and has authority from Jesus Christ to baptize" (D&C 20:73; see also 3 Ne. 11:25).

The organization of the LDS Church in 1830 was strikingly similar to contemporary evangelical denominations with which Joseph was familiar. Richard Bushman observes: "Nothing in this initial organization would have surprised a Methodist, save for the absence of a bishop to superintend the whole."[42] The duties of LDS elders were initially spelled out in terms similar to those prescribed for elders in the Methodist Church: overall supervision, ordaining priests and teachers, and performing ordinances. The early LDS Church, like the Methodist church, had both "traveling" elders (D&C 124:39) with no jurisdictional restriction and "standing" elders assigned to a particular locale (D&C 124:137).

The title of apostle in the early LDS church was not initially an office but was simply another name for an elder (D&C 20:38),[43] at least until 1835 when the Twelve were ordained. These apostles or elders, not priests, were initially given the responsibility "to baptize" (D&C 18:29).

The first bishop in the Church was Edward Partridge who was ordained on February 4, 1831 (D&C 41:9). The office of bishop is mentioned nowhere in the Book of Mormon, though it appears in the New Testament (1 Tim. 3:1–7). According to Gregory Prince, "The evidence suggests that Sidney Rigdon, a convert from Campbellism, played the pivotal role in bringing the matter [of the New Testament precedent for the office of bishop] to Joseph Smith's attention."[44] Prince notes that a key tenet of Campbellism was that "there were only two legitimate offices in the ancient church, bishop and deacon." Within the Campbellite movement, Rigdon had "risen to the office of bishop. Eventually he and Campbell parted ways over gifts of the spirit. Shortly thereafter . . . [Mormon missionaries] converted Rigdon. Within weeks Rigdon and fellow Campbellite Edward Partridge journeyed to New York to meet Joseph Smith, arriving in December 1830." Rigdon immediately became Joseph's confidant and scribe. "It is significant," says Prince, "that the first bishop of the Restoration was Partridge and that he was ordained by Rigdon in Smith's presence."[45]

Although bishops in the New Testament had ministerial duties that were spiritual in nature (they were presiding elders in the Church), in the early LDS Church the role of bishop was confined to "administering all temporal things" (D&C 107:68).

As already discussed, priesthood callings in the Book of Mormon—and initially in the Church—weren't directly linked to spiritual powers. Prince argues that Rigdon not only prompted the creation of the office of bishop, but also influenced Joseph's decision to add the concept of power to the priesthood.[46] While yet a Campbellite minister, Rigdon evidently believed that ministers of Christ should be vested with spiritual gifts. According to LDS scholars Jill Mulvay Derr and Karen Lynn Davidson, "In August of 1830, three months before he was baptized by Mormon elders, Sidney rigdon had had a doctrinal falling out with Alexander Campbell over the importance of spiritual gifts and communal property."[47] Rigdon arrived in New York in December 1830 and, within days, acted as Joseph's scribe in receiving a revelation enhancing the nature of priesthood callings to include "power." Elders would now "be endowed with power from on high" to more effectively bear testimony among the nations (D&C 38:32). It was shortly after receiving this revelation that Joseph Smith, with Sidney Rigdon as scribe, revised Genesis 14 so that it attributed extraordinary, outward manifestations of power to those like Melchizedek who are "ordained . . . after the order of the son of God" (JST Gen. 14:26–32). This development contrasts with earlier teachings in the Book of Mormon which depict Melchizedek as "having exercised mighty faith," but only to the extent that he "received the office of the high priesthood" (Alma 13:18) and was effective in preaching repentance.

In June 1831, a new "order" called the order of the high priesthood was introduced and conferred upon elders for the first time. This office added an endowment of power to the authority they already held as elders. The Prophet remarked "that the order of the high-priesthood is that they have the power given them to seal up the

Saints unto eternal life. And said it was the privilege of every elder present to be ordained to the high priesthood."[48] Within two weeks, elders exercised their new power by sealing entire congregations to eternal life.[49]

By October 1831, high priesthood seemed to mean the office of high priest with no further reference to a spiritual endowment. Today the high priesthood is understood to mean the higher or Melchizedek Priesthood and not the office of high priest as it did during the life of the Prophet. LDS scholar Lyndon Cook explains: "Joseph Smith and his associates did not equate high priesthood with Melchizedek Priesthood. Only high priests held the high priesthood; as such they were recognized as the elite of the priesthood. . . . After the Prophet's death the significance began to diminish, and eventually the term high priesthood became synonymous with Melchizedek Priesthood and 'higher priesthood.'"[50]

With most of the priesthood offices being in place by the middle of 1831, in November 1831 Joseph introduced the Old Testament notion of a hereditary or lineal right to the office of bishop, stating that "no man has a legal right to this office, to hold the keys of this priesthood, except he be a literal descendant of Aaron" (D&C 68:18). Lineal privileges also appeared in connection with the patriarchal priesthood which was the "right of the firstborn" (Abr. 1:2–4), which "rightly belongs to the literal descendants of the chosen seed" (D&C 107:40). What motivated this reinstitution of ancient lineal priesthood rights? According to Bushman, "The return to ancient lineage priesthood appears to be another manifestation of Joseph's penchant for Hebrew religion."[51] Like his adoption of the belief that ancient sacrifices would be reinstated, Joseph was evidently drawn to Old Testament lineal privileges.

Nauvoo Period

During the Nauvoo period, Joseph Smith gave almost exclusive attention to the power or authority restored by Elijah when speaking of priesthood authority, equating it with what has come to be known as "the fulness of the priesthood." The fulness of the priesthood was reserved for those who received their second anointing. Speaking to a congregation of Saints in Philadelphia on Sunday, August 6, 1843, Brigham Young explained, "For any person to have the fullness of that priesthood, he must be a king and priest."[52] Ordinances conferring this authority were instituted on September 28, 1843, and over the next five months were received by twenty men and their wives.[53]

The Prophet taught that the conferral of the fulness of the priesthood was a "sealing . . . on top of the head,"[54] and that it fulfills the prophecy in Revelation 7:2–3 describing God's servants being "sealed in their foreheads."⁵⁵ Furthermore, Joseph taught that this ordinance would qualify men to be part of the special missionary force in the last days—144,000 high priests (D&C 77:8–11). This number comes from Revelation 7:4 which states, "And I heard the number of them which were sealed: and there were sealed an hundred and forty and four thousand of all the tribes of the children of Israel." The Prophet conferred these blessings on at least seventeen men prior to his death.⁵⁶

Contemporary Mormonism

The organization and operation of the priesthood have continued to undergo changes since the time of Joseph Smith. Most notable are the addition and deletion of administrative positions and modification of certain duties. For years the Church had a Church patriarch, assistants to the Twelve, and stake seventies, but these have been discontinued. Minimum age requirements have now been set for offices in the Aaronic Priesthood and for the office of elder. The Aaronic Priesthood, which was earlier considered to be a calling for mature adults, is now given to all worthy males at age twelve.⁵⁷ The Melchizedek Priesthood is currently given to worthy male adults eighteen years of age and older regardless of lineage. Members today don't think so much in terms of "voting" (D&C 20:65) to *approve* individual callings in the priesthood (the revelations call this principle "common *consent*"), but rather tend to talk more in terms of "sustaining" individuals to callings in the sense of pledging support to them.

It should be noted that ministerial callings in the Book of Mormon and early LDS Church were specified as spiritual callings to be made "according to the gifts and callings of God unto him" (Moro. 3:4; D&C 20:60). In contrast, today these same ordinations, from deacon to elder, are generally made as a matter of course with no consideration for whether the individual possesses the spiritual gift of the calling, only that age and worthiness requirements have been met.

Where Joseph Smith emphasized lineal rights to the priesthood, such as patriarch, bishop and even elder, today there is no inherent benefit in being of any particular lineage when it comes to priesthood. In fact, in current practice no priesthood offices or callings are granted based on lineal considerations.

Today, the fulness of the priesthood is generally not thought of as being received when one has been sealed up to eternal life. Rather, every individual who receives the ordinances of the temple is assumed to have received the fulness of the priesthood. Joseph Fielding Smith taught, "Every man who is faithful and will receive these ordinances and blessings [in the temple] obtains a fulness of the priesthood, and the Lord has said that 'he makes them equal in power, and in might, and in dominion.'"[58]

Blacks and the Priesthood

The most dramatic change in the priesthood in recent years occurred in June 1978 when President Spencer W. Kimball announced that the priesthood was now available to "all worthy male members of the church . . . without regard for race or color" (D&C Official Declaration 2). This declaration ended the nearly 130-year ban on blacks from holding the priesthood.

There is no indication in the Bible that blacks were *cursed* pertaining to the priesthood or any other blessings of the gospel. Though Jesus initially confined his preaching to the Jews (Matt. 10:5–6), Peter was later shown that gentiles (i.e., non-Jews) were now privileged to receive the same blessings previously limited to the Jews (Acts 10:9–18). Peter states, "Of a truth I perceive that God is no respecter of persons: But in every nation [i.e., regardless of race or ethnicity] he that feareth him, and worketh righteousness, is accepted with him" (Acts 10:34–35). Even the Book of Mormon expressly states that there is no distinction in privilege between "black and white," but "all are alike unto God" (2 Ne. 26:33).

When the priesthood was first introduced in the Church, it doesn't appear to have been withheld from any males who were worthy. Joseph Smith's sanction of the ordination of Elijah Abel, a free black, to the office of elder in March 1836, and later in the same year to seventy, is evidence that the Prophet was at least initially unopposed to free blacks holding the priesthood.[59]

The first recorded statement on the priesthood ban appears to be by Parley P. Pratt who said of a black Church member on April 25, 1847, he "was a black man with the blood of Ham in him which linege was cursed as regards the priesthood."[60] On February 13, 1849, Brigham Young echoed a popular folklore linking blacks to descendants of Cain when he remarked in a private conversation, "The Lord had cursed Cain's seed with blackness and prohibited them the Priesthood."[61] Then, in 1852, he issued a public proclamation that blacks could not hold the priesthood, saying, "Any man having one drop of the seed of Cain in him cannot receive the priesthood."[62]

Various Church leaders from the time of Brigham Young to the middle of the twentieth century have made pronouncements to the effect that blacks would never hold the priesthood until after the millennium. Brigham Young, for example, declared that blacks could "never" hold the priesthood "until the last ones of the residue of Adam's posterity are brought up to that favorable position."[63] He made it clear that this would be after all others had been redeemed and resurrected.[64] In the mid-twentieth century, Joseph Fielding Smith similarly taught, "Not only was Cain called upon to suffer, but because of his wickedness he became the father of an inferior race. A curse was placed upon him and that curse has been continued through his lineage and must do so while time endures."[65] Of course, these pronouncements were all nullified with the revelation granting the priesthood to blacks in 1978. Shortly after the priesthood ban was lifted, Bruce R. McConkie gave this explanation for past misspoken declarations: "We spoke with limited understanding and without the light and knowledge that has now come into the world."[66]

Why blacks were denied the priesthood in the first place has been and continues to be a bit controversial.[67] Some have concluded that the priesthood was withheld from them because they were presumed to be of the lineage of Cain through Ham who, according to LDS scripture, was "cursed . . . as pertaining to the Priesthood" (Abr. 1:26–27). Recognizing that God would not punish children for the sins of their fathers, it became commonly held that it was denied them in consequence of their lack of valiancy in the preexistence.[68] As early as 1844, LDS apostle Orson Hyde attributed the "accursed lineage of Canaan" to a premortal lack of valor. "Those spirits in heaven that lent an influence to the devil," he stated, "were required to come into the world and take bodies in the accursed lineage of Canaan; and hence the Negro or African race."[69]

More liberal-minded Saints have seen the ban as largely the influence of popular folk myths that were in circulation at the time to discriminate against blacks and justify slavery. Armand Mauss, an LDS emeritus professor of sociology at Washington State University, states: "Much of the conventional 'explanation' for the priesthood restriction was simply borrowed from the racist heritage of nineteenth-century Europe and America, especially from the justifications for slavery used in the ante-bellum South."[70] In a 2008 issue of BYU Studies commemorating the thirtieth year since the priesthood ban was lifted, Edward L. Kimball, son of Spencer W. Kimball, and Marcus H. Martins, BYU-Hawaii chair of religious education and son of Helvécio Martins, the first black LDS General Authority, effectively confirmed this same conclusion.[71]

In the early nineteenth century, it was widely speculated that a black skin was given as the mark of the curse of Cain which was believed to have continued through Canaan, the son of Ham.[72] In Genesis 9:25–27, the Lord cursed Canaan, the son of Ham, saying, "Cursed be Canaan; a servant of servants shall he be unto his brethren" (Gen. 9:25). Mauss notes that "many Mormons and other Christians (of a fundamentalist variety) have given the far-fetched interpretation that this curse was the origin of the postdiluvian Negro race and its troubles, including persecution, discrimination, and (for Mormons) the withholding of the priesthood."[73] LDS scholar Lester Bush observes that "Mormon scripture [i.e., the book of Abraham] and the contemporary proslavery arguments are striking" in their perpetuation of this lore.[74]

The book of Abraham implies that Cain was barred from the priesthood and that this curse continued from Cain through Ham: "From Ham sprang the race which preserved the curse in the land" (Abr. 1:24). According to Bruce R. McConkie, "Noah's son Ham married Egyptus, a descendant of Cain, thus preserving the Negro lineage through the flood."[75] The story of Egyptus appears in Abraham 1:20–25.

Given the LDS notion that Ham was the one through whom the "Negro lineage" continued after the flood,[76] some Mormon critics have considered it ironic that Joseph Smith, whom Brigham Young called a "pure Ephraimite,"[77] would not have also been cursed as to the priesthood since, according to LDS scholar Hugh Nibley, "Joseph [of the Old Testament] married Asenath [an Egyptian], who was the daughter of the high priest of Heliopolis and a direct descendant of Ham."[78] This would make both Ephraim and Manasseh—from whom the majority of Church members have been told they descend—half Hebrew and half Egyptian, carrying the blood of Ham.

In contrast to traditional LDS teachings, many Old Testament scholars see Noah's curse on Canaan as having had historic fulfillment in the Old Testament itself in a way that shows a clear bias in favor of Shem over Canaan. The Israelites, who descended from Shem, were commanded to march into the land of Canaan and utterly destroy its inhabitants. These biblical Canaanites were not black, by the way, but were culturally, religiously, and ethnically very close to the Israelites themselves. The descendants of Japeth, were "the people of the North" (the Assyrians, Medes, and Persians) who eventually ruled the land of Canaan and subjugated not only the descendants of Ham, but occupied Shem's dwelling place, thus fulfilling the part of the curse that "God shall enlarge Japheth, and he shall dwell in the tents of Shem; and Canaan shall be his servant" (Gen. 9:27). Biblical scholar Scott Foutz notes: "To look beyond this obvious fulfillment of Noah's curse in the biblical narrative of the Old Testament and seek rather to claim its relevance to various epochs of institutionalized slavery or racial discrimination is to employ a hermeneutic [i.e., method of interpretation] which relies much more heavily on subjective commentary than upon the text."[79]

Despite the fact that McConkie later repudiated authoritative pronouncements extending the priesthood ban until after the millennium, he made no effort to renounce the doctrine that blacks were less valiant in the preexistence or that their skin color still preserves the mark of their curse. Armand Mauss notes,

> Ironically, the doctrinal folklore that many of us thought had been discredited, or at least made moot, through the 1978 revelation continued to appear in Elder McConkie's own books written well after 1978, and continues to be taught by well-meaning teachers and leaders in the Church to this very day. The tragic irony is that the dubious doctrines in question are no longer even relevant, since they were contrived to "explain" a Church policy that was abandoned a quarter century ago.[80]

The Church's apparent unwillingness to disavow the doctrinal basis for denying blacks the priesthood has been a thorn in the side of many black members. As African American Mormon David Jackson expressed, "What [the 1978 revelation] doesn't say is we're no longer of the lineage of Cain, that we no longer did these things in preexistence. It does not say we are not cursed with black skin."[81] As a result of this lingering doctrinal legacy, a tendency persists among many Latter-day Saints to view the 1978 revelation on the priesthood much as they view the Manifesto: It is a change in practice only but doesn't overturn the underlying doctrine. Just as many Latter-day Saints still believe polygamy to be an eternal principle, the belief still seems to linger that blacks were less valiant spirits in the preexistence.

This reticence to repudiate past doctrinal explanations for the priesthood is beginning to change. Apostle Jeffrey R. Holland, in a March 4, 2006 PBS interview, called such explanations "folklore" and said, they "must never be perpetuated." Referring to earlier Church leaders who promoted this folklore he said, "I'm sure, in their own way, [they] were doing the best they knew to give shape to [the ban], to give context for it, to give even history to it. All I can say is however well intended the explanations were, I think almost all of them were inadequate and/or wrong." According to Elder Holland, "We just don't know, in the historical context of the time, why it was practiced."[82]

Whatever the reason for the priesthood ban, Martins observes that the lifting of this ban has reestablished "doctrinal consistency," since it is more in conformance with the original teachings of Joseph Smith. According to Martins, "the revelations given to Joseph Smith . . . establishing the orders of the priesthood in the modern era are broad and all-inclusive in scope, meaning that they established no restrictions regarding which tribes or lineages could hold the priesthood in this last dispensation."[83] Today, priesthood inclusivity for worthy men is once again enthroned as the doctrine of the church.

Notes

1. *Gospel Principles* (2009), 67.
2. Andrew F. Ehat and Lyndon W. Cook, *The Words of Joseph Smith*, 8.
3. Ibid.
4. Bruce R. McConkie, *Mormon Doctrine*, 140.
5. John A. Tvedtnes, *The Church of the Old Testament*, iv.
6. J. Bergman, H. Ringren, and W. Dommershausen, "Kohen," 66.
7. McConkie, *Here We Stand*, 146.
8. Ehat and Cook, *The Words of Joseph Smith*, 59.
9. Though the principle that only those with a physical body can ordain others having physical bodies is implied in Doctrine and Covenants 129, later LDS teachings have made it explicit. Oscar W. McConkie, writing in the *Encyclopedia of Mormonism* states, "Spirits can convey information, but they cannot confer priesthood upon mortal beings, because spirits do not lay hands on mortals." Oscar W. McConkie, "Angels," 1:41.
10. Joseph Pohle, "Priesthood," 411.
11. Latter-day Saints have become accustomed to assuming Aaron was ordained through the laying on of hands and therefore interpret Hebrews 4:5 ("No man taketh this honor [of being a high priest] unto himself, but he that was called of God, as was Aaron") to mean that one can only receive the priesthood by the laying on of hands. It should be noted, however, that this is nowhere implied in Hebrews, which emphasizes only *the fact* that Aaron was "called of God," not *the manner* in which God called him.
12. At least twice, two contemporary men were called high priests (1 Chron. 15:11; Luke 3:2), but only one was the legal high priest.
13. Alan K. Parrish, "Seventy," 3:1301.
14. Raymond E. Brown, *An Introduction to the New Testament*, 283 note 8.
15. Clement, "Epistles of Clement," 1.42–43.
16. See Luke Timothy Johnson, *Among the Gentiles: Greco-Roman Religion and Christianity*, 237.
17. Phillip Schaff, *History of the Christian Church*, 1:491.
18. F. F. Bruce, *The New International Commentary on the New Testament: The Book of Acts*, 415.
19. Brown, *An Introduction to the New Testament*, 646.
20. Ehat and Cook, *The Words of Joseph Smith*, 6. Richard L. Bushman expressed bewilderment as to "why 'evangelical minister' was ever used [to designate Patriarchs], considering the title suggested a gospel preacher." His only explanation was that it allowed Joseph to introduce a new office in the Church while still adhering to the New Testament "model for Church organization." Richard L. Bushman, *Joseph Smith: Rough Stone Rolling*, 261.
21. James D. G. Dunn, *Unity and Diversity in the New Testament: An Inquiry into the Character of Earliest Christianity*, 122.
22. George Brinkerhoff, "Gifts of the Spirit," 2:544–46, lists only charismatic gifts (healing, tongues, etc.) as gifts of the Spirit with no mention of or consideration given to administrative gifts such as the gift of being an apostle or an evangelist.
23. Charles S. Buck, *A Theological Dictionary*, 373.

24. Deborah Vansau McCauley, *Appalachian Mountain Religion: A History*, 102.

25. Bostwick Hawley, *Manual of Methodism*, 172.

26. Ibid.

27. "History of the Shakers," 339. Alexander Campbell, "A Restoration of the Ancient Order of Things—No. XIX," *Christian Baptist* 4, no. 10 (May 7, 1827): 335. Disciples preferred to call their elders "bishops." See also Mark Lyman Staker, *Hearken, O Ye People: The Historical Setting for Joseph Smith's Ohio Revelations*, 31–33.

28. David Whitmer, one of the three witnesses, explained that Alma 13 "is speaking of the order of the High Priests before Christ. . . . [B]ut when Christ came into the world, he then claimed his own holy order of priesthood and power on earth, doing away with all types and shadows under the old law, himself alone being our great and last High Priest unto whom we can go to obtain mercy and find grace to help in time of need." David Whitmer, *An Address to All Believers in Christ*, 64.

29. Gregory A. Prince, *Power from On High: The Development of Mormon Priesthood*, 16 note 46.

30. Joseph Fielding Smith, *Answers to Gospel Questions*, 3:203.

31. W. Ladd Hollist, "Priest, Aaronic Priesthood," 3:1132.

32. Smith, *Answers to Gospel Questions*, 1:124.

33. Ibid., 1:127.

34. The lone reference to the priesthood in Moses 6:7 is a later emendation appearing in Sidney Rigdon's handwriting. Kent P. Jackson, *The Book of Moses and the Joseph Smith Translation Manuscripts*, 102.

35. Prince, *Power from On High*, 48.

36. D. Michael Quinn, *The Mormon Hierarchy: Origins of Power*, 11.

37. William G. Hartley, "From Men to Boys: LDS Aaronic Priesthood Offices, 1829–1996," 85.

38. Prince, *Power from On High*, 48.

39. Bushman, *Joseph Smith: Rough Stone Rolling*, 253.

40. Prince, *Power from On High*, 2.

41. Scott H. Faulring, "The Book of Mormon: A Blueprint for Organizing the Church," 60–71.

42. Bushman, *Joseph Smith: Rough Stone Rolling*, 254.

43. Quinn notes that several early LDS missionaries were given titles of "apostle" and "prophet," but without the significance they have today. Prior to 1834, "charismatic or visionary experience" and "missionary service" were sufficient to qualify one as an "apostle." Quinn, *The Mormon Hierarchy: Origins of Power*, 9–14.

44. Prince, *Power from On High*, 63.

45. Ibid., 63–64.

46. Ibid., 15–18.

47. Jill Mulvay Derr and Karen Lynn Davidson, "A Wary Heart Becomes 'Fixed Unalterably' Eliza R. Snow's Conversion to Mormonism," 118.

48. Joseph Smith, quoted in Donald Q. Cannon and Lyndon W. Cook, *Far West Record: Minutes of the Church of Jesus Christ of Latter-day Saints, 1830–1844*, 20–21.

49. Prince, *Power from On High*, 20.

50. Lyndon W. Cook, *The Revelations of the Prophet Joseph Smith: A Historical and Biographical Commentary of the Doctrine and Covenants*, 136–37.

51. Bushman, *Joseph Smith: Rough Stone Rolling*, 261. According to David Whitmer, "This matter of two orders of priesthood in the Church of Christ, and lineal priesthood of the old law being in the church, all originated in the mind of Sidney Rigdon." Whitmer, *An Address to All Believers*, 64.

52. *History of the Church*, 5:527.

53. Ehat and Cook, *The Words of Joseph Smith*, 241.

54. Ibid.

55. Ibid., 240.

56. Ibid., 297.

57. For the history of this change, see Hartley, "From Men to Boys," 80–136.

58. Joseph Fielding Smith, *Doctrines of Salvation: Compiled Sermons of Joseph Fielding Smith*, 3:132–33.

59. Lester E. Bush Jr., "Mormonism's Negro Doctrine: An Historical Overview," 17.

60. General Minutes, April 25, 1847, quoted in Ronald K. Esplin, "Brigham Young and Priesthood Denial to the Blacks," 395.

61. Brigham Young, Journal History, February 13, 1849, quoted in Bush, "Mormonism's Negro Doctrine," 25.

62. Brigham Young, quoted in Matthias Cowley, comp. and ed., *Wilford Woodruff: His Life and Labors*, 351.

63. Brigham Young, October 9, 1859, *Journal of Discourses*, 7:291.

64. Brigham Young, December 3, 1854, *Journal of Discourses*, 2:143 and August 19, 1866, 11:272.

65. Joseph Fielding Smith, *The Way to Perfection*, 101–2.

66. Bruce R. McConkie, "All Are Alike unto God."

67. For a recent treatment on the history of blacks and the priesthood, see Armand L. Mauss, *All Abraham's Children: Changing Mormon Conceptions of Race and Lineage*.

68. McConkie, *Mormon Doctrine*, 527; Smith, *Doctrines of Salvation*, 1:66–67.

69. Orson Hyde, "Speech of Orson Hyde, Delivered before High Priests Quorum, in Nauvoo, April 27, 1845 . . .," quoted in Bush, "Mormonism's Negro Doctrine," 27.

70. Armand L. Mauss, "Dispelling the Curse of Cain: Or How to Explain the Old Priesthood Ban without Looking Ridiculous," 57.

71. Edward L. Kimball, "Brigham Young and Priesthood Denial to the Blacks: An Alternate View," 10–19; Marcus H. Martins, "Thirty Years after the 'Long-Promised Day': Reflections and Expectations," 81.

72. Bush, "Mormonism's Negro Doctrine," 16.

73. Armand L. Mauss, "Mormonism and the Negro: Faith, Folklore, and Civil Rights," 25–26.

74. Lester E. Bush Jr., "A Commentary on Stephen G. Taggart's 'Mormonism's Negro Policy: Social and Historical Origins'," 93.

75. McConkie, *Mormon Doctrine*, 527.

76. For an informative work on the interpretive tradition of the biblical story of Ham, see Stephen R. Haynes, *Noah's Curse: The Biblical Justification for American Slavery*.

77. Brigham Young, April 8, 1855, *Journal of Discourses*, 2:268.

78. Hugh W. Nibley, *Teachings of the Book of Mormon—Semester 1: Transcripts of Lectures Presented to an Honors Book of Mormon Class at Brigham Young University, 1988–1990*, 1:20.

79. Scott Foutz, "Theology of Slavery: Western Theology's Role in the Development and Propagation of Slavery."

80. Armand L. Mauss, "The LDS Church and the Race Issue: A Study in Misplaced Apologetics."

81. David Jackson, quoted in Larry B. Stammer, "Mormons May Disavow Old Views on Blacks," A-1.

82. Jeffrey R. Holland, quoted in "The Mormons: Interview, Jeffrey Holland."

83. Martins, "Thirty Years after the 'Long-Promised Day,'" 81.

~ 18 ~

The Gathering of Israel and Establishment of Zion

In LDS theology, the principal way in which the millennial kingdom will be realized is through the gathering of Israel and establishment of Zion. The tenth Article of Faith states: "We believe in the literal gathering of Israel and in the restoration of the Ten Tribes; that Zion (the New Jerusalem) will be built upon the American continent; that Christ will reign personally upon the earth; and, that the earth will be renewed and receive its paradisiacal glory" (A of F 10). As evidenced in this 1842 declaration of beliefs, early Latter-day Saints had a rather literalistic understanding of the gathering with all of Israel, including the ten lost tribes, being restored to their homelands, and with a holy city called Zion being built in preparation for Christ's millennial reign. Today, the gathering is spoken of more in terms of drawing converts into the stakes and wards of the Church throughout the world, and the expression "building Zion" is used more as a way to designate how the world-wide Church is increasing in size and strength.[1] Here we explore how the doctrine of the gathering and establishment of Zion appears to have developed since ancient times.

Biblical Prophecies of the Gathering

At the time of Joseph Smith, Christians had heightened expectations regarding the gathering of Israel, particularly the gathering of the Jews. Furthermore, many Protestants believed that America would play a key role in facilitating this gathering.[2] Beginning with the Puritans in the mid-seventeenth century, there was a growing perception that biblical prophecies concerning the end of days were beginning to be fulfilled, and many Christians were anxiously awaiting, among other impending events, the mass conversion of the Jews.

Old Testament

The gathering of Israel is a theme that originated in the Old Testament after the scattering and captivity of Israel. The northern kingdom of Israel was taken captive by the Assyrians ca. 722 B.C. followed by the captivity of the southern kingdom of Judah by the Babylonians ca. 587 B.C. Prophets of both kingdoms spoke of their return to the lands of their inheritance (Jer. 31:7–12, 32:37–40; Ezek. 36:24). This return wasn't spoken of as a distant future event, nor did Old Testament prophets predict multiple gatherings and remote gathering places. They merely reassured scattered Israel that God had not forsaken them but would deliver them from their oppressors and bring them back to their Palestinian homeland. Robert Carroll, a lecturer in Old Testament at the University of Glasgow, notes that Old Testament prophets "did not talk about last things but about a day or period in the near future when the present troubles would be over and the more positive aspects of Israelite life would be enjoyed without hindrance from any source."[3] Despite hopes of a renewed kingdom, the Persian king Cyrus permitted only a remnant of Jews to return. Although these few Jews were allowed to rebuild their temple and their city, they never became an independent nation in their own land. They acted as mere tributaries, first to the Persians, then to the Greeks, and finally to the Romans, under whose iron yoke they were when Jesus was born. Hence came the wistful query of his disciples: "Lord, wilt thou at this time restore again the kingdom to Israel?" (Acts 1:6).

New Testament

In contrast to the Old Testament, the New Testament says very little about any future gathering of Israel. Only one New Testament scripture is listed in the LDS Topical Guide under "Israel, Gathering of," and it refers to a gathering of the "children of God" (presumably Christian believers) rather than of Israelites and mentions no gathering location, only that they are to be gathered "in one" (John 11:51–52).

A more familiar New Testament passage often interpreted as a prophecy of the latter-day gathering is Matthew 24:28: "For wheresoever the carcase is, there will the eagles be gathered together." An LDS interpretation is that the carcass is the church or kingdom of God and the gathering of the eagles is the gathering of Israel.[4] At first glance, this seems like a plausible interpretation and was one way

Christians understood this passage at the time of Joseph Smith.[5] The Prophet effectively canonized this interpretation by appending the following explanation to this verse: "so likewise shall mine elect be gathered from the four quarters of the earth" (JST Matt. 24:28; see also JS–M 1:27; JST Luke 17:37).

However, when this passage is read carefully and in context, one wonders if Jesus might have rather envisioned the dead carcass as representative of the wicked being smitten in judgment. Luke places this passage in the context of the destruction of the wicked, comparing it to "the days of Noe [Noah]" (Luke 17:26) and "the days of Lot" (Luke 17:29). Jesus explains that people will be "taken" without warning from their beds and while working in their fields (Luke 17:34–36). When asked where they will be taken, Jesus gives the enigmatic response, "Wheresoever the body is, thither will the eagles be gathered together" (Luke 17:37). Given the context and suddenness of the event, it implies a swift destruction rather than a gradual or even accelerated gathering.

According to most scholarly commentaries, those being "taken" correspond to the dead carcass, not to the eagles. Some scholars see the reference to "eagles" as an allusion to the insignia of the Roman army and therefore as a reference to the Roman overthrow of Jerusalem in A.D. 70.[6] Interestingly, the Greek word translated "eagles" is the same word for "vultures" which, in this context, many scholars, as well as the NASB and NIV translations, agree is the intended meaning, since eagles aren't generally known to flock.[7] In either case, the image isn't one of righteous souls gathering around the living Christ or standard of truth, but of menacing predators converging upon their prey. According to one New Testament commentary, "Jerusalem is like a dead and putrid corpse. Its life is gone, and it is ready to be devoured. The Roman armies will find it out, as the vultures do a dead carcass, and will come around it, to devour it."[8]

Biblical Prophecies of Latter-day Missionary Work

Latter-day Saints consider missionary work to be the principal means of spiritually gathering Israel in the last days, and several Old Testament passages are cited as prophecies of this effort. One of these is Isaiah 18:1–2 which reads: "Woe to the land shadowing with wings, which is beyond the rivers of Ethiopia: That sendeth ambassadors by the sea, even in vessels of bulrushes upon the waters, saying, Go, ye swift messengers, to a nation scattered and peeled, to a people terrible from their beginning hitherto; a nation meted out and trodden down, whose land the rivers have spoiled!" In 1825, Ethan Smith published his popular *View of the Hebrews* which interpreted "the land shadowing with wings" as the western hemisphere where "the two great wings of North and South America meet, as at the body of a great eagle."[9] Early LDS expositors adopted this same popular, literalistic interpretation as evidenced in a February 1843 editorial in the *Latter-day Saints Millennial Star*, which stated that the passage has reference "to the two continents of America, which in their general formation as laid down upon the maps, have a resemblance to expanded wings."[10] Apostle Orson Pratt frequently cited this passage as a reference to North and South America which, he noted, "has the appearance of shadowing with wings."[11] Nearly a century later, Joseph Fielding Smith not only interpreted the wings as the Americas, but replaced "Woe" with "Hail," so that the passage reads as a salutation rather than a malediction.[12] In this interpretation, America is to be hailed in the last days for sending LDS missionaries as "swift messengers" into the world.

Scholars view this passage in a completely different light, for they see it as depicting political turmoil in the region of ancient Israel. Joseph Blenkinsopp, writing in the Anchor Bible commentaries, explains that "the initial [Hebrew] *hôy* can be a simple exclamation demanding attention (as Isa. 17:12) but in this instance it introduces a woe-saying directed against Nubia [i.e., Ethiopia]."[13] The Hebrew expression translated in the KJV as "land shadowing with wings" is rendered "land of whirring wings" in the NRSV or "land of buzzing insect wings" in the Anchor Bible, which is said to refer to Ethiopia's ancient notoriety as a land infested with insects.[14] The NRSV, like other modern translations, refers in verse 2 to a "land the rivers divide" and inhabited by people who are "tall and smooth." J. J. M. Roberts, writing in *The HarperCollins Study Bible*, explains that "Ethiopia or Nubia [was] divided by branches of the Nile."[15] Moreover, "the Nubians of ancient Ethiopia were black, tall and . . . clean shaven," thus answering the description "tall and smooth."[16]

Roberts explains that the ambassadors in this passage have reference to Ethiopian messengers soliciting support "for Ashdod's revolt against Assyria in 714 B.C.E. In opposition to the Ethiopian messengers encouraging Judah to join this revolt (see Isa. 14:32; 20:1–6), Isaiah insists that one must wait for God's appointed time of harvest."[17] In short, scholars view this passage as describing contemporary conflicts in the region, not modern missionaries being sent out from America. This makes the lifting of the "ensign" and blowing of the trumpet in verse 3 a literal call to arms, not an invitation to receive the gospel.

Jeremiah 16:16 is another oft-cited Old Testament passage presumed to be a reference to latter-day missionary work: "Behold, I will send for many fishers, saith the LORD, and they shall fish them; and after will I send for many hunters, and they shall hunt them from every mountain, and from every hill, and out of the holes of the rocks." The chapter heading in the LDS edition of the King James Bible explains that "fishers and hunters shall gather [Israel]," and the footnote for this verse references "missionary work." This interpretation overlooks the context in which these words are spoken, which is one of condemnation. The Lord threatens to scatter Israel and bring judgment upon the people for their wickedness. The reason for sending fishers and hunters in verse 16 is explained in the very next verse: "For mine eyes are upon all their [Israel's] ways: they are not hid from my face, neither is their iniquity hid from mine eyes" (v. 17). So the fishers and hunters are actually "Gentiles" (v. 19) that the Lord sends to invade and destroy Israel, consuming them "by the sword" (v. 4; see also vv. 17–18; Lam. 4:18). As one Old Testament scholar explains, the image of the fishermen and hunters was used "to emphasize the impossibility of escaping the coming punishment."[18] Leo Perdue, professor of Hebrew Bible at Brite Divinity School, indicates that "the fishermen and hunters may represent, respectively, the Egyptians (Isa. 19:5–10) and Babylonians (Lam. 4:18–19)."[19] Thus, the imagery portends a dual onslaught on the Israelites as a consequence of their waywardness.

In turning to the New Testament, one passage commonly cited in LDS discourse as a prophecy of latter-day missionary work is Matthew 24:14: "And this gospel of the kingdom shall be preached in all the world for a witness unto all nations; and then shall the end come." Read in context, this preaching appears to refer to proselytizing activities then going on and coincides with the destruction of Jerusalem in A.D. 70 (vv. 15–16). Joseph Smith, however, amended it to read that the gospel will be preached "again" indicating a later, second missionary period (JS–M 1:31). This change creates support for the latter-day restoration of the gospel, but it seems inconsistent with the text and with the eschatological view expressed elsewhere in the New Testament, which has Christ's gospel being preached uninterruptedly to all nations of the then-known world, followed by "the end" (see Chapter 2).

That New Testament writers saw the gospel as having already been preached to the world is evidenced by Paul's remark that "their sound went into all the earth, and their words unto the ends of the world. . . . The preaching of Jesus Christ . . . now is . . . made known to all nations" (Rom. 10:18; 16:25–26). To the Colossians he wrote, "The gospel . . . is come unto you, as it is in all the world" (Col. 1:5–6). Several verses later he reemphasizes that "the gospel, which ye have heard . . . was preached to every creature which is under heaven" (Col. 1:23). The sense one gets from the composite New Testament teachings is that the end was in sight—not two millennia in the future after yet another round of gospel preaching.

Spiritual vs. Temporal Gathering

In colonial America, Christians understood the gathering of the Jews primarily as a spiritual gathering to Christ rather than a literal gathering to their homeland. "At first" observes Grant Underwood, an LDS scholar in early Mormon history, "many held to this spiritual 'calling' of the Jews but not to a physical return to Israel." He notes, however, that "by the time Increase Mather delivered his famous sermon 'The Mystery of Israel's Salvation,' [1667] the idea of a temporal restoration was commonplace."[20]

Latter-day Saints shared popular views regarding the temporal and spiritual gathering of the Jews. Debates among millennialists at the time of Joseph Smith addressed two main issues: (1) whether the Jews would be converted (spiritually gathered) prior to or after Christ's coming, and (2) whether the gathering to their homelands (temporal gathering) would occur before or after their conversion.

Presbyterian clergyman Elias Boudinot (1740–1821) and Congregationalist Reverend Ethan Smith (1762–1849) believed that the second coming was imminent and that the Jews must be converted before he comes.[21] Stephen Epperson, a student of early Mormon teachings pertaining to Jews, relates: "More literalistic Christian views of the Millennium . . . led [some Christians] to anticipate that the last days were imminent and that they would live to witness the inauguration of the millennial reign of Christ with his saints. Linked to these beliefs was the conviction that restoring the Jewish people to a nation in the Holy Land and converting them *en masse* to Christianity were necessary precursor events to the Millennium."[22]

Christians who believed that the conversion and gathering of the Jews would precede Christ's second coming tended also to believe that the conversion or spiritual "restoration" of the Jews would precede their temporal "restoration." Toward the end of his 1815 treatise on the second coming, Boudinot devotes several pages in a plea to the Jews to convert to Christianity. He believed that this was the only possible way the Jewish portion of the "House of Israel" would ever become acceptable to God and be blessed to return to Jerusalem and the Holy Land.[23]

Other Christians believed that the Jews would be physically gathered to Israel before becoming converted and that their conversion wouldn't occur until after Christ sets foot on the earth again. This view was based largely on the Christian millenarian interpretation of Zechariah 12–14, which describes the battle at Armageddon in which the gathered Jews are besieged by hostile gentiles and, at the crucial moment of the battle, are delivered by the Lord whom, according to the millenarian interpretation, they would not recognize as Jesus until he showed them the wounds in his hands and feet. Jews would then repent and accept Christ as their savior.

This interpretation seems to confuse two unrelated passages. While scholars agree that Zechariah 14 refers to the Lord coming to rescue the Jews from their enemies, which is the oft-prophesied "day of the Lord" (Zech. 14:1), they don't see the Lord as being the same individual whose wounds are spoken of earlier in Zechariah 13. Indeed, the question asked in Zechariah 13:6, "What are these wounds in thine hands?" isn't addressed to the Lord who later (Zech. 14:4) stands on the Mount of Olives, but rather to "the prophets [who] . . . deceive" (Zech. 13:4). Thus, the NRSV more clearly renders verse 6 as a question put to "them," i.e., the false prophets. W. Sibley Towner, professor of biblical interpretation at Union Theological Seminary, explains that the response these prophets give—that the wounds were received in the house of friends (Zech. 13:6)—is effectively a "denial that the wounds [were inflicted as] . . . punishment for prophesying."[24] Biblical scholars, therefore, see Zechariah 13 as a rebuke of false prophets followed later in Zechariah 14 by the dreaded day of the Lord.

As for the popular Christian notion that the Lord in Zechariah 14 is Christ and that the Jews will be converted *en masse* at his appearance, it should be observed that the chapter speaks of the Lord in the same ordinary sense of the God whom the Jews had always worshipped, with no wounds or other tell-tale marks. There is no indication of any change of belief or practice in the Jews after the Lord's appearance, much less a full-scale conversion of any kind. On the contrary, Zechariah 14:18–20 indicates that, after the Lord appears, Jewish festivals and sacrifices will continue to be observed in the same traditional fashion.

Congruent with many early nineteenth-century views, the Book of Mormon also speaks of a latter-day "temporal and spiritual" gathering of Israel (1 Ne. 22:3). The gathering is to be first spiritual and then temporal (2 Ne. 30:5–7; 3 Ne. 20:30–33, 21:26–28). According to the Book of Mormon, to be gathered spiritually is to be "restored to the true church and fold of God" (2 Ne. 9:2). The temporal gathering occurs when these converts are then "gathered home to the lands of their inheritance, and . . . established in all their lands of promise" (2 Ne. 9:2; see also 25:15–18; Jer. 16:14–21). Thus, in the Book of Mormon, modern Israelites are to become converted to the gospel while yet scattered (2 Ne. 25:15–16).

In the Book of Mormon, conversion to the gospel is not only a precursor, but a precondition to being temporally gathered. According to 2 Nephi 6:11, "When they [the Jews] shall come to the knowledge of their Redeemer, they shall be gathered together again to the lands of their inheritance" (see also 2 Ne. 9:1–2, 10:7). It is as though the blessing of receiving their lands of inheritance is predicated on their acceptance of Christ.

LDS teachings after the Book of Mormon are mixed when addressing the issue of whether the Jews would be converted to Christ before or after their return to Palestine. This ambivalence is due largely to what appears to be conflicting revelations on the subject. At least one revelation reinforces the popular Christian interpretation of Zechariah by placing the conversion of the Jews after their gathering (D&C 45:51–53), while Book of Mormon passages (cited above) have the Jews converting before their gathering to Palestine.

Even though most current LDS doctrinal expositors acknowledge that the Book of Mormon indeed teaches that conversion precedes the gathering,[25] an exception is made when specifically considering the Jews who have already begun to return to Palestine yet show little inclination to convert to Mormonism.[26] The general view as it relates to the Jews is based on Zechariah 12–14 and Revelation 11, which both Latter-day Saints and evangelicals interpret to mean that the Jews will be converted in the wake of the second coming. According to this popular Christian view, the Jews will gather to their homeland, be besieged by gentile hordes, and at the crucial moment in this battle, called Armageddon, be delivered by a messiah whom they will not recognize until he shows them the wounds in his hands and feet (see D&C 45:51–53). Any uncertainty about their deliverer's identity will then be swept away. McConkie states that the Jews "will then weep for the sins of their ancestors, be converted, and become the valiant souls that the children of the prophets should be."[27] Fourth Church president Wilford Woodruff expressed this view in 1873, declaring, "They [i.e., the Jews] do not believe in Jesus of Nazareth now, nor ever will until he comes and sets his foot on Mount Olivet and it cleaves in twain."[28]

To reconcile Book of Mormon prophecies of a pre-gathering conversion of the Jews with later teachings of a post-gathering conversion, Bruce R. McConkie appeals to 2 Nephi 30:7: "And it shall come to pass that the Jews which are scattered also shall begin to believe in Christ; and they shall begin to gather in upon the face of the land; and as many as shall believe in Christ shall also become a delightsome people." The interpretation he gives is that the Jews will only "begin" to believe before their gathering, with their real conversion to follow.[29] The passage suggests, however, that when the Jews "begin to believe," only to that extent will they "begin to gather." The implication, particularly in light of the Book of Mormon passages cited above, is that the Jews will be gathered only as they come to believe in Christ.

For some LDS commentators, the clarity of the Book of Mormon teaching that conversion precedes gathering—even for the Jews—is incontrovertible. BYU Hebrew professor Donald Parry and his brother

Jay, a prolific LDS expositor, repudiate the common LDS view that Jews will be converted after their gathering. Citing Book of Mormon passages noted above, they argue that "the gathering of the Jews will follow the same pattern as that of everyone else;" so that for "all the house of Israel, the spiritual gathering precedes and leads to the temporal gathering."[30] Three other LDS scholars stop short of acknowledging the prior conversion of "all" Jews who gather to Israel, stating that, "although according to Elder Wilford Woodruff a certain number of the Jews will 'gather to their own land in unbelief,'. . . the Book of Mormon makes it clear that the greater part will gather only after they have come to believe in Jesus as the Messiah."[31] In point of fact, the referenced Wilford Woodruff sermon doesn't confine the number of Jews who will gather to Palestine in unbelief to only "a certain number," but rather states without exception: "The Jews have got to gather to their own land in unbelief."[32] As previously indicated, Wilford Woodruff taught that only Christ's personal appearance would convert the Jews. Moreover, the Book of Mormon nowhere suggests that only "the greater part" of those Jews who gather will first be converted. Such harmonizing tendencies seem to be symptomatic of a uniformist view of LDS doctrine.

Lamanite Role in the Gathering

Another aspect of the gathering that has doctrinal significance in LDS theology pertains to the role of the Lamanites, whom Latter-day Saints have traditionally understood as being inclusive of essentially all Native Americans.[33] Many early nineteenth-century Christians believed that Native Americans were descendants of the house of Israel and that it was the role of Christians to restore them to the gospel. This was the view of Ethan Smith, a Congregational clergyman who published *View of the Hebrews: or, the Tribes of Israel in America* in 1823 and 1825. "If our natives be indeed from the tribes of Israel," he wrote, "American Christians may well feel, that one great object of their inheritance here, is, that they may have a primary agency in restoring those 'lost sheep of the house of Israel.'"[34]

The emphasis on the Lamanites as the primary focus of gospel preaching and recognition of their divinely appointed leadership role in the gathering has diminished since the time of Joseph Smith. The Book of Mormon taught that a "remnant of Jacob" (i.e., the Lamanites) would be the main focus of the gathering in America and that the gentiles (i.e., non-Lamanites) would have the privilege of being "numbered among" the Lamanites if they repent. If the gentiles don't repent, they will be "beat[en] in pieces" and "cut off" from the land which has been "given [to the Lamanites] . . . . for their inheritance" (3 Ne. 16:14–15,

20:15–20, 21:11–13, Morm. 5:20–24). In the Book of Mormon account of Christ's visit to America, he prophesied to the descendants of Lehi using language from Micah:

> And my people who are a remnant of Jacob [i.e., Lamanite descendants] shall be among the Gentiles, yea, in the midst of them as a lion among the beasts of the forest, as a young lion among the flocks of sheep, who, if he go through both treadeth down and teareth in pieces, and none can deliver.
> Their hand shall be lifted up upon their adversaries, and all their enemies shall be cut off. . . .
> And I will cut off the cities of thy land, and throw down all thy strongholds. (3 Ne. 21:12–13; see also Micah 5:7–11).

Commenting on this passage, Parley P. Pratt explained, "This destruction includes an utter overthrow, and desolation of all our Cities, Forts, and Strong holds—an entire annihilation of our race, except such as embrace the Covenant and are numbered with Israel."[35] Joseph Smith's prophecy on war given in 1832 predicted that, when slaves rise up against their masters in the United States, "it shall come to pass also that the remnants [i.e., Lamanites] who are left of the land will marshal themselves, and shall become exceedingly angry, and shall vex the Gentiles with a sore vexation" (D&C 87:1–5).

The Book of Mormon also has the Lamanites taking the leadership role in building the city of New Jerusalem, while converted gentiles "shall assist my people, the remnant of Jacob, and also as many of the house of Israel as shall come, that they may build a city, which shall be called the New Jerusalem" (3 Ne. 21:23). According to Book of Mormon witness David Whitmer, "Christ says that the 'remnant of Jacob' (the seed of Lehi, unto whom this land was consecrated) are the people who shall build that city, and the gentiles are only to assist them to build it. The other people who shall also assist them to build that city are 'as many of the house of Israel as shall come' into the covenant."[36] In 1837, Parley P. Pratt similarly wrote, "the remnant of Joseph, (the Indians) . . . will finally build a New Jerusalem; a city of Zion; with the assistance of the believing Gentiles."[37]

Not surprisingly, the first missionaries of the LDS Church were called to take the message of the restored gospel to the Lamanites. In September 1830, a revelation was given to Oliver Cowdery through Joseph Smith stating, "You shall go unto the Lamanites and preach my gospel unto them" (D&C 28:8). Just four months earlier, Andrew Jackson, president of the United States, signed the "Indian Removal Act" aimed at relocating all Native Americans west and southwest of the Missouri State border. W. W. Phelps considered it "marvelous" to see "the gathering of the Indians . . . through the instrumentality of the government of the United States."[38] Coincidentally, the later revealed location of the prophesied city of Zion turned out to be convenient to the area where these "Lamanites," who were to take the lead in building this city, had been gathered. The times of the gentiles was coming to a close, and now was the time of the fulfillment of the promises to the remnant of Jacob.

The Saints initially saw themselves as gentiles, which was in line with the general understanding of the time that the gentiles would play a key role in facilitating the gathering of Israel.[39] Notably, the title page of the Book of Mormon states that the book would come forth among the Lamanites and Jews "by way of the Gentile."[40]

By 1831, however, the Saints had begun thinking of themselves as literal descendants of Israel and not just adopted gentiles. A revelation in 1831 implied that, unless they were "rebellious," the Saints could consider themselves as actual descendants of Joseph through Ephraim (D&C 64:36).[41] Another revelation in 1833 foretold of "the tribes of Israel" being "crowned with glory . . . by the hands of . . . the children of Ephraim" (D&C 133:30–34). The Saints' perception of themselves as lineal descendants of Abraham was further reinforced when Joseph Smith Sr., ordained as the Church's first patriarch in December 1833, began giving patriarchal blessings declaring that their blood lines came directly through Abraham. On April 15, 1837, for example, he blessed Wilford Woodruff saying, "Thou art of the Blood of Ephraim [and] . . . all of thy relatives . . . are of the blood of Ephraim."[42]

While Mormonism holds that those not of the blood of Israel become Israelites through embracing the gospel,[43] such an adoption is seldom necessary as most converts, regardless of their nationality, are considered to be literal blood descendents of the House of Israel already. This teaching was reaffirmed in 1991 when the following question was sent to the *Ensign* magazine: "Are most members of the Church literal descendants of Abraham, Isaac, and Jacob, or are they Gentiles who have been adopted into the house of Israel?" In response, Church educator Daniel H. Ludlow explained that "the lineages declared in patriarchal blessings are almost always statements of actual blood lines; they are not simply tribal identifications by assignment." After quoting several Church authorities he concludes, "The clear teaching of the prophets is that few persons *not* of the blood of Abraham have become members of the Church in this dispensation."[44]

The shift in the Saints' self-understanding, going from gentile to literal descendant of Israel, seems to have impacted their perception of who would take the leadership role in building the New Jerusalem. Armand Mauss, an LDS professor emeritus of sociology and religious studies at Washington State University, notes that, for Mormonism's first century, "Mormons had acquired a new understanding of themselves as literal Israelites . . . and had taken over the responsibility for building the New Jerusalem."[45] At the end of the twentieth century, Brian L. Smith, writing in the *Encyclopedia of Mormonism*, stated unequivocally that "Ephraim's descendants . . . have the responsibility of preparing the way for the gathering of the other tribes."[46] He quoted John A. Widtsoe who remarked that "the tribe of Ephraim [is] the tribe to which has been committed the leadership of the Latter-day work."[47]

LDS commentators have been faced with the challenge of reconciling Book of Mormon references to the Lamanites' leadership role in the gathering with these later teachings emphasizing the role of the Ephraimites. Joseph Fielding Smith dealt with this issue by giving a loose interpretation of the Book of Mormon reference to the "remnant of Jacob" in 3 Nephi 21:12–13:

> There is nothing in the passage as I read it which should convey this thought [that the remnant of Jacob refers predominantly to the Lamanites]. . . . I take it we, the members of the Church, most of us of the tribe of Ephraim, are of the remnant of Jacob. . . . It is Ephraim who is to be endowed with power to bless and give to the other tribes, including the Lamanites, their blessings.[48]

While this interpretation is consistent with the current LDS understanding that most non-Lamanites who join the Church are also descendants of Jacob through the tribe of Ephraim, it is nowhere implied in the Book of Mormon nor is it suggested in initial LDS teachings. In the Book of Mormon, European Americans are gentiles who will be numbered with the Lamanites (descendants of Lehi) only if they repent.

McConkie also referred to the remnant of Jacob as any who are "righteous," whether Lamanite or otherwise. He rejected the idea that the Lamanites would literally tread upon and tear to pieces the unrepentant gentiles—he calls it "prophetic imagery"—and asserts that "these words . . . have reference to the desolations and ultimate burning that shall destroy the wicked at the Second Coming."[49] In contrast to this modern view, and as evidenced in the references previously cited, early Latter-day Saints took this prophetic imagery quite literally and fully anticipated a destructive offensive by the Lamanites on the gentiles. This more literal interpretation is not at all inconsistent with the Book of Mormon narrative, in which God used the Lamanites to periodically punish and purge the Nephites when they fell into disobedience.

The interpretation by Joseph Fielding Smith and McConkie—that the "remnant of Jacob" spoken of in 3 Nephi 21 comprises the entire house of Israel, and that the thrashing of the gentiles by this remnant is merely the destruction of the wicked at the second coming—has gained the support of many LDS doctrinal expositors.[50] Other LDS commentators, however, find it difficult to ignore the straightforward reading of the text and assert that the "remnant of Jacob" is an unambiguous reference to the descendants of the people of the Book of Mormon who will literally rise up and thrash the gentiles if they don't repent.[51] Elder Jeffrey Holland, for example, equates the "remnant of Jacob" in this passage with "the children of Lehi" and observes that the "tread[ing] down and tear[ing] in pieces" spoken of in 3 Nephi 21:12–13 is a prophecy of what "*could* come to the Gentiles at the hands of the remnant of Jacob."[52]

A related concept that has changed since its appearance in the Book of Mormon is the curse of a dark skin upon the Lamanites and their prophesied latter-day transformation to a "white and delightsome" people upon their acceptance of the gospel (2 Ne. 30:6, first edition). In the 1840 edition "white and delightsome" was changed to "pure and delightsome" implying a spiritual purity rather than a white skin pigment. Most editions between 1840 and 1981, however, used the original wording of "white and delightsome." Saints actually anticipated a change in skin color among the Lamanites as they embraced the gospel. Joseph Smith, apparently anxious for the Book of Mormon prophecy to be fulfilled, at one point advocated that certain elders take Indian women as plural wives to accelerate the change of their skin color. He even received a revelation to that effect:

> Verily, I say unto you, that the wisdom of man, in his fallen state, knoweth not the purposes and the privileges of my holy priesthood, but ye shall know when ye receive a fulness by reason of the anointing: For it is my will, that in time, ye should take unto you wives of the Lamanites and Nephites, that their posterity may become white, delightsome and just, for even now their females are more virtuous than the gentiles.[53]

In the October 1960 general conference, Spencer W. Kimball, then an apostle, declared that the Book of Mormon prophecy regarding the skin transformation of the Lamanites was becoming fulfilled and that the Indians "are fast becoming a white and delightsome people." According to Elder Kimball, "The [Indian] children in the home placement program in Utah are often lighter than their brothers and sisters in the hogans on the reservation."[54]

In the 1981 edition of the Book of Mormon, 2 Nephi 30:6 was changed again to "pure"[55] paralleling a growing tendency in the Church to reject the notion of skin color as a curse or indicator of one's spiritual stature. Though many Latter-day Saints now maintain that the Book of Mormon speaks of the Lamanites becoming pure and delightsome only in a spiritual sense, it seems fairly clear from related passages in the Book of Mormon explicitly mentioning skin color that more than a spiritual transformation was anticipated (2 Ne. 5:19–25; Jacob 3:8–9; Alma 3:6–19; 3 Ne. 2:15–16). These residual passages alluding to changes in skin color based on one's sinfulness or righteousness have fueled numerous discussions on the exact nature of the Lamanite transformation that should be anticipated.

Latter-day Gathering Places

The earliest revelations of Joseph Smith make no mention of a specific gathering place for Mormon converts although the Book of Mormon spoke of converted gentiles, along with the Lamanites, possessing America as their land of inheritance (1 Ne. 14:2; 2 Ne. 10:18–19; 3 Ne. 16:13–16, 21:20–24). Terryl L. Givens observes that, in the earliest years of Mormonism, any mention of converts being gathered was spoken of in general terms and likely understood figuratively.[56] In the summer of 1828, for example, the Lord revealed, "I will gather them [i.e., those who receive the restored gospel] as a hen gathereth her chickens" (D&C 10:65). It was in October 1830 that the Saints were first informed of an actual gathering place. A revelation stated, "The decree hath gone forth from the Father that they [i.e., the elect] shall be gathered in unto one place upon the face of this land" (D&C 29:8).

When Independence, Missouri, was identified as the place of Mount Zion or the New Jerusalem, Saints were anxious to migrate there, and in July 1831 (D&C 57:1–2) they received a commandment to gather to Zion in Missouri. Even converted Jews were instructed to gather to Zion instead of Jerusalem.[57]

Though Missouri was viewed by the Saints as the place where they would escape the judgments poured out on the wicked and be prepared for Christ's imminent return (D&C 29:8–11), this vision was short lived, as within only a few years, they were forced to flee to Illinois. After gathering for a brief time in Nauvoo, the Saints were eventually driven west to the Rockies. Salt Lake City and surrounding areas became the new places of gathering in perceived fulfillment of the Old Testament prophecy that "the mountain of the LORD's house shall be established in the top of the mountains . . . and all nations shall flow unto it" (Isa. 2:2–3; Micah 4:1–2). The Salt Lake Valley was only to be a temporary gathering place until "the redemption of Zion" (D&C 105:9).

Beginning in the 1890s and continuing into the twentieth century, the Church discouraged Saints from migrating to Utah, largely for financial reasons.[58] For the most part, this new policy to stay put wasn't intended to be taken as a change of gathering place to one's homeland, but was merely a deferment of their gathering to Zion. Some Church leaders opposed this change in policy, viewing it as a direct contradiction of the Lord's commandment to gather to Zion. In 1939, for example, Joseph Fielding Smith protested, "I do not know when the Lord reversed his commandment (D&C 29:8 and 133:1–16), that his people should be gathered out from Babylon."[59] He lamented the fact that the Church was spending money to build up stakes in foreign lands instead of urging and assisting converts to gather to Zion. In August 1962 he remarked, "Our spending everywhere is to me alarming . . . . We are constantly creating stakes in Europe, the islands of the Pacific, and on the American continent. I wonder if we have forgotten the commandment to gather. To come to Zion."[60] However, nine years later as president of the Church, he evidently had a change of heart, for he declared in a Church area conference in Manchester, England, "We are and shall be a world church. This is our destiny. It is part of the Lord's program."[61]

In the latter half of the twentieth century, the counsel to temporarily remain in one's homeland began shifting to a directive to permanently *gather* to one's homeland. LDS biographer Heidi Swinton writes, "In 1955 when Elder Spencer W. Kimball visited Europe for six months, stopping at every mission on the continent and in England, his message was clear: 'The days of gathering [to Zion in America] are over, and now we've got to establish Zion in all areas of the world. We need you here. Stay in your homeland and build up The Church of Jesus Christ of Latter-day Saints.'"[62] The current emphasis that Saints should gather to their own home stakes has required reinterpreting Book of Mormon passages which speak of the tribe of Judah gathering to Jerusalem and all others, including converted Gentiles, gathering to America. As late as 1966 McConkie was still stressing in *Mormon Doctrine* that, to be "gathered home to the lands of their inheritance, and . . . established in all their lands of promise" (2 Ne. 9:2) meant "that the house of Joseph will be established in America, the house of Judah in Palestine, and that the Lost Tribes will come to Ephraim in America to receive their blessings in due course."[63] In an area conference held in Mexico in 1972, McConkie turned this same Book of Mormon passage around to justify the increasing Church directive to have Latter-day Saints of every nation gather to their *own* lands. "[The] revealed words," he said, referring to 2 Nephi 9:2, "speak of . . . there being congregations of the covenant people of the Lord in every nation, speaking every tongue, and among every people when the Lord comes."[64] This proof-text has since provided the perceived scriptural justification for the current practice of having Saints remain in their homelands. In April 1973, Harold B. Lee, eleventh president of the Church, quoted McConkie's interpretation in general conference.[65] Elder Boyd K. Packer then observed that President Lee had, "in effect, [officially] announced that the pioneering phase of gathering was now over. The gathering is now to be out of the world into the Church in every nation."[66]

Gathering the Ten Lost Tribes

A major phase of the gathering of Israel in the last days is the gathering of the ten lost tribes. These are believed to be members of the Northern Kingdom of Israel who were deported *en masse* to Assyria in 721 B.C. and who, according to legend, later migrated northward to become the lost tribes of Israel. The Bible gives little information about these tribes; however, numerous myths have cropped up over the centuries to explain their whereabouts.

At the time of Joseph Smith, it was popularly held that the ten lost tribes were largely intact. Among the various theorized populations that had been identified prior to 1830 as the ten tribes were the British, the Afghans, the Abyssinians, the Japanese, the Karaites of Russia, and the Native American Indians.[67] There was even speculation that the earth was hollow and contained a spacious territory in which the ten tribes dwelled. In 1822, John Cleves Symmes applied, without success, to Congress and the government of Russia for funds to find the entrance.[68] It was speculated at the time that there was a wide opening near the North Pole.[69] The one element these theories all had in common was that the lost tribes were together in a single body.

Many of these theories also situated the tribes in the land of the north. Early LDS teachings made similar claims. The Book of Mormon states "that the other tribes hath the Father separated from them [i.e., the Jews]" (3 Ne. 15:20), indicating that they were not interspersed among the Jews. Jesus was to visit these "other tribes" who were not in any of the lands he had visited (3 Ne. 16:1–4). The Book of Mormon further explains that these "lost tribes" kept records which would eventually come forth (2 Ne. 29:12–13). A revelation received in November 1831 alludes to the ten tribes "who are in the north countries" with "prophets" of their own who shall one day "smite the rocks, and the ice shall flow down at their presence. And an highway shall be cast up in the midst of the great deep" (D&C 133:26–27). The revelation then explains that they are to come to Zion as a body and be crowned with glory by the tribe of Ephraim (D&C 133:28–30). In April 1836 Moses restored "the keys of . . . the leading of the ten tribes from the land of the north" (D&C 110:11). In January 1833 Joseph wrote a letter to a newspaper editor in Rochester stating that the ten tribes wouldn't return until after the destruction of the wicked and that they would come "from the north country."[70]

Early Latter-day Saints had their own pet theories regarding the location of the ten tribes. Included were beliefs that they were in the north polar region, inside the earth, or on a fragment broken off from the earth.[71] Early LDS scripture provided much of the fodder that fed these speculative ideas with references to the ten tribes being in "the north countries" and "ice flow[ing] down at their presence" (D&C 133:26–27). The Book of Mormon allegory of the olive tree in Jacob 5 refers to certain "natural branches" of Israel that were "hid" in the "nethermost part of the vineyard," which is also described as the "poorest spot" in the Lord's vineyard. This imagery, understood by early Saints as an allusion to the ten lost tribes,[72] reinforced the popular theory that the ten tribes were hid from the rest of the world in the frozen "north countries."

In an 1835 letter to Oliver Cowdery, W. W. Phelps postulated:

> There may be a continent at the north pole, of more than 1300 square miles, containing thousands of millions of Israelites, who, after a highway is cast up in the great deep, may come to Zion, singing songs of everlasting joy.... This idea is greatly strengthened by reading Zenos' account of the tame olive tree in the Book of Mormon. The branches planted in the nethermost parts of the earth, "brought forth much fruit," and no man that pretends to have pure religion, can find "much fruit" among the Gentiles, or heathen of this generation.[73]

The return of the ten tribes as a single body was the predominant view in the Church until the latter part of the twentieth century.[74] As alternative explanations to the single-body view became increasingly voiced, Joseph Fielding Smith remarked, "There are many members of the Church who think that these 'lost tribes' were scattered among the nations and are now being gathered out and are found through all the stakes and branches of the Church.... [The Lord] has ... made it very clear and definite that these lost people are separate and apart from the scattered Israelites now being gathered out." Citing scriptures and pronouncements of Joseph Smith as supporting evidence, he concluded as "fact that these people are now in a body in preparation for their return."[75]

Surprisingly, after Joseph Fielding Smith's presidency, the "scattered view" he had so strongly repudiated began gaining currency, with Bruce R. McConkie, his son-in-law, as one of its most vocal proponents. In 1982, he pronounced:

> The Ten Tribes were first taken as a body into Assyria . . . [and] went out from Assyria, northward, in a body, under prophetic guidance. . . . [T]hey were then splintered and driven and scattered into all places and among all peoples. These Ten Tribes . . . are in nations and places known in the days of Isaiah and Jeremiah and the ancient prophets as the north countries. Hence, their return to Palestine at least will be from the land of the north.[76]

This view of the ten tribes being scattered among the nations, though contradictory to earlier teachings, does avoid the scientifically untenable idea that some thriving, unknown civilization exists somewhere in the frozen North.

According to biblical scholars, the idea that a majority of the ten tribes were deported from Palestine and then migrated to a distant north country is without historical basis.[77] First of all, only a minority of the population was deported from Palestine. After rehearsing ancient recorded historical accounts of the Assyrian siege, H. G. May, professor in the Oberlin Graduate School of Theology, states, "Evidence shows conclusively that the number of Israelites deported could not have been more than one twentieth or one fiftieth of the total population. The ten tribes of Israel were therefore never 'lost' because they were never deported."[78] The exiles numbered 27,290 and represented only the relatively small district of Samaria in the Northern Kingdom.[79] They were taken to Assyria and Media in what is now northwestern Iran and assimilated into this new culture. In *A History of the Jews*, historian Paul Johnson states that the ten tribes "lived in later Jewish legend, but in reality they were simply assimilated into the surrounding Aramaean population, losing their faith and their language; and the spread of Aramaic westwards, as the common language of the Assyrian empire, helped to conceal their evanescence."[80] The greater portion of the ten tribes that remained in Palestine intermarried with Jews and alien settlers that took possession of much of Samaria, thereby losing their tribal distinction and becoming "lost" or no longer identifiable as "the ten tribes."

Latter-day Zion

The term "Zion" has acquired a range of meanings in LDS theology, from an ideal movement to a synonym for the city of New Jerusalem to a geographical region encompassing North and South America. Historically, Zion was the name of the fortified hill of pre-Israelite Jerusalem, and David's accomplishment was conquering the "stronghold of Zion" (2 Sam. 5:6–10). This name gradually became associated with Jerusalem itself; hence, biblical scholars recognize most Old Testament references to Zion as simply references to Jerusalem. When both Jerusalem and Zion are mentioned together in the same verse (see 2 Kgs. 19:31; Isa. 4:3–4), it is usually in the form of a repetitive or synonymous parallelism denoting the same place. For example, Joel prophesied that the Lord shall "roar from Zion" and "utter his voice from Jerusalem" (Joel 3:16–17). Isaiah similarly proclaims that "out of Zion shall go forth the law, and the word of the LORD from Jerusalem" (Isa. 2:2–4; see also Micah 4:1–2). Biblical scholars explain that these parallelisms convey the single idea that the Lord's voice, which is synonymous with his word or law, shall go forth from Jerusalem, which is synonymous with Zion. Thus, Old Testament prophets anticipated a renewal of the city of Jerusalem, also called Zion.

In Old Testament history, the Israelites' theology of Zion transformed from a current place, i.e., Jerusalem—that they believed God had chosen and permanently secured for them—to a future idealized city that served as a beacon of hope. According to Donald E. Gowan, professor of Old Testament at Pittsburgh Theological Seminary, when the city of Jerusalem was destroyed in 587 B.C. "that should have been the end of Zion theology (cf. Lamentations 1 and 2). The events of history had thoroughly demonstrated the falseness of any belief in invulnerability." He goes on to explain, however, that "instead of repudiating Zion theology, exilic Judaism had corrected it, had eschatologized it, had found a way to take account of judgment and express their hope for a divinely accomplished future that would take all they had once believed to be present-tense truth about Jerusalem and make that, and more, come true in the days that are coming."[81]

Unlike Old Testament prophecies, the New Testament scarcely mentions Zion, perhaps because the New Testament emphasizes a heavenly rather than earthly paradise. Hebrews speaks of the saints coming unto a "heavenly" Jerusalem or Zion (Heb. 12:22). The only New Testament reference to a latter-day Zion is found in Revelation which describes a vision of Jesus standing "on the mount Sion [Zion], and with him an hundred forty and four thousand, having his Father's name written in their foreheads" (Rev. 14:1). According to scholars, this Zion of the Lord's appearance could be referring to either the earthly Jerusalem or the heavenly New Jerusalem that descends. Notably, neither the Old nor the New Testament gives any indication of the prophesied Zion on earth as being any place or society outside of Palestine.

Gowan notes that Christian writings dating to the Patristic era show an increasing tendency to spiritualize Zion as referring to God's kingdom—symbolized on earth by the Church. He states, "There has been an extensive transcendentalizing of the new Jerusalem in Christianity, so that it most often represents Christian hopes for the coming kingdom of God on earth, already foreshadowed in the Church, or for a blissful life of the believer in heaven. The expectation of a future restoration of the physical city of Jerusalem as the center of the new world hasn't disappeared, but it holds much less significance than in Jewish eschatology."[82]

As America became colonized, many Christian settlers anticipated that the promised Zion, which they perceived to be the biblically prophesied new Jerusalem (Rev. 21:2), would be set up in America. LDS General Authority Milton R. Hunter observes, "After the United States had obtained its independence from England and was fast becoming a nation, religious leaders and social reformers from various lands looked upon America as the place to establish a new Zion, the New Jerusalem. . . . Prominent among these new societies were the Shakers, the Perfectionists of Oneida, the Dukhobors, Owenite Colonies, Fourierist Colonies, the Free Society of Vaux, the Aiglemont Colony, Robinson's Colonies and numerous other groups who were looking forward for the coming of the Savior."[83] In 1697 Puritan magistrate Samuel Sewall stated that the "New Jerusalem" would come down in "the Heart of America" where the Indians lived. He further declared that God would rather "Tabernacle in our Indian Wigwam" than in the magnificent cathedrals of Europe.[84] Congregationalist minister Timothy Dwight (1752–1817) likewise preached that America was "both a new Eden and a latter-day Zion" and designated this country as "the favorite land of heaven."[85]

A Google Book Search for the years 1800 to 1830 shows that Zion was most frequently used in early American religious discourse in the spiritualized sense of God's church or kingdom on earth. A sermon delivered by Congregationalist pastor Samuel Austin, published in 1808, defined Zion as "that holy community commonly styled the Church," and "every person who is sanctified in heart is a subject of this community."[86] Thus, Zion was also thought of as the "sanctified in heart" (cf. D&C 97:21). Protestants gave Christ the title "Zion's king" and referred to the work of sanctifying believers and spreading the kingdom as "the cause of Zion."[87]

In the Book of Mormon, "Zion" is used in this traditional Protestant sense of the work of God's kingdom on earth (see 1 Ne. 13:37; 22:14, 19; 2 Ne. 6:12–13; 8:15; 10:13–16; 26:29–31; 28:21; 3 Ne. 21:1). The Zion of prophecy isn't, as yet, spoken of as a city or other geographical location. Several early revelations prior to the organization of the Church also referred to God's latter-day work as Zion (D&C 6:6, 11:6, 12:6, 14:6). On the day the Church was organized, the Lord said of Joseph, "Him have I inspired to move the cause of Zion in mighty power for good. . . . Yea, his weeping for Zion I have seen" (D&C 21:7–8). This same symbolic usage occurs in the late 1830 writing of the book of Moses where "the Lord called his people ZION" (Moses 7:18) and Christ is the "King of Zion" (Moses 7:53).

While Book of Mormon prophets spoke of the latter-day Zion as a spiritual cause, they spoke of the latter-day New Jerusalem as an actual city with the land of America being "the place of the New Jerusalem" (3 Ne. 20:22; Ether 13:3). The term "Zion" doesn't appear to have been directly connected with the city of New Jerusalem until June 1830 when Joseph brought to light a revelation given to Enoch concerning the last days which states: "Righteousness and truth will I cause to sweep the earth as with a flood, to gather out mine elect from the four quarters of the earth, unto a place which I shall prepare, an Holy City, that my people may gird up their loins, and be looking forth for the time of my coming; for there shall be my tabernacle, and it shall be called Zion, a New Jerusalem" (Moses 7:62). So early on in Mormonism, Zion became associated with both the church or kingdom of God and the city of the New Jerusalem, which was to be "a place which I [the Lord] shall prepare."

More specific information regarding the location of Zion or the New Jerusalem came in September 1830, just five months after the Church was organized. A revelation in September 1830 informed the Saints that, although "no man knoweth where the city Zion shall be built," they could at least know that "it shall be on the borders by the Lamanites" (D&C 28:9). This designation was a common way to identify the edge of white settlement in the United States which, at this time, was demarked by the Mississippi River.[88] Another revelation that same month enjoined the Saints to "bring to pass the gathering of [the Lord's] elect" emphasizing that the Saints should be "gathered in unto one place" (D&C 29:7–8). This command to gather was undoubtedly considered in light of the new knowledge received regarding the place of Zion, the New Jerusalem.

In June 1831, the Lord commanded Joseph Smith and other leading brethren of the Church to "journey to the land of Missouri" and there it would "be made known unto them the land of your inheritance" (D&C 52:3–5). The next month, a revelation identified "the land of Missouri" as "the land of promise, and the place for the city of Zion" (D&C 57:1–2), and that "the place which is now called Independence is the center place" (D&C 57:3).

This revelation of the exact place where Zion or the city of the New Jerusalem was to be built caused great excitement among the Saints who were cautioned in August 1831 not to gather there "in haste, lest there should be confusion" (D&C 63:24). In January 1833, however, the Prophet called upon the "Christian world" to "embrace the everlasting covenant, and flee to Zion before the overflowing scourge overtake you."[89] A revelation in September 1832 once again equated Zion with the "New Jerusalem" to be built (D&C 84:2–4). Circumstances, however, prevented the city of Zion from being built: persecutions forced the Saints to flee from Missouri, first from Jackson County in 1833, and then from northern Missouri in the winter of 1838–39. They were encouraged, though, by a revelation in August 1833: "Surely Zion is the city of our God, and surely Zion cannot fall, neither be moved out of her place" (D&C 97:19). While Zion had taken on the meaning of a specific city, it continued to retain a spiritual significance as, in the same revelation, the Lord referred to Zion as all who are "PURE IN HEART" (D&C 97:21).

With no prospect of the city of Zion being redeemed any time soon, in July 1840, the Prophet expanded the geography of Zion to include "all [of] N[orth] & S[outh] America."[90] The tenth Article of Faith originally read, "We believe . . . that Zion will be built upon this continent." This was later modified to read, "We believe . . . that Zion (the New Jerusalem) will be built upon the American continent." The addition of "the New Jerusalem" would have been unnecessary for early Saints who were accustomed to thinking of Zion as a city.

Though Old Testament prophets seem to have envisioned Zion as a restored and revitalized Jerusalem, Latter-day Saints have interpreted Old Testament prophecies of Zion as the Lord's base of operation in America, separate and distinct from Jerusalem. McConkie explains, "During the Millennial era there are two great world capitals—one in the Zion of America, the New Jerusalem, whence the law shall proceed, and the other in the Zion of old, the Old Jerusalem, whence the word of the Lord shall go forth."[91] He interpreted the "law" as civil law and different from the "word of the Lord," even though, as a Hebrew parallel, they would have been synonymous. Several twentieth-century Church presidents have taught that the U.S. Constitution has fulfilled the ancient prophecy of Isaiah that "out of Zion shall go forth the law."[92] Zion, in this interpretation, presumably signifies the United States of America.

With the cessation of physical gathering coupled with the growth and establishment of the Church throughout the world, it is predominantly the spiritualized use of Zion as "THE PURE IN HEART" (D&C 97:21) that is now emphasized.[93] Thus, Zion has come to be equated with the Church's stakes worldwide. The realization of Zion as a city or center place is generally considered to be reserved for the millennium.[94]

New Jerusalem

As noted above, in LDS theology, the city of New Jerusalem is to be built in Jackson County, Missouri. It is to serve as the center of government, together with the Jerusalem in Palestine, for the millennial kingdom of Christ.

The term "New Jerusalem" doesn't appear in the Old Testament, although Old Testament writers did prophesy that Jerusalem of old would be "redeemed" (Isa. 52:9) and become "a praise in the earth" (Isa. 62:7). Scholars note that ancient Jews didn't anticipate a heavenly city coming down from the sky; rather they expected to see their captive city liberated and reestablished as the city of the living God. However, as history deferred this anticipated restoration, the hope for a glorious, rebuilt Jerusalem (Hag. 2:9) was eventually transformed into a belief in a heavenly Jerusalem which, in turn, expanded to become equated with heaven itself. In *A Brief History of Heaven*, historical theologian Alister McGrath explains,

> Initially the prophetic vision of a new Jerusalem was understood to apply to a future earthly city—a reconstructed city of bricks and mortar, which would rise from the ruins of the old city with the return of its people from their exile in Babylon. The Old Testament books of Nehemiah and Ezra document attempts to restore Jerusalem to its former glory, and fulfill the hopes of a renewed presence of the glory of the Lord. Yet with the passing of time, Jewish hopes began to crystallize around the idea of a heavenly Jerusalem—a future city, beyond this world, filled with the "glory of the Lord," in which God is seated on a throne.[95]

In the book of Revelation, a Jewish-Christian apocalyptic text, John envisions this heavenly Jerusalem coming down "out of heaven" (Rev. 3:12). He refers again to this city's descent in Revelation 21:2, which states, "I John saw the holy city, new Jerusalem, coming down from God out of heaven, prepared as a bride adorned for her husband." In verse 10 he again sees in vision "that great city, the holy Jerusalem, descending out of heaven from God" (v. 10). This new city of Jerusalem is enormous by any earthly standard. The foundation alone is 1,500 miles by 1,500 miles—roughly half the size of the United States of America. It also has a height of 1,500 miles making it a perfect cube. Was the "new Jerusalem" John saw intended to be a city located in the United States unrelated to the old Jerusalem, or was he envisioning merely a heavenly replacement for the old Jerusalem (as anticipated by ancient Jews)? And because John refers to a city descending in both Revelation 21:2 and 21:10, was he seeing two separate cities and events; namely, the descent of both a New Jerusalem and a renewed old Jerusalem? Scholars see these two passages as referring to the same event, with the new Jerusalem being merely "a heavenly counterpart to the earthly Jerusalem."[96]

It was common for early American evangelicals to differentiate between the place of the New Jerusalem, which they believed would be located in America, and the old biblical Jerusalem of Palestine. Many early American Puritans viewed America as the land where the New Jerusalem would be built.[97] Cotton Mather proclaimed in 1710 that the "Lord will have an holy city in America; a city, the street whereof will be pure gold."[98] In his research on developing conceptions of New Jerusalem in America, Craig S. Campbell writes that in early colonial America, "the New Jerusalem, true to the verse in Revelation, was almost always seen as 'coming down' from heaven," and "New Englanders rarely thought of it as being built on earth by people." As America started becoming a nation, however, "more emphasis was given to building up the new country, so ideas of a tangible millennial construction became popular."[99]

While the book of Revelation speaks of a "new Jerusalem," as simply a heavenly version of old Jerusalem, early American Christians spoke of it as "New Jerusalem" with a capital 'N' (like New England, New York, etc.), as though it would take its namesake from Jerusalem of old, but be set up in the New World. Millenarians at the time of Joseph Smith expressed the view that the New Jerusalem would consist of the righteous who are resurrected from the dead as well as the righteous living who are lifted up to meet Christ in the clouds at his second coming.[100] It was believed that all these individuals would descend with Christ as the New Jerusalem.[101]

From the beginning, LDS scriptures reflected the notion of an earthly construction as well as a literal descent of the New Jerusalem and distinguished between old Jerusalem and the New Jerusalem in ways similar to popular millenarian views at the time. Latter-day Saints, like many of their contemporaries, placed the New Jerusalem on American soil. According to the Book of Mormon, not only would old Jerusalem "be built up again, a holy city unto the Lord," but also "a New Jerusalem should be built upon this land" (Ether 13:4–8). "When the earth shall pass away . . . there shall be a new heaven and a new earth. . . . And then cometh the New Jerusalem. . . . And then cometh also the Jerusalem of old" (Ether 13:8–11). In John's vision, there was no earthly construction of the New Jerusalem and only a single "holy city, new Jerusalem" descended following the creation of "a new heaven and a new earth" (Rev. 21:1–2).

The current LDS understanding of Revelation is that a New Jerusalem will be built in Independence, Missouri, and the old Jerusalem will be rebuilt in Palestine. Both will have a temple erected by Latter-day Saints to which the Lord will come. At the start of the millennium, the old Jerusalem and the New Jerusalem will be caught up to meet Christ and then will descend to the earth to operate as two world capitals during the millennium. After the millennium and the earth's glorification, a celestial Jerusalem (which is neither the old nor New Jerusalem) will descend to the earth.[102]

Notes

1. Ronald D. Dennis, "Gathering," 2:537.
2. Elias Boudinot, *A Star in the West*, 297.
3. Robert P. Carroll, *When Prophecy Failed*, 38.
4. Bruce R. McConkie, *Doctrinal New Testament Commentary*, 2:173.
5. This interpretation was given by Calvin and several other reformers. See James Morrison, *Commentary on the Gospel According to Matthew*, 520-21.
6. Joseph A. Fitzmyer, *The Gospel According to Luke*, 1173.
7. See virtually any one of the more than twenty online Bible commentaries listed at studylight.org website, "Commentaries," http://www.studylight.org/com/ (accessed December 27, 2004). For a modern scholarly analysis, see John Topel, "What Kind of Sign Are Vultures?" 404.
8. Albert Barnes, *Notes on the New Testament*, under Matthew 24:28.
9. Ethan Smith, *View of the Hebrews: 1825 Second Edition Complete Text*, 184.
10. "The Work of the Lord in the Last Days," 171.
11. Orson Pratt, *Journal of Discourses*, March 26, 1871, 14:67; April 7, 1872, 15:49; June 15, 1873, 16:84–85; February 28, 1875, 17:318.
12. Joseph Fielding Smith, *Signs of the Times*, 45–46.
13. Joseph Blenkinsopp, *Isaiah 1–39*, 309.
14. Ibid.
15. J. J. M. Roberts, "Isaiah," 1038.
16. Ibid.
17. Ibid.
18. F. B. Huey Jr., *Jeremiah, Lamentations*, 169.
19. Leo G. Perdue, "Jeremiah," 1144–45.
20. Grant Underwood, *The Millenarian World of Early Mormonism*, 64.
21. See Dale R. Broadhurst, "Transcriber's Comments: The Second Advent." Broadhurst notes that "it was . . . common for American Calvinists to make mention of a 'restoration' of 'Israel' prior to the second coming of Christ."
22. Steven Epperson, *Mormons and Jews*, 8.
23. Elias Boudinot, *The Second Advent*, 556-64.
24. W. Sibley Towner, "Zechariah," 1425.
25. See, for example, Bruce R. McConkie, *Mormon Doctrine*, 280; Terry L. Niederhauser, "Israel: The Gathering of Israel," 2:710.
26. There is a difference of opinion among LDS authorities as to whether the modern gathering of the Jews to Palestine fulfills ancient prophecy. Joseph Fielding Smith taught, "The Jews today are gathering in Palestine in fulfillment of the predictions of the ancient prophets. Why are they gathering

to their homeland? Because of the restoration of the keys for the gathering of Israel." Joseph Fielding Smith, *Doctrines of Salvation: Compiled Sermons of Joseph Fielding Smith*, 3:257. Bruce R. McConkie, however, wrote that "this gathering of the Jews to their homeland, and their organization into a nation and a kingdom, is not the gathering promised by the prophets. It does not fulfill the ancient promises." Bruce R. McConkie, *The Millennial Messiah: The Second Coming of the Son of Man*, 229.

27. Bruce R. McConkie, *A New Witness for the Articles of Faith*, 632.

28. Wilford Woodruff, *Journal of Discourses*, January 12, 1873, 15:278.

29. McConkie, *The Millennial Messiah*, 228. See also Robert L. Millet, *Selected Writings of Robert L. Millet*, 268–69.

30. Donald W. Parry and Jan A. Parry, *Understanding the Signs of the Times*, 50.

31. David B. Galbraith, D. Kelly Ogden, and Andrew C. Skinner, *Jerusalem: The Eternal City*, 358–59; citing *Journal of Discourses* 15:278.

32. Wilford Woodruff, *Journal of Discourses*, January 12, 1873, 15:278.

33. Until the recent controversy over DNA research and Jewish ancestry of American Indians, it has been generally believed and taught in the Church that American Indians are the direct descendants of the Lamanites who, according to the Book of Mormon, are literal Israelites. This claim is also implicit in Book of Mormon prophecies regarding the Lamanites. The title page of the Book of Mormon states that it was "written to the Lamanites, who are a remnant of the house of Israel." In 1830 several revelations were given through Joseph Smith sending elders to preach to the American Indians whom the revelations designated as "the Lamanites" (D&C 28:8, 30:6, 32:2). The introduction to the 1981 edition of the Book of Mormon stated, "The Lamanites are the principal ancestors of the American Indians." This wording was changed in the 2006 Doubleday edition and subsequent editions published by the LDS Church, stating only that the Lamanites "are among the ancestors of the American Indians." See Peggy Fletcher Stack, "Single Word Change in Book of Mormon Speaks Volumes."

34. Smith, *View of the Hebrews*, 196.

35. Parley P. Pratt, *Mormonism Unveiled: Zion's Watchman Unmasked, and Its Editor, Mr. L. R. Sunderland, Exposed . . .* , 15. In the first edition of *Voice of Warning* Pratt told Indians that, unless the Gentiles repent, "the very places of their dwellings will become desolate except such of them as are gathered and numbered with you. . . . And your children will only know, that the Gentiles once conquered this country, and became a great nation here, as they read it in history." Parley P. Pratt, *A Voice of Warning and Instruction to All People, Containing a Declaration of the Faith and Doctrine of the Church . . .* , 191. Writing in 1838, Pratt said, "Now, Mr. Sunderland. . . . I will state as a prophecy [sic], that there will not be an unbelieving Gentile upon this continent 50 years hence; and if they are not greatly scourged, and in a great measure overthrown, within five or ten years from this date, then the Book of Mormon will have proved itself false." Pratt, *Mormonism Unveiled*, 15.

36. David Whitmer, *An Address to All Believers in Christ*, 71.

37. Pratt, *Voice of Warning*, 186.

38. William W. Phelps, "The Indians," 54.

39. Armand L. Mauss, *All Abraham's Childen: Changing Mormon Conceptions of Race and Lineage*, 21.

40. Joseph Smith may have considered himself excluded from being a gentile as the Book of Mormon prophesies that he would be a descendant of the ancient biblical Joseph (2 Ne. 3:6-15). That the gentiles spoken of in the Book of Mormon were considered to be, in general, non-Israelites is evidenced by the fact that they could only be "numbered among the House of Israel" by embracing the gospel (1 Ne. 14:2; 2 Ne. 10:18; 3 Ne. 16:13, 21:6, 30:2).

41. Ibid., 42. George P. Lee, the only American Indian (Navajo) to ever have been a General Authority, felt that Mormon Church leaders were deliberately trying to overturn what God had ordained. In a letter he wrote to the Church hierarchy on September 1, 1989, he stated, "You have set yourself up as a literal seed of Israel when the Lord Jesus designated you as Gentiles or 'adopted' Israel. . . . This has resulted in great confusion, misinterpretations and misunderstandings of the scriptures as they relate to Gentiles and Israel. . . . It is not God's but man-inspired. . . . It is getting to the point where every Gentile that is baptized is told and taught that he is literal seed of Ephraim unless he is a Jew, Indian or Black." George P. Lee, Letter to the First Presidency, et al; Sept. 1, 1989, 13-16. Quoted in Jerald Tanner and Sandra Tanner, "Excommunication."

42. Wilford Woodruff, *Wilford Woodruff's Journal, 1833-1898*, 1:143.

43. V. Ben Bloxham, "Law of Adoption," 2:810.

44. Daniel H. Ludlow, "Of the House of Israel," 51-54.

45. Mauss, *All Abraham's Children*, 42.

46. Brian L. Smith, "Ephraim," 2:461.

47. Ibid., 462.

48. Smith, *Doctrines of Salvation*, 2:250-51.

49. McConkie, *The Millennial Messiah*, 248.

50. Joseph Fielding McConkie and Robert L. Millet, *Doctrinal Commentary on the Book of Mormon*, 4:111, 451. Although he proffers no explanation of how the Lamanites are to tread the gentiles, Spencer W. Kimball does state: "The Lamanite is not wholly and exclusively the remnant of Jacob which the Book of Mormon talks about. We are all of Israel! We are of Abraham and Isaac and Jacob and Joseph through Ephraim and Manasseh. We are all of us remnants of Jacob." Spencer W. Kimball, *The Teachings of Spencer W. Kimball*, 600-601.

51. Bruce A. Chadwick and Thomas Garrow, "Native Americans," 3:981. Monte S. Nyman and Farres H. Nyman, *The Words of the Twelve Prophets: Messages to the Latter-day Saints*, 84; Hoyt W. Brewster Jr., *Doctrine and Covenants Encyclopedia*, 459; Daniel H. Ludlow, *A Companion to Your Study of the Old Testament*, 381-82.

52. Jeffrey R. Holland, *Christ and the New Covenant: The Messianic Message of the Book of Mormon*, 288; emphasis mine.

53. Quoted in H. Michael Marquardt, *Joseph Smith Revelations: Text and Commentary*, 374-76. W. W. Phelps reported that "about three years after this [prophecy] was given, I asked brother Joseph, privately, how 'we,' that were mentioned in the revelation could take wives from the 'natives' as we were all married men? He replied, instantly 'In the same manner that

Abraham took Hagar and Keturah; and Jacob took Rachel, Bilhah [and] Zilpah; by revelation—the saints of the Lord are always directed by revelation.'" Ibid.

54. Spencer W. Kimball, "The Day of the Lamanites," 922–23.

55. Douglas Campbell, "'White' or 'Pure,'" 119–35.

56. Terryl Givens, *People of Paradox: A History of Mormon Culture*, 102.

57. Dean C. Jessee, comp. and ed., *The Personal Writings of Joseph Smith*, 521. Ironically, this instruction to have Jews gather to Nauvoo was sent to Orson Hyde by the Prophet as Hyde was on his way to dedicate Jerusalem for the gathering of the Jews.

58. Orson F. Whitney, "Stay Where You Are!" 585.

59. Joseph Fielding Smith Jr. and John J. Stewart, *The Life of Joseph Fielding Smith*, 283.

60. Ibid., 326–27.

61. Joseph Fielding Smith, quoted in ibid., 365.

62. Heidi S. Swinton, *In the Company of Prophets*, 91.

63. Bruce R. McConkie, *Mormon Doctrine*, 305–6.

64. Bruce R. McConkie, quoted in Harold B. Lee, "Strengthening the Stakes of Zion," 4–5.

65. Ibid., 4–5.

66. Boyd K. Packer, "To Be Learned Is Good If . . . ," 71.

67. Joseph Jacobs, "Tribes, Lost Ten," 249–52. See also H. G. May, "Archeological News and Views," 55–60.

68. David Standish, *Hollow Earth: The Long and Curious History of Imagining Strange Lands, Fantastical Creatures, Advanced Civilizations, and Marvelous Machines below the Earth's Surface*, 81.

69. For example, the sixteenth-century cartographer Gerard Mercator created a map, "Mercator Septentrionalium Terrarum descriptio," showing the entrance of the earth at the north pole.

70. Jessee, *The Personal Writings of Joseph Smith*, 298. Joseph had earlier related that John the Revelator was with the ten tribes, preparing them for their return. *History of the Church*, 1:176 note 4.

71. R. Clayton Brough, *The Lost Tribes*, 41–91. Brough discusses several LDS theories explaining the location of the ten tribes including the "unknown planet" theory, the "narrow neck" proposition (a subtheory of the unknown planet theory), the "hollow earth" theory, the "North Pole" theory, and the "dispersion" theory.

72. William W. Phelps, "The Ten Tribes," 33–34.

73. William W. Phelps, "Letter No. 11," 194.

74. Standard Church publications presented the lost tribes as being preserved in a single body and returning together as a group. For example, see James E. Talmage, *Articles of Faith*, 308

75. Smith, *Signs of the Times*, 158–60.

76. McConkie, *The Millennial Messiah*, 320–22. Interestingly, sixteen years earlier, in 1966, McConkie was asserting that the ten lost tribes "were still a distinct people" at the time of Christ and makes no mention of them being scattered prior to returning in the latter days "with 'their prophets' and their scriptures." McConkie, *Mormon Doctrine*, 457–58.

77. For a list of scholarly sources repudiating the mass exile of the ten tribes, see H. G. May, "Archeological News and Views," 55.
78. Ibid., 58.
79. Ibid.
80. Paul Johnson, *A History of the Jews,* 70.
81. Donald E. Gowan, *Eschatology in the Old Testament,* 8–9.
82. Ibid., 19.
83. Milton R. Hunter, *The Gospel through the Ages,* 276.
84. Samuel Sewall, quoted in Gustav H. Blanke and Karen Lynn, "God's Base of Operations: Mormon Variations on the American Sense of Mission," 86. This article gives a good background of the early nineteenth-century sense of American mission which provided not only the beliefs, but the rhetoric and imagery that would be taken up by Mormonism.
85. Stephen E. Berk, *Calvinism versus Democracy: Timothy Dwight and the Origins of American Evangelical Orthodoxy,* 21.
86. Samuel Austin, "God Glorified in Building Up Zion," 27.
87. See, for example, "The Nature and Importance of the Pastoral Office," 199.
88. Milton V. Backman Jr., *The Heavens Resound: A History of the Latter-day Saints in Ohio, 1830–1838,* 43.
89. *History of the Church,* 1:315–16.
90. Jessee, *The Personal Writings of Joseph Smith,* 533.
91. McConkie, *A New Witness for the Articles of Faith,* 540.
92. Harold B. Lee, "The Way to Eternal Life," 15; George Albert Smith, "Dedicatory Prayer for the Idaho Falls Temple," 564; Ezra Taft Benson, *The Teachings of Ezra Taft Benson,* 595.
93. Givens, *People of Paradox,* 103.
94. A. D. Sorensen, "Zion," 4:1624–26.
95. Alister E. McGrath, *A Brief History of Heaven,* 9.
96. David E. Aune, "Revelation," 2335
97. Paul Boyer, "The Puritans."
98. Cotton Mather, *Theopolis Americana,* 43–44.
99. Craig S. Campbell, *Images of the New Jerusalem: Latter Day Saint Faction Interpretations of Independence, Missouri,* 9.
100. Underwood, *The Millenarian World of Early Mormonism,* 114.
101. Ibid.
102. McConkie, *The Millennial Messiah,* 1:95–96.

≈ 19 ≈

The Second Coming and Millennium

Latter-day Saints, like many Christians, believe that the resurrected Christ will return gloriously to earth to usher in a millennial kingdom on earth. This event, referred to as the *parousia* (Greek = coming), is to be preceded by visible signs and wonders. This chapter looks at scriptures and teachings related to Christ's second coming and the inauguration of his millennial reign.

To fully appreciate the historical development of the doctrine of the second coming and millennium, it is helpful to understand the nature of the apocalyptic literature on which millennial expectations are based. It is also worthwhile to realize that the faithful of virtually every generation have anticipated the Lord's coming in glory as imminent—ever near, but never here.

Apocalyptic Literature and Millennial Expectations

Old Testament prophecies concerning God's intervention to deliver captive Israel and New Testament prophecies of Christ's second coming to deliver the Saints from sorrow and sin were embellished and often encrypted in a class of sacred writings called apocalyptic. (Greek *apokalypsis* means an unveiling or revealing.) Apocalyptic literature has an eschatological (i.e., end-time) orientation and predicts how everything including humankind, the earth, and the cosmos will ultimately wind up. The eschatological view portrayed in apocalyptic literature is generally pessimistic about humankind's ability to solve social ills and end human conflict. The only hope of deliverance is through God's cataclysmic intervention in human history. It is God who will ultimately defeat the forces of evil and bring about lasting peace.

According to biblical scholars, apocalyptic writings first appeared in early Judaism at the beginning of the third century B.C. and extended into the second century A.D. Included are the books of Daniel, Revelation, and sections of Isaiah, Ezekiel, and Zechariah. Several extracanonical writings are also apocalyptic, including the Assumption of Moses, 1 Enoch (or the book of Enoch), and 4 Ezra (or 2 Esdras in the Apocrypha). Many Bible scholars see apocalypticism as a way ancient Jews were able to explain the apparent lapse in prophetic promises that God would reclaim Israel from exile after the destruction of the temple. To vindicate God's prophets, these promises were pushed into the future, thus preserving hope in their eventual fulfillment. Eric Meyers, professor of Judaic studies at Duke University, explains: "Unable to bring sixth- and fifth-century [B.C.] realities into alignment with the more uninhibited visions of earlier generations, the latter prophets were forced to express themselves in more eschatological and apocalyptic language. . . . Hence, Israel's glorious hopes were transferred to the eschatological realm, and only by supernatural and trans-historical means could such a restoration be envisioned."[1] Thus, disappointed expectations spurred apocalyptic predictions which recast earlier unfulfilled prophecies to an eschatological setting.

Scholars note that New Testament Christians, who believed that the coming kingdom was imminent, experienced similar disappointments and likewise readjusted their expectations to a future time and setting. Michael White, professor of classics and Christian origins at the University of Texas, notes that between A.D. 70 and A.D. 100 "the early Christians, who [were] . . . largely still within the larger framework of Judaism, also . . . reinterpret[ed] their understanding of history. Some of their expectations for the war did not come to pass. Many of them apparently thought that this was going to be the return of Jesus, and that Jesus was at this time going to restore the kingdom to Israel."[2] It is during this time of challenged faith that a Christian apocalyptic tradition emerged in the book of Revelation and several other New Testament writings.

The book of Revelation, composed during a period of persecution in the first century, borrowed heavily from Jewish apocalyptic literature—especially Daniel—to explain the Christian situation. Daniel's "Son of man" became Christ, numerological formulas were restated, and the dualistic world of good and evil acquired a new set of characters. The document's essential apocalyptic nature is evident in its prediction of God's imminent intervention to reverse human history and overpower evil. This prophecy of triumph and deliverance was written specifically for early Christians who were suffering persecution under imperial Rome. As New Testament scholar Raymond Brown states, "It was addressed to the seven churches and its details and historical context pertain to the first century rather than to the twentieth or twenty-first century."³ M. Eugene Boring, writing for *The New Interpreter's Study Bible*, is equally assertive in this regard: "That John is writing 'prophecy' does not mean that he is predicting historical events of the long-range future, but that he is presenting an inspired interpretation of contemporary events for the Christians of his own time. . . . John does not predict any historical event beyond his own generation."⁴ While the message of Revelation is timeless, its symbolic narrative should be first understood in its original context of early Christian struggle and persecution.

Christian ideas of a millennium were, therefore, based in part on Jewish apocalypticism recast in a Christian setting. Later Christians combined Old Testament prophecies of a kingdom of peace, New Testament prophecies of the second coming, and the lone reference to a thousand-year period of Christ's reign in Revelation (Rev. 20:1–6) to formulate a uniquely Christian millennial eschatology. LDS scholar Grant Underwood notes, "By linking the commencement of the millennium to the return of Christ in glory, the early fathers provided a peculiarly Christian twist to the doctrine of the final period of peace and prosperity on the earth."⁵

One's view of apocalyptic literature inevitably impacts one's perception of the second coming and millennium. Those who view apocalyptic predictions as the infallible word of God are likely to look forward with an eye of faith to an end of corruption and the advent of a new era of peace and glory with a certain urgent sense of fulfillment. They also tend to literalize apocalyptic teachings rather than recognize the pervasive symbolism, including the symbolic use of numbers. Perhaps most significantly, they treat the entire body of apocalyptic writings as though it presents a single, unified eschatology, disregarding the fact that different writers had different visions with different sequences of events—all of which have some variation from the eschatological expectations of Latter-day Saints today.

Those who view apocalyptic literature as inspiring yet embellished messages of hope to those who were experiencing crises are usually willing to allow for what they perceive to be errors in judgment and lapses in fulfillment. For them, these prophecies served a useful purpose for the time they were written and should not be taken as prophecies awaiting literal fulfillment. This doesn't mean, of course, that the essential message of these prophecies can't be a source of hope and encouragement for the faithful in all ages.

Imminence of the Lord's Coming

True to the apocalyptic spirit, the Lord's coming in judgment has been portrayed in all ages as an imminent event in which those currently suffering oppression are rescued and inherit a place in God's glorious kingdom on the earth.

Old Testament

For Old Testament people, it was God (not Christ) who would manifest his power to free Israel and pour out wrath on its enemies. And it was widely perceived that the deliverance was to happen soon. Isaiah declared that it would come in "a very little while" (Isa. 10:25), and told Israel's captors, "Howl ye; for the day of the LORD is at hand" (Isa. 13:6; see also Joel 1:15). Ezekiel also proclaimed that "the day is near, even the day of the LORD is near" (Ezek. 30:3). Joel sent out an immediate alert: "Blow ye the trumpet in Zion, and sound an alarm in my holy mountain let all the inhabitants of the land tremble for the day of the LORD cometh, for it is nigh at hand" (Joel 2:1). Daniel wrote to the Israelites in distress, imploring them to stand firm as God would soon decisively end their oppression; "Blessed is he that waiteth, and cometh to the thousand three hundred and five and thirty days" (Dan. 12:12). This elusive day of the Lord seems to have been always near but never arriving.

The Lord's coming is often couched in apocalyptic language as evidenced in Isaiah 13:9–11, 13:

> Behold, the day of the LORD cometh, cruel both with wrath and fierce anger, to lay the land desolate and he shall destroy the sinners thereof out of it.
>
> For the stars of heaven and the constellations thereof shall not give their light the sun shall be darkened in his going forth, and the moon shall not cause her light to shine.
>
> And I will punish the world for their evil, and the wicked for their iniquity; and I will cause the arrogancy of the proud to cease, and will lay low the haughtiness of the terrible. . . .
>
> Therefore I will shake the heavens, and the earth shall remove out of her place, in the wrath of the LORD of hosts, and in the day of his fierce anger.

Though this passage speaks of the day of the Lord as a time when both heaven and earth tremble and quake, it appears to have in mind the near-term fall of Babylon to the Medo-Persian Empire in 539 B.C. The explanation of its fulfillment is given in verses 17–19:

> Behold, I will stir up the Medes against them, which shall not regard silver; and as for gold, they shall not delight in it.

Their bows also shall dash the young men to pieces; and they shall have no pity on the fruit of the womb; their eye shall not spare children.

And Babylon, the glory of kingdoms, the beauty of the Chaldees' excellency, shall be as when God overthrew Sodom and Gomorrah.

What Isaiah seems to have been predicting was Babylon's imminent overthrow by the Medes, whom the Lord would use as his agents in executing his wrath. The destruction would be of such magnitude that it would impact heaven and earth. To look at this as an event in the distant future, literally cosmic in nature, disregards what scholars consider as the essential characteristic of apocalyptic utterances, not to mention the historical context which incited it. Though Mormons, like other Christians, tend to look forward to this prophecy being fulfilled in the not too distant future, the ancients appear to have anxiously anticipated its fulfillment in their own time.

New Testament

New Testament writers also eagerly anticipated the Lord's coming; however, they understood the Lord to be Jesus Christ. As discussed in Chapter 2, early Christians believed they were living in the last days and that Christ's coming was nigh. In the synoptic Gospels Christ tells his disciples that he will come in glory with his kingdom before the people then living have all died. "This generation shall not pass away," he declared, "till all be fulfilled" (Luke 21:32). In Matthew 10:23, he sends out his disciples saying, "Verily, I say unto you, Ye shall not have gone over the cities of Israel, till the Son of man be come." He later assured his disciples: "There be some standing here, which shall not taste of death, till they see the Son of man coming in his kingdom" (Matt. 16:28).[6] Catholic New Testament scholar Hans Küng observes, "There is not a single saying of Jesus which postpones the end-event to the distant future. On the contrary, it is clear from the oldest stratum of the Synoptic tradition that Jesus expects the kingdom of God in the immediate future."[7]

Paul's writings also evidence a perception that the second coming was near at hand. "Now is our salvation nearer than when we [first] believed" (Rom. 13:11). He informed the Corinthians that "the time [before judgment] is short" (1 Cor. 7:29) when "the fashion of this world passeth away" (v. 31). He admonished Timothy to "put the brethren in remembrance" of the fact that they are now living in the "latter times" and warns them of the "seducing spirits" and "doctrines of devils" which would be manifested (1 Tim. 4:1, 6). Timothy was later instructed that, "in view of his appearing and kingdom [i.e., Christ's second coming]" (NRSV 2 Tim. 4:1), he was to "exhort with all longsuffering and doctrine" (2 Tim. 4:2). He encouraged the Thessalonians "to wait for [God's] Son from heaven" (1 Thess. 1:10) and refers to the faithful (himself included) as "we which are alive and remain unto the coming of the Lord" (1 Thess. 4:15; see also v. 17). New Testament scholar James Dunn remarked, "Paul strongly believed that Jesus' resurrection and the gift of the Spirit were the beginning (the first-fruits) of the end-time harvest (1 Cor. 15:20, 23; Rom. 8:23); and for most of his ministry Paul proclaimed the imminence of the parousia and the end (1 Thess. 1:10; 4:13–18; 1 Cor. 7:29–31). Particularly worthy of notice is his preservation in 1 Cor. 16:22 of an Aramaic cry from the earliest church—'Maranatha, Our Lord, come!'"[8]

Latter-day Saints often point to 2 Thessalonians 2:2 as evidence that Paul understood the second coming to be a distant event, for he counseled the Saints not to be "shaken in mind, or be troubled . . . as that the day of Christ is at hand." But according to modern translations, as well as New Testament scholarship, Paul was actually attempting to dispel a disturbing rumor that "the day of Christ *has already come*" (NIV 2 Thess. 2:2; emphasis mine). Paul assures the Thessalonians that Christ won't come until there is an "apostasy" (*apostasia* = a turning away or rebellion) and "that man of sin . . . the son of perdition" is revealed (2 Thess. 2:3). At the height of this rebellion, Christ will appear to straighten things out and destroy the man of sin (2 Thess. 2:2–8). Paul asserts that this sequence of events would be consummated shortly, "for the mystery of iniquity doth already work" (2 Thess. 2:7). And when it can no longer be held back, the lawless one will be revealed "whom the Lord shall consume . . . with the brightness of his coming" (2 Thess. 2:8). In short, Paul is dispelling a rumor that Christ had already come, not that his coming was soon at hand.

Other New Testament writers also alluded to the imminence of Christ's return. James wrote, "The coming of the Lord draweth nigh. . . . [He] standeth before the door" (James 5:8–9). Peter expressed confidence that the second coming would take place in "these [i.e., Peter's] days" or, as the New English Bible translation states, "this present time" (Acts 3:24) and gave assurance that "the end of all things is at hand" (1 Pet. 4:7). Hebrews describes the saints then living as being at "the end of the world" (Heb. 9:26) and proclaims that "the Day of the Lord is coming near" (Today's Eng. Ver. Heb. 10:25), for "in just a very little while, He who is coming will come and will not be late" (NIV Heb. 10:37). John the Revelator, who saw in vision that the winding-up scene of the world was to "shortly come to pass" (Rev. 1:1), testified that the hour was "at hand" (Rev. 1:3). The angel told John not to even bother sealing up the prophecy of his book "for the time is at hand . . . and, behold, I [Jesus] come quickly" (Rev. 22:10–12). In sum, the overwhelming sense one gets from a straightforward reading of the New Testament is that Christ's coming was very near with many first-century Christians expecting him to return while they were still alive.[9]

Christ's failure to return as anticipated is commonly referred to in the Christian world as the "delay of the parousia." Christians who hold to the inerrancy of the scriptures face the challenge of reconciling promises of Christ's imminent literal return with the lapse of two millennia. Most Christians today are unwilling to concede that New Testament writers could have been so greatly mistaken and propose other explanations for this apparent delay. Many take New Testament prophecies at their word, leading them to conclude that Christ must have already returned, but in a non-literal sense. Preterists, for example, maintain that Christ's coming had a spiritual fulfillment and that he is already reigning in the hearts of the righteous.[10] John Humphrey Noyes, founder of the Oneida community (1811–86), contended that the second coming occurred as early as A.D. 70. However, those who espouse this explanation have difficulty explaining biblical passages which portray his return as being both personal and visible (Matt. 26:64; Acts 1:4–11; 1 Thess. 4:16; Titus 2:11–14).

After an extensive analysis of what Jesus might have intended by his declaration: "This generation shall not pass, till all these things be fulfilled" (Matt. 24:34), R. C. Sproul, a Calvinist professor of systematic theology, conceded, "If both 'this generation' and 'all these things' are taken at face value, then either all the content of Jesus' Olivet Discourse, including the parousia he describes here, have already taken place (in some sense), or at least some of Jesus' prophecy failed to take place within the time-frame assigned to it."[11]

While composing his own version of the New Testament, Joseph Smith revised the language of several prophecies to give them a much later horizon, thus rescuing them from failure. For example, while Matthew 24:34 reads: "This generation [i.e., the generation living at the time of Christ] shall not pass, till all these things [i.e., the signs preceding his second coming] be fulfilled," the JST reads: "This generation, *in which these things shall be shown forth*, shall not pass away until all I have told you shall be fulfilled" (JS–M 1:34, emphasis mine).[12] The KJV correspondingly states that "ye [i.e., the disciples] shall see all these things" (Matt. 24:33), but in the JST "they [i.e., the elect] shall see all these things" (JS–M 1:39).

John the Baptist came preaching that "the kingdom of heaven is at hand" (Matt. 3:2), and declared that even "now . . . the axe is laid at the root of the trees" which are ready to be "hewn down, and cast into the fire" (Matt. 3:10). Scholarly exegetes see this as an unmistakable reference to the final judgment and appearance of the eschatological kingdom which John perceived as imminent.[13] Joseph Smith, however, viewed this kingdom as a spiritual kingdom, which was close "at hand," not in the sense of being close in time, but close by "in the hands of John" who granted entry to the kingdom through baptism.[14]

In Luke 3, John the Baptist's ministry is presented as the fulfillment of Isaiah's end-time prophecy:

> The voice of one crying in the wilderness [saying] Prepare ye the way of the Lord, make his paths straight.
> Every valley shall be filled, and every mountain and hill shall be brought low; and the crooked shall be made straight, and the rough ways shall be made smooth. (Luke 3:4–5)

Joseph Smith, who understood the lowering of the mountains and raising of the valleys as events attending the second coming (D&C 49:23), inserted five additional verses before verse 5, which placed the leveling of the land in a latter-day context—though this seems to disrupt the natural flow of the original text where the leveling of the land was simply meant as a metaphorical prophecy of John making Jesus's paths straight.

Joseph Smith revised several New Testament epistles to remove any sense of delay in the parousia. For example, where Paul writes to the Corinthians that Old Testament stories of God's judgments on the disobedient "are written for our [Paul's and his contemporaries'] admonition, upon whom the ends of the world are come" (1 Cor. 10:11), the JST instead reads: "They were written for our admonition also, and for an admonition for those upon whom the end of the world shall come." While the KJV has Paul saying "*we* which are alive and remain" when the Lord comes (1 Thess. 4:15), the JST has him referring to "*they* who are alive."[15] And instead of announcing that "the time is short" until the end comes (1 Cor. 7:29), in the JST Paul announces that "the time that remaineth is but short, that ye shall be sent forth unto the ministry." Finally, JST Hebrews 9:26 has Christ being sacrificed "in the meridian of time" instead of "in the end of the world" as in the KJV.

Early Nineteenth-Century Christianity

By the early 1800s many Protestants had come to believe "that mankind was living in the last days, that the 'midnight cry' might soon be heard, and that the coming of the Messiah might be expected shortly. Such beliefs . . . were part and parcel of everyday evangelical religion."[16] Seekers and restorationists believed that Christ's coming was fast approaching and that signs signaling his return were everywhere evident. Seekers believed that the restoration of the ancient gospel was a necessary precursor to the second coming of Christ, which many were certain would occur within their own lifetimes.[17] Early American colonists were intrigued by the apocalyptic writings of the Bible and saw themselves as participants in apocalyptic fulfillment. For example, Baptist preacher William Miller (1783–1849), founder of the Millerites, convinced a large following in 1839 that the second coming would occur in 1843 and prepared his followers to meet the Lord.[18]

Early Mormonism

Latter-day Saints shared the same enthusiastic anticipation of an imminent return of the Savior in glory. The Doctrine and Covenants repeatedly affirmed that Christ would "come quickly" (D&C 33:18; 34:12; 35:27; 39:24; 41:4; 49:28; 51:20; 54:10; 68:35; 87:8; 88:126; 99:5; 112:34) and that his return was "nigh" or "at hand" (D&C 1:12, 35; 29:9, 10; 33:10; 34:7; 35:15, 16, 26; 39:19, 21; 42:7; 43:17; 45:37–39; 49:6; 58:4; 63:53; 104:59; 106:4; 128:24; 133:17). Joseph Smith initially seemed convinced that Christ would return in the generation in which he lived.

On January 4, 1833, he prophesied "by the authority of Jesus Christ, that not many years shall pass away before . . . pestalence hail famine and earthquake will sweep the wicked of this generation from off the face of this Land to open and prepare the way for the return of the lost tribes of Israel from the north country." He then observed, "There are those now living upon the earth whose eyes shall not be closed in death until they see all these things which I have spoken fulfilled."[19] On March 30, 1834, after the Saints were expelled from Jackson County, he told Edward Partridge, their bishop, "God will strike through kings in the days of his wrath but what he will deliver his people in Jackson County, where, ere long, he will set his feet, when earth and heaven shall tremble!"[20] It has been reported that in more than a third (37 percent) of a sample of sixty-two patriarchal blessings given by Joseph Smith Sr. between 1835 and 1844, he promised the recipient that he or she would not die before Christ's second coming.[21]

In February 1835, the Prophet apparently realized he had misjudged the time of the Lord's coming and therefore extended the time saying, "Fifty-six years should wind up the scene."[22] In April 1843, he remarked, "I prophesy in the name of the Lord God—and let it be written—that the Son of Man will not come in the heavens till I am 85 years old, 48 years hence or about 1890."[23] These statements pushed the predicted time of the second coming back to 1890–91, a time which many Saints anticipated with mounting expectation, especially since it coincided with maximum federal efforts to suppress the practice of polygamy. Soon after the U.S. Supreme Court upheld antipolygamy legislation in the Reynolds ruling of 1878, Apostle Wilford Woodruff declared to a conference of Saints in northern Arizona that "there will be no United States in the year 1890."[24] When the cleansing of the earth and Second Coming did not materialize, many were understandably disappointed. Most Saints, however, simply re-extended their millennial expectations to a more distant future.

Much of the expectation of Christ's imminent return in the early LDS Church stemmed from an 1832 revelation which announced that the temple in Jackson County, Missouri, to which the Savior would return in person,

> shall be reared in this generation.
> For verily this generation shall not all pass away until an house shall be built unto the Lord, and a cloud shall rest upon it, which cloud shall be even the glory of the Lord, which shall fill the house. (D&C 84:4–5)

Brigham Young and other General Authorities throughout the nineteenth century expressed confidence that this prophecy would soon be fulfilled since they viewed themselves as the generation spoken of.[25] For example, in April 1845 Brigham Young vowed to a congregation of Saints in Nauvoo: "As the Lord lives we will build up Jackson county in this generation."[26] In 1862 after the Saints moved west, he again assured them that it wouldn't be long before "we have to go back to Jackson County, [Missouri,] which I expect will be in seven years."[27] In May 1870, Orson Pratt reassured the Saints saying, "God promised in the year 1832 that we should, *before the generation then living had passed away*, return and build up the City of Zion in Jackson County. . . . We believe in these promises as much as we believe in any promise ever uttered by the mouth of Jehovah. . . . Why? Because *God cannot lie.* He will fulfill all His promises. He has spoken, it must come to pass. This is our faith."[28]

One year later he again spoke unwaveringly, "The generation [spoken of in D&C 84:5] has not passed away; all the people that were living thirty-nine years ago have not passed away; but before they do pass away this [i.e., the building of the temple and coming of the Savior] will be fulfilled."[29] Wilford Woodruff, fourth president of the Church, said on June 27, 1875, the thirty-first anniversary of Joseph Smith's assassination: "I believe there are many children now living in the mountains of Israel [Utah] who will never taste death, that is, they will dwell on the earth at the coming of the Lord Jesus Christ."[30] In general conference in 1898 and in 1900, Lorenzo Snow, fifth LDS Church president, affirmed: "There are many—hundreds and hundreds within the sound of my voice—that will live to go back to Jackson County (Missouri) and build a holy temple to the Lord our God."[31]

THE SECOND COMING AND MILLENNIUM   437

The fading prospect of an imminent second coming caused Church leaders to again readjust their projections. Putting lapsed predictions into perspective, eighty-five-year-old Benjamin F. Johnson, who was converted in 1831, wrote in 1903, "We were over seventy years ago taught by our leaders to believe that the coming of Christ and the millennial reign was much nearer than we believe it to be now."[32] Christ's promised coming in "this generation" as stated in Section 84 has since been explained by either redefining "generation" to mean this last dispensation of the gospel,[33] or reasoning that the redemption could have indeed occurred at that time, but, due to internal and external circumstances, "the real time" for building the temple was postponed.[34]

Contemporary Mormonism

Through most of the twentieth century, Latter-day Saints expected that the second coming would occur at or near the century's end. This understanding was based largely on Doctrine and Covenants 77, which states that the earth's "continuance, or its temporal existence" will last seven thousand years (D&C 77:6). Since the millennium is to last one thousand years, it would necessarily have to start at the end of the sixth thousand years. Revelations further state that Christ's coming will inaugurate the millennium (D&C 29:11; 43:29–30; 130:16; 88:95–98). As Doctrine and Covenants 77:12 explains:

> In the beginning of the seventh thousand years will the Lord God sanctify the earth, and complete the salvation of man, and judge all things . . . and the sounding of the trumpets of the seven angels are the preparing and finishing of his work, in the beginning of the seventh thousand years—the preparing of the way before the time of his coming.

According to the Bible's chronology, Adam fell in 4004 B.C.[35] which would make the end of the twentieth century roughly six thousand years since the fall. Accordingly, Bruce R. McConkie commented in 1966 that Doctrine and Covenants 77 "states categorically that Christ will come 'in the beginning of the seventh thousand years' of the earth's temporal continuance."[36] Twenty years later, however, McConkie revised his outlook stating that Christ would not come at the beginning of the seventh thousand years but rather at some unspecified time afterward. Citing the same verses in Doctrine and Covenants 77 he stated: "They speak of events destined to occur 'in the beginning of the seventh thousand years,' which events will be 'the preparing of the way before the time of his coming' (D&C 77:12). This revealed word can only mean that the Lord will come sometime after the beginning of the named time, but whether that coming will be ten or a hundred years thereafter, we are left to wonder."[37] This is a good example of how changing prospects influence the way prophecy is interpreted.

How do current LDS commentators explain the apparent delay of the parousia? The near-term projections of the New Testament are often explained as being relative; and since a thousand years for human beings is one day with the Lord (2 Pet. 3:8), it shouldn't be surprising for the Lord to speak of a distant event as being close at hand (D&C 63:53). McConkie comments: "We conclude that in the eternal perspective the coming of the Lord is nigh, but that from man's viewpoint many years may yet pass away before that awesome and dreadful day."[38] This view, however, doesn't explain how passages are to be taken which expressly state that those then alive would remain until he comes. With respect to the repeated phrase "I come quickly" (Rev. 3:1, 22:7, 22:20), McConkie explains that "quickly" doesn't mean "soon, but in a quick manner; that is, with speed and suddenness after all of the promised conditions precedent have occurred."[39] The problem with this interpretation is that virtually all modern translations suggest that the more accurate reading is "I come soon." Remember that John was commanded not to even bother sealing up his writings "for the time is at hand" (Rev. 22:10). Another challenge for LDS commentators is dealing with the unmistakable impression evidenced among New Testament writers that they themselves were living in the last days. BYU religion professor Kent Jackson suggests that New Testament references to the last days pertained to the last days of the church, and not to the last days of the world.[40] A challenge for this interpretation, however, is that many of the New Testament passages just cited explicitly refer to the second coming of Christ and the end-time judgment, not the end of the church.

According to LDS scripture, the righteous will be able to discern the signs of Christ's coming since the Lord promised, "Unto you it shall be given to know the signs of the times, and the signs of the coming of the Son of Man" (D&C 68:11). Historically, however, it seems that the faithful have been no more discerning of the time of Christ's coming than others of their day. Indeed, faithful believers of virtually every age seem to have been persuaded that the signs in their time portended the end of the world.

Spirit Poured Out on All Flesh

To illustrate the changing understanding of end-time signs, consider the prophecy in Joel 2:28–29:

> And it shall come to pass afterward, that I will pour out my spirit upon all flesh; and your sons and your daughters shall prophesy, your old men shall dream dreams, your young men shall see visions:
>
> And also upon the servants and upon the handmaids in those days will I pour out my spirit.

According to Old Testament scholar Richard Henshaw, the message of Joel is a call to ancient Israel to repent, "for 'the day of the Lord' predicted of old has come." And when judgment has been poured out on their oppressors and their former days of glory restored, "all will be prophets."[41] To relate this prophecy to his own day, Peter changed the word "afterward" (i.e., after the kingdom of Israel is restored) to "in the last days," which, for Peter, was his own time, and declared it to have been fulfilled by manifestations of the Spirit on the day of Pentecost (Acts 2:16–21). To the contrary, Joseph Smith related that he was informed by the angel Moroni in 1823 that Joel's prophecy had not yet been fulfilled (JS–H 1:41). Revelations in the Doctrine and Covenants which speak of the outpouring of God's Spirit invariably refer to the Holy Ghost and speak of this event in the future tense (D&C 19:38, 27:18, 44:2, 95:4). The consistent view expressed in the Church before 1870 was that the Spirit that would be poured out on all flesh was the Holy Ghost and that this event would not occur until the millennium. In August 1871, however, Brigham Young stated: "The time has come when the Lord is commencing to pour out his Spirit upon the people," which he defined as "the Spirit of Christ."[42]

Today, building upon Brigham Young's interpretation that the Lord's spirit in Joel 2:28–29 refers to the light of Christ, the Lord's spirit is seen as having been poured out on all flesh for several centuries through scientific discoveries and other advancements preparing the way for the restoration of the gospel.[43] Although some Latter-day Saints may argue that, in some peculiar sense, all of these claims of fulfillment are true, each of the interpretations given seems to have been motivated by changes in theological perspective and suggests a certain degree of subjectivity in interpreting end-time prophecies.

Millennialism

Scriptures pertaining to the latter-day millennium or thousand-year reign of Christ on earth have been progressively reinterpreted over time to create the perception of a unified, harmonious picture. Grant Underwood notes, "From the beginning such harmonization of diverse texts has been an exercise in interpretation and elaboration."[44]

Old Testament

According to critical scholars, eschatological or end-time prophecies in the Old Testament do not speak of latter-day events in a millennial context as understood by Latter-day Saints, even though they focus on an earthly and sometimes heavenly kingdom of God. In the Old Testament the kingdom of God is the anxiously anticipated, not-too-distant establishment of God's rule upon the earth and the liberation of Israel from captivity. Old Testament prophecies describe this period as an anticipated era in which "the Lord of hosts shall reign" (Isa. 24:23), "Israel shall dwell safely" (Jer. 23:6), "the wolf . . . shall dwell with the lamb" (Isa. 11:6), "swords" will be beaten "into plowshares" (Isa. 2:4), and none "shall . . . hurt nor destroy" (Isa. 11:9). Old Testament scholar David P. Wright characterized the rather "imminent orientation" of these Old Testament prophecies stating that "prophetic books [of the Old Testament] share the common expectation of an imminent return to the land of Israel and consequent abundant and even enduring blessing after [the] Babylonian captivity."[45] Ezekiel described the return of Israel as being "at hand" (Ezek. 36:8), and Jeremiah foretold that the Babylonian captivity would last only seventy years (Jer. 25:11–12, 29:10) and would be followed by the Lord's wrath being poured out on "all the nations" (Jer. 25:17) and on "all the inhabitants of the earth" (Jer. 25:29, 30).

Nowhere do Old Testament prophecies mention a millennial period of righteousness followed by either an end-time battle with Satan or a final judgment. In the Old Testament, the Lord is prophesied to come at the final judgment day, bringing in a new heaven and new earth (Isa. 65:17, 66:22). This "newness" would be the earth's final state, a state which many Christians (including Latter-day Saints) now consider to be an interim millennial period. Old Testament texts make no discernable distinction between the restored kingdom of Israel reestablished on the earth and the eternal state of the earth. (See, for example, the intermingling of the two in Isaiah 65:17–25.)

Ancient Jewish prophets don't seem to have considered heaven as a place where the righteous would someday dwell. Rather, they envisioned a restoration of the kingdom of Israel followed by an endless era of righteousness upon the earth. In the Old Testament, this endless era of peace and prosperity was the final reward for the righteous. According to Wright,

> These prophets collectively say that after the people's punishment in the foreign land the people . . . would be forgiven and renewed (e.g., given a new heart) and return to their land. . . . The restoration to the land would begin a period of regeneration when

the people would no longer be troubled by their enemies and would have . . . prosperity. Jerusalem would be rebuilt and become glorious. The temple in Jerusalem, which was destroyed by the Babylonians, would also be rebuilt, and its priesthood and sacrificial worship would be reestablished. . . . With the temple and Jerusalem rebuilt, God would come and again make his abode in the temple (or the city).[46]

In short, Old Testament prophets spoke of only a single renovation, which would be the final state of the earth. Latter-day Saints interpret this state as a millennial period preceding a far more glorious final state of the earth. It was only in later Judaism, closer to the time of Christ, that a millennial period prior to the end appears in Jewish literature. According to the *Jewish Encyclopedia*, "This concept is expressed in Jewish literature in Enoch, xiii., xci. 12-17; in the apocalypse of the ten weeks, in Apoc. Baruch, xl. 3 ('And his dominion shall last forever, until the world doomed to destruction shall perish'); and in II Esdras vii. 28-29."[47] Scholars explain that it is this intertestamental Jewish concept of a millennial period that would influence the millennial language of the book of Revelation.

New Testament

In the New Testament, the basic Old Testament eschatological themes reappear; however, Christ is now the one who comes at the end of time to judge the world and rule over the righteous. Christians connected apocalypticism with Jesus's repeated proclamation of the coming kingdom. The Gospel of Matthew alone has more than fifty-five references to this kingdom. Jesus taught his disciples to pray for the arrival of this kingdom (Matt. 6:10), and Luke records how people "thought that the kingdom of God should immediately appear" (Luke 19:11). James and John, at the insistence of their mother, sought positions of power in the kingdom which they believed Jesus would soon establish (Matt. 20:20–21). As in the Old Testament, this kingdom is not described in terms of an interim millennial kingdom followed by a celestialized earth, but as the final kingdom of God.

Aside from an isolated reference to the millennium in Revelation 20:2–7, the New Testament, like the Old Testament, makes no mention of a millennial period preceding the end time. In fact, most New Testament passages which prophesy of final events do not allow for a millennial period. According to New Testament descriptions, Christ's second coming will be accompanied by a final judgment resulting in either salvation or damnation for each of the earth's inhabitants (1 Cor. 1:7, 8; Philip. 1:6, 10; 1 Jn. 2:28; 1 Tim. 4:8; 2 Tim. 4:1). When

Christ returns, a rapture (literally "caught up") of the living and the dead in resurrection leads to uninterrupted communion with the Lord from that day forward (1 Thess. 4:13–18). As one biblical scholar summarizes, "Reading the Bible chronologically reveals that the millennial kingdom is not clearly distinguished from the eternal state until the last book of the Bible."[48]

In the New Testament, the second coming is to be followed immediately by a permanently renewed earth, the final resurrection, and the final judgment of all humankind. Peter, for example, identifies Christ's coming as "the day of judgment" (2 Pet. 2:9, 3:7). This "day of the Lord will come as a thief in the night; in the which the heavens shall pass away with a great noise, and the elements shall melt with fervent heat, the earth also and the works that are therein shall be burned up" (2 Pet. 3:10). This is all to be followed by "new heavens and a new earth, wherein dwelleth righteousness" (2 Pet. 3:13). There is no mention of a subsequent judgment or of any other succeeding events, such as a second resurrection. The implication is that, following the resurrection and judgment at Christ's second coming, the righteous will live forever on the glorified earth while the wicked will be cast out.

The apostle Paul taught that Christ's coming would initiate the resurrection, "then," he states, "cometh the end, when he shall have delivered up the kingdom to God, even the Father" (1 Cor. 15:24). Once again, no succeeding events are mentioned. The resurrection and judgment consummate God's work on earth. In the Gospels the righteous and the wicked are separated at Christ's coming (Matt. 13:41, 24:37–41, 25:31–46, Luke 17:29–35). It is then, not a thousand years later, that the final judgment of both Saints and sinners occurs.

So where did the idea of a millennial era of peace followed by a final judgment day come from? New Testament scholar Raymond Brown offers the following explanation:

> If one reviews the history of Messianism (e.g., NJBC 77:152–63), an anticipation that survived the Babylonian exile was that one day God would restore the kingdom of David under a model anointed king, the Messiah; indeed, earlier Scripture was reread with this understanding (e.g., Amos 9:11). Even though idealized and pictured as definitive, this would be an earthly, historical kingdom, and most often its relation to the endtime was not specified. On the other hand, in a pessimistic view of history, some apocalyptic literature pictured God's direct final intervention without any mention of the restoration of the Davidic kingdom (Isa. 24–27; Dan.; Assumption of Moses; Apocalypse of Abraham).

One way of combining the two expectations was to posit two divine interventions: (1) a restoration of an earthly kingdom or period of blissful prosperity to be followed by (2) God's endtime victory and judgment.[49]

The book of Revelation seems to incorporate this combined perspective in its graphic depiction of final events. Here John outlines the establishment of God's kingdom in two phases: a millennial phase (Rev. 19:11–20:6) and a final phase (Rev. 20:7–22:5). In the millennial phase, the angels destroy wickedness and imprison Satan, locking him away in a bottomless pit where he can do no harm. The righteous are no longer deceived, and the resurrected martyrs reign with Christ for a thousand years. After this millennial period, Satan and his angels are released from their chains and allowed to mount a final, though futile, attack against God's kingdom. Satan attempts "to deceive the nations" (Rev. 20:8) as he battles against "the camp of the saints, and the beloved city [Jerusalem]," but "fire came down from God out of heaven, and devoured them" (Rev. 20:9). Satan himself is thrown into a lake of fire and brimstone where he is "tormented day and night for ever and ever" (Rev. 20:10).

The second or final phase of God's kingdom begins with a general resurrection of the dead. A final judgment ensures that anyone whose name is not written in the Book of Life is thrown into the burning lake. All others will be granted eternal life on a renewed earth whose capital city is the new Jerusalem. The natural sequence of events in the last three chapters of Revelation seems to be the establishment of a millennial kingdom, a general resurrection and final judgment, the creation of a new heaven and earth, and the righteous taking up an eternal abode in the New Jerusalem which descends from heaven.

Revelation 20, which prophesies of Christ's thousand-year reign, leaves important issues unresolved. For example, it doesn't actually say that Christ will return to earth or that he will reign personally during this thousand years. In fact, Christ's kingdom is depicted as descending literally from heaven after the millennium (Rev. 21:2). No mention is made of a general resurrection at the millennium's commencement, only a resurrection of "the souls of them that were beheaded for the witness of Jesus, and for the word of God" (Rev. 20:4). "But the rest of the dead lived not again until the thousand years were finished" (Rev. 20:5). The raising of the beheaded martyrs seems to compose the sum total of "the first resurrection," and they become "priests of God and of Christ, and shall reign with him a thousand years" (Rev. 20:6). It is as though they are rewarded for martyrdom with an advance resurrection and position of honor with Christ. Even non-Christian Jews at the time of Christ believed that martyrs would receive special consideration in the resurrection.[50] Another conclusion drawn from the text is that no actual judgment, other than the destruction poured out on the wicked, occurs until after the "thousand years" (Rev. 20:11–15).

The notion of the thousand-year period in Revelation is believed to have come from Jewish apocalypticism, which some scholars suggest was likely influenced, directly or indirectly, by Zoroastrianism, a religion of the Persians.[51] In a summary of scholarly views regarding possible sources for the millennial language found in Revelation 20, Jack T. Sanders, professor of religious studies at the University of Oregon, concludes that there is "widespread, albeit not universal, agreement that the idea of the millennium comes in one way or another from Ps. 90:4, 'A thousand years in your eyes are like a yesterday' . . . , combined with the Jewish notion of an interim messianic period at the divine conclusion to history or with the Jewish notion that history plays out over a cosmic week that, under the influence of Ps. 90:4, is thought to be a period of 6000 years followed by a Sabbath of 1000 years."[52] James Tabor, professor of religious studies at the University of North Carolina, asserts that, "despite its Christ-centered formulation, Revelation clearly tapped into a concept that had been developing among Jews for centuries. A division of 6,000 years of human time is described in the Babylonian Talmud in a conversation between two rabbis. Rabbi Kattina taught: 'Six thousand years shall the world exist, and one thousand, the seventh, it shall be desolate, as it is written, 'And the Lord alone shall be exalted in that day' . . . . Just as the seventh year is one year of release in seven [a reference to the sabbatical year (Deut. 15:1)], so is the world: one thousand years out of seven shall be fallow.'"[53]

Early Nineteenth-Century Christianity

Given that the Bible contains only a single reference to a thousand-year period, which could be taken figuratively, and because a literal second coming failed to materialize, it is little wonder that the predominant Christian view until the time of the Reformation was Amillennialism. Amillennialists view the kingdom of God, not as a literal kingdom, but as Christ's reign in the hearts of the righteous. Hence, they anticipate no future literal millennium. Amillennialists are able to reconcile millennial language with their view of a present spiritual reign by citing passages showing that Christ has reigned since his resurrection (1 Cor. 15:22–28; Rev. 1:9) and now sits "on his throne" (Acts 2:30; Heb. 1:3, 8; 10:12–13), while the Saints likewise reign with Christ in his spiritual kingdom (Eph. 2:5–6; Rev. 5:9–10; Rom. 5:17).

Millennialism, or the belief in a future literal millennial period on earth, was becoming increasingly popular at the time of Joseph Smith. Millennialists were divided into two major camps: premillennialists ("catastrophic millennialists") and postmillennialists ("progressive millennialists)." Premillennialists believed that Christ would come to a largely degenerate world before (pre-) the millennium and, through a major catastrophe, destroy the wicked, usher in his personal reign, and rule the earth for the next thousand years. Postmillennialists, in contrast, believed that Christ's second coming would occur after (post) the millennium, and that the millennium itself would be established progressively by Christianizing the world through preaching the gospel. In November 1830, the great revivalist preacher Charles Grandison Finney told an audience in Rochester, New York, that if Christians would unite they could "convert the world and bring on the millennium in three months."[54] Premillenialists believed that "there would be two comings, two judgments, and two resurrections—one at the time of Christ's coming and one after [the millennium]."[55] Postmillennialists espoused one general resurrection and one day of judgment, both to "coincide with Christ's return to earth at the end of the thousand years."[56]

Promoted in eighteenth-century America by Jonathan Edwards and Samuel Hopkins, postmillennialism had become the dominant view among Protestants by the nineteenth century. Premillennialism, however, was gaining popularity in the early 1800s as many began anticipating Christ's literal return as being imminent, in spite of, and perhaps even because of, the wicked state of the world.

Mormonism

The earliest LDS views regarding the second coming appear, though sketchily, in the Book of Mormon and seem to have a postmillennial orientation. Postmillennialists, unlike premillenialists, were generally non-literalists and therefore did not necessarily view the millennium as literal thousand-year period, nor did they insist on a literal binding of Satan or a personal reign of Christ on the earth. Significantly, the Book of Mormon mentions neither a thousand-year millennial period nor a literal binding of Satan. Furthermore, Christ is not prophesied to appear at the start of a millennial period nor is he supposed to reign personally on the earth prior to the final judgment. The Book of Mormon prophesies that Jews will convert to Christ through gospel preaching, not through Christ's sudden millennial appearance as in later revelations (see Chapter 18).

Interestingly, the LDS Topical Guide lists more than a dozen passages each for the Old and New Testaments under "Jesus Christ,

Second Coming," but has only two Book of Mormon citations, both of which simply restate Old Testament prophecies concerning the final-judgment day of the Lord.

The first citation is 3 Nephi 24:2, in which the resurrected Christ quotes Malachi 3:2, asking, "Who may abide the day of his coming?" In interpreting this passage, Jesus explains that it refers to "the time when he [Christ] should come in his glory" (3 Ne. 26:3). But this is also the time when "the earth should be wrapt together as a scroll, and the heavens and the earth should pass away." It will occur at "the great and last day, when all people, and all kindreds, and all nations and tongues shall stand before God, to be judged of their works" (3 Ne. 26:4). Thus, Christ's coming is depicted as coinciding with the very end of the earth's history, and therefore doesn't seem to allow for a millennial period to follow.

The second Book of Mormon passage listed in the LDS Topical Guide is 3 Nephi 27:16, which speaks of "that day when [Christ] shall stand to judge the world." This judgment day will be "at the last day" (vv. 6, 20) when "all men" are resurrected (vv. 14–15)—and, hence, is not premillennial. At this time, the wicked will be "cast into the fire, from whence they can no more return" (v. 17), while the righteous enter into the kingdom of heaven (vv. 6, 19). Once again, this passage doesn't provide for a millennial period following this judgment; all are resurrected, and their judgment is final.

In the Book of Mormon, the timing of the second coming, the universal resurrection, and final judgment is much more consistent with a postmillennial view of the second coming—which was the dominant eschatological view of the early nineteenth century. The eschatological picture portrayed in the Book of Mormon is that the gospel will progressively spread while God increasingly blesses the righteous and pours out destruction on the wicked. Christ's only manifestation before the final judgment day is the increasing display of his power in destroying the wicked (2 Ne. 6:14) and blessing the righteous (2 Ne. 26:13). During this period of cleansing, the faithful will be gathered to their lands of inheritance while the wicked are destroyed by fires, plagues, etc. Eventually, only the righteous will remain; and because of their righteousness, Christ will "reign in dominion, and might, and great glory" (1 Ne. 22:24),[57] while Satan has no power over them "for a long time" (1 Ne. 30:18; Jacob 5:76), even "for the space of many years" (1 Ne. 22:26). This scenario is not unlike the way many postmillennialists in Joseph Smith's time viewed events: Satan would be bound by "the power of the gospel" that would bear sway in the lives of all men, and the millennial period would last simply "a long time."[58] After this lengthy but indefinite period, the Book of Mormon has the Lord allegorically saying, "Evil fruit shall again come into my vineyard, then will I cause the good and the bad to be gathered; and the good will I preserve unto myself, and the bad will I cast away into its own place. And then cometh the season and the end; and my vineyard will I cause to be burned with fire" (Jacob 5:77).[59]

According to the sequence evident in the Book of Mormon, at the very end of time Christ will "come in his glory" (3 Ne. 26:3), "the heavens and the earth should pass away" (3 Ne. 26:3), and all will be resurrected and brought to "stand before God, to be judged of their works, whether they be good or whether they be evil" (3 Ne. 26:4). Those with good works enter "endless life and happiness" while those whose works are evil are "delivered up to the devil, who hath subjected them, which is damnation" (Mosiah 16:10–11). This is the essence of Book of Mormon eschatology.

Early revelations in the Doctrine and Covenants are surprisingly quiet regarding Christ's second coming and millennial reign. None of the revelations in the Doctrine and Covenants received before September 1830 (twenty-five in total) mentions a millennium or Christ's second coming. Although Doctrine and Covenants 5:19 and 27:18 now refer to Christ's coming, neither verse was in the original 1833 *Book of Commandments*. Other passages in these early sections refer to "the last day" but in terms of the final judgment day when the righteous are saved and the wicked damned (D&C 4:2, 5:35, 6:13, 9:14, 10:23, 17:8, 18:24–25, 19:3).

Doctrine and Covenants 5:35 ends with the promise that the righteous "shal[l] be lifted up at the last day." Today, Latter-day Saints would interpret this event as occurring prior to the millennium at Christ's second coming. In the Book of Mormon, however, the "last day," in its more than fifty occurrences, appears to always refer to the final judgment day—literally the earth's last day. Related passages in the Book of Mormon which speak of the righteous being "lifted up at the last day" are also spoken in reference to the end time when all the dead are raised to be judged (1 Ne. 13:37; 2 Ne. 9:22; Mosiah 23:22; Alma 13:29; Ether 4:19).

The first unambiguous LDS reference to the second coming and millennial reign of Christ on the earth doesn't appear until September 1830, in a revelation to Joseph Smith: "For I [the Lord] will reveal myself from heaven with power and great glory, with all the hosts thereof, and dwell in righteousness with men on earth a thousand years, and the wicked shall not stand" (D&C 29:11). Near this same time, the Prophet received a revelation explaining that Enoch "saw the day of the coming of the Son of Man, in the last days [no longer "at the last day"], to dwell on the earth in righteousness for the space of a thousand years" (Moses 7:65). Interestingly, these revelations referring to Christ's coming and millennial reign say nothing of a resurrection and judgment occurring at this time. On the contrary, it isn't until after the millennium and after the earth is destroyed that

> Michael, mine archangel, shall sound his trump, and then shall all the dead awake, for their graves shall be opened, and they shall come forth—yea, even all.
> And the righteous shall be gathered on my right hand unto eternal life; and the wicked on my left hand will I be ashamed to own before the Father. (D&C 29:26–27).

These first revelations referring to the millennium make explicit the fact that Christ will appear physically on the earth at the start of the millennium (rather than reigning spiritually in the hearts of the righteous as implied in D&C 1:36), and that the era of peace and righteousness will last a thousand years. The resurrection and final judgment, however, still occur at the end of the earth.

Merging these later premillennialist teachings with earlier postmillennialist language created a sort of hybrid form of millennialism. It wasn't long (March 1831) before a first resurrection was identified as occurring at the start of the millennium (D&C 45:54).

Shifting to a premillennialist eschatology created the need to rethink certain notions that seem to be more attached to a postmillennialist perspective. For example, biblical and Book of Mormon passages referring to the coming of the Lord situate it at the final judgment when all but the righteous will be destroyed (Old Testament) or condemned (New Testament and Book of Mormon). In 1841 Joseph Smith introduced the provocative idea that the "wicked" will not be entirely destroyed at the coming of Christ, but will remain on earth during the millennium.[60] Even if Joseph was only referring to those who abide a terrestrial law (see D&C 84:49–53), this was still a departure from earlier teachings that seemed to suggest that only righteous Mormons would abide the day of his coming. Underwood notes that this new teaching "represented an abrupt about-face from a decade of Mormon consensus to the contrary, and it would be at least another decade before the idea really caught hold even among church leaders."[61]

The New Heaven and Earth

With the introduction of the idea that Christ's return would precede the end time by at least a thousand years, events traditionally associated with the Lord's coming at the end of time became confused in LDS thought. In the Old Testament, the "day of the Lord" coincided with the end of time which culminated in a new heaven and a new earth. With the current separation in time between the second coming and the end time, the creation of a new heaven and earth is now depicted as occurring twice or in two stages, first when Christ comes at the start of the millennium and then again at the end of time.[62]

According to biblical scholars, eschatological or end-time prophecies in the Old Testament include a new creation and new way of life. This was to be an end-time occurrence that would last indefinitely. Not only would all forms of evil and suffering be eliminated, including Israel's oppressors, but the earth itself would return to an Edenic state. In this glorious new age, the kingdom of God would rule, replacing all earthly empires forever. To emphasize the cosmic magnitude of this transformation, it was extended to include even a new heaven. Old Testament prophets spoke of the creation of this new heaven and earth as being an end-time event in which the Lord comes and pronounces final judgment, all things become new, and the righteous dwell indefinitely with God (Isa. 24:19–23; 34:1–6; 65:16–20; 66:22–24).

Ancient prophets described this envisioned golden age using what was a familiar three-tiered cosmology while still preserving traditional boundaries of habitation. The heavens and earth would become new and improved but still serve the same purposes. James Tabor observes that, in all prophecies of the end time, "the cosmos is still basically the same. Humans stay on earth. The normal cycles of nature continue. Generations still come and go, and the dead of past ages remain in Sheol, thoroughly 'dead.'"[63] It is a "new" heaven and earth in the sense that all things become glorious and a new era of righteousness begins. Isaiah speaks of the righteous who remain saying, "And they shall go forth, and look upon the carcases of the men that have transgressed against me for their worm shall not die, neither shall their fire be quenched; and they shall be an abhorring unto all flesh" (Isa. 66:24). Thus, the flesh of the dead would still remain for the righteous to look upon.

As already noted, the New Testament presents a view of the last days that is similar to that found in the Old Testament, particularly in regard to the judgment at the end of time and the creation of a new heaven and earth (2 Pet. 3:5–13; Rev. 21:1–7). The book of Revelation—which is the only place that expressly speaks of a millennial period prior to the Lord's coming—still has the millennium (Rev. 20) preceding the creation of a new heaven and earth (Rev. 21). Thus, the "new heaven and earth" spoken of in the New Testament is the final state of the earth.

As noted earlier, the Book of Mormon also speaks of heaven and earth passing away as events of the final judgment unfold (3 Ne. 26:3–4). The New Jerusalem and old Jerusalem descend as part of the new heaven and new earth to become the abode of the redeemed (Ether 13:9–11). This scenario reflects a postmillennial perspective popular at the time of Joseph Smith. When the millennium is first introduced in LDS scriptures, the creation of the new heaven and earth is kept as an end-time event and, therefore, occurs after the millennium (see D&C 29:22–24).[64] In August 1832, the Prophet said of the ancient righteous, "They saw the end of the glorious thousand years, when Satan was loosed for a little season; they saw the day of judgment when all men received according to their works, and they saw the heaven and the earth flee away to make room for the city of God, when the righteous receive an inheritance in eternity."[65] This view of the new heaven and earth occurring at the final judgment of the world was a common understanding of many Christians in the early 1800s.

As Latter-day Saints began reinterpreting Old Testament prophecies of latter-day glories as having a millennial setting rather than being the final state of the earth, the Old Testament pronouncement of a new heaven and earth at the beginning of this glorious state naturally came to be viewed as occurring at the start of the millennium. One can see the two roads that had to converge here. On the one hand, Old Testament prophecies became interpreted as depicting a new heaven and earth at the start of the millennium. On the other hand, the book of Revelation and the Prophet himself placed the new heaven and earth after the millennium.

To resolve this conflict, Bruce R. McConkie would later posit two new creations, one at the beginning of the millennium and one at the end of the earth. Invoking the principle of multiple fulfillment—which was often his way of resolving conflicting claims of fulfillment—McConkie remarked that, at the second coming, "This old earth and this old heaven, with all their evil and corruption and worldliness, shall come to an end; and there will be new heavens and a new earth whereon dwelleth righteousness. . . . Then after the Millennium, plus a little season . . . there will again be new heavens and a new earth, but this time it will be a celestial earth."[66]

Not surprisingly, in addition to placing the creation of the new heaven and earth both before and after the millennium, other events traditionally associated with the end time also had to be placed both before and after the millennium to resolve related conflicts. These include the judgment, resurrection, and coming of the New Jerusalem. Even the great battle of Armageddon is seen as occurring both before and after the millennium.[67]

Notes

1. E. M. Meyers, "The Crisis of the Mid Fifth-Century B.C.E. Second Zechariah and the 'End' of Prophecy," 718-19.
2. L. Michael White, "The Political History of the Jewish People."
3. Raymond E. Brown, *An Introduction to the New Testament*, 810.
4. M. Eugene Boring, "Revelation," 2233.
5. Grant Underwood, *The Millenarian World of Early Mormonism*, 15.
6. "Some" implies more than just John whom Latter-day Saints believe was privileged to remain alive until the second coming.
7. Hans Küng, *On Being a Christian*, 216.
8. James D. G. Dunn, *Unity and Diversity in the New Testament: An Inquiry into the Character of Earliest Christianity*, 19.
9. For additional passages in the New Testament indicating Christ's imminent return, see Mark 14:62; Acts 1:6-7; 1 Cor. 1:7-8, 15:51-53, 16:22; Phil. 1:6, 10; 4:5; 1 Thess. 1:9-10; 5:1-7, 23; 2 Thess. 2:1; 1 Tim. 6:14; 2 Pet. 3:3-4, 9-10; Rev. 1:1, 3, 7; 2:25; 3:3, 11; 22:7, 10, 12, 20.
10. Preterism, from the Latin praeter, meaning "past," is the belief that the events prophesied in the New Testament have already happened; namely, that the great war of Armageddon in Revelation occurred near 70 A.D. when the temple in Jerusalem was destroyed and many Jews were killed or scattered. According to Preterists, when Jesus talked about the end of the world, he did not mean that the physical world would be no more, but that the old worldview held by various contemporary Jewish groups was coming to an end, to be replaced by a new concept—the Kingdom of God. Thus, all of the major elements in Revelation (tribulation, Armageddon, rapture, etc.) are seen as having actually taken place in the first century A.D. Preterism as a defined movement began in the seventeenth century. It is an eschatological perspective rather than a formal religion or denomination. See Dennis Todd, "Doctrinal Classifications and Color Key."
11. R. C. Sproul, *The Last Days According to Jesus*, 64-65.
12. Many scholars assert that there was to be no significant time lapse between the destruction of the temple and the second coming in this prophecy. James D. Tabor, a professor of religious studies at the University of North Carolina, explains, "Jesus connects the destruction of the Jerusalem Temple to the more general 'signs of the end of the age': false prophets, war and disruptions, earthquakes, famines, pestilence, persecution, and a world-wide proclamation of his message. . . . The scheme is very tightly connected, and Jesus declares at the end that 'this generation shall not pass away until all these thing are fulfilled.'" James D. Tabor, "The Future," 48. The word "immediately" in Matthew 24:29 suggests that the cosmic disasters and coming of Christ were to follow on the heels of the destruction of Jerusalem. It appears that Jesus presented an uninterrupted chronological succession of events leading up to his second coming that was to all be witnessed by those then alive.
13. See, for example, Dunn, *Unity and Diversity in the New Testament*, 346.
14. Andrew F. Ehat and Lyndon W. Cook, *The Words of Joseph Smith*, 157.

15. The JST further associates the word "remain" with those "who are asleep" so that it is not the living but the dead who "remain." This, however, poses difficulties given the context of verses 15 and 17.

16. J. F. C. Harrison, *The Second Coming: Popular Millenarianism*, 5.

17. James B. Allen and Glen M. Leonard, *The Story of the Latter-day Saints*, 17.

18. L. Michael White, "Prophetic Belief in the United States." When Christ failed to appear in 1843, Miller realized that he had calculated the date wrong by assuming there was a year 0, which actually doesn't exist. He then changed his prediction to 1844 which also failed, resulting in what was referred to as the Great Disappointment when many defected.

19. Dean C. Jessee, comp. and ed., *Personal Writings of Joseph Smith*, 298. In May 1843, Joseph also prophesied "in the name of the Lord God of Israel" that "in a few years the government [of the United States] will be utterly overthrown and wasted, and there will not be so much as a potsherd left." *History of the Church*, 5:394.

20. Jessee, *Personal Writings of Joseph Smith*, 338.

21. Gregory A. Prince, *Power from On High: The Development of Mormon Priesthood*, 176–77. H. Michael Marquardt, comp. *Early Patriarchal Blessings of the Church of Jesus Christ of Latter-day Saints* (Salt Lake City: Smith-Pettit Foundation, 2009), presents a much larger sample (more than 700) by the first three patriarchs (Joseph Sr., Hyrum, and William) which, although too late for inclusion in this study, should shed light on early Mormon understanding of the Second Coming.

22. *History of the Church*, 2:182. Interestingly, the expression from Revelation, "I come quickly" (Rev 3:11; 22:7, 12; 22:20), appears ten times in the Doctrine and Covenants prior to 1835, but only once afterwards.

23. Ehat and Cook, *The Words of Joseph Smith*, 180.

24. Quoted in Dan Erickson, *As a Thief in the Night: The Mormon Quest for Millennial Deliverance*, 188.

25. See *Journal of Discourses*: George Q. Cannon, August 23, 1864, 10:345; Orson Pratt, May 5, 1870, 13:362; Orson Pratt, June 14, 1874, 17:112.

26. Brigham Young, "Speech," *Times and Seasons* 6 (July 1, 1845): 956.

27. Brigham Young, qtd. in *Journal History*, August 22, 1862.

28. Orson Pratt, May 5, 1870, *Journal of Discourses*, 13:362.

29. Orson Pratt, April 9, 1871, *Journal of Discourses*, 14:276.

30. Wilford Woodruff, June 27, 1845, *Journal of Discourses*, 18:37.

31. Wilford Woodruff, *Conference Report*, April 1898, 14, 64; quoted in Klaus J. Hansen, "The Metamorphosis of the Kingdom of God: Toward a Reinterpretation of Mormon History," 231.

32. Benjamin F. Johnson, Letter to George F. Gibbs, 1903, qtd. in E. Dale LeBaron, "Benjamin Franklin Johnson: Colonizer, Public Servant and Church Leader," 343.

33. Wilford Woodruff considered "generation" in Doctrine and Covenants 84:4 to be synonymous with this last dispensation of the gospel, saying Christ's coming "will take place in this generation, when the Gospel of Christ has again been offered to the inhabitants of the earth." Wilford Woodruff, July 3, 1880, *Journal of Discourses*, 21:195. Most LDS scriptural commentators follow

President Woodruff's lead in equating "generation" in Doctrine and Covenants 84 with the current gospel dispensation. See, for example, Richard O. Cowan, *Answers to Your Questions about the Doctrine and Covenants*, 97; Robert L. Millet, "A Revelation on Priesthood," 311; Daniel H. Ludlow, *A Companion to Your Study of the Four Gospels*, 114; and Joseph Fielding Smith, *Church History and Modern Revelation*, 2:102-3.

34. In 1963 Apostle Spencer W. Kimball stated that the reason the Jackson County temple hadn't yet been built as promised was "because we haven't converted the Indians in large enough numbers; never shall we go to Jackson County until we have converted and brought into this church great numbers of Lamanites. Now you just as well set that down as a basic fact." Quoted in *Book of Mormon Student Manual: Religion 121–122*, 428. Doctrine and Covenants 124:59–51 effectively acknowledges that the building of the temple in New Jerusalem was hindered by external persecution; this commandment was therefore postponed.

35. James Ussher is credited with developing this generally accepted calculation in 1654. Dan Smail, "In the Grip of Sacred History," 1343.

36. Bruce R. McConkie, *Mormon Doctrine*, 624.

37. Bruce R. McConkie, *A New Witness for the Articles of Faith*, 635; see also Bruce R. McConkie, D*octrinal New Testament Commentary*, 3:499. For a similar view see Joseph Fielding McConkie, *Answers: Straightforward Answers to Tough Gospel Questions*, 116.

38. Bruce R. McConkie, *The Millennial Messiah: The Second Coming of the Son of Man*, 30.

39. McConkie, *Doctrinal New Testament Commentary*, 3:591.

40. Kent P. Jackson, *From Apostasy to Restoration*, 23.

41. Richard A. Henshaw, "Joel," 1348, 1352.

42. Brigham Young, August 13, 1871, *Journal of Discourses*, 14:201-2. For examples of LDS teachings prior to 1870 that have Joel's prophecy being fulfilled by the Holy Ghost being poured out on all flesh in the millennium, see "Millennium. No. III," *Evening and Morning Star* 2 (February 1834): 131; "Millennium. No. XIII," *Latter Day Saints' Messenger and Advocate* 1 (March 1835): 87; John Taylor, *The Government of God*, 86–87; Orson Pratt, July 25, 1852, *Journal of Discourses*, 1:292.

43. Joseph Fielding Smith, *Doctrines of Salvation: Compiled Sermons of Joseph Fielding Smith*, 1:53, 176, 182. See also McConkie, *Mormon Doctrine*, 716; Gordon B. Hinckley, *Conference Report*, April 1961, 88. Of course, the view that it is the light of Christ rather than the Holy Ghost being poured out on all flesh runs contrary to the Lord's pronouncement that he is withdrawing his spirit from the inhabitants of the earth (D&C 63:32), which LDS authorities have also identified as the light of Christ. Joseph Fielding Smith, *Signs of the Times*, 94–95.

44. Underwood, *The Millenarian World of Early Mormonism*, 149 note 15.

45. David P. Wright, "Historical Criticism: A Necessary Element in the Search for Religious Truth," 31.

46. Ibid., 31–32.

47. Joseph Jacobs and A. Biram, "Millennium," 9:593.

48. Daniel B. Wallace, "New Testament Eschatology in Light of Progressive Revelation." Wallace is a professor of New Testament studies at Dallas Theological Seminary.

49. Brown, *Introduction to the New Testament*, 800.

50. George A. Barton and Kaufmann Kohler, "Resurrection," 10:383.

51. Norman Cohn, *Cosmos, Chaos, and the World to Come: The Ancient Roots of Apocalyptic Faith*, 77–104.

52. Sanders, "Whence the First Millennium?" 444.

53. James D. Tabor, "Why 2K?" 18.

54. Charles G. Finney, quoted in Underwood, *The Millenarian World of Early Mormonism*, 8.

55. Ibid., 4.

56. Ibid.

57. 1 Nephi 22:24 does not say that Christ will personally appear or reign on the earth as is sometimes assumed. See *Gospel Principles* (2009), 267.

58. Ted Peters, *Futures: Human and Divine*, 29–30.

59. The binding and loosing of Satan in Revelation 20:1–3 is another example of how Mormonism's earliest teachings followed popular nineteenth-century figural interpretations (1 Ne. 14:12–17; 22:24–28; 30:5–18; 2 Ne. 30:18; Jacob 5:71–77; 3 Ne. 20:22; 21:20–29) while later teachings treat it more literally (D&C 43:31; 45:55; 84:100; 88:110–11; 101:28). Interestingly, Bruce R. McConkie initially appealed to Joseph's later teachings to interpret the binding of Satan as literal, but then later changed his mind asserting, based on Joseph's earlier teachings, that the binding of Satan would be figurative. McConkie, *Mormon Doctrine*, 495–96; and McConkie, *The Millennial Messiah*, 668.

60. Ehat and Cook, *The Words of Joseph Smith*, 65. See also *History of the Church*, 5:212.

61. Underwood, *The Millenarian World of Early Mormonism*, 168 note 67.

62. Thomas J. Riskas Jr., "New Heaven and New Earth," 3:1009; McConkie, *Mormon Doctrine*, 531.

63. James D. Tabor, "What the Bible Says about Death, Afterlife, and the Future."

64. The only reference that might possibly imply a new heaven and earth at the start of the millennium is Doctrine and Covenants 63:49: "When the Lord shall come . . . old things shall pass away, and all things [shall] become new." The context, however, is only that of the dead rising to a newness of life. This scripture echoes Paul's pronouncement that, "if any man be in Christ, he is a new creature: old things are passed away; behold, all things are become new" (2 Cor. 5:17).

65. Joseph Smith Jr., "Present Age of the World," 22.

66. McConkie, *The Millennial Messiah*, 535–36.

67. According to Bruce R. McConkie, not only will the battle of Armageddon be fought prior to the millennium, but after the millennium "the battle of Gog and Magog, another Armageddon, as it were, will be fought again." McConkie, *A New Witness for the Articles of Faith*, 651. Joseph Smith, however, stated that "the battle of Gog and Magog will be after the millennium" and does not mention a premillennial Armageddon battle. *History of the Church*, 5:298.

≈ 20 ≈

The Resurrection

Latter-day Saints, like most other Christians, believe that the dead will rise from the grave through the resurrection of Christ. In Mormon doctrine, the resurrection is physical in nature, universal in scope, and eternal in duration. Furthermore, not all are raised at the same time or with the same glory; rather, individuals rise at a time and with a glory commensurate with their righteousness in mortality.

History of the Resurrection

The Judeo-Christian doctrine of the resurrection begins late in the Old Testament during the second temple period. Initial teachings on the resurrection are obscure and seem to depict a resurrection of only the righteous. Beliefs about the resurrection have expanded over the centuries, and current LDS teachings on the subject are quite extensive, leaving little left to the imagination.

Old Testament

As pointed out in Chapter 11, ancient Israelites didn't think of humans as dual beings composed of a body and a spirit. Instead they believed the body was only animated by the breath of life. In the Old Testament, life essentially ended at death and the "spirit" or impersonal breath of life returned to God who gave it (Eccl. 12:7).

The realms of existence in ancient Semitic cosmology consisted of the upper realm of the Gods located above the earth (heaven), a middle world of humans (earth), and a lower realm located beneath the earth (the netherworld or Sheol). Sheol was considered to be the end of any meaningful existence; and therefore, ancient Hebrews believed that the dead faded away in Sheol. Psalm 115:17 notes that "the dead praise not the Lord" since "in that very day [of death] his thoughts perish" (Ps. 146:4). Thomas P. Rausch, a professor of theology at Loyola Marymount University, explains:

> The idea of life beyond the grave entered very late into the Jewish tradition. For most of the period reflected in the Old Testament, death meant simply the end of life. The spirit (*ruah*) or principle of life and activity departed and the self (*nepes*) went down to Sheol, the underworld or abode of the dead. In the ancient Near East, Sheol is a place of darkness and dust, the final destination of the human person from which there is no release (cf. Job 17:13–16). But in Jewish thought Sheol was not a place of another kind of life but rather the negation of everything that life represents.[1]

In Ecclesiastes, Sheol is depicted as a place of annihilation, equivalent to the grave, where all souls, both the righteous and the wicked, end up (Eccl. 9:3). In Sheol "there is no work, nor device, nor knowledge, nor wisdom" (Eccl. 9:10). Having no more consciousness, "the dead know not any thing" (Eccl. 9:5). The LDS Bible Dictionary (s.v. "Ecclesiastes") minimizes the nihilistic outlook of Ecclesiastes by saying that it "must be read in the light of one of its key phrases: 'under the sun' (1:9), meaning 'from a worldly point of view.'" In Ecclesiastes, however, all people are "under the sun . . . while they live, and after that they go to the dead" (Eccl. 9:3), where the aforementioned conditions prevail. In his commentary on Ecclesiastes, Old Testament scholar Tremper Longman states, "The list of things absent after death, *actions*, *thought*, *knowledge* and *wisdom*, suggest both physical and mental processes coming to a complete end. . . . We thus see that 'under the sun' [i.e., life on earth] entails the entirety of human possibility."[2]

In ancient Hebrew thought, one's life continued on through one's children, hence the importance attached to having a continuing posterity. Old Testament scholar H. Wheeler Robinson notes that, in the Old Testament, "it is not said to the good man that he shall be rewarded in some future life, but 'thou shalt know . . . that thy seed shall be great, and thine offspring as the grass of the earth' (Job 5:25)."[3] One of the most damning things that could occur would have been the termination of one's offspring (see 2 Sam. 14:7).

Herman Bavinck, a theologian of the Dutch Reformed churches writing in the *International Standard Bible Encyclopaedia*, attributes emerging ideas of a continued existence after death to "the Greek, Platonic idea that the body dies, yet the soul is immortal." According to Bavinck, the idea of an afterlife is utterly contrary to the Israelite consciousness and is nowhere found in the Old Testament. The whole man dies, when in death the spirit (Ps. 146:4; Eccl. 12:7), or soul (Gen. 35:18; 2 Sam. 1:9; 1 Kgs. 17:21; Jonah 4:3), goes out of a man. Not only his body, but his soul also returns to a state of death and belongs to the nether-world; therefore the Old Testament can speak of a death of one's soul (Gen. 37:21; Num. 23:10; Deut. 22:21; Judg. 16:30; Job 36:14; Ps. 78:50).[4]

Many biblical scholars see the idea of a continued life of the soul and resurrection of the body as a late development in Judaism, resulting largely from disappointed expectations for a restored kingdom of Israel.[5] As a consolation for their suffering and sacrifices, the faithful were assured of everlasting life in God's kingdom instead of languishing in Sheol. Jewish scholar Simcha Paull Raphael writes, "It is likely that the Maccabean revolt of 167 B.C.E. was the historical context that led to the rapid emergence of the concept of resurrection. . . . Since they [the Jews] were fighting for God's justice, it strengthened belief that they would eventually be vindicated for their life sacrifice, and would be delivered up from the realm of the dead."[6]

According to James Tabor, a professor of Christian origins and ancient Judaism at the University of North Carolina, "The first references to the idea of the dead being raised occur only in very late portions of the Hebrew Bible (Daniel 12:1–3). It was a doctrine that was emerging in certain Jewish circles from the 2nd century B.C.E. down through the 1st century C.E."[7] Significantly, only those portions of the Old Testament that many scholars believe were written in the second century B.C. (during the Hellenistic period) allude to a bodily resurrection. They include Isaiah 24–27 (often referred to as the little Apocalypse) and Daniel. But even then, the resurrection wasn't necessarily understood as being universal. Speaking to the Lord's people, Isaiah declares, "Thy dead men shall live, together with my dead body shall they rise" (Isa. 26:19). Speaking of Israel's enemies, however, Isaiah exults saying, "[They] are dead, they shall not live; they are deceased, they shall not rise" (Isa. 26:14). It is as though resurrection is a reward in itself for the righteous, while the wicked are denied this blessing. Daniel 12, which also dates from this period, describes the end-time deliverance of "every one that shall be found written in the book" (Dan. 12:1), stating, "Many of them that sleep in the dust of the earth shall awake, some to everlasting life, and some to shame and everlasting contempt" (Dan. 12:2). The fact that Daniel saw *many* has led "almost all commentators" to interpret this passage as advancing a limited resurrection.[8] F. F. Bruce, professor of biblical criticism and exegesis at the University of Manchester, further questions whether this verse allows at all for a resurrection of the wicked: "It is possible to render these words otherwise: 'many who sleep in the dust of the earth will wake, and these are (destined) to everlasting life; but those (the others, who do not wake) are (destined) to the reproach of eternal abhorrence.'"[9] In addition to these two apocalyptic entries in the Old Testament, which most scholars regard as the only references to a literal resurrection in the Old Testament, several non-biblical apocalyptic writings from the second century B.C. to the time of Christ also suggest a limited resurrection.[10]

Latter-day Saints, like many other Christians, see references to the resurrection in several Old Testament passages creating an unwarranted impression that it was a widely held Hebrew belief. Perhaps the most frequently cited passage is Job 19:26: "And though after my skin worms destroy this body, yet in my flesh shall I see God." The Book of Mormon, like traditional Christianity, universalizes the language of this passage: "*our* flesh must waste away and die; nevertheless, in *our* bodies *we* shall see God" (2 Ne. 9:4; emphasis mine; cf. Moses 5:10). So in the Book of Mormon, everyone will stand before God in the flesh at judgment day.

Christians and Jews have traditionally clashed on the meaning of Job's expression "in my flesh shall I see God." In the Jewish Bible, Job 19:26 reads, "then *without* my flesh shall I see God."[11] This reading gives it a meaning which is exactly the opposite of the idea conveyed in the KJV. This contrary rendering is possible because of the ambiguity of the Hebrew. Even the LDS Old Testament Institute manual acknowledges that "the Hebrew text says, 'from my flesh,' and this can be interpreted in either sense."[12] From the context itself, it is questionable whether Job was alluding to a resurrection. First, when Job says in verse 25, "I know that my redeemer liveth," he is not bearing witness to the redeeming power of Jesus Christ. James Crenshaw, Duke University professor of Old Testament, explains that the Hebrew word translated "redeemer" should actually be rendered "vindicator" or "avenger" and "the issue here is revenge."[13] As emphasized by Edwin M. Good, professor of religious studies at Stanford University, "the word is not 'redeemer,' much less 'Redeemer.' Job is not referring to a divine savior or to Jesus."[14] Second, Job had earlier (14:12) declared that the dead "shall not awake, nor be raised out of their sleep." He thereby takes a direct stance against the resurrection of the dead. Summarizing what he perceived to be a misguided Christian tendency to read the doctrine of the resurrection into Job 19:26, Marvin Pope, professor of semitic languages and literatures at Yale University, states, "Many Christian interpreters since Origen have tried to read here an affirmation of immortality or resurrection, but without success: Chrysostom quite correctly refuted this interpretation with the citation of 14:12 [the dead 'shall not awake, nor be raised']."[15]

Another Old Testament passage often seen as a reference to the resurrection is Ezekiel 37:1–10 in which Ezekiel is commanded to prophesy to a valley of bones: "Behold, I will cause breath to enter into you, and ye shall live." Thus, the dead of Israel shall live again and "know that I am the Lord" (vv. 5–6). Although this description sounds like a literal resurrection, one need only read on to discover that the dead bones symbolize the spiritually dead Israelites (vv. 11–14). God promises that he will put his spirit in them, and they shall again become spiritually alive. Ezekiel 36:26–27 similarly states, "I will put my spirit within you, and cause you to walk in my statutes." The subject of both chapters is Israel's hardheartedness and God's plan to infuse them with new spiritual life.[16] To interpret this passage as a literal resurrection goes beyond the stated interpretation provided by the text itself.

New Testament

Jews at the time of Christ were divided on the subject of the resurrection. The Pharisees, who were more open to progressive doctrinal developments, embraced the idea of a resurrection, but evidently only for the righteous.[17] The more traditional Sadducees rejected the resurrection altogether as unscriptural (Matt. 22:23).

The New Testament isn't always consistent in its portrayal of who will be resurrected. Although later New Testament writers tend to speak of the resurrection as universal, one earlier writer gives the impression that only the righteous will be resurrected. The earliest New Testament writings are the letters of Paul, a converted Pharisee, who emphasized that resurrection was a reward for righteousness. He observed that those Saints who had received Christ's spirit are now "waiting for the adoption, to wit, the redemption of [their] body" (Rom. 8:23). He assured the Saints: "If the Spirit of him that raised up Jesus from the dead dwell in you, he that raised up Christ from the dead shall also quicken your mortal bodies by his Spirit that dwelleth in you" (Rom. 8:11). For Paul, the resurrection is promised only "if the Spirit of him [i.e., God] . . . dwell in you." It was Paul's personal hope that he "might attain unto the resurrection of the dead" (Philip. 3:10–11). Thus, the resurrection was seen as a prize that was discriminately bestowed—not unconditionally and universally granted. In Paul's writings, only the righteous would have their "vile" bodies "fashioned like unto his [i.e., Christ's] glorious body" (Philip. 3:21).[18]

Though Paul writes that "the dead in Christ shall rise first" (1 Thess. 4:16), this wasn't intended to suggest that those who are not "in Christ" shall rise later. Rather, Paul teaches that this would be followed by the rising of those Saints "which are [still] alive," for they "shall be caught up" (1 Thess. 4:17). Paul states, "In a moment, in the twinkling of an eye, at the last trump . . . the dead shall be raised incorruptible, and we [referring to the living Saints] shall be changed" (1 Cor. 15:52). For Paul, only a single general resurrection was to occur, which would be at the end of time when the righteous dead are raised, followed immediately by the righteous living.[19]

A passage from one of Paul's epistles that is frequently cited as evidence that the resurrection is universal is 1 Corinthians 15:22: "For as in Adam all die, even so in Christ shall all be made alive." Though use of the word "all" may seem to imply a universal resurrection, many New Testament scholars point out that "all" is restricted by the phrase "in Christ." In other words, it is all who are "in Christ" that are resurrected. The phrase, "in Christ," or its equivalent, occurs 176 times in the writings of Paul and conveys the idea of being spiritually connected to Christ.[20] Significantly, the expression "in Christ" appears twice in verses 18–19 leading up to verse 22, and in both places it has reference to those who are spiritually connected to Christ. According to many scholars, Paul's analogy in verse 22 is that, just as all who are "in" (i.e., biologically linked to) Adam shall die, so also shall all those who are "in" (i.e., spiritually linked to) Christ be made alive.[21] *The Living Bible* translates this passage: "Everyone dies because they are related to Adam . . . but all who are related to Christ will rise again." Of course the implication is that those who are not "in Christ" will not be resurrected, which is precisely the implication of the very next verse where Paul gives the order of the resurrection as follows: first, Christ who is "the firstfruits," and then "they that are Christ's [i.e., those whom he claims as his] at his coming" (1 Cor. 15:23). After this "cometh the end" (1 Cor. 15:24) with no mention of any subsequent resurrection after those that are "in Christ."

It isn't until New Testament writings subsequent to Paul's that a universal resurrection of both the just and the unjust emerges (Matt. 25:31–46; John 5:29; Rev. 20:11–15).[22] Even then, however, there is no indication that there will be more than one time of resurrection. Except for a lone reference in Revelation 20:4–13 which alludes to the resurrection at the start of the millennium of those who had been martyred for their testimony of Jesus,[23] the New Testament speaks of only one future resurrection which will occur at the final judgment (John 5:29, 11:24; 1 Cor. 15:23–24; Heb. 9:27). Although the current LDS view holds that the resurrection of the Saints precedes the resurrection of sinners by at least a thousand years, New Testament teachings place the resurrection of the righteous at the very "last day" (John 6:40; see also 1 Thess. 4:16–17), which is the day that marks the close of God's work on earth and the beginning of the eternal age to come. Paul had to contend against false teachers who were "saying that the resurrection is past already" (2 Tim. 2:18). He clarified that this one and only resurrection won't occur until the sound of the very "last trump" (1 Cor. 15:52)—implying that there are to be no more trumpets signaling subsequent resurrections. "Then," Paul says, "cometh the end" (v. 24).[24]

Early Nineteenth-Century Christianity

At Joseph Smith's time, most Protestants believed in a single, universal resurrection that would occur at the time of final judgment (i.e., postmillennialism). The 1647 Westminster Confession of Faith declared, "At the last day . . . all the dead shall be raised up, with the self-same bodies . . . which shall be united again to their souls forever."[25] Premillennialism, which was less common, looked forward to two major resurrections: one at the beginning of the millennium and one at the end.

Early Mormonism

Like the Westminster Confession, the Book of Mormon explicitly teaches a bodily resurrection that is both universal and irreversible (Alma 11:45).[26] Those in the Book of Mormon living before Jesus's ministry in the Old World, referred to the time of Christ's resurrection as the first resurrection (Mosiah 15:21–25; Alma 40). According to the prophet Abinadi, this first resurrection would include all who are righteous as well as the ignorant (which, of course, would preclude the need for vicarious ordinances to be performed) and little children "that have been, and who are, and who shall be, even until the resurrection of Christ" (Mosiah 15:21–26). Righteous Nephites living before Christ, therefore, looked forward to being numbered in the "first resurrection" (Mosiah 18:9), which they believed would coincide with the resurrection of Christ. Indeed, both the New Testament and the Book of Mormon refer to the resurrection of "the saints" at the time of Christ's resurrection (Matt. 27:52–53; Hel. 14:25).

For all who are resurrected in latter times, the Book of Mormon essentially echoes the New Testament teaching of an end-time general resurrection consisting of the "resurrection of life" and the "resurrection of damnation" (compare Mosiah 16:11 with John 5:29). Like the New Testament, the Book of Mormon doesn't see these as two distinct resurrection events, but only as two separate groups of people in the same resurrection event. At the final judgment "all shall rise from the dead and stand before God, and be judged according to their works" (Mosiah 11:41).[27]

In the first recorded revelation referring explicitly to a millennium and the events that are to precede and follow it, there is no mention of a resurrection at the start of the millennium. Instead it describes a resurrection occurring only after the "little season" (D&C 29:22) following the millennium when "Michael, mine archangel, shall sound his trump, and then shall all the dead awake, for their graves shall be opened, and they shall come forth—yea, even all. And the righteous shall be gathered on my right hand unto eternal life; and the wicked on my left hand will I be ashamed to own before the Father" (D&C 29:26–27). The sense one gets is that this will be a great, general resurrection of both the righteous and the wicked occurring at the end of time.

Later Mormonism

The doctrine of a single general resurrection at the end of time as recorded in the Bible, Book of Mormon, and early LDS revelations was soon changed to include two distinct resurrection events and eventually more. The first indication of more than one resurrection occurred in March 1831 when the Prophet received a revelation identifying a "first resurrection" which would occur just before "Satan shall be bound" (D&C 45:54), presumably at the start of the millennium. Evidently, the Prophet's shift to a premillennialist view of the second coming (see chap. 19) necessitated a corresponding premillennial resurrection.

Interestingly, this first resurrection, which is premillennial, will include "the Saints" (D&C 45:46) followed immediately by "the heathen nations . . . and they that knew no law" (v. 54). At this stage in LDS literature, there is no mention of either the heathen or those ignorant of the law receiving any lesser reward than the Saints. In identifying those who "shall not have part in the first resurrection," Doctrine and Covenants 63:17–18 lists "the fearful, and the unbelieving, and all liars . . . , and the whoremonger, and the sorcerer." In other words, there will be a resurrection of the righteous and the ignorant who are saved, followed sometime later by the resurrection of the disbelievers and the disobedient (regardless of degree) who suffer eternal torment.

A revelation given in February 1832 gave more specific information on the timing of the second resurrection: They "shall not be redeemed from the devil until the last resurrection, until the Lord, even Christ the Lamb, shall have finished his work" (D&C 76:85)—that is, when everything is complete and there is no more business to take care of on earth. This passage does not suggest, as is frequently assumed, the idea of a resurrection occurring at the end of the millennium, which is then followed by a short season and, finally, the resurrection of sons of perdition.[28] In fact, Doctrine and Covenants 76 makes no mention of the resurrection of the latter.[29] However, a revelation ten months later has all who are wicked—including sons of perdition—resurrecting as one event at the end of the earth when Christ's work is finished (D&C 88:100–102).

To summarize, latter-day scriptures prior to 1831 depict a single general resurrection at the end of the earth which will include both the just and the unjust. In March 1831, however, two resurrection events began to be delineated: the first resurrection occurring at the start of the millennium for the righteous and the ignorant (the resurrection of eternal life), and a second resurrection occurring at the end of the earth for all the wicked (the resurrection of damnation), with no inclusion of sons of perdition in the latter. In February 1832, the ignorant became differentiated from the righteous and were assigned a lesser degree of salvation—the terrestrial kingdom (D&C 76:50–80). Those coming forth in the last resurrection at the end of the earth would no longer suffer eternal torment as in earlier revelations, but would inherit what Joseph Smith termed a "telestial" glory (D&C 76:81–85). By December 1832, this last resurrection included sons of perdition (D&C 88:102), who would be cast, with their resurrected bodies, into outer darkness.

In current LDS discourse, these two resurrections are further subdivided into four stages. Where Doctrine and Covenants 45:45–54 refers to the first resurrection occurring in two waves, one right after the other, and separated only by the length of time it takes Christ to alight upon the earth, it is now customary to speak of the "morning" and "afternoon" of the first resurrection as though there were an appreciable time separating the two. The current scheme of the resurrection, as articulated by McConkie, has a "morning" and "afternoon" of the first resurrection starting at Christ's appearance and continuing throughout the millennium followed by a "morning" and "afternoon" of the second resurrection starting at the end of the millennium and culminating at the end of the world some season of time later.[30] This morning-afternoon bifurcation derives from an alteration in meaning of the traditional Christian colloquialism "morning of the first resurrection," or more commonly just "morning of the resurrection," which was originally intended to convey the image of waking up from the sleep of death as one wakes up in the morning.[31] In Mormonism, its meaning shifted to refer to the first wave of resurrection rather than to the resurrection itself.

In the Bible and Book of Mormon, the expression "firstfruits of the resurrection" refers exclusively to Christ and simply means that he was the first to be resurrected (1 Cor. 15:20; 2 Ne. 2:8–9). Paul spoke of the resurrection as consisting of "Christ the firstfruits" and then "afterward they that are Christ's at his coming" (1 Cor. 15:23). The Doctrine and Covenants defines "firstfruits" differently, stating that it consists of those "who shall descend with him first" when he comes at the beginning of the millennium. They include all the righteous "who are on the earth [the living] and in their graves [the dead], who are first caught up to meet him" (D&C 88:98). These two groups, however, were the ones Paul referred to as "Christ's at his coming," which he distinguished from Christ who alone was "the firstfruits."

The inclusion of living mortals in the firstfruits of the resurrection (D&C 88:98) has led to conflicting views about whether they would actually be resurrected or merely translated and still retain their mortal status. James E. Talmage took the view that they would be resurrected.[32] Although consistent with Paul's teachings (1 Cor. 15:51–54) and the plain sense of Doctrine and Covenants 88:98, this position is problematic because LDS revelations make it clear that the righteous living will continue to remain mortal (apparently this is necessary for them to be tested and continue propagating mortal species) until they reach "the age of man" (D&C 63:50), or, as later revealed, "the age of a tree" (D&C 101:30), at which time they are "changed in the twinkling of an eye" from mortality to immortality (D&C 63:51). Current LDS commentators, therefore, usually assert that the righteous living will only be translated or transfigured, not immortalized.[33] Of course Paul's statement, that both the dead and the living will be changed to immortality at Christ's coming (1 Cor. 15:51–52), would have made perfect sense to him since he understood Christ's coming as signaling the end of time, not the start of the millennium.

In addition to changing the meaning of "firstfruits," LDS scripture also alters the meaning of Paul's reference to those who are "Christ's at his coming" (1 Cor. 15:23). Paul uses it to refer to the righteous, both living *and* dead, who are resurrected when Christ comes and who will "meet the Lord in the air" (1 Thess. 4:17), again without any mention of multiple trumps being sounded. The Doctrine and Covenants uses the phrase "at his coming" to refer only to the resurrection of the dead who inherit the terrestrial kingdom (D&C 88:99). According to Joseph Fielding Smith, "'At his coming,' apparently meaning after he has established his government and holy order, those will come forth who have kept the terrestrial law."[34] Elder Smith thus construed "at his coming" to mean an appreciable length of time after Christ's coming and involving a lesser glory, a meaning different in both timing and degree from Paul's.

Paul taught that, at Christ's coming, the righteous dead would be raised first followed immediately by the righteous living.[35] He never referred to a resurrection of those whom Latter-day Saints would see as telestial candidates. To the Thessalonians, Paul wrote, "The dead in Christ shall rise first: Then we [the righteous] which are alive and remain shall be caught up together with them in the clouds, to meet the Lord in the air" (1 Thess. 4:16–17; see also 1 Cor. 15:52). Doctrine and Covenants 88:96–98 seems to reverse this sequence, stating that "the Saints that are upon the earth, who are alive, shall be quickened and be caught up to meet him,"[36] and then "they who have slept in their graves shall come forth, for their graves shall be opened; and they also shall be caught up to meet him."

Resurrection as a Process

In current LDS theology, the process of the resurrection is more involved than what is described in the scriptures. In all discussions of the resurrection in the standard works, the dead come forth simultaneously at a single signal variously designated as Christ's appearance, his voice, or the sound of the trump. Accordingly, the Prophet "saw in vision" everyone rising together "when the trump of God should sound & the voice of God should say ye Saints arise."[37] Though the belief that all rise in unison was widely held in early Mormonism, the resurrection is now explained as occurring successively through individual priesthood ordinances performed by priesthood bearers as they themselves are resurrected. Brigham Young explained, "We have not, neither can we receive here, the ordinance and the keys of the resurrection. They will be given to those who have passed off this stage of action and have received their bodies again. . . . They will be ordained, by those who hold the keys of the resurrection, to go forth and resurrect the Saints, just as we receive the ordinance of baptism, then the keys to baptize others for the remission of sins."[38] According to this scheme, Joseph Smith will be the first to be resurrected by one already holding the keys of the resurrection. He will then be ordained to resurrect others and so on. Thus, the resurrection is a process carried out individually by ordinance followed by ordination—a process that logistically would take considerable time.

One interesting LDS doctrine related to the resurrection is the belief that, at the moment of resurrection, all who rise from the dead will appear physically just as they did when they died, and only gradually will bodily imperfections disappear.[39] This view differs from the traditional Christian understanding that we will be resurrected as fully grown adults with perfect bodies. It also seems to contradict the Book of Mormon teaching "concerning the resurrection of the mortal body," which states that "the spirit and the body shall be reunited again in its perfect form; both limb and joint shall be restored to its proper frame" without "so much as a hair of their heads be[ing] lost" (Alma 11:43–45).[40]

The current concept that individuals will rise just as they died is traceable to a late teaching of Joseph Smith regarding those who die in youth or infancy. In March 1842, he stated: "As concerning the resurrection I will merely say that all men will come from the grave as they lie down, whether old or young will not be added unto their stature one cubit neither taken from it."[41] Later, Joseph is said to have taught that little children, when resurrected, will have the opportunity to be raised to adulthood by their resurrected parents.[42] The belief that parents would be able to raise their deceased children in the resurrection happened also to be a popular view among many contemporary Christians.[43]

In LDS theology, the idea of individuals rising from the grave "as they lie down" was expanded from initially applying only to infants to later include those with physical imperfections. Joseph F. Smith, for example, taught in June 1909 that people will be resurrected just as they died with scars, lost limbs, old age, etc. "Not that a person will always be marred by scars, wounds, deformities, defects or infirmities, for these will be removed in their course, in their proper time, according to the merciful providence of God."[44] His son, Apostle Joseph Fielding Smith, later confirmed this idea but accelerated the process, explaining that the perfection process, though not immediate, "will not cover any appreciable extent of time."[45] So while initial LDS teachings suggest that bodily imperfections disappear immediately in the resurrection, later teachings suggest a more gradual disappearance, then yet later assert a near immediate disappearance.

Resurrection of All Life Forms

Mormonism is one of the few religions to affirm the resurrection of all plant and animal life forms. This doctrine stems from the broader belief that all life forms had their existence as spirits in the preexistence and are eternal in nature. According to Bruce R. McConkie, "Animals, birds, fowls, fishes, plants, and all forms of life occupy an assigned sphere and play an eternal role in the great plan of creation, redemption, and salvation. They were all created as spirit entities in pre-existence (Moses 3:1–9)." In the end, he states, "all these forms of life will come up in the resurrection, 'in their destined order or sphere of creation, in the enjoyment of their eternal felicity' (D&C 77:3)."[46] Thus, all life forms that were first created spiritually (including the earth itself) and that subsequently entered mortality are destined to progress to a resurrected state for all eternity.

There is no indication in the Bible that any life forms other than humans will be resurrected. In describing his vision of the resurrection, John the Revelator spoke only of humans coming forth (Rev. 20:13). Joseph Fielding Smith's explanation for this silence is that "the Bible as it has come to us through numerous translations and copies does not contain the information concerning the immortality of the animal world in the clearness which, without any doubt, it was invested with the pure inspiration of the revelations of the Lord."[47]

One chapter Joseph Smith quotes from as evidence of an animal resurrection is Revelation 4, which speaks of "four beasts full of eyes before and behind" (v. 6) who gave "honor and glory and thanks" (v. 9) to God. The Prophet explained that these animals were "individual beasts ... in their destined order or sphere of creation, in the enjoyment of their eternal felicity" (D&C 77:3). According to Joseph, "John saw curious beasts in heaven . . . that had been saved from ten thousand times ten thousand earths like this, strange beasts of which we have no conception."[48] New Testament scholars, however, usually interpret these four beasts surrounding the throne of God as "four strange animal-shaped spirits—each with six wings, multiple eyes, and various faces. These seem to be the spirits who guard the throne."[49] It should also be remembered that beasts were symbolic creatures in John's vision.

Traditional Christianity has tended to reject assertions that animals will be resurrected. However, according to Josiah Priest, "many" held to a belief in the resurrection of animals in the early 1800s. Priest wrote, "Much learned labour has been bestowed, to render the subject of an animal resurrection plausible."[50] Priest himself repudiated the idea as being unscriptural.

The idea of a resurrection of non-human life forms does not appear in the Book of Mormon. That they existed spiritually before they were created temporally was taught in 1830 in the book of Moses, but not their continued existence in the hereafter. The book of Moses speaks of God's work and glory being only to bring to pass the immortality and eternal life of "man" (Moses 1:39). Indication of an animal resurrection first appears in a September 1830 revelation which states that, after the millennium and little season have ended, "the earth will be consumed and pass away" (D&C 29:23). Then "all things shall become new, even the heaven and the earth, and all the fulness thereof, both men and beasts, the fowls of the air, and the fishes of the sea" (D&C 29:24).

The current LDS understanding of a universal resurrection of animals, insects, and every plant that ever grew is mind boggling. C. S. Lewis wittily suggested that "a heaven for mosquitoes and a hell for men could very conveniently be combined."[51] The resurrection of the billions upon billions of insects that die daily staggers the imagination. And what of the incredibly vast number of noxious weeds that have fulfilled the measure of their creation over the past millions of years of their generations? These weeds alone would completely blanket any earth-sized sphere in the hereafter many times over.

Notes

1. Thomas P. Rausch, *Who Is Jesus? An Introduction to Christology*, 53.
2. Tremper Longman, *The Book of Ecclesiastes*, 231. Though he acknowledges that the New Testament responds to the the pessimistic outlook of Ecclesiastes, Longman maintains that there is "absolutely no concept of life after death" in Ecclesiastes and is adamant that "those who wish to argue otherwise are reduced to special pleading of the most obvious kind."
3. H. Wheeler Robinson, *The Religious Ideas of the Old Testament*, 91. Robinson suggests that it may have been the strong corporate personality of ancient Israel that retarded the emergence of the idea of an afterlife.
4. Herman Bavinck, "Death," 2:812; scriptural abbreviations standardized.
5. Colleen McDannell and Bernhard Lang, *Heaven: A History*, 15. Geza Vermes, *The Resurrection*, 1.
6. Simcha Paull Raphael, *Jewish Views of the Afterlife*, 110.
7. James D. Tabor, "The Signs of the Messiah: 4Q521."
8. George W. E. Nickelsburg, *Resurrection, Immortality, and Eternal Life in Intertestamental Judaism and Early Christianity*, 37 note 63.
9. F. F. Bruce, *Paul: Apostle of the Heart Set Free*, 301.
10. Charles C. Torrey, "Apocalypse," 672.
11. Job 19:26, Jewish Publication Society Translation, 1917.
12. Keith Meservy, quoted in *Old Testament: Genesis–2 Samuel (Religion 301) Student Manual*, 30.
13. James L. Crenshaw, "Job," 771.
14. Edwin M. Good, "Job," 418.
15. Marvin Pope, *Job*, 147.
16. David L. Petersen, "Ezekiel," 1281–82.
17. See Everett Ferguson, *Backgrounds of Early Christianity*, 516. According to Josephus, the Pharisees held that "the soul of the good alone passes into another body," quoted in McDannell and Lang, *Heaven: A History*, 20.
18. Though Latter-day Saints may interpret Christ's "glorious body" as being celestially glorious (thus explaining why only the righteous would receive a like resurrection), Paul never spoke of any other type of resurrected body than the kind that Jesus had; rather, he said that all who would be resurrected would be transformed into the image and likeness of Christ (see Chapter 21).
19. It is true that a secondhand account of Paul's ministry, written a couple of decades after his death, has Paul declaring before Felix "that there shall be a resurrection of the dead, both of the just and unjust" (Acts 24:15). This statement, however, may not have reflected Paul's actual understanding—or at least his earliest understanding. None of Paul's own writings leave any room for a resurrection of those who are not "in Christ."
20. D. A. Hayes, *Paul and His Epistles*, 393.
21. See Hans Conselmann, *I Corinthians*, 269; Gordon D. Fee, *The First Epistle to the Corinthians*, 751; and Anthony C. Thiselton, *The First Epistle to the Corinthians*, 1225–28.
22. While John 5:29 speaks of a universal resurrection of both the good and the evil, other references suggest a resurrection of only the righteous (John 6:39–40, 44, 54).

23. According to Geza Vermes, "the first resurrection is linked to the return of Christ and benefits only the martyrs." Vermes, *The Resurrection*, 131. Some Christians argue that the resurrection spoken of here is only figurative, since a bodily resurrection is referred to later (Rev. 20:11–13). Interestingly, the Book of Mormon also speaks of the spirit's returning at death to the presence of God as a "resurrection" (Alma 40:15).

24. If, in fact, Paul held to the idea of a single resurrection which was yet to occur, one wonders if Paul was unaware of the resurrection of the righteous at the time of Christ's resurrection, later recorded by Matthew (Matt. 27:52–53). Perhaps Paul saw the resurrection as already in progress and soon to be completed with Christ's imminent return. According to New Testament scholar John Dominic Crossan, "As a Pharisee, Paul believed in such an apocalyptic resurrection and concluded that it had already begun with Jesus. We often say that for Paul the end of the world was imminent. It is more accurate to say that for Paul the end had *already begun*; only its final consummation was imminent." John Dominic Crossan, *The Birth of Christianity*, xix; emphasis mine.

25. "Westminster Confession of Faith."

26. One Book of Mormon passage that calls the permanency of the resurrection into question is 2 Nephi 1:22 which states that the wicked face "the eternal destruction of both soul and body." This may simply be a not-so-appropriate (for Book of Mormon theology) appropriation of Matthew 10:28 which reads, "And fear not them which kill the body, but are not able to kill the soul: but rather fear him which is able to destroy both soul and body in hell." For a comparsion of Alma 11:45 with 1 Corinthians 15:42–44 see Brant Gardner, *Second Witness*, 4:192–93.

27. A somewhat distinctive view of the resurrection is expressed by Alma, who confesses ignorance regarding the number of resurrections but asserts confidently that those who die after Christ cannot be resurrected until both the righteous and wicked who died before Christ are resurrected (Alma 40:19). This perception is not inconsistent with a postmillennial view where the wicked and righteous are resurrected at nearly the same time anyway.

28. Bruce R. McConkie asserts that sons of perdition come forth "in the *latter end* of the resurrection of damnation." Bruce R. McConkie, *Mormon Doctrine*, 640; emphasis mine. However, this notion of sons of perdition being resurrected after those inheriting a telestial glory is nowhere found or implied in the standard works or Joseph Smith's teachings.

29. Doctrine and Covenants 76 gives the impression that sons of perdition will not be resurrected, for they are "the only ones who shall not be redeemed in the due time of the Lord. . . . . For all the rest shall be brought forth by the resurrection of the dead." (D&C 76:38–39). It may have made sense to the Prophet at this stage in his doctrinal thinking to exclude sons of perdition from the resurrection and instead see everyone else as gifted with salvation both in terms of resurrection and reward. Ten months later, however, Doctrine and Covenants 88:32 would include them in the resurrection. Brigham Young later taught that, although sons of perdition will be resurrected, it will not be permanent: "The first death is the separation of the spirit from the body; the second death is . . . the dissolution of the organized particles which compose the spirit, and their return to their native elements."

January 12, 1862, *Journal of Discourses*, 9:149. Young felt that God is determined to eventually make something out of these "native elements" and therefore decomposes them for later reuse. As part of Young's notion of recycling wasted life forms, he taught that "the rebellious will be thrown back into their native element [spirit and physical matter], there to remain myriads of years before their dust will again be revived, before they will be re-organized." February 27, 1853, *Journal of Discourses*, 1:118.

30. Bruce R. McConkie, *Doctrinal New Testament Commentary*, 1:196.

31. See, for example, Andrew F. Ehat and Lyndon W. Cook, *The Words of Joseph Smith*, 195–96.

32. James E. Talmage, *Jesus the Christ: A Study of the Messiah and His Mission According to Holy Scriptures Both Ancient and Modern*, 787.

33. Joseph Fielding Smith, *The Way to Perfection*, 298–99; see also Robert L. Millet, "Life in the Millennium," 170–71; and Hoyt W. Brewster Jr., *Behold, I Come Quickly: The Last Days and Beyond*, 206.

34. Ibid., 86; see also McConkie, *Mormon Doctrine*, 639–40.

35. Though this distinction between the time of the resurrection of the dead and of the living may seem inconsequential—inasmuch as only a small moment seems to separate the two—Paul evidently wanted those who had lost loved ones to know that their loved ones will have some recompense by preceding the living in the resurrection (1 Thess. 4:13–14).

36. In September 1839, Smith actually expanded those who would be caught up to meet Christ to include "all" the living. When that occurs, he explained, "the righteous will remain with him in the cloud whilst all the proud and all that do wickedly will have to return to the earth, and suffer his vengeance which he will take upon them." Dean C. Jessee, Mark Ashurst-McGee, and Richard L. Jensen, *Journals, Volume 1: 1832–1839*, 352.

37. See, for example, Ehat and Cook, *The Words of Joseph Smith*, 195, 197.

38. Brigham Young, August 24, 1872, *Journal of Discourses*, 15:137.

39. Douglas L. Callister, "Resurrection," 3:1223; Victor L. Ludlow, *Principles and Practices of the Restored Gospel*, 231.

40. Joseph Fielding Smith, harmonizing this passage with later teachings of a gradual restoration, averred that it "expresses the thought that the body will come forth as it was laid down . . . , that it will take time to adjust the body from the condition of imperfections." Joseph Fielding Smith, *Doctrines of Salvation: Compiled Sermons of Joseph Fielding Smith*, 2:293–94.

41. Ehat and Cook, *The Words of Joseph Smith*, 109.

42. The only contemporary recorded teaching of the Prophet on the subject was that resurrected children would be enthroned with their childhood stature throughout all eternity. Ibid., 109, 136 note 22, 342, 347, 369, 372. Mormon parents may have found it disconcerting that their children would never grow, possibly explaining why Joseph reportedly later stated that they could raise their children in the hereafter. Ibid., 136 note 22. According to Wilford Woodruff, Brigham Young "herd Joseph Smith say that children would not Grow after death & at another time that they would grow[,] & he hardly knew how to reconcile it." Wilford Woodruff, *Wilford Woodruff's Journal, 1833–1898*, 6:363.

43. McDannell and Lang, *Heaven: A History*, 268.

44. Joseph F. Smith, *Gospel Doctrine: Selections from the Sermons and Writings of Joseph F. Smith*, 23.
45. Smith, *Doctrines of Salvation*, 2:294.
46. McConkie, *Mormon Doctrine*, 38; see also Sandra Bradford Packard, "Animals," 1:42.
47. Joseph Fielding Smith, *Answers to Gospel Questions*, 2:48.
48. Ehat and Cook, *The Words of Joseph Smith*, 185.
49. McDannell and Lang, *Heaven: A History*, 39.
50. Josiah Priest, A *View of the Expected Christian Millennium*, 305, 313.
51. C. S. Lewis, *The Problem of Pain*, 141.

~ 21 ~

Final Judgment

Closely associated with the doctrine of the resurrection is the doctrine of the final judgment with its rewards and punishments. In LDS theology there are several major judgments that occur at different stages in one's existence. One is the premortal judgment which determines who is worthy to come to earth and under what conditions. Another is the judgment that occurs at death as one is assigned to either paradise or hell in the spirit world. Yet another judgment occurs at the resurrection when everyone receives either a glorified body (celestial, terrestrial, or telestial) or a body with no glory at all. Finally, there is the judgment which occurs at the end of time after every soul has been resurrected. This judgment is said to make final the eternal state of all who have ever lived on the earth.[1]

Judgment Day

The concept of a final judgment day at the end of history is found in Judaism, Christianity, Islam, and Zoroastrianism. It is a prominent theme in the Old Testament where God's judgment is regarded as operative both within history and at its end. Belief in a judgment day carries over into the New Testament as well as in later Christianity and Mormonism, each having its own particular ideas on the subject.

Old Testament

The Old Testament speaks of the consummation of history in what it refers to as "the day of the Lord." There are at least twenty-five references to this day or event in the Old Testament (see, for example, Isa. 2:12; 13:6, 9; 34:8; Jer. 46:10; Ezek. 13:5, 30:3; Joel 1:15, 2:1). Initially, it was spoken of as a punitive event—God would pour out destruction on all who provoked his wrath. "All nations" (Joel 3:2,

12–19) including Israel (Amos 9:10; Mal. 3:2–5) would be targets of this judgment. Gerald O'Collins notes,

> The day of Yahweh was the day when God was to intervene decisively in judgment against the wickedness of Israel (Jer. 16:16–18; Amos 5:18–20; 8:9–10; Ezek. 7:1–27; Zeph. 1:14–18; Joel 2:1–2), of Babylon (Isa. 13:6, 9), and of Egypt (Ezek. 30:3). On this doomsday God would judge sinners and manifest the divine glory (Isa. 2:11–12) . . . . [He would both] destroy evildoers and spare the good (Mal. 3:13–4:3).[2]

Because the emphasis was more on punishing the wicked than rewarding the righteous, it was referred to as a "day of vengeance" (Jer. 46:10) and a "great and dreadful day" (Mal. 4:5)—not, as some infer, "a great day (for the righteous) and a dreadful day (for the wicked)."[3] Joel 2:11 proclaimed, "The day of the Lord is great and very terrible, and who can abide it?" Thus, the greatness lay in the magnitude of its terribleness.

Biblical scholars point out that Old Testament promises made to God's people as well as prophesied judgments were mostly temporal in nature and pertained to this earthly existence.[4] When God gave the Ten Commandments to the children of Israel, the promised blessing for obedience was "that ye may live, and that it may be well with you, and that ye may prolong your days in the land which ye shall possess" (Deut. 5:33). God threatened the Israelites with temporal punishment for disobedience, not with hell or damnation in the hereafter.

Until at least the Babylonian captivity, judgment was not for the purpose of determining one's status in the hereafter; rather it was God's intervention at the end of the world to rectify injustices upon the earth. It was targeted at the living, not the dead. Most of the Old Testament period had no notion of a soul existing as a separate entity from the body that is able to survive the death of the physical body (see Chapter 20.) All of the dead, both good and evil, ended up in the shadowy and silent underworld of Sheol.

Little attention is given in the Old Testament to the judgment of individuals. Prophecies of impending judgment pertained more to nations as a whole. Jewish scholar Kaufmann Kohler explains, "It was the future destiny of the nation which concerned the Prophets and the people; and the hope voiced by prophet, psalmist, and liturgical poet was simply that the Lord as the Only One will establish His kingdom over the whole earth."[5]

New Testament

The New Testament employs Old Testament expressions regarding the coming of the Lord in judgment, but applies them to Christ's second coming (1 Thess. 5:2). For example, in the Synoptic Gospels, Jesus announces *himself* "coming in the clouds of heaven" as the eschatological judge (Mark 14:62). All judgment is thus committed to him (John 5:22, 27; Acts 17:31). Paul states that God "will judge the world . . . by that man [i.e., Christ] whom he hath ordained" (Acts 17:31); and in one of his epistles, the Old Testament "day of the Lord"—which to ancient Jews meant God the Father—now becomes "the day of our Lord Jesus Christ" (1 Cor. 1:8). According to other New Testament passages, during Christ's return he will judge the whole race of Adam, none excepted (Matt. 25:31–46; 2 Cor. 5:10; Rev. 20:11–15). This would even include the fallen angels who have been "reserved unto judgment" (2 Pet. 2:4; see also Jude 6). Furthermore, saints are to assist Christ in this judgment (1 Cor. 6:2–3).[6]

The New Testament builds on Old Testament eschatology and draws upon the language and imagery of contemporaneous Jewish teachings in its graphic description of rewards and punishments that are to come upon both the quick and the dead. In his *Backgrounds of Early Christianity*, Everett Ferguson explains that, by New Testament times, Jewish writings show "a tendency to use Sheol or Hades for the place of punishment for the wicked." He further relates that "fire was the usual form of punishment" and that "normally the punishment was considered eternal, but occasionally one comes across the idea of extermination of the wicked at the judgment."[7]

The New Testament book of Hebrews calls the final judgment an "eternal judgment" (Heb. 6:2), suggesting that the rewards and punishments of the afterlife are fixed forever. Similarly, Paul speaks of the righteous, both living and dead, being raised at Christ's coming to "ever be with the Lord" (1 Thess. 4:17); i.e., that is their final state. The book of Revelation describes the wicked being cast into the lake of fire where they "shall be tormented day and night for ever and ever" (Rev. 20:10; see also Rev. 14:10–11).

In the New Testament, the righteous are received to celestial glory while the wicked are condemned to hell. There is no middle ground. The New Testament completely separates the righteous (i.e., the sheep) from the wicked (i.e., the goats) at the time of judgment. The wicked "go away into eternal punishment but the righteous into eternal life" (Matt. 25:46). The "eternal punishment" spoken of here is equated with "outer darkness [where] there shall be weeping and gnashing of teeth" (v. 30). It is also referred to as an "everlasting fire, prepared for the devil and his angels" (v. 41; see also Matt. 8:11–12).

As shown in the previous chapter, aside from a single reference in Revelation 20:4–6, there are no multiple resurrections predicted in New Testament writings. Similarly, only one judgment is mentioned, which will occur at the time of the resurrection. God "hath appointed a day, in the which he will judge the world in righteousness by that man whom he hath ordained" (Acts 17:31). When Christ comes, the dead will be resurrected and final judgment rendered once and for all (Rev. 20:11–15; Matt. 16:27, 24:41–46; Rom. 2:5–6; 1 Cor. 3:13; 1 Thess. 5:1–10; 2 Thess. 1:1–10; 2 Tim. 4:1).

Although the New Testament teaches the concept of a single heaven and a single hell, certain passages can be taken as intimations that people receive varying rewards and punishments in this heaven or hell depending on what they have done in this life (Matt. 6:19–21, 11:20–24; Luke 12:47–48; 1 Cor. 3:8; 2 Cor. 9:6; Heb. 10:26–31; Rev. 22:12). This doesn't appear to be the same, however, as inheriting separate kingdoms in heaven or hell.

A passage that Latter-day Saints frequently cite as evidence of tiered kingdoms in the hereafter is John 14:2: "In my Father's house are many mansions. . . . I go to prepare a place for you." Although the Prophet left this verse unchanged in the JST, in January 1844 he modified this passage in light of the doctrine of celestial marriage saying, "House here named should have been translated kingdom; and any person who is exalted to the highest mansion has to abide a celestial law, and the whole law to[o]."[8] Two months later, he referred to this passage as teaching multiple "kingdoms," stating that the correct translation "should be—'In my Father's kingdom are many kingdoms.'"[9] Most modern translations read "rooms" instead of "mansions" so that the verse is rendered, "In my Father's house are many rooms." The general consensus among biblical scholars is that the reference to many mansions (i.e., rooms) is intended only to convey that there is ample space available in the one house (i.e., kingdom) of Jesus's Father so that all of his disciples would live together with him —"that where I am, there ye may be also" (v. 2).[10] To infer that the rooms Christ went to prepare included rooms for non-believers who would not dwell with him (cf. D&C 76:112) seems incongruous with the sense of the passage. Indeed, New Testament writers speak of individuals dwelling only in either God's kingdom with God and Christ, or in outer darkness with Satan.

Another passage viewed by Latter-day Saints as evidence of the doctrine of three degrees of glory is 1 Corinthians 15. In answer to the question, "How are the dead raised up? and with what body do they come?" (1 Cor. 15:35), Paul responds by first giving a brief lesson on nature:

Thou fool, that which thou sowest is not quickened, except it die:

And that which thou sowest, thou sowest not that body that shall be, but bare grain, it may chance of wheat, or of some other grain:

But God giveth it a body as it hath pleased him, and to every seed his own body.

All flesh is not the same flesh: but there is one kind of flesh of men, another flesh of beasts, another of fishes, and another of birds.

There are also celestial bodies, and bodies terrestrial: but the glory of the celestial is one, and the glory of the terrestrial is another.

There is one glory of the sun, and another glory of the moon, and another glory of the stars: for one star differeth from another star in glory. (vv. 36–41)

Paul then draws an analogy between these natural phenomena and the resurrected body:

So also is the resurrection of the dead. It is sown in corruption; it is raised in incorruption:

It is sown in dishonour; it is raised in glory: it is sown in weakness; it is raised in power:

It is sown a natural body; it is raised a spiritual body. There is a natural body, and there is a spiritual body. (vv. 42–44)

Note that up to verse 42 Paul has said nothing explicitly concerning bodies in the resurrection. He has only referred to different bodies as seen in nature. Verses 38–41, which describe different celestial and terrestrial bodies, isn't a reference to bodies in the resurrection (as suggested in Doctrine and Covenants 76:78); rather it simply points to the fact that the everyday world is composed of celestial (NRSV = "heavenly") types of bodies (the sun, stars, angels, etc.) and terrestrial (NRSV = "earthly") types of bodies (humans, birds, fish, etc.). Joseph Smith's addition of a "telestial" type of body (JST 1 Cor. 15:40)—as if there is something besides heavenly and earthly bodies—doesn't really fit into Paul's division of the world.

Paul's analogy seems only intended to show that bodies are adapted to the purposes for which God intended and, therefore, one should not be surprised to learn that resurrected bodies are different from mortal bodies. Jamieson, Fausset and Brown's Bible commentary explains, "The analogy is not to prove different degrees of glory among the blessed (whether this may be, or not, indirectly hinted at), but this: As the various fountains of light, which is so similar in its aspect and properties, differ (the sun from the moon, and the moon from the stars; and even one star from another star, though all seem so much alike); so there is nothing unreasonable in the doctrine that our present bodies differ from our resurrection bodies, though still continuing bodies."[11] It should be remembered that Paul is responding to the question, "How are the dead raised up? and with what body do they come?" (1 Cor. 15:35). It is not a question about differences *between* bodies in the resurrection.

Drawing an analogy to the way a small seed, when planted, transforms into a more abundant stalk of grain (vv. 36–37), Paul explains that the weak, corrupt, non-glorious, natural body of mortality is transformed in the resurrection into a powerful, incorrupt, glorious, spiritual body (vv. 42–44). When considered against the backdrop of Paul's composite writings, which allow only for the resurrection of the righteous, this seems to be just another allusion to the anticipated time when the "vile body" of the flesh will be transformed into a "glorious body" like Christ's (Phil. 3:21).

The Latter-day Saint understanding of 1 Corinthians 15 as a reference to three degrees of bodily glory is certainly not without precedent. As early as the third century, Origen taught that the sun, moon, and stars represent differences in bodily glory among the Saints in the resurrection, although he gives no intimation of multiple "kingdoms" of glory.[12] He further saw the "birds" and "fishes" (1 Cor. 15:39) as representing differences among "sinners." So Origen saw degrees of damnation as well as degrees of glory in Paul's analogy. In the eighteenth and early nineteenth centuries, John Wesley, Thomas Dick, and others gave the following modified reading of 1 Corinthians 15:41–42 to support degrees of glory: "For *as* one star differeth from another star in glory, so also is the resurrection from the dead."[13] Note that this modification adds the word "as" and changes the period after the word "glory" to a comma, thus implying that resurrected bodies vary like stars in their glory. Notably, an identical rendering of these two verses is also given in Doctrine and Covenants 76:98 with the same intent of supporting the doctrine of varying degrees of glory in the resurrection. Certainly Paul's descriptive analogy lends itself to a range of interpretations, but any interpretation involving multiple degrees of glory, much less differentiated *kingdoms* of glory, goes beyond any explicit teachings of Paul.

What about Paul's vision in which he was caught up to the "third heaven" (2 Cor. 12:2)? Doesn't that imply multiple heavens? The answer is yes, but most likely in a different sense from the LDS concept of degrees of glory in the hereafter. It was a familiar Hebrew tradition that there were three different heavens.[14] The first heaven was the atmospheric heaven of clouds, birds, etc. (Gen. 1:20; Ps. 77:17–18, 79:2, 104:12). The second was the starry heaven of the moon and stars (Gen. 1:14, 22:17; Ps. 8:3; Isa. 13:10). The third heaven was the heaven where God dwelt, also referred to as the heaven of heavens (Deut. 10:4; 1 Kgs. 8:27).

When the Bible speaks of the "heavens" passing away (2 Pet. 3:10), it is presumably referring to the first and second heavens, but not the third heaven. Paul says that he was caught up to the third heaven where God is (2 Cor. 12:2), and verse 4 calls that place "paradise." Many scholars find his ascent to the third heaven a carryover into Christianity of Jewish mystic visions that were common at the time.[15] In short, though the New Testament teaches that every man will be rewarded "according to his deeds" (Rom. 2:6), there is no unambiguous reference to three degrees of glory for resurrected beings in the hereafter.

Early Nineteenth-Century Christianity

At the time of Joseph Smith, Christian beliefs regarding judgment day were based largely on creedal interpretations of relevant New Testament passages. Mainstream Christianity held that there would be a single time or "great day" in which all who ever lived would be judged. The 1647 Westminster Confession of Faith announced that "God hath appointed a day" in which "all persons, that have lived upon earth, shall appear before the tribunal of Christ, to give an account of their thoughts, words, and deeds; and to receive according to what they have done in the body, whether good or evil."[16] This description of a single, universal, end-time judgment is consonant with a postmillennial perspective.

Premillennialists, as discussed in Chapter 19, saw two judgments in the scriptures. The first, they believed, would occur at the start of the millennium when Christ returns. The righteous would then resurrect while the wicked would be banished with the devil and his angels until the thousand years of Christ's reign are ended. According to Joseph Smith's contemporary, William Miller, the start of the millennium signals "the first resurrection and the first judgment."[17] With respect to the second judgment, Miller explained, "After the 1000 years shall have passed away . . . the sea, death and hell will give up their dead. . . . The Saints will judge them, the justice of God will drive them from the earth into the lake of fire and brimstone where they will be tormented day and night, forever and ever."[18] Thus, the judgment of the wicked follows the judgment of the righteous by a thousand years, and just as the righteous are given an eternal reward in heaven, the wicked are condemned eternally to hell.

Although most Christians believed that many souls would end up in hell, a growing body of Universalists in the early 1800s also popularized the doctrine of a universal restoration to holiness and happiness. Universalists could not conceive of God condemning any of his creations to eternal misery and therefore saw everyone being given some degree of happiness. Most evangelicals sternly opposed Universalism, asserting that it takes away individual accountability for sin and suggests that Christ saves people regardless of whether they are righteous or not. Anti-Universalists argued that Christ came to save people *from* their sins, not *in* them. Itinerant Methodist preacher Lorenzo Dow, for example, declared in 1804 that "Jesus shall save his people (not in) but from their sins."[19] Even closer to Joseph Smith—around 1819 and about ten miles from the Smith home in Manchester—Charles Marford, a lay Methodist preacher from Victor, New York, similarly attested, "Christ is a Savior to save his people from their sins, and not in them."[20]

Though Protestants of the early 1800s spoke of a single heaven, many understood there to be multiple degrees of glory in that heaven.[21] Eighteenth-century Puritan Jonathan Edwards stated, "There are many mansions in God's house because heaven is intended for various degrees of honor and blessedness." He encouraged Christians to "seek high degrees of glory in heaven."[22] John Wesley, a contemporary of Edwards, also spoke of a "difference between the degrees of glory" in heaven.[23] Eighteenth-century Swedish mystic Emanuel Swedenborg (1688–1772), whose works were known to Joseph Smith,[24] taught that heaven consists of three degrees or levels "entirely distinct from each other." The highest level he called the "celestial kingdom" where the inhabitants are the most fully developed in their spiritual capabilities and must be joined in heterosexual marriage. He further stated that the glory of the inhabitants of these three heavens corresponded to the "sun, moon and stars."[25]

Many of Joseph's contemporaries no longer saw heaven as a place where the sole focus of thought and action was on God as expressed in the New Testament and in classical Christianity, often referred to as the beatific vision. As discussed in Chapter 15, many clergymen in the early 1800s depicted heaven as a place of continual learning and improvement. American family ideals and the humanistic thinking of the Enlightenment gave people new ways of thinking about the afterlife. They began viewing heaven as an extension of the same relationships and activities valued here on earth. There was a growing belief at the time of Joseph Smith that many of life's experiences on earth (family relationships, social interactions, acquiring new knowledge, etc.) are fundamentally good and would extend into the next life.[26] Emanuel Swedenborg wrote several volumes relating visions and dreams of the hereafter in which he described in great detail the geography, habitations, culture, and activities one would find there, noting parallels to earth life. For Swedenborg, marriage relationships continue into heaven. In answer to the question, "Is there a similar love between consorts in the heavens and in the earths?" two angels told Swedenborg that "it was altogether similar, but much more blessed, because angelic perception and sensation are much more exquisite than human perception and sensation." In answer to the question of whether "offspring were born there," Swedenborg was further instructed that "there were not any natural offspring, but spiritual offspring," which, he was informed, consisted of "love and wisdom."[27]

Early Mormonism

The earliest LDS teachings regarding the final judgment and consignment of individuals to either heaven or hell are reminiscent of traditional Christian views. Just as the 1647 Westminster Confession of Faith speaks of everyone being brought before "the tribunal of Christ, to give an account of their thoughts, words, and deeds,"[28] the Book of Mormon also speaks of the great judgment day when all will "be arraigned before the bar of Christ" (Alma 11:44; cf. Morm. 3:20) and will have to account for their "thoughts, . . . words, and . . . deeds" (Mosiah 4:30; cf. Alma 12:12–14). In this sense, the Book of Mormon is decidedly anti-Universalist, proclaiming that God holds all people accountable for their actions and that Christ saves people "from" their sins, not "in" their sins (Alma 11:34–37; 21:16).

In the Book of Mormon, much as in the Bible and traditional Christianity, the choice is nearly always between good and evil, light and darkness. Accordingly, one inherits either eternal life or eternal damnation. No middle ground is offered. One is either "clean" or "unclean" (1 Ne. 10:20–21), either a member of the "church of the Lamb" or the "church of the devil" (1 Ne. 14:10), either "carnal, sensual, and devilish" (Alma 42:10) or "a saint through the atonement of Christ" (Mosiah 3:19), either "sheep of the good shepherd" or sheep of "the devil" (Alma 5:39). In the end, one receives either "never-ending happiness" or "endless wo" (Alma 28:11–12), "peace and life eternal" or "captivity and . . . destruction" (1 Ne. 14:7). There is no acknowledgment of a spectrum of righteousness at the final judgment; and correspondingly, there is no gradation of salvation.

Just as evangelical creeds spoke of a never-ending suffering of the wicked, the Book of Mormon also depicts the wicked as suffering "endless torment, from whence they can no more return" (Mosiah 3:25). Their "final doom is to endure a never-ending torment" (Mosiah 2:39). When Jesus appeared to the Nephites, he emphasized more than once that the wicked are "hewn down and cast into the fire, from whence there is no return" (3 Ne. 27:11, 17). Thus, the judgment pronounced in the Book of Mormon upon the wicked, as well as on the righteous, is irrevocable; souls end up either endlessly in hell or endlessly in heaven (1 Ne. 15:29–36; 2 Ne. 2:27–29, 9:11–19; Mosiah 5:8–11, 26:23–27; Alma 3:26, 40:11–26, 41:3–5).

Early revelations in the Doctrine and Covenants speak of the same bipolar judgment as that expressed in the Book of Mormon. A revelation given September 1830 states that, at judgment day, when all are resurrected, "the righteous shall be gathered on my right hand unto eternal life; and the wicked on my left hand will I be ashamed to own before the Father" (D&C 29:26–29). A revelation in 1831 characterizes all people as either obedient or disobedient, meriting either eternal life or eternal damnation:

> And unto him that repenteth and sanctifieth himself before the Lord shall be given eternal life.
> And upon them that hearken not to the voice of the Lord shall be fulfilled that which was written by the prophet Moses, that they should be cut off from among the people. (D&C 133:62–63)

This latter group, the revelation continues, "shall go away into outer darkness, where there is weeping, and wailing, and gnashing of teeth" (D&C 133:73). Thus, before 1832, Mormon thought expressed no gradation of glory in the hereafter—only two polarized outcomes.

An early shift in the LDS doctrine of judgment pertains to the duration of hell. After emphatic teachings in the Book of Mormon that the wicked are punished endlessly in hell, a revelation given the same month as the book's publication (March 1830) softens this view, declaring that "eternal" and "endless" are descriptive of the *kind* of reward or punishment rather than its duration. Specifically, "Eternal punishment is God's punishment" and "Endless punishment is God's punishment" (D&C 19:11–12). In spite of clear New Testament and Book of Mormon passages to the contrary, the revelation asserts that "it is not written [anywhere in scripture] that there shall be no end to this torment" (D&C 19:6). Notably, Universalists also used the argument that "eternal" should be understood qualitatively to refute the belief that God's punishment has no end. In 1805, Universalist preacher Hosea Ballou declared: "I say the word *eternal* is not applied to the *duration* of happiness, but to the nature of that life which is brought to light through the gospel."[29] This revelation (D&C 19) marks the beginning of what LDS scholar and Joseph Smith biographer Richard Bushman terms "a perplexing reversal,"[30] as Joseph seemingly discards the doctrine of never-ending punishment taught in the Book of Mormon in favor of a more Universalist perspective.

A common belief in Joseph Smith's day was that, once individuals die, their spirits remain in a state of happiness or misery until the resurrection, after which they are consigned eternally to that same state. In 1776, anti-Universalist John Cleveland declared, "The time of life here on earth is our only probation-time for eternity." He added: "After death . . . while our bodies are in the grave our souls will be in a fixed state of happiness or misery, according to the state we were in when we gave up the ghost . . . and after the resurrection and final judgment the wicked will be in a state of punishment in soul and body forever and ever."[31] The Book of Mormon similarly makes no essential distinction between the state of the soul in the spirit world and its final state after the resurrection. After death, "the spirits of those who are righteous are received into a state of happiness, which is called paradise, a state of rest, a state of peace, where they shall rest from all their troubles and from all care, and sorrow" (Alma 40:12). The spirits of the wicked, in contrast, "shall be cast out into outer darkness; there shall be weeping, and wailing, and gnashing of teeth, and this because of their own iniquity, being led captive by the will of the devil" (Alma 40:13). This consignment to a state of either happiness or misery is fixed, with no prospect of being reclaimed through hearing and accepting the gospel in the spirit world.

In the Book of Mormon, individuals do not and cannot repent once they pass into the spirit world, "for that same spirit [i.e., either "the spirit of the devil" or "the Spirit of the Lord" (Alma 34:35)][32] which doth possess your bodies at the time that ye go out of this life . . . will have power to possess your body in that eternal world" (Alma 34:34). For at death either Christ will "seal you his" (Mosiah 5:15), or you will be "constrained to exclaim: . . . the devil hath obtained me" (2 Ne. 9:46). And "this is the final state" of the righteous and the wicked (Alma 34:35). It is precisely because our eternal state is fixed at death that Amulek warns, "If we do not improve our time while in this life, then cometh the night of darkness wherein there can be no labor performed" (Alma 34:33).

According to current LDS theology, one's eternal state is not fixed at death since one can respond to the saving truths of the gospel even in the spirit world and be saved. Conversely, the righteous can still succumb to temptation in the spirit world.[33] To accommodate this later doctrine of salvation for the dead, varying interpretations have been given of the phrase "the day of this life" in Alma 34:32. Some commentators have suggested that "the day of this life" extends into the spirit world.[34] Joseph Fielding Smith acknowledged that Amulek's remarks pertained to mortality but states that they were confined to the Zoramites who "had rebelled against the truth" and were therefore on the verge of becoming sons of perdition for whom there is no repentance in this world or the spirit world.[35] McConkie's explanation was that Amulek was actually teaching that no one who rejects the gospel in this life will get a second chance in the spirit world.[36] All of these various harmonizing explanations have some merit; however, the plain sense of the passage seems to be that the day of this life ends for all at death, after which the night of darkness follows when no one can do anything to change his or her state (Alma 41:5–7).

Book of Mormon teachings regarding the concept of the resurrection and final judgment parallel New Testament passages and employ similar language. The Book of Mormon has the resurrected Christ saying that at

> the great and last day . . . all people, and all kindreds, and all nations and tongues shall stand before God, to be judged of their works, whether they be good or whether they be evil—
>
> If they be good, to the resurrection of everlasting life; and if they be evil, to the resurrection of damnation. (3 Ne. 26:4–5; see also John 5:29; Rev. 20:12–13)

The general idea one gets from the Book of Mormon is that the resurrection and final judgment won't occur until the end time. In the words of Alma (which seems to recall Hebrews 9:27), "It was appointed unto men that they must die; and after death, they must come to judgment, even that same judgment of which we have spoken, which is the end" (Alma 12:27). At this final judgment, the righteous will come forth in "the resurrection of life" and those who have done evil in "the resurrection of damnation" (3 Ne. 26:5). In his visit to the Nephites, the resurrected Savior spoke of this "great and last day, when all people, and all kindreds, and all nations and tongues shall stand before God, to be judged of their works, whether they be good or whether they be evil" (3 Ne. 26:4).

Early revelations in the Doctrine and Covenants also place this final judgment at the very end of earth's history. A revelation given in March 1830 states that Christ has "all power, even to the destroying of Satan and his works at the end of the world, and the last great day of judgment" when "every man" will be judged "according to his works and the deeds which he hath done" (D&C 19:3). Six months later, a September 1830 revelation declared that, just before the earth shall pass away,

> Michael, mine archangel, shall sound his trump, and then shall all the dead awake, for their graves shall be opened, and they

shall come forth—yea, even all.

And the righteous shall be gathered on my right hand unto eternal life; and the wicked on my left hand will I be ashamed to own before the Father. (D&C 29:26–27)

Thus at this end-time resurrection "all" will come forth—both "the righteous" and "the wicked"—to be judged.

In addition to paralleling many New Testament teachings on judgment and the resurrection, the Book of Mormon reflects familiar early nineteenth-century interpretations of New Testament teachings. Consider, for instance, John 12:32, which reads, "And I, if I be lifted up from the earth, will draw all men unto me." At the time of Joseph Smith, Universalists used this passage as evidence that "all men" will be saved. Anti-Universalists countered that men would not be drawn to Christ in salvation, but rather in judgment. In 1819, Methodist minister D. Isaac wrote that, just as Christ was judged by men and lifted up, so will he lift up all men unto him to be judged.[37] The Book of Mormon effectively canonizes this anti-Universalist understanding in Christ's explanation to the Nephites, "And for this cause have I been lifted up . . . [to] draw all men unto me, that they may be judged according to their works" (3 Ne. 27:14–15).[38]

Later Mormonism

Where initial LDS revelations presented a bifurcated picture of the hereafter, later revelations and teachings shifted to a graduated view in which the righteous and wicked are to receive varying rewards based on beliefs and behavior. The Book of Mormon denounced Universalism, but later LDS scriptures all but embraced it averring that Christ "saves all the works of his hands, except . . . sons of perdition" (D&C 76:43)—an exception that even full-fledged Universalists had difficulty refuting because of its solid biblical grounding. Along with embracing a more Universalist model of salvation, the image of a single final judgment began evolving into multiple judgments. The Book of Mormon and early revelations make no distinction between one's state of blessedness or torment in the spirit world and one's subsequent state in the resurrection. Later teachings, however, make a clear distinction on this point, proclaiming that the suffering in hell of the wicked will end when they are eventually resurrected to a telestial glory.

Doctrine and Covenants 76, revealed in February 1832, states that heaven consists of three degrees or kingdoms of glory: celestial, terrestrial, and telestial.[39] Celestial beings obey the first principles and ordinances of the gospel and are "valiant in the testimony of Jesus" (D&C 76:79). Little children were added to this group in

January 1836 (D&C 137:10). Terrestrial candidates are both "honorable men of the earth" who are not Latter-day Saints (D&C 76:75), and Latter-day Saints who are not honorable. Those who inherit a telestial glory are blatant sinners: "liars, and sorcerers, and adulterers, and whoremongers" (D&C 76:103).

In an apparent allusion to Hebrews 1:14, which speaks of spirits (i.e., angels) ministering to mortals who are heirs of salvation (intended to show that saints are higher than angels), Doctrine and Covenants 76 has resurrected beings of a higher kingdom ministering to those of a lower kingdom. (Those in the telestial kingdom evidently minister to no one.) It is noteworthy that ministering to the inhabitants of the terrestrial kingdom is the only activity identified for those who inherit the celestial kingdom. There is, as yet, no mention of continued family relationships nor the creation and peopling of worlds as gods.

In 1843 Joseph Smith received a revelation further subdividing the celestial kingdom into three additional realms with only those entering the new and everlasting covenant of marriage qualifying for the highest glory in the celestial kingdom (D&C 131:1–2). There, they are promised a continuation of spirit offspring throughout all eternity (D&C 132:19–20). By implication, those who enter the two bottom tiers of the celestial kingdom would be those who overcome the world by faith in Christ, are valiant in the testimony of Jesus (D&C 76:53, 79), but, for whatever reason, choose not to marry.

Those who enter the celestial kingdom but fall short of exaltation "are appointed angels in heaven . . . to minister for those who are worthy of a far more, and an exceeding, and an eternal weight of glory" (D&C 132:16–17). In contrast to resurrected beings of a higher order ministering to those of a lower order as described in Doctrine and Covenants 76, the ministration is now reversed so that those of a lower order become ministering servants to those of a higher order. This scenario is actually more consistent with Hebrews 1:14, although it moves this ministration to the afterlife instead of in mortality, as implied in Hebrews.

Latter-day Saints are prone to read the current doctrine of multiple degrees of glory back into Book of Mormon texts even though it is an awkward fit. Book of Mormon references to eternal life are thus interpreted as referring to the highest degree in the celestial kingdom. Conversely, being cast out with the devil and his angels is no longer seen as applying to all run-of-the-mill wicked individuals who suffer in hell at death and continue in this state through eternity. It is now considered a fate reserved only for those who become sons of perdition in the resurrection, having committed the unpardonable sin.[40]

Attempts to harmonize the Book of Mormon with current salvation theology have proven to be challenging. For example, the Book of

Mormon teaching that those who die without the law have "eternal life" (Mosiah 15:24; see also Mosiah 3:11; Moro. 8:22) is now taken to mean that they inherit only the terrestrial kingdom (D&C 76:72). However, little children, who also have eternal life in the Book of Mormon (Mosiah 15:25), are seen as being exalted in the celestial kingdom.

Conversely, the Book of Mormon consigns all unbelievers to "outer darkness" where they suffer the "second death." According to the current LDS understanding of these terms, all unbelievers would therefore be sons of perdition; however, this differs from the current doctrine that unbelievers will inherit at least a telestial glory. The resurrection of damnation spoken of in the Bible and Book of Mormon (Mosiah 16:11; 3 Ne. 26:5), which referred to the excruciating torment in the resurrection, is now understood as including those who inherit the telestial kingdom,[41] even though the glory of this kingdom "surpasses all understanding" (D&C 76:89).

During the Savior's visit to the Nephites after his resurrection, he spoke of the final judgment of the righteous and the wicked (3 Ne. 27:24–32,) stating: "Enter ye in at the strait gate; for strait is the gate, and narrow is the way that leads to life, and few there be that find it; but wide is the gate, and broad the way which leads to death, and many there be that travel therein, until the night cometh, wherein no man can work" (3 Ne. 27:33). With today's understanding of those who finally enter into "life" (i.e., eternal life) or "death" (i.e., the second death), this pronouncement of the Savior would need to be taken to mean that few obtain eternal life while the majority of people become sons of perdition. When read in context, it appears that the "second death" spoken of in the Book of Mormon (Jacob 3:11; Alma 12:16; Hel. 14:17–18) can't be speaking of sons of perdition because it applies to all but the very most righteous—even those who are guilty of only minor infractions. According to Doctrine and Covenants 76:30–37, however, only sons of perdition suffer the second death. To be consistent with this teaching, Joseph Fielding Smith concluded that Book of Mormon references to the "second death" must pertain exclusively to sons of perdition,[42] even though the Book of Mormon itself teaches that the second death comes on all transgressors who die in their sins.

In current LDS thought, the second coming is no longer "the" day of judgment as depicted in the Bible and Book of Mormon, but only "a" day of judgment in that the righteous dead—and the righteous living as soon as they reach the "age of a tree" (D&C 101:30)—are rewarded with a glorious resurrection, while the wicked continue their confinement in spirit prison until the end of the millennium when they come forth to receive either a telestial glory or a kingdom of no glory. This premillennial judgment is followed by a final judgment at the end of the earth. Bruce R. McConkie explains that the final judgment is "the formal occasion when every living soul will stand before the judgment bar, an event that will not take place until the last soul has been resurrected—to learn their status and the degree of glory they are to receive in eternity."[43] Placing this final judgment day at the end of the earth rather than at the coming of Christ as depicted in earlier LDS scriptures is essential if one is to maintain consistency with the later-developed idea of an ongoing resurrection and judgment even after the second coming.

Later LDS teachings seemingly disregard the doctrine of eternal or never-ending punishment as taught in the Bible and Book of Mormon. In spite of the clear presence of this doctrine in these scriptures, Apostle James E. Talmage asserts, "The false doctrine that the punishment to be visited upon erring souls is endless, that every sentence for sin is of interminable duration, must be regarded as one of the most pernicious results of misapprehension of scripture. It is but a dogma of unauthorized and erring sectaries, at once unscriptural, unreasonable, and revolting to one who loves mercy and honors justice."[44] How this doctrine is "unscriptural" is puzzling at best.

In addition to limiting the duration of damnation, later scriptures also reduce the number of those suffering the second death. A revelation given August 1831 states that liars and other sinners suffer the second death (D&C 63:17), a teaching consistent with the Bible, Book of Mormon, and earlier sections of the Doctrine and Covenants. Six months later, however, another revelation modified this teaching so that the second death affects only sons of perdition who deny the Holy Ghost as well as the Son, effectively "crucify[ing] him unto themselves" (D&C 76:35–37). This continues to be the prevailing understanding in Mormonism.[45]

A subtle shift in LDS thought pertains to the nature of heaven itself. In early Mormonism, it was understood that the earth would "die," but then "be quickened again" (D&C 88:26) and become the eternal abode of the righteous (D&C 88:20)—an Eden-like paradise, an idyllic dwelling place. An 1831 revelation spoke of "a land flowing with milk and honey" that Saints would inherit "while the earth shall stand, and ye shall possess it again in eternity, no more to pass away" (D&C 38:18–20). Later the same year the Lord referred to the land of Zion as being an inheritance that the righteous would "possess . . . from generation to generation, forever and ever" (D&C 69:8). However, in 1843 this concept of the earth being parceled out among the righteous for their eternal abode was replaced by a more rarefied one as Joseph characterized heaven as "a sea of glass and fire" (D&C 130:7), adding that "this earth, in its sanctified and immortal state, will be made like unto crystal" (D&C 130:9). Richard Bushman observes: "The view of heaven as a crystalline sea of glass seemed like a departure from Joseph's earlier ideas," which were "in the tradition of heavenly speculators [such as Emanuel Swedenborg] who saw heaven more as an extension of earth."[46]

The Unpardonable Sin

Latter-day Saints believe that sinning against the refulgent light of the Holy Ghost is a sin of such magnitude that there is no possibility of forgiveness in this world or in the world to come. Such individuals are said to effectively consent to Christ's death. Those who commit this unpardonable sin are condemned to suffer the wrath of God throughout eternity and are labeled sons of perdition. Joseph Smith said: "Jesus Christ will save all except the sons of perdition."[47]

In the Old Testament, there is no mention of an unpardonable sin because there is very little concept of rewards and punishments in a hereafter. In spite of this understandable absence, Joseph Smith's revised account of Genesis has Cain becoming "Perdition" and ruling over Satan himself (Moses 5:23–24), all as a result of his refusal to obey God's commandments (Moses 5:23–25).

The LDS notion of sinning against the Holy Ghost has its closest biblical parallel in the New Testament book of Hebrews, which states that it is "impossible" to renew souls unto repentance who "fall away" after they "were once enlightened, and have tasted of the heavenly gift, and were made partakers of the Holy Ghost" (Heb. 6:4–6). Most New Testament scholars concur that the basic idea being expressed here is that those who apostatize after fully partaking of the enlightenment of the Holy Ghost can no longer be brought to repentance. Other New Testament passages used in LDS discourse to corroborate this idea of sinning against the Holy Ghost appear to be less clearly related.

One of these passages is in Matthew which has Jesus discussing the sin of speaking against the Holy Ghost:

> All manner of sin and blasphemy shall be forgiven unto men: but the blasphemy against the Holy Ghost shall not be forgiven unto men.
> And whosoever speaketh a word against the Son of man, it shall be forgiven him: but whosoever speaketh against the Holy Ghost, it shall not be forgiven him, neither in this world, neither in the world to come. (Matt. 12:31–32)

Notice that Jesus isn't talking about *sinning* against the light or witness of the Holy Ghost, but rather *speaking out* against the Holy Ghost (i.e., profaning the name of the Holy Ghost or saying evil things about the Holy Ghost), although disrespect can be manifested in other ways as well. The *Encyclopedia of Mormonism* defines "blasphemy against the Holy Ghost" as "knowingly . . . sin[ning] against the Holy Ghost by denying its influence after having received it."[48] That Jesus was talking about speaking actual words against the Holy Ghost is confirmed four verses later where he declares that "every idle word that men shall speak, they shall give account thereof in the day of judgment" (Matt. 12:36). Amy Donaldson, a researcher in Christianity and Judaism in antiquity at Notre Dame, explains that, in light of contemporaneous Jewish teachings regarding blasphemy, "both 'speak a word against' and 'blaspheme' bear the same meaning, namely, to speak against God or his representative in an irreverent way that may pose a challenge to God's ability or authority."[49]

From an LDS perspective of the Godhead, one might wonder why speaking against Christ is forgivable while speaking against the Holy Ghost (the third member of the Godhead) is not. As noted in Chapter 8, the synoptic Gospels never portray Christ as deity or on a par with God. Indeed, he refers to himself in Matthew 12:31 as "the Son of Man," most likely an Aramaic idiom for "human."[50] The Holy Ghost, on the other hand, is spoken of in the ordinary Jewish sense of God's own Spirit or power, not in the sense of the third person of the Godhead. Consequently, to blaspheme against the Holy Ghost was to literally blaspheme against God.[51]

It is noteworthy that, while Jesus states that speaking against the Holy Ghost is unforgivable, he doesn't say that the punishment for such a sin is any different from other types of sins one may commit. As previously mentioned, the New Testament doesn't differentiate between degrees of punishment for the wicked; all are cast into outer darkness where there is "weeping and gnashing of teeth" (Matt. 8:12). In the case of those who speak against the Holy Ghost, it seems as though their punishment simply becomes guaranteed in advance.

In addition to the sin of speaking out against the Holy Ghost, John 1 mentions a "sin unto death" (1 Jn. 5:16) that cannot be expunged by prayer. Many Latter-day Saints also understand this passage as referring to the unpardonable sin of "blasphemy against [i.e., sinning against] the Holy Ghost."[52] Biblical scholars, however, are less certain about both the nature of this sin and the type of "death" it brings.[53] David Rensberger, professor of New Testament at the Interdenominational Theological Center in Atlanta, states that "this is not the same as the sin mentioned in Mark 3:29 [i.e., Jesus's reference to blasphemy against the Holy Ghost]."[54] From John's text, it doesn't appear to be one particular sin, for John also says that "there is a sin not unto death" (1 Jn. 5:16). Though unexplained, the "sin unto death" may hark back to the doctrine taught earlier in John's epistle that "he that loveth not his brother abideth in death" (1 Jn. 3:14). Thus, hatred would be a sin unto death.

The title "son of perdition" appears only twice in the Bible, both in the New Testament. In the Gospel of John, it is an epithet applied to Judas Iscariot (John 17:12) while Paul applies it to an unidentified "man of sin" (2 Thess. 2:3). "Son of perdition" carries the connotation of being lost or fallen ("perdition" derives from Greek and means "lost"). To be a son of perdition is to be a son of darkness as opposed to a son of light. Nowhere in the Bible is "son of perdition" associated with the commission of an unpardonable sin, though clearly it is associated with wicked and abominable behavior. In the New Testament those who don't obtain salvation are faced with the only other alternative, which is perdition (Philip. 1:28; 1 Tim. 6:9; Heb. 10:39; 2 Pet. 3:7), thus becoming in effect, sons of perdition.

In LDS theology, sons of perdition are those—and exclusively those—who suffer the "second death" (D&C 76:30–38). "Second death" is believed to refer to the banishment of sons of perdition to outer darkness after the resurrection.[55] In the New Testament, the term "second death" appears only in the book of Revelation and applies to all whose names are not recorded in the "book of life" (Rev. 20:14–15). This category is not limited to those who commit what Latter-day Saints consider as the unpardonable sin, but includes "the fearful, and unbelieving, and the abominable, and murderers, and whoremongers, and sorcerers, and idolaters, and all liars" (Rev. 21:8; cf. 22:15).

The Book of Mormon uses New Testament phraseology, while imposing a modern Christian understanding when speaking of the unpardonable sin. It is defined as lying to God by denying what one knows to be true through the power of the Holy Ghost (Jacob 7:19; Alma 39:5–6). Like both New Testament and evangelical traditions, the Book of Mormon maintains that sons of perdition suffer the second death along with all others who are wicked (Jacob 3:11; Alma 12:16, 32; 13:30; Hel. 14:18–19). Thus, the punishment of those who commit the unpardonable sin is not materially different from those who commit any other sin and don't repent. The only difference seems to be that their fate is sealed prior to the judgment day.

In the Book of Mormon, the second death is defined in a traditional Christian way as "a spiritual death" in which one dies "as to things pertaining unto righteousness" (Alma 12:16). It is a second death because it follows the first spiritual death which comes upon everyone through the Fall (Hel. 14: 16–17). Thus, after all are redeemed by the resurrection from the first spiritual death, "there cometh upon them [the sinners] again a spiritual death, yea, a second death, for they are cut off again as to things pertaining to righteousness" (Hel. 14:18).

Furthermore, all who are worldly and thereby figuratively sell or exchange Christ for silver and gold are compared to "*the* son of perdition," a direct reference to Judas Iscariot (3 Ne. 27:32; emphasis mine).[56] In another reference to Judas, the Book of Mormon prophesies of those living in the last days saying, "Wo unto him that shall say at that day, to get gain, that there can be no miracle wrought by Jesus Christ; for he that doeth this shall become like unto the son of perdition, for whom there was no mercy, according to the word of Christ!" (3 Ne. 29:7). Thus, in the Book of Mormon, a son of perdition (or one like *the* son of perdition) is any sinful or deceitful person.

As noted above, the book of Moses subsequently personalized the meaning of sons of perdition calling Cain "Perdition." Thus, he is the father of lies and all who hearken unto his lies become his sons (Moses 5:24). Still, sons of perdition are not just those few who commit egregious sins but include all who seek after worldly gain and listen to Satan's lies.

Joseph Smith gave increased emphasis to the topic of the "unpardonable sin" and "sons of perdition" during the final months of his life as he was also revisioning the doctrine of hell and the afterlife. His teachings at that time focused more on apostate Mormons becoming sons of perdition. The Prophet taught that to "sin against the Holy Ghost," one "must receive the Holy Ghost, have the heavens opened unto him, and know God, and then sin against him."[57] He further declared, "This is the case with many apostates in this Church, . . . they have got the same spirit the devil had, you cannot save them, they make open war like the devil."[58] Isolating sons of perdition largely to militant apostates seems to further narrow the category formerly covered by the title "son of perdition." LDS scholar Grant Underwood notes, "Before the late Nauvoo period there was little explanatory discussion of the term unpardonable sin. Therefore, even if the early Saints had talked of damnation coming in its fullest sense only to 'sons of perdition,' there were then no conceptual restraints limiting that category to apostate Mormons alone."[59]

So while the Bible, Book of Mormon, and other early LDS scriptures speak of all unrighteous people becoming sons of perdition and suffering the second death, by February 1832, most of these individuals (liars, whoremongers, etc.) were considered worthy of a place in the telestial kingdom and therefore escape the punishment of outer darkness (D&C 76:98–103). Sons of perdition are those who have "denied the Holy Spirit after having received it" (D&C 76:35). In the later Nauvoo period, Joseph Smith taught that such individuals inevitably become hostile apostates. Today, LDS teachings tend to paint sons of perdition as being restricted to a very few who turn against the fulness of the light of the Holy Ghost.[60] Ironically,

President Joseph F. Smith questioned whether Judas himself, who was expressly designated as *the* son of perdition, really possessed enough light to qualify as a son of perdition, since the Holy Ghost wasn't given to New Testament Saints until the day of Pentecost.[61]

Murderers

One class of grievous transgression expressly condemned in LDS theology is murder. Joseph Smith taught that "a murderer . . . cannot have forgiveness [in this life]. David sought repentance at the hand of God carefully with tears, for the murder of Uriah; but he could only get it through hell."[62] "No murderer hath eternal life," he averred, explaining that murderers "cannot be forgiven, until they have paid the last farthing."[63]

In the Old Testament, where rewards and punishments were confined to this life, the penalty for murder was death (Gen. 9:5–6; Lev. 24:17). It took the New Testament to assign a punishment in the hereafter to murderers, but even so it was a punishment no different than that inflicted on any other sinner (Rev. 21:8). 1 John 3:15 states that anyone "who hates his brother is a murderer," and Jesus himself ranked angry thoughts on a par with murder (Matt. 5:21–22).

Though the New Testament never singles out murder as any more punishable than other sins, Joseph Smith appropriated two passages from Acts to support the assertion that murderers cannot be forgiven in this life.

The first passage is from Acts 3 where Peter reproves the Jews for "kill[ing] the Prince of life" (Acts 3:15) saying, "I wot [i.e., I know] that through ignorance ye did it, as did also your rulers" (Acts 3:17). In a sermon delivered in May 1841, Joseph Smith redirected Peter's entire remark to the Jewish rulers rather than to the Jewish masses. According to the Prophet, "Peter preached repentance and baptism for the remission of sins to the Jews who had been led to acts of violence and blood by their leaders; but to the rulers he said, 'I wot that through ignorance ye did it, as did also your rulers.'"[64] Joseph then changed the wording from "I wot" to "I would" so that "to the Rulers he said, 'I would that through ignorance ye did it, as did also those ye ruled.'"[65] Joseph's alterations to this verse are particularly interesting given that he had earlier corroborated the original meaning by changing "I wot" to "I know" (JST Acts 3:17). Thus, an ignorant transgression on the part of the general Jewish populace is transformed into a deliberate act of cold-blooded murder carried out by the Jewish leaders.

Returning to the account in Acts we find Peter subsequently calling upon the Jews to repent saying, "Repent ye therefore, and be converted, that your sins may be blotted out, when the times of refreshing shall come from the presence of the Lord" (Acts 3:19). Commenting on this passage, the Prophet explained, "He did not say to them, 'Repent and be baptized for the remission of your sins' [because] . . . they could not be baptized for the remission of sins, for they had shed innocent blood."[66] Was Peter really condemning the Jewish leaders as murderers and refraining from telling them to be baptized because there was no forgiveness for them except through suffering in hell? Standard translations, including the KJV, give a completely different sense. Instead of a statement of condemnation directed only at the Jewish leaders, Peter is reaching out to the larger Jewish populace, saying in effect that, since they had acted in ignorance, they are eligible for redemption and encouraged to repent with the promise that their sins will be remitted like everyone else's when Christ comes to reclaim sinners from sin.

The second passage cited by the Prophet to justify the irredeemability of murderers is Acts 2 where Peter refers to David who killed Uriah after first committing adultery with his wife. Peter quotes Psalms 16:10 which he attributes to David who said, "Thou wilt not leave my soul in hell, neither wilt thou suffer thine Holy One to see corruption" (Acts 2:27). Peter then explains why it should be evident that this was a prophecy of Christ and not a statement about David. First, Peter explains that David "is both dead and buried, and his sepulchre is with us unto this day" (Acts 2:29). Thus, he remained in hell and his flesh saw the corruption and decay of death. In contrast, Christ's "soul was not left in hell, neither [did] his flesh . . . see corruption [i.e., his body wasn't in the tomb long enough to decay]" (Acts 2:31). Second, Peter points out that the individual spoken of in Psalms was told "Sit thou on my right hand," but David "is not ascended into the heavens" (Acts 2:34). Christ, on the other hand, has ascended to heaven and now sits on the right hand of God's throne. The apostle Paul gives essentially the same interpretation of Psalms 16:10 as Peter arguing that it couldn't possibly have reference to David because he "saw corruption [i.e., decay]: But he, whom God raised again [i.e., Christ], saw no corruption" (Acts 13:35–37).

Joseph Smith, in contradistinction to both Peter and Paul, argued that it was David—not Christ—who received the promise that his soul would not be left in hell. "David sought repentance at the hand of God carefully with tears, for the murder of Uriah," said the Prophet, "but he could only get it through hell: he got a promise that his soul should not be left in hell."[67] The Prophet further understood Peter to be saying that, because David was a murderer, he missed having part in the resurrection at the time of Christ, and would have to wait until Christ comes again to be redeemed.[68]

The fact that Joseph Smith misconstrued Peter's exposition of Psalms doesn't make him any less of a prophet than Peter or Paul. In fact, his interpretation of Psalms is probably more accurate than theirs as it at least recognizes that the subject was the psalmist himself and not Christ. According to Philip Johnston, professor of Old Testament at Wycliffe Hall in Oxford, "Modern scholarship emphatically rejects this exegesis [given by Peter and Paul]. . . . For a start, the psalmist was hardly David. Secondly, he was referring to himself, not some unknown future figure. And thirdly, he was asserting deliverance from imminent mortal danger, not proclaiming belief in life beyond death."[69] Part of Peter's misunderstanding of Psalm 16 is his dependency on the Septuagint version, which is different from the Hebrew. Paul Achtemeier explains, "Whereas the Hebrew speaks of God keeping the faithful servant from the 'pit' [i.e., the grave itself], the Septuagint translation speaks of keeping the 'Holy One' from 'corruption' [i.e., decaying in the grave], a change that lies at the heart of the point Peter is making in this sermon."[70] The general scholarly interpretation can be summarized as follows: the psalmist is confident that Yahweh will preserve him and deliver him *from* (not *out of*) death, because he is Yahweh's loyal one who has chosen Yahweh as his portion. If this interpretation is correct, it essentially means that the interpretations of Peter, Paul, and Joseph Smith are all flawed, though for different reasons.

In the Book of Mormon, murder is placed second only to the unpardonable sin of denying the Holy Ghost (Alma 39:5). It is a sin for which "it is not easy . . . to obtain forgiveness" (Alma 39:6). This is different from saying murderers *cannot* obtain forgiveness. Within a year of the publication of the Book of Mormon, however, a revelation was received stating, "He that kills shall not have forgiveness in this world, nor in the world to come" (D&C 42:18).

This designation of murder as an unforgivable sin was softened in 1832 when the doctrine of three degrees of glory was revealed, and it was made known that murderers are eventually "saved" (D&C 76:43) and permitted to enter the telestial kingdom (D&C 76:85) where they inherit the same glory as liars, etc. (v. 103). Some LDS commentators reconcile the revelation that murderers can *never* be forgiven (D&C 42:18) with this later revelation that they are eventually "redeemed" (D&C 76:85) by redefining the term "unforgivable" to mean that they are pardoned but still barred from exaltation. To differentiate between murderers who are pardoned but not exalted and sons of perdition who have no pardon of any kind, murder has come to be termed an "unforgivable" sin, while the sin against the Holy Ghost is designated an "unpardonable" sin.[71]

In 1857, Brigham Young spoke of certain grievous sins including murder "that cannot be atoned for without the shedding of their [the perpetrator's] blood." He stated that there are "plenty of instances where men, have been righteously slain, in order to atone for their sins."[72] Apostle Heber C. Kimball echoed this same understanding in 1859, "If a man has shed innocent blood, he will have to pay the atonement, or he never can atone for his sin."[73] Early in the twentieth century, Apostle Joseph Fielding Smith reiterated that "man may commit certain grievous sins—according to his light and knowledge—that will place him beyond the reach of the atoning blood of Christ. If then he would be saved he must make sacrifice of his own life to atone—so far as in his power lies—for that sin, for the blood of Christ alone under certain circumstances will not avail."[74] As late as 1966, McConkie was still affirming this doctrine: "There are some serious sins for which the cleansing of Christ does not operate, and the law of God is that men must then have their own blood shed to atone for their sins."[75] This doctrine of "blood atonement" is one reason the state of Utah had the firing squad as a legal means of execution, along with hanging and, later, lethal injection, until 2004.[76]

In recent years, the Church has been more reticent in teaching the doctrine of blood atonement. Lowell M. Snow, writing in the 1992 *Encyclopedia of Mormonism*, explains that if a person "commits a grievous sin such as the shedding of innocent blood, the Savior's sacrifice alone will not absolve the person of the consequences of the sin. Only by voluntarily submitting to whatever penalty the Lord may require can that person benefit from the Atonement of Christ."[77] There is a notable absence of the express requirement to shed one's blood or forfeit one's own life. Snow adds that Brigham Young's teaching (that a murderer's blood must be shed to atone for his sin) "is not a doctrine of the Church." In a letter dated September 20, 1978, and addressed to LDS Church president Spencer W. Kimball, Thomas B. McAffee, then editor of the *Utah Law Review*, asked about the Church's view on the death penalty as it relates to blood atonement. Responding on official letterhead at the request of the First Presidency, Apostle Bruce R. McConkie wrote: "We do *not* believe that it is necessary for men in this day to shed their own blood to receive a remission of sins. This is said with a full awareness of what I and others have written and said on this subject in times past." He continued: "There simply is no such thing among us as a doctrine of blood atonement that grants a remission of sins or confers any other benefit upon a person because his own blood is shed for sins."[78]

FINAL JUDGMENT 497

Notes

1. Bruce R. McConkie, *Mormon Doctrine*, 404.
2. Gerald O'Collins, *Christology: A Biblical, Historical, and Systematic Study of Jesus*, 140.
3. Daniel H. Ludlow, *A Companion to Your Study of the Book of Mormon*, 284.
4. Thomas B. Thayer, *The Origin and History of the Doctrine of Endless Punishment*, 34–38. Geza Vermes, *The Resurrection*, 136.
5. Kaufmann Kohler, "Eschatology," 6:210.
6. It is unclear whether the saints in this passage are to judge in the sense of sitting in final judgment or in the sense of ruling in the final kingdom. A similar ambiguity exists with the twelve apostles acting as judges where the sense shifts from ruling in the New Testament (Matt. 19:28; cf. JST Matt. 25:34; Rev. 21:14) to judging in the Book of Mormon (Mormon 3:18–19; cf. 1 Ne. 12:8–10; 3 Ne. 27:27) and back to ruling in the Doctrine and Covenants (D&C 29:12).
7. Everett Ferguson, *Backgrounds of Early Christianity*, 555.
8. Andrew F. Ehat and Lyndon W. Cook, *The Words of Joseph Smith: The Contemporary Accounts of the Nauvoo Discourses of the Prophet Joseph Smith*, 319.
9. Ibid., 367–68.
10. For scholarly references, see David L. Paulsen, "The Redemption of the Dead: A Latter-day Saint Perspective on the Fate of the Unevangelized," 290 note 9.
11. Robert Jamieson, A. R. Fausset, and David Brown, *A Commentary, Critical and Explanatory, on the Old and New Testaments*, 2:294–95.
12. Origen, *De Principiis*, 2.10.2.
13. One need only do an internet book search for the phrase "for as one star differeth" between the year 1780 and 1830 to see how frequently this modified rendering was given. The origin of this modified rendering goes back to at least Saint Augustine (A.D. 354–430).
14. The Hebrew idea of three heavens was sometimes expanded to include seven heavens, and, in some traditions, more. Victor Paul Furnish, *II Corinthians*, 525; Philip Edgecumbe Huges, *Paul's Second Epistle to the Corinthians*, 432–34.
15. Hughes, *Paul's Second Epistle to the Corinthians*, 435–36; C. R. A. Morray-Jones, "Paradise Revised," 265–292.
16. "Westminster Confession of Faith."
17. William Miller, quoted in Grant Underwood, *The Millenarian World of Early Mormonism*, 114.
18. Ibid.
19. Lorenzo Dow, *The Opinion of Dow; or, Lorenzo's Thoughts, On Different Subjects, in an Address to the People of New-England*, 101.
20. Quoted in Dan Vogel, *Joseph Smith: The Making of a Prophet*, 182.
21. Charles S. Buck, *A Theological Dictionary*, 210.
22. Jonathan Edwards, quoted in Bruce Wilkinson, *A Life God Rewards: Why Everything You Do Today Matters Forever*, 119.

23. John Wesley, quoted in ibid., 120–21.

24. The writings of Emanuel Swedenborg were quite popular in Smith's day and were frequently advertised in the *Ontario Repository*, a newspaper that was printed in Canandaigua, New York, just twelve miles from the Smith home in Palmyra. Edward Hunter, a convert to Mormonism from Swedenborgism, noted the Prophet's familiarity with Swedenborg and claimed that in 1839 he heard him remark: "Emanuel Sweadenburg had a view of the world to come but for daily food he perished." Edward Hunter, "Copy of Record Written by Edward Hunter," 5; see also E. M. Meyers, "Death in Swedenborgian and Mormon Eschatology," 58–64.

25. For parallels and contrasts between Smith's and Swedenborg's beliefs, see Craig Miller, "Did Swedenborg Influence (LDS) Mormon Doctrine?"

26. Colleen McDannell and Bernhard Lang, *Heaven: A History*, 181–99.

27. Emanuel Swedenborg, *Delights of Wisdom Concerning Conjugial Love; After Which Follow: Pleasures of Insanity Concerning Scortatory Love*, 45–46.

28. "Westminster Confession of Faith."

29. Hosea Ballou, *A Treatise on the Atonement*, 161–62; emphasis his. See also Woodbury M. Fernald, *Universalism against Partialism*, 2–81; Dan Vogel, "'The Prophet Puzzle' Revisited," 55.

30. Richard L. Bushman, *Joseph Smith: Rough Stone Rolling*, 200.

31. John Cleveland, quoted in Dan Vogel, *Joseph Smith: The Making of a Prophet*, 245.

32. The "spirit" in this passage is often interpreted as one's own spirit. For example, see Bruce R. McConkie, *Mormon Doctrine*, 762; Joseph Fielding McConkie and Robert L. Millet, *Doctrinal Commentary on the Book of Mormon*, 3:256; *Gospel Principles* (2009), 242. The idea seems rather to be that it is the spirit of Satan or the Spirit of God that does the possessing (see Alma 34:35). This clarification is made in Bruce C. Hafen and Marie K Hafen, *The Belonging Heart: The Atonement and Relationships with God and Family*, 140.

33. Joseph Fielding Smith, *Answers to Gospel Questions*, 3:194.

34. Rodney Turner, "Two Prophets: Abinadi and Alma," 252; Ludlow, *A Companion to Your Study of the Book of Mormon*, 216.

35. Smith, *Answers to Gospel Questions*, 4:3.

36. McConkie, *Mormon Doctrine*, 686.

37. Daniel Isaac, *The Doctrine of Universal Restoration Examined and Refuted*, 71.

38. Many scholarly Bible commentaries concur with at least the general sense of the Universalist interpretation of John 12:32; not the Universalist view that all will be saved, but that Christ's salvation extends to people of all nationalities and, therefore, draws all classes of people to him in salvation. It is pointed out that Jesus's remark is directed to his disciples who had, evidently reluctantly, brought him a message that a certain group of Greeks wanted to have an audience with him (John 12:20). Of course, they presumed that Jesus would have nothing to do with Greeks. See David K. Rensberger, "The Gospel According to John," 2038; Raymond E. Brown, *John*, 477; Ernest De Witt Burton, "The Biblical Doctrine of the Atonement: VII," 23; Adam Clarke, *Commentary on the Bible*, s.v. John 12.

39. Brigham Young postulated more kingdoms, stating, "There are mil-

lions of such kingdoms . . . as many degrees of glory as there are degrees of capacity." Brigham Young, *The Essential Brigham Young*, 140

40. McConkie, *Mormon Doctrine*, 237, 746.

41. Ibid., 642.

42. Smith, *Answers to Gospel Questions*, 1:74. On a separate occasion, the flipside of this question was submitted to Joseph Fielding Smith asking essentially what the scriptural meaning of "eternal life" is. His response was, "Those who obtain eternal life will dwell with the Father and the Son. They become joint heirs with Jesus Christ in receiving the fulness of the Father's Kingdom." Ibid., 2:6. The implication is that "eternal life" as spoken of in the Book of Mormon refers only to the highest (celestial) kingdom.

43. McConkie, *Mormon Doctrine*, 404. It isn't clear what purpose a final judgment will serve individuals like Abraham who has already "entered into his exaltation and sitteth upon his throne" (D&C 132:29).

44. James E. Talmage, *Articles of Faith*, 55.

45. Rodney Turner, "Sons of Perdition," 3:1391–92.

46. Bushman, *Joseph Smith: Rough Stone Rolling*, 487.

47. Ehat and Cook, *The Words of Joseph Smith*, 347; see also Rodney Turner, "Unpardonable Sin," 4:1499; McConkie, *Mormon Doctrine*, 816.

48. Turner, "Unpardonable Sin," 4:1499.

49. Amy M. Donaldson, "Blasphemy against the Spirit and the Historical Jesus," 170.

50. Dennis L. Duling, "Matthew," 1880.

51. Donaldson, "Blasphemy against the Spirit," 167–68.

52. Smith, *Answers to Gospel Questions*, 1:70; Richard M. Romney, "Spiritual Death," 3:1407.

53. Several alternative interpretations are provided in Raymond E. Brown, *The Epistles of John*, 611–20.

54. David K. Rensberger, "The First Letter of John," 2298.

55. Joseph Fielding Smith, *Doctrines of Salvation: Compiled Sermons of Joseph Fielding Smith*, 2:220; Turner, "Sons of Perdition," 3:1391.

56. It seems odd that Jesus would allude to the son of perdition (i.e., Judas) to the Nephites who presumably would have had no knowledge of Judas Iscariot and his betrayal of Christ.

57. Ehat and Cook, *The Words of Joseph Smith*, 347.

58. Ibid.

59. Grant Underwood, "Saved or Damned: Tracing a Persistent Protestantism in Early Mormon Thought," 96.

60. Turner, "Sons of Perdition," 3:1392.

61. Joseph F. Smith, *Gospel Doctrine: Selections from the Sermons and Writings of Joseph F. Smith*, 433, 435.

62. Ehat and Cook, *The Words of Joseph Smith*, 331.

63. Ibid., 73.

64. Ibid. This rendering is awkward because it has Peter comparing the Jewish rulers to themselves.

65. Ibid.; cf 331.

66. Ibid., 331.

67. Ibid.

68. Ibid., 73. The interpretation Joseph Smith gives of Acts 2:27 is problematic in that he places the time of the redemption and resurrection of these murderers at the "times of refreshing," which he understood as referring to the time of the second coming. Doctrine and Covenants 76, however, places their redemption after the millennium.

69. Philip P. Johnston, "'Left in Hell'? Psalm 16, Sheol and the Holy One," 214.

70. Paul Achtemeier, *The Inspiration of Scripture*, 64.

71. H. Dean Garrett, "The Three Most Abominable Sins," 169–70; Ludlow, *A Companion to Your Study of the Book of Mormon*, 221–22.

72. Brigham Young, February 8, 1857, *Journal of Discourses* 4:220, see also Young, March 16, 1856, *Journal of Discourses* 3:247.

73. Heber C. Kimball, August 28, 1859, *Journal of Discourses* 7:236.

74. Smith, *Doctrines of Salvation*, 1:134.

75. McConkie, *Mormon Doctrine*, 92; Smith, *Doctrines of Salvation*, 1:134.

76. Smith, *Doctrines of Salvation*, 1:136. For an analysis of the influence the doctrine of blood atonement had on Utah's method of capital punishment, see Martin R. Gardner, "Mormonism and Capital Punishment," 9–26. Executions by firing squad in Utah were prohibited in March 2004. When the state of Utah was studying forms of capital punishment in 2003, the Church issued a statement at the request of the Utah Sentencing Commission. It said only that the Church "has no objection to the elimination of the firing squad in Utah." Quoted in Linda Thomson, "Church Not against a Firing Squad Ban." In 2010, Ronnie Lee Gardner was executed by firing squad in Utah. He was given this option because his capital sentencing occured before the 2004 prohibition.

77. Lowell M. Snow, "Blood Atonement," 1:131.

78. Quoted in L. Kay Gillespie, *The Unforgiven: Utah's Executed Men*, 14.

Epilogue

Mormon theology, though distinctive in many ways, shares the same legacy of change and cultural accommodation that was characteristic of early Christian and earlier Israelite religions. Judaism, Christianity, and Mormonism emerged in succession as inspired reformulations of the theological traditions preceding them, each borrowing from contemporary ideologies (the convergence stage) and adding their own peculiar enhancements (the differentiation stage). Mormonism, in particular, initially adopted many doctrines in common with early nineteenth-century evangelicalism, but soon began introducing doctrines that were not only distinctive but, in some cases, disdained by orthodox Christians.

In light of the long history of theological change and scriptural adaptation dating back to Old Testament times, it would be naive to suppose that all the major doctrinal kinks have been worked out, and that we now have the final word of God on all important doctrinal matters. It has been suggested that the very notion of continuing revelation resists theological finality. According to BYU professor James Faulconer, "Since Latter-day Saints insist on continuing revelation, they cannot have a dogmatic theology that is any more than provisional and heuristic, for a theology claiming to be more than that could always be trumped by new revelation."[1] Add to this the fact that revelation is always mediated through finite and fallible humans and the result is a theology that is, by its very nature, imperfect and therefore ever subject to revision. Given such an open theology, Blake Ostler may be correct in stating that, when it comes to religion, "there is no final, once and for all, statement of the truth."[2]

Firm—Yet Flexible—in the Faith

In light of the incomplete and dynamic nature of Mormon theology, how firm and fixed should Latter-day Saints be in holding to the doctrines taught by the Church? Can members sustain Church leaders and accept their teachings as the word of God, yet allow for imperfections and variations in their precepts? When one considers that Brigham Young's Adam-God doctrine has not only been abandoned but labeled heresy (see chap. 7); that plural marriage—at one time considered essential for exaltation—is no longer deemed necessary (see chap. 15); that the teaching that blacks were less noble in the preexistence is now being dismissed as folklore (see chap. 17); and that a host of other doctrines have been similarly changed, reversed, or discarded, there are certainly enough precedents to warrant a more flexible posture toward Church teachings. This does not mean, however, that one can't be supportive of Church leaders or thoroughly committed to the aims of the church. BYU religion professor Robert L. Millet advises, "[W]e can sustain with all our hearts the prophets and apostles without believing that they are perfect or that everything they say or do is exactly what God wants said and done."[3]

Significantly, the doctrines the Church expects its members to embrace for temple worthiness are fairly basic and few in number, amounting essentially to whether God exists, Jesus is our redeemer, and the Church has been restored and continues to be guided by a living prophet. Beyond these core professions of belief, Saints presumably have some latitude in what they can believe. Early Latter-day Saints held to the maxim: "In essentials there should be unity, in nonessentials liberty, and in all things charity."[4] Differing views or reluctance to go with the status quo on non-essential doctrines is no more an indication of a weak or underdeveloped testimony than indiscriminate acceptance of all popularly held LDS doctrines is a sign of a mature testimony.

Having a Scriptural Leg to Stand On

If, in fact, many of the passages used to support LDS doctrines today had other meanings in their original context, how does this affect the validity of these doctrines? Does it mean that they are unfounded and therefore false, or could it merely suggest that we need not always expect to find scriptural justification for every belief taught in the church?

Certainly doctrines can be true on grounds other than having scriptural sanction. LDS scripture itself teaches, for instance, that the witness of the Holy Ghost provides the only incontrovertible evidence of the truth (Moro. 10:5). To be sure, Doctrine and Covenants 50:17–20 states that confirming evidence that comes any other way "is not of God." For many Saints, the rational appeal or resonance of Mormon theology is convincing evidence of its truthfulness ("truth is reason").[5] Still others have embraced Mormon doctrine because of its commendable fruits ("by their fruits ye shall know them" [Matt. 7:20]).[6] In sum, the absence of scriptural validation, and even the scriptural negation of a belief, does not in itself falsify the belief. Therefore, appealing to scripture to substantiate Mormon truth claims should be seen as a secondary rather than a primary basis of justification for LDS beliefs.

Interestingly, many biblical scholars today are asking if it is even desirable to embrace doctrines simply because they are found in the Bible.[7] Their reasoning is that the doctrines expressed in the Old and New Testaments partially reflect or were adapted to the cultural paradigms of the time. If this is the case, they argue, why would one feel more vindicated in his or her beliefs by imitating modes of thought that don't really fit current, more enlightened paradigms? With its emphasis on continuing revelation, Mormonism has a built-in mechanism for redefining doctrines as times change.

The Crisis of Doctrinal Exclusivity

Since its inception, many Mormons have taken an exclusivist stance towards other belief systems, acknowledging that, while other religions have a portion of the truth (mingled with error), only Mormonism contains the full and undiluted truth. This has sometimes led to feelings, and certainly an external perception, of doctrinal superiority and elitism among Latter-day Saints.[8] But if Mormon theology is itself still evolving and partially reflects the imperfect understanding of its expounders, the fallacy of theological exclusivity should be apparent. There is nothing wrong with proclaiming one's church to be "true" in the sense of it being sanctioned and even led by God, but it doesn't necessarily follow that all the doctrines taught in the church are *ipso facto* the absolute truth. And even if Mormonism does possess more of the correct pieces of the theological puzzle than other religions, it certainly doesn't warrant an attitude of theological exclusivity or superiority.

A similar exclusivist attitude is sometimes seen with respect to spirituality. Many Latter-day Saints have the impression that they alone have the "gift" of the Holy Ghost, since only LDS Melchizedek priesthood bearers can confer this gift. Consequently, members presume that they are—or at least should be—more spiritual than non-Latter-day Saints. Saints who interact with other faithful Christians soon realize, however, that there are many good people who are not only as exemplary in Christian living as Latter-day Saints, but also have comparable spiritual experiences. According to a 2002 U.S. poll, 90 percent of all Christians have experienced the same types of spiritual experiences that are typically reported by Latter-day Saints.[9] BYU religion professor Roger Keller, who also happens to be a former Presbyterian minister, has observed, "The Holy Ghost that I knew before I was a Latter-day Saint is the same Holy Ghost I know as a Latter-day Saint. And the experience is no different."[10] Refuting the notion that Saints have spiritual superiority over those of other faiths, he affirmed, "We find amongst our Evangelical Pentecostal brothers and sisters virtually the same spiritual gifts that we find among ourselves."[11]

The point to be made is that doctrines, just like spiritual experiences, don't have to originate in the LDS Church to be legitimate or have theological value. There is much that Mormons can learn from the theological insights of those in other faiths. As BYU religion professors Robert L. Millet and Lloyd D. Newell observed: "We need only become acquainted with individuals of other religious persuasions to recognize their goodness and the truths that they possess. It would be blatant arrogance to suppose that the Latter-day Saints are the only people on earth with whom our Heavenly Father is concerned or to whom he seeks to make known his mind and will."[12]

In his *Stages of Faith*, Protestant scholar James Fowler identifies several levels to which individuals may attain in their faith journey. He defines a mature faith as one in which individuals are able to look beyond the bounds of their own familiar traditions and listen to what the larger reality has to say, whatever that message might be. Individuals in this stage are characterized as being cognizant of the pluralistic and human-conditioned nature of religious truth. According to Fowler, one's consciousness at this stage "accepts as axiomatic that truth is more multidimensional and organically interdependent than most theories or accounts of truth can grasp. Religiously, it knows that the symbols, stories, doctrines and liturgies offered by its own or other traditions are inevitably partial, limited to a particular people's experience of God and incomplete."[13] A mature faith accepts God's sovereignty in the universe while at the same time recognizing that no one possesses the holy grail of absolute and unerring truth. It compels one to identify less with theological dogma than with God's universal love and immanence in the world. Such individuals see evidence of God working on multiple fronts, and that "it is the same God which worketh all in all" (1 Cor. 12:6).

The Future of Mormon Theology

In light of the provisional nature of Mormon theology, one wonders how and at what pace it will continue to evolve. Since the middle of the nineteenth century, LDS doctrinal orthodoxy has shifted ever so slowly towards more culturally acceptable norms. Certain radical doctrines of the past have fallen by the wayside and there are indications that other distinctive doctrines are becoming marginalized. In a *Time Magazine* interview in 1997, President Gordon B. Hinckley marginalized the teaching that God the Father was once a man saying, "I don't know that we teach it. I don't know that we emphasize it."[14] Compare this to Joseph Smith's bold declaration: "It is the first principle [of the Gospel] to know . . . that he [God] once was a man like us."[15]

Although current LDS doctrines are unlikely to undergo radical change, subtle shifts in emphasis and interpretation will undoubtedly influence the way they are understood (just as in the past), especially as more figurative meanings are applied. Consider, for example, what might be intended when one says that God is a personal being, that Jesus Christ is the Son of God, that Joseph Smith was a prophet, and that the Book of Mormon is the word of God. Each of these assertions can be taken literally or, to varying degrees, more figuratively. Is God a personal being in the sense that he has a human body and even the quirks and idiosyncrasies of humans, or is he a personal being only because he relates to humans on a personal level? Is Jesus Christ the Son of God because he was literally the begotten offspring of God in the flesh or because he emulated qualities associated with God and, as Paul taught, became considered as God's Son? Was Joseph Smith a prophet in the stereotypical sense of one who speaks the absolute mind and will of God, or in the sense in which ancient prophets appear to have operated—speaking for God as they perceived they were "moved upon" by his Spirit? Is the Book of Mormon the word of God in the literal sense of being his infallible word, or only in the sense that it bears a divine imprint and inspires one to be more Christ-like? Can the more figurative responses to these questions still qualify as legitimate expressions of Mormon faith?

Beyond Theology

A final yet no less significant question for Latter-day Saints has to do with the importance of theology relative to other aspects of Mormonism. Is one's theology, for instance, to be valued above having an active religious lifestyle? Theological matters tend to be merely contemplative, whereas Christian living is transformative. Overemphasis on doctrine can lead to divisiveness and exclusivity; compassionate Christian service dissolves denominational barriers and brings people of diverse beliefs together in purposeful activity. It is interesting that Jesus himself never left a systematized theology, but rather it was said of him that he "went about doing good" (Acts 10:38). He told his disciples that they would be known by their "love one to another" (John 13:35), not by their theological superiority.

Many Latter-day Saints would agree that adhering to the basic principles of love, integrity, and faith in God is much more important than whether one happens to have embraced the right theological teachings. Apostle James E. Talmage observed, "Honesty of purpose, integrity of soul, individual purity, freedom of conscience, willingness to do good to all men even enemies, pure benevolence—these are some of the fruits by which the religion of Christ may be known, far exceeding in importance and value the promulgation of dogmas and the enunciation of theories."[16] It is true that one's theology provides a rational framework for carrying out a Christian life, but it isn't the theology that makes one a saint. Speaking to a diverse Christian audience, BYU religion professor Roger Keller remarked, "Not one of our theologies will ever save a soul. Not one of our theologies can ever change a life. All they can do is to explain, and then only poorly, the work of the One in whom we all have faith."[17]

For many, the practical value of any religious ideology is its ability to give meaning to life, sustain one in trials, and inspire love and compassion. Theological historian Karen Armstrong observed, "Despite its otherworldliness, religion is highly pragmatic," and "it is far more important for a particular idea of God to work than for it to be logically or scientifically sound."[18] Regardless of how one chooses to view Mormon theology, it will continue to remain vibrant and viable for one simple reason: it works.

Notes

1. James E. Faulconer, "Rethinking Theology: The Shadow of the Apocalypse," 179.

2. Blake T. Ostler, *Exploring Mormon Thought: The Attributes of God*, 69.

3. Robert L. Millet, "What Do We Really Believe? Identifying Doctrinal Parameters within Mormonism," 268.

4. This motto, which was also popular among restorationists in Joseph Smith's day, has been attributed to Peter Meiderlin, an irenic Lutheran theologian and pastor living in Augsburg during the early seventeenth century. See Hans Rollman, "In Essentials Unity: The Pre-history of a Restoration Movement Slogan."

5. In his research on early Mormon conversion, Steven Harper notes that "one finds the word 'reasonable' and its relatives used frequently by writers trying to describe what it was in Mormon theology that caused conversion in them." Steven Harper, "Infallible Proofs, Both Human and Divine: The Persuasiveness of Mormonism for Early Converts," 101

6. The pioneering American psychologist and philosopher William James averred that pragmatism is the only reliable way to evaluate the "truthfulness" of religious beliefs stating, "By their fruits ye shall know them, not by their roots." William James, *The Varieties of Religious Experience: A Study in Human Nature*, 24.

7. Euan Cameron calls this inability to point to a time in history when doctrines were pure and unmediated the "historical problem" of Christianity. Euan Cameron, *Interpreting Christian History: The Challenge of the Churches' Past*, 164.

8. Eric-Jon K. Marlowe, "The Only True Church: Boldness without Overbearance," 27.

9. Jeffery L. Sheler, "Faith in America," 40f.

10. Roger R. Keller, "The Apostasy."

11. Ibid.

12. Robert L. Millet and Lloyd D. Newell, *Draw Near unto Me*, 9.

13. James W. Fowler, *Stages of Faith*, 186. Fowler notes that the strength of this stage comes from one's "capacity to see and be in one's or one's group's most powerful meanings, while simultaneously recognizing that they are relative, partial and inevitably distorting apprehensions of transcendent reality. Its danger lies in the direction of a paralyzing passivity or inaction, giving rise to complacency or cynical withdrawal, due to its paradoxical understanding of truth" (198).

14. David Van Biema, "Kingdom Come," 56.

15. Andrew F. Ehat and Lyndon W. Cook, *The Words of Joseph Smith*, 344.

16. James E. Talmage, *Articles of Faith*, 389.

17. Roger R. Keller, "Jesus Christ: Priest, King, and Prophet," 346.

18. Karen Armstrong, *A History of God: The 4000-Year Quest of Judaism, Christianity, and Islam*, xxi.

Bibliography

Achtemeier, Paul J. *I Peter: A Commentary on First Peter.* Minneapolis: Fortress Press, 1996.
_____, ed. *Harper's Bible Dictionary.* San Francisco: Harper and Row, 1985.
_____. *The Inspiration of Scripture.* Philadelphia: Westminster Press, 1980.
Ackerman, Susan. "Isaiah." In *The New Interpreter's Study Bible.* Edited by Walter J. Harrelson, 955–1049. Nashville, Tenn.: Abingdon Press, 2003.
Adams, Hannah. *A Dictionary of All Religions and Religious Denominations.* 1817. Rpt. Atlanta: Scholars Press, 1992.
Adams, Robert Merihew. "Middle Knowledge and the Problem of Evil." *American Philosophical Quarterly* 14 (April 1977): 109–117.
Albright, William Foxwell. "What Were the Cherubim?" In *The Biblical Archaeologist Reader.* Edited by G. Ernest Wright and David Noel Freedman, 95–97. Chicago: Quadrangle Books, 1961.
Alexander, Caleb. *An Essay on the Real Deity of Jesus Christ. To Which Are Added Strictures on Extracts From Mr. Emlyn's Humble Inquiry Concern-ing the deity of Jesus Christ.* Boston: Joseph Bumstead, 1791
Alexander, Thomas G. *Mormonism in Transition: A History of the Latter-day Saints, 1890–1930.* 3rd edition. Salt Lake City: Greg Kofford Books, 2011.
_____. "The Reconstruction of Mormon Doctrine: From Joseph Smith to Progressive Theology." *Sunstone* 5 (July/August 1980): 24–33.
Allen, Ethan. *Reason: The Only Oracle of Man; or a Compendius System of Natural Religion.* 1784. Rpt, Boston: J. P. Mendum, 1854.
Allen, James B. "The Significance of Joseph's 'First Vision' in Mormon Thought." *Dialogue: A Journal of Mormon Thought* 1 (Autumn 1966): 29–46.
Allen, James B., and Glen M. Leonard. *The Story of the Latter-day Saints.* 2d ed. rev. Salt Lake City: Deseret Book Co., 1992.
Allison, Dale C., Jr. "The Historians' Jesus and the Church." In *Seeking the Identity of Jesus.* Edited by Beverly Roberts Gaventa and Richard B. Hays, 79–95. Grand Rapids, Mich.: Eerdmans Publishing Co., 2008.
Anderson, Francis I., and David Noel Freedman. *Amos: A New Translation with Introduction and Commentary.* Anchor Bible Series. New York: Doubleday, 1989.
Anderson, Lavina Fielding, ed. *Lucy's Book: A Critical Edition of Lucy Smith's Family Memoir.* Salt Lake City: Signature Books, 2001.
Andrus, Hyrum L. *Doctrinal Commentary on the Pearl of Great Price.* Salt Lake City: Deseret Book, 1967.
_____. *Doctrines of the Kingdom.* Salt Lake City: Bookcraft, 1973.
_____. *God, Man, and the Universe.* Salt Lake City: Bookcraft, 1968.
"The Answer." *Times and Seasons* 4 (February 1843): 82–85.
The Ante-Nicene Fathers. Edited by Alexander Roberts and James Donaldson. 1885. 6 vols. Rpt., Grand Rapids, Mich.: Eerdmans Publishing Co., 1975.
Armstrong, Karen. *The Great Transformation: The World in the Time of Buddha, Socrates, Confucius, and Jeremiah.* New York: Alfred A. Knopf, 2006.

_____. *A History of God: The 4000-Year Quest of Judaism, Christianity, and Islam.* Rpt., New York: Ballantine Books, 1994.

"An Attempt to Explain Several of the Principal Texts, Which are Brought Forward by Those Who Hold to a Universal Restoration, In Support of Their System." *Connecticut Evangelical Magazine* 6 (September 1805): 83–84.

Attridge, Harold W. "Hebrews." In *HarperCollins Study Bible: Fully Revised and Updated.* Edited by Harold W. Attridge, 2035–50. San Francisco: Harper, 2006.

Aune, David E. "Revelation." *The HarperCollins Study Bible.* Edited by Wayne A. Meeks, 2307–37. New York: HarperCollins, 1993.

Austin, Samuel. "God Glorified in Building up Zion." In *The Columbian Preacher vol. 1.* Edited by Nathan Elliot, 27–45. Catskill, N.Y.: Nathan Elliot, 1808.

Avis, Paul. "Church." In *The Encyclopedia of Christianity.* Edited by John Bowden. Oxford, Eng.: Oxford University Press, 2005.

Bacchiocchi, Samuele. "The Survival of the Soul: A Historical Glimpse of the Belief in the Survival of the Soul." *Endtime Issues*, No. 4, January 12, 1999. Biblical Perspectives. http://www.biblicalperspectives.com/endtimeissues/eti_04.pdf (accessed May 17, 2010).

Bachman, Danel, and Ronald K. Esplin. "Plural Marriage." In *Encyclopedia of Mormonism.* 4 vols., 3:1095. New York: Macmillan Publishing, 1992.

Backman, Milton V., Jr. *The Heavens Resound: A History of the Latter-day Saints in Ohio, 1830–1838.* Salt Lake City: Deseret Book, 1983.

_____. *Joseph Smith's First Vision: The First Vision in Historical Context.* Salt Lake City: Bookcraft, 1971.

_____. "Preparing the Way: The Rise of Religious Freedom in New England." *Ensign*, January 1989, 16–19.

Bacon, Leonard. *Baxter's Works.* 2 vols. New Haven, Conn.: Durrie and Peck, 1835.

Bagatti, Bellarmino. *The Church from the Circumcision.* Jerusalem: Franciscan Printing Press, 1971.

Bailey, Elijah. *America in Primitive Trinitarianism Examined and Defended.* Bennington, Vt.: Darius Clark, 1826.

Ballard, M. Russell. "Learning the Lessons of the Past." *Ensign*, May 2009, 31–34.

Ballif, Jae R. "Melchizedek Priesthood." *In Encyclopedia of Mormonism.* 4 vols., 2:882–87 New York: Macmillan Publishing, 1992.

Ballou, Adin. *The Autobiography of Adin Ballou, 1803–1890.* Completed and edited by William S. Heywood. Lowell, Mass.: Vox Populi Press, 1896.

Ballou, Hosea. *A Treatise on Atonement.* Randolph, Vt.: Sereno Wright, 1805.

"The Baptist Confession of Faith." Available on the The Center for Reformed Theology and Apologetics (CRTA) website. http://www.reformed.org/documents/baptist_1689.html (accessed June 2, 2010).

Barker, Margaret. *The Great Angel: A Study of Israel's Second God.* Louisville, Ky.: Westminster/John Knox Press 1992.

Barlow, Philip L. *Mormons and the Bible: The Place of Latter-day Saints in American Religion.* New York: Oxford University Press, 1991.

Barnes, Albert. *Notes on the New Testament.* Grand Rapids, Mich.: Baker Publishing Group House, 1949.

Barnett, P. W. "Apostasy." In *Dictionary of the Later New Testament and Its Developments.* Edited by Ralph P. Martin and Peter H. Davids. Downers Grove, Ill.: InterVarsity Press, 1997.

Barnett, W. F. "Satan." In *New Catholic Encyclopedia.* Edited by Thomas Carson and Joann Cerrito. 2d ed. 15 vols. Detroit, Mich.: Gale, 2003.

Barney, Kevin L. "Examining Six Key Concepts in Joseph Smith's Understanding of Genesis 1:1." *BYU Studies* 39, no. 3 (2000): 107–124.
———. "Footnotes: 'Line upon Line.'" Email to Scripture-L, October 30, 1998, www.wnetc.com/scripture-l (accessed January 10, 2005).
———. "Introduction to Luke's Gospel." Available for download from Feast upon the Word. http://feastupontheword.org/images/f/fa/09_Luke.pdf (accessed May 5, 2009).
———. "Reflections on the Documentary Hypothesis." *Dialogue: A Journal of Mormon Thought* 33, no. 1 (Spring 2000): 57–99.
———. "A Seemingly Strange Story Illuminated." *FARMS Review of Books* 13, no. 1 (2001): 1–20.
———. "Understanding Old Testament Poetry." *Ensign,* June 1990, 51–54.
Barr, James. *Fundamentalism*. London: SCM Press, 1977.
———. Letter to David C. C. Watson, April 23, 1984. Transcription. http://members.iinet.net.au/~sejones/barrlett.html (accessed July 23, 2005).
Barton, George A., and Kaufmann Kohler. "Resurrection." In *The Jewish Encyclopedia*. 12 vols., 10:382–85. New York: Funk and Wagnalls, 1901–06.
Barton, John. "Amos." In *The New Interpreter's Study Bible*. Edited by Walter J. Harrelson, 1279–91. Nashville, Tenn.: Abingdon Press, 2003.
Bateman, Merrill J. "A Pattern for All." *Ensign,* November 2005, 74–76.
Bavinck, Herman. "Death." In *The International Standard Bible Encyclopedia*. Edited by James Orr, 5 vols., 2:811–13. Chicago: Howard-Severance Co., 1915.
Beale, G.K. *The Erosion of Inerrancy in Evangelicalism: Responding to New Challenges to Biblical Authority*. Wheaton, Ill.: Crossway Books, 2008.
Becker, Joachim. *Messianic Expectation in the Old Testament*. Translated by David E. Green. Philadelphia: Fortress, 1980.
Beecher, Edward. *The Conflict of the Ages*. 5th ed. Boston: Phillips, Samson, 1854.
Beegle, Dewey M. *Scripture: Tradition and Infallibility*. Rev. ed. Grand Rapids, Mich.: Eerdmans Publishing Co., 1973.
Bellamy, Joseph Bellamy. *True Religion Delineated; or, Experimental Religion, as Distinguished from Formality on the One Hand, and Enthusiasm on the other, set in a scriptural and rational light*. Boston, 1750. Rpt., Morris-Town, N.J.: Henry P. Russell, 1804.
Bennett, Samuel. *A Few Remarks by Way of Reply to an Anonymous Scribbler, Calling Himself a Philanthropist, Disabusing the Church of Jesus Christ of Latter-day Saints of the Slanders and Falsehoods which he has Attempted to Fasten Upon It*. Philadelphia: Brown, Bicking & Guilbert Printers, 1840.
Bennion, Lowell L. *An Introduction to the Gospel*. Salt Lake City: Deseret Sunday School Union Board, 1959.
———. "The Mormon Christianizing of the Old Testament: A Response." *Sunstone* 5 (November/December 1980): 40.
———. Oral History, 80–81, 193. James H. Moyle Oral History Program. LDS Church History Library, Church of Jesus Christ of Latter-day Saints, Salt Lake City.
Benson, Ezra Taft. *The Teachings of Ezra Taft Benson*. Salt Lake City: Bookcraft, 1988.
Bergey, Ronald. "The Rhetorical Role of Reiteration in the Suffering Servant Poem (Isa 52:13–53:12)." *Journal of the Evangelical Theological Society* 40, no. 2 (June 1997): 177–88.
Bergman, J., H. Ringren, and W. Dommershausen. "*Kohen.*" In *Theological Dictionary of the Old Testament*. Edited by G. Johannes Botterweck, Helmer

Ringgren, and Heinz-Josef Fabry. Translated by David E. Green, 60–75. Grand Rapids, Mich.: Eerdmans Publishing Co., 1995.

Berk, Stephen E. *Calvinism versus Democracy: Timothy Dwight and the Origins of American Evangelical Orthodoxy.* Hamden, Conn.: Archon, 1974.

Berkouwer, G. C. *Man: The Image of God.* Grand Rapids, Mich.: Eerdmans Publishing Co., 1962.

Biblos. "On Despair of the Divine Mercy." *The Christian Specter* 2, no. 12 (December 1820): 620–25.

Biema, David Van. "Kingdom Come." *Time Magazine*, August 4, 1997, 51–57.

Blanke, Gustav H., and Karen Lynn. "God's Base of Operations: Mormon Variations on the American Sense of Mission." *BYU Studies* 20 (Fall 1979): 83–92.

Blenkinsopp, Joseph. *Isaiah 1–39.* New York: Doubleday, 2000.

Blomberg, Craig L. "Is Mormonism Christian?" In *The New Mormon Challenge.* Edited by Francis J. Beckwith, Carl Mosser, and Paul Owen, 315–32. Grand Rapids, Mich.: Zondervan, 2002.

Blomberg, Craig L,. and Stephen E. Robinson. *How Wide the Divide? A Mormon and an Evangelical in Conversation.* Downers Grove, Ill.: InterVarsity Press, 1997.

Bloom, Harold. *The American Religion: The Emergence of the Post-Christian Nation.* New York: Simon & Schuster, 1992.

Bloxham, V. Ben. "Law of Adoption." In *Encyclopedia of Mormonism.* 4 vols., 2:810. New York: Macmillan Publishing, 1992.

Bokovoy, David E. "'Ye Really *Are* Gods': A Response to Michael Heiser Concerning the LDS Use of Psalm 82 and the Gospel of John." *FARMS Review* 19, no. 1 (2007): 304–8.

Boles, John B. *The Great Revival, 1787–1805.* Lexington, Ky.: University Press of Kentucky, 1972.

The Book of Common Prayer and Other Rites and Ceremonies of the Church, According to the Protestant Episcopal Church in the United States of America. Charleston, N. C.: W.P. Young, 1808.

Book of Mormon Student Manual: Religion 121–122. 2d ed. Salt Lake City: The Church of Jesus Christ of Latter-day Saints, 1979.

Boring, M. Eugene. "Revelation." In *The New Interpreter's Study Bible.* Edited by Walter J. Harrelson, 2211–40. Nashville, Tenn.: Abingdon Press, 2003.

Boudinot, Elias. *The Second Advent.* Trenton, N.J.: D. Fenton and S. Hutchinson, 1815.

———. *A Star in the West.* Trenton N.J.: D. Fenton, S. Hutchinson, and J. Dunham, 1816.

Boyer, Paul. "The Puritans." In *Apocalypse!* Frontline. http://www.pbs.org/wgbh/pages/frontline/shows/apocalypse/explanation/puritans.html (accessed October 8, 2006).

Bradbury, Thomas. *The Duty and Doctrine of Baptism.* New York: William Barlas, 1810.

Brewster, Hoyt W., Jr. *Doctrine and Covenants Encyclopedia.* Salt Lake City: Deseret Book, 1988.

———. *Behold, I Come Quickly: The Last Days and Beyond.* Salt Lake City: Deseret Book, 1994.

Brinkerhoff, George. "Gifts of the Spirit." In *Encyclopedia of Mormonism.* 4 vols., 2:544–46. New York: Macmillan Publishing, 1992.

Broadhurst, Dale R. "Transcriber's Comments: The Second Advent." Oliver's Bookshelf. http://olivercowdery.com/texts/boud1815.htm#comments (accessed May 17, 2010).

Brooke, John L. *Refiner's Fire: The Making of Mormon Cosmology, 1644–1844.* Cambridge, Mass.: Cambridge University Press, 1996.

Brothers, Richard. *A Revealed Knowledge of the Prophecies and Times*. W. Springfield, Mass: Edward Gray, 1797. Electronic selections at The Oliver Cowdery Memorial. http://olivercowdery.com/texts/brot1797.htm (accessed May 17, 2006).

Brough, R. Clayton. *The Lost Tribes*. Bountiful, Utah: Horizon Publishers, 1979.

Brown, Colin. *The New International Dictionary of New Testament Theology*. Grand Rapids, Mich.: Zondervan, 2004.

———. "Trinity and Incarnation: In Search of Contemporary Orthodoxy." *Ex Auditu* 7 (1991): 83–100.

Brown, John. *A Compendious View of Natural and Revealed Religion*. Philadelphia: David Hogan, 1819.

Brown, John Newton. "Pre-existiani." In *The Encyclopedia of Religious Knowledge*, 964. Brattlesboro, Vt.: Brattleboro, Pesenden, and Co., 1836.

Brown, Raymond E. *The Birth of the Messiah*. New York: Doubleday, 1977.

———. *The Epistles of John*. Garden City, N.Y.: Doubleday, 1982.

———. *The Gospel According to John*. New York: Doubleday and Company, 1970.

———. "The Holy Ghost as Paraclete: The Gift of John's Gospel." 1988. *Scripture from Scratch*. http://www.americancatholic.org/Newsletters/ SFS/an0598.asp (accessed November 20, 2006).

———. *Introduction to the New Testament*. New York: Doubleday Press, 1996.

———. *John*. Anchor Bible Series, Vol. 29. New York: Doubleday, 1966.

Brown, S. Kent, C. Wilfred Griggs, and H. Kimball Hansen. "Review of *April Sixth* by John C. Lefgren." *BYU Studies* 22 (Summer 1982): 375–83.

Brown, Samuel M. "The Prophet Elias Puzzle." *Dialogue: A Journal of Mormon Thought* 39 (Fall 2006): 1-17.

Bruce, F. F. *The New International Commentary on the New Testament: The Book of Acts*. Grand Rapids, Mich.: Eerdmans Publishing Co., 1954.

———. *New Testament History*. Garden City, New York: Doubleday, 1980.

———. *Paul: Apostle of the Heart Set Free*. Grand Rapids, Mich.: Eerdmans Publishing Co., 1977.

———. "Paul on Immortality." *Scottish Journal of Theology* 24 (November 1971): 457–72.

———, ed. *Vine's Expository Dictionary of Old and New Testament Words*. Old Tappan, N.J.: Fleming H. Revel Company, 1985.

Brueggemann, Walter. *An Introduction to the Old Testament: The Canon and Christian Imagination*. Louisville, Ky.: Westminster John Knox Press, 2003.

———. *Isaiah 40–66*. Louisville, Ky.: Westminster John Knox, 1998.

Bruening, Ari D., and David L. Paulsen. "The Development of the Mormon Understanding of God: Early Mormon Modalism and Other Myths." *FARMS Review of Books* 13, no. 2 (2001): 109–69.

Bryant, William Cullen, ed. *Picturesque America, or the Land We Live In*. 2 vols. New York: D. Appleton and Co., 1872–74.

Buchanan, George Wesley. *To the Hebrews: Translation, Comment and Conclusions*. Garden City, N. Y.: Doubleday, 1972.

Buck, Charles S. *A Theological Dictionary*. 2 vols. Philadelphia: James Kay and Co., 1830.

Buerger, David John. "The Adam-God Doctrine." *Dialogue: A Journal of Mormon Thought* 15, no. 1 (Spring 1982): 14–58.

———. *The Mysteries of Godliness: A History of Mormon Temple Worship*. San Francisco: Smith Research Associates, 1994.

Bullinger, E. W. *Figures of Speech used in the Bible*. Grand Rapids, Mich.: Baker Publishing Groups, 1968.

Burton, Alma P. "Salvation." In *Encyclopedia of Mormonism,* 4 vols., 4:1256–57. New York: Macmillan Publishing, 1992.

Burton, Ernest De Witt. "The Biblical Doctrine of the Atonement: VII, Atonement in the Teaching of Jesus." *The Biblical World* 32, no. 1 (July 1908): 19–25.

Bush, Lester E. Jr. "A Commentary on Stephen G. Taggart's 'Mormonism's Negro Policy: Social and Historical Origins.'" *Dialogue: A Journal of Mormon Thought* 4 (Winter 1969): 86–103.

――――. "Mormonism's Negro Doctrine: An Historical Overview." *Dialogue: A Journal of Mormon Thought* 7, no. 1 (Spring 1973): 11–68.

Bushinski, L. A. "Spirit (in the Bible)." In *New Catholic Encyclopedia.* Edited by Thomas Carson and Joann Cerrito. 2d ed. 15 vols. Detroit, Mich.: Gale, 2003.

――――. "Spirit of God." In *New Catholic Encyclopedia.* Edited by Thomas Carson and Joann Cerrito, 2d ed., 15 vols. Detroit, Mich.: Gale, 2003.

Bushman, Richard L. "Joseph Smith and the Creation of the Sacred." In *Joseph Smith Jr. Reppraisals after Two Centuries.* Edited by Reid L. Neilson and Terryl L. Givens, 93–106. New York: Oxford University Press, 2009.

――――. *Joseph Smith and the Beginnings of Mormonism.* Urbana: University of Illinois Press, 1984.

――――. "A Joseph Smith for the Twenty-first Century." *BYU Studies* 40, no. 3 (2001): 155–71.

――――. *Joseph Smith: Rough Stone Rolling.* New York: Alfred A. Knopf, 2005.

Buttrick, George Arthur. et al. *The Interpreters Bible.* 12 vols. New York: Abington Press, 1957.

Byrne, Brendan. "Sons of God." In *Anchor Bible Dictionary.* Edited by David Noel Freedman. 6 vols., 6:156–59. New York: Doubleday, 1992.

Callister, Douglas L. "Resurrection." In *Encyclopedia of Mormonism.* 4 vols., 3:1222–23. New York: Macmillan Publishing, 1992.

Callister, Tad R. *The Inevitable Apostasy and the Promised Restoration.* Salt Lake City: Deseret Book, 2006.

Calvin, John. *Calvin's Bible Commentaries: Matthew, Mark, and Luke, Part III.* Translated by John King. 1857. Rpt., N.p.: Forgotten Books, 2007.

――――. *Institutes of the Christian Religion.* 2 vols. Translated by John Allen Book. Philadelphia: Presbyterian Board of Publication, 1813.

Cameron, Euan. *Interpreting Christian History: The Challenge of the Churches' Past.* Malden, Mass: Blackwell Publishing, 2005.

Campbell, Alexander. *Christian Baptism: With Its Antecedents and Consequents.* London: Arthur Hall, Virtue and Co., 1853.

――――. "Delusions." *Millennial Harbinger* 2 (February 7, 1831): 93. Electronic reprint at The Restoration Movement Pages. http://www.mun.ca/rels/restmov/texts/ acampbell/mh1831/DELUSION.HTM (accessed March 22, 2005).

――――. "A Restoration of the Ancient Order of Things—No. I." *Christian Baptist* 2, no. 7 (February 7, 1825): 126–28.

――――. "A Restoration of the Ancient Order of Things—No. XIX." *Christian Baptist* 4, no. 10 (May 7, 1827): 335–36.

Campbell, Craig S. *Images of the New Jerusalem: Latter Day Saint Faction Interpretations of Independence, Missouri.* Knoxville: University of Tennessee Press, 2004.

Campbell, Douglas. "'White' or 'Pure': Five Vignettes." *Dialogue: A Journal of Mormon Thought* 29, no. 4 (Winter 1996): 119–35.

Cannon, Donald Q., and Lyndon W. Cook, eds. *Far West Record: Minutes of the Church of Jesus Christ of Latter-day Saints, 1830–1844.* Salt Lake City: Deseret Book, 1983.

Cannon, Elaine Anderson. "Mother in Heaven." In *Encyclopedia of Mormonism*. 4 vols., 2:961. New York: Macmillan Publishing, 1992.

Carroll, Robert P. "Eschatological Delay in the Prophetic Tradition?" *Zeitschrift für die alttestamentliche Wissenschaft* 94, no. 1 (1982): 47–58.

———. *When Prophecy Failed*. New York: Seabury, 1979.

———. *Wolf in the Sheepfold: The Bible as Problem for Christianity*. London: SCM Press, 1991.

Carson, D. A. *Exegetical Fallacies*. Grand Rapids, Mich.: Baker Publishing Group House, 1984.

Carter, Warren. "Matthew." In *The New Interpreter's Study Bible*. Edited by Walter Harrelson, 1745–1800. Nashville, Tenn.: Abingdon Press, 2003.

"Caswall's Prophet of the Nineteenth Century." *Millennial Star* 3 (April 1843): 197.

The Catechism of the Council of Trent. Translated by J. Donovan. Baltimore: Fielding Lucas, Jr., 1829.

Catlin, Jacob. *A Compendium of the System of Divine Truth*. Hartford, Conn.: George Goodwin and Sons, 1818.

Chadwick, Bruce A., and Thomas Garrow. "Native Americans." In *Encyclopedia of Mormonism*. 4 vols., 3:981. New York: Macmillan Publishing, 1992.

Chandler, Ted. "Alma 42 and the Atonement." MormonThink. http://mormonthink.com /mormonstudiesatone.htm (accessed May 18, 2010).

Charles, Melodie Moench. "The Book of Mormon Christology." In *New Approaches to the Book of Mormon: Explorations in Critical Methodology*. Edited by Brent Lee Metcalfe, 81–114. Salt Lake City: Signature Books, 1993.

Charles, R. H. *A Critical and Exegetical Commentary on the Revelation of St. John, with Introduction, Notes, and Indices, Also the Greek Text and English Translation*, 2 vols. New York: Charles Scribner's Sons, 1920.

Chisholm, Robert B. "The Everlasting Covenant and the City of Chaos: Intentional Ambiguity and Irony in Isaiah 24." *Criswell Theological Review* 6 (1992–93): 23–53.

Christensen, Michael J. "The Problem, Promise, and Process of Theosis." In *Partakers of the Divine Nature: The History and Development of Deification*. Edited by Michael J. Christensen and Jeffery A. Wittung, 23–30. Grand Rapids, Mich.: Baker Academic, 2008.

Christensen, Ryan C. "Appendix D: Bibliographical Note on LDS Writings." In *Early Christians in Disarray: Contemporary LDS Perspectives on the Christian Apostasy*. Edited by Noel B. Reynolds, 371–85. Provo, Utah: FARMS and BYU Press, 2005.

"The Christian Education of Children." *The Christian Advocate* 5 (August 1827): 344–47.

"Christian Union—No. 1." *Christian Baptist* 2 (July 4, 1825): 237

"The Church of Christ." *Evening and Morning Star* 1 (March 1833): 73–80.

Clark, J. Reuben, Jr. "When Are Church Leader's Words Entitled to Claim of Scripture?" *Church News,* July 31, 1954, 2, 9–11.

Clark, James R., ed. *Messages of the First Presidency of the Church of Jesus Christ of Latter-day Saints, 1833–1964*. 6 vols. Salt Lake City: Bookcraft, 1965–75.

Clark, R. M. "Words Relating to the Lord Jesus Christ." *Bible Translator* 13 (April 1962): 81–90.

Clark, Robert E. "Baptism for the Dead and the Problematic of Pluralism." *Dialogue: A Journal of Mormon Thought* 30, no. 1 (Spring 1997): 105–16.

Clarke, Adam. *Christian Theology*, 2d ed. Edited by Samuel Dunn. London: James Nichols, 1835.

_____. *A Collection of Discourses on Various Subjects.* New York: M. Bangs and J. Emory, 1827.

_____. *Commentary on the Bible.* New York: Abingdon-Cokesbury Press, multiple editions 1810–25. A fully digitized and searchable version of the Clarke's commentary is available on the GodRules.NET website. http://www.godrules.net/library/clarke/clarke.htm (accessed March 16, 2005).

Clarke, John, ed. *The Works of Samuel Clarke, D. D., Late Rector of St. James's Westminster.* 4 vols. London: John Clarke, D. D., 1788.

Clement. "The Epistles of Clement." Translated by John Keith. In *The Ante-Nicene Fathers. Translations of the Writings of the Fathers Down to A.D. 325.* 5th ed. Edited by Allan Menzies. 10 vols., 9:226–56. New York: Charles Scribner's Sons, 1912.

Clements, Ronald E. "Deuteronomy." In *The New Interpreter's Study Bible.* Edited by Walter J. Harrelson, 241–302. Nashville, Tenn.: Abingdon Press, 2003.

Cloward, Robert. "Isaiah 29 in the Book of Mormon." In *Isaiah in the Book of Mormon.* Edited by Donald W. Parry and John W. Welch, 191–247. Provo, Utah: Foundation for Ancient Research and Mormon Studies, 1998.

Cohen, A. *The Psalms.* London: Soncino Press, 1945.

Cohn, Norman. "The Book of Daniel." In *Apocalypse!* Frontline. http://www.pbs.org/wgbh/pages/frontline/shows/apocalypse/explanation/bdaniel.html (accessed October 23, 2004).

_____. *Cosmos, Chaos, and the World to Come: The Ancient Roots of Apocalyptic Faith.* New Haven, Conn.: Yale University Press, 1993.

Collins, John J. "Daniel, Book of." In *The Anchor Bible Dictionary.* Edited by David Noel Freedman, 6 vols., 2:29–37. New York: Doubleday, 1992.

Colton, Eleanor. "Virgin Birth." In *Encyclopedia of Mormonism.* 4 vols., 4:1510. New York: Macmillan Publishing, 1992.

"Comparison between Heathenism and Christianity." *Evening and Morning Star* 1 (October 1832): 35–36.

Compton, Todd M. "Apostasy." In *Encyclopedia of Mormonism.* 4 vols., 1:56–58. New York: Macmillan Publishing, 1992.

_____. *In Sacred Loneliness: The Plural Wives of Joseph Smith.* Salt Lake City: Signature Books, 1997.

_____. "The Sermon at the Temple and the Sermon on the Mount." *FARMS Review of Books on the Book of Mormon* 3 (1991): 319–22.

Condie, Spencer J. "The Savior's Visit to the Spirit World." *Ensign,* July 2003, 32–36.

"Conference Minutes," *Times and Seasons* 2 (February 1841): 307.

Conference Reports of the Church of Jesus Christ of Latter-day Saints. Salt Lake City: Church of Jesus Christ of Latter-day Saints, 1880– [Semi–annual series.]

A Confession of Faith Put Forth by the Elders and Brethren of Many Congregations of Christians (Based Upon Profession of Their Faith,) in London and the Country. September 25, 1742. Rpt., Philadelphia: John Gray, 1829.

"Confessions of Faith of the Calvinistic Methodists or the Presbyterians of Wales." Creeds of Christendom. http://www.creeds.net/cmwales/ (accessed February 5, 2005).

Conselmann, Hans. *I Corinthians.* Translated by James W. Leitch. Philadelphia: Fortress Press, 1975.

Constable, Thomas L. *Notes on Zechariah.* 2009. Dr. Constable's Expository (Bible Study) Notes. http://www.soniclight.com/constable/notes/pdf/zechariah.pdf (accessed May 14, 2010).

Cook, Lyndon W. *The Revelations of the Prophet Joseph Smith: A Historical and Biographical Commentary of the Doctrine and Covenants.* Salt Lake City:

Deseret Book, 1985.
Cook, Roger D. "Hebrew, Early Judaic, and Early Christian Thought." Version 4.9. Unpublished manuscript available at http://www.angelfire.com/az3/LDC/hebrewthought.pdf (accessed May 14, 2010).
Cooke, Parson. "Review of 'Commendation and Reproof of Unitarians.'" *The Spirit of the Pilgrims* 3 (April 1830): 224.
Corrill, John. *A Brief History of the Church of Christ of Latter Day Saints (Commonly Called Mormons;) Including An Account of Their Doctrine and Discipline; With the Reasons of the Author for Leaving the Church.* St. Louis, Mo.: Author, 1839
Cowan, Richard O. *Answers to Your Questions about the Doctrine and Covenants.* Salt Lake City: Deseret Book, 1996.
Cowdery, Oliver. "To John Whitmer Esq." *Latter Day Saints' Messenger and Advocate* 2 (December 1835): 233–37.
———. "To W. W. Phelps." *Latter Day Saints' Messenger and Advocate* 1 (February 1835): 77–80.
Cowdery, Warren A. Letter. *Latter Day Saints' Messenger and Advocate* 1 (April 1835): 97–99.
Cowley, Matthias, comp. and ed. *Wilford Woodruff: His Life and Labors.* Salt Lake City: Deseret News, 1916.
Crapo, Richley H. "An Anthropologist Looks at the Judeo-Christian Scriptures." Utah State University. http://cc.usu.edu/~fath6/bible.htm (accessed March 6, 2005).
Crenshaw, James L. "Job." In *The HarperCollins Study Bible.* Edited Wayne A. Meeks, 749–96. New York: HarperCollins, 1993.
Cross, Frank L., and Elizabeth A. Livingstone, eds. *The Oxford Dictionary of the Christian Church,* 3rd ed. Oxford, Eng.: Oxford University Press, 1997.
Crossan, John Dominic. *The Birth of Christianity.* New York: HarperCollins, 1998.
Crowe, Michael J. *The Extraterrestrial Life Debate, 1750–1900: The Idea of a Plurality of Worlds from Kant to Lowell.* Cambridge, Eng.: Cambridge University Press, 1986.
———. "A History of the Extraterrestrial Life Debate." *Zygon: Journal of Science and Religion* 32 (June, 1997): 147–162.
Cryer, Frederick H. *In Search of God.* Translated by Tryggve N. D. Mettinger. Philadelphia: Fortress, 1988.
Dahl, Larry E., and Charles D. Tate Jr., eds. *The Lectures on Faith in Historical Perspective.* Provo, Utah: BYU Religious Studies Center, 1990.
Davies, W. D., and D. C. Allison Jr. *A Critical and Exegetical Commentary on the Gospel According to St. Matthew.* Edinburgh: T. and T. Clark, 1991.
Davison, Lisa. "Job." In *The New Interpreter's Study Bible.* Edited by Walter J. Harrelson, 703–48. Nashville, Tenn.: Abingdon Press, 2003.
Day, John. "Rahab." In *Anchor Bible Dictionary.* Edited by David Noel Freedman, 6 vols., 5:610. New York: Doubleday, 2003.
Deist, F., and I. Du Plessis. *God and His Kingdom.* Pretoria, South Africa: J. L. van Schaik, 1982.
Dennis, Ronald D. "Gathering," In *Encyclopedia of Mormonism.* 4 vols., 2:536–37. New York: Macmillan Publishing, 1992.
Derr, Jill Mulvay, and Karen Lynn Davidson. "A Wary Heart Becomes 'Fixed Unalterably': Eliza R. Snow's Conversion to Mormonism." *Journal of Mormon History* 30, no. 2 (Fall 2004): 98–128.
Dever, William G. *Did God Have a Wife? Archeology and Folk Religion in Ancient Israel.* Grand Rapids, Mich.: Eerdmans Publishing Co., 2005.
Dick, Thomas. *The Christian Philosopher.* New York: G. & C. Carvill, 1826.

———. *The Philosophy of a Future State*. Glasgow, Eng: William Collins, 1825.
Doctrines of the Gospel Student Manual: Religion 430 and 431. Salt Lake City: Church of Jesus Christ of Latter-day Saints, 2000.
Donaldson, Amy M. "Blasphemy against the Spirit and the Historical Jesus." In *Society of Biblical Literature Seminar Papers* 139 (2003): 157–71.
Donofrio, Thomas E. "Early American Influences on the Book of Mormon." MormonThink. http://www.mormonthink.com/influences.htm (accessed May 18, 2010).
Dow, Lorenzo. *The Opinion of Dow; or, Lorenzo's Thoughts, On Different Subjects, in an Address to the People of New-England*. Windham, Conn.: J. Byrne, 1804.
Drum, Walter. "Incarnation." In *The Catholic Encyclopedia*. Edited by Charles G. Herbermann et al. 15 vols., 7:706–15. New York: Universal Knowledge Foundation, Inc., 1913.
Duerden, Richard Y. "Review of David Daniell, *The Bible in English: Its History and Influence*." *BYU Studies* 46, no. 1 (2007): 143–47.
Duling, Dennis L. "Matthew." In *The HarperCollins Study Bible*. Edited by Wayne A. Meeks, 1857–1914. New York: HarperCollins, 1993.
Dulles, Avery. *The Assurance of Things Hoped For: A Theology of Christian Faith*. New York: Oxford University Press, 1994.
Dunn, James D. G. *Christology in the Making*, 2d ed. London: SCM Press, 1989.
———. *The Theology of Paul the Apostle*. Grand Rapids, Mich.: Eerdmans Publishing Co., 1998.
———. *Unity and Diversity in the New Testament: An Inquiry into the Character of Earliest Christianity*. 3rd ed. London: SCM Press, 2006.
Dursteler, Eric R. "Inheriting the 'Great Apostasy.'" In *Early Christians in Disarray: Contemporary LDS Perspectives on the Christian Apostasy*. Edited by Noel B. Reynolds, 29–65. Provo, Utah: FARMS and BYU Press, 2005.
Dyer, Alvin R. *The Refiner's Fire*. Salt Lake City: Deseret Book, 1960.
Edgerton, Dow. "The Exegesis of Tears." *Theology Today* 46 (April 1989): 21–38.
Edwards, Jonathan. "The Necessity of the Atonement, and the Consistency between That and Free Grace, in Forgiveness." In *Sermons, Essays, and Extracts by Various Authors; Selected with Special Respect to the Great Doctrine of Atonement*. New York: George Forman, 1811.
———. *The Works of Jonathan Edwards: With an Essay on His Genius by Henry Rogers and Memoir by Sereno E. Dwight*. 2 vols. London: John Childs and Son, 1839.
The Eerdmans Bible Dictionary. Edited by Allen C. Myers. Grand Rapids, Mich: Eerdmans Publishing Co., 1987.
Ehat, Andrew F. "'They Might Have Known That He Was Not a Fallen Prophet': The Nauvoo Journal of Joseph Fielding." *BYU Studies* 19 (Winter 1979): 133–66.
Ehat, Andrew F., and Lyndon W. Cook, eds. *The Words of Joseph Smith: The Contemporary Accounts of the Nauvoo Discourses of the Prophet Joseph Smith*. Provo, Utah: BYU Religious Studies Center, 1980.
Ehrman, Bart. *Lost Christianities: The Battle for Scripture and the Faiths We Never Knew*. New York: Oxford University Press, 2003.
"Elder Bruce R. McConkie: 'Preacher of Righteousness,'" *Ensign*, June 1985, 15–21.
England, Eugene, ed. "George Laub's Nauvoo Journal." *BYU Studies* 18, no. 2 (Winter 1978): 151–78.
Epperson, Steven. *Mormons and Jews*. Salt Lake City: Signature Books, 1992.
Erickson, Dan. *As a Thief in the Night: The Mormon Quest for Millennial*

Deliverance. Salt Lake City: Signature Books, 1998.
Ericson, Loyd. "The Challenge of Defining Mormon Doctrine." *Element: The Journal for the Society for Mormon Philosophy and Theology* 3, no. 1/2 (Spring/Fall 2007): 69–90.
Esplin, Ronald K. "Brigham Young and Priesthood Denial to the Blacks: An Alternate View." *Brigham Young University Studies* 19 (Spring 1979): 394–402.
Esplin, Scott C. "The Fall of Kirtland: The Doctrine and Covenants' Role in Reaffirming Joseph." *The Religious Educator: Perspectives on the Restored Gospel* 8, no. 1 (2007): 18–24.
Eusebius of Caesarea. *The History of the Church from Christ to Constantine.* Translated by G. A. Williamson. London: Penguin, 1989.
Evans, Craig A. "Jesus' Self-Designation: 'The Son of Man' and the Recognition of His Divinity." In *The Trinity: An Interdisciplinary Symposium on the Trinity.* Edited by Stephen T. Davis, D. Kendall, and G. O'Collins, 29–47. Oxford: Oxford University Press, 1999.
Evenson, William E., and Duane E. Jeffrey, eds. *Mormonism and Evolution: The Authoritative LDS Statements.* Salt Lake City: Greg Kofford Books, 2006.
"The Family: A Proclamation to the World," *Ensign*, November 1995, 102.
Farmer, Molly. "Premortal Existence Is Not a New Concept, Author Says." *Deseret News*, March 12, 2009, M3.
Faulconer, James E. "Rethinking Theology: The Shadow of the Apocalypse." *Farms Review* 19, no. 1 (2007): 175–99.
_____. "Review of Francis J. Beckwith and Stephen E. Parrish, *The Mormon Concept of God: A Philosophical Analysis.*" In *BYU Studies* 32, no. 4 (1992): 185–95.
Faulring, Scott H. "The Book of Mormon: A Blueprint for Organizing the Church." *Journal of Book of Mormon Studies* 7, no. 1 (1998): 60–71.
Faust, James E. "Dear Are the Sheep That Have Wandered." *Ensign,* May 2003, 61–68.
_____. "The Restoration of All Things." *Ensign,* May 2006, 61–62, 67–68.
Fee, Gordon D. *The First Epistle to the Corinthians.* Grand Rapids, Mich.: Eerdmans Publishing Co., 1987.
Ferguson, Everett. *Backgrounds of Early Christianity.* 3d ed. Grand Rapids, Mich.: Eerdmans Publishing Co., 2003.
Fernald, Woodbury M. *Universalism against Partialism.* Boston: N. pub., 1840.
Fillerup, Robert C., comp. "William Clayton's Nauvoo Diaries and Personal Writings." Robert Fillerup website. http://www.code-co.com/rcf/mhistdoc/clayton.htm (accessed January 5, 2005).
Firmage, Edwin, Jr. "Historical Criticism and the Book of Mormon: A Personal Encounter." *Sunstone* 16 (July 1993): 58–64.
Firmage, Edwin B. *An Abundant Life: The Memoirs of Hugh B. Brown.* Salt Lake City: Signature Books, 1999.
Fisk, Wilbur. *Calvinist Controversy.* New York: T. Mason and G. Lane, 1837.
Fitzmyer, Joseph A. *The Biblical Commission's Document: "The Interpretation of the Bible in the Church."* Rome: Pontificium Institutum Biblicum, 1995.
_____. *The Gospel According to Luke.* Anchor Bible Commentaries, Vol. 28. Edited by William F. Albright and David Noel Freedman. Garden City, N. Y.: Doubleday & Co., 1985.
Fortman, Edmund J. *The Triune God: A Historical Study of the Doctrine of the Trinity.* Philadelphia: Westminster Press, 1972.
Foutz, Scott. "Theology of Slavery: Western Theology's Role in the Development and Propagation of Slavery." *Quodlibet Journal* 2, no. 1 (January 2000).

http://www.quodlibet.net/foutz-slavery.shtml (accessed March 23, 2005).

Fowler, James W. *Stages of Faith: The Psychology of Human Development and the Quest for Meaning.* New York: HarperCollins, 1981.

Friedman, Richard E. *Who Wrote the Bible?* New York: Harper and Row, 1987.

Funk, Robert W., and Roy W. Hoover. *The Five Gospels: The Search for the Authentic Words of Jesus.* New York: Macmillan Publishing, 1993.

Furnish, Victor Paul. "1 Corinthians." In *HarperCollins Study Bible.* Edited by Wayne A. Meeks, 2139–63. New York: HarperCollins, 1993.

———. *II Corinthians.* Anchor Bible Series, Vol. 32A. Garden City, N.Y.: Doubleday, 1984.

G. W. J. "Essay on Future Punishment." *Presbyterian Magazine* 2 (October 1822): 444–51.

Gaebelein, Frank E., ed. *The Expositor's Bible Commentary.* 12 vols. Grand Rapids, Mich.: Zondervan, 1978.

Galbraith, David B., D. Kelly Ogden, and Andrew C. Skinner. *Jerusalem: The Eternal City.* Salt Lake City: Deseret Book, 1996.

Gardner, Brant A. *The Gift and Power: Translating the Book of Mormon.* Salt Lake City: Kofford Books, 2011.

———. *Second Witness: Analytical and Contextual Commentary on the Book of Mormon.* 6 Vols. Salt Lake City: Kofford Books, 2007.

Gardner, Martin R. "Mormonism and Capital Punishment: A Doctrinal Perspective, Past and Present." *Dialogue: A Journal of Mormon Thought* 12 (Spring 1979): 9–26.

Garrett, H. Dean. "The Three Most Abominable Sins." In *Alma: The Testimony of the Word.* Edited by Monte S. Nyman and Charles D. Tate Jr., 157–71. Provo, Utah: BYU Religious Studies Center, 1992.

Gaventa, Beverly Roberts. "Acts." In *The HarperCollins Study Bible.* Edited by Wayne A. Meeks, 2056–112. New York: HarperCollins, 1993.

Giles, Kevin. *Jesus and the Father: Modern Evangelicals Reinvent the Doctrine of the Trinity.* Grand Rapids, Mich.: Zondervan, 2006.

Gill, John. *Gill's Complete Body of Doctrinal Divinity: Being a System of Evangelical Truths, Deduced from the Ancient Scriptures.* Abridged and edited by William Straughton. Philadelphia: B. Graves, 1810.

Gillespie, L. Kay. *The Unforgiven: Utah's Executed Men.* Salt Lake City: Signature Books, 1995.

Ginzberg, Louis. *The Legends of the Jews.* Translated by Henrietta Szold, 4 vols. Philadelphia: Jewish Publication Society of America, 1913.

Girardeau, John L. *Calvinism and Evangelical Arminianism.* 1890. Rpt., Harrisonburg, Va.: Sprinkle Publications, 1984.

Givens, Terryl L. *By the Hand of Mormon: The American Scripture that Launched a New World Religion.* New York: Oxford University Press, 2002.

———. "Joseph Smith: Prophecy, Process, and Plenitude." *BYU Studies* 44, no. 4 (2005): 55–68.

———. *People of Paradox: A History of Mormon Culture.* New York: Oxford University Press, 2007.

———. *When Souls Had Wings: Pre-mortal Existence in Western Thought.* New York: Oxford University Press, 2010.

Godfrey, Kenneth W. "A Note on the Nauvoo Library and Literature Institute." *BYU Studies* 14 (Spring 1974): 386–89.

———. "The History of Intelligence in Latter-day Saint Thought." In *The Pearl of Great Price: Revelations from God.* Edited by Donl Peterson and Charles D. Tate Jr. Provo, Utah: BYU Religious Studies Center, 1989.

Goergen, Donald J. *The Death and Resurrection of Jesus.* Collegeville, Minn.:

Liturgical Press, 1988.
Good, Edwin M. "Job." In *Harper's Bible Commentary*. Edited by James L. Mays, 369–93. San Francisco: Harper Row, 1988.
Goodsell, Buel. "Campmeetings on the Champlain District." *Methodist Magazine* 8 (December 1825): 483–86
Goodwin, Scott. "Joseph's Ladder: Principles of Eternal Progression in Three Theological Traditions." In *Archive of Restoration Culture: Summer Fellows' Papers 1997–1999,* 101–9. Provo, Utah: Joseph Fielding Smith Institute for Latter-day Saint History, 2000.
Goodwin, Thomas. *The Works of Thomas Goodwin.* 12 vols. Edited by W. Lyndsay Alexander et al. Edinburgh: James Nichol, 1861.
Gospel Principles. Salt Lake City: Church of Jesus Christ of Latter-day Saints, 1979. Reprinted 1981, 1985, 1986, 1988, 1992, 1995, 1997, and 2009.
Gottstein, Alon. "The Body as Image of God in Rabbic Literature." *Harvard Theological Review* 87 no. 2 (April, 1994): 171–95.
Gowan, Donald E. "The Book of Amos: Introduction, Commentary, and Reflections." In *The New Interpreter's Bible.* Edited by Leander E. Keck, 12 vols., 7:337–431. Nashville, Tenn.: Abingdon Press, 1996.
———. *Eschatology in the Old Testament.* Philadelphia: Fortress Press, 1986.
Grant, David M. "Creation." In *Encyclopedia of Mormonism.* 4 vols., 1:868. New York: Macmillan Publishing, 1992.
Grant, Richard G. "Isaiah in the Book of Mormon." Come to Zarahemla. http://www.cometozarahemla.org/isaiah/isaiah-in-the-bofm.html (accessed January 5, 2005).
Green, Calvin, and Seth Youngs Wells. *A Summary View of the Millennial Church or United Society of Believers, (Commonly Called Shakers).* Albany, N. Y.: Packard & Van Benthuysen, 1823.
Green, Joel B. *1 Peter: Two Horizons New Testament Commentary.* Grand Rapids, Mich.: Eerdmans Publishing Co., 2007.
Greenhow, John. "To the Editor of the Times and Seasons." *Times and Seasons* 4, no. 15 (June 1, 1843): 228–32.
Grenz, Stanley J. *Theology for the Community of God.* Grand Rapids, Mich.: Eerdmans Publishing Co., 2000.
Griffin, Edward D. *Sermons by the Late Edward D. Griffin, D.D.* Vol. 2. Albany, New York: Packard, Van Benthuysen & Co., 1838.
Griffith, Michael T. *One Lord, One Faith: Writings of the Early Christian Fathers as Evidences of the Restoration.* Bountiful, Utah: Horizon, 1996.
Guthrie, Shirley C. *Christian Doctrine.* Richmond, Va.: CLC Press, 1968.
H. N. "Sermon." *Hopkinsian Magazine* 3 (November 1828): 241–48.
Hafen, Bruce C., and Marie K. Hafen. *The Belonging Heart: The Atonement and Relationships with God and Family.* Salt Lake City: Deseret Book, 1994.
Hagner, Donald. *Matthew 14–28.* In *Word Biblical Commentary.* Edited by Bruce Metzger, David Hubbard, and Glenn W. Barker, 33:471. Dallas, Tex.: Word Publishers, 1995.
Haines, Victor Yelverton. "Felix Culpa." In *A Dictionary of Biblical Tradition.* Edited by David L. Jeffrey. Grand Rapids, Mich.: Eerdmans Publishing Co., 1992.
Hale, Van. "Defining the Contemporary Mormon Concept of God." In *Line upon Line: Essays on Mormon Doctrine.* Edited by Gary James Bergera, 7–15. Salt Lake City: Signature Books, 1989.
———. "The Origin of the Human Spirit in Early Mormon Thought." In *Line upon Line: Essays in Mormon Doctrine.* Edited by Gary J. Bergera, 115–26. Salt Lake City: Signature Books, 1989.

Hales, Brian C. *Modern Polygamy and Mormon Fundamentalistm: The Generations after the Manifesto.* Salt Lake City: Greg Kofford Books, 2006.
Hamblin, William J. "Joseph Smith and Kabbalah: The Occult Connection." *Farms Review of Books* 8, no. 2 (1996): 251–325.
Hansen, Klaus J. "The Metamorphosis of the Kingdom of God: Toward a Reinterpretation of Mormon History." In *The New Mormon History: Revisionist Essays on the Past.* Edited by D. Michael Quinn, 221–46. Salt Lake City: Signature Books, 1992.
Hanson, Paul D. "Zechariah 9 and the Recapitulation of an Ancient Ritual Pattern." *Journal of Biblical Literature* 92 (March 1973): 37–59.
Harley, Timothy. *Moon Lore.* London: Swan Sonnenschein, Le Bas & Lowry, 1885.
Harper, Steven. "Infallible Proofs, Both Human and Divine: The Persuasiveness of Mormonism for Early Converts." *Religion and American Culture* 10 (Winter 2000): 99–118.
Harrell, Charles R. "The Development of the Doctrine of Preexistence: 1830–1844." *BYU Studies* 28 (1988): 75–96.
Harrison, J. F. C. *The Second Coming: Popular Millenarianism.* London: Routledge and Kegan, 1979.
Hart, D. G., and John R. Muether. "Turning Points in American Presbyterian History—Part 5: The Plan of Union, 1801." *New Horizons,* May 2005.
Hartley, William G. "From Men to Boys: LDS Aaronic Priesthood Offices, 1829–1996." *Journal of Mormon History* 22 (Spring 1996): 80–136.
Hasel, Gerhard F. "The 'Days' of Creation in Genesis 1: Literal 'Days' or Figurative 'Periods/Epochs' of Time." *Origins* 21 (1994): 5–38.
Hatch, John P., ed. *Anthon H. Lund, Danish Apostle: Diaries of Anthon H. Lund, 1890–1921.* Salt Lake City: Signature Books, 2006.
Hatch, Nathan O. *The Democratization of American Christianity.* New Haven, Conn.: Yale University Press, 1989.
Hauglid, Brian. "Searching for God's Word in New Testament Textual Criticism." *The Religious Educator: Perspectives on the Restored Gospel* 8, no. 2 (2007): 101–14.
Hawley, Bostwick. *Manual of Methodism.* New York: Carlton and Lanahan, 1868.
Hayden, A. S. *History of the Disciples in the Western Reserve, Ohio.* Cincinnati: Chase & Hall, 1876.
Hayes, D. A. *Paul and His Epistles.* Grand Rapids, Mich.: Baker Publishing Group House, 1969.
Haynes, Stephen R. *Noah's Curse: The Biblical Justification for American Slavery.* New York: Oxford University Press, 2002.
Haze, Craig J. "The Apologetic Impulse in Early Mormonism: The Historical Roots of the New Mormon Challenge." In *The New Mormon Challenge.* Edited by Francis J. Beckwith, Carl Mosser, and Paul Owen., 31–57. Grand Rapids, Mich.: Zondervan, 2002.
Heath, Harvard S. "Smoot Hearings." In *Encyclopedia of Mormonism.* 4 vols., 3:1363–64. New York: Macmillan Publishing, 1992.
The Heidelberg Catechism. London: N. pub., 1720.
Heim, Knut. "The Perfect King of Psalm 72." In *The Lord's Anointed: Interpretation of Old Testament Messianic Texts.* Edited by Philip E. Satterthwaite, Richard S. Hess, and Gordon J. Wenham, 223–48. Grand Rapids, Mich.: Baker Publishing Groups, 1995.
Hendel, Ronald. "Genesis." In *The HarperCollins Study Bible: Fully Revised and Updated.* Edited by Harold W. Attridge, 3–82. San Francisco: HarperSanFrancisco, 2006.

Henshaw, Richard A. "Joel." In *The HarperCollins Study Bible*. Edited by Wayne A. Meeks, 1347–1354. New York: HarperCollins, 1993.

Henze, Matthias. "Daniel." In *The New Interpreter's Study Bible*. Edited by Walter J. Harrelson, 1231–52. Nashville, Tenn.: Abingdon Press, 2003.

Herrick, Greg. "Baalism in Canaanite Religion and Its Relation to Selected Old Testament Texts." Biblical Studies Foundation. http://bible.org/article/baalism-canaanite-religion-and-its-relation-selected-old-testament-texts (accessed May 14, 2010).

———. "Is the Bible the Only Revelation from God?" Biblical Studies Foundation. http://bible.org/article/bible-only-revelation-god (accessed May 20, 2010).

Herschel, William. "On the Nature and Construction of the Sun and Fixed Stars." *Philosophical Transactions of the Royal Society of London* 85 (1795): 46–72.

Hicks, Elias. "Sermon by Elias Hicks, Delivered at Darby, November 15, 1826." *The Quaker* 1, no. 6 (1827): 1–20.

———. "Sermon by Elias Hicks, Delivered in Wilmington, Del. Sunday Morning, December 3, 1826." *The Quaker* 1, no. 6 (1827):177–211.

Hicks, Michael. "Joseph Smith, W. W. Phelps, and the Poetic Paraphrase of 'The Vision.'" *Journal of Mormon History* 20, no. 2 (Fall 1994): 63–84.

Hiebert, Theodore. "Genesis." In *The New Interpreter's Study Bible*. Edited by Walter J. Harrelson, 1–84. Nashville, Tenn.: Abingdon, 2003.

Hill, Marvin S. *Quest for Refuge: The Mormon Flight from American Pluralism*. Salt Lake City: Signature Books, 1989.

Hinckley, Gordon B. *Be Thou an Example*. Salt Lake City: Deseret Book, 1981.

———. "Closing Remarks." *Ensign*, November 2004, 104–5.

———. "The Great Things Which God Has Revealed." *Ensign*, May 2005, 80–83.

History of the Church. Smith, Joseph, Jr. et al. *History of the Church of Jesus Christ of Latter-day Saints*, edited by B. H. Roberts. 2d ed. rev. Salt Lake City: Deseret News Press, 6 vols. published 1902–12, Vol. 7 published 1932.

"History of the Shakers." *The Port Folio* 8 no. 4 (October 1812): 329–343.

Hobbes, Thomas. *Leviathan or the Matter, Forme, & Power of a Common-wealth: Ecclesiasticall and Civill*. London: Andrew Crooke, 1651. Electronic reprint. McMaster University Archive for the History of Economic Thought. http://socserv.mcmaster.ca/econ/ugcm/3ll3/hobbes/ Leviathan.pdf (accessed March 7, 2009).

Hoekema, Anthony A. *The Bible and the Future*. Grand Rapids, Mich.: Eerdmans Publishing Co., 1979.

Holifield, E. Brooks. *Theology in America: Christian Thought from the Age of Puritans to the Civil War*. New Haven, Conn.: Yale University Press, 2003.

Holland, Jeffrey R. "Atonement of Jesus Christ." In *Encyclopedia of Mormonism*, 4 vols., 1:82–86. New York: Macmillan Publishing, 1992.

———. *Christ and the New Covenant: The Messianic Message of the Book of Mormon*. Salt Lake City: Deseret Book, 1997.

Hollist, W. Ladd. "Priest, Aaronic Priesthood." In *Encyclopedia of Mormonism*. 4 vols., 3:1132–33. New York: Macmillan Publishing, 1992.

Homer, Michael W. "Similarity of Priesthood in Masonry: The Relationship between Freemasonry and Mormonism." *Dialogue: A Journal of Mormon Thought* 27 (Fall 1994): 1–113.

Hooker, Morna D. *A Commentary on the Gospel According to St Mark*. Black's New Testament Commentaries. London: Continuum, 2006.

Hooker, Richard. "Backgrounds." Washington State University – World

Civilizations. http://www.wsu.edu/~dee/CHRIST/CHRIST.HTM (accessed January 25, 2005).

―――. "Monolatry ~1300–1000 BC." Washington State University – World Civilizations. http://www.wsu.edu/~dee/HEBREWS/MONOL.HTM (accessed October 30, 2004).

Horrell, David G. "Who are 'The Dead' and When was the Gospel Preached to Them?: The Interpretation of 1 Pet 4.6." *New Testament Studies* 49 (January 2003): 70–89.

Hoskisson, Paul Y. "Update: The 'Familiar Spirit' in 2 Nephi 26:12." *Insights* 26, no. 6 (2008): 7.

House, Paul R. *Old Testament Theology*. Downers Grove, Ill.: InterVarsity Press, 1998.

Huey, F. B., Jr. *Jeremiah, Lamentations*. Nashville, Tenn.: Boardman Press, 1993.

Huges, Philip Edgecumbe. *Paul's Second Epistle to the Corinthians*. Grand Rapids, Mich.: Eerdmans Publishing Co., 1962.

Hughes, Richard T. "Joseph Smith as an American Restorationist." *Brigham Young University Studies* 44, no. 4 (2005): 31–39.

Hunter, Edward. "Copy of Record Written by Edward Hunter." Photocopy at "Bishop" Edward Hunter Family website. http://www.www.georgeqcannon.com/Family%20History%20Database/All%20Family%20History%20Files/Cannon%20Family/Edward%20Hunter%20Family/Documents/Edward%20Hunter%20Self%20History.pdf (accessed May 19, 2010).

Hunter, Howard W. *The Teachings of Howard W. Hunter, Fourteenth President of the Church of Jesus Christ of Latter-day Saints*. Edited by Clyde J. Williams. Salt Lake City: Bookcraft, 1997.

Hunter, Milton R. *The Gospel through the Ages*. Salt Lake City: Stevens & Wallis, 1945.

Huntington, Oliver B. "Our Sunday Chapter: The Inhabitants of the Moon." *Young Woman's Journal* 3, no. 6 (March 1892): 263–64.

Hutchinson, Anthony A. "A Mormon Midrash? LDS Creation Narratives Reconsidered." *Dialogue: A Journal of Mormon Thought* 21 (Winter 1988): 11–74.

Hyde, Paul Nolan. "Intelligences." In *Encyclopedia of Mormonism*. 4 vols., 2:692–93. New York: Macmillan Publishing, 1992.

"An Interview with Brevard S. Childs." Philosophy and Religion. http://www.philosophy-religion.org/bible/childs-interview.htm (accessed May 24, 2010).

Irving, Gordon. "Law of Adoption." *BYU Studies* 14, no. 3 (Spring 1974): 291–314.

Isaac, Daniel. *The Doctrine of Universal Restoration Examined and Refuted*. New York: J. Soule and T. Mason, 1819.

J. K. "The Origin of Sin." *The Sentinel and Star in the West* 1 (October 17, 1829): 9–11.

Jackson, Kent P. *The Book of Moses and the Joseph Smith Translation Manuscripts*. Provo, Utah: BYU Religious Studies Center, 2005.

―――. *From Apostasy to Restoration*. Salt Lake City: Deseret Book, 1996.

―――. "I Have a Question," *Ensign,* August 1999, 66.

―――. "The Lord Is There (Ezekiel 37–48)." In *Studies in Scripture: 1 Kings to Malachi*. Edited by Kent P. Jackson and Robert L. Millet, 300–319. Salt Lake City: Deseret Book, 1993.

―――. *Lost Tribes and Latter Days: What Modern Revelation Tells Us about the Old Testament*. Salt Lake City: Deseret Book, 2005.

Jacob, Edmond. "Death." In *Interpreters' Dictionary of the Bible*. Edited by George Arthur Buttrick. 4 vols., 1:802. Nashville, Tenn.: Abington Press, 1962.

Jacobs, Joseph. "Tribes, Lost Ten." In *The Jewish Encyclopedia*. 12 vols. 12:249–53. New York: Funk and Wagnalls, 1901–06.
Jacobs, Joseph and A. Biram, "Millennium." In *The Jewish Encyclopedia*. 12 vols. 9:593. New York: Funk and Wagnalls, 1901–06.
James, William. *The Varieties of Religious Experience: A Study in Human Nature*. New York: Modern Library, 2002.
Jamieson, Robert, A. R. Fausset, and David Brown. *A Commentary, Critical and Explanatory, on the Old and New Testaments*. 2 vols. New York: S. S. Scranton, 1875.
Jeffrey, Duane E. "Noah's Flood: Modern Scholarship and Mormon Traditions." *Sunstone*, no. 134 (October 2004): 27–45.
Jenson, Phillip P. "Models of Prophetic Prediction and Matthew's Quotation of Micah 5:2." In *The Lord's Anointed: Interpretation of Old Testament Messianic Texts*. Edited by Philip E. Satterthwaite, Richard S. Hess, and Gordon J. Wenham, 189–211. Grand Rapids, Mich.: Baker Publishing Group, 1995.
Jerome, Saint. *Commentary on Daniel*. 407 A.D. Translated by Gleason L. Archer, 1958. The Tertullian Project. http://tertullian.org/fathers/jerome_daniel_02_text.htm (accessed May 18, 2006).
Jessee, Dean C., ed. "The Kirtland Diary of Wilford Woodruff." *BYU Studies* 12, no. 4 (Summer 1972): 365–99.
———, ed. *The Papers of Joseph Smith: Autobiographical and Historical Writings*. 2 vols. Salt Lake City: Deseret Book, 1989.
———, comp. and ed. *The Personal Writings of Joseph Smith*. Rev. ed. Salt Lake City: Deseret Book, 2002.
Jessee, Dean C., Mark Ashurst-McGee, and Richard L. Jensen, eds. *Journals, Volume 1: 1832–1839*. Vol. 1 of the Journals series of *The Joseph Smith Papers*. Edited by Dean C. Jessee, Ronald K. Esplin, and Richard Lyman Bushman. Salt Lake City: Church Historian's Press, 2008.
Johnson, Charles A. *The Frontier Camp Meeting*. Dallas: Southern Methodist University Press, 1955.
Johnson, Luke Timothy. *Among the Gentiles: Greco-Roman Religion and Christianity*. New Haven, Conn.: Yale University Press, 2009.
Johnson, Paul. *A History of the Jews*. New York: Harper & Row, 1817.
Johnston, Philip P. "'Left in Hell'? Psalm 16, Sheol and the Holy One." In *The Lord's Anointed: Interpretation of Old Testament Messianic Texts*. Edited by Phillip E. Satterthwaite, Richard S. Hess, and Gordon J. Wenham, 213–22. Grand Rapids, Mich.: Baker Publishing Group, 1995.
Josephus. *The Antiquities of the Jews*. In *Josephus: Complete Works*. Translated by William Whiston . Grand Rapids, Mich.: Kregel Publications, 1973.
———. *The Works of Flavius Josephus in Four Volumes*. Translated by William Whitson. Grand Rapids, Mich.: Baker Publishing Group, 1984.
Journal of Discourses, 26 vols. Liverpool: F. D Richards, 1855–86.
Judah, "The Everlasting Gospel," *Christian Magazine* 1 (January 1824): 1–8.
Judd, Frank F., Jr. "Prophets 'Like unto Moses.'" *BYU Religious Studies Center Newsletter* 21, no. 3 (2006): 7.
Just, Felix. "New Testament Theology: Introductory Glossaries." Catholic Resources for Bible, Liturgy, Art, and Theology. http://catholic-resources.org/Bible/NT-Theology.htm(accessed June 4, 2010).
Juster, Susan. *Doomsayers: Anglo-American Prophecies in the Age of Revolution*. Philadelphia: University of Pennsylvania Press, 2003.

Kapelrud, Arvid S. *The Ras Shamra Texts and the Old Testament.* Translated by G. W. Anderson. Norman: University of Oklahoma Press, 1963.

Katich, Samuel. "A Tale of Two Marriage Systems: Perspectives on Polyandry and Joseph Smith." Foundation for Apologetic Information & Research (FAIR). http://www.fairlds.org/pubs/polyandry.pdf (accessed February 15, 2006).

Kearney, Greg. "Ask the Apologist." The Foundation for Apologetic Information & Research (FAIR). http://www.fairlds.org/Misc/Similarities_between_Masonic_and_Mormon_Temple_Ritual.html (accessed May 17, 2010).

Keating, Joseph. "Christianity." In *The Catholic Encyclopedia.* Edited by Charles G. Herbermann et al. 15 vols., 3:712–20. New York: Universal Knowledge Foundation, Inc., 1913.

Keck, Brian E. "Ezekiel 37, Sticks, and Babylonian Writing Boards: A Critical Reappraisal." *Dialogue: A Journal of Mormon Thought* 23 (Spring 1990): 126–38.

Keck, Leander E. "Romans." In *The HarperCollins Study Bible.* Edited by Wayne A. Meeks, 2114–38. New York: HarperCollins, 1993.

Keener, Craig S. *The IVP Bible: Background Commentary.* Downers Grove, Ill: InterVarsity Press, 1993.

Keller, Roger R. "The Apostasy." Presented at the Foundation for Apologetic Information & Research (FAIR) 1999 conference. Available on the FAIR website. http://www.fairlds.org/pubs/conf/2004KelR.html (July 31, 2005).

———. "Jesus Christ: Priest, King, and Prophet." In *Salvation in Christ.* Edited by Roger R. Keller and Robert L. Millet, 345–364. Provo, Utah: Brigham Young University Press, 2005.

Kent, W. H. "Devil." In *The Catholic Encyclopedia.* Edited by Charles G. Herbermann et al. 15 vols., 4:764–67. New York: Universal Knowledge Foundation, Inc., 1913.

Kessler, Edward. *An Introduction to Jewish Christian Relations.* Cambridge, Eng.: Cambridge University Press, 2010.

Kimball, Edward L. "Brigham Young and Priesthood Denial to the Blacks: An Alternate View." *Brigham Young University Studies* 47, no. 2 (2008): 10–19.

Kimball, Spencer W. "The Day of the Lamanites." *Improvement Era,* December 1960, 922–23.

———. *The Teachings of Spencer W. Kimball.* Edited by Edward L. Kimball. Salt Lake City: Bookcraft, 1982.

Kimball, Stanley B. *Heber C. Kimball: Mormon Patriarch and Pioneer.* Urbana: University of Illinois Press, 1981.

Kinkade, William. *The Bible Doctrine of God, Jesus Christ, the Holy Spirit, Atonement, Faith and Election.* New York: H. R. Piercy, Printer, 1829.

Kirkland, Boyd. "The Development of the Mormon Doctrine of God." In *Line upon Line: Essays in Mormon Doctrine.* Edited by Gary James Bergera, 35–52. Salt Lake City: Signature Books, 1989.

Kittel, G., and G. Friedrich, eds. *Theological Dictionary of the New Testament.* Translated and edited by Geoffrey W. Bromiley. 10 vols. Grand Rapids, Mich.: Eerdmans Publishing Co., 1968.

Knight, Douglas A. "Cosmology." In *Mercer Dictionary of the Bible.* Edited by Watson E. Mills, 175–76. Macon, Ga.: Macon University Press, 1990.

Kofford, Greg. "The First Vision: Doctrinal Developments and Analysis." Presented at the 1988 Sunstone Symposium in Salt Lake City Utah. August 18, 1988.

Kohler, Kaufmann. "Eschatology." In *The Jewish Encyclopedia.* 12 vols. 6:209–218. New York: Funk and Wagnalls, 1901–06.

———. "Kingdom of God." In *The Jewish Encyclopedia.* 12 vols. 7:502–503. New York: Funk and Wagnalls, 1901–06.

Kohler, Kaufmann, Isaac Broyde, and Ludwig Blau. "Soul." In *The Jewish Encyclopedia*. 12 vols. 11:472–76. New York: Funk and Wagnalls, 1901–06.
Kohler, Kaufmann, and Samuel Krauss. "Baptism." In *The Jewish Encyclopedia*. 12 vols. 2:499–500. New York: Funk and Wagnalls, 1901–06.
Kostenberger, Andreas J. "Jesus the Good Shepherd Who Will Also Bring Other Sheep (John 10:16): The Old Testament Background of a Familiar Metaphor." *Bulletin for Biblical Research* 12, no. 1 (2002): 67–96.
Kraus, Hans-Joachim. *Psalms 1–59: A Commentary*. Translated by Hilton C. Oswald. Minneapolis: Augsburg, 1988.
Küng, Hans. *On Being a Christian*. Garden City, New York: Doubleday, 1976.
Ladd, George E. *A Theology of the New Testament*. Grand Rapids, Mich.: Eerdmans Publishing Co., rev. 1993.
Lang, B. "*Kipper*." In *Theological Dictionary of the Old Testament*. Edited by G. Johannes Botterweck, Helmer Ringgren, Heinz-Josef Fabry. Translated by David E. Green, 288–303. Grand Rapids, Mich,: Eerdmans Publishing Co., 1995.
Larsen, Stan. "The King Follett Discourse: A Newly Amalgamated Text." *BYU Studies* 18 (Winter 1978): 193–208.
Larson, Stan and Samuel J. Passey, eds. *The William E. McLellin Papers: 1854–1880*. Salt Lake City: Signature Books, 2008.
Lathrop, Joseph. *The Angel Preaching the Everlasting Gospel*. Springfield, Mass.: Thomas Dickman, 1812.
Law, William. *A Practical Treatise on Christian Perfection*. Portsmouth, Va.: Charles Morgridge, 1822.
LDS Newsroom. "Approaching Church Doctrine." May 4, 2007. LDS Newsroom: The Official News Source for Media, Opinion Leaders, and the Public. http://newsroom.lds.org/ldsnewsroom/eng/commentary/ approaching-mormon-doctrine (accessed August 29, 2009).
LeBaron, E. Dale. "Benjamin Franklin Johnson: Colonizer, Public Servant and Church Leader." M.A. thesis, Brigham Young University, 1967.
"Lecture Series Explores the Book of Mormon." *Sunstone* (February 1989): 52–55.
Lectures on Faith. Salt Lake City: Deseret Book, 1985 printing.
"Lectures on the Shorter Catechism of the Westminster Assembly of the Divines—Addressed to Youth." *Christian Advocate* 3 (December, 1825): 529–32.
Lee, Harold B. "Strengthening the Stakes of Zion." *Ensign*, July 1973, 4–5.
———. *Teachings of Harold B. Lee*. Edited by Clyde J. Williams. Salt Lake City: Bookcraft, 1996.
———. "The Way to Eternal Life." *Ensign*, November 1971, 9–17.
———. *Ye Are the Light of the World*. Salt Lake City: Deseret Book, 1979.
Leeming, David Adams, and Margaret Adams Leeming. *Encyclopedia of Creation Myths*. Santa Barbara, Calif.: ABC-CLIO, 1994.
Lenski, R. C. H. *The Interpretation of St Matthew's Gospel*. Columbus, Ohio: Wartburg Press, 1943.
Leonard, Glen L. *Nauvoo: A Place of Peace, a People of Promise*. Salt Lake City: Deseret Book/Brigham Young University Press, 2002.
"Letters from W. W. Phelps to his Wife, Sally Phelps." Book of Abraham Project. http://www.boap.org/LDS/Early-Saints/Phelps-letters.html (accessed November 4, 2007).
"Letters on the Atonement." *The Religious Monitor or Evangelical Repository* 3 (August 1826): 141.
Levenson, Jon E. *Creation and the Persistence of Evil*. San Francisco: Harper & Row, 1988.

Lewis, C. S. *The Problem of Pain.* 1940. Rpt., New York: HarperCollins, 2001.

Lewis, Jack P. "'The Gates of Hell Shall Not Prevail Against It' (Matt 16:18): A Study of the History of Interpretation." *Journal of Evangelical Theology* 38, no. 3 (September 1995): 349–67.

Lincoln, Andrew T. "'Born of the Virgin Mary': Creedal Affirmation and Critical Reading." In *Christology and Scripture: Interdisciplinary Perspectives.* Edited by Andrew T. Lincoln and Angus Paddison, 84–103. London: T&T Clark International, 2007.

———. *Paradise Now and Not Yet: Studies in the Role of the Heavenly Dimension in Paul's Thought with Special Reference to His Eschatology.* Cambridge, Eng.: Cambridge University Press, 1981.

Lindsay, Jeff. "Questions about the LDS Temple Ceremony and Masonry." LDS FAQ: Mormon Answers. http://www.jefflindsay.com/LDSFAQ/FQ_masons.shtml (accessed March 16, 2005).

"The Living Christ: The Testimony of the Apostles, The Church of Jesus Christ of Latter-day Saints." *Ensign,* April 2000, 2–3.

Lohse, Eduard. *Colossians and Philemon.* Translated by William R. Poehlmann and Robert J. Karris. Philadelphia: Fortress Press, 1971.

———. *The New Testament Environments.* Translated by John E. Steely. Nashville, Tenn.: Abingdon, 1976.

Longman, Tremper. *The Book of Ecclesiastes.* Grand Rapids, Mich.: Eerdmans Publishing Co., 1998.

Loveley, E., and H. J. Sorenson. "Creation." In *New Catholic Encyclopedia.* Edited by Thomas Carson and Joann Cerrito. 2d ed.. 15 vols. Detroit, Mich.: Gale, 2003.

Lowe, Abraham T. *The Columbian Class Book, Consisting of Geographical, Historical and Biographical Extracts, Compiled from Authentic Sources, and Arranged on a Plan Different from Any Thing before Offered the Publick. Particularly Designed for the Use of Schools.* 2d ed. Worcester, Mass.: Dorr & Howland, 1825.

Ludlow, Daniel H. *A Companion to Your Study of the Book of Mormon.* Salt Lake City: Deseret Book, 1976.

———. *A Companion to Your Study of the New Testament: The Four Gospels.* Salt Lake City: Deseret Book, 1982.

———. *A Companion to Your Study of the Old Testament.* Salt Lake City: Deseret Book, 1981.

———. "Of the House of Israel." *Ensign,* January, 1991, 51–54.

Ludlow, Victor L. *Principles and Practices of the Restored Gospel.* Salt Lake City: Deseret Book, 1992.

Luther, Martin. *A Commentary on St. Paul's Epistle to the Galatians.* London: James Cundee, 1807.

Mackay, Thomas W. "Early Christian Millenarianist Interpretation of the Two Witnesses in John's Apocalypse 11:3–13." In *By Study and Also by Faith: Essays in Honor of Hugh W. Nibley on the Occasion of His Eightieth Birthday, 27 March 1990.* Edited by John M. Lundquist and Stephen D. Ricks, 2 vols. Salt Lake City: Deseret Book and Foundation for Ancient Research and Mormon Studies, 1990.

Madison, John V. "English Versions of the New Testament." *Journal of Biblical Literature* 44 nos. 3/4 (1925): 273–75, 261–88.

Maier, Paul L. "The Times and Places of Jesus." *The Lutheran Witness.* October 1999. Reprinted online by Issues, Etc.. http://www.mtio.com/articles/aissar30.htm (accessed May 15, 2010).

Mallett, Robert. "What Do You Mean, Restoration Movement?" The Christian Restoration Association. http://www.thecra.org/restmovement.html (accessed January 3, 2005).

Mannock, John. *The Poor Man's Catechism; or, the Christian Doctrine Explained.* Baltimore, Md.: J. Robinson, 1815.

Marais, J. I. "Psychology." *The International Standard Bible Encyclopedia.* Edited by James Orr, 5 vols., 4:2494–99. Chicago: Howard-Severance Co., 1915.

Marlowe, Eric-Jon K. "The Only True Church: Boldness without Overbearance." *The Religious Educator: Perspectives on the Restored Gospel* 7, no. 3 (2006): 23–37.

Marquardt, H. Michael. "The Book of Abraham Revisited." Mormon Origins. http://www.xmission.com/~research/about/abraham.htm (accessed January 12, 2006).

———. *Joseph Smith Revelations: Text and Commentary.* Salt Lake City: Signature Books, 1999.

Martins, Marcus H. "Thirty Years After the 'Long-Promised Day': Reflections and Expectations." *BYU Studies* 47, no. 2 (2008): 79–85.

Martyr, Justin. "First Apology." In *The Ante-Nicene Fathers: Translations of the Writings of the Fathers down to A.D. 325.* Edited and translated by Alexander Roberts and James Donaldson, 10 vols. Buffalo, New York: Christian Literature Publishing, 1885. Available on the Early Christian Writings website, http://www.earlychristianwritings.com/text/justinmartyr-firstapology.html (accessed March 20, 2006).

Mather, Cotton. *Theopolis Americana.* Boston: B. Green, 1710.

Matthews, Robert J. *A Bible! A Bible!.* Salt Lake City: Bookcraft, 1990.

———. "Joseph Smith's Efforts to Publish His Bible 'Translation.'" *Ensign,* January 1983, 57–64.

———. "The 'New Translation' of the Bible, 1830–1833: Doctrinal Development during the Kirtland Era." *BYU Studies* 11 (Summer 1971): 400–422.

———. *"A Plainer Translation": Joseph Smith's Translation of the Bible, a History and Commentary.* Provo, Utah: Brigham Young University Press, 1975.

Mauss, Armand L. *All Abraham's Children: Changing Mormon Conceptions of Race and Lineage.* Urbana: University of Illinois Press, 2003.

———. "Dispelling the Curse of Cain: Or How to Explain the Old Priesthood Ban without Looking Ridiculous." *Sunstone* (October 2004): 56–60.

———. "The LDS Church and the Race Issue: A Study in Misplaced Apologetics." Presented at the Foundation for Apologetic Information & Research (FAIR) 2003 conference. Available on the FAIR website. http://www.fairlds.org/FAIR_Conferences/ 2003_LDS_Church_and_the_Race_Issue.html (accessed September 13, 2006).

———. "Mormonism and the Negro: Faith, Folklore, and Civil Rights." *Dialogue: A Journal of Mormon Thought* 2 (Winter 1967): 19–39.

Maxwell, Neal A. *All These Things Shall Give Thee Experience.* Salt Lake City: Deseret Book, 1979.

———. *Even As I Am.* Salt Lake City: Deseret Book, 1982.

———. "How Choice a Seer!" *Ensign,* November 2003, 99–101.

———. *"Not My Will, But Thine."* Salt Lake City: Bookcraft, 1989.

———. "Plow in Hope." *Ensign,* May 2001, 59–60.

———. "Testifying of the Great and Glorious Atonement." *Ensign,* October 2001, 10–15.

———. *Things as They Really Are.* Salt Lake City: Deseret Book, 1978.

May, H. G. "Archeological News and Views: The Ten Lost Tribes." *Biblical Archaeologist* 6 (September 1943): 55–60.

Mays, James L. "Prayer and Christology: Psalm 22 as Perspective on the Passion." *Theology Today,* October 1985, 322–331.
McCauley, Deborah Vansau. *Appalachian Mountain Religion: A History.* Urbana: University of Illinois Press, 1995.
McConkie, Bruce R. "All Are Alike unto God." An address to a Book of Mormon Symposium for Seminary and Institute teachers, Brigham Young University, August 18, 1978, BYU Speeches. http://speeches.byu.edu/reader/reader.php?id=11017 (accessed February 19, 2010).
———. "Christ and the Creation." *Ensign,* June 1982, 9–15.
———. *Doctrinal New Testament Commentary.* 3 vols. Salt Lake City: Bookcraft, 1965–1973.
———. Letter to Eugene England, February 19, 1981.
———. *Mormon Doctrine,* 2d ed. Salt Lake City: Bookcraft, 1966.
———. *Mortal Messiah: From Bethlehem to Calvary.* 4 vols. Salt Lake City: Deseret Book, 1979–81.
———. *The Millennial Messiah: The Second Coming of the Son of Man.* Salt Lake City: Deseret Book, 1982.
———. "A New Commandment: Save Thyself and Thy Kindred!" *Ensign,* August 1976, 7–12.
———. *A New Witness for the Articles of Faith.* Salt Lake City: Deseret Book, 1985.
———. *The Promised Messiah: The First Coming of Christ.* Salt Lake City, Deseret Book, 1978.
———. "The Salvation of Little Children." *Ensign,* April 1977, 3–7.
———. "The Seven Deadly Heresies." In *1980 Devotional Speeches of the Year.* 74–80. Provo, Utah: Brigham Young University Press, 1981.
———. "Who Shall Declare His Generation?" *BYU Studies* 16, no. 4 (1975–76): 553–560.
McConkie, Joseph Fielding. *Answers: Straightforward Answers to Tough Gospel Questions.* Salt Lake City: Deseret Book, 1998.
———. *Gospel Symbolism.* Salt Lake City: Bookcraft, 1999.
———. *Here We Stand.* Salt Lake City: Deseret Book, 1995.
———. *Seeking the Spirit.* Salt Lake City: Deseret Book, 1978.
———. "Premortal Existence, Foreordinations, and Heavenly Councils." In *Apocryphal Writings and the Latter-day Saints.* Edited by C. Wilford Griggs, 173–98. Provo, Utah: BYU Religious Studies Center, 1986. Rpt., Greg Kofford Books, 2007.
McConkie, Joseph Fielding, and Robert L. Millet. *Doctrinal Commentary on the Book of Mormon.* 4 vols. Salt Lake City: Bookcraft, 1987–92.
McConkie, Oscar W. "Angels." In *Encyclopedia of Mormonism.* 4 vols., 1:41. New York: Macmillan Publishing, 1992.
McCown, Wayne G. "Holiness in Hebrews." *Wesleyan Theological Journal* 16, no. 2 (Spring 1981): 58–78.
McDannel, Colleen, and Bernhard Lang. *Heaven: A History.* 2d ed. New Haven, Conn.: Yale University Press, 2001.
McDowell, Josh. *The New Evidence that Demands a Verdict.* Nashville, Tenn.: Thomas Nelson, 1999.
McGrath, Alister E. *A Brief History of Heaven.* Oxford, Eng.: Blackwell Publishers, 2003.
———. *Christian Theology: An Introduction.* 3rd ed. Oxford, Eng.: Blackwell Publishers, 2001.
———. *A Scientific Theology. Vol. 1: Nature.* Edinburgh: T. & T. Clark, 2001.

McKim, Donald K. *Theological Turning Points: Major Issues in Christian Thought.* Atlanta, Ga.: John Knox Press, 1988.
McMurrin, Sterling M. *The Theological Foundations of the Mormon Religion.* Salt Lake City: University of Utah Press, 1965.
Merritt, Timothy. "Divinity." *Methodist Magazine* 6 (September 1823): 241–48, 321–27.
_____. "Divinity." *Methodist Magazine* 6 (September 1823): 321–27.
Meservy, Keith H. "Ezekiel's Sticks and the Gathering of Israel." *Ensign,* February 1987, 4–13.
_____. "God Is with Us (Isaiah 1–17)." In *Studies in Scripture, Vol. 4: 1 Kings to Malachi.* Edited by Kent P. Jackson, 86–107. Salt Lake City: Deseret Book, 1993.
_____. "Lord = Jehovah." *Ensign,* June 2002, 29.
Messadie, Gerald. *A History of the Devil.* Translated by Mare Romano. New York: Kodansha International, 1997.
Metcalfe, Brent Lee. "The Priority of Mosiah: A Prelude to Book of Mormon Exegesis." In *New Approaches to the Book of Mormon: Explorations in Critical Methodology.* Edited by Brent Lee Metcalfe, 395–444. Salt Lake City: Signature Books, 1993.
_____. "Whence and Whither the Five Points of Fellowship?" Mormon Scripture Studies. http://mormonscripturestudies.com/tem/blm/fpof.asp January 1, 2002 (accessed August 16, 2006).
Meyers, E. M. "The Crisis of the Mid Fifth-Century B.C.E. Second Zechariah and the 'End' of Prophecy." In *Pomegranates and Golden Bells: Studies in Biblical, Jewish, and Near Eastern Ritual, Law, and Literature in Honor of Jacob Milgrom.* Edited by D. P. Wright, D. N. Freedman, & A. Hurvitz. Winona Lake, Ind.: Eisenbrauns, 1995.
Meyers, Mary Ann. "Death in Swedenborgian and Mormon Eschatology." *Dialogue: A Journal of Mormon Thought* 14, no. 1 (Spring 1981): 58–64.
Millard, David. *The True Messiah Exalted, or Jesus Christ Really Is the Son of God, Vindicated in Three Letters to a Presbyterian Minister.* Canandaigua, N.Y.: J. D. Bennis, 1818.
"The Millennium," *Times and Seasons* 3, no. 7 (February 1, 1842): 672.
"Millennium. No. III." *Evening and Morning Star* 2 (February 1834): 131
"Millennium. No. XIII." *Latter Day Saints' Messenger and Advocate* 1 (March 1835): 84–87
Miller, Craig. "Did Swedenborg Influence (LDS) Mormon Doctrine?" Presented at the 2002 Sunstone Symposium in Salt Lake City Utah. August 7, 2002. Available at author's website. http://craigwmiller.tripod.com/interest.htm (accessed December 27, 2004).
Millet, Robert L. "Joseph Smith and Modern Mormonism: Orthodoxy, Neo-orthodoxy, Tension, and Tradition." *BYU Studies* 29, no. 3 (1989): 49–68.
_____. "Life in the Millennium." In *Watch and Be Ready: Preparing for the Second Coming of the Lord.*167–190. Salt Lake City: Deseret Book, 1994.
_____. *The Mormon Faith: A New Look at Christianity.* Salt Lake City: Shadow Mountain Press, 1998.
_____. "A New and Everlasting Covenant (D&C 132)." In *Studies in Scripture, Vol. 1: The Doctrine and Covenants.* Edited by Robert L. Millet and Kent P. Jackson, 512–25. Salt Lake City: Deseret Book, 1989.
_____. "A Revelation on Priesthood." In *Studies in Scripture, Vol. 1: The Doctrine and Covenants.* Edited by Robert L. Millet and Kent P. Jackson. Salt Lake City: Deseret Book, 1989.
_____. *Selected Writings of Robert L. Millet.* Salt Lake City: Deseret Book, 2000.

———. "What Do We Really Believe? Identifying Doctrinal Parameters within Mormonism." In *Discourses in Mormon Theology: Philosophical and Theological Possibilities*. Edited by James M. McLachlan and Loyd Ericson, 265–81. Salt Lake City: Greg Kofford Books, 2007.

———. *Within Reach*. Salt Lake City: Deseret Book, 1995.

Millet, Robert L., and Lloyd D. Newell. *Draw Near unto Me*. Salt Lake City: Deseret Book, 2004.

Milton, John. *Paradise Lost, Illustrated with Texts of Scripture*. 3d edition. Edited by John Gillies. London: W. Flint, 1788.

"Miltoniana." *The Baptist Magazine* 17 (November 1825): 463–67.

Moffat, James, *Grace in the New Testament*. New York: Ray Long and Richard R. Smith, 1932.

Moore, Jacob. "Divinity." *Methodist Magazine* 8 (August 1825): 289–96.

"The Mormons: Interview, Jeffrey Holland." April 30, 2007. American Experience and Frontline. http://www.pbs.org/mormons/interviews/holland.html (accessed June 7, 2008).

Morray-Jones, C. R. A. "Paradise Revised (2 Cor. 12:1–12): The Jewish Mystical Background of Paul's Apostalate. Part 2: Paul's Heavenly Ascent and Its Significance." *Harvard Theological Review* 86 (July 1993): 265–92.

Morrison, James. *Commentary on the Gospel According to Matthew*. London: Hamilton, Adams & Co., 1870.

Mowinckel, Sigmund. *He That Cometh*. New York: Abingdon Press, 1956.

Myer, Isaac. *Qabbalah*. Philadelphia: Privately printed, 1888.

"The Nature and Importance of the Pastoral Office," *The American Baptist Magazine* 5 (July 1825), 199–202.

Nelson, Russell M. "The Creation." *Ensign*, May 2000, 84–86.

———. "The Gathering of Scattered Israel." *Ensign*, Nov 2006, 79–82.

———. *Perfection Pending, and Other Favorite Discourses*. Salt Lake City: Deseret Book, 1998.

———. "The Spirit of Elijah." *Ensign*, November 1994, 84–86.

NET Bible. Biblical Studies Foundation website. http://bible.org/netbible/index.htm?textwelc.htm (accessed May 14, 2010).

New American Bible. Iowa Falls, Iowa: Catholic World Press/World Bible Publishers, 1990.

"New and Old Calvinism." *Methodist Magazine and Quarterly Review (1830–1840)* 13 (January 1831): 222–27.

The New Standard Dictionary of the English Language. (New York: Funk & Wagnalls, 1945).

Newquist, Jerreld L., comp. and ed. *Gospel Truth: Discourses and Writings of President George Q. Cannon*. 2 vols. Salt Lake City: Zion's Book Store, 1957.

Nibley, Hugh W. "On the Sacred and the Symbolic." In *Temples of the Ancient World: Ritual and Symbolism*. Edited by Donald W. Parry, 535–622. Salt Lake City: Deseret Book, 1994.

———. *Teachings of the Book of Mormon—Semester 1: Transcripts of Lectures Presented to an Honors Book of Mormon Class at Brigham Young University, 1988–1990*. Provo, Utah: Foundation for Ancient Research and Mormon Studies, 1993.

Nickelsburg, George W. E. *Resurrection, Immortality, and Eternal Life in Intertestamental Judaism and Early Christianity, Expanded Edition*. Cambridge, Eng.: Harvard University Press, 2006.

Niederhauser, Terry L. "Israel: The Gathering of Israel." In *Encyclopedia of Mormonism*. 4 vols., 2:709–11. New York: Macmillan Publishing, 1992.

Nielson, F. Kent, and Stephen D. Ricks. "Creation, Creation Accounts." In *Encyclopedia of Mormonism*, 4 vols., 1:340–43. New York: Macmillan Publishing, 1992.

Noll, Mark A. "The Enlightenment and Evangelical Intellectual Life in the Nineteenth Century." In *Ideas, Ideologies, and Social Movements: The United States Experience since 1800*. Edited by Peter A. Coclanis and Stuart Bruchey, 42–59. Columbia: University of South Carolina Press, 1999.

Norman, Keith E. "Deification: The Content of Athanasian Soteriology." *FARMS Occasional Papers* 1 (2000): 1–30.

———. "The Mark of the Curse: Lingering Racism in Mormon Doctrine." *Dialogue: A Journal of Mormon Thought* 32, no. 1 (Spring 1999): 119–36.

———. "Mormon Cosmology: Can It Survive the Big Bang?" *Sunstone* 10 (December 1985): 18–23.

Nyman, Monte S. "Hope, Faith, and Charity." In *Studies in Scriptures, Vol. 8: Alma 30 to Moroni*. Edited by Kent P. Jackson, 293–301. Salt Lake City: Deseret Book, 1988.

Nyman, Monte S., and Farres H. Nyman. *The Words of the Twelve Prophets: Messages to the Latter-day Saints*. Salt Lake City: Deseret Book, 1990.

O'Collins, Gerald. *Christology: A Biblical, Historical, and Systematic Study of Jesus*. New York: Oxford University Press, 1995.

O'Meara, Thomas F. "Christian Theology and Extraterrestrial Intelligent Life." *Theological Studies* 60 (March 1999): 3–30.

Oaks, Dallin H. "The Great Plan of Happiness." *Ensign*, November 1993, 72–76.

Ogden, D. Kelly. "The Book of Amos." In *Studies in Scripture, Vol. 4: 1 Kings to Malachi*. Edited by Kent P. Jackson, 52–60. Salt Lake City: Deseret Book , 1993.

Old Testament: Genesis–2 Samuel (Religion 301) Student Manual. 3rd ed. Salt Lake City: Church of Jesus Christ of Latter-day Saints, 1981.

Old Testament: Gospel Doctrine Teacher's Manual. Salt Lake City: Church of Jesus Christ of Latter-day Saints, 2001.

Olsen, Roger E. *Arminian Theology: Myths and Realities*. Downers Grove, Ill.: InterVarsity Press, 2006.

———. *The Story of Christian Theology*. Downers Grove, Ill.: InterVarsity Press, 1999.

Origen. *De Principiis*. Translated by Frederick Crombie. In *The Ante-Nicene Fathers. Translations of the Writings of the Fathers down to A.D. 325*. Edited by Alexander Roberts and James Donaldson. 10 vols., 4:239–384. Buffalo, N. Y.: The Christian Literature Publishing Company, 1885.

Ostler, Blake T. "The Book of Mormon as a Modern Expansion of an Ancient Source." *Dialogue: A Journal of Mormon Thought* 20 (Spring 1987): 66–123.

———. "Bridging the Gulf." *FARMS Review of Books* 11, no. 2 (1999): 103–77.

———. "Re-vision-ing the Mormon Concept of Deity." *Element: The Journal for the Society for Mormon Philosophy and Theology* 1, no. 1 (Spring 2005). Society for Mormon Philosophy and Theology. http://smpt.org/ docs/ostler_element1-1.html (accessed March 1, 2010).

———. *Exploring Mormon Thought: The Attributes of God*. Salt Lake City: Greg Kofford Books, 2001.

———. *Exploring Mormon Thought: The Problems of Theism and the Love of God*. Salt Lake City: Greg Kofford Books, 2006.

———. *Exploring Mormon Thought: Of God and Gods*. Salt Lake City: Greg Kofford Books, 2008.

Owens, Lance S. "Joseph Smith and Kabbalah: The Occult Connection." *Dialogue: A Journal of Mormon Thought* 27, no. 3 (Fall 1994): 117–94.
Packard, Sandra Bradford. "Animals." In *Encyclopedia of Mormonism*. 4 vols., 1:42–43. New York: Macmillan Publishing, 1992.
Packer, Boyd K. "Scriptures." *Ensign,* November 1982, 51–53.
———. "To Be Learned Is Good If . . . ." *Ensign,* November 1992, 71–73.
———. "The Twelve." *Ensign,* May 2008, 83–87.
Packer, Rand H. "Dispensation of the Fulness of Times." In *Encyclopedia of Mormonism*. 4 vols., 1:387–88. New York: Macmillan Publishing, 1992.
Pagels, Elaine. *Beyond Belief: The Secret Gospel of Thomas*. New York: Random House, 2003.
———. *The Origin of Satan*. New York: Vintage Books, 1996.
Paine, Thomas. *Age of Reason: In Two Parts*. New York: G. N. Devries, 1827.
Palmer, Grant H. *An Insider's View of Mormon Origins*. Salt Lake City: Signature Books, 2002.
Parrish, Alan K. "Seventy." In *Encyclopedia of Mormonism*. 4 vols., 3:1300–1303. New York: Macmillan Publishing, 1992.
Parry, Donald W., and Jay A. Parry, *Understanding the Signs of the Times*. Salt Lake City: Deseret Book, 1999.
Parry, Donald W., and Stephen C. Ricks. *The Dead Sea Scrolls: Questions and Responses for Latter-day Saints*. Provo, Utah: FARMS, 2000.
Paul, Erich Robert. *Science, Religion, and Mormon Cosmology*. Urbana: University of Illinois Press, 1992.
Paulsen, David L. "Joseph Smith and the Problem of Evil," *BYU Speeches,* September 21, 1999. http://speeches.byu.edu/reader/reader.php?id=1644 (accessed October 25, 2005).
———. "The Redemption of the Dead: A Latter-day Saint Perspective on the Fate of the Unevangelized." In *Salvation in Christ*. Edited by Roger R. Keller and Robert L. Millet, 263–97. Provo, Utah: BYU Religious Studies Center, 2005.
Perdue, Leo G. "Jeremiah." In *The HarperCollins Study Bible*. Edited by Wayne A. Meeks, 1110–1207. New York: HarperCollins, 1993.
"Perfection." *Latter Day Saints' Messenger and Advocate* 2 (May 1836): 310–12.
Peters, John L. *Christian Perfection & American Methodism*. Grand Rapids, Mich.: Francis Ashbury Press, 1985.
Peters, Ted. *Futures: Human and Divine*. Atlanta: John Knox Press, 1978.
———. *Science, Theology, and Ethics*. Burlington, Vt.: Ashgate Publishing Co., 2003.
Petersen, David L. "Ezekiel." In *The HarperCollins Study Bible*. Edited by Wayne A. Meeks, 1222–1301. New York: HarperCollins Publishers, 1993.
Peterson, Daniel C. "Nephi and His Asherah." *Journal of Book of Mormon Studies* 9, no. 2 (2000), 16–25.
———. "Ye Are Gods: Psalm 82 and John 10 as Witnesses to the Divine Nature of Humankind." In *The Disciple as Scholar: Essays on Scripture and the Ancient World in Honor of Richard Lloyd Anderson*. Edited by Stephen D. Ricks, Donald W. Parry, and Andrew H. Hedges, 471–594. Provo, Utah: FARMS, 2000.
Phelps, William W. "The Answer." *Times and Seasons* 5 (January 1, 1845): 757–61.
———. "Despise Not Prophesyings." *Times and Seasons* 2 (February 1, 1841): 297–99.
———. "The Indians." *Evening and Morning Star* 1 (December 1832): 54.
———. "Letter No. 11." *Latter Day Saints' Messenger and Advocate* 2 (October 1835): 193–95.
———. "The Ten Tribes." *Evening and Morning Star* 1 (October 1832): 33–34.

———. "To Oliver Cowdery, Esq." *Latter Day Saints' Messenger and Advocate* 1 (May 19, 1835): 114–15.

———. "A Voice from the Prophet: 'Come to Me.'" *Times and Seasons* 6 (January 15, 1845): 783.

Pike, Dana. "Is the Plan of Salvation Attested in the Dead Sea Scrolls?" In *LDS Perspectives on the Dead Sea Scrolls*. Edited by Donald W. Parry and Dana M. Pike, 73–94. Provo, Utah: FARMS, 1997.

Planet News. "A Discussion with Dr. James H. Charlesworth, George L. Collord Professor of New Testament Language and Literature at Princeton Theological Seminar." Quartz Hill School of Theology. http://www.theology.edu/revelation/revappen.htm (accessed May 17, 2005).

Pohle, Joseph. "Priesthood." In *The Catholic Encyclopedia*. Edited by Charles G. Herbermann et al. 15 vols., 4:409–20. New York: Universal Knowledge Foundation, Inc., 1913.

Poll, Richard D. "What the Church Means to People like Me." In *Faith and History: Reflections of a Mormon Historian*. Edited by Richard D. Poll, 1–13. Salt Lake City: Signature Books, 1989.

Pontifical Biblical Commission. "The Interpretation of the Bible in the Church." Presented to Pope John Paul II on April 23, 1993. Available on the Catholic Resources for Bible, Liturgy, Art, and Theology website. http://catholic-resources.org/ChurchDocs/PBC_Interp.htm (accessed May 14, 2010).

Pope, Marvin. *Job*. Anchor Bible. New York: Doubleday, 1979.

Porter, Larry. "Dating the Melchizedek Priesthood." *Ensign*, June 1979, 5–10.

Porter, Perry L. "Anson Call: Excerpts from His Autobiography." Mormon Church History. http://www.xmission.com/~plporter/lds/ansoncall.htm (accessed May 20, 2010).

Pratt, Orson. "Celestial Marriage." *The Seer* 1, no. 2 (February 1853): 25–32.

———. "The Fall and Atonement." *The Latter-day Saints' Millennial Star* 28 (September 22, 1866): 593–96.

———. *An Interesting Account of Several Remarkable Visions*. Edinburgh: Ballantyne and Hughes, 1840.

———. "The Pre-Existence of Man." *The Seer* 1, no. 4 (April 1853): 49–57.

———. "The Pre-Existence of Man." *The Seer* 1, no. 7 (July 1853): 97–104.

———. "The Pre-Existence of Man." *The Seer* 1, no. 9 (September 1853): 132–35.

———. *Prophetic Almanac for 1845*. New York: Prophet's Office, 1845.

———. "Questions for the Latter-day Saints. By the Rev. F. Austin, A Roman Catholic Minister." *The Latter-day Saints' Millennial Star* 11 (August 1, 1849): 234–39.

Pratt, Parley P. *An Answer to Mr. William Hewitt's Tract against the Latter-day Saints*. Manchester, Eng.: W. R. Thomas, 1840.

———. *An Appeal to the Inhabitants of the State of New York, Letter to Queen Victoria (Reprinted from the Tenth European Edition,) The Fountain of Knowledge; Immortality of the Body, and Intelligence and Affection*. Nauvoo, Ill: John Taylor, 1844.

———. *Autobiography of Parley P. Pratt*. Salt Lake City: Deseret Book Company, 1874.

———. "The Gospel Illustrated in Questions and Answers." *Latter-day Saints' Millennial Star* 1 (June 1840): 25–28.

———. *Key to the Science of Theology: Designed as an Introduction to the First Principles of Spiritual Philosophy, Religion, Law and Government, as Delivered by the Ancients, and as Restored in this Age, for the Final Development of Universal Peace, Truth, and Knowledge*. Liverpool, Eng.: F. D. Richards, 1855.

_____. *Mormonism Unveiled: Zion's Watchman Unmasked, and its Editor, Mr. L.R. Sunderland, Exposed: Truth Vindicated: the Devil Mad, and Priestcraft in Danger!* New York: 1838.

_____. "To the Editor of the Latter Day Saints Messenger and Advocate." *Latter Day Saints' Messenger and Advocate* 2 (May 1836): 317–18.

_____. "The True God and His Worship Contrasted with Idolatry." *Millennial Star* 2 (April 1842): 184–89.

_____. *Voice of Warning and Instruction to All People, Containing a Declaration of the Faith and Doctrine of the Church of the Latter Day Saints, Commonly Called Mormons.* Manchester, Eng.: 1837.

"Preamble." *Nauvoo Expositor* 1, no. 1 (June 7, 1844): 1–2.

Price, Robert M. "Joseph Smith: Inspired Author of the Book of Mormon." In *American Apocrypha: Essays on the Book of Mormon.* Edited by Dan Vogel and Brent Lee Metcalf, 321–366. Salt Lake City: Signature Books, 2002.

Priest, Josiah. *The Anti-Universalist: or Fallen Angels of the Scriptures; Proofs of the Being of Satan and of Evil Spirits.* Albany, N. Y.: J. Munsell, 1837.

_____. *A View of the Expected Christian Millennium.* 2d. ed. Albany, N. Y.: Loomis Press, 1827.

Priestly, Joseph. *Disquisitions Relating to Matter and Spirit.* London: J. Johnson, 1777.

Prince, Gregory A. *Power from On High: The Development of Mormon Priesthood.* Salt Lake City: Signature Books, 1995.

Quinn, D. Michael. *Early Mormonism and the Magic World View.* Rev. ed. Salt Lake City: Signature Books, 1998.

_____. *The Mormon Hierarchy: Origins of Power.* Salt Lake City: Signature Books, 1994.

Rad, Gerhard Von. *Old Testament Theology.* New York: Harper Brothers, 1962.

Ramm, Bernard. *Offense to Reason: A Theology of Sin.* Vancouver, B. C.: Regent College Publishing, 2000.

Raphael, Simcha Paull. *Jewish Views of the Afterlife.* 2nd ed. Lanham, Md.: Rowman & Littlefield, 2009.

Rasband, Ronald A. "'Moses, My Son.'" *Ensign,* January 2010, 42–45.

Rausch, Thomas P. *Who Is Jesus? An Introduction to Christology.* Collegeville, Minn.: Liturgical Press, 2003.

Rensberger, David K. "The First Letter of John." In *The HarperCollins Study Bible.* Edited by Wayne A. Meeks, 2292–99. New York: HarperCollins, 1993.

_____. "The Gospel According to John." In *The HarperCollins Study Bible.* Edited by Wayne A. Meeks, 2011–55. New York: HarperCollins, 1993.

"Review of New Publications." *The Christian Observer* 27 (January 1827): 29–51.

Reynolds, George, and Janne M. Sjodahl. *Commentary on the Pearl of Great Price.* Salt Lake City: Deseret Book, 1965.

Reynolds, Noel B. "The Case for Sidney Rigdon as Author of the Lectures on Faith." *Journal of Mormon History* 31 (Fall 2005): 1–41.

Rhodes, Michael D. "Teaching the Book of Abraham Facsimiles." *The Religious Educator: Perspectives on the Restored Gospel* 4, no. 2 (2003): 115–123.

Rhymer, David. "Between Text & Sermon: Jeremiah 31:31–34." *Interpretation* 59 (2005): 294–297.

Richards, Franklin D. "Happiness and Joy in the Temple." *Ensign,* November 1986, 70–71.

Richards, LeGrand. *A Marvelous Work and a Wonder.* Salt Lake City: Deseret Book, 1950.

Ridderbos, Herman N. *Paul: An Outline of His Theology.* Translated by John Richard De Witt. Grand Rapids, Mich.: Eerdmans Publishing Co., 1975.
Riskas, Thomas J., Jr. "New Heaven and New Earth." In *Encyclopedia of Mormonism,* 4 vols., 3:1009. New York: Macmillan Publishing, 1992.
Roberts, B. H. *A Comprehensive History of the Church of Jesus Christ of Latter-day Saints.* 6 vols. Salt Lake City: Deseret News Press, 1930.
_____. *Mormon Doctrine of Deity.* Salt Lake City: Horizon Books, 1982.
_____. *Outlines of Ecclesiastical History.* Salt Lake City: Deseret Book, 1927.
_____. "Seventies Council Table." *Improvement Era* 11 (May 1908): 558–59.
Roberts, J. J. M. *The Bible and the Ancient Near East.* Winona Lake, Ind.: Eisenbrauns, 2002.
_____. "Isaiah." In *The HarperCollins Study Bible.* Edited by Wayne A. Meeks, 1011–1109. New York: HarperCollins, 1993.
Robertson, A. T. *Word Pictures in the New Testament.* Nashville, Tenn.: Broadman Press, 1932. Available online at the StudyLight website. http://www.studylight.org/com/rwp/ (accessed May 14, 2010).
Robinson, H. Wheeler. *The Religious Ideas of the Old Testament.* New York: Charles Schribner's Sons, 1913.
Robinson, Parker Pratt, ed. *Writings of Parley P. Pratt.* Salt Lake City: Privately published, 1952.
Robinson, Stephen E. "The Expanded Book of Mormon?" In *Second Nephi: The Doctrinal Structure.* Edited by Monte S. Nyman and Charles D. Tate Jr., 391–414. Salt Lake City: Greg Kofford Books, 2007.
Rollman, Hans. "In Essentials Unity: The Pre-history of a Restoration Movement Slogan." *Restoration Quarterly* 38, no. 3 (1997). Restoration Quarterly website. http://www.acu.edu/sponsored/restoration_quarterly/archives/1990s/vol_39_no_3_contents/ rollmann.html (accessed May 19, 2010).
Romney, Marion G. *Look to God and Live.* Salt Lake City: Deseret Book, 1971.
_____. "Records of Great Worth." *Ensign,* September 1980, 3–8.
_____. "Why the Church of Jesus Christ of Latter-day Saints." *Ensign,* January 1973, 30–33.
Romney, Richard M. "Spiritual Death." In *Encyclopedia of Mormonism.* 4 vols., 3:1407–8. New York: Macmillan Publishing, 1992.
Rose, H. J. *A Handbook of Greek Mythology,* 6th ed. London: Taylor and Francis, 1958.
Rosenberg, Joel W. "Genesis." In *The HarperCollins Study Bible.* Edited by Wayne A. Meeks, 3–76. New York: HarperCollins, 1993.
Salmon, Douglas F. "Parallelomania and the Study of Latter-day Scripture: Confirmation, Coincidence, or the Collective Unconscious?" *Dialogue: A Journal of Mormon History* 33, no. 2 (Summer 2000): 129–56.
Sandberg, Karl C. "Knowing Brother Joseph Again: The Book of Abraham and Joseph Smith as Translator." *Dialogue: A Journal of Mormon Thought* 22 (Winter 1989): 17–38.
Sanders, G. "Cosmology." In *Catholic Encyclopedia.* Edited by Thomas Carson and Joann Cerrito, 2d ed., 15 vols, 4:283–84. Detroit: Gale, 2003.
Sanders, Jack T. "Whence the First Millennium? The Sources behind Revelation 20." *New Testament Studies* 50 (July 2004): 444–56.
Sanders, James A. "From Isaiah 61 to Luke 4." In *Luke and Scripture: The Function of Sacred Traditions in Luke–Acts.* Edited by James A. Sanders and Craig Evans, 46–59. Minneapolis: Fortress Press, 1993.
Sanders, John P. *No Other Name: An Investigation into the Destiny of the Unevangelized.* Grand Rapids, Mich.: Eerdmans Publishing Co., 1992.

———. "Those Who Have Never Heard: A Survey of the Major Positions." In *Salvation in Christ*. Edited by Roger R. Keller and Robert L. Millet, 299–325. Provo, Utah: BYU Religious Studies Center, 2005.

Sandoz, Ellis. *Political Sermons of the American Founding Era: 1730–1805*. 2 vols. Indianapolis: Liberty Fund, 1998.

Sawyer, John. *The Fifth Gospel: Isaiah in the History of Christianity*. Cambridge, Eng.: Cambridge University Press, 1996.

Scannell, T. B. "Confirmation." In *The Catholic Encyclopedia*. Edited by Charles G. Herbermann et al. 15 vols., 4:215–22. New York: Universal Knowledge Foundation, Inc., 1913.

Schaff, Philip. *The Creeds of the Evangelical Protestant Churches*. London: Hodder and Stoughton, 1877.

———. *History of the Christian Church*. 8 vols. Grand Rapids, Mich.: Eerdmans Publishing Co., 1979.

Scharffs, Gilbert W. "Apostate." In *Encyclopedia of Mormonism*. 4 vols., 1:59. New York: Macmillan Publishing, 1992.

Schibler, Daniel. "Isaiah 1–12 and 28–33." In *The Lord's Anointed: Interpretation of Old Testament Messianic Texts*. Edited by Philip E. Satterthwaite, Richard S. Hess, and Gordon J. Wenham, 87–104. Grand Rapids, Mich.: Baker Publishing Group, 1995.

Schindler, Marc. "Deutero-Isaiah in the Book of Mormon?" The Foundation for Apologetic Information and Research (FAIR). http://www.fairlds.org/Book_of_Mormon/Deutero-Isaiah_in_the_Book_of_Mormon.html (accessed September 15, 2007).

Schreiner, Thomas. "Head Coverings, Prophecies, and the Trinity." In *Recovering Biblical Manhood and Womanhood*. Edited by W. Grudem and J. Piper. Westchester, Ill.: Crossway, 1991.

Seely, Paul H. "The Firmament and the Water Above." *The Westminster Theological Journal* 53 (1991): 227–40.

Seitz, Christopher R. *Isaiah 1–39*. Louisville, Ky.: Westminster/John Knox, 1993.

"Selected." *Evening and the Morning Star* 1, no. 1 (June 1832): 3.

"Sermon on 1 Corinthians 15:41–42." *Churchman's Magazine* 4 (July 1825): 83–84, 101–6.

Sewall, Samuel. *Phaenomena quaedam Apocalyptica ad aspectum Novi Orbis configurata. Or, some few lines towards a description of the New Heaven*. Boston: Bartholomew Green and John Allen, 1697.

Shand, Mark L. "A Presbyterian View of Covenant Children." *Protestant Reformed Theological Journal* 38, no. 1 (November 2004):70–95.

Shapiro, R. Gary. "Book Review of *Mormonism and Evolution: The Authoritative Statements* by William E. Evenson and Duane E. Jeffery." No Death Before the Fall. http://ndbf.net/review.htm (accessed June 15, 2007).

Sheets, Kerry A. "The 'Adat El, 'Council of the Gods' and Bene Elohim, 'Sons of God': Ancient Near Eastern Concepts in the Book of Abraham." Mormonism Researched, http://www2.ida.net/graphics/shirtail/council.htm (accessed January 25, 2005).

Sheler, Jeffery L. "Faith in America." *U.S. News & World Report*, May 6, 2002, 40–44, 46, 48–49.

Shepherd, David J. *Village Enlightenment in America: Popular Religion and Science in the Nineteenth Century*. Urbana: University of Illinois Press, 2000.

Sherlock, Richard. "'We Can See No Advantage to a Continuation of the Discussion': The Roberts/Smith/Talmage Affair." *Dialogue: A Journal of Mormon Thought* 13 (Fall 1980): 63–78.

Sherry, Thomas E., and Jeffrey Marsh. "Precious Truths Restored: Joseph Smith Translation Changes Not Included in Our Bible." *The Religious Educator: Perspectives on the Restored Gospel* 5, no. 2 (2004): 57–75.

Shillitoe, Thomas. *An Address to Friends in Great Britain and Ireland.* London: Harvey and Darton, 1823.

Shipps, Jan. *Mormonism: The Story of a New Religious Tradition.* Urbana: University of Illinois Press, 1987.

———. *Sojourner in the Promised Land: Forty Years among the Mormons.* Urbana: University of Illinois Press, 2000.

Simmons, Menno. *Complete Writings.* Edited by John C. Wenger. Scottdale, Penn.: Herald Press, 1956.

Skinner, Andrew C. "Birth of Jesus Christ." In *Encyclopedia of Mormonism.* 4 vols., 2:729. New York: Macmillan Publishing, 1992.

Skousen, Royal. "Textual Variants in the Isaiah Quotations in the Book of Mormon." In *Isaiah in the Book of Mormon.* Edited by Donald W. Parry and John W. Welch, 369–90. Provo, Utah: FARMS, 1998.

Smail, Dan. "In the Grip of Sacred History." *The American Historical Review* 110 (December 2005): 1337–61.

Smart, William B. *Messages for a Happier Life: Inspiring Essays from the Church News.* Salt Lake City: Deseret Book, 1989.

Smith, Brian L. "Ephraim." In *Encyclopedia of Mormonism.* 4 vols., 2:461. New York: Macmillan Publishing, 1992.

Smith, Cynthia Ann Miller. "Shadows of Things to Come: The Theological Implications of Intelligent Life on Other Worlds." M.A. thesis, Georgia State University, 2004. Reprint available on author's website. http://www.roman-catholic.org/th.html (accessed July 23, 2005).

Smith, Ethan. *Dissertation on the Prophecies Relative to AntiChrist and the Last Times; Exhibiting the Rise, Character, and Overthrow of That Terrible Power; and a Treatise of the Seven Apocalyptic Vials.* Charleston, Mass.: Samuel T. Armstrong, 1811.

———. *A Key to the Figurative Language Found in the Scriptures.* Exeter, N. H.: C. Norris & Co., 1814.

———. *View of the Hebrews: 1825 Second Edition Complete Text.* Edited by Charles D. Tate Jr. Provo, Utah: BYU Religious Studies Center, 1996.

———. *View of the Trinity: A Treatise on the Character of Jesus Christ, and on the Trinity in Unity of the Godhead, with Quotations from the Primitive Fathers.* 2d ed. Poultney, Vt.: Smith & Shute, 1824.

Smith, George Albert. "Dedicatory Prayer for the Idaho Falls Temple." *Improvement Era,* October 1945, 562–65.

Smith, Joseph, Jr. [no title]. *Elders Journal* 1 (July 1838): 42–44.

———. "The Answer." *Times and Seasons* 4 (February 1, 1843): 82–85.

———. "Baptism for the Dead." *Times and Seasons* 3 (April 15, 1842): 759–61.

———. "Baptism." *Times and Seasons* 3 (September 1, 1842): 903–05.

———. "Church History." *Times and Seasons* 3 (March 1, 1842): 706–10.

———. "Present Age of the World." *Evening and the Morning Star 1* (August 1832): 21–22.

———. "The Elders of the Church in Kirtland, to their Brethren Abroad." *Evening and Morning Star* 2 (March 1834): 143.

———. "To the Elders of the Church of the Latter Day Saints." *Latter Day Saints' Messenger and Advocate* 2 (November 1835): 209–12.

———. "To the Elders of the Church of the Latter Day Saints." *Latter Day Saints' Messenger and Advocate* 3 (December 1835): 225–30.

———. "To the Saints Scattered Abroad." *Latter Day Saints' Messenger and Advocate* 1 (June 1835): 137–38.

———. "Try the Spirits." *Times and Seasons* 3. no. 11 (April 1, 1842): 743–48.

Smith, Joseph Jr., et al. *History of the Church of Jesus Christ of Latter-day Saints*, edited by B. H. Roberts, 2d ed. rev. 6 vols., 1902–12, Vol. 7, 1932; rpt., Salt Lake City: Deseret Book, 1980 printing.

Smith, Joseph F. *Gospel Doctrine: Selections from the Sermons and Writings of Joseph F. Smith.* Edited by John A. Widtsoe. 5th ed. Salt Lake City: Deseret Book, 1939.

Smith, Joseph F., John R. Winder, and Anthon H. Lund. "The Origin of Man." *Improvement Era* 13 (November 1909): 75–18.

Smith, Joseph Fielding. *Answers to Gospel Questions.* 5 vols. Salt Lake City: Deseret Book, 1957–66.

———. *Church History and Modern Revelation.* 2 vols. Salt Lake City: Deseret Book, 1953.

———. *Doctrines of Salvation: Compiled Sermons of Joseph Fielding Smith.* Compiled by Bruce R. McConkie. 3 vols. Salt Lake City: Bookcraft, 1954–56.

———. *Elijah the Prophet and His Mission.* Salt Lake City: Deseret Book, 1957.

———. Letter to Thales A. Derrick, September 25, 1961.

———. *Life of Joseph F. Smith.* Salt Lake City: Deseret News Press, 1938.

———. *Man: His Origin and Destiny.* Salt Lake City: Deseret Book, 1954.

———. "The Most Important Knowledge." *Ensign,* May 1971, 2–3.

———. *The Progress of Man.* Salt Lake City: Deseret Book, 1964.

———. *The Restoration of All Things.* Salt Lake City: Deseret Book, 1973.

———. *Signs of the Times.* Salt Lake City: Deseret Book, 1952.

———. *Take Heed to Yourselves.* Salt Lake City: Deseret Book 1966.

———., comp. and ed. *Teachings of the Prophet Joseph Smith.* Salt Lake City: Deseret Book, 1976.

———. *The Way to Perfection.* Salt Lake City: Deseret Book, 1935.

Smith, Joseph Fielding, Jr., and John J. Stewart. *The Life of Joseph Fielding Smith.* Salt Lake City: Deseret Book, 1972.

Smith, Mark S. *The Early History of God: Yahweh and the Other Deities in Ancient Israel.* 2d ed. Grand Rapids, Mich.: Eerdmans Publishing, 2002.

———. *The Origins of Biblical Monotheism: Israel's Polytheistic Background and the Ugaritic Texts.* New York: Oxford University Press, 2000.

Snow, Eliza R. *Biography and Family Record of Lorenzo Snow.* Salt Lake City: Deseret News, 1884.

———. "My Father in Heaven." *Times and Seasons* 6 (November 15, 1845): 1039.

Snow, Erastus E. *E. Snow's reply to the Self-Styled Philanthropist, of Chester County.* Philadelphia: N. pub. 1840.

Snow, LeRoi C. "Devotion to a Divine Inspiration." *Improvement Era* 22 (June 1919): 653–63.

Snow, Lowell M. "Blood Atonement." In *Encyclopedia of Mormonism.* 4 vols., 1:131. New York: Macmillan Publishing, 1992.

Snow, R. J. "Natural Man,"In *Encyclopedia of Mormonism.* 4 vols., 3:985. New York: Macmillan Publishing, 1992.

Sorensen, A. D. "Zion." In *Encyclopedia of Mormonism.* 4 vols., 4:1624–26. New York: Macmillan Publishing, 1992.

Sperry, Sidney B. *Book of Mormon Compendium.* Salt Lake City: Bookcraft, 1968.

Sproul, R. C. *The Last Days According to Jesus.* Grand Rapids, Mich.: Baker House Books, 1998.

Spurgeon, Charles H. *Sermons of C. H. Spurgeon of London*. New York: Sheldon, Blakeman, and Company, 1857.

Stack, Peggy Fletcher. "Single Word Change in Book of Mormon Speaks Volumes." *Salt Lake Tribune*, November 8, 2007. Online copy available on Free Republic website. http://www.freerepublic.com/focus/f-religion/1923110/posts (accessed June 24, 2010).

Staker, Mark Lyman. *Hearken, O Ye People: The Historical Setting for Joseph Smith's Ohio Revelations*. Salt Lake City: Greg Kofford Books, 2009.

Stammer, Larry B. "Mormons May Disavow Old Views on Blacks." *Los Angeles Times,* May 18, 1998, A-1.

Standish, David. *Hollow Earth: The Long and Curious History of Imagining Strange Lands, Fantastical Creatures, Advanced Civilizations, and Marvelous Machines Below the Earth's Surface*. Cambridge, Mass.: De Capo Press, 2006.

Stendahl, Krister. "Baptism for the Dead, Ancient Sources." In *Encyclopedia of Mormonism*, 4 vols., 1:97. New York: Macmillan Publishing, 1992.

Stevenson, Joseph Grant. *Stevenson Family History*. Provo, Utah: Stevenson Publishing Co., 1955.

Stricker, Barry. "Anthropology." *Holman Bible Dictionary*. Nashville, Tenn.: Holman Bible Publishers, 1991.

Stutz, Howard C. *"Let the Earth Bring Forth": Evolution and Scripture*. Salt Lake City: Greg Kofford Books, 2010.

Stuy, Brian H., ed. *Collected Discourses Delivered by President Wilford Woodruff, His Two Counselors, The Twelve Apostles, and Others*. 5 vols. Woodland Hills, Utah.: B.H.S. Publishing, 1987–92.

Swanson, Vern G. "The Development of the Concept of a Holy Ghost in Mormon Theology." In *Line upon Line: Essays on Mormon Doctrine*. Edited by Gary James Bergera, 89–101. Salt Lake City: Signature Books, 1989.

Swedenborg, Emanuel. *Delights of Wisdom Concerning Conjugial [sic] Love; After Which Follow: Pleasures of Insanity Concerning Scortatory Love*. Boston: John Allen, 1833.

_____. *The True Christian Religion: Containing the Universal Theology of the New Church Foretold by the Lord in Daniel VII:13–14; and in Revelation XXI:1–2*. Boston: Otis Clapp, 1851.

Swinton, Heidi S. *In the Company of Prophets*. Salt Lake City: Deseret Book, 1993.

Tabor, James D. "The Future." In *What the Bible Really Says*. Edited by Morton Smith and R. Joseph Hoffman. Buffalo, N.Y.: Prometheus Books, 1989.

_____. "The Message and Mission of Paul." University of North Carolina Charlotte, The Jewish Roman World of Jesus. http://www.religiousstudies.uncc.edu/jdtabor/paul.html (accessed January 25, 2005).

_____. "The Signs of the Messiah: 4Q521." University of North Carolina Charlotte. The Jewish Roman World of Jesus. http://www.religiousstudies.uncc.edu/jdtabor/ 4q521.html (October 25, 2005).

_____. "What the Bible Says about Death, Afterlife, and the Future." University of North Carolina Charlotte, The Jewish Roman World of Jesus. http://www.religiousstudies.uncc.edu/jdtabor/future.html (accessed November 29, 2004).

_____. "Why 2K?" *Bible Review* 15 (December 1999): 16–27.

Talmage, James E. *Articles of Faith*. 1899. Rpt., Salt Lake City: Church of Jesus Christ of Latter-day Saints, 1981.

_____. *The Great Apostasy*. Salt Lake City: Deseret Book, 1909.

_____. *The House of the Lord*. 1912. Rpt., Salt Lake City: Deseret Book, 1968.

———. *Jesus the Christ: A Study of the Messiah and His Mission According to Holy Scriptures Both Ancient and Modern.* Salt Lake City: Deseret News, 1915.
———. *The Vitality of Mormonism.* Boston: Gorham Press, 1919.
Tanner, Jerald, and Sandra Tanner. "Covering Up Mormon Polygamy." *Salt Lake City Messenger*, no. 94 (August 1998). Utah Lighthouse Ministry. http://www.utlm.org/newsletters/no94.htm#COVERING UP MORMON POLYGAMY (accessed May 17, 2010).
———. "Excommunication." *Salt Lake City Messenger*, no. 73 (October 1989). Utah Lighthouse Ministry. http://www.utlm.org/newsletters/no73.htm (accessed September 23, 2006).
Tanner, Martin S. "Is There Anti-Universalist Rhetoric in the Book of Mormon?" *FARMS Review* 6, no. 1 (1994): 21–52.
Tate, George S. "Prayer Circles." In *Encyclopedia of Mormonism.* 4 vols., 3:1120–21. New York: Macmillan Publishing, 1992.
Taylor, John. *The Government of God.* Liverpool: S. W. Richards, 1852.
———. *The Mediation and Atonement.* Salt Lake City: Deseret Book, 1882.
———. "Reflections." *Times and Seasons* 5 (September 2, 1844): 633–35.
Taylor, Nathaniel W. *Essays, Lectures, Etc. upon Selected Topics in Revealed Theology* (1850). Edited by Bruce Kuklick. New York: Garland Publishing, 1987.
Taylor, Thomas. *The Six Books of Proclus: The Platonic Successor, on the Theology of Plato.* 2 vols. London: A. J. Valpy, 1816.
"The Ten Tribes." *Evening and the Morning Star* 1 (October 1832): 33–34.
Thayer, Joseph Henry. *A Greek-English Lexicon of the New Testament.* New York: American Book, 1889.
Thayer, Thomas B. *The Origin and History of the Doctrine of Endless Punishment.* Boston, Mass.: James M. Usher, 1858.
Theissen, Gerd. *A Theory of Primitive Christian Religion.* London: Eng.: SCM Press, 1999.
Theophilus. "On the Value of the Soul." *Christian Magazine* 1 (April 1824): 107–11.
Thiselton, Anthony C. *The First Epistle to the Corinthians.* Grand Rapids, Mich.: Eerdmans Publishing Co., 2000.
Thomas, M. Catherine. "Hell." In *Encyclopedia of Mormonism.* 4 vols., 2:585–86. New York: Macmillan Publishing, 1992.
———. "Paradise." In *Encyclopedia of Mormonism.* 4 vols., 3:1062–63. New York: Macmillan Publishing, 1992.
Thomas, Mark D. *Digging in Cumorah: Reclaiming Book of Mormon Narratives.* Salt Lake City: Signature Books, 1999.
———. "Listening to the Voice from the Dust: Moroni 8 as Rhetoric." *Sunstone* 4 (January–February 1979): 22–24.
———. "A Mosaic for a Religious Counterculture: The Bible in the Book of Mormon." *Dialogue: A Journal of Mormon Thought* 25 (Winter 1996): 47–68.
Thompson, Stephen E. "Messiah in Context." *Sunstone*, no. 94 (February 1994): 75–76.
Thomson, Linda. "Church Not against a Firing Squad Ban." *Deseret Morning News*, September 4, 2003. http://deseretnews.com/dn/view/0,1249,510051735,00.html (accessed October 16, 2006).
"Thoughts on 1 Peter 3:19." *Methodist Magazine* 2 (October 1819): 375–80.
"To the Church of Christ Abroad in the Earth." *Evening and the Morning Star* 1, no. 1 (June 1832): 6.
Todd, Dennis. "Doctrinal Classifications and Color Key." The Preterist Archive.

http:// www.preteristarchive.com/Administrative/index.html (accessed May 18, 2010).
Tommaso, Lorenzo Di. *The Book of Daniel and the Apocryphal Daniel Literature.* Leiden, Holland: Brill, 2005.
Top, Brent L. *The Life Before.* Salt Lake City: Bookcraft, 1988.
_____. "War in Heaven." In *Encyclopedia of Mormonism.* 4 vols., 4:1546–47. New York: Macmillan Publishing, 1992.
Topel, John. "What Kind of Sign Are Vultures? Luke 17, 37b." *Biblica* 84, no. 3 (2003): 403–11.
Torrey, Charles C. "Apocalypse." In *The Jewish Encyclopedia.*12 vols. 1:669–75. New York: Funk and Wagnalls, 1901–06.
Tov, Emanuel. *Textual Criticism of the Hebrew Bible.* Minneapolis, Minn.: Fortress Press, 1992.
Towner, W. Sibley. "Malachi." In *The HarperCollins Study Bible.* Edited by Wayne A. Meeks, 1428–32. New York: HarperCollins, 1993.
_____. "Zechariah." In *The HarperCollins Study Bible.* Edited by Wayne A. Meeks, 1412–27. New York: HarperCollins, 1993.
Trumbower, Richard. *Rescue for the Dead.* Oxford, Eng.: Oxford University Press, 2001.
Turner, Rodney. "The Doctrine of the Firstborn and Only Begotten." In *The Pearl of Great Price: Revelations from God.* Edited by H. Donl Peterson and Charles D. Tate Jr., 91–119. Provo, Utah: BYU Religious Studies Center, 1989.
_____. "Sons of Perdition." In *Encyclopedia of Mormonism.* 4 vols., 3:1391–92. New York: Macmillan Publishing, 1992.
_____. "Two Prophets: Abinadi and Alma." In *Studies in Scripture, Vol. 7: 1 Nephi to Alma 29.* Edited by Kent P. Jackson, 240–58. Salt Lake City: Deseret Book, 1987.
_____. "Unpardonable Sin." In *Encyclopedia of Mormonism.* 4 vols., 4:1499. New York: Macmillan Publishing, 1992.
Tvedtnes, John A. *The Church of the Old Testament.* Salt Lake City: Deseret Book, 1980.
_____. "Early Christian and Jewish Rituals Related to Temple Practices." Presented at the Foundation for Apologetic Information & Research (FAIR) 1999 conference. Available on the FAIR website. http://www.fairlds.org/pubs/conf/1999TveJ.html (accessed July 23, 2005).
_____. "Knowledge of Christ to Come." *Journal of Book of Mormon Studies* 5, no. 1 (Spring 1996): 159–61.
_____. "A Much Needed Book that Needs Much." *FARMS Review of Books* 9, no. 1 (1997): 33–42.
_____. "Review of Michael T. Griffith, *One Lord, One Faith: Writings of the Early Christian Fathers as Evidences of the Restoration.*" *FARMS Review of Books* 9, no. 1 (1997): 33–42.
Underwood, Grant. "Attempting to Situate Joseph Smith." *BYU Studies* 44, no. 4. Special Issue — The Worlds of Joseph Smith (2005): 41–52.
_____. "A 'Communities of Discourse' Approach to Early LDS Thought." In *Discourses in Mormon Theology: Philosophical and Theological Possibilities.* Edited by James M. McLachlan and Loyd Ericson, 27–38. Salt Lake City: Greg Kofford Books, 2007.
_____. *The Millenarian World of Early Mormonism.* Urbana: University of Illinois Press, 1993.

———. "Revelation, Text, and Revision: Insights from the Book of Commandments and Revelations." *BYU Studies* 48, no. 3 (2009): 67–84.

———. "Saved or Damned: Tracing a Persistent Protestantism in Early Mormon Thought." *BYU Studies* 25 (Summer 1985): 85–103.

The Universalist Register: Containing the Statistics of the Church, with an Almanac for 1874. Boston: Universalist Publishing House, 1874.

Van Orden, Bruce A. "Redeeming the Dead As Taught in the Old Testament." In *Witness of Jesus Christ: The 1989 Sperry Symposium on the Old Testament*. Edited by Richard D. Draper, 261–69. Salt Lake City: Deseret Book, 1990.

Van Wagoner, Richard S., Steve C. Walker, and Allen D. Roberts. "The 'Lectures on Faith': A Case Study in Decanonization." *Dialogue: A Journal of Mormon Thought* 20 (Fall 1987): 71–77.

Vermes, Geza. *The Resurrection*. London: Penguin Books, 2006.

Vine, W. E. *Vine's Expository Dictionary of Old and New Testament Words*. Edited by F. F. Bruce, 5 vols. Grand Rapids, Mich.: Fleming H. Revell, 1981.

"A Visit to Joe Smith." *Times and Seasons* 3 (September 15, 1842): 926.

Vlach, Michael J. "What Is Dispensationalism?" TheologicalStudies.org. http://www.theologicalstudies.org/dispen.html (accessed April 28, 2006).

Vogel, Dan. "Anti-Universalist Rhetoric in the Book of Mormon." In *New Approaches to the Book of Mormon: Explorations in Critical Methodology*. Edited by Brent Lee Metcalfe, 21–52. Salt Lake City: Signature Books, 1993.

———. "The Earliest Mormon Concept of God." In *Line upon Line: Essays in Mormon Doctrine*. Edited by Gary J. Bergera, 17–33. Salt Lake City: Signature Books, 1989.

———, comp. and ed. *Early Mormon Documents*. 5 vols. Salt Lake City: Signature Books, 1996–2003.

———. *Indian Origins and the Book of Mormon*. Salt Lake City: Signature Books, 1986.

———. *Joseph Smith: The Making of a Prophet*. Salt Lake City: Signature Books, 2004.

———. "'The Prophet Puzzle' Revisited." In *The Prophet Puzzle: Interpretive Essays on Joseph Smith*. Edited by Bryan Waterman, 49–68. Salt Lake City: Signature Books, 1999.

Walker, Steven C. "Mankind." In *Encyclopedia of Mormonism*, 4 vols., 2:853–54. New York: Macmillan Publishing, 1992.

Wallace, Daniel B. "New Testament Eschatology in Light of Progressive Revelation." Biblical Studies Foundation. http://www.bible.org/page.asp?page_id=404 (accessed February 10, 2006).

———. "The Translation of 2 Peter 1:19a." February 28, 2004. Biblical Studies Foundation. http://www.bible.org/page.asp?page_id=3 (accessed August 22, 2006).

Wallace, Howard. "Leviathan and the Beast in Revelation." *Bible Archeaologist* 11, no. 3 (1948): 61–68.

Walton, Michael T. "Professor Seixas, the Hebrew Bible, and the Book of Abraham." *Sunstone* 6 (March–April 1981): 41–43.

Ward, James M. *Thus Says the Lord: The Message of the Prophets*. Nashville, Tenn.: Abingdon Press, 1991.

Ward, Roy B. "The Restoration Principle: A Critical Analysis." *Restoration Quarterly* 8, no. 4 (Fall 1965): 197–210.

Ward, Thomas. "General Conference." *Millennial Star* 4 (July 1843): 33–36.

Warfield, Benjamin. "The Divine and Human in the Bible." In *The Princeton*

Theology. Edited by Mark A. Noll, 268–88. Grand Rapids, Mich.: Baker Publishing Group, 2001.

Warner, C. Terry. "Agency." In *Encyclopedia of Mormonism*. 4 vols., 1:26–27. New York: Macmillan Publishing, 1992.

Watson, Elden J. "Different Thoughts - #7: Adam-God." May 2002. Elden Watson's website. http://www.eldenwatson.net/7AdamGod.htm (accessed May 15, 2010).

———. "The 'Prognostication' of Asa Wild." *BYU Studies* 37, no. 3 (1998): 223–30.

Watson, Richard. *Theological Institutes; or A View of the Evidences, Doctrines, Morals and Institutions of Christianity*. 2 vols. New York: T. Mason and G. Lane, 1836.

———. *The Works of the Rev. Richard Watson*. 12 vols. London: John Mason, 1834–37.

Wayment, Thomas A. *To Teach as Jesus Taught: 11 Attributes of a Master Teacher*. Springville, Utah: Cedar Fort, 2009.

Welch, John W. "Isaiah 53, Mosiah 14, and the Book of Mormon." In *Isaiah in the Book of Mormon*. Edited by Donald W. Parry and John W. Welch, 293–312. Provo, Utah: FARMS, 1999.

———. "Modern Revelation: A Guide to Research about the Apostasy." In *Early Christians in Disarray: Contemporary LDS Perspectives on the Christian Apostasy*. Edited by Noel B. Reynolds, 109–27. Provo, Utah: FARMS and BYU Press.

———. *The Sermon at the Temple and the Sermon on the Mount: A Latter-day Saint Approach*. Salt Lake City: Deseret Book and FARMS, 1990.

———. *The Worlds of Joseph Smith: A Bicentennial Conference at the Library of Congress*. Provo, Utah: Brigham Young University Press, 2006.

Wesley, John. "John Wesley's Notes on the Bible." Wesley Center for Applied Theology. http://wesley.nnu.edu/john_wesley/notes/ (accessed May 14, 2010).

———. *Sermons on Several Occasions*. 2 vols. New York: B. Waugh and T. Mason, 1836.

"Westminster Confession of Faith." Center for Reformed Theology and Apologetics. http://www.reformed.org/documents/wcf_with_proofs/ (accessed May 14, 2010).

"What Is Truth?" *The Candid Examiner* 2 (November 6, 1826): 86–87.

White, L. Michael. "The AntiChrist: A Historical Puzzle." In *Apocalypse!* Frontline. http://www.pbs.org/wgbh/pages/frontline/shows/apocalypse/antichrist/white.html, (accessed November 27, 2004).

———. "The Political History of the Jewish People." In *Apocalypse!* Frontline. http://www.pbs.org/wgbh/pages/frontline/shows/apocalypse/explanation/jews.html (accessed October 8, 2006).

———. "Prophetic Belief in the United States." In *Apocalyse!* Frontline. http://www.pbs.org/wgbh/pages/frontline/shows/apocalypse/explanation/amprophesy.html (accessed July 23, 2005).

White, O. Kendall, Jr., *Mormon Neo-orthodoxy: A Crisis Theology*. Salt Lake City: Signature Books, 1987.

Whitefield, George. *The Works of the Reverend George Whitefield, M.A.* Vol. 6. London: 1772.

Whitmer, David. *An Address to All Believers in Christ*. Richmond, Mo.: 1887.

Whitney, Orson F. *Gospel Themes*. Salt Lake City: N.p, 1914.

———. "Stay Where You Are!" *Millennial Star* 83 (September 15, 1921): 585.

Widmer, Kurt. *Mormonism and the Nature of God: A Theological Evolution, 1830–1915*. Jefferson, N. C.: McFarland, 2000.

Widstoe, John A. *Priesthood and Church Government*. Salt Lake City: Deseret Book, 1939.

Wilkinson, Bruce. *A Life God Rewards: Why Everything You Do Today Matters Forever*. Sisters, Ore.: Multnomah Publishers, 2002.

Williams, Clyde J. "The JST and the New Testament Epistles." In *Joseph Smith Translation: The Restoration of Plain and Precious Things*. Edited by Monte S. Nyman and Robert L. Millet, 215–34. Provo, Utah: BYU Religious Studies Center, 1985.

Williams, Roger. *George Fox Digg'd out of His Burrowes*. Boston, 1676.

_____. *The Hireling Ministry None of Christ's*. London, 1652.

Winchester, Benjamin. "The Divinity of Christ—The Object of His Mission—The Kingdom of God, or Church Militant, and the Gospel." *Gospel Reflector* 1 (January 1841): 32–42.

_____. "The Millennium." *Gospel Reflector* 1 (May 1841): 246–48.

Winchester, Elhanan. *A Course of Lectures on the Prophecies*. 2 vols. Walpole, N. H.: Carlisle, 1800.

Wood, Gordon S. "Evangelical America and Early Mormonism." *New York History* 61, no. 4 (1980): 359–86.

Wood, Leon James. *The Bible & Future Events: An Introductory Survey of Last-day Events*. Grand Rapids, Mich.: Zondervan, 1973.

Woodruff, Wilford. *Wilford Woodruff's Journal, 1833–1898*. Typescript, 9 vols., edited by Scott G. Kenney. Midvale, Utah: Signature Books, 1983–84.

Worcester, Noah. *Bible News, or Sacred Truths Relating to the Living God, His Only Son, and Holy Spirit*, 2d ed. Boston: Bradford and Read, 1812.

"The Work of the Lord in the Last Days." *Latter-day Saints' Millennial Star* 3 (February 1843):169–72.

Wray, T. J., and Gregory Mobley. *The Birth of Satan: Tracing the Devil's Biblical Roots*. New York: Palgrave Macmillan Publishing, 2005.

Wright, David P. "Historical Criticism: A Necessary Element in the Search for Religious Truth." *Sunstone* 16 (September 1992): 28–38.

_____. "Joseph Smith's Interpretation of Isaiah in the Book of Mormon." *Dialogue: A Journal of Mormon Thought* 31 (Winter 1998): 181–206.

_____. "Sex and Death in the Garden of Eden." *Sunstone* 12, no. 2 (June 1998): 33–39.

Wright, G. Ernest. *The Old Testament against Its Environment*. Chicago: H. Regnery, 1962.

Wright, Nicholas Thomas. *Jesus and the Victory of God*. Minneapolis, Minn.: Fortress Press, 1996.

Wright, Richard. *The Anti-satisfactionist: or, the Salvation of Sinners by the Free Grace of God*. Liverpool, Eng.: F. B. Wright, 1805.

Young, Brigham. *The Essential Brigham Young*. Edited by Eugene E. Campbell. Salt Lake City, Signature Books, 1992.

_____. "Hearken, O Ye Latter-day Saints." August 23, 1865. In *Messages of the First Presidency of the Church of Jesus Christ of Latter-day Saints, 1833–1964*. Compiled by James R. Clark. 6 vols., 2:229–35. Salt Lake City: Bookcraft, 1965.

_____. "Speech." *Times and Seasons* 6 (July 1, 1845): 953–57.

Young, Brigham, and Willard Richards. "Election and Reprobation." *Millennial Star* 1 (January 1841): 217–25.

Zucker, Louis C. "Joseph Smith as a Student of Hebrew." *Dialogue: A Journal of Mormon Thought* 3 (Summer 1968): 41–55.

Scripture Index

OLD TESTAMENT

Genesis

Gen. 1:4 — 229
Gen. 1:5 — 228
Gen. 1:7–8 — 227
Gen. 1:14 — 140
Gen. 1:14 — 479
Gen. 1:16 — 106
Gen. 1:20 — 479
Gen. 1:26 — 105–6, 131, 229, 267
Gen. 2:1 — 227
Gen. 2:1–3 — 206
Gen. 2:3–4 — 241
Gen. 2:5–6 — 246n. 6
Gen. 2:7 — 200, 256
Gen. 2:8 — 227
Gen. 2:9 — 256
Gen. 2:10–14 — 246n. 2
Gen. 2:16 — 256
Gen. 2:16–17 — 251
Gen. 2:17 — 255, 269n. 17, 370n. 79
Gen. 3:1 — 193
Gen. 3:4–6 — 252
Gen. 3:5 — 253
Gen. 3:8 — 178
Gen. 3:14–15 — 193–94
Gen. 3:15 — 276
Gen. 3:16–19 — 259
Gen. 3:17 — 255
Gen. 3:19 — 256
Gen. 3:22 — 229, 253, 256
Gen. 3:24 — 251
Gen. 4:3–5 — 274
Gen. 4:6 — 258
Gen. 4:9 — 258
Gen. 4:14 — 258
Gen. 4:15 — 258
Gen. 4:16 — 258
Gen. 6:1–2 — 218
Gen. 6:1–5 — 351
Gen. 6:4 — 218
Gen. 6:6–7 — 126
Gen. 6:9 — 327
Gen. 7:11 — 228
Gen. 8:2 — 228
Gen. 8:20 — 374
Gen. 8:21 — 260
Gen. 9:1–7 — 32
Gen. 9:5–6 — 493
Gen. 9:8–17 — 43n. 5
Gen. 9:13 — 246n. 6
Gen. 9:25–27 — 389
Gen. 9:27 — 390
Gen. 9:31 — 131
Gen. 10 — 116
Gen. 11:7 — 106
Gen. 12:7 — 374
Gen. 16:7 — 106
Gen. 17:1 — 178, 327
Gen. 17:1–8 — 43n. 5
Gen. 17:7–13 — 335n. 16
Gen. 17:11 — 331
Gen. 18:1 — 136
Gen. 18:13 — 327
Gen. 22:10–12 — 126
Gen. 22:16 — 125
Gen. 22:17 — 349, 479
Gen. 24:60 — 349
Gen. 28:12–13 — 178
Gen. 32:24 — 178
Gen. 32:30 — 136
Gen. 33:6 — 229
Gen. 33:9 — 229
Gen. 35:18 — 457
Gen. 37:21 — 457
Gen. 49:22–26 — 93–94

Exodus

Ex. 3:1–17 — 376
Ex. 3:2 — 178
Ex. 4:11 — 194
Ex. 4:22 — 168, 170
Ex. 7:1 — 117
Ex. 7:2–3 — 194
Ex. 7:13 — 94
Ex. 9:12 — 194, 245
Ex. 9:16 — 245
Ex. 10:1 — 194
Ex. 10:20 — 194
Ex. 11:10 — 194
Ex. 12:14 — 32, 298
Ex. 12:17 — 32, 298
Ex. 12:24 — 32, 298
Ex. 14:8 — 194
Ex. 15:20 — 375
Ex. 20:13 — 32
Ex. 20:17 — 300
Ex. 21:12–17 — 300
Ex. 24:9–10 — 136
Ex. 30:18–21 — 297
Ex. 30:22–30 — 311
Ex. 33:11 — 131, 136
Ex. 33:20 — 136
Ex. 34:6–7 — 275
Ex. 40:9 — 375
Ex. 40:12–15 — 311
Ex. 40:15 — 375

Leviticus

Lev. 3:17 — 32, 298
Lev. 4:1–35 — 275
Lev. 5:11–13 — 274
Lev. 10:11 — 375
Lev. 16:34 — 32, 298
Lev. 17:7 — 32, 298
Lev. 19:2 — 328, 329
Lev. 24:17 — 493

Numbers

Num. 3:6–12 — 374
Num. 8:10 — 375
Num. 9:12 — 375
Num. 13:33 — 218

Num. 15:27–31 — 275
Num. 23:10 — 457
Num. 27:20 — 376
Num. 27:23 — 375, 376
Num. 31:16–18 — 125
Num. 35:31–34 — 32

Deuteronomy

Deut. 1:10 — 316
Deut. 2:10–11 — 218
Deut. 2:20–21 — 218
Deut. 3:11 — 218
Deut. 5:22 — 299
Deut. 5:33 — 474
Deut. 6:4 — 173–74
Deut. 10:4 — 479
Deut. 10:22 — 316
Deut. 13 — 300
Deut. 14:2 — 125
Deut. 15:1 — 444
Deut. 18:9–22 — 56
Deut. 18:15 — 55, 56
Deut. 18:15–20 — 61–62
Deut. 18:23 — 62
Deut. 18:26 — 62
Deut. 22:21 — 457
Deut. 28:45–46 — 298
Deut. 28:59 — 84
Deut. 28:62 — 316
Deut. 32:5 — 155
Deut. 32:7–8 — 212
Deut. 32:8–9 — 116
Deut. 32:39 — 194
Deut. 33:15 — 94
Deut. 33:27 — 126

Joshua

Josh. 11:4 — 316
Josh. 12:4 — 218
Josh. 17:15 — 218

Judges

Judg. 4:4 — 375
Judg. 5:2 — 229
Judg. 7:12 — 316
Judg. 16:30 — 457

1 Samuel

1 Sam. 13:5 — 316
1 Sam. 15:3 — 125
1 Sam. 15:11 — 126
1 Sam. 16:14 — 194
1 Sam. 22:12 — 156
1 Sam. 22:17 — 156
1 Sam. 24:10 — 156
1 Sam. 25:26 — 156
1 Sam. 25:30 — 156
1 Sam. 28:6–9 — 51

2 Samuel

2 Sam 17:11 — 316
2 Sam. 1:9 — 457
2 Sam. 5:6–10 — 414
2 Sam. 7:14 — 139, 155
2 Sam. 11:5 — 260
2 Sam. 14:7 — 456
2 Sam. 23:5 — 43n. 5

1 Kings

1 Kgs. 4:20 — 316
1 Kgs. 6:23–28 — 131
1 Kgs. 7:23 — 297
1 Kgs. 8:7 — 126
1 Kgs. 8:27 — 479
1 Kgs. 17:21 — 457
1 Kgs. 22:19–23 — 106, 195

2 Kings

2 Kgs. 2:13–14 — 376
2 Kgs. 19:31 — 415
2 Kgs. 22:14 — 375

1 Chronicles

1 Chr. 18:11–19 — 297

2 Chronicles

2 Chr. 2:4 — 298
2 Chr. 4:2–6 — 297

Ezra

Ezra 8:1–8 — 375

Nehemiah

Neh. 6:14 — 375
Neh. 9:23 — 316

Job

Job 1:1 — 327
Job 1:1–7 — 106
Job 1:5 — 374
Job 1:6 — 155, 203
Job 1:6–12 — 195, 217
Job 1:7 — 126
Job 1:21 — 194
Job 2:1 — 155, 195
Job 2:1–6 — 217
Job 2:10 — 194
Job 5:25 — 456
Job 14:12 — 458
Job 17:13–16 — 456
Job 19:26 — 458
Job 25:6 — 171
Job 27:3 — 200
Job 32:8 — 200
Job 36:14 — 457
Job 38:4 — 228
Job 38:4–7 — 203
Job 38:7 — 155
Job 38:17 — 349

Psalms

Ps. 2:7 — 155, 158, 173
Ps. 2:11–12 — 155
Ps. 8:3 — 479
Ps. 9:13 — 349
Ps. 16:10 — 494
Ps. 22:1 — 276
Ps. 22:7 — 276
Ps. 22:8 — 276
Ps. 22:15 — 276
Ps. 22:18 — 276
Ps. 29:1 — 155
Ps. 51:5 — 260
Ps. 77:17–18 — 479
Ps. 78:50 — 457
Ps. 79:2 — 479
Ps. 82:1 — 117
Ps. 82:5–6 — 118
Ps. 82:6 — 116–17, 119
Ps. 84:11 — 151
Ps. 85:11 — 94
Ps. 89:26–27 — 155
Ps. 89:27 — 168
Ps. 90:2 — 126
Ps. 90:4 — 237, 444
Ps. 93:2 — 126
Ps. 104:12 — 479
Ps. 105:25 — 194
Ps. 110:1 — 173
Ps. 110:4 — 155–56
Ps. 115:16–18 — 228
Ps. 115:17 — 455–56
Ps. 146:3 — 171
Ps. 146:4 — 456, 457
Ps. 147:4–5 — 126
Ps. 148:2–5 — 197

SCRIPTURE INDEX

Proverbs

Prov. 20:27 — 200

Ecclesiastes

Eccl. 1:9 — 456
Eccl. 9:3 — 456
Eccl. 9:5 — 456
Eccl. 9:10 — 456
Eccl. 12:7 — 200, 455, 457

Isaiah

Isa. 1:2 — 68n. 25
Isa. 1:15 — 32
Isa. 1:21 — 32
Isa. 1:26–27
Isa. 2:11–12 — 474
Isa. 2:12 — 473
Isa. 2:2–3 — 154, 410
Isa. 2:2–4 — 415
Isa. 2:4 — 440
Isa. 4:3–4 — 415
Isa. 4:4 — 32
Isa. 5:26–29 — 83
Isa. 6:1 — 136
Isa. 7:14 — 167
Isa. 7:18–20 — 83
Isa. 8:7 — 83
Isa. 8:19 — 51
Isa. 9:6 — 147n. 81, 175–76
Isa. 10:5–6 — 83
Isa. 10:25 — 430
Isa. 11:1–13 — 54
Isa. 11:6 — 440
Isa. 11:9 — 440
Isa. 11:12 — 82, 83
Isa. 13:6 — 430, 473, 474
Isa. 13:9 — 473, 474
Isa. 13:9–11 — 430
Isa. 13:10 — 479
Isa. 13:13 — 430
Isa. 13:17–19 — 430–31
Isa. 14:12–16 — 195–96
Isa. 14:32 — 400
Isa. 17:12 — 400
Isa. 18:1–2 — 399
Isa. 18:3 — 400
Isa. 19:5–10 — 401
Isa. 20:1–6 — 400
Isa. 22:3–6 — 276
Isa. 22:11 — 276
Isa. 22:23 — 276
Isa. 22:25 — 276
Isa. 24:5 — 43n. 5
Isa. 24:5–6 — 32
Isa. 24:19–23 — 449
Isa. 24:20–22 — 354
Isa. 24:23 — 440
Isa. 25:6–9 — 154
Isa. 26:2 — 297
Isa. 26:14 — 457
Isa. 26:19 — 457
Isa. 27:1 — 194
Isa. 28:10 — 8–9
Isa. 29 — 50–52
Isa. 29:4 — 68n. 23
Isa. 29:9–12 — 92–93
Isa. 29:10 — 33
Isa. 29:11 — 101n. 3
Isa. 29:13–14 — 84
Isa. 29:15 — 84
Isa. 34:1–6 — 449
Isa. 34:8 — 473
Isa. 35:3–4 — 229
Isa. 40:1–8 — 229
Isa. 41:8–9 — 276
Isa. 42:5 — 200
Isa. 43:7 — 245
Isa. 44:1–2 — 276
Isa. 44:21 — 276
Isa. 44:24 — 229
Isa. 44:28 — 15
Isa. 45:4 — 276
Isa. 45:5 — 116
Isa. 45:5–7 — 194
Isa. 45:11 — 155
Isa. 45:21 — 116
Isa. 46:10 — 202
Isa. 48:1 — 306
Isa. 48:20 — 276
Isa. 49:3 — 276
Isa. 49:5 — 245
Isa. 51:9 — 217
Isa. 51:12 — 171
Isa. 52:9 — 419
Isa. 52:13 — 279
Isa. 52:13–14 — 57
Isa. 53 — 154
Isa. 53:1 — 279
Isa. 53:4 — 280
Isa. 53:8 — 156
Isa. 53:10 — 173
Isa. 61:1 — 186
Isa. 61:1–2 — 153, 343, 344
Isa. 61:4 — 343
Isa. 62:7 — 419
Isa. 63:1 — 280
Isa. 63:1–6 — 281
Isa. 63:17 — 194
Isa. 65:16–20 — 449
Isa. 65:17–25 — 440
Isa. 66:2 — 440
Isa. 66:22–24 — 449
Isa. 66:24 — 449

Jeremiah

Jer. 1:5 — 212
Jer. 16:4 — 401
Jer. 16:14–21 — 403
Jer. 16:16 — 400
Jer. 16:16–18 — 474
Jer. 16:17–19 — 401
Jer. 17:9 — 260
Jer. 23:6 — 440
Jer. 23:18 — 106
Jer. 23:22 — 106
Jer. 23:24 — 130
Jer. 25:11–12 — 440
Jer. 25:17 — 440
Jer. 25:29–30 — 440
Jer. 29:10 — 440
Jer. 31:7–12 — 398
Jer. 31:9 — 139, 168
Jer. 31:15 — 10
Jer. 31:16 — 10
Jer. 31:31–32 — 299
Jer. 31:31–33 — 298
Jer. 32.17 — 126
Jer. 32:37–40 — 398
Jer. 46:10 — 473, 474

Lamentations

Lam. 3:37–38 — 194
Lam. 4:18–19 — 401

Ezekial

Ezek. 2:1–2 — 186
Ezek. 3:17 — 14
Ezek. 13:5 — 473
Ezek. 30:3 — 430, 473, 474
Ezek. 36:8 — 440
Ezek. 36:24 — 398

Ezek. 36:26–27 — 459
Ezek. 37:1–14 — 200, 459
Ezek. 37:4–14 — 260
Ezek. 37:16–23 — 93

Daniel

Dan. 2:28 — 80
Dan. 2:31–45 — 80–81
Dan. 3:25 — 155, 156–57
Dan. 3:28 — 157
Dan. 7:13 — 81, 171
Dan. 7:15 — 172
Dan. 10:20 — 82
Dan. 12:1–3 — 457
Dan. 12:12 — 430
Dan. 21:2 — 457

Hosea

Hosea 11:1 — 10

Joel

Joel 1:15 — 430, 473
Joel 2:1 — 430, 473
Joel 2:1–2 — 474
Joel 2:11 — 474
Joel 2:28 — 19
Joel 2:28–29 — 438–39
Joel 3:2 — 473
Joel 3:12–19 — 474
Joel 3:16–17 — 415

Amos

Amos 3:1–7 — 14
Amos 5:18–20 — 474
Amos 7:10–17 — 14
Amos 7:11 — 33
Amos 8:9–10 — 474
Amos 8:11–12 — 32–33
Amos 9:10 — 474
Amos 9:11 — 442

Obadiah

Obad. 1:21 — 345

Jonah

Jonah 4:3 — 457

Micah

Micah 3:8 — 186
Micah 4:1–2 — 154, 410, 415
Micah 5:7–11 — 406

Nahum

Nahum 3:16 — 316

Zephaniah

Zeph. 1:14–18 — 474

Haggai

Hag. 2:9 — 419

Zechariah

Zech. 2:1 — 195
Zech. 7:12 — 186
Zech. 9:1–10 — 10
Zech. 12–14 — 402–4
Zech. 12:1 — 200
Zech. 13 — 26n. 44
Zech. 13:2–6 — 9–10
Zech. 13:4 — 403
Zech. 13:6 — 403
Zech. 14:1 — 403
Zech. 14:4 — 403
Zech. 14:18–20 — 403

Malachi

Mal. 1:16 — 53
Mal. 1:6–2 — 53
Mal. 3:1 — 52, 53
Mal. 3:2 — 446
Mal. 3:2–4 — 53
Mal. 3:2–5 — 474
Mal. 3:6 — 126
Mal. 3:6–12 — 53
Mal. 3:10 — 228
Mal. 3:13–4:3 — 474
Mal. 4:2 — 150–51
Mal. 4:5 — 53, 78, 474
Mal. 4:5–6 — 65, 74, 77, 79, 346, 367n. 18
Mal. 4:6 — 88n. 9

Matthew

Matt. 1:18 — 166
Matt. 1:21 — 152
Matt. 1:23 — 178
Matt. 2:15 — 10
Matt. 3:2 — 433
Matt. 3:10 — 433
Matt. 3:16 — 301
Matt. 4:1–11 — 196
Matt. 5:17 — 299
Matt. 5:17–18 — 304
Matt. 5:20 — 328
Matt. 5:21 — 304
Matt. 5:21–22 — 493
Matt. 5:45 — 139
Matt. 5:48 — 328, 331, 341n. 149
Matt. 6:10 — 441
Matt. 6:19–21 — 476
Matt. 7:20 — 503
Matt. 8:11–12 — 475
Matt. 8:12 — 490
Matt. 8:17 — 280
Matt. 10:5–6 — 388
Matt. 10:22 — 321
Matt. 10:28 — 469n. 26
Matt. 10:35–37 — 316
Matt. 11:10 — 53
Matt. 11:14 — 53
Matt. 11:20–24 — 476
Matt. 12:31 — 490
Matt. 12:31–32 — 489
Matt. 12:36 — 490
Matt. 13:24–26 — 35
Matt. 13:31–32 — 46–37
Matt. 13:33 — 37
Matt. 13:37–43 — 36
Matt. 13:38–30 — 36
Matt. 13:41 — 442
Matt. 15:24 — 95
Matt. 16:14 — 205
Matt. 16:17–19 — 350
Matt. 16:18 — 35, 85, 349
Matt. 16:19 — 77
Matt. 16:27 — 476
Matt. 16:28 — 431
Matt. 17:11 — 65, 79
Matt. 17:11–12 — 53
Matt. 17:12–13 — 65, 79
Matt. 18:17 — 85
Matt. 19:9–12 — 316
Matt. 19:28 — 377
Matt. 20:20–21 — 441
Matt. 21:2–7 — 10
Matt. 22:23 — 459
Matt. 22:24 — 147n. 81
Matt. 22:44 — 155
Matt. 24:13 — 321
Matt. 24:14 — 56
Matt. 24:14–16 — 401
Matt. 24:28 — 398
Matt. 24:33 — 433
Matt. 24:34 — 433
Matt. 24:37–41 — 442

SCRIPTURE INDEX

Matt. 24:41–46 — 476
Matt. 25:30 — 475
Matt. 25:31–46 — 460, 475
Matt. 25:41 — 475
Matt. 25:46 — 475
Matt. 26:64 — 433
Matt. 27:39 — 276
Matt. 27:43 — 276
Matt. 27:46 — 276
Matt. 27:52–53 — 461
Matt. 27:53–53 — 469n. 24
Matt. 28:19 — 301
Matt. 28:20 — 35

Mark

Mark 2:10 — 172
Mark 2:28 — 172
Mark 3:20–35 — 159
Mark 3:29 — 490
Mark 6:1–6 — 159
Mark 9:4 — 71n. 86
Mark 10:14 — 331, 322
Mark 10:42–44 — 154
Mark 12:18–25 — 316
Mark 13 — 17
Mark 14:61–62 — 172
Mark 14:62 — 475

Luke

Luke 1:17 — 53, 65–66, 74
Luke 1:19 — 65
Luke 1:24–26 — 205
Luke 1:35 — 159, 166
Luke 3:4–5 — 434
Luke 3:21–22 — 188
Luke 3:22 — 158
Luke 3:38 — 244
Luke 4:21 — 153, 344
Luke 6:13 — 377
Luke 10:1 — 377
Luke 10:9 — 381
Luke 10:10–12 — 325
Luke 10:17–20 — 381
Luke 10:22 — 111
Luke 10:23 — 431
Luke 12:47–48 — 476
Luke 16:22–23 — 347, 348
Luke 16:26 — 347
Luke 16:43 — 347
Luke 17:26 — 399
Luke 17:29 — 399
Luke 17:29–35 — 442

Luke 17:34–37 — 399
Luke 18:29–30 — 316
Luke 19:11 — 441
Luke 21:32 — 431
Luke 22:19–20 — 281
Luke 22:24–27 — 154
Luke 23:43 — 348
Luke 24:49 — 186, 310
Luke 25:31–46 — 442

John

John 1:1 — 17, 107, 178, 295
John 1:1–4 — 178
John 1:2 — 159, 163, 224n. 30
John 1:3 — 126, 229, 232
John 1:12 — 141, 204
John 1:13 — 163
John 1:14 — 159, 162, 163
John 1:16 — 162
John 1:18 — 107, 136, 137, 163
John 1:30 — 163, 205
John 3:3–5 — 300, 336n. 33
John 3:13 — 205
John 3:16–18 — 163
John 3:17 — 159
John 3:31 — 163, 205
John 4:24 — 132, 145n. 42
John 4:32 — 107
John 5:19 — 128
John 5:22 — 475
John 5:26 — 127
John 5:27 — 475
John 5:28–29 — 349
John 5:29 — 460, 461, 468n. 22, 484
John 6:39–40 — 468n. 22
John 6:40 — 460
John 6:44 — 468n. 22
John 6:54 — 468n. 22
John 7:17 — 216
John 7:38 — 323
John 8:23 — 163
John 8:32–33 — 216
John 8:42 — 139, 163
John 8:44 — 139
John 8:58 — 178
John 9:2 — 204
John 10:16 — 95
John 10:17–18 — 127

John 10:18 — 282
John 10:27 — 216
John 10:30 — 178
John 10:34–36 — 117
John 11:24 — 460
John 11:51–52 — 398
John 12:20 — 498n. 38
John 12:32 — 485, 498n. 38
John 12:45 — 137
John 13:35 — 505
John 14:2 — 476
John 14:9 — 128, 137
John 14:15–26 — 323
John 14:16 — 322
John 14:16–17 — 186
John 14:26 — 322
John 14:28 — 178
John 15:16 — 377
John 15:26 — 186, 323
John 15:7–8 — 322
John 16:8 — 186
John 16:13–14 — 323
John 16:13–16 — 186
John 17:3 — 107, 178
John 17:12 — 491
John 18:37 — 216
John 19:23 — 276
John 19:28 — 276
John 19:30 — 323
John 20:17 — 139, 175, 177
John 20:22 — 301, 323
John 20:28 — 107, 178

Acts

Acts 1:4–11 — 433
Acts 1:5 — 301
Acts 1:6 — 398
Acts 1:8 — 310
Acts 1:12–22 — 377
Acts 1:26 — 377
Acts 2:4 — 310
Acts 2:16–21 — 439
Acts 2:23 — 213
Acts 2:27 — 494, 500n. 68
Acts 2:29 — 494
Acts 2:30 — 158, 444
Acts 2:31 — 494
Acts 2:33 — 186
Acts 2:34 — 494
Acts 2:38 — 300, 301
Acts 3:13 — 177, 276

Acts 3:15 — 493
Acts 3:17 — 493
Acts 3:18 — 150
Acts 3:19 — 300, 493–94
Acts 3:19–21 — 61
Acts 3:21 — 60, 62, 63, 65
Acts 3:22–26 — 55
Acts 3:24 — 432
Acts 3:26 — 276
Acts 4:27 — 276
Acts 4:30 — 276
Acts 7:38 — 55
Acts 8:12–17 — 301
Acts 8:14–17 — 307
Acts 8:32–35 — 279
Acts 10:9–18 — 388
Acts 10:34–35 — 388
Acts 10:38 — 50
Acts 10:43 — 150
Acts 10:48 — 301
Acts 13:32–33 — 158
Acts 13:33 — 158
Acts 13:35–37 — 494
Acts 14:23 — 378
Acts 15:1–5 — 17, 299
Acts 15:5–11 — 335n. 16
Acts 15:24 — 17, 299
Acts 17:25–26 — 140
Acts 17:26 — 213
Acts 17:28–29 — 139
Acts 17:29 — 105
Acts 17:31 — 475, 476
Acts 19:1–6 — 307
Acts 19:1–7 — 301
Acts 20:17 — 379
Acts 20:28 — 379, 380
Acts 20:29–30 — 37

Romans

Rom. 1:1 — 378
Rom. 1:4 — 158
Rom. 1:20 — 105
Rom. 2:5–6 — 476
Rom. 2:6 — 479
Rom. 4:15 — 331, 332, 359
Rom. 4:17 — 232
Rom. 4:24–25 — 282
Rom. 5 — 253
Rom. 5:12 — 256, 263
Rom. 5:17 — 444
Rom. 5:19 — 252, 260
Rom. 6:3 — 301
Rom. 6:4 — 282
Rom. 7:1–5 — 59
Rom. 7:4 — 282
Rom. 7:7 — 300
Rom. 7:9–10 — 304
Rom. 7:10 — 260
Rom. 7:12 — 304
Rom. 7:18 — 266
Rom. 7:23 — 266
Rom. 8:6 — 260
Rom. 8:9–10 — 323
Rom. 8:11 — 282, 350, 459
Rom. 8:16 — 140
Rom. 8:17 — 245
Rom. 8:19 — 169
Rom. 8:23 — 432, 459
Rom. 8:28–29 — 170
Rom. 8:29 — 132, 168
Rom. 8:29–30 — 213
Rom. 8:38 — 214
Rom. 9:22–23 — 245
Rom. 9:23 — 207
Rom. 10:9 — 282
Rom. 10:18 — 401
Rom. 11:2 — 213
Rom. 11:5 — 213, 214
Rom. 11:21 — 37
Rom. 12:3–8 — 380
Rom. 13:8–10 — 300
Rom. 13:11 — 431
Rom. 16:7 — 378
Rom. 16:25–26 — 401

1 Corinthians

1 Cor. 1:5 — 301
1 Cor. 1:7–8 — 441
1 Cor. 1:8 — 321, 475
1 Cor. 1:13 — 301, 355
1 Cor. 1:17 — 355
1 Cor. 2:2 –17
1 Cor. 3:8 — 476
1 Cor. 3:13 — 476
1 Cor. 6:2–3 — 475
1 Cor. 6:11 — 301
1 Cor. 6:14 — 282
1 Cor. 7:1–9 — 318
1 Cor. 7:25 — 3
1 Cor. 7:26 — 318
1 Cor. 7:27 — 318
1 Cor. 7:29 — 318, 431, 434
1 Cor. 7:29–31 — 432
1 Cor. 7:31 — 431
1 Cor. 7:32–33 — 318
1 Cor. 8:4–6 — 117–18
1 Cor. 8:6 — 107, 109, 119, 126
1 Cor. 9:5–6 — 378
1 Cor. 9:19 — 140
1 Cor. 10:2 — 294
1 Cor. 10:11 — 34, 434
1 Cor. 11:1–12 — 317
1 Cor. 11:30 — 347
1 Cor. 12:6 — 504
1 Cor. 12:28 — 379–80
1 Cor. 13:12 — viii
1 Cor. 15:3–4 — 281
1 Cor. 15:6 — 347
1 Cor. 15:15 — 282
1 Cor. 15:18 — 347
1 Cor. 15:20 — 281, 432, 463
1 Cor. 15:21 — 281
1 Cor. 15:22–24 — 460
1 Cor. 15:22–28 — 444
1 Cor. 15:23 — 432, 463, 464
1 Cor. 15:23–24 — 460
1 Cor. 15:24 — 442, 461
1 Cor. 15:29 — 355, 363
1 Cor. 15:35 — 476, 478
1 Cor. 15:36–37 — 478
1 Cor. 15:36–41 — 477
1 Cor. 15:39 — 478
1 Cor. 15:41–42 — 478
1 Cor. 15:42–44 — 477, 478
1 Cor. 15:44–45 — 145n. 46
1 Cor. 15:51 — 347
1 Cor. 15:51–52 — 38
1 Cor. 15:51–54 — 464
1 Cor. 15:52 — 460, 461, 465
1 Cor. 16:15 — 380
1 Cor. 16:22 — 432

2 Corinthians

2 Cor. 1:3 — 140
2 Cor. 1:22 — 322
2 Cor. 3:14 — 150
2 Cor. 4:14 — 282
2 Cor. 5:5 — 322
2 Cor. 5:10 — 475
2 Cor. 9:6 — 476
2 Cor. 11:2 — 316
2 Cor. 11:3 — 194

2 Cor. 11:31 — 118
2 Cor. 12:2 — 478, 479
2 Cor. 12:4 — 348
2 Cor. 13:11 — 328

Galatians

Gal. 1:1 — 282
Gal. 1:4 — 281
Gal. 1:19 — 378
Gal. 3:8 — 294
Gal. 4:4 — 59

Ephesians

Eph. 1:3 — 118
Eph. 1:4 — 207
Eph. 1:5 — 214
Eph. 1:7 — 281
Eph. 1:10 — 58, 59, 60
Eph. 1:11 — 214
Eph. 1:13 — 321
Eph. 1:13–14 — 322
Eph. 1:17 — 140
Eph. 1:20 — 282
Eph. 2:1 — 260
Eph. 2:5–6 — 444
Eph. 2:14–15 — 300
Eph. 2:16 — 281
Eph. 2:19–20 — 378, 380
Eph. 2:21 — 310
Eph. 2:22 — 323
Eph. 3:1 — 59
Eph. 3:5 — 59
Eph. 3:6–8 — 59
Eph. 3:9 — 229, 232
Eph. 4:6 — 107
Eph. 4:11 — 379, 380
Eph. 4:30 — 321

Philippians

Philip. 1:6 — 441
Philip. 1:10 — 441
Philip. 1:28 — 491
Philip. 3:4 — 347
Philip. 3:10–11 — 459
Philip. 3:21 — 459, 478

Colossians

Col. 1:3 — 118
Col. 1:5–6 — 401
Col. 1:14 — 281
Col. 1:15 — 132, 169

Col. 1:16 — 126, 197, 229, 232
Col. 1:17 — 169
Col. 1:18 — 169
Col. 1:20 — 281
Col. 1:23 — 401
Col. 2:9 — 105
Col. 2:11 — 335n. 16
Col. 2:12 — 282
Col. 2:13–14 — 300

1 Thessalonians

1 Thess. 1:10 — 282, 432
1 Thess. 2:18 — 196
1 Thess. 4:13–15 — 347
1 Thess. 4:13–18 — 432, 442
1 Thess. 4:15 — 432, 434
1 Thess. 4:16 — 433, 459
1 Thess. 4:16–17 — 460, 464–65
1 Thess. 4:17 — 38, 432, 475
1 Thess. 5:1–10 — 476
1 Thess. 5:2 — 475
1 Thess. 5:23 — 201

2 Thessalonians

2 Thess. 1:1–10 — 476
2 Thess. 2:2–3 — 37–38
2 Thess. 2:2–8 — 432
2 Thess. 2:3 — 491
2 Thess. 2:8 — 38
2 Thess. 2:13–14 — 38

1 Timothy

1 Tim 2:5 — 376
1 Tim. 1:17 — 136
1 Tim. 2:5 — 107, 109
1 Tim. 2:14 — 252
1 Tim. 3:1–7 — 379, 384
1 Tim. 3:8–13 — 379
1 Tim. 4:1 — 37, 431
1 Tim. 4:1–4 — 318
1 Tim. 4:6 — 431
1 Tim. 4:8 — 441
1 Tim. 4:14 — 380
1 Tim. 5:10 — 324
1 Tim. 6:9 — 491
1 Tim. 6:15–16 — 136

2 Timothy

2 Tim. 1:6 — 380
2 Tim. 1:9 — 214
2 Tim. 2:18 — 461
2 Tim. 3:1–12 — 34–35
2 Tim. 4:1 — 441, 476
2 Tim. 4:1–2 — 432
2 Tim. 9:11 — 214

Titus

Titus 1:5–9 — 379
Titus 2:11–14 — 433
Titus 2:13 — 107

Hebrews

Heb. 1:1–2 — 177
Heb. 1:2 – 59
Heb. 1:3 — 132–33, 444
Heb. 1:3–5 — 158
Heb. 1:6 — 169
Heb. 1:7 — 351
Heb. 1:8 — 107, 444
Heb. 1:13 — 158
Heb. 1:14 — 140, 351, 486
Heb. 2:6–10 — 172
Heb. 2:9 — 132
Heb. 2:18 — 280
Heb. 3:1–2 — 378
Heb. 3:6 — 321
Heb. 3:14 — 321
Heb. 4:1–2 — 294
Heb. 4:5 — 392n. 11
Heb. 4:6 — 294
Heb. 4:12 — 201
Heb. 4:14–16 — 35, 310
Heb. 5:5–10 — 158
Heb. 5:6–10 — 376
Heb. 6:1 — 328
Heb. 6:2 — 369n. 69, 475
Heb. 6:4–6 — 489
Heb. 6:11 — 321
Heb. 7:3 — 376
Heb. 7:15 — 376
Heb. 7:23–24 — 376
Heb. 7:27 — 66
Heb. 7:28 — 158
Heb. 8:8–13 — 299
Heb. 9:3 — 375
Heb. 9:7 — 375
Heb. 9:10 — 59
Heb. 9:24 — 310

Heb. 9:26 — 34, 432
Heb. 9:27 — 460
Heb. 10:8–9 — 66
Heb. 10:12–13 — 444
Heb. 10:25 — 432
Heb. 10:26–31 — 476
Heb. 10:37 — 432
Heb. 10:39 — 491
Heb. 11:3 — 129
Heb. 11:13 — 356, 357
Heb. 11:39–40 — 356–57
Heb. 12:9 — 140
Heb. 12:22 — 415
Heb. 13:20 — 282

James

James 1:17 — 140
James 5:3 — 34
James 5:8 — 34
James 5:8–9 — 432

1 Peter

1 Pet. 1:2 — 207, 213
1 Pet. 1:3 — 118
1 Pet. 1:5 — 35
1 Pet. 1:15–16 — 329
1 Pet. 1:16 — 328
1 Pet. 1:20 — 34, 59, 213
1 Pet. 1:21 — 282
2 Pet. 2:4 — 219
1 Pet. 2:5 — 377
1 Pet. 2:9 — 377
1 Pet. 2:24 — 281
1 Pet. 3:18 — 281
1 Pet. 3:18–20 — 350–54, 363
1 Pet. 4:6 — 351–52, 363
1 Pet. 4:7 — 432
1 Pet. 5:1–3 — 379
1 Pet. 5:1–10 — 320
1 Pet. 5:13 — 320

2 Peter

2 Pet. 1:1 — 107
2 Pet. 1:5–7 — 337n. 54
2 Pet. 1:11 — 320
2 Pet. 1:16 — 321
2 Pet. 1:19–21 — 321
2 Pet. 2:4 — 475
2 Pet. 2:4–9 — 351
2 Pet. 2:9 — 35, 422
2 Pet. 3:1–4 — 321

2 Pet. 3:4 — 347
2 Pet. 3:5–13 — 449
2 Pet. 3:7 — 442, 491
2 Pet. 3:8 — 236–37, 438
2 Pet. 3:10 — 442, 479
2 Pet. 3:12–14 — 321
2 Pet. 3:13 — 442
2 Pet. 3:16 — 8

1 John

1 Jn. 2:12 — 342n. 165
1 Jn. 2:18 — 34
1 Jn. 2:28 — 441
1 Jn. 3:2–3 — 329
1 Jn. 3:14 — 491
1 Jn. 3:15 — 493
1 Jn. 4:4 — 35
1 Jn. 4:9 — 163
1 Jn. 4:12 — 136
1 Jn. 5:7 — 121n. 14
1 Jn. 5:16 — 490

Jude

Jude 1:6 — 219
Jude 1:14 — 218
Jude 1:17–19 — 34
Jude 1:24 — 35

Revelation

Rev. 1:1 — 220, 432
Rev. 1:13 — 81, 172
Rev. 1:3 — 432
Rev. 1:5 — 169, 281
Rev. 1:6 — 118, 120, 376–77
Rev. 1:9 — 444
Rev. 1:18 — 349
Rev. 2:7 — 348
Rev. 2:26 — 321
Rev. 3:1 — 438
Rev. 3:10 — 35
Rev. 3:12 — 419
Rev. 4:6 — 22, 467
Rev. 4:9 — 467
Rev. 5:9–10 — 444
Rev. 7:2–3 — 386
Rev. 9:1 — 219
Rev. 9:11 — 40
Rev. 11 — 404
Rev. 12:1–17 — 38–39
Rev. 12:3–4 — 220
Rev. 12:4 — 196

Rev. 12:7 — 196
Rev. 12:8 — 44n. 28
Rev. 12:9 — 194
Rev. 12:12–13 — 220
Rev. 13:1–14 — 196
Rev. 14:1 — 72n. 90, 415
Rev. 14:6–7 — 95–97
Rev. 14:10–11 — 475
Rev. 14:18–20 — 281
Rev. 17:5 — 40
Rev. 17:8 — 287
Rev. 19:10 — 150
Rev. 19:13–15 — 281
Rev. 20:1–3 — 454n. 59
Rev. 20:1–6 — 429
Rev. 20:2 — 194
Rev. 20:2–7 — 441
Rev. 20:3 — 196
Rev. 20:4–15 — 460
Rev. 20:4–6 — 443, 476
Rev. 20:8–10 — 443
Rev. 20:10 — 221, 475
Rev. 20:11–13 — 469n. 23
Rev. 20:11–15 — 444, 460, 475, 476
Rev. 20:12 — 357
Rev. 20:12–13 — 358, 485
Rev. 20:13 — 466
Rev. 20:14–15 — 491
Rev. 21:1–2 — 420
Rev. 21:1–7 — 449
Rev. 21:2 — 316, 416, 419, 443
Rev. 21:8 — 491, 493
Rev. 21:10 — 419
Rev. 21:14 — 377
Rev. 22:7 — 438
Rev. 22:10 — 18, 438
Rev. 22:10–12 — 433
Rev. 22:12 — 476
Rev. 22:15 — 491
Rev. 22:18 — 8
Rev. 22:20 — 438

JOSEPH SMITH TRANSLATION

JST Gen. 1:2 — 151
JST Gen. 1:27 — 151
JST Gen. 1:29 — 151
JST Gen. 6:53 — 152
JST Gen. 6:60 — 152

SCRIPTURE INDEX

JST Gen. 7:57 — 152
JST Gen. 8:7 — 374
JST Gen. 8:11 — 153
JST Gen. 14:26–32 — 385
JST Gen. 14:30–33 — 374
JST Gen. 17:6–7 — 331
JST Gen. 17:11 — 265, 331, 335n. 16
JST Gen. 50:26–32 — 57
JST Gen. 50:28 — 101
JST Ex. 33:20 — 137
JST Ex. 34:1 — 374
JST Ex. 34:1–2 — 297
JST Mal. 4:4–5 — 75
JST Matt. 17:10 — 65
JST Matt. 17:14 — 65
JST Matt. 24–28 — 399
JST Mark 9:4 — 71n. 86
JST Luke 10:22 –111
JST Luke 11:53 — 98
JST Luke 17:37 — 399
JST John 1:1 — 295
JST John 1:19 — 137
JST John 1:21–28 — 65
JST John 1:22–26 — 65
JST John 2:24 — 25n. 13
JST John 4:26 — 145n. 42
JST John 13:10 — 325
JST Acts 3:17 — 493
JST Rom. 8:29 — 170
JST 1 Cor. 7:29 — 434
JST 1 Cor. 10:11 — 434
JST 1 Cor. 15:40 — 477
JST 1 Thess. 4:15 — 434
JST 1 Tim. 2:4 — 163
JST 1 Tim. 6:15–16 — 137
JST Heb. 7:3 — 376
JST Heb. 9:26 — 434
JST Heb. 11:40 — 356
JST 1 Pet. 3:20 — 354
JST 2 Pet. 2:19 — 321
JST 1 Jn. 4:12 — 137
JST Rev. 12:7 — 38
JST Rev. 13:1 — 22

BOOK OF MORMON

Title Page — 4, 407

1 Nephi

1 Ne. 10:4 — 151
1 Ne. 10:18 — 287
1 Ne. 10:20–21 — 481
1 Ne. 10:22 — 382
1 Ne. 11:11 — 187, 191n. 13
1 Ne. 11:15 — 167
1 Ne. 11:16 — 285
1 Ne. 11:18 — 111
1 Ne. 11:21 — 111
1 Ne. 11:26 — 285
1 Ne. 11:27 — 187
1 Ne. 11:32 — 111
1 Ne. 12:13 — 180n. 15
1 Ne. 13:6–9 — 42
1 Ne. 13:23–28 — 98
1 Ne. 13:26–28 — 42
1 Ne. 13:29 — 41
1 Ne. 13:34–35 — 91
1 Ne. 13:37 — 416, 447
1 Ne. 13:40 — 97, 111
1 Ne. 14:2 — 22
1 Ne. 14:7 — 84, 481
1 Ne. 14:10 — 42, 85–86, 481
1 Ne. 14:12 — 42, 410, 423n. 40
1 Ne. 14:12–17 — 454n. 59
1 Ne. 15:29–36 — 482
1 Ne. 19:23 — 26n. 41, 51
1 Ne. 19:6 — 4
1 Ne. 19:8 — 151
1 Ne. 20:1 — 306
1 Ne. 22:1–11 — 52
1 Ne. 22:3 — 403
1 Ne. 22:14 — 416
1 Ne. 22:19 — 416
1 Ne. 22:21 — 55
1 Ne. 22:24 — 446
1 Ne. 22:24–28 — 454n. 59
1 Ne. 22:26 — 446
1 Ne. 30:5–18 — 454n. 59
1 Ne. 30:18 — 446

2 Nephi

2 Ne. 1:15 — 305
2 Ne. 1:22 — 469n. 26
2 Ne. 2:3 — 59
2 Ne. 2:5 — 295
2 Ne. 2:8–9 — 463
2 Ne. 2:17 — 221
2 Ne. 2:17–18 — 196, 197
2 Ne. 2:21 — 262, 360
2 Ne. 2:22 — 2, 234, 256
2 Ne. 2:22–23 — 254
2 Ne. 2:23 — 253, 257, 258
2 Ne. 2:24 — 255, 269n. 16
2 Ne. 2:25 — 246, 255, 258
2 Ne. 2:26 — 59
2 Ne. 2:27 — 193
2 Ne. 2:27–29 — 482
2 Ne. 3:6–15 — 423n. 40
2 Ne. 3:7–8 — 101
2 Ne. 3:9–10 — 55–56
2 Ne. 3:14–15 — 57
2 Ne. 5:10 — 304, 381
2 Ne. 5:16 — 310
2 Ne. 5:19–25 — 409
2 Ne. 6:5 — 51
2 Ne. 6:11 — 403
2 Ne. 6:12–13 — 416
2 Ne. 6:14 — 446
2 Ne. 8:15 — 416
2 Ne. 9:1–2 — 403
2 Ne. 9:2 — 411
2 Ne. 9:4 — 458
2 Ne. 9:6 — 256
2 Ne. 9:7 — 284
2 Ne. 9:11–19 — 482
2 Ne. 9:13 — 348
2 Ne. 9:22 — 447
2 Ne. 9:46 — 483
2 Ne. 10:7 — 403
2 Ne. 10:13–16 — 416
2 Ne. 10:18 — 22, 423n. 40
2 Ne. 10:18–19 — 410
2 Ne. 10:3 — 152
2 Ne. 11:7 — 230
2 Ne. 21:11–12 — 83
2 Ne. 22:2 — 174
2 Ne. 25:7 — 51
2 Ne. 25:12 — 164
2 Ne. 25:15–16 — 403
2 Ne. 25:15–18 — 403
2 Ne. 25:16 — 286
2 Ne. 25:17–18 — 84
2 Ne. 25:19 — 151
2 Ne. 25:22 — 87
2 Ne. 25:25 — 381
2 Ne. 26:9 — 179n. 8
2 Ne. 26:12 — 52
2 Ne. 26:13 — 446
2 Ne. 26:16 — 51
2 Ne. 26:22 — 87
2 Ne. 26:29–31 — 416

2 Ne. 26:33 — 388
2 Ne. 27:7 — 92
2 Ne. 27:9 — 51
2 Ne. 27:15–20 — 92, 102n. 2
2 Ne. 28:3–5 — 87
2 Ne. 28:4–15
2 Ne. 28:21 — 416
2 Ne. 28:22 — 197
2 Ne. 28:26 — 381
2 Ne. 28:30 — 9
2 Ne. 29:1 — 84
2 Ne. 29:2 — 83
2 Ne. 29:3 — 83
2 Ne. 29:7 — 84
2 Ne. 29:11–12 — 358
2 Ne. 29:12–13 — 412
2 Ne. 30:5–7 — 403
2 Ne. 30:6 — 409
2 Ne. 30:7 — 404
2 Ne. 30:18 — 454n. 59
2 Ne. 31:8 — 187
2 Ne. 31:11 — 306
2 Ne. 31:13–4 — 306
2 Ne. 31:17–21 — 306
2 Ne. 31:21 — 109, 118
2 Ne. 32:1–6 — 306
2 Ne. 32:5 — 187

Jacob

Jacob 1:17 — 310
Jacob 2:24 — 340n. 115
Jacob 2:30 — 147n. 81
Jacob 3:11 — 487, 491
Jacob 3:8–9 — 410
Jacob 4:4 — 150, 295
Jacob 4:5 — 304
Jacob 4:9 — 230, 233
Jacob 5:71–77 — 454n. 59
Jacob 5:76 — 446
Jacob 5:77 — 447
Jacob 6:5 — 305
Jacob 7:11 — 150
Jacob 7:19 — 491

Mosiah

Mosiah 2:25 — 230
Mosiah 2:27 — 161
Mosiah 2:39 — 481
Mosiah 3:5 — 151
Mosiah 3:8 — 176
Mosiah 3:11 — 21, 332, 333, 360, 487
Mosiah 3:16 — 333
Mosiah 3:19 — 262, 267, 303
Mosiah 3:21 — 176
Mosiah 3:25 — 481
Mosiah 4:2 — 230, 267
Mosiah 4:5 — 305
Mosiah 4:5–8 — 306
Mosiah 4:6–7 — 287
Mosiah 4:11 — 267
Mosiah 4:30 — 481
Mosiah 5:2 — 305
Mosiah 5:7 — 175
Mosiah 5:8–11 — 482
Mosiah 5:15 — 323, 483
Mosiah 7:17 — 310
Mosiah 7:27 — 110, 134, 135, 176, 230
Mosiah 11:41 — 461
Mosiah 13:27 — 381
Mosiah 13:28 — 285
Mosiah 13:33 — 150
Mosiah 13:34 — 285
Mosiah 13:34–35 — 279
Mosiah 14:1–2 — 57
Mosiah 15:1 — 279
Mosiah 15:2–5 — 110, 161
Mosiah 15:10–13 — 156
Mosiah 15:19 — 287
Mosiah 15:21–26 — 461
Mosiah 15:24 — 21, 360, 487
Mosiah 15:3 — 176
Mosiah 15:4 — 109, 141, 175, 176
Mosiah 15:4–5 — 109, 118
Mosiah 16:1–4 — 262, 303
Mosiah 16:3 — 262, 253
Mosiah 16:10–11 — 447
Mosiah 16:11 — 461, 487
Mosiah 16:12 — 305
Mosiah 16:15 — 109
Mosiah 17:8 — 285
Mosiah 18:9 — 461
Mosiah 18:10 — 306
Mosiah 18:12 — 306
Mosiah 18:13 — 111, 287, 360
Mosiah 18:13–14 — 382
Mosiah 18:14 — 306
Mosiah 18:16 — 306
Mosiah 23:22 — 447
Mosiah 26:20 — 323
Mosiah 26:21 — 216
Mosiah 26:23 — 230
Mosiah 26:23–27 — 482
Mosiah 26:4 — 303
Mosiah 27:13 — 86
Mosiah 29:20 — 305

Alma

Alma 3:6–19 — 410
Alma 3:26 — 482
Alma 4:4 — 86
Alma 4:7 — 383
Alma 5:9 — 305
Alma 5:12 — 305
Alma 5:14 — 267, 305
Alma 5:15 — 230
Alma 5:26 — 305
Alma 5:28 — 151
Alma 5:33 — 305
Alma 5:48 — 164
Alma 5:50 — 151
Alma 6:1 — 382, 383
Alma 7:7 — 151
Alma 7:10 — 161, 166
Alma 7:11 — 280
Alma 7:12 — 280
Alma 9:26 — 151, 164
Alma 11:28–29 — 118
Alma 11:34–37 — 481
Alma 11:38 — 175
Alma 11:38–39 — 176
Alma 11:43–50 — 465
Alma 11:44 — 481
Alma 11:45 — 461
Alma 12:12–14 — 481
Alma 12:14 — 358
Alma 12:16 — 487, 491
Alma 12:23 — 2
Alma 12:23–24 — 295
Alma 12:24 — 360
Alma 12:25 — 287
Alma 12:27 — 484
Alma 12:30 — 287
Alma 12:31–32 — 295
Alma 12:32 — 491
Alma 12:36 — 253
Alma 12:37 — 295
Alma 13:1–3 — 216
Alma 13:2–12 — 287

SCRIPTURE INDEX

Alma 13:3 — 207, 382
Alma 13:3–4 — 214
Alma 13:5 — 287
Alma 13:7 — 334n. 15
Alma 13:16 — 334n. 15
Alma 13:18 — 381, 385
Alma 13:19 — 376
Alma 13:20 — 8
Alma 13:21 — 151
Alma 13:25 — 151
Alma 13:29 — 447
Alma 13:30 — 491
Alma 14:5 — 111
Alma 15:13 — 382, 383
Alma 16:13 — 310
Alma 17:4 — 305
Alma 18:4–5 — 134
Alma 18:26–29 — 134
Alma 18:39 — 287
Alma 18:42 — 305
Alma 19:17–18 — 305
Alma 21:16 — 481
Alma 22:8–11 — 134
Alma 22:13 — 287
Alma 22:13–14 — 303
Alma 25:15 — 381
Alma 26:13 — 305
Alma 26:15 — 305
Alma 28:11–12 — 481
Alma 31:15 — 134
Alma 31:15–17 — 134
Alma 31:16–18 — 304
Alma 31:28–30 — 134
Alma 34:8 — 286
Alma 34:10–11 — 284
Alma 34:12 — 285, 286
Alma 34:14 — 66, 294
Alma 34:32–36 — 483
Alma 34:33 — 360
Alma 34:35–36 — 323
Alma 34:38 — 187
Alma 38:39 — 109
Alma 39:5–6 — 491, 495
Alma 39:6 — 187
Alma 40 — 461
Alma 40:8 — 237
Alma 40:11–14 — 360
Alma 40:12 — 483
Alma 40:12–13 — 352
Alma 40:12–14 — 348
Alma 40:15 — 469n. 23
Alma 40:19 — 460n. 27

Alma 40:20 — 3
Alma 40:22 — 63
Alma 40:24 — 63
Alma 41:1 — 8, 63
Alma 41:2 — 63
Alma 41:3–5 — 482
Alma 41:4 — 63
Alma 41:5–7 — 484
Alma 41:6 — 63
Alma 41:10 — 63
Alma 42:4 — 358, 360
Alma 42:7 — 258, 261
Alma 42:9 — 261
Alma 42:10 — 262
Alma 42:15 — 285
Alma 42:21–31 — 283
Alma 45:22–23 — 382

Helaman

Hel. 6:26 — 252
Hel. 10:6–7 — 382
Hel. 12:7 — 267
Hel. 12:15 — 238
Hel. 14:12 — 176
Hel. 14:16 — 262
Hel. 14:16–18 — 491
Hel. 14:17–18 — 487
Hel. 14:18 — 262
Hel. 14:18–19 — 491
Hel. 14:25 — 461
Hel. 16:18 — 176

3 Nephi

3 Ne. 1:14 — 161
3 Ne. 2:8 — 152
3 Ne. 2:15–16 — 410
3 Ne. 7:25 — 382
3 Ne. 8:5 — 152
3 Ne. 9:14 — 305
3 Ne. 9:15 — 230
3 Ne. 9:19–20 — 66
3 Ne. 11:25 — 384
3 Ne. 11:31–39 — 306
3 Ne. 11:40 — 21, 305
3 Ne. 12:17–18 — 304
3 Ne. 12:48 — 329
3 Ne. 15:11–24 — 95
3 Ne. 15:20 — 412
3 Ne. 16:1–4 — 412
3 Ne. 16:13 — 22, 423n. 40
3 Ne. 16:13–16 — 410
3 Ne. 16:14–15 — 405

3 Ne. 18:31 — 216
3 Ne. 20:11 — 52
3 Ne. 20:15–20 — 405
3 Ne. 20:22 — 417, 454n. 59
3 Ne. 20:26 — 283
3 Ne. 20:30–33 — 403
3 Ne. 20:43–44 — 57–58
3 Ne. 21:1 — 416
3 Ne. 21:6 — 423n. 40
3 Ne. 21:9–10 — 57
3 Ne. 21:11–13 — 406
3 Ne. 21:12–13 — 21, 408, 409
3 Ne. 21:20–24 — 410
3 Ne. 21:20–29 — 454n. 59
3 Ne. 21:23 — 406
3 Ne. 21:26–28 — 403
3 Ne. 24:2 — 446
3 Ne. 25:2 — 151
3 Ne. 25:5–6 — 75
3 Ne. 26:3–4 — 446, 447, 449
3 Ne. 26:4–5 — 484
3 Ne. 26:5 — 111, 487
3 Ne. 27:6 — 446
3 Ne. 27:8 — 48
3 Ne. 27:8–11 — 87
3 Ne. 27:11 — 482
3 Ne. 27:13–14 — 111
3 Ne. 27:14–15 — 485
3 Ne. 27:14–17 — 446
3 Ne. 27:17 — 482
3 Ne. 27:19–20 — 446
3 Ne. 27:24–26 — 358
3 Ne. 27:24–32 — 487
3 Ne. 27:27 — 329
3 Ne. 27:32 — 492
3 Ne. 27:33 — 487
3 Ne. 29:6 — 381
3 Ne. 29:7 — 492
3 Ne. 30:2 — 22, 423n. 40

Mormon

Morm. 2:15 — 302
Morm. 3:20 — 481
Morm. 3:21 — 178
Morm. 5:20–24 — 406
Morm. 7:5 — 283
Morm. 7:7 — 109, 118
Morm. 8:15–16 — 51
Morm. 8:17 — 4

Morm. 8:23–25 — 52
Morm. 8:26–31 — 42
Morm. 8:36 — 86
Morm. 9:12 — 110, 176
Morm. 9:17 — 230

Ether

Ether 3:2 — 262
Ether 3:13 — 287
Ether 3:14 — 110, 111, 176
Ether 3:15–16 — 135, 230
Ether 4:7 — 175, 176
Ether 4:19 — 447
Ether 9:22 — 179n. 8
Ether 13:3 — 417
Ether 13:4–8 — 420
Ether 13:8–11 — 420
Ether 13:9–11 — 449

Moroni

Moro. 2:1–3 — 306
Moro. 3:2–3 — 382
Moro. 3:4 — 387
Moro. 7:22 — 128
Moro. 7:24 — 149
Moro. 8:6 — 332
Moro. 8:8 — 265, 333, 335n. 16
Moro. 8:9 — 332
Moro. 8:12 — 265, 333
Moro. 8:18 — 127
Moro. 8:19 — 332
Moro. 8:19–20 — 265, 333
Moro. 8:22 — 21, 365, 333, 487
Moro. 8:22–23 — 360
Moro. 10:5 — 502
Moro. 10:32–33 — 329
Moro. 10:34 — 174

DOCTRINE AND COVENANTS

D&C 1:12 — 435
D&C 1:24 — 25n. 19
D&C 1:30 — 31
D&C 1:35 — 435
D&C 1:36 — 448
D&C 2:1–2 — 75
D&C 4:1 — 84
D&C 4:2 — 447
D&C 4:3 — 383
D&C 5:4 — 101
D&C 5:6 — 383
D&C 5:14 — 38
D&C 5:17 — 383
D&C 5:19 — 447
D&C 5:35 — 447
D&C 6:1 — 84
D&C 6:4 — 383
D&C 6:6 — 416
D&C 6:13 — 447
D&C 6:26 — 101
D&C 9:14 — 447
D&C 10:23 — 447
D&C 10:52–57 — 86
D&C 10:59 — 95
D&C 10:65 — 410
D&C 10:67 — vii
D&C 10:67–68 — 305
D&C 10:68 — 87
D&C 10:69 — 349
D&C 11:1 — 84
D&C 11:4 — 383
D&C 11:6 — 416
D&C 11:20 — 219
D&C 12:1 — 84
D&C 12:4 — 383
D&C 12:6 — 416
D&C 12:7 — 221
D&C 13 — 72n. 90
D&C 13 — 73
D&C 14:1 — 84
D&C 14:4 — 383
D&C 14:6 — 416
D&C 17:8 — 349
D&C 17:23 — 447
D&C 18:5 — 349
D&C 18:11 — 308
D&C 18:24–25 — 447
D&C 18:29 — 384
D&C 18:44 — 84
D&C 19:3 — 447, 484
D&C 19:6 — 482
D&C 19:11–12 — 482
D&C 19:18 — 112
D&C 19:38 — 439
D&C 19:41 — 308
D&C 20:1 — 48, 151
D&C 20:9 — 304
D&C 20:12 — 127
D&C 20:17 — 127, 284
D&C 20:20 — 262
D&C 20:26 — 150, 295
D&C 20:28 — 107, 109, 284
D&C 20:38 — 384
D&C 20:38–64 — 383
D&C 20:42–51 — 381
D&C 20:59 — 308
D&C 20:60 — 387
D&C 20:65 — 380, 387
D&C 20:73 — 384
D&C 20:77 — 110
D&C 20:79 — 110
D&C 21:6 — 349
D&C 21:7–8 — 416
D&C 21:11 — 334n. 15
D&C 27:18 — 439, 447
D&C 27:5 — 102n. 6, 304
D&C 27:6 — 64, 65
D&C 27:6–9 — 71n. 86
D&C 27:9 — 75
D&C 28:2 — 55
D&C 28:8 — 406, 422n. 33
D&C 29:1 — 175
D&C 29:7–8 — 417
D&C 29:8 — 411
D&C 29:8–11 — 410
D&C 29:9 — 435
D&C 29:11 — 437, 447
D&C 29:22 — 462
D&C 29:22–24 — 450
D&C 29:23–24 — 467
D&C 29:26–27 — 448, 462, 484–85
D&C 29:26–29 — 482
D&C 29:30–32 — 208
D&C 29:31 — 230
D&C 29:31–32 — 241
D&C 29:36 — 221
D&C 29:37 — 221
D&C 29:40 — 197, 252
D&C 29:42 — 175, 360
D&C 29:46 — 165, 175
D&C 29:47 — 265, 333
D&C 30:4 — 31
D&C 30:6 — 422n. 33
D&C 32:2 — 422n. 33
D&C 33:10 — 435
D&C 33:13 — 349
D&C 33:18 — 435
D&C 34:3 — 219
D&C 34:12 — 435
D&C 35:2 — 219
D&C 35:15–16 — 435

SCRIPTURE INDEX

D&C 35:20 — 98–99
D&C 35:26 — 435
D&C 35:27 — 435
D&C 37:3 — 310
D&C 38:18–20 — 488
D&C 38:32 — 310, 385
D&C 39:15 — 310
D&C 39:19 — 435
D&C 39:21 — 435
D&C 39:24 — 435
D&C 41:4 — 435
D&C 41:9 — 384
D&C 42:12 — 304
D&C 42:18 — 495
D&C 42:7 — 435
D&C 43:17 — 435
D&C 43:29–30 — 437
D&C 43:31 — 454n. 59
D&C 44:1 — 310
D&C 44:2 — 439
D&C 44:2–3 — 310
D&C 45:1 — 230
D&C 45:9 — 52
D&C 45:17 — 344
D&C 45:37–39 — 435
D&C 45:45–54 — 463
D&C 45:46 — 462
D&C 45:51–52 — 9
D&C 45:51–53 — 404
D&C 45:54 — 448, 462
D&C 45:55 — 454n. 59
D&C 49 — 50
D&C 49:5– 165
D&C 49:6 — 435
D&C 49:17 — 208
D&C 49:23 — 434
D&C 49:28 — 435
D&C 50:17–20 — 502
D&C 50:24 — 302
D&C 51:20 — 435
D&C 52:3–5 — 417
D&C 54:10 — 435
D&C 57:1–2 — 410, 417
D&C 57:3 — 417
D&C 58:4 — 435
D&C 63:17 — 488
D&C 63:17–18 — 462
D&C 63:24 — 417
D&C 63:32 — 453n. 43
D&C 63:49 — 454n. 64
D&C 63:50 — 464
D&C 63:51 — 464

D&C 63:53 — 435, 438
D&C 64:36 — 407
D&C 65:2–6 — 81
D&C 67:13 — 329
D&C 68:11 — 438
D&C 68:18 — 386
D&C 68:27 — 265
D&C 68:35 — 435
D&C 69:8 — 488
D&C 74:7 — 333
D&C 76:13 — 162, 165
D&C 76:23–25 — 165
D&C 76:24 — 141, 147n. 81, 286, 288
D&C 76:25 — 162, 197
D&C 76:28–29 — 221
D&C 76:30–38 — 491
D&C 76:35 — 187, 492
D&C 76:35–37 — 488
D&C 76:38–39 — 460n. 29
D&C 76:42 — 230, 231
D&C 76:43 — 485, 495
D&C 76:50–80 — 463
D&C 76:51–53 — 307
D&C 76:53 — 486
D&C 76:55–59 — 307
D&C 76:58 — 119, 124n. 61
D&C 76:69 — 329
D&C 76:71 — 170
D&C 76:72 — 487
D&C 76:72–74 — 361
D&C 76:73 — 361
D&C 76:73–74 — 353, 362, 364
D&C 76:77 — 354
D&C 76:78 — 477
D&C 76:79 — 485, 486
D&C 76:81–85 — 463
D&C 76:85 — 462, 495
D&C 76:89 — 487
D&C 76:98 — 478
D&C 76:98–103 — 492
D&C 76:103 — 486, 495
D&C 76:106–7 — 281
D&C 76:112 — 476
D&C 77:2 — 22, 208, 348
D&C 77:3 — 246, 466, 467
D&C 77:5 — 348
D&C 77:6 — 236, 437
D&C 77:8–11 — 387

D&C 77:9 — 65
D&C 77:12 — 236, 242, 437
D&C 77:13 — 334n. 15
D&C 77:14 — 65
D&C 84:2–4 — 418
D&C 84:4–5 — 436
D&C 84:6–16 — 374
D&C 84:17–27 — 297
D&C 84:21–22 — 137
D&C 84:25 — 297, 309
D&C 84:25–27 — 374
D&C 84:33–44 — 307–9
D&C 84:49–53 — 448
D&C 84:100 — 454n. 59
D&C 86:3 — 36
D&C 86:8–10 — 42
D&C 87:1–5 — 406
D&C 87:8 — 435
D&C 88:2–4 — 322
D&C 88:3 — 187
D&C 88:5 — 170
D&C 88:12 — 239
D&C 88:20 — 488
D&C 88:21 — 300
D&C 88:26 — 488
D&C 88:27 — 145n. 46
D&C 88:32 — 460n. 29
D&C 88:37 — 239
D&C 88:66 — 230
D&C 88:95–98 — 437
D&C 88:96–98 — 465
D&C 88:98 — 464
D&C 88:98–99 — 361
D&C 88:99 — 464
D&C 88:100–102 — 463
D&C 88:102 — 463
D&C 88:110–11 — 454n. 59
D&C 88:113 — 221
D&C 88:114 — 221
D&C 88:126 — 435
D&C 88:139 –341n. 134
D&C 93:3 — 224n. 30
D&C 93:4 — 161
D&C 93:9 — 190
D&C 93:10 — 230, 231
D&C 93:11– 165
D&C 93:12 — 161, 162
D&C 93:14 — 162
D&C 93:15 — 187
D&C 93:21–22 — 170

D&C 93:22– 165
D&C 93:23 — 208, 233
D&C 93:26 — 190
D&C 93:29 — 202, 208, 224n. 30
D&C 93:30 — 209
D&C 93:33 — 202, 233
D&C 93:33–34 — 189
D&C 93:36 — 208
D&C 93:38 — 208, 264, 287
D&C 95:4 — 439
D&C 95:8 — 310
D&C 97:19 — 418
D&C 97:21 — 416, 418
D&C 98:12 — 9
D&C 98:16–17 — 75
D&C 98:22 — 349
D&C 99:5 — 435
D&C 101:28 — 454n. 59
D&C 101:30 — 464
D&C 101:30 — 487
D&C 104:11 — 310
D&C 104:59 — 435
D&C 105:9 — 410
D&C 105:12 — 310
D&C 106:4 — 435
D&C 107:40 — 386
D&C 107:40–53 — 374
D&C 107:91 — 55
D&C 109:4 — 174
D&C 109:22 — 311
D&C 109:34 — 174
D&C 109:42 — 174
D&C 109:56 — 174
D&C 109:68 — 174
D&C 109:72 — 81
D&C 109:77 — 127
D&C 110 — 73
D&C 110:3 — 184n. 105
D&C 110:11 — 412
D&C 110:12 — 65
D&C 110:13–16 — 74, 75, 77
D&C 110:45–46 — 71n. 86
D&C 112:34 — 435
D&C 113:1–4 — 54
D&C 115:4–5 — 83
D&C 117:8 — 246n. 2
D&C 121:28 — 114, 115
D&C 121:32 — 115
D&C 122:23 — 31

D&C 124:39 — 384
D&C 124:123– 165
D&C 124:134 — 334n. 15
D&C 124:137 — 384
D&C 128:6–7 — 357
D&C 128:17 — 346, 367n. 18
D&C 128:17–18 — 77
D&C 128:18 — 58, 77, 356
D&C 128:21 — 9, 73
D&C 128:22 — 344
D&C 128:24 — 435
D&C 129:3 — 329
D&C 130:3 — 323
D&C 130:7 — 488
D&C 130:9 — 488
D&C 130:16 — 437
D&C 130:22 — 130, 136
D&C 130:22–23 — 188–89
D&C 131:1–2 — 486
D&C 131:2–4 — 189
D&C 131:5 — 321
D&C 131:7 — 202
D&C 132:1 — 340n. 115
D&C 132:1–4 — 318
D&C 132:15–16 — 317
D&C 132:19 — 325, 326
D&C 132:19–20 — 486
D&C 132:26 — 325
D&C 132:26–27 — 326
D&C 132:30 — 315
D&C 133:26–27 — 412
D&C 133:64 — 52
D&C 133:1–16 — 411
D&C 133:17 — 435
D&C 133:26–27 — 413
D&C 133:26–30 — 412
D&C 133:30–34 — 407
D&C 133:36–39 — 96
D&C 133:38–50 — 281
D&C 133:54–56 — 366
D&C 133:57–58 — 52
D&C 133:62–63 — 482
D&C 133:73 — 482
D&C 135:3 — 304
D&C 137:6 — 361–62
D&C 137:7 — 362
D&C 137:9 — 362
D&C 137:10 — 333, 486
D&C 138:12 — 364, 366
D&C 138:18 — 344

D&C 138:18–19 — 365
D&C 138:20 — 364
D&C 138:28–29 — 363
D&C 138:28–30 — 350
D&C 138:30 — 365, 366
D&C 138:32–33 — 365
D&C 138:36 — 365
D&C 138:37 — 364
D&C 138:42 — 344
D&C 138:45–46 — 71n. 86
D&C 138:46–47 — 367n. 18
D&C 138:49–50 — 365, 366
D&C 138:50 — 344
D&C 138:57 — 366
D&C 138:57–58 — 365
D&C 143:16–17 — 486
Official Declaration–2 — 388

PEARL OF GREAT PRICE

Moses

Moses 1:1–6 — 175
Moses 1:3 — 179
Moses 1:6 — 112, 119, 164
Moses 1:6–33 — 179
Moses 1:11 — 137
Moses 1:13 — 141, 164
Moses 1:16 — 141
Moses 1:19 — 164
Moses 1:29 — 238
Moses 1:32 — 164
Moses 1:32–33 — 230
Moses 1:33 — 238, 288
Moses 1:34 — 235
Moses 1:39 — 467
Moses 1:41 — 55, 99
Moses 2:1 — 230
Moses 2:4–31 — 236
Moses 2:26–27 — 118–19
Moses 2:27 — 135
Moses 3:1–7 — 208, 241
Moses 3:1–9 — 466
Moses 3:5 — 243
Moses 3:5–9 — 242
Moses 3:7 — 243, 244
Moses 3:17 — 254
Moses 3:23 — 243
Moses 4:1 — 199, 222

Moses 4:1–3 — 197
Moses 4:3 — 222
Moses 4:3–4 — 221
Moses 4:6–7 — 197
Moses 4:19 — 252
Moses 4:21 — 193
Moses 4:26 — 235
Moses 5:10 — 458
Moses 5:11 — 254, 258
Moses 5:13 — 262
Moses 5:14 — 383
Moses 5:23–25 — 489
Moses 5:24 — 208, 241, 492
Moses 5:4 — 258
Moses 5:7 — 164, 273
Moses 5:54–55 — 141
Moses 5:57 — 287
Moses 5:58 — 383
Moses 5:59 — 295, 334n. 15
Moses 6:7 — 373
Moses 6:9 — 135
Moses 6:22 — 244
Moses 6:36 — 208, 241
Moses 6:48 — 2, 258
Moses 6:49 — 262
Moses 6:51 — 208, 241, 243
Moses 6:52 — 153, 164
Moses 6:54 — 264
Moses 6:55 — 262
Moses 6:57 — 153, 171
Moses 6:59 — 2
Moses 6:63 — 208, 241
Moses 6:64–66 — 297, 298

Moses 7:1 — 141
Moses 7:11 — 297
Moses 7:18 — 417
Moses 7:33 — 353
Moses 7:36 — 288
Moses 7:36–39 — 353
Moses 7:47 — 173, 287
Moses 7:50 — 153
Moses 7:53 — 417
Moses 7:54–56 — 173
Moses 7:56 — 353
Moses 7:57 — 354
Moses 7:59 — 164
Moses 7:62 — 417
Moses 7:65 — 173
Moses 7:65 — 447
Moses 8:13–15 — 219
Moses 8:14 — 141
Moses 8:23–24 — 297
Moses 8:24 — 153
Moses 8:62 — 94

Abraham

Abr. 1:2 — 374
Abr. 1:2–4 — 386
Abr. 1:20–25 — 390
Abr. 1:26–27 — 389
Abr. 3:2 — 238
Abr. 3:2–4 — 237
Abr. 3:9 — 238
Abr. 3:18 — 209, 231
Abr. 3:19 — 115, 259
Abr. 3:22 — 209
Abr. 3:22–23 — 215–16
Abr. 3:24 — 231
Abr. 3:26 — 218
Abr. 3:28 — 222
Abr. 4–5 — 242
Abr. 4:1 — 115, 233
Abr. 4:8 — 237
Abr. 4:26–27 — 119, 231
Abr. 4:27 — 231
Abr. 5:7 — 223n. 6
Abr. 5:10 — 246n. 2
Abr. 5:13 — 236, 237, 259
Abr. Fac. 2:1 — 236
Abr. Fac. 2:5 — 239
Abr. Fac. 2:7 — 189

Joseph Smith–Matthew

JS–M 1:27 — 399
JS–M 1:31 — 56, 401
JS–M 1:34 — 433
JS–M 1:39 — 433

Joseph Smith–History

JS–H 1:18 — 18, 41
JS–H 1:18–19 — 49
JS–H 1:38–39 — 75
JS–H 1:40 — 55
JS–H 1:41 — 439
JS–H 1:63–65 — 51
JS–H 1:69 — 79
JS–H 1:74–75 — 80

Articles of Faith

A of F 2 — 265
A of F 4 — 296, 305, 337n. 54
A of F 8 — 25n. 9
A of F 9 — 91
A of F 10 — 397, 418

Index

A

A Treatise on the Atonement, 241–42
Aaronic priesthood
  and Book of Mormon, 21, 381, 383
  and John the Baptist, 75
  restoration of, 73, 79–80
Abel, Elijah, 388
Abraham, 315–16
Achtemeier, Paul, 350
Adam
  begotten, 231
  creation of, 234, 243–44
  and Eve receive gospel, 294
  fall of. See fall of Adam.
  made in image of Christ, 133
  son of God, 244
Adam-God doctrine, 23, 142–43
adoption, 30n. 114, 140, 158, 181n. 56
afterlife
  degrees of glory. See degrees of glory.
  in Old Testament, 297, 298, 456
  judgment. See final judgment.
  paradise, 348
  resurrection. See resurrection.
age of accountability, 263, 265
Age of Reason, 238
Alexander, Caleb, 160
Alexander, Thomas G.
  on God in the Book of Mormon, 134
  on godhead in early Mormonism, 112
  on human nature, 266
  on Mormon tritheism, 114
  on multiple Mormon theologies, 6
Alger, Fanny, 319
Allen, Ethan, 239
Allen, James B., 49–50
Allison, Dale C., Jr., 349
Althaus, Paul, 347
Amana Community. See True Inspiration Society.
Anderson, Lavina Fielding, x

Andrus, Hyrum L.
  on first flesh, 244
  on creation, 236
angels, 218
animals, 467
Anselm, 282, 283
Anthon, Charles, 92, 102n. 2
anthropomorphism. See God the Father, corporeality of.
apocrypha, 22
apostasy. See Great Apostasy.
apostle
  in early Mormonism, 383–84, 393n. 43
  in New Testament, 377–78
  twelve, 19
  women, 378
Arianism, 164
Arminianism, 213–14, 215, 245, 263, 269n. 16, 285, 302. See also foreordination.
Arminius, Jacob, 213
Armstrong, Karen
  on Jesus and contemporary Jews, 16
  on Jesus as God's son, 157
  on theology, x, 506
Athanasian Creed, 108
Atonement, 273–88
  in early nineteenth-century Christianity, 282
  infinite, 283–86
  in Mormonism, 282–83
  in New Testament, 281–82
  in Old Testament, 274–81
  retroactive redemption, 286–87
  satisfaction theory, 282, 283
  universal effects, 287–88
Attridge, Harold, 299
Augustine, St.
  on everlasting gospel, 294
  on Satan, 197
  on unbaptized children, 331
Augustus, Caesar, 157

Aune, David, 97
Austin, Samuel, 416
authority. *See* priesthood authority.
Avis, Paul, 85

B

Bagatti, Bellarmino, 10
Bailey, Elijah, 108
Ballou, Adin, 359
Ballou, Hosea
  on creation of humans, 208
  on eternal punishment, 482
  on infinite atonement, 284
  on restorationism, 62
  on two creations, 241–42
baptism
  of infants, 332–33
  and Jewish temple, 335n. 21
  in New Testament, 300–301
  in Old Testament, 297–98
  replaces circumcision, 342n. 172
baptism for the dead, 348, 355, 362–63.
  connects dispensations, 77–78
  saviors on mount Zion, 345
  See also salvation for the dead;
    temples; work for the dead.
Baptist Confession of Faith, 262
Barlow, Philip
  on Joseph Smith Translation, 99
  on Mormonism and biblical theology, 5
  on multiple Mormon theologies, 5–6
Barnes, Albert, 264
Barnett, Paul, 35
Barney, Kevin L., x
  on baptism, 298, 301
  on creation, 232
  on Jesus entering Jerusalem, 10
  on "line upon line," 9
Barr, James
  on creation, 236
  on God as changeable, 25n. 10
Barton, John, 14
Bateman, Merrill, 60
Bavinck, Herman, 456–57
Baxter, Richard, 201
Becker, Joachim
  on messianic prophecies, 154
  on proof-texting, 11
Beecher, Edward, 202
Beegle, Dewey, 11
Bennett, Samuel, 135

Bennion, Lowell
  on Jehovah, 175
  on preexistence, 203
  and theological liberalism, 2
Berkouwer, Gerrit C.
  on body-spirit dualism, 266, 346–47
  on death, 347
  on soul, 201
Bible
  authorship, ix, 43n. 12, 70n. 56, 82,
    136–37, 146n. 61, 250n. 81, 298, 350
  critical analysis, viii, 12–18
  multiple theological perspectives, 5
  preservation of, 97–98
binitarianism, 111–12, 187. *See also*
    godhead; modalism; trinitarian-
    ism; tritheism.
bishop
  in early Christianity, 378–79
  in early Mormonism, 383–85
  in nineteenth-century Christianity, 381
Blau, Ludwig, 200
Blekinsopp, Joseph, 400
blood atonement, 496. *See also* murder;
    unpardonable sin.
Bloom, Harold, 211
Book of Abraham, 99–100
Book of Commandments, 20–21, 48, 79,
    101, 383, 447
Book of Common Prayer, 164, 261
Book of Mormon
  on age of accountability, 265
  anti-Unitarian, 108
  anti-Universalist, 197
  and apostasy, 41–42, 86
  and Calvinism, 303–4
  and classical trinitarianism, 109
  and priesthood, 79, 381–83
  changes to, 111
  coming forth of, 92–97
  on creation, 230, 233, 246
  on death before fall, 234
  dictation sequence, 306
  on fall of Adam, 253
  fulness of gospel, 304–5
  on fulness of time, 59
  on God as father, 141
  on godhead, 109
  on heathens, 360
  on Holy Ghost, 187
  on Jehovah, 174
  on Jesus as Father, 176

on Jesus's conception, 161, 167
on Jesus's sonship, 161
lack of higher ordinances, 20–21
and law of Moses in, 304
lost manuscript, 151
on messiah, 180n. 15
and modalism, 109–11, 178
and modern salvation theology, 486–87
monotheistic, 118
on name of Christ's church, 48
on nature of God, 134–35
on Only Begotten, 164
"other sheep," 95
on preexistence, 207
on preservation of Bible, 98
on prevenient grace, 303
prophecies in, 21
prophecies of
  in New Testament, 95–97
  in Old Testament, 51, 92–94
on race, 388
renewed source for theology, 24. See also neo-orthodoxy.
on restoration, 62, 63, 85
on Satan, 221
on sealing, 323
on Second Coming, 446–47
similarity to evangelicalism, 20
stick of Ephraim, 93
temples, 310
on unbaptized children, 332
Boring, M. Eugene
  on book of Revelation, 429
  on war in heaven, 220
Boudinot, Elias
  on conversion of Jews, 402
  on Elias and John the Baptist, 88n. 5
Brothers, Richard, 88n. 6
Brown, Colin, 178
Brown, Hugh B., 7–8
Brown, John, 245
Brown, Raymond E.
  on biblical criticism, 13
  on book of Revelation, 428–29
  on Jesus's conception, 166
  on Jesus's sonship, 158
  on millennialism, 442–43
  on Old Testament prophecies, 14–15, 149
  on sinning in the womb, 204
  on sons of God, 155
  on twelve apostles, 377
  on virgin birth, 167

Broyde, Isaac, 200
Bruce, F. F.
  on elders and bishops, 379
  on fulfillment of the law, 300
  on resurrection, 457–58
  on Son of Man, 172
  on the immortal soul, 347
Brueggeman, Walter
  on creation, 228
  on suffering servant, 279
Buck, Charles
  on Adam, 133
  on intelligences, 115
  on ordinances, 334n. 15
  on spirit, 201
Buerger, David, 142
Bush, Lester, 390
Bushinski, L. A., 185, 186
Bushman, Richard L.
  on body of God, 136
  on Book of Mormon expansion theory, 20
  on early Church organization, 384
  on eternal punishment, 482–83
  on Freemasonry and temple endowment, 313
  on heaven as a sea of glass, 488–89
  on Kirtland Temple endowment, 312
  on nineteenth-century Christian prophets, 50
  on patriarchs, 392n. 20
  on priesthood, 87n. 1, 386
  on restoration of priesthood, 80
Byrne, Brendan – on sons of God, 203

C

Cain, 389–90
calling and election made sure
  in Bible, 320–23
  in contemporary Mormonism, 326
  in early Mormonism, 323–25
  Holy Spirit of promise, 321–22
  in Nauvoo period, 325
callings, 380–81
Calvin, John, 266
Calvinism, 213–214, 245, 263, 269n. 16, 285, 300, 303–4. See also foreordination.
Cameron, Euan, 49
Campbell, Alexander
  on apostasy, 40
  on Book of Mormon, 20
  and ecclesiastical authority, 380

on name of Christ's church, 48
restorationist, 41
Campbell, Craig S., 420
Campbellism, 134, 385
Canaanite religions
  gods, 106
  influences on Old Testament theology, 13, 125
Cannon, George Q.
  on gift of the Holy Ghost, 308
  on infallibility, 7
  on oath and covenant, 337n. 63
Carroll, Robert
  on gathering of Israel, 398
  on prophecy, 16
Catholicism, 42, 307
celestial marriage. *See* eternal marriage.
  See also polygamy.
Chandler, Ted, 283
Charles, R. H., 196
Charlesworth, James H.
  on book of Revelation, 18
  on messianic prophecy, 154
cherubim, 268n. 1
children
  die in infancy, 332–33
  infant baptism, 332
  of sealed parents. *See* eternal marriage.
  resurrection of, 466, 470n. 42
  salvation of, 331–34, 342n. 165, 359
    in Methodism, 332
  unable to sin, 333
Childs, Brevard, 4
Christ. *See* Jesus.
Christensen, Ryan C., 43
Christian theology
  cultural influences of, ix
  development of, ix
Church of Jesus Christ of Latter-day Saints
  before organization, 86
  ensign to nations, 82–83
  name of, 48
  organization of, 87
  restoration of
    in early LDS teachings, 85–87
    in New Testament, 84–85
    in Old Testament, 80–84
circumcision, 335n. 16
  replaced by baptism, 342n. 172
Clark, J. Reuben, 6

Clarke, Adam
  on God's eternality, 144
  on infinite atonement, 284, 285
  on inhabited worlds, 239, 240
  on messianic prophecy, 153
  on misreading scripture, 9–10
  on Nebuchadnezzar's dream, 81
  on perfectionism, 329
  on restoration, 65, 70n. 70
  on saviors on mount Zion, 345
  on Satan, 196
Clarke, Samuel, 126–27
Clayton, William, 319
Clement of Rome
  on apostasy, 33
  on succession of authority, 378
Cleveland, John, 358
Cohen, Abraham, 277
Collins, John, 81
Colton, Eleanor, 167
Coltrin, Zebedee
  on dispensations, 59
  on preaching to the dead, 364
Comforter
  Holy Ghost, 322. *See also* Holy Ghost.
  Jesus, 322. *See also* calling and election made sure.
  paraclete, 186
Compton, Todd C., 31
confirmation. *See* gift of the Holy Ghost.
Cook, Lyndon W.
  on D&C 130:22, 188
  on high priesthood, 386
  on Nauvoo endowment, 315
Council of Nicaea, 164
Cowdery, Oliver
  on Moroni's visit to Joseph Smith, 88n. 9
  second elder, 384
Cowdery, Warren, 202
creation
  agent and method, 229–31
  by God, 229
  by Jesus, 229–30
  evolution. *See* evolution.
  ex material, 231–34
  ex nihilo, 231–34
  first flesh, 243–44
  Genesis, 227–29
  length of days, 235–38, 246n. 2, 248n. 49, 269n. 17
  other worlds, 238–41, 249n. 80
  purpose of, 245–46

similarities with other myths, 228
spiritual, 241–42
creeds, 1
Crenshaw, James, 458
Crossan, John Dominic, 469n. 24
Crowe, Michael, 240

D

Darby, John D., 58
Dark Ages, 31, 42. *See also* Great Apostasy.
David
  and murder, 493–94
  and stem of Jesse, 54, 55
Davidson, Karen Lynn, 385
Davies, W. D., 349
deacon
  in early Christianity, 378
  in early Mormonism, 383
  in nineteenth-century Christianity, 381
Dead Sea Scrolls, 104n. 45, 116
death. *See* afterlife. *See also* resurrection.
degrees of glory
  and Book of Mormon
  celestial, 480, 485–86
    Alvin Smith in, 361–62
  outer darkness, 490
  son of perdition. *See* son of perdition.
  telestial, 486, 487
    resurrection to, 463
  terrestrial, 486
    for heathens and ignorant, 361
    resurrection to, 464
Derr, Jill Mulvay, 385
Deutero-Isaiah, 28n. 74
Dever, William, 116
devil. *See* Satan.
Dick, Thomas, 239–40
Disciples of Christ, 381. *See also* Campbellism.
dispensationalism, 58–59
  definition of dispensation, 58.
  gospel taught in every dispensation, 293
  in New Testament, 59
  seven dispensations, 58
  See also fulness of times.
divine council, 106, 115. *See also* godhead.
doctrine
  abandoning, 24
  changing, vii
  definitions of, viii
  exclusivity, 503–4
  myth of uniformity, 5–7

no official systematic theology, 1
restoration of, 91–104
sources of, vii, 1
Donaldson, Amy, 490
Dow, Lorenzo
  on creation of spirits, 206
  on heathens, 359
  on Universalism, 480
Dulles, Avery, 297
Dunn, James D. G.
  on body-spirit dualism, 266
  on early Christian church, 48, 49
  on fulfillment of the law, 299
  on Holy Spirit of promise, 323
  on Jesus's sonship, 158
  on proof-texting, 11
  on spirit, 186
Dursteler, Eric, 42
Dwight, Timothy, 416
dyophysitism, 160. *See also* Jesus.

E

early Christian church, 48, 49, 85. *See also* New Testament theology
Earth.
  moved during fall of Adam, 258–59
  resurrection of, 488
  See also creation.
Edwards, Jonathon
  on degrees of heaven, 480
  and millennium, 445
  and restored truths, 97
  similarities to Book of Mormon, 283
  on universe, 239
Ehrman, Bart, 48, 49
elder
  in Book of Mormon, 382
  in early Christianity, 378–79
  in early Mormonism, 87n. 1, 383–85
  in nineteenth-century Christianity, 381
  traveling and standing, 384
element. *See* matter.
Elias
  different from Elijah, 66
  Greek for Elijah, 65–66, 79
  John the Baptist, 65, 88n. 5
  John the Revelator, 65
  role in restoration, 64–65, 73
  See also Elijah.
Elijah
  forerunner, 53
  John the Baptist, 74–75

at mount of transfiguration, 65.
and restoration, 73
restores sealing power, 75, 76, 78, 324, 346
and work for the dead, 77–79
See also Elias.
Elohim
  God the Father, 174–75. *See also* God the Father.
  name of God, 106, 125, 138
  plural form of "god," 114–15, 124n. 63, 138
Encyclopedia of Mormonism, 1
endowment, 20, 198n. 2
  in Book of Mormon, 338n. 74
  in early Mormonism, 310–12
  and Freemasonry, similarities to 313–14. *See also* Freemasonry.
  and Gnostic sects, 310
  Holy Order, 313
  Kirtland Temple, 312
  in later Mormonism, 315
  in Nauvoo period, 312
  in New Testament, 309–10
  not found in early Mormonism, 20
  in Old Testament, 309
  spiritual, 311
  women, 312
ensign, 82–83
  and gathering of Israel, 83
  See also Church of Jesus Christ of Latter-day Saints.
Ephrata Society, 355
Episcopalians, 380
Epperson, Stephen, 402
Ericson, Loyd, x
Esplin, Scott, 69
eternal generation, 164
eternal life, 499n. 42
eternal marriage
  in contemporary Mormonism, 319–20
  in later Mormonism, 319
  in Nauvoo period, 318–19
  in New Testament, 316
  in Old Testament, 315–16
  not found in early Mormonism, 20, 21
  and salvation, 476, 486
  seals children to eternal life, 326–27
  seals couples to eternal life, 77
eternal progress, 330–31. *See also* perfectionism.
Eusebius, 294
everlasting covenant, 31, 43n. 5
evolution, 234–35
  no death before fall, 234
  pre-Adamites. *See* pre-Adamites.
ex materia. See creation.
ex nihilo. See creation.
Expositor's Bible Commentary, 59

F

fall of Adam
  length of day, 269n. 17
  no death before, 2–3, 25n. 8
  original guilt. *See* original guilt.
  physical banishment, 258
  physical death, 256–57
  power of procreation, 257–58
  removal of the Earth, 258–59
  spiritual consequences, 259–65
  spiritual death, 259–63
  transgression, 252–55
familiar spirit, 51, 68n. 23
"Family: A Proclamation to the World," 142
Faulconer, James E.
  on continuing revelation, 7, 501
  on Mormonism as a-theological, 1
Faust, James E.
  on angel in Revelation, 96
  on children of sealed parents, 327
Ferguson, Everett, 475
final judgment
  degrees of glory. *See* degrees of glory.
  in early Mormonism, 481–85
  in early nineteenth-century Christianity, 479–81
  endless punishment, 482
  in later Mormonism, 485
  in New Testament, 475–79
  in Old Testament, 473–75
  second death, 487–88
  son of perdition. *See* son of perdition.
  unpardonable sin. *See* unpardonable sin.
Finney, Charles Grandison, 445
First Vision, 49–50, 132, 136
  and apostasy, 41
  as evidence of God's corporeality, 145n. 58
foreordination
  in Bible, 212–13
  in contemporary Mormonism, 215–17
  in early Mormonism, 214–15

    in early nineteenth-century
        Christianity, 213–14
    in Nauvoo period, 215
    See also preexistence.
Foutz, Scott, 390
Fowler, James, 504
Free Will Baptists, 381
Freemasonry, 22, 312–14. *See also* endowment.
fulness of the gospel, 304–5
fulness of time, 58–60
    as Christ's first coming, 59
    See also restoration.

G

Gabriel, 65
Garden of Eden, 22, 193, 243, 251–55
gates of hell, 35, 349. *See also* apostasy; salvation for the dead.
gathering of Israel
    conversion of Jews. *See* Jews, conversion of.
    and ensign, 83
    and Irvingites, 18
    Lamanites, 405–10
    Latter-day missionary work, 399–401
    location, 410–12
    lost tribes, 412–14
    in New Testament, 398–99
    in Old Testament, 398
    and Second Coming, 408, 402
    spiritual vs. temporal, 402–3
Gaventa, Beverly, 61
gift of the Holy Ghost
    in Book of Mormon, 306
    in New Testament, 301
    laying on of hands, 300, 308, 336n. 33, 382
gifts of the spirit, 19
Gill, John – on everlasting gospel, 295
Givens, Terryl L.
    on Book of Mormon expansion theory, 20
    on gathering, 410
    on Joseph Smith, 91
    on syncretism, 1–2
glory. *See* degrees of glory.
God
    absolute vs. finite
        in Bible, 126
        in early Mormonism, 126–27
        in later Mormonism, 127–30
    body of, 22
    cause of evil, 194
    creator, 229
    in early Old Testament, 13–14
    eternal, 128
    finite, 129
    fulness of truth, 128
    knowledge, 129, 207, 216, 144n. 32
    spirit, 132
    unchanging, 127
    See also Elohim; God the Father; godhead; Jehovah; Jesus; modalism; Trinity.
God the Father
    body of flesh and bone, 135
    capable of seeing, 136–38
        requires Melchizedek priesthood, 137, 146n. 65
        with spiritual eyes, 137
    corporeality of
        in early Mormonism, 134–36
        in early nineteenth century Christianity, 133–34
        in Nauvoo period, 136
        in New Testament, 131–33
        in Old Testament, 130–31
    Elohim, 125, 138, 174–75
    father of spirits
        in early Mormonism, 141
        in later Mormonism, 141–42
        in New Testament, 139–40
        in Old Testament, 139
    Jehovah 174–5
    personage of spirit, 133–34, 135
    once a man, 127, 505
God the Mother, 124n. 59, 207
godhead
    in contemporary Mormonism, 114
    definitions of, 105
    in early Mormonism, 109–11
    in early nineteenth-century Christianity, 107–9
    in Kirtland period, 112–13
    in Nauvoo period, 113–14
    in New Testament, 107
    names of, 106
    in Old Testament, 105–7
    royal "we," 246n. 7
    three gods, 114
    three personages, 113–14
    two personages, 111–12
gods, plurality of
    in early Mormonism, 118

hierarchy, 115
in New Testament, 117–18
in Old Testament, 116–17
polytheism, 122n. 36
royal "we," 246n. 7
Good, Edwin M., 458
Goodsell, Buel, 302
gospel
everlasting, 293–96
fulness of. *See* fulness of the gospel.
Gospel Principles, 1
on children of God, 211
on creation, 247n. 13
on Elijah, 74
on fall of Adam, 235
on foreordination, 216
on God, body of, 130
on Holy Ghost, body of, 191n. 1
on preaching to dead, 366
Gottstein, Alan, 132
Gowan, Donald, 415–16
grace, prevenient, 302, 303
Graham, Billy, 249n. 80
Grant, David, 233
Grant, Heber J., 320
Great Apostasy
in contemporary Mormonism, 42–43, 45
in early Mormonism, 41–42
great and abominable church, 42
necessitates a restoration, 31
New Testament prophecies, 33–40
Old Testament prophecies of, 32
priesthood, 42
Protestant views, 40–41
Green, Joel B., 352
Griffen, Edward D., 330.
Gunkel, Herman, 276–77
Guthrie, Shirley, 261

H

Hades, 35, 475. *See also* hell.
Hale, Van, 210–11
Harrell, Charles R., viii–ix
Harrell, Daniel, x
Harrell, Thomas, x
Harrell, Yvonne, x
Harris, Martin
on apostasy, 40
on biblical criticism, 12
and Charles Anthon, 102n. 2
lost manuscript, 151

heathens
resurrection of, 462
salvation for the dead, 359–62
heaven
sea of glass, 488–89
three kingdoms, 476–80. *See also* degrees of glory.
See also afterlife.
Heavenly Father. *See* God the Father. *See also* God.
Heavenly Mother. *See* God the Mother.
Heim, Knut, 155
hell, 475
endless punishment, 482
See also afterlife; Hades; judgment; Sheol; outer darkness.
Hendel, Ronald
on creation, 244
on early Old Testament theology, 14
Henze, Matthias
on Nebuchadnezzar's dream, 82
on Son of Man, 171–72
hermeticism, 22
Herrick, Greg, 13
Herschel, William, 240
Hicks, Elias
on everlasting gospel, 294
on original guilt, 264
Hicksites, 134
Hiebert, Theodore
on divine council, 106
on fall of Adam, 256
on Satan, 194
high priest, 383, 386
high priesthood. *See* priesthood.
Hill, Marvin, 22
Hinckley, Gordon B.
on God as once man, 505
on Jesus, 149
Hobbes, Thomas, 201
Holland, Jeffrey R.
on Atonement, 286, 289n. 29
on racist folklore, 391
on remnant of Jacob, 409
Holy Ghost
body of, 189–90
Comforter, 186, 322. *See also* Comforter.
conceives Jesus, 161, 166
in contemporary Mormonism, 190
in early Mormonism, 187–88

in early nineteenth-century Christianity, 186–87
gift of. *See* gift of the Holy Ghost.
in Nauvoo period, 188–89
in New Testament, 186
in Old Testament, 185–86
receiving, 301. *See also* gift of Holy Ghost.
sin against, 489–90. *See also* final judgment; murder; unpardonable sin.
Spirit of the Lord, 185
Holy Spirit. *See* Holy Ghost.
Hooker, Richard
  on early Christianity, 16
  on plurality of gods in Old Testament, 123n. 46
Hopkins, Samuel, 445
Hoskisson, Paul Y., 52
Hughes, Richard
  on Joseph Smith, 47
Hughes, Richard, 47
humans
  body-spirit dualism, 266–68, 346–47
  offspring of God, 139–40
  sinful nature, 260. *See also* original guilt.
Humphrey, John, 433
Hunter, Edward, 498
Hunter, Milton R., 416
Hutchinson, Anthony
  on fall of Adam, 269n. 17
  on Joseph Smith and proof-texting, 12
Hyde, Orson, 389

I

Ignatius, 378
infallibility. *See* prophetic infallibility.
intelligence, 209
  aid in creation, 231
  eternal, 242
  independent of spirit, 211
  and plurality of gods, 115
  See also soul; spirit; spirit birth.
Irvingites, 18–19
Isaac, Daniel
  on final judgment, 485
  on inhabited worlds, 239
Israelite theology, 13–16
  and Canaanite traditions, xin. 8, 13, 125, 296–97
  cosmology, 455

cultural influences of, ix

J

Jackson, David, 391
Jackson, Kent P.
  on Jesus in the Old Testament, 149
  on last days, 438
  on Son of God, 157
Jacob, Edmond, 346
James, William, 507n. 6
Jefferson, Thomas, 45n. 36
Jeffery, Duane, 234–35
Jehovah
  God the Father, 174–5
  God of Israel, 212
  Jesus, 106, 131, 173–75
  meaning of, 173–74
  one God, 177
Jenson, Phillip P., 180n. 18
Jerome, St.
  and Lucifer, 195
  on eternal generation, 164
  on Nebuchadnezzar's dream, 89n. 35
Jerusalem Community, 50
Jesus
  atonement of. *See* Atonement.
  chooses apostles, 377
  Christ (name), 152–53.
  Comforter, 322. *See also* calling and election made sure; Comforter.
  conceived by Holy Ghost, 161, 166
  creator, 229–30
  date of birth, 151, 179n. 9
  elder brother. *See* Jesus, firstborn.
  Elias, 65
  Father, 109–10, 175–77
  firstborn, 168–71
  God of the Old Testament, 177–79
  Jehovah, 106, 131, 173–75
  last commission, 35
  member of godhead, 107
  messiah, 153–54
  millennial reign of, 19, 443–44
  name, meaning of, 152
  Only Begotten Son, 162–66
    eternally, 163–64
    in the flesh, 162, 164, 166, 181n. 55
    in New Testament, 163
  prophecies of
    in Book of Mormon, 150
    in Old Testament, 149–50
  receives Holy Ghost, 187–88

resembles God the Father, 132
resurrection, 350
second coming of. *See* Second Coming. *See also* millennium.
sexually conceived, 166
similarities with contemporary Pharisees, 16
Son of God
  in early Mormonism, 161–62
  in New Testament, 157–159
  in nineteenth-century evangelicalism, 159–61
  in Old Testament, 154–57
  two natures, 159–60
Son of Man, 171–73. *See also* Son of Man.
Spirit of the Lord, 191n. 13
suffering servant, 278–80
virgin birth, 17, 166–67, 182n. 72
visits spirit world, 350–54, 364
word of God, 17
Jesus Seminar, 27n. 56
Jewish midrash, 22
Jews
  at time of Jesus, 16, 34, 107, 153–54, 178, 186, 316–17, 459
  conversion of, 75, 402–4
  See also gathering of Israel.
John the Baptist
  and Aaronic priesthood, 75
  and baptism, 300–301
  as Elias, 65, 88n. 5
  as Elijah, 53, 74–75
  restores priesthood, 73, 79
John the Revelator, 65
Johnson, Benjamin F., 437
Johnson, Charles, 302
Johnson, Paul, 414
Jones, Abner, 47
Joseph Smith Translation, 98–99
  and Book of Mormon, 68n. 29
  completion and publication, 104n. 32
  See also standard works.
Josephus
  on giants, 218
  on God, 132
Judaism. *See* Israelite theology; Jews.
Judd, Frank, 55
judgment. *See* final judgment.
Just, Felix, 5

K

kapar, 274. *See also* Atonement.
Kapelrud, Arvid, 13
Keck, Leander, 232
Keller, Roger
  on godhead, 120
  on Holy Ghost, 504
  on theology, 506
Kent, William, 196
Key to the Science of Theology, 52
  revised by Charles Penrose, 189
keys. *See* priesthood.
Kimball, Edward L., 389
Kimball, Heber C.
  on blood atonement, 496
  on Freemasonry and temple endowment, 313
  on Holy Ghost, 190
Kimball, Spencer W.
  on gathering, 411
  on Native American skin color, 409
  on remnant of Jacob, 423n. 50
  on Zion, 453
King Follet discourse, 127–28, 224n. 52. *See also* God the Father, once a man.
kingdom of God, 80. *See also* the Church of Jesus Christ of Latter-day Saints.
kingdoms. *See* degrees of glory.
Kinkade, William, 134
Kirkland, Boyd
  on God in early Mormonism, 126
  on Jehovah, 174
Kirtland Temple
  dedicatory prayer, 174, 312
  endowment, 312
  House of God, 312
  preparatory temple, 314
  restoration of keys, 73, 74
Kohler, Kaufmann
  on Jewish baptism, 298
  on Old Testament prophets, 474
  on the soul, 200
Kolob, 259
Kostenberger, Andreas J., 103n. 8
Kraus, H. J., 276
Kraus, Samuel, 298
Küng, Hans
  on biblical authorship, 3, 350
  on imminent millennium, 431
  on Jesus, 180n. 23

on resurrection, 282

L

Ladd, George, 168
Lamanites
  ancestors of Native Americans, 405
  remnant of Jacob, 408–9, 423n. 50
  white and delightsome, 409
Lang, Bernhard, 347
Langton, Stephen, 279
last days
  imminent prophecies of
    by Joseph Smith, 23
    in New Testament, 17
    in New Testament, 34
Lathrop, Joseph, 39
law of Moses, 274–75
  eternal, 298. *See also* everlasting covenant.
  in Book of Mormon, 304
  murder, 32
  old dispensation, 59
laying on of hands. *See* gift of the Holy Ghost, laying on of hands; priesthood, laying on of hands.
LDS Newsroom, 7
Lectures on Faith
  authorship, 121n. 21
  canonization of, 4
  on creation, 119, 129, 230
  decanonization of, 4, 122n. 22, 145n. 45
  on God as absolute, 129
  on God's body, 133
  on godhead, 4, 111–12
  on Holy Ghost, 188
  on Jesus's sonship, 162
  on perfection, 329–30
  on unchanging God, 127
Lee, Ann, 50
Lee, Harold B., 411
Lenski, R. C. H., 35
Levenson, Jon, 246n. 7
Lewis, C. S., 467
limbo, 331. *See also*, afterlife, spirit world.
Lincoln, Andrew, 157, 159
Lohse, Eduard
  on firstborn, 169
  on messianic prophecies, 275
Longman, Tremper, 456
lost tribes. *See* gathering of Israel, lost tribes.
Lovely, E., 232

Lucifer. *See* Satan.
Ludlow, Daniel H., 407
Lund, Anthon H.
  on Joseph F. Smith's revelation of the spirit world, 365
  on Son of Man, 173
Luther, Martin
  on baptizing children, 332
  on Jesus, 150

M

Maier, Paul, 151–52
Mallet, Robert, 47
Mannock, John, 165
Marais, J. I., 202, 204, 205
Marford, Charles, 480
Martins, Marcus H., 389, 391
marvelous work and wonder, 84
Mather, Cotton, 420
matter
  eternal, 233
  immaterial substance, 201
  refined. *See* spirit, refined matter.
Matthews, Robert J.
  on Joseph Smith Translation, 104n. 32
  on Joseph Smith's polygamy, 318
Mauss, Armand
  on Abrahamic lineage, 407
  on priesthood ban, 389–90, 91
Maxwell, Neal A.
  on God's knowledge, 216
  on Jesus's suffering, 290n. 33
  on messianic prophecies, 281
  on universe, 238
May, H. G., 414
Mays, James, 277
McConkie, Bruce R.
  on Adam, 244, 247n. 14, 257
  on Adam-God doctrine, 142, 147n. 91
  on angel in Revelation, 97
  on blacks and the priesthood, 6, 389, 390
  on blood atonement, 496
  on calling and election made sure, 326
  on Church organization, 373–74
  on continuing revelation, vii–viii, 6
  on conversion of Jews, 404
  on creation, 231, 236, 237–38
  on day of Pentecost, 310
  on death of children, 333–34
  on doctrinal discernment, 7
  on doctrine and truth, xin. 4, 24n. 6

on Elias, 79
on Elijah, 74
on evolution, 2, 235
on final judgment, 488
on foreordination 216–17
on fulness of gospel, 304–5
on gathering, 411
on God's knowledge, 129
on God's spirit body, 145n. 46
on Holy Ghost, 190
on infinite atonement, 286–86
on intelligence, 211.
on Jehovah, 174
on Jesus as God of Israel, 177
on Jesus as Jehovah, 173
on Jewish temple baptisms, 335n. 21
on laying on of hands, 336n. 33
on little children, 342n. 178
on lost tribes, 413–14, 424n. 76
on messianic prophecies, 156, 277
on millennium, 454n. 59
on new heaven and earth, 450
on Only Begotten, 166
on perfectionism, 328
on plants and animals, 466
on polygamy, 320
on preaching to the dead, 349
on pre-Adamites, 234
on preexistence, 211
on priesthood, 44n. 30
on resemblance of Father and Son, 132
on restoration of blood sacrifice, 67
on resurrection, 349
on second chances for salvation, 366
on Second Coming, 408, 437–38
on Son of Man, 173
on sons of God, 219
on sons of perdition, 469n. 28
on soul after death, 484
on spirit birth, 140
on Spirit of the Lord, 191n. 13
on spirit prison, 367n. 7
on spiritual creation, 242
on Ten Commandments, 300
and theological conservatism
on virgin birth, 167
on war in heaven, 220
on Zion, 418
McConkie, Joseph Fielding
 on Book of Mormon, 303
 on Book of Mormon prophecy of
  Joseph Smith, 57–58
 on Jewish temple baptisms, 335n. 21
McConkie, Oscar W., 392n. 9
McCown, Wayne G., 357
McDannell, Colleen, 347
McGrath, Alister
 on creation, 232
 on New Jerusalem, 419
McKim, Donald, 260
McLellin, William E., 79–80, 89n. 25
McMurrin, Sterling, 129–30
Melchizedek Priesthood
 and Book of Mormon, 21, 381, 382
 in early Mormonism, 20
 high priesthood, 386
 in New Testament, 310
 ordination essential for exaltation, 307–9
 and prophets, 374
 required to see God, 137
 restoration of, 73, 79–80, 87n. 1, 89n. 25
 and sacrifice, 71n. 90
Merritt, Timothy
 on Atonement, 282
 on fall of Adam, 256
 on probationary state, 359
Meservy, Keith, 173
Messadie, Gerald, 194
messiah, 275. *See* Jesus.
messianic prophecies, 275–81
Metcalfe, Brent Lee, 306
Methodism, 381, 384
Metz, Christian, 50
Meyers, Eric, 428
Millard, David
 on Holy Ghost, 113, 187
 on modalism, 108
millennium
 amillennialism, 444
 apocalyptic literature, 427–29
 in Apocrypha, 441
 Armageddon, 454n. 67
 and Irvingites, 19
 in Mormonism, 445–48
 in nineteenth-century Christianity, 444–45
 new heaven and earth, 448–50
 in New Testament, 441–44
 Old Testament, 440–41
 postmillennialism, 445, 448
 premillennialism, 445, 448, 462
 and resurrection, 462–63
Miller, William
 on Second Coming, 435

on the millennium, 479
Millet, Robert L.
  on doctrinal exclusivity, 504
  on God's eternality, 143n. 11
  on godhead in Book of Mormon, 111
  on prophetic fallibility, 502
  on redemptive theology, 24
  on fall of Adam, 258
Mobley, Gregory, 196
modalism, 108, 160–61
  in Book of Mormon, 109–11
  in early Mormonism, 178
  See also godhead; tritheism; trinitarianism.
Molinism, 359
monophysitism, 160. See also Jesus.
monotheism
  in Book of Mormon, 118
  in Doctrine and Covenants, 119
  in early Mormonism, 118–19
  in New Testament, 117, 178
  in Old Testament, 116, 178
moon, 240
Moore, Jacob, 160
Mormon theology
  eclectic religion, 19
  conservatism and liberalism, 2–3
  cultural influences of, ix
  early
    and Book of Mormon, 19–20
    lack of higher ordinances, 20–21
  future of 504–5
  myth of doctrinal uniformity, 5–7
  Nauvoo, 21–23
  relationship to Christianity and Judaism, x
Moroni
  angel in Revelation, 96
  visits Joseph Smith, 88n. 9
mortality. See probationary state.
Moses
  restores keys of gathering, 73
  sees God, 136
Mowinckel, Sigmund, 276
murder
  capital punishment in Utah, 500n. 76
  judgment of, 493–96
  law of Moses, 32
  See also blood-atonement; unpardonable sin.

N

Native Americans
  changing skin color, 409
  Lamanites, 405, 422n. 33. See also Lamanites.
Nauvoo temple, 314. See also endowment; temple.
Nebuchadnezzar's dream, 80–82.
Nelson, Russell M.
  on creation, 248n. 49
  on saviors on mount Zion, 345–46
neshamah, 223n. 6. See also spirit; soul.
New Jerusalem, 416–21, 443
  Independence, Missouri, 420
  See also Zion.
New Testament theology, 16–18
  and contemporary Jewish beliefs, 16
  multiple theological perspectives, 17
  non-Jewish converts, 17
Newell, Lloyd D., 504
Nibley, Hugh
  on Joseph of Egypt, 390
  and writings on the apostasy, 43n. 2
Nielsen, F. Kent, 237
Noll, Mark, 18
Norman, Keith
  on infallibility, 7
  on modern cosmology, 240

O

"O My Father," 139
Oaks, Dallin H., 252
O'Collins, Gerald
  on baptism, 301
  on biblical theologies, 5
  on messianic prophecies, 154
  on Son of God, 155
  on suffering servant, 278, 279
  on the spirit, 185
Ogden, D. Kelley – on Amos, 33
O'Kelly, James, 47
Oliver, W.H., x
Olson, Roger, 266
ordinances
  baptism. See baptism.
  calling and election made sure. See calling and election made sure.
  definition of, 334n. 15
  in early Mormonism, 20–21, 303
  endowment. See endowment.

eternal marriage. *See* eternal marriage.
gift of the Holy Ghost. *See* gift of the Holy Ghost.
Melchizedek Priesthood. *See* Melchizedek Priesthood.
necessary in Book of Mormon, 21
in New Testament, 299
in nineteenth-century Christianity, 301–3
in Old Testament, 296–99
second anointing, 320, 326, 341n. 134. *See also* temple endowment.
washing of feet, 311, 341n. 134
See also baptism for the dead; priesthood; temple; work for the dead.
Origen
on eternal generation, 164
on spirits in prison, 352
original guilt, 259, 263–65
original sin. *See* original guilt.
Osiander, 133
Ostler, Blake T.
on Arminianism in Mormon scripture, 304
on biblical theologies, 5
Book of Mormon expansion theory, 20
on continuing revelation, 501
on divorce in New Testament, 17
on human authorship of scripture, 3, 4
on infinite atonement, 286
on plurality of gods, 115

P

Packer, Boyd K.
on Book of Mormon, 93
on gathering, 411
Paine, Thomas, 238
parable of the leaven, 37
parable of the mustard seed, 36–37
parable of the wheat and tares, 35–36
paraclete, 186. *See also* Holy Ghost.
Paradise Lost, 258
paradise. *See* afterlife.
Parry, Donald, 404–5
Parry, Jay, 404–5
Partridge, Edward, 384
patriarch, 392n. 20
patriarchal blessings, 407
Paul, Erich Robert
on Enlightenment cosmologies, 238
on other worlds, 240

Penrose, Charles, 189
Perdue, Leo, 401
perfectionism
complete, 328
in early Mormonism, 329–30
in later Mormonism, 330–31
in Nauvoo period, 330
in New Testament, 328
in nineteenth-century Evangelicalism, 328–29
in Old Testament, 327–28, 357
Peter, James, and John
date of Melchizedek priesthood restoration, 87n. 1
restore priesthood, 73, 77, 79, 89n. 25
Phelps, William W.
on gathering of Native Americans, 406–7
on Jesus as elder brother, 171
on Jesus's sonship, 165
on lost tribes, 413
on spirit birth, 142
on war in heaven, 222
Philadelphia Confession of Faith, 286, 358
Phillips, J. B., 188
Philosophy of a Future State, 240
pneuma, 185, 186, 223n. 6. *See also* Holy Ghost; soul; spirit.
Pohle, Joseph, 375
polygamy, 318–320.
in Book of Mormon, 340n. 115
essential for salvation, 319
Manifesto, 319
polyandry, 319.
See also eternal marriage.
polytheism. *See* gods, plurality of.
Pontifical Biblical Commission, ix, 11
Pope, Marvin, 458
Porter, Larry, 87n. 1
postmortem evangelization. *See* salvation for the dead.
Pratt, Orson
on creation of spirits, 206
disagrees with Brigham Young, 129
on gathering of Israel, 400
on God as fulness of truth, 128
on hierarchy of gods, 123n. 42
on Holy Ghost, 189, 191n. 23
on infinite atonement, 284
on intelligence, 211
on Jesus as elder brother, 168, 170–71
on marriage sealing, 325

on original guilt, 265
on preexistence in Book of Mormon, 207
on receiving priesthood, 308
on spirit birth, 141, 147n. 81
on spiritual creation, 242
on war in heaven, 222
on Zion, 436
Pratt, Parley P.
  on blacks and priesthood, 388
  on God's spirit body, 135
  on Irvingites, 18–19
  on Joseph Smith, 52
  on Lamanites, 406
  on matter and spirit, 233
  on ordinances, 335n. 15
  on restoration, 64
  on sons of God, 204
  on spirit, 208
prayer circles, Masonic, 313
pre-Adamites, 234–35. See also creation; evolution.
predestination. See foreordination.
preexistence
  ability to sin, 271n. 50
  creation, 231
  in contemporary Mormonism, 211–12
  and early church Fathers, 205
  in early Mormonism, 207–8
  in early nineteenth-century Christianity, 206–7
  foreordination. See foreordination.
  in Kirtland period, 208–9
  in New Testament, 204–5
  in Nauvoo period, 209–11
  in Old Testament, 203–4
  war in heaven. See war in heaven.
preterism, 451n. 10
Price, Robert M., 21
priest
  in Book of Mormon, 382
  in early Christianity, 376–77
  in early Mormonism, 87n. 1, 383
  in Old Testament, 374–85
Priest, Josiah
  on Elijah, 75
  on resurrection of animals, 467
  on retroactive redemption, 287
priesthood. See also Aaronic priesthood; Melchizedek priesthood.
  age requirements, 387
  authority, 19
  and blacks, 388–91
  in Book of Mormon, 381–83
  in contemporary Mormonism, 387
  in early Mormonism, 383
  fulness of, 387–88
  given to Adam, 373
  high priesthood, 385–86
  laying on of hands, 382.
  loss of. See Great Apostasy.
  in Nauvoo period, 386
  in New Testament, 376
  in nineteenth-century Christianity, 380
  oath and covenant, 337n. 63
  in Old Testament, 374–76
  ordination, 374, 377–78, 382, 392n. 11
  restoration, 66, 73–80
    in early Mormonism, 79–80
    in New Testament, 79
    in Old Testament, 74–79
  revealing, 88n. 10
Priestley, Josiah, 201–2, 233
primitivism. See restorationism.
Prince, Gregory
  on early Church organization, 384–85
  on early endowment, 312
  on Joseph Smith and Freemasonry, 338n. 81
  on Nauvoo temple architecture, 314
  on priesthood in Book of Mormon, 381
  on sealing power, 324
probationary state, 358, 360
proof-texting, 8–12, 183n. 83
  in Bible, 10–11
  by Christians, 9
  goes beyond "likening," 26n. 41
prophecy
  after the fact, 15, 17
  in Book of Mormon, 21
  in later Mormonism, 28n. 70
  in Old Testament, 14
  specific, in Mormonism, 28n. 70
  unfulfilled, 15
prophet
  discernment, 23
  in early Mormonism, 393n. 43
  and Melchizedek Priesthood, 374
  in New Testament, 379–80
  in nineteenth century Christianity, 50
  in Old Testament, 14
prophetic infallibility, 7–8
prototokos, 168. See also Jesus.

Q

Quinn, D. Michael
  on early Church organization, 383
  on restoration of priesthood, 87n. 1
Qumran, 27n. 54

R

Rad, Von, 131
Raphael, Simcha Paull, 457
Rapp, George, 50
Rappites, 50
Ras Shambra tablets, 116
Rausch, Thomas P., 456
reincarnation – 205
Rensberger, David, 490
restitution of all things. *See* restoration
restoration
  of all things, 60–67
  animal sacrifice, 66, 67
  in Book of Mormon, 63
  in contemporary Mormonism, 66–67
  doctrines, 91–104
  in early Mormonism, 63–66
  of Israel, 61
  in Nauvoo period, 66
  in New Testament, 61–62
  in nineteenth-century Christianity, 62–63
  in Old Testament, 60–61
  priesthood, 64, 66, 73–80
  See also Book of Mormon; Church of Jesus Christ of Latter-day Saints; Joseph Smith; priesthood.
restorationism, 47–48
  and Catholicism, 40–41
  dates for, 44n. 28
  movements, 47
resurrection
  of all forms of life, 466–67
  of children, 333, 466, 470n. 42
  in early Mormonism, 461–62
  in early nineteenth-century Christianity, 461
  of Earth, 488
  of heathens, 462
  with imperfections, 465
  in later Mormonism, 462–65
  in New Testament, 459–61
  in Old Testament, 455–59
  and millennium, 462–63
  process, 465–66

sons of perdition, 469n. 28
three kingdoms, 476–80
revelation, 25n. 19
Revelation, book of, 18
Rhodes, Michael, 100
Rhymer, David, 299
Richards, LeGrand, 342n. 165
Richards, Willard, 214
Ridderbos, Herman N, 60
Rigdon, Sidney, 385
Roberts, B. H.
  on God as community of intelligences, 128
  on name of the Church, 48
  on unfulfilled prophecy, 23
Roberts, J. J. M.
  on gathering of Israel, 400
  on Jesus as Father, 176
  on messianic prophecies, 153
  on similarities between Israelites and neighbors, 296
Robertson, A.T., 35
Robinson, H. Wheeler, 456
Robinson, Stephen E.
  on Book of Mormon, 303
  on corporeality of God, 131
  on "gods," 120
  on preservation of Bible, 97–98
  on proof-texting, 8
  on two churches, 85–86
Romney, Marion G.
  on pre-Adamites, 235
  on virgin birth, 182n. 72
Rowley, H. H., 278
ruah, 185. *See also* Holy Ghost.

S

sacrifice
  blood, 22
  in Old Testament, 274–78
  restoration of, 66, 67, 71n. 90
salvation for the dead
  baptism for the dead. *See* baptism for the dead.
  in contemporary Mormonism, 366–67
  in early Mormonism, 21, 360–61
  ignorant and heathens, 359–62
  in later Mormonism, 361
  in New Testament, 346–58
  in Old Testament, 343–46
  nineteenth-century Christianity, 358–60

preaching to the dead, 363–66
Sanders, Jack T., 444
Sanders, James, 153
Satan
  in early Mormonism, 197
  in early nineteenth-century
      Christianity, 197
  and fall of Adam. 252–53, 276. See
      also fall of Adam.
  Lucifer, 195–96
  meaning of name, 194–95
  and millennium, 443, 454n. 59
  in New Testament, 196–97
  in Old Testament, 193–96
  second heir, 198n. 19
  similarities to other myths, 194
  unable to tempt children, 333
  Universalist, 222
  and war in heaven, 217–18, 221–22
saviors on mount Zion, 345–46. See also
    baptism for the dead.
Schaff, Phillip, 379
School of the Prophets, 311, 324
Schreiner, Thomas, 317
Scott, Walter
  on gospel ordinances, 301
  restorationist, 47
scripture
  human authorship of, 3
  and inerrancy, 3
  source of theology, 12–24
sealing power, 77–79
  in Book of Mormon, 323
  restoration of, 74, 76
  See also eternal marriage; Elijah;
      priesthood.
Second Coming
  in Book of Mormon, 446–47
  forerunner, 53
  and gathering, 402
  imminent
    in contemporary Mormonism, 437
    in early Mormonism, 435–37
    in early nineteenth-century
        Christianity, 434–35
    in New Testament, 33, 431–34
    in Old Testament, 430–31
  and Irvingites, 19
  and Lamanites, 408
  and millennialism, 441–43
Second Great Awakening, ix–x, 19
Seventh-day Adventists, 50

seventy, 377
Sewall, Samuel
  on "other sheep," 95
  on New Jerusalem, 416
Seixas, Joshua, 114.
Shakers, 50, 352, 381
Sheol, 228, 455–56, 475. See also hell.
Shindler, Marc, 28n. 74
Shipps, Jan, 61
Skousen, Royal, 68n. 29
Smith, Alvin
  in celestial kingdom, 361–62
  sealed to parents, 79
Smith, Azael, 81
Smith, Brian L., 408
Smith, Elias, 47
Smith, Emma, 312
Smith, Ethan
  on conversion of Jews, 402
  on gathering of Israel, 399–400
  on infant baptism, 332
  on messianic prophecy, 156
  on Native Americans, 295, 405
  views on Elijah, 53
Smith, Joseph, Jr., 47–72
  on Adam, 231
  and Alvin Smith in celestial kingdom,
      361–62
  angel in Revelation, 96
  apocrypha, use of, 22
  on apostasy, 39, 41
  on Atonement, 273
  and baptism for the dead, 362
  on biblical inerrancy, 25n. 9
  on body of God, 136
  on Book of Mormon, 4
  Book of Mormon prophecies of, 56–58
  on book of Revelation, 22, 467
  on calling and election made sure,
      320, 321
  on changeable God, 127
  on children of sealed parents, 326
  on creation, 233–34
  on creeds, 1
  on David's repentance, 494
  on death of children, 333, 334
  on doctrinal authority, vii
  on Elias and Elijah, 66
  on Elijah, 75, 77, 78, 357
  and Elijah Abel, 388
  on everlasting gospel, 295
  on everlasting priesthood, 373

on faith, 129
family, 41
first elder, 384
First Vision. *See* First Vision.
on foreordination, 215
and Freemasonry, 338n. 81
on fulness of times, 58
on gift of the Holy Ghost, 306–7
on God as father of spirits, 140
on God as once man, 505
on godhead, 105, 113
on Holy Ghost, 188–90
on human nature, 266
on inhabited moon, 240
on intelligences, 115
on interpreting scripture, 22
on Irvingites, 19
on Jehovah, 174–75
on Jesus as second Comforter, 322
on Jesus's sonship, 162
on key words and signs, 313
King Follet Discourse, 127–28
on kingdoms of heaven, 476
on length of day, 269n. 17
on "man of sin," 44n. 23
on material spirit, 202
on Melchizedek Priesthood
on millennium, 448
and monotheism, 118
on murder, 493
on Native American skin color, 409
and Nauvoo theology, 21
on Nebuchadnezzar's dream, 81
on new heaven and earth, 450
New Testament prophecies of, 56
Old Testament prophecies of, 50–56
on ordinances, 335n. 15
on parable of the leaven, 37
on parable of the mustard seed, 37
on parable of the wheat and tares, 36
on plurality of gods, 117–18, 119–20, 124n. 61
on preexistence, 209–10
on preservation of Bible, 98
and proof-texting, 12
prophecies of, 23
on redemption of Earth, 270n. 30
on resemblance of Father and Son, 132
on restoration of all things, 63, 64
on restoration of blood sacrifice, 67
on restoration of priesthood, 77, 80
on restoration, 66

on resurrection, 465, 470n. 36
on salvation for the dead, 344, 356, 364
on salvation of heathens, 362
on Satan, 222
on sealing, 77–78
on Second Coming, 435
on sin against Holy Ghost, 492
on sons of God, 219
on sons of perdition, 489
on spirit matter, 233
on spirits in prison, 354
studies Hebrew, 23, 100, 113, 138, 174
on three gods, 114
translator, 101–102
on unchanging ordinances, 293–94
on Zion, 418
Smith, Joseph Sr., 407
Smith, Joseph F.
 on Adam, 244
 on becoming children of God, 147n. 83
 on children, 333
 on Elohim, 138
 on Jesus as elder brother, 168
 on Jesus's sonship, 166
 on marriage, 317
 on polygamy, 319
 on preexistence, 199
 on resurrection, 466
Smith, Joseph Fielding
 on animals, 466–67
 on apostasy, 39
 on blacks and the priesthood, 6, 389
 on blood atonement, 496
 on children, 342n. 178
 on children of sealed parents, 327
 on creation, 236
 on dinosaurs, 235
 on Elijah, 77
 on eternal life, 248n. 39, 499n. 42
 on evolution, 146n. 80
 on fall of Adam, 254
 on fulness of gospel, 304
 on fulness of priesthood, 387–88
 on gathering of Israel, 400, 411, 421n. 26
 on God speaking to humans, 179
 on God's knowledge, 129
 on infinite atonement, 291n. 52
 on intelligence, 211
 on Jesus as Jehovah, 131
 on Jesus's sonship, 162
 on Joseph Smith, 52
 on lost tribes, 413

on marriage, 317, 327
on marvelous work and wonder, 84
on Mount of Transfiguration, 310
on perfectionism, 327
on preexistence, 225n. 53
on priesthood in the Book of Mormon, 382–83
on remnant of Jacob, 408
on restoration of blood sacrifice, 67
on resurrection, 466, 470n. 40
on second death, 487
on Son of Man, 171
on soul after death, 483–84
on spiritual creation, 242
on sun, inhabited, 240
on terrestrial kingdom, 464
Smith, Lucy Mack, 41
Smith, Mark S., 116
Snow, Eliza R., 142
Snow, Erastus, 135
Snow, Lorenzo
  couplet on eternal progression, 119, 124n. 62
  on salvation for the dead, 363
  on spirits in prison, 368n. 51
  on Zion, 436
Snow, Lowell M., 496
social trinitarianism. *See* trinitarianism.
Son of Man, 81, 490. *See also* Jesus.
son of perdition, 486–87
  resurrection of, 462, 469n. 28
sons of God, 141, 218–19. *See also* divine council; godhead.
Sorenseon, H. J., 232
soul
  creation of, 206
  in early nineteenth-century Christianity, 201–2
  in Mormonism, 202
  in New Testament, 201
  neshamah, 223n. 6
  in Old Testament, 200
  pneuma, 223n. 6
  preexistence of. *See* preexistence.
See also spirit.
spirit
  body-spirit dualism, 266–68, 346–47
  immortal, 346–48
  material, 201
  refined matter, 233
spirit birth, 210–11
  in Book of Mormon, 109

Spirit of the Lord. *See* Holy Ghost.
spirit world, 348–66, 370n. 78. *See also* afterlife.
spiritual gifts. *See* gifts of the spirit.
Sproul, R. C., 433
Spurgeon, Charles, 113
Stages of Faith, 504
standard works, vii, 1, 68n. 29
  canonization, 4
standard. *See* ensign.
stem of Jesse, 54–55
Stendahl, Krister, 355
Stone, Barton W., 47
Strong, A. Brent, x
Stuart, Moses, 236
sun, 240
Swedenborg, Emanuel
  on godhead, 122n. 27
  on levels of heaven, 480
Symmes, John Cleves, 412

T

Tabor, James D.
  on destruction of temple, 451
  on millennialism, 444
  on new heaven and earth, 449
  on resurrection, 457
Talmage, James E.
  on endless punishment, 488
  on fall of Adam, 254–55
  on foreordination, 215–16
  on fruits of Christianity, 506
  on Jesus as God of the Old Testament, 179
  on marriage, 317
  on resurrection, 464
  on Son of Man, 171, 173
Tate, George S., 313
Taylor, John
  on Book of Mormon prophecy of Joseph Smith, 57
  on Cain's sacrifice, 288n. 4
  on human nature, 267
  on infinite atonement, 285
  on Son of Man, 173
  on spirit birth, 142
Taylor, Nathaniel W., 264
Taylor, Thomas, 239
teacher
  in Book of Mormon, 382
  in early Christianity, 380
  in early Mormonism, 383

temple
  in Book of Mormon, 310
  for modern blood sacrifice, 67
  in Old Testament, 297–98
  See also endowment.
Ten Commandments, 300
Tertullian
  on baptism for the dead, 355
  and original sin, 263
Thayer, Thomas, 204–5
The Christian Baptist, 48
theology
  beyond, 505–6
  definition of, 1
  and human involvement, 1–30
Thomas, M. Catherine
  on gates of hell, 349
  on paradise, 348
Thomas, Mark D.
  on Book of Mormon, 20
  on Elijah, 53
  on First Vision, 49
  on proof-texting in the Book of Mormon, 11
  on spiritual ecstasy, 302
Towner, W. Sibley
  on Malachi, 53
  on proof-texting, 10
traducianism, 206. See also Adam; creation.
trinitarianism, 107–9
  and atonement, 284
  and creation, 229
  and Holy Ghost, 187
  in New Testament, 107
  social, 113
  See also godhead; modalism; tritheism.
tritheism, 108. See also godhead; modalism; trinitarianism.
True Inspiration Society, 50
Turner, Rodney
  on Only Begotten, 165
  on other worlds, 291n. 63
Tvedtnes, John
  on Emmanuel, 178
  on first begotten, 169, 170
  on restoration, 60

U

Underwood, Grant
  on authorship of scripture, 4
  on gathering, 402
  on influences on Mormonism, 29n. 92
  on millennialism, 429, 439, 448
  on nineteenth-century Christianity, 18
  on revelation, 25n. 19
  on unpardonable sin, 492
Unitarianism, 107–8, 187. See also godhead.
Universalism, 62–63, 352, 480, 498n. 38
  and mortality as probationary, 359
  and sin, 284
unpardonable sin
  and blood atonement, 496
  and Holy Ghost, 489–90
  murder, 495
  and second death, 487, 491–92

V

vaticinium ex eventu, 15. See also prophecy, after the fact.
Victorinus, 220
Vine, W. E., 163
Vine's Expository Dictionary, 59
virgin birth. See Jesus, virgin birth.
Vogel, Dan, 110–11
Voice of Warning, 64

W

Wallace, Daniel, 321
war in heaven
  in early Mormonism, 221
  in later Mormonism, 222
  in Nauvoo period, 221–22
  in New Testament, 218
  in Old Testament, 217–18
  See also preexistence.
Ward, James M., 289n. 17
Ward, Roy, 34, 38
Ward, Thomas
  on evangelicalism, 19
  on intelligence, 208–9
Warfield, Benjamin, 4
Watson, Richard
  on angel in Revelation, 96–97
  on Jehovah, 174
Wayment, Thomas, 152
Welch, John W.
  on Isaiah in Book of Mormon, 279
  on parable of the wheat and tares, 36
  on temple in Book of Mormon, 338n. 74
welding link, 77
Wesley, John
  on apostasy, 40, 44n. 28

on degrees of glory, 480
on fall of Adam, 254, 261
on foreordination, 214
on free-will, 302
on gifts of the spirit, 40
on Jesus as Father, 176–77
on original guilt, 264
on perfectionism, 328
on resurrection, 478
on saviors on mount Zion, 345
on seeing God, 137
Westminster Confession of Faith
on covenants of works and grace, 294
on creation, 232
on God, 122n. 28, 133
on Jesus's suffering, 280
on judgment, 479, 481
on original guilt, 263
White, Ellen G., 50
White, Kendall, 24
White, L. Michael
on apocalyptic language, 428
on Nebuchadnezzar's dream, 82
Whitmer, David
on Lamanites, 406
on priesthood, 79–80, 89n. 25, 89n. 27, 393n. 28, 394n. 51
Whitney, Orson F., 326–27
Whitney, Sarah Ann, 325
Widmer, Kurt, 161
Widstoe, John A.
on descendants of Ephraim, 408
on restoration of blood sacrifice, 67
Wild, Asa, 97
Wilkinson, Jemima, 50
Williams, John, 40
Williams, Roger, 39, 44n. 28
Winchester, Benjamin, 259, 262
Winchester, Elhanan, 352
Woodruff, Wilford W.
on conversion of Jews, 404, 405
on destruction of United States, 436
on exaltation through the priesthood, 308
on law of adoption, 30n. 114
patriarchal blessing, 407
on polygamy, 319
on salvation for the dead, 363
on Second Coming, 436
on vicarious sealing to parents, 370n. 88
Worcester, Noah, 187
work for the dead. *See* salvation for the dead.

worlds. *See* creation, other worlds.
Wray, T. J., 196
Wright, David P.
on millennialism, 440–41
on prophecy, 15–16
Wright, Ernest, 106
Wright, John, 47
Wright, N. T.
on apostasy, 34
on suffering servant, 279

Y

Yahweh. *See* Jehovah.
Young, Brigham
on Adam-God, 23, 142
on blacks and the priesthood, 6, 388
on blood atonement, 496
on children of sealed parents, 327
on creation, spiritual, 242
disagrees with Orson Pratt, 129
on fall of Adam, 259
on foreordination, 214
on fulness of priesthood, 386
on God's knowledge, 129
on human nature, 267, 268, 270n. 41
on imperfect language in revelation, viii
on infinite atonement, 285
on sun and moon, inhabited, 240
on Jesus as elder brother, 171
on law of adoption, 30n. 114
on other worlds, 288
on perfectionism, 331
on polygamy, 319
on pouring out of Spirit, 439
on preaching scripture, 23
on preaching to the dead, 364–65
on resurrection, 465
on saviors on mount Zion, 345
on spirit birth, 142
on spirit world, 370n. 78
on temple endowment, 314, 315
on Zion, 436

Z

Zion, 414–18
in America, 416
Missouri, 417
western Hemisphere, 418
and U. S. Constitution, 418
See also New Jerusalem.

About the Cover Image

The Painter

Born in 1576, Leonello Spada, also known as Lionello Spada, was an Italian painter from Bologna. He apprenticed with Cesare Baglioni and went on to become a follower of Michelangleo Merisi da Caravaggio. He excelled at quadratura painting, a style of ceiling painting that creates the illusion of continuing the existing architecture, and he was even part of a specialized team, along with Girolamo Curti. Later he gravitated toward the Carracci Academy and his canvas paintings reflected this shift in style. A few of his most famous works include a large canvas entitled *Saint Dominic Burning the Books of the Heretics* (1616) in the Basilica of San Domenico, the frescoes in the dome of Basilica della Ghiara (1616), and *Return of the Prodigal Son* (after 1615) and *Aeneas and Anchises* (1615), both on display at the Louvre. Spada died May 17, 1622 in Parma, Italy.

The Painting

San Girolamo (1614-1616) - oil on canvas, 175.5 x 166.5 cm

Basilica di San Domenico in Bologna, Italy

The painting depicts Saint Jerome, San Girolamo in Italian, a saint recognized by both the Catholic Church and the Eastern Orthodox Church. He was an Illyrian Catholic priest from a town called Stridon in the Roman province, Dalmatia (the actual location of Stridon is unknown, but it was most likely located in either today's Croatia or Slovenia). Born circa 347, Saint Jerome was not baptized until sometime between 360 and 366 in Rome while studying rhetoric and philosophy. He would often visit the sepulchers of martyrs and apostles in the catacombs, an experience he described as entering hell and perhaps one reason he is often pictured with a skull. After finishing his studies, he went on to become a Doctor of the Church, a title given to only the most renowned theologians, and produce numerous texts. He is most famous for translating the Bible from Hebrew into Latin, a feat that required a great deal of correspondence with Jewish Christians. He eventually moved to Jerusalem to further his understanding of Jewish scripture commentary and continue writing. Throughout his life Saint Jerome was an apologist, something that was ever apparent in his work. He sought for truth in religion by using reason and historical evidence. His translation of the Bible, for example, was widely popular because he spent a great deal of time studying its history, as well as the history of Judaism. He also was not afraid to directly address attacks on orthodox doctrine, often using a polemic argument. He produced a number of scriptural commentaries, catalogued many of the Christian authors, and even wrote a dialogue against the Pelagians that caused violent riots, thus demonstrating his passion for argument and truth. He is traditionally, although incorrectly, credited with the discovery of spectacles which were actually discovered some nine centuries after his death. Classical painters none the less include glasses as a tribute to Saint Jerome's higher education and learning. He died near Bethlehem in 420 on September 30, a date that is now celebrated as the feast day of Saint Jerome. He is remembered as not only having immense amount of knowledge but also an unquenchable thirst for learning. His writings are considered some of the finest in Christian antiquity and he is often referred to as the quintessential scholar.

Also available from
GREG KOFFORD BOOKS

Mormonism in Transition: A History of the Latter-day Saints, 1890–1930, 3rd ed.

Thomas G. Alexander

Paperback, ISBN: 978-1-58958-188-3

More than two decades after its original publication, Thomas G. Alexander's Mormonism in Transition still engages audiences with its insightful study of the pivotal, early years of the Church of Jesus Christ of Latter-day Saints. Serving as a vital read for both students and scholars of American religious and social history, Alexander's book explains and charts the Church's transformation over this 40-year period of both religious and American history.

For those familiar with the LDS Church in modern times, it is impossible to study Mormonism in Transition without pondering the enormous amount of changes the Church has been through since 1890. For those new to the study of Mormonism, this book will give them a clear understanding the challenges the Church went through to go from a persecuted and scorned society to the rapidly growing, respected community it is today.

Praise for Mormonism in Transition:

"A must read for any serious student of this 'peculiar people' and Western history." – STANLEY B. KIMBALL, *Journal of the West*

"Will be required reading for all historians of Mormonism for some time to come." – WILLIAM D. RUSSELL, *Journal of American History*

"This is by far the most important book on this crucial period in LDS history." – JAN SHIPPS, author of *Mormonism: The Story of a New Religious Tradition*

"A work of careful and prodigious scholarship." – LEONARD J. ARRINGTON, author of *Brigham Young: American Moses*

"Clearly fills a tremendous void in the history of Mormonism." – Klaus J. Hansen, author of *Mormonism and the American Experience*

Re-reading Job: Understanding the Ancient World's Greatest Poem

Michael Austin

Paperback, ISBN: 978-1-58958-667-3

Job is perhaps the most difficult to understand of all books in the Bible. While a cursory reading of the text seems to relay a simple story of a righteous man whose love for God was tested through life's most difficult of challenges and rewarded for his faith through those trials, a closer reading of Job presents something far more complex and challenging. The majority of the text is a work of poetry that authors and artists through the centuries have recognized as being one of--if not the--greatest poem of the ancient world.

In *Re-reading Job: Understanding the Ancient World's Greatest Poem*, author Michael Austin shows how most readers have largely misunderstood this important work of scripture and provides insights that enable us to re-read Job in a drastically new way. In doing so, he shows that the story of Job is far more than that simple story of faith, trials, and blessings that we have all come to know, but is instead a subversive and complex work of scripture meant to inspire readers to rethink all that they thought they knew about God.

Praise for *Re-reading Job*:

"In this remarkable book, Michael Austin employs his considerable skills as a commentator to shed light on the most challenging text in the entire Hebrew Bible. Without question, readers will gain a deeper appreciation for this extraordinary ancient work through Austin's learned analysis. Rereading Job signifies that Latter-day Saints are entering a new age of mature biblical scholarship. It is an exciting time, and a thrilling work." — David Bokovoy, author, *Authoring the Old Testament*

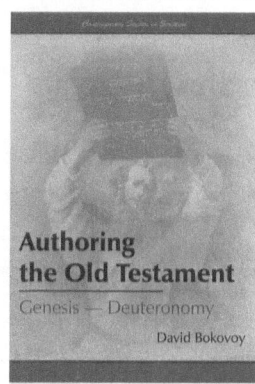

Authoring the Old Testament: Genesis–Deuteronomy

David Bokovoy

Paperback, ISBN: 978-1-58958-588-1

For the last two centuries, biblical scholars have made discoveries and insights about the Old Testament that have greatly changed the way in which the authorship of these ancient scriptures has been understood. In the first of three volumes spanning the entire Hebrew Bible, David Bokovoy dives into the Pentateuch, showing how and why textual criticism has led biblical scholars today to understand the first five books of the Bible as an amalgamation of multiple texts into a single, though often complicated narrative; and he discusses what implications those have for Latter-day Saint understandings of the Bible and modern scripture.

Praise for *Authoring the Old Testament*:

"*Authoring the Old Testament* is a welcome introduction, from a faithful Latter-day Saint perspective, to the academic world of Higher Criticism of the Hebrew Bible. . . . [R]eaders will be positively served and firmly impressed by the many strengths of this book, coupled with Bokovoy's genuine dedication to learning by study and also by faith." — John W. Welch, editor, *BYU Studies Quarterly*

"Bokovoy provides a lucid, insightful lens through which disciple-students can study intelligently LDS scripture. This is first rate scholarship made accessible to a broad audience—nourishing to the heart and mind alike." — Fiona Givens, co-author, *The God Who Weeps: How Mormonism Makes Sense of Life*

"I repeat: this is one of the most important books on Mormon scripture to be published recently. . . . [*Authoring the Old Testament*] has the potential to radically expand understanding and appreciation for not only the Old Testament, but scripture in general. It's really that good. Read it. Share it with your friends. Discuss it." — David Tayman, The Improvement Era: A Mormon Blog

Joseph Smith's Polygamy, 3 Vols.

Brian Hales

Hardcover
Volume 1: History 978-1-58958-189-0
Volume 2: History 978-1-58958-548-5
Volume 3: Theology 978-1-58958-190-6

Perhaps the least understood part of Joseph Smith's life and teachings is his introduction of polygamy to the Saints in Nauvoo. Because of the persecution he knew it would bring, Joseph said little about it publicly and only taught it to his closest and most trusted friends and associates before his martyrdom.

In this three-volume work, Brian C. Hales provides the most comprehensive faithful examination of this much misunderstood period in LDS Church history. Drawing for the first time on every known account, Hales helps us understand the history and teachings surrounding this secretive practice and also addresses and corrects many of the numerous allegations and misrepresentations concerning it. Hales further discusses how polygamy was practiced during this time and why so many of the early Saints were willing to participate in it.

Joseph Smith's Polygamy is an essential resource in understanding this challenging and misunderstood practice of early Mormonism.

Praise for *Joseph Smith's Polygamy*:

"Brian Hales wants to face up to every question, every problem, every fear about plural marriage. His answers may not satisfy everyone, but he gives readers the relevant sources where answers, if they exist, are to be found. There has never been a more thorough examination of the polygamy idea."
—Richard L. Bushman, author of *Joseph Smith: Rough Stone Rolling*

"Hales's massive and well documented three volume examination of the history and theology of Mormon plural marriage, as introduced and practiced during the life of Joseph Smith, will now be the standard against which all other treatments of this important subject will be measured." —Danel W. Bachman, author of "A Study of the Mormon Practice of Plural Marriage before the Death of Joseph Smith"

Women at Church: Magnifying LDS Women's Local Impact

Neylan McBaine

Paperback, ISBN: 978-1-58958-688-8

Women at Church is a practical and faithful guide to improving the way men and women work together at church. Looking at current administrative and cultural practices, the author explains why some women struggle with the gendered divisions of labor. She then examines ample real-life examples that are currently happening in local settings around the country that expand and reimagine gendered practices. Readers will understand how to evaluate possible pain points in current practices and propose solutions that continue to uphold all mandated church policies. Readers will be equipped with the tools they need to have respectful, empathetic and productive conversations about gendered practices in Church administration and culture.

Praise for *Women at Church*:

"Such a timely, faithful, and practical book! I suggest ordering this book in bulk to give to your bishopric, stake presidency, and all your local leadership to start a conversation on changing Church culture for women by letting our doctrine suggest creative local adaptations—Neylan McBaine shows the way!" — Valerie Hudson Cassler, author of *Women in Eternity, Women of Zion*

"A pivotal work replete with wisdom and insight. Neylan McBaine deftly outlines a workable programme for facilitating movement in the direction of the 'privileges and powers' promised the nascent Female Relief Society of Nauvoo." — Fiona Givens, co-author of *The God Who Weeps: How Mormonism Makes Sense of Life*

"In her timely and brilliant findings, Neylan McBaine issues a gracious invitation to rethink our assumptions about women's public Church service. Well researched, authentic, and respectful of the current Church administrative structure, McBaine shares exciting and practical ideas that address diverse needs and involve all members in the meaningful work of the Church." — Camille Fronk Olson, author of *Women of the Old Testament* and *Women of the New Testament*

Discourses in Mormon Theology: Philosophical and Theological Possibilities

Edited by
James M. McLachlan and Loyd Ericson

Hardcover, ISBN: 978-1-58958-103-6

A mere two hundred years old, Mormonism is still in its infancy compared to other theological disciplines (Judaism, Catholicism, Buddhism, etc.). This volume will introduce its reader to the rich blend of theological viewpoints that exist within Mormonism. The essays break new ground in Mormon studies by exploring the vast expanse of philosophical territory left largely untouched by traditional approaches to Mormon theology. It presents philosophical and theological essays by many of the finest minds associated with Mormonism in an organized and easy-to-understand manner and provides the reader with a window into the fascinating diversity amongst Mormon philosophers. Open-minded students of pure religion will appreciate this volume's thoughtful inquiries.

These essays were delivered at the first conference of the Society for Mormon Philosophy and Theology. Authors include Grant Underwood, Blake T. Ostler, Dennis Potter, Margaret Merrill Toscano, James E. Faulconer, and Robert L. Millet

Praise for *Discourses in Mormon Theology*:

"In short, *Discourses in Mormon Theology* is an excellent compilation of essays that are sure to feed both the mind and soul. It reminds all of us that beyond the white shirts and ties there exists a universe of theological and moral sensitivity that cries out for study and acclamation."
-Jeff Needle, Association for Mormon Letters

Rube Goldberg Machines: Essays in Mormon Theology

Adam S. Miller

Paperback, ISBN: 978-1-58958-193-7

"Adam Miller is the most original and provocative Latter-day Saint theologian practicing today."

—Richard Bushman, author of *Joseph Smith: Rough Stone Rolling*

"As a stylist, Miller gives Nietzsche a run for his money. As a believer, Miller is as submissive as Augustine hearing a child's voice in the garden. Miller is a theologian of the ordinary, thinking about our ordinary beliefs in very non-ordinary ways while never insisting that the ordinary become extra-ordinary."

—James Faulconer, Richard L. Evans Chair of Religious Understanding, Brigham Young University

"Miller's language is both recognizably Mormon and startlingly original.... The whole is an essay worthy of the name, inviting the reader to try ideas, following the philosopher pilgrim's intellectual progress through tangled brambles and into broad fields, fruitful orchards, and perhaps a sacred grove or two."

—Kristine Haglund, editor of *Dialogue: A Journal of Mormon Thought*

"Miller's Rube Goldberg theology is nothing like anything done in the Mormon tradition before."

—Blake Ostler, author of the EXPLORING MORMON THOUGHT series

"The value of Miller's writings is in the modesty he both exhibits and projects onto the theological enterprise, even while showing its joyfully disruptive potential. Conventional Mormon minds may not resonate with every line of poetry and provocation—but Miller surely afflicts the comfortable, which is the theologian's highest end."

—Terryl Givens, author of *By the Hand of Mormon: The American Scripture that Launched a New World Religion*

Fire on the Horizon: A Meditation on the Endowment and Love of Atonement

Blake T. Ostler

Paperback, ISBN: 978-1-58958-553-9

Blake Ostler, author of the groundbreaking Exploring Mormon Thought series, explores two of the most important and central aspects of Mormon theology and practice: the Atonement and the temple endowment. Utilizing observations from Søren Kierkegaard, Martin Buber, and others, Ostler offers further insights on what it means to become alienated from God and to once again have at-one-ment with Him.

Praise for *Fire on the Horizon*:

"*Fire on the Horizon* distills decades of reading, argument, and reflection into one potent dose. Urgent, sharp, and intimate, it's Ostler at his best." — Adam S. Miller, author of *Rube Goldberg Machines: Essays in Mormon Theology*

"Blake Ostler has been one of the most stimulating, deep, and original thinkers in the Latter-day Saint community. This book continues and consolidates that status. His work demonstrates that Mormonism can, and indeed does, offer profound nourishment for reflective minds and soul-satisfying insights for thoughtful believers." — Daniel C. Peterson, editor of *Interpreter: A Journal of Mormon Scripture*

For Zion: A Mormon Theology of Hope

Joseph M. Spencer

Paperback, ISBN: 978-1-58958-568-3

What is hope? What is Zion? And what does it mean to hope for Zion? In this insightful book, Joseph Spencer explores these questions through the scriptures of two continents separated by nearly two millennia. In the first half, Spencer engages in a rich study of Paul's letter to the Roman to better understand how the apostle understood hope and what it means to have it. In the second half of the book, Spencer jumps to the early years of the Restoration and the various revelations on consecration to understand how Latter-day Saints are expected to strive for Zion. Between these halves is an interlude examining the hoped-for Zion that both thrived in the Book of Mormon and was hoped to be established again.

Praise for *For Zion*:

"Joseph Spencer is one of the most astute readers of sacred texts working in Mormon Studies. Blending theological savvy, historical grounding, and sensitive readings of scripture, he has produced an original and compelling case for consecration and the life of discipleship." — Terryl Givens, author, *Wrestling the Angel: The Foundations of Mormon Thought*

"*For Zion: A Mormon Theology of Hope* is more than a theological reflection. It also consists of able textual exegesis, historical contextualization, and philosophic exploration. Spencer's careful readings of Paul's focus on hope in Romans and on Joseph Smith's development of consecration in his early revelations, linking them as he does with the Book of Mormon, have provided an intriguing, intertextual avenue for understanding what true stewardship should be for us—now and in the future. As such he has set a new benchmark for solid, innovative Latter-day Saint scholarship that is at once provocative and challenging." — Eric D. Huntsman, author, *The Miracles of Jesus*

"Let the Earth Bring Forth" Evolution and Scripture

Howard C. Stutz

Paperback, ISBN: 978-1-58958-126-5

A century ago in 1809, Charles Darwin was born. Fifty years later, he published a scientific treatise describing the process of speciation that launched what appeared to be a challenge to the traditional religious interpretation of how life was created on earth. The controversy has erupted anew in the last decade as Creationists and Young Earth adherents challenge school curricula and try to displace "the theory of evolution."

This book is filled with fascinating examples of speciation by the well-known process of mutation but also by the less well-known processes of sexual recombination and polyploidy. In addition to the fossil record, Howard Stutz examines the evidence from the embryo stages of human beings and other creatures to show how selection and differentiation moved development in certain favored directions while leaving behind evidence of earlier, discarded developments. Anatomy, biochemistry, and genetics are all examined in their turn.

With rigorously scientific clarity but in language accessible to a popular audience, the book proceeds to its conclusion, reached after a lifetime of study: the divine map of creation is one supported by both scientific evidence and the scriptures. This is a book to be read, not only for its fascinating scientific insights, but also for a new appreciation of well-known scriptures.

www.ingramcontent.com/pod-product-compliance
Lightning Source LLC
Chambersburg PA
CBHW020216240426
43672CB00006B/331